PROGRESS IN BRAIN RESEARCH

VOLUME 95

THE VISUALLY RESPONSIVE NEURON: FROM BASIC NEUROPHYSIOLOGY TO
BEHAVIOR

Other volumes in PROGRESS IN BRAIN RESEARCH

PROGRESS IN BRAIN RESEARCH

VOLUME 95

THE VISUALLY RESPONSIVE NEURON: FROM BASIC NEUROPHYSIOLOGY TO BEHAVIOR

EDITED BY

T.P. HICKS

Departments of Biology and Psychology, College of Arts and Sciences, The University of North Carolina at Greensboro, Greensboro, NC 27412-5001, U.S.A.

S. MOLOTCHNIKOFF

Department of Biological Sciences, University of Montreal, Montreal, P.Q., Canada, H3C 3J7

T. ONO

Department of Physiology, Faculty of Medicine, Toyama Medical and Pharmaceutical University, Toyama 930-01, Japan

ELSEVIER
AMSTERDAM – LONDON – NEW YORK – TOKYO
1993

ISBN 0-444-89492-6 (volume)
ISBN 0-444-80104-9 (series)

Elsevier Science Publishers B.V.
P.O. Box 211
1000 AE Amsterdam
The Netherlands

Library of Congress Cataloging-in-Publication Data

The Visually responsive neuron : from basic neurophysiology to
  behavior / edited by T.P. Hicks, S. Molotchnikoff, and T. Ono.
       p.   cm. -- (Progress in brain research ; v. 95)
    Includes bibliographical references and index.
    ISBN 0-444-89492-6 (alk. paper)
    1. Visual pathways. 2. Visual cortex. 3. Visual perception.
  I. Hicks, T. Philip. II. Molotchnikoff, S. III. Ono, Taketoshi.
  IV. Series.
    [DNLM: 1. Neurons--physiology.   W1 PR667J v.95 1992 / WL 102.5
  V834 1992]
  QP376.P7 vol. 95
  [QP383.15]
  612'.82 s--dc20
  [612.8'4]
  DNLM/DLC
  for Library of Congress   92-48461
                                                           CIP

Printed on acid-free paper

Printed in The Netherlands

List of Contributors

D. Albrecht, Institut für Physiologie, Bereich Medizin (Charité) der Humboldt-Universität zu Berlin, Hessische Straße 3 – 4, 0-1040 Berlin, Germany.

J.A. Baro, School of Optometry, University of Missouri-St. Louis, 8001 Natural Bridge Road, St. Louis, MO 63131-4499, U.S.A.

G.P. Biral, Istituto di Fisiologia Umana, Via Campi 287, 41100 Modena, Italy.

S. Bisti, Istituto di Neurofisiologia C.N.R., Università di Pisa, via S. Zeno 51, 56127, Pisa, Italy.

M.W. Brown, Department of Anatomy, University of Bristol, Bristol, BS8 lTD, U.K.

P. Buisseret, Laboratoire de Neurophysiologie, Collège de France, 11 place Marcelin Berthelot, 75231 Paris, Cedex 05, France.

J. Bullier, Vision et Motricité, INSERM U94, 16 avenue du doyen Lépine, 69500 Bron, France.

J.P. Burke, Neurobiology Research Center and Department of Physiology and Biophysics, University of Alabama at Birmingham, Volker Hall G-78B, Birmingham, AL 35294, U.S.A.

P. Buser, Institut des Neurosciences, Département de Neurophysiologie Comparée, CNRS et Université Pierre et Marie Curie, 9 Quai Saint-Bernard, 75230 Paris Cedex 05, France.

C. Casanova, Département d'Opthalmologie, Faculté de Médecine, Université de Sherbrooke, Sherbrooke, P.Q., Canada, JIH 5N4.

C. Cavada, Departamento de Morfología, Facultad de Medicina, Universidad Autónoma de Madrid, Arzobispo Morcillo 2, s/n 28029 Madrid, Spain.

L. Cervetto, Istituto Policattedra di Discipline Biologiche, Università di Pisa, via Bonnano 6, 56100 Pisa, Italy.

L.M. Chalupa, Departments of Psychology and Neurology and the Center for Neurobiology, University of California, Davis, CA 95616, U.S.A.

C.L. Colby, Laboratory of Sensorimotor Research, National Eye Institute, Bldg. 10, Room 10C – 101, National Institutes of Health, Bethesda, MD 20892, U.S.A.

A. Cowey, Department of Experimental Psychology, Oxford University, South Parks Road, Oxford OX1 3UD, U.K.

O.D. Creutzfeldt, Max-Planck-Institut für biophysikalische Chemie, Abteilung Neurobiologie, Postfach 2841, W-3400 Göttingen, Germany.

H. Davidowa, Institut für Physiologie, Bereich Medizin (Charité) der Humboldt-Universität zu Berlin, Hessische Straße 3-4, O-1040 Berlin, Germany.

P. Dean, Department of Psychology, The University of Sheffield, P.O. Box 603, Western Bank, Sheffield S10 2UR, U.K.

D. Debanne, Laboratoire de Neurobiologie et Neuropharmacologie du Développement, Bât. 440, Université de Paris XI, F-91405 Orsay, Cedex, France.

G.C. Demontis, Istituto Policattedra di Discipline Biologiche, Università di Pisa, Istituto di Neurofisiologia C.N.R., via Bonanno 6, 56100 Pisa, Italy.

P. DeWeerd, Laboratorium voor Neuro- en Psychofysiologie, Faculteit der Geneeskunde, Katholieke Universiteit Leuven, B-3000 Louvain, Belgium.

J.-R. Duhamel, Laboratory of Sensorimotor Research, National Eye Institute, Bldg. 10, Room 10C – 101, National Institutes of Health, Bethesda, MD 20892, U.S.A.

D.D. Dunning, Department of Physiology, Medical College of Virginia, Virginia Commonwealth University, Box 551, MCV Station, Richmond, VA 23298, U.S.A.

F.L. Fahy, Department of Anatomy, University of Bristol, Bristol, BS8 1TD, U.K.

Y. Frégnac, Laboratoire de Neurobiologie et Neuropharmacologie du Développement, Bât. 440, Université de Paris XI, F-91405 Orsay, Cedex, France.

M.J. Friedlander, Neurobiology Research Center and Department of Physiology and Biophysics, University of Alabama at Birmingham, Volker Hall G-78B, AL 35294, U.S.A.

M. Fukuda, Department of Physiology, Faculty of Medicine, Toyama Medical and Pharmaceutical University, Sugitani 2630, Toyama 930-01, Japan.

Y. Fukuda, Department of Psychology, Osaka University Medical School, 2-2 Yamadaoka Suita, Osaka 565, Japan.

P. Girard, Vision et Motricité, INSERM U94, 16 avenue du doyen Lepine, 69500 Bron, France.

M.E. Goldberg, Laboratory of Sensorimotor Research, National Eye Institute, Bldg.10, Room 10C – 101, National Institutes of Health, Bethesda, MD 20892, U.S.A.

P.S. Goldman-Rakic, Section of Neurobiology, Yale University School of Medicine, New Haven, CT 06510, U.S.A.

M.A. Goodale, Department of Psychology, The University of Western Ontario, London, Ont., Canada N6A 5C2.

J.-P. Guillemot, Groupe de Recherche en Neuropsychologie Expérimentale, Département de Kinanthropologie, Université de Québec à Montréal, CB 8888, Succ. "A", Montréal, P.Q., Canada, H3C 3P8.

Y. Hayashi, Department of Physiology, Hyogo College of Medicine, Hyogo, Japan.

T.P. Hicks, Departments of Biology and Psychology, 267 Bruce Eberhart Building, College of Arts and Sciences, The University of North Carolina at Greensboro, Greensboro, NC 27412 – 5001, U.S.A.

K.-I. Ito, Departments of Biology and Psychology, 267 Bruce Eberhart Building, College of Arts and Sciences, The University of North Carolina at Greensboro, NC 27412 – 5001, U.S.A.

J.J. Kulikowski, Visual Sciences Laboratory, UMIST, P.O. Box 88, Manchester M60 1QD, U.K.

C. Kusmic, Dipartimento di Fisiologia e Biochimica, Università di Pisa, via S. Zeno 31, Pisa 56100, Italy.

B.B. Lee, Abteilung Neurobiologie, Max-Planck-Institut für biophysikalische Chemie, W-3400 Göttingen, Germany.

F. Lepore, Groupe de Recherche en Neuropsychologie Expérimentale, Département de Psychologie, Université de Montréal, 90 Vincent D'Indy Ave., Montréal, P.Q. Canada H2V 259.

P.L. Marchiafava, Dipartimento di Fisiologia e Biochimica, Università di Pisa, via S. Zeno 31, Pisa 56100, Italy.

C.A. Marzi, Istituto di Fisiologia Umana, Università Degli Studi di Verona, Strada le Grazie 37134, Verona, Italy.

R. Masuda, Department of Physiology, Faculty of Medicine, Toyama Medical and Pharmaceutical University, Sugitani 2630, Toyama 930-01, Japan.

J.G. McHaffie, Department of Physiology, Medical College of Virginia, Richmond, VA 23298, U.S.A.

M.A. Meredith, Department of Anatomy, Medical College of Virginia, Virginia Commonwealth University, Box 551, MCV Station, Richmond, VA 23298, U.S.A.

C. Milleret, Collège de France, Laboratoire de Neurophysiologie, 11 Place Marcelin Berthelot, 75231 Paris, Cedex 05, France.

A.D. Milner, Department of Psychology, University of St. Andrews, St. Andrews, Fife KY16 9JU, U.K.

S. Molotchnikoff, Department of Biological Sciences, University of Montreal, C.P. 6128, Succ. "A", Montreal, P.Q., Canada, H3C 3J7.

R.D. Mooney, Department of Anatomy, Medical College of Ohio, CS #10008 Toledo, OH 43699, U.S.A.

K. Nakamura, Department of Physiology, Faculty of Medicine, Toyama Medical and Pharmaceutical University, Sugitani 2630, Toyama 930-01, Japan.

H. Nishijo, Department of Physiology, Faculty of Medicine, Toyama Medical and Pharmaceutical University, Sugitani 2630, Toyama 930-01, Japan.

M. Norita, Department of Anatomy, Niigata University School of Medicine, Asahimachi, Niigata 951, Japan.

Y. Okada, Department of Physiology, School of Medicine, Kobe University, 7-5-1 Kusunoki-cho, Chuo-ku, Kobe 650, Japan.

T. Ono, Department of Physiology, Faculty of Medicine, Toyama Medical and Pharmaceutical University, Sugitani 2630, Toyama 930-01, Japan.

G.A. Orban, Laboratorium voor Neuro- en Psychofysiologie, Faculteit der Geneeskunde, Katholieke Universiteit Leuven, B-3000 Louvain, Belgium.

C.K. Peck, School of Optometry, University of Missouri-St. Louis, 8001 Natural Bridge Road, St. Louis, MO 63121-4499, U.S.A.

H.M. Petry, Department of Psychology, Life Sciences Building, University of Louisville, Louisville, KY 40292, U.S.A.

M. Ptito, Groupe de Recherche en Neuropsychologie Expérimentale, Département de Psychologie, Université de Montréal, B.P. 6128, Succ. "A", Montréal, P.Q., Canada H3C 3J7.

P. Redgrave, Department of Psychology, The University of Sheffield, P.O. Box 603, Western Bank, Sheffield S10 2UR, U.K.

B.E. Reese, Department of Psychology and Neuroscience Research Institute, University of California, Santa Barbara, CA 93106, U.S.A., and Department of Human Anatomy, University of Oxford, Oxford, U.K.

R.W. Rhoades, Department of Anatomy, Medical College of Ohio, CS #10008, Toledo, OH 43699, U.S.A.

L. Richer, Groupe de Recherche en Neuropsychologie Expérimentale, Département de Kinanthropologie, Université de Québec à Montréal, C.P. 8888, Succ. "A", P.Q. Canada, H3C 3P8.

I.P. Riches, Department of Anatomy, University of Bristol, Bristol, BS8 LTD, U.K.

D.L. Robinson, Section on Visual Behavior, Laboratory of Sensorimotor Research, National Eye Institute, National Institutes of Health, Bethesda, MD 20892, U.S.A.

P.-A. Salin, Vision et Motricité, INSERM U94, 16 avenue du doyen Lépine, 69500 Bron, France.

H. Sasaki, Department of Physiology, Hyogo College of Medicine, Hyogo, Japan.

R.P. Scobey, Departments of Psychology and Neurology and the Center for Neurobiology, University of California, Davis, CA 95616, U.S.A.

D. Shulz, Laboratoire de Neurobiologie et Neuropharmacologie du Développement, Bât. 440, Université de Paris XI, F-91405 Orsay, Cedex, France.

S.I. Shumikhina, Institute of Higher Nervous Activity and Neurophysiology, Academy of Sciences of the U.S.S.R., 5a Butlerova St, 117865 Moscow, Russia.

W. Singer, Max-Planck-Institut für Hirnforschung, Deutschordenstraße 46, D-6000 Frankfurt/Main 71, Germany.

I. Skaliora, Departments of Psychology and Neurology and the Center for Neurobiology, University of California, Davis CA 95616, U.S.A.

J.M. Sprague, Department of Anatomy, The School of Medicine, Philadelphia, PA 19104-6058, U.S.A.

B.E. Stein, Department of Physiology, Medical College of Virginia, Virginia Commonwealth University, Box 551, MCV Station, Richmond, VA 23298, U.S.A.

P. Stoerig, Institut für medizinische Psychologie, Ludwig-Maximilians-Universität München, Goethestrasse 31, W-8000 Munich 2, Germany.

E. Tabuchi, Department of Physiology, Faculty of Medicine, Toyama Medical and Pharmaceutical University, Sugitani 2630, Toyama 930-01, Japan.

R. Tamura, Department of Physiology, Faculty of Medicine, Toyama Medical and Pharmaceutical University, Sugitani 2630, Toyama 930-01, Japan.

G. Tassinari, Istituto di Fisiologia Umana, Università Degli Studi di Verona, Strada Le Grazie, 37134, Verona, Italy.

C. Trimarchi, Istituto di Neurofisiologia C.N.R., via S. Zeno 51, 56127 Pisa, Italy.

E. Vandenbussche, Laboratorium voor Neuro- en Psychofysiologie, Faculteit der Geneeskunde, Katholieke Universiteit Leuven, B-3000 Louvain, Belgium.

R. Vogels, Laboratorium voor Neuro- en Psychofysiologie, Faculteit der Geneeskunde, Katholieke Universiteit Leuven, B-3000 Louvain, Belgium.

M.T. Wallace, Department of Physiology, Medical College of Virginia, Virginia Commonwealth University, Box 551, MCV Station, Richmond, VA 23298, U.S.A.

V. Walsh, Visual Sciences Laboratory, UMIST, P.O. Box 88, Manchester M60 1QD, U.K.

S.M. Warder, School of Optometry, University of Missouri-St. Louis, 8001 Natural Bridge Road, St. Louis, MO 63121-4499, U.S.A.

M. Westby, Department of Psychology, The University of Sheffield, P.O. Box 603, Western Bank, Sheffield S10 2UR, U.K.

From left to right, top row: Group scene, S. Shumikhina, S. Molotchnikoff; *second row:* L. Chalupa, P. Stoerig, D. Robinson, W. Singer, L. Pelltier, Y. Michaud, R. Vogels, J. Bullier; *third row:* K. Kubota, M. Goodale, D. Schulz, C. Peck; *fourth row:* D. Robinson, J.-P. Guillemot, Y. Okada, I. Shevelev; *fifth row:* L. Cervetto, P. Marchiafava, C. Milleret, P. Hicks, B. Lee, M. Goldberg, J.-P. Guillemot, D. Albrecht; *bottom row:* C. Marzi, H. Petry, T. Ono, P. Stoerig.

From left to right, top row: P. Redgrave, M. Brown, M. Goldberg, J. Kulikowski; *second row:* S. Bisti, R. Mooney, C. Milleret, B. Stein; *third row:* M. Fukuda, B. Lee, group scene; *fourth row:* C. Cavada, P. Hicks, M. Friedlander, V. Durand, J. Bullier; *fifth row:* J. Sprague, P. Stoerig, H. Sasaki; *bottom row:* C. Casanova, W. Singer, P. Buisseret, W. Singer, S. Molotchnikoff.

Preface

It is probably no exaggeration, or at least not much of one, to state that the vast majority of what we now know about the form and function of sensory systems of the brain, comes to us through the results of experiments performed on one aspect or another of the visual system. This statement remains true, irrespective of whether the knowledge derives from behavioral studies, evoked-potential level of electrophysiological analysis, single unit recording or even at the electron microscope, or patch-clamp level of investigation. Thus it seems quite appropriate to introduce a new volume dedicated solely to this very important subject in conjunction with the Third International Brain Research Organization World Congress of Neuroscience, for publication in the Progress in Brain Research series.

It has been five years since the previous volume on a related topic appeared in this series − and that conference proceedings concentrated exclusively on extrageniculostriate vision. The present volume presents a much broader context for the contributions on all aspects on vision; indeed, it is interesting to note that the first and last chapters of the book deal with or mention the pineal body, so the topics covered here are broad-based and wide-ranging.

To attempt to try to present vision to readers in a logical fashion, we have grouped our material for presentation into 5 main themes (see Contents). While the inclusion of one or two chapters in one thematic section rather than another may seem a bit arbitrary, largely the division came about quite naturally and seems appropriate. The material indeed spans from molecules to cognition. Many chapters deal with overt behavior − including the study of man − while others concentrate completely on synaptic or membrane levels of analysis. The species studied also range over diverse phyla, and our contributors formed a very diverse group as well, coming from all over Europe, North America and Asia.

It is with deep regret and a great sadness, that we recognize that Otto Creutzfeldt's contribution to this book was probably the last paper he penned. His untimely passing just a few short months after the completion of the conference, was an emotional blow to us all. He will be missed keenly for many years to come.

While thinking about Dr. Creutzfeldt's contribution to this book one's thoughts are drawn to the problem of retinal handling of light stimuli, and one is reminded again that everything we see in the world comes to us from a few cells at the receptor level. Barry Lee makes this point well in his chapter, that the visual system really is only as good as the receptors in the retina. As we scan through many of the other early chapters, we are reminded again that even though we may believe we are focussing on one single object, the presence of other, adjacent objects will be exerting their influences on our perception. These "external" distractors, or influences, may take the form of remote targets, may be manifested by the observational conditions, or they may present as built-in influences, such as relating to the specific task involved in our gaze direction. These and other factors have an important bearing on our response to central, foveal targets (see chapters by Milner and Goodale, and by Colby, Duhamel and Goldberg).

Parallel processing as a viable component of visual system modelling still seems alive and well, both as regards within-system (e.g. magnocellular or parvocellular) or across-system processing (e.g. striate, extrastriate systems). The analysis of modality properties of cells in diverse areas of the visual pathways remains a highly important topic of investigation and of broad interest, relating to integration of responses to different aspects of single objects. Likewise, the whole issue of salience seems increasingly to be indivisible from sensation and perception, as evinced by the work of Robinson, and Fahy, Riches and Brown, among others.

More and more as one reads over these new chapters authored by the most leading and prominent investigators in the area, one is reminded how similar the basic mechanisms of vision, or of neuronal processing in general are, across all species (Casanova-Robinson; rabbits-monkeys-rat-cat, etc.). Whether one looks at plasticity of synaptic transmission, or photic transduction, or modelling at a systems level, one cannot help but draw on knowledge gained from experiments performed on a plethora of species and this in itself is an important message to emanate from a group such as was brought together here.

The Québec ambience was warm and friendly, as it always is. The food and wine were such as only the francophone community within Canada can provide with panache, and make it all seem routine. The speakers worked hard to submit their manuscripts promptly and for their cooperative efforts and their enthusiastic, yet friendly, discussions at the meeting, we offer our gratitude.

Magog, August 1991

T.P. Hicks
S. Molotchnikoff
T. Ono

List of Financial Supporters

– Natural Sciences and Engineering Research Council of Canada (NSERC)/Conseil de la Recherche en Sciences Naturelles et en Génie du Canada (CRSNG)

– Medical Research Council of Canada (MRC)/Conseil des Recherches Médicales du Canada (CRM)

– Fonds pour la Formation de Chercheurs et l'Aide à la Recherche (FCAR) du Québec

– Nihon Koden (Japan)

– Kurokawa Seisakusho (Japan)

– Université de Montréal

– Département des Sciences biologiques – U. de M.

Contents

Section I – Peripheral Processing

Section II – Sensory Integration in Superior Colliculus

SECTION I

Peripheral Processing

T.P. Hicks, S. Molotchnikoff and T. Ono (Eds.)
Progress in Brain Research, Vol. 95
© 1993 Elsevier Science Publishers B.V. All rights reserved.

CHAPTER 1

The electrical responses of the trout pineal photoreceptors to brief and prolonged illumination

Pier Lorenzo Marchiafava and Claudia Kusmic

Dipartimento di Fisiologia e Biochimica, Università di Pisa, Pisa 56100, Italy

Introduction

The pineal body in lower vertebrates contains photoreceptors which may be identified by their morphological and ultrastructural analogies with retinal receptor cells (Oksche and Hartwig, 1979; Oksche, 1986). The structural framework of the pineal body, however, is different from the retina in that receptor cells may be directly connected to ganglion cells with no interposed cells except for the presence of irregularly distributed, ill-defined interneurons (Dowling and Boycott, 1966; Boycott and Dowling, 1969; Wake et al., 1974; Oksche, 1986).

It is conceivable to attribute special operating properties to pineal photoreceptors when considering that the pineal body is situated on the dorsal side of the animal head thus becoming a permanent target of direct sun rays, contrary to the lateral eyes centered at, or below the horizon. Furthermore, pineal photoreceptors are covered by optically opaque tissue layers which impede any spatial discrimination (Van de Kamer, 1965). The purpose of the present paper was to analyze whether such peculiar attributes are correlated to some differences, with respect to the retina, about either the nature of the pineal receptors photoresponse or their light adaptation properties.

There are already reports of hyperpolarizing photoresponses recorded intracellularly from pineal photoreceptors of lower vertebrates (Hanyu et al., 1969; Tabata et al., 1975; Pu and Dowling, 1981; Nakamura et al., 1986; Meissl and Ekstrom, 1988; Ekstrom and Meissl, 1988; Kusmic et al., 1988). The nature of the phototransduction mechanism underlying the light-induced hyperpolarization is still debated, however, since it may be produced by at least two different mechanisms involving membrane conductance changes of opposite sign (McReynolds and Gorman, 1970).

Here we report experiments of intracellular recording from pineal photoreceptors of the trout. We confirm the hyperpolarizing nature of their photoresponses, similar to retinal photoreceptors, and we present evidence that they are the result of a membrane conductance decrease, as reported in preliminary form by Kusmic and Marchiafava (1989). In addition, 3-isobutyl-1-methylxantine (IBMX), a potent phosphodiesterase inhibitor, alters the photoresponses in accordance with the effects observed by other authors in the amphibian retina (Capovilla et al., 1983). We have found, however, a significant difference between the two photoreceptor types with regard to their light adaptation properties. Thus, pineal photoreceptors produce constant amplitude responses to prolonged illumination, without showing the characteristic, time-dependent membrane potential changes measured in retinal receptor cells under similar circumstances (Fain, 1976).

4

These results will be discussed in relation to the pineal photoreceptor role in the synthesis and secretion of indolamines.

Methods

Preparation

Adult trouts (*Salmo irideus*) weekly supplied by a local nursery were used for the experiments. Immediately after removal from the water, the animals were decapitated by an oblique section cutting the brain at prepontine level. The excised head was firmly pinned to expose the pineal gland after ablation of the parietal bones. The epiphysis is situated superficially over the dorsomedial portion of the diencephalon and appeared as a rounded structure of about $1.5 - 2$ mm diameter, engulfed in an abundant matrix of intensely vascularized ependyma. The gland was isolated from the brain and placed on a small perfusion chamber, continuously supplied with oxygenated fish saline (NaCl 153 mM; KCl 2.6 mM; $CaCl_2$ 2 mM; $MgCl_2$ 0.5 mM; Hepes 20 mM; glucose 10 mM at pH 7.4), at a temperature of about $18°C$. The preparation was mounted on the stage of an inverted microscope and illuminated with either white or monochromatic light of different intensities obtained by interposing interference and neutral density filters along the optic path. The unattenuated irradiance of the light source at the surface of the epiphysis, measured as described in Marchiafava and Torre (1978), was 4.95×10^2 μW/cm^2.

Electrophysiological recording

Glass microelectrodes (Clark Electronic Instruments, 1.2 mm/0.50 mm, outer and inner diameter) with a resistance of about 100 MΩ were used. The electrodes were obtained with a manual Livingston-type puller just prior to the experiments and filled with a solution of 2 M KCl in double-distilled water, occasionally replaced by a solution of 6% (by volume) Procion yellow in 0.1 M LiCl. Microelectrodes were positioned with the aid of a Huxley micromanipulator. The site of the penetration was identified on a high-resolution TV image of

the preparation illuminated by light at 715 nm. Signals were fed into a "Biologic" single-electrode current-voltage-clamp system. The amplified signals were stored on a digital tape recorder and analyzed by DATAC (a data analysis program generously given and installed into an IBM AT computer by Dr. Daniel Bertrand).

Cell identification

Nineteen cells producing photoresponses similar to Fig. 1 were successfully injected with Procion yellow (500 msec at 1/sec, -1 nA, 1 min) during intracellular recording. At the end of the experiment the preparation was fixed in a solution of 4% paraformaldehyde in phosphate buffer (pH 7.4) at $4°C$ for 2 h, than rinsed in buffer, dehydrated, clarified and mounted on a cover slip for direct observation at the fluorescence microscope where micrographs were obtained (Plate I). Photoreceptors were distinguished from other pineal cells by the presence of the outer segment and of varicose end-

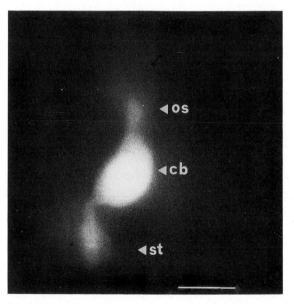

Plate I. Fluorescence micrographs of a typical pineal receptor cell injected intracellularly with Lucifer yellow. The cell looks like a typical retinal cone, buth with a much shorter outer segment. The cell represented here produced the photoresponses shown in Fig. 1A. OS, Outer segment; CB, cell body; ST, synaptic terminal. Calibrating bar is 10 μm.

ings at the two cell extremes, respectively. Other morphological parameters could vary among photoreceptors, such as the terminal ramifications and the total cell size.

Results

The average membrane potential recorded from 36 pineal photoreceptors, dark-adapted for about 15 min was -22 mV ($\pm$ 6 mV S.D.).

Fig. 1A shows a series of responses to white flashes of increasing intensity recorded from an anatomically identified photoreceptor. The responses to low light intensity show a time to peak of about 1.5 sec, a value which rarely drops to less than 0.25 sec, in the case of saturating responses (lower trace). The responses to strong flashes show a slow recovery and an occasional initial sag of small amplitude. The average peak amplitude of saturating responses was 18 mV ($\pm$ 4 mV S.D.).

The time course of the photoresponses could be influenced by increased inner segment conductance during hyperpolarization, as occurs in retinal receptor cells. A simple test to verify such eventuality was to superimpose both the voltage and the current responses to a series of identical flashes, recorded under either current- or voltage-clamp, respectively. In Fig. 1B the two sets of responses have been normalized to their maximal amplitude resulting in a very satisfactory match of their time course, thus denoting negligible membrane non-linearities within the recorded potential range.

The relationship between time to peak and stimulus intensity obtained from ten photoreceptors is illustrated in Fig. 2. It is evident that by decreasing the flash intensity from saturation to threshold, the time to peak shows a six-fold increase, up to more than 1400 msec.

The curve A in Fig. 3 illustrates the relationship between the peak amplitude of the responses to a 50 msec flash and the light intensity. The relation is fitted by the equation:

$$r = I^{0.82}/(I^{0.82} + Is) \qquad (1)$$

where r is the normalized response amplitude, I represents the light intensity and Is half the saturating intensity. The exponent indicates that the dynamic range of pineal photoreceptors spreads over about five log units of light intensity, i.e., a

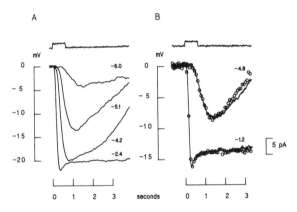

Fig. 1. Intracellular recording from pineal receptor cells of the responses to 650 msec pulses of white light. A. Family of superimposed photoresponses recorded from the cell illustrated in Plate I. Numbers to the right indicate log units of attenuation of the light source. Upper trace indicates time of illumination. Zero in the ordinate represents dark membrane potential. B. The responses of a single morphologically identified pineal photoreceptor to two 650 msec pulses of white light, whose intensity is attenuated as indicated by the numbers to the right (see above). Recordings were obtained in current clamp (continuous line represents membrane voltage) and in voltage clamp (circles represent membrane current). The traces were normalized to their saturation amplitude. The outward current is represented as a downward deflection.

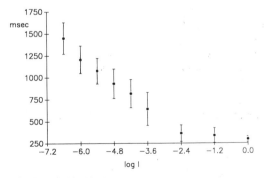

Fig. 2. Relationship between the response time to peak and the intensity of 50 msec flashes, measured in ten cells. Abscissae indicate log unit of attenuation of the light source. Bars are S.D. values.

substantially wider range than for retinal cells (Baylor and Fuortes, 1970; Cervetto et al., 1977; Baylor et al., 1979). Response-intensity relations were also obtained by measuring the voltage response at fixed intervals shorter than the time to peak. The instantaneous relationship obtained at a 250 msec delay from the beginning of a 50 msec flash is shown by curve B in Fig. 3. Here the curve may be fitted by the exponential equation:

$$r = 1 - e^{-kI} \qquad (2)$$

where r is the normalized flash response amplitude, I is the flash intensity and k is a proportionality constant indicating the cell light sensitivity. The discrepancy between the two curves may be interpreted by assuming that at short delays after the flash, such as 250 msec, the photoresponse is due to the superposition of single invariant events, but a process of light adaptation develops later on influencing the kinetics of the photoresponse.

Light adaptation in retinal photoreceptors is

associated with a progressive amplitude decay of the response to sustained illumination. It was thought to be particularly interesting to measure the parameter of light adaptation in pineal photoreceptors owing to their anatomical location which makes them uninterruptedly exposed to solar irradiance.

Fig. 4 illustrates the responses of a photoreceptor to a sustained illumination with two different light intensities. It is evident that the membrane potential maintains the same negative value throughout the whole stimulation, independently of the light intensity used. Such steady responses represent a consistent, specific property of all pineal photoreceptors tested, and indicate that there is no time-dependent change of the cell sensitivity to light other than that occurring at the beginning of the steady illumination. This point was also investigated by superimposing brief flash responses of various intensity to a steady illumination. Fig. 5A shows a family of responses to flashes of increasing intensity presented in the dark. Figs. 5B and C show that the amplitude of the responses to the same series of flashes may be decreased by background illuminations producing hyperpolarization of 5 and 10 mV, respectively. However, the amplitude of the flash responses is not modified by the duration of the

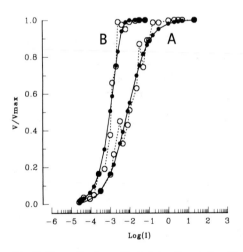

Fig. 3. Normalized amplitude-intensity relationships obtained from 19 cells by recording photoresponses to brief white flashes (50 msec). Empty circles represent the average of the responses to the various light intensities. Black dots indicate the function expressed by Eqns. 1 and 2 relative to curve A and B, respectively. Curve B represents the instantaneous relationship at 250 msec from the onset of illumination. Curve A refers to the peak amplitude. Abscissae indicate logarithmic units of light intensity where zero represents saturation intensity.

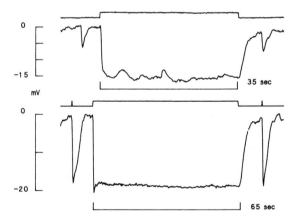

Fig. 4. Pineal photoreceptor responses to brief and prolonged illumination with white light. Lines above the traces indicate time of illumination. Light was attenuated by 4.8 and 3.6 log units for the upper and lower responses, respectively. Note that the steady responses maintain the same amplitude throughout.

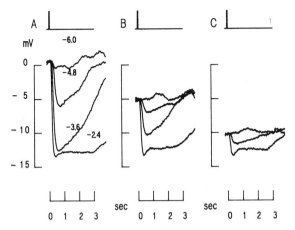

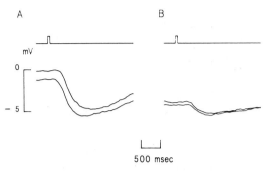

Fig. 5. Series of superimposed responses of a pineal receptor cell to brief flashes of white light in the dark and during background illumination. The background light produces a steady hyperpolarization (B and C) and a progressive amplitude reduction of the test flash photoresponses in comparison to the responses in the dark (A). In B and C the background light was attenuated by 7.2 and 6.0 log units, respectively. The upper lines indicate the time of illumination. The attenuation of the light source was 6.0, 4.8, 3.6 and 2.4 log units in order for the responses shown in A, B and C, from top to bottom. Zero in the voltage calibration indicates membrane potential in the dark.

Fig. 6. Brief flash responses in the dark and superimposed at various times from the beginning of a sustained illumination. Traces are averages of two responses each. A. Responses to a 50 msec flash delivering 17.5 photons/μm^2 per second at 521 nm before and after 60 sec of sustained background illumination. B. The average responses to the same test flash recorded at 4 and 7 sec (lower trace) and at 55 and 58 sec (upper trace), respectively, after the beginning of a continuous illumination with 5.82×10^{-2} photons/μm^2 per second. Note that time of background illumination does not affect the test response.

background illumination (Fig. 6), contrary to what has been observed by other authors in retinal receptor cells whose flash responses recover to about 40% of the dark value within 10 – 20 sec after the onset of the background (Fain, 1976).

The relationship between the peak amplitude of the responses to flashes of increasing intensity and the background light intensity are plotted in the diagram of Fig. 7. Here it is evident that the background-induced incremental threshold is not associated with variations of the saturating intensity, whereby the range of intensities producing flash responses is gradually compressed. By further increasing the background intensity (– 3.6) the cell becomes totally unresponsive (Fig. 7, lower curve).

The kinetics of the responses to a given flash intensity were examined under various backgrounds, as illustrated in Fig. 8. The photoresponses attenuated by the background (Fig. 8A, the two uppermost traces) can be multiplied by their respective

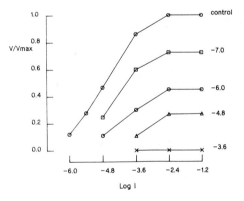

Fig. 7. The average stimulus-response relationship obtained from two pineal photoreceptors in the dark and during background illumination. The ordinate represents the normalized amplitude of the flash responses, as measured from the background-induced potential level. The photoresponses of each cell were normalized to their maximal response amplitude recorded in the dark. The upper curve was obtained with dark background; the background light intensity used to obtain each of the lower curves is indicated by the numbers to the right, representing log units of attenuation of the light source. White light has been used for both flash and background illumination. Note that response saturation may be reached by flashes of similar intensity, independently of the background.

attenuation factors $(V_{\text{peak(background)}}/V_{\text{peak(dark)}})$ to produce curves which satisfactorily match the rising phase of the response in the dark (Fig. 8B), but not the depolarizing phase which is clearly faster.

Spectral and absolute sensitivity

The action spectrum obtained from 12 photoreceptors shows two populations of cells characterized by peak sensitivity at ca. 495 and 521 nm, respectively (Fig. 9). Photoresponses to different wavelengths and light intensity, recorded from the same receptor cell could be matched by their amplitude and time course, thus showing univariance with respect to the number of photons, independently of the wavelength (Fig. 10).

The absolute sensitivity to dim light flashes of monochromatic light at the peak of the spectrum obtained from 12 cells is shown in Table I. The average value, derived from about 1 mV criterion responses is 202 ($\pm$ 96 S.D.) μV photon^{-1} μm^2.

It is interesting to note that these values are of the same order of magnitude as those obtained from dissociated retinal cone cells of another teleost (Marchiafava, 1985). Unfortunately there is no in-

formation about the absolute sensitivity of retinal rod cells in teleosts to compare with the present results.

Membrane properties

The passive properties of the photoreceptor membrane were analyzed by recording the voltage

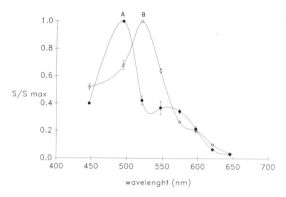

Fig. 9. The average action spectra obtained from 12 pineal photoreceptors. Curve A represents eight cells with maximal sensitivity at 495 nm; Curve B refers to four cells peaking at 520 nm. Bars indicate standard deviation. The curves were derived from families of $V/\log I$ functions obtained with a 50 msec monochromatic illumination of the isolated epiphysis every 6 sec and not exceeding $1.2 - 1.8$ logarithmic units above threshold. Ordinate represents relative quantum sensitivity obtained by dividing the amplitude of a criterion response, not exceeding 3 mV, by the number of photons falling on the pineal body.

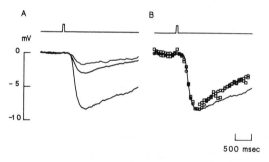

Fig. 8. The effect of background light on the amplitude and time course of the flash responses. A. Superimposed responses to a 50 msec flash delivering 140.6 photons/μm^2 per second at 521 nm given in the dark (lower trace) and during background illumination with 9.3×10^{-1} photons/μm^2 per second (middle trace) and with 58 photons/μm^2 per second (upper trace). The membrane potential just prior to the upper two photoresponses has been shifted to zero level for the sake of comparison. B. Matching the response in the dark with those obtained with two backgrounds (empty squares and circles, respectively), each multiplied by its attenuation factor ($V_{\text{peak(background)}}/V_{\text{peak(dark)}}$. Upper line indicates time of flash illumination.

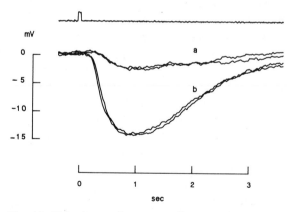

Fig. 10. Univariance of receptor cell responses to 50 msec monochromatic flashes. (a) and (b) represent two sets of superimposed responses to 521 and 597 μm. In (a), the stimulus flux was 15.4 and 41.6 photons/μm^2, in (b) it was 245 and 665 photons/μm^2, for the two wavelengths, respectively.

TABLE I

Absolute and peak spectral sensitivity of pineal photoreceptors

Cell		Sensitivity (μV photon^{-1} μm^2)	Wavelength (nm)
Type A	1	266	495
	2	140	495
	3	200	495
	4	80	495
	5	133	495
	6	223	495
	7	95	495
	8	111	495
Type B	9	360	521
	10	170	521
	11	273	521
	12	380	521

response to brief pulses of constant current injected in the dark and during illumination (Fig. 11A). The current-induced voltage drops in the dark (within ± 18 mV from the resting potential) indicate a membrane resistance of about 530 MΩ, which increases to 566 MΩ during illumination with about half saturating light intensity. The membrane time constant is about 1.09 msec; this value, however, may be significantly contaminated by errors due to the high electrode impedance.

To reduce the possibility that occasional voltage-dependent membrane rectification may contribute to the measured resistance changes during illumination, the photoresponses were recorded under voltage clamp. The peak photocurrent values measured (88 pA) were comparable to those recorded from retinal receptor cells (Baylor et al., 1979).

The photocurrents elicited by flashes of moderate intensity (about 1.2 log units above threshold) were recorded at several values of membrane holding potentials. The current values obtained by subtracting the peak photocurrent from the dark value preceding the test flash are plotted on the graph shown in Fig. 11B. Here the slope conductance shows a significant decrease, corresponding to a conductance decrease of about 10% of the absolute

dark value. The extrapolated value of membrane potential at which the current reversed was around 60 mV above dark potential. These results are in good agreement with those obtained during current clamp and are qualitatively similar to those obtained from retinal photoreceptors (Toyoda et al., 1969; Baylor and Fuortes, 1970).

The effect of inhibiting phosphodiesterase activity

The membrane conductance decrease observed during the photoresponse suggests the possibility of further analogies between pineal and retinal receptor cells with regard to the mechanism controlling the permeability changes. In retinal rod cells, the addition of 3-isobutyl-1-methylxantine (IBMX), a phosphodiesterase activity inhibitor, is known to increase the intracellular concentration of cGMP which in turn leads to the opening of a greater

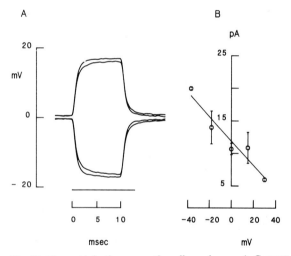

Fig. 11. Current injection across the cell membrane. A. Current clamp recording. The voltage responses to pulses of constant current (± 3 × 10^{-11}A) delivered in the dark (inner traces) and during illumination (outer traces). Dark and light membrane potentials are artificially superimposed to better pronounce the amplitude differences. B. Voltage clamp. I/V relationship at various levels of holding potentials (zero in the abscissa represents dark resting potential). The points represent the average peak photocurrents, following a moderate intensity flash, minus the dark current indicated by zero in the ordinate. The slope of the regression line represents a membrane conductance decrease at the peak of the photoresponse of about 187 pS. The peak photocurrent, averaged from four dark-adapted photoreceptors was 16 (± 8 S.D.) pA.

number of membrane channels in the dark (Fesenko et al., 1985; Zimmerman and Baylor, 1986).

To check whether a similar model is also compatible with the electrical properties of pineal receptor cells, 50 μM of IBMX were added to the perfusate.

About 120 sec after the addition of IBMX, the dark level of membrane potential depolarized by about 6 mV and the photoresponses to dim and intermediate intensities showed an approximately two-fold increase in amplitude (Fig. 12B) with respect to the control in normal saline (Fig. 12A). In addition, IBMX may increase the time of the responses to dim flashes to peak by up to about 25% (Fig. 12D), but this effect disappears by increasing the flash intensity.

Discussion

General considerations

In this work we have examined some electrical

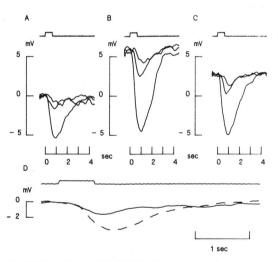

Fig. 12. The effect of IBMX (50 μM) on the membrane potential in the dark and during the photoresponses. A. Superimposed responses to flashes attenuated by 6.6, 6.0 and 4.8 log units before the addition of IBMX to the perfusion medium. B. Three minutes after the addition of IBMX. C. Ten minutes after wash out. Zero in the ordinate represents dark membrane potential before the addition of IBMX. D. The effect of IBMX (50 μM) on the time course and the amplitude of the responses to dim flash intensity (attenuation was 6.6 log units). The response in normal saline is indicated by the continuous line, the dashed line represents the response 2 min after the addition of 50 μm IBMX.

properties of pineal photoreceptors in the dark and during illumination. Our results are qualitatively similar to those obtained by others from retinal receptor cells (Baylor and Fuortes, 1970; Cervetto et al., 1977; see Attwell, 1986), with the exception of the light-adaptive behavior which in pineal cells possesses specific features which may be relevant to their secretory function (see below).

A specific property of the pineal cell photoresponses consists of a relatively long time to peak which, in the case of very dim flashes may be as long as 1500 msec, i.e., about 1150 msec longer than an equivalent retinal rod response (Cervetto et al., 1977) or about 1350 msec longer than in retinal cone cells (Baylor and Hodgkin, 1974). The minimal pineal time to peak is about 270 msec compared to 50 msec of the retinal rod saturated responses.

The slow kinetics of the pineal photoresponses allow poor temporal resolution of light stimuli with respect to the retinal receptor cells. Indeed, as will be discussed later, pineal photoreceptors are provided with other special properties which make them adequate to regulate the endogenous hormonal synthesis and secretion in relation to the slow varying levels of daily luminance.

Spectral and absolute sensitivity

Two different action spectra have been found peaking at about 495 and 521 nm, as expected by the presence of the same chromophores, 11-cis-retinal and 11-cis-3-dehydroretinal, compared to the trout retina (Tabata et al., 1985) whose photoreceptor pigments absorb maximally at 505 and 527 nm (Bridges, 1956; Muntz and Beatty, 1965). The action spectrum of pineal photoreceptors in vivo, however, should be influenced by the supraepiphyseal tissues whose absorbance decreases progressively from 450 to 650 nm (Hartwig and van Veen, 1979). In this respect, the chromatic filtering of hemoglobin at 530 nm (Rumen and Chance, 1969) is also relevant, owing to the dense vascularization of the pineal gland. A definite answer about the relative efficacy of these two factors to determine the actual spectrum of pineal photoreceptors could come from recording in vivo.

Membrane properties

The observed light-induced membrane conductance decrease suggests that hyperpolarization of pineal response is a consequence of a decrease in Na^+ permeability, as in the case of retinal photoreceptors (Toyoda et al., 1969; Baylor and Fuortes, 1970; Baylor et al., 1979). This hypothesis is supported by a reversal potential of about 30 mV, and by the disappearance of the photoreceptor response in a Na^+-free solution (Samejima and Morita, 1988).

The effects observed by inhibiting phosphodiesterase activity are qualitatively comparable to those observed in the retina of other species (Capovilla et al., 1983). Thus the hypothesis of a cyclic nucleotide controlling plasma membrane permeability to Na ions (Fesenko et al., 1985; Haynes et al., 1986; Lamb et al., 1986; see Stryer, 1986) is also applicable to pineal photoreceptors.

Light adaptation

The fact that the relation between the peak amplitude response and the flash intensity is fitted by a modified Michaelis-Menten equation indicates that the receptor cell is undergoing a process of light adaptation (see for a discussion Nakatani et al., 1991). The adaptive mechanism, however, is activated not earlier than 250 msec after the flash onset, since the instantaneous amplitude-intensity relationship within such interval may be fitted by Eqn. 2, typically describing non-adaptive behavior. The 86% decrease of the response time to peak (Fig. 2), obtained by increasing a dim flash intensity to saturation level, is a further evidence in support of the existence of an adaptive process. Thus, the light adaptation properties revealed by pineal photoresponses to brief flashes are qualitatively similar to those of retinal receptors which light adapt within a time interval shorter than the time to peak (Nakatani et al., 1991).

Pineal photoreceptors, however, are clearly distinguishable from the retinal receptor cells by their steady responses to prolonged illumination, and by the changes induced upon superimposed flash responses. A consequence of such property is that the saturating light intensity for pineal photoreceptors does not vary with time of illumination but it remains locked to its dark value, whereby superimposed brief flash responses are solely depressed as an hyperbolic function of the background intensity. As a result the pineal receptor dynamic range is gradually compressed, as shown in Fig. 7.

This latter result contrasts with the observed recovery of both the membrane potential and the superimposed flash responses occurring in light-adapted retinal receptor cells (Baylor and Hodgkin, 1974; Fain, 1976), whereby these cells can adjust over an additional 3 log units with respect to the dark value. In this respect, the pineal photoreceptor at least partially compensates by showing a dark dynamic range by about 2.4 log units broader than the average retinal receptor cell (Fain and Dowling, 1973; Baylor and Hodgkin, 1973; Cervetto et al., 1977).

The present results may be interpreted by assuming a similar light-adaptive mechanism for both pineal and retinal receptor cells. There are strong evidences in the retina that it consists of a calcium-dependent regulation of cytosolic levels of cyclic GMP (McNaughton et al., 1986; Torre et al., 1986; Fain et al., 1989; Matthews et al., 1990). In pineal photoreceptors, however, one can postulate the existence of an intracellular calcium concentration lower than in the retina or, alternatively, a lower guanilate cyclase affinity for Ca. Thus the drop of Ca concentration obtained at the peak of the responses to even very low light intensity may be sufficient, by itself, to set the cyclase activity to a maximal level which can not be further enhanced by any subsequent decrease of calcium concentration such as that, for instance, produced during prolonged illumination by the Na-Ca exchanger (Hodgkin et al., 1987; Lagnado et al., 1988).

The evidence that pineal receptors maintain a constant potential during steady illumination may have a relevant significance in view of the fact that pineal photoreceptors both synthetize and secrete indolamines, at the level of the inner segment by means of a Ca-dependent mechanism (Elks et al., 1979; Ekstrom and Meissl, 1990). By analogy with the nerve cells, the Ca^{2+} entry should be regulated by the cell membrane potential (Carbone and Lux, 1984). Thus, a constant relationship between the membrane potential and the actual level of light irradiance allows the pineal photoreceptors to maintain the seric melatonin level in a steady proportion with the intensity of the ambient illumination.

Summary and conclusions

Intracellular recordings from 103 photoreceptors in the excised pineal body of adult trouts were obtained by using single electrode current- and voltage-clamp techniques.

The photoresponses to brief flashes showed the same polarity but a slower time course than those previously recorded from retinal photoreceptors of lower vertebrates. Pineal photoreceptors showed spectral sensitivity peaks at about 495 and 521 nm and absolute sensitivity comparable to retinal cone cells of the same species.

The photoreceptor membrane conductance, measured under voltage clamp during moderate illumination was about 10% lower than in the dark, and the extrapolated reversal potential of the response was at 60 mV above the dark membrane potential.

The addition of 3-isobutyl-1-methylxantine (IBMX) to the perfusate was followed by a receptor depolarization in the dark and by a slow-down of the response kinetic.

Pineal receptor cells produce constant amplitude responses during steady illumination, without displaying the delayed slow depolarization typically associated with light adaptation of retinal photoreceptors.

Photoresponses to brief flashes superimposed on a steady illumination are decreased in amplitude by an amount directly related to the background intensity. Increase of the background intensity leads to threshold increments without significant changes of the saturation intensity, resulting in a gradual compression of the cell dynamic range.

These results were discussed relative to light adaptation in retinal photoreceptors. The conclusion can be drawn that the response properties of pineal photoreceptors during steady illumination are part of an unknown, self-regulating mechanism to lock the rate of metabolism and secretion of indolamines to the absolute level of diurnal light.

References

Attwell, D. (1986) Ionic channels and signal processing in the outer retina. *J. Exp. Physiol.,* 71: 497 – 536.

Baylor, D.A. and Fuortes, M.G.F. (1970) Electrical responses of single cones in the retina of turtle. *J. Physiol. (Lond.),* 207: 77 – 92.

Baylor, D.A. and Hodgkin, A.L. (1973) Detection and resolution of visual stimuli by turtle photoreceptors. *J. Physiol. (Lond.),* 234: 163 – 198.

Baylor, D.A. and Hodgkin, A.L. (1974) Changes in the time scale and sensitivity in turtle photoreceptors. *J. Physiol. (Lond.),* 242: 729 – 758.

Baylor, D.A., Lamb, T.D. and Yau, K.W. (1979) The membrane current of single rod outer segments. *J. Physiol. (Lond.),* 288: 589 – 611.

Boycott, B.B. and Dowling, J.E. (1969) Organization of the primate retina: light microscopy. *Philos. Trans. R. Soc. Lond. (Biol.),* 255: 109 – 184.

Bridges, C.D.B. (1956) The visual pigment of the rainbow trout (*Salmo Irideus*). *J. Physiol. (Lond.),* 134: 620 – 629.

Capovilla, M., Cervetto, L. and Torre, V. (1983) The effect of phosphodiesterase inhibitors on the electrical activity of the toad rods. *J. Physiol. (Lond.),* 343: 277 – 294.

Carbone, E. and Lux, H.D. (1984) A low voltage-activated calcium conductance in embryonic chick sensory neurons. *Biophys. J.,* 46: 413 – 418.

Cervetto, L., Pasino, E. and Torre, V. (1977) Electrical responses of rods in the retina of *Bufo. J. Physiol. (Lond.),* 267: 17 – 51.

Dowling, J.E. and Boycott, B.B. (1966) Organization of the primate retina: electron microscopy. *Proc. R. Soc. Lond. (Biol.),* 166: 80 – 111.

Ekstrom, P. and Meissl, H. (1988) Intracellular staining of physiologically identified photoreceptor cells and hyperpolarizing interneurons in the teleost pineal organ. *Neuroscience,* 25: 1061 – 1070.

Ekstrom, P. and Meissl, H. (1990) Electron microscopic analysis of S-antigen and serotonin-immunoreactive neural and sensory elements in the photosensory pineal organ of the salmon. *J. Comp. Neurol.,* 292: 73 – 82.

Elks, M.L., Youngblood, W.W. and Kizer, J.S. (1979) Synthesis and release of serotonin by brain slices: effect of ionic manipulations and cationic ionophores. *Brain Res.,* 172: 461 – 469.

Fain, G.L. (1976) Sensitivity of toad rods: dependence on wavelength and background illumination. *J. Physiol. (Lond.), 261:* 71 – 101.

Fain, G.L. and Dowling, J.E. (1973) Intracelluar recordings from single rods and cones in the mudpuppy retina. *Science,* 180: 1178 – 1181.

Fain, G.L., Lamb, T.D., Matthews, H.R. and Murphy, R.L.W. (1989) Cytoplasmic calcium as the messenger for light adaptation in salamander rods. *J. Physiol. (Lond.),* 416: 215 – 243.

Fesenko, E.E., Kolensnikov, S.S. and Lyubarsky, A.L. (1985) Induction by cyclic GMP of cation conductance in plasma membrane of retinal rod outer segment. *Nature,* 313: 310 – 313.

Hanyu, I., Niwa, H. and Tamura, T. (1969) A slow potential from the epiphysis cerebri of fishes. *Vision Res.,* 9: 621 – 623.

Hartwig, H.G. and Van Veen, T. (1979) Spectral characteristics of visible radiation penetrating into the brain and stimulating extraretinal photoreceptors. *J. Comp. Physiol. A,* 130: 277 – 282.

Haynes, L.W., Kay, A.R. and Yau, K.W. (1986) Single cyclic GMP-activated channel activity in excised patches of rod outer segment membranes. *Nature,* 321: 66 – 70.

Hodgkin, A.L., McNoughton, P.A. and Nunn, B.J. (1987) Measurement of sodium-calcium exchange in salamander rods. *J. Physiol. (Lond.),* 391: 347 – 370.

Kusmic, C. and Marchiafava, P.L. (1989) Membrane resistance properties of pineal photoreceptors in the trout. *Exp. Biol.,* 48: 183 – 186.

Kusmic, C., Marchiafava, P.L. and Strettoi, E. (1988) A new type of photoresponse by cells of the isolated trout pineal body. *J. Physiol. (Lond.),* 407: 84P.

Lagnado, L., Cervetto, L. and McNaughton, P.A. (1988) Ion transport by the Na-Ca exchange in isolated rod outer segments. *Proc. Natl. Acad. Sci. U.S.A.,* 85: 4548 – 4552.

Lamb, T.D., Matthews, H.R. and Torre, V. (1986) Incorporation of calcium buffers into salamander retinal rods: a rejection of the calcium theory of phototransduction. *J. Physiol. (Lond.),* 372: 315 – 349.

Marchiafava, P.L. (1985) Cell coupling in doubles cones of the fish retina. *Proc. R. Soc. Lond. (Biol.),* 226: 211 – 215.

Marchiafava, P.L. and Torre, V. (1978) The responses of amacrine cells to light and intracellularly applied currents. *J. Physiol. (Lond.),* 276: 83 – 102.

Matthews, H.R., Fain, G.L., Murphy, R.L.W. and Lamb, T.D. (1990) Light adaptation in cone photoreceptors of the salamander: a role for cytoplasmic calcium. *J. Physiol. (Lond.),* 420: 447 – 469.

McNaughton, P.A., Cervetto, L. and Nunn, B.J. (1986) Measurement of the intracellular calcium concentration in salamander rods. *Nature,* 322: 261 – 263.

McReynolds, J.S. and Gorman, A.L. (1970) Membrane conductance and spectral sensitivity of Pecten photoreceptors. *J. Gen. Physiol.,* 56: 392 – 406.

Meissl, H. and Ekstrom, P. (1988) Photoreceptor responses to light in the isolated pineal organ of the trout, *Salmo gairdneri. Neuroscience,* 25: 1071 – 1076.

Muntz, F.W. and Beatty, D.D. (1965) A critical analysis of the visual pigment of salmon and trout. *Vision Res.,* 5: 1 – 17.

Nakamura, T., Thiele, G. and Meissl, H. (1986) Intracellular responses from the photosensitive pineal organ of the teleost, *Phoxinus phoxinus. J. Comp. Physiol. A,* 159: 325 – 330.

Nakatani, K., Tamura, T. and Yau, K.W. (1991) Light adaptation in retinal rods of the rabbit and two other non-primate mammals. *J. Gen. Physiol.,* 97: 413 – 435.

Oksche, A. (1986) Historical perspectives of photoneuroendocrine systems. In: P.J. O'Brein and D.C. Klein (Eds.), *Pineal and Retinal Relationships,* Academic Press, New York, 114 pp.

Oksche, A. and Hartwig, H.G. (1979) Pineal sense organs – components of photoneuroendocrine systems. *Prog. Brain Res.,* 52: 113 – 130.

Pu, G.A. and Dowling, J.E. (1981) Anatomical and physiological characteristics of pineal photoreceptor cells in the larval lamprey, *Petromyzon marinus. J. Neurophysiol.,* 46: 1018 – 1038.

Rumen, N.M. and Chance, B. (1969) A correlation between spin states and light absorption spectra of ferric lamprey hemoglobin at room and low temperature. *Biochim. Biophys. Acta,* 175: 242 – 247.

Samejima, M. and Morita, Y. (1988) External sodium ions are required for light response in pineal photoreceptors. *Vision Res.,* 28: 251 – 258.

Stryer, L. (1986) Cyclic GMP cascade of vision. *Annu. Rev. Neurosci.,* 9: 87 – 119.

Tabata, M., Tamura, T. and Niwa, H. (1975) Origin of the slow potential in the pineal organ of the rainbow trout. *Vision Res.,* 15: 737 – 740.

Tabata, M., Susuki, T. and Niwa, H. (1985) Chromophores in the extraretinal photoreceptors (pineal organ) of teleosts. *Brain Res.,* 338: 173 – 176.

Torre, V., Matthews, H.R. and Lamb, T.D. (1986) Role of calcium in regulating the cyclic GMP cascade of phototransduction in retinal rods. *Proc. Natl. Acad. Sci. U.S.A.,* 83: 7109 – 7113.

Toyoda, J., Nosaki, H. and Tomita, T. (1969) Light-induced resistance changes in single photoreceptors of *Necturus* and *Gekko. Vision Res.,* 9: 453 – 463.

Van De Kamer, J.C. (1965) Histological structure and cytology of the pineal complex in fishes, amphibians and reptiles. *Prog. Brain Res.,* 10: 30 – 48.

Wake, K., Ueck, M. and Oksche, A. (1974) Acetylcholinesterase-containing nerve cells in the pineal complex and subcommissural area of the frogs. *Cell Tissue Res.,* 154: 423 – 442.

Zimmerman, A.L. and Baylor, D.A. (1986) Cyclic GMP-sensitive conductance of retinal rods consists of aqueous pores. *Nature,* 321: 70 – 72.

T.P. Hicks, S. Molotchnikoff and T. Ono (Eds.)
Progress in Brain Research, Vol. 95
© 1993 Elsevier Science Publishers B.V. All rights reserved.

CHAPTER 2

Light sensitivity, adaptation and saturation in mammalian rods

Gian Carlo Demontis, Silvia Bisti and Luigi Cervetto

Istituto Policattedra di Discipline Biologiche, Università di Pisa, Istituto di Neurofisiologia C.N.R, Pisa, Italy

Introduction

The vertebrate visual system performs with remarkable efficiency over a range of light intensities exceeding 10 log units. The same system which in dark-adapted conditions detects a few photons scattered over a time interval of about 1 sec, is not overloaded by a radiant flux delivering up to billions of photons per second. This stunning flexibility is usually referred to as light-adaptation.

Although light-adaptation most likely reflects the existence of efficiently tuned gain control mechanisms operating at more than one level in the visual system (Shapley and Enroth-Cugell, 1984; Green, 1986), there is little doubt that a good deal of adaptation is laid out in photoreceptors (Fain, 1976; Tamura et al. 1989; Matthews, 1991; Nakatani et al., 1991).

The presence in the same retina of two different classes of receptors (rods and cones) with clear-cut differences in temporal and spatial summation contributes to an expansion of the dynamic range of the visual system (see Barlow, 1972). The absolute sensitivity to incident light of optimum wavelength of rods exceeds that of cones about two orders of magnitude (Lasansky and Marchiafava, 1974; see also Lamb and Pugh, 1990). Conversely, bright lights optimal for cone stimulation induce saturation in rods. For this reason it is generally believed that rods contribute little to vision at high luminance levels (Aguilar and Stiles, 1954).

Previous work on amphibian rods (Cervetto et al., 1985) has shown that the loss of responsiveness induced by saturating lights may partially recover with time , while the saturating conditions are kept unchanged. A similar phenomenon has also been observed psychophysically in human subjects (Adelson, 1982). On this account one may suppose that the extent of the rod contribution to vision is larger than previously believed.

In this paper we analyze the absolute sensitivity, background desensitization and saturation in guinea-pig rods. The principal purpose of this study is to establish the extent and the conditions for rod adaptation in mammals and compare them with those of lower vertebrates. In agreement with a recent report (Matthews, 1991), we find that guinea-pig rods possess adaptation properties qualitatively similar to those of amphibian rods. We also find that light-adapted guinea-pig rods may efficiently signal light changes up to background levels that for a human subject would be equivalent to ambient illuminations of over 10^3 candles (cd)/m^2. Considering that a dark-adapted rod may generate a detectable response to the absorption of a few photons, the range of light intensity over which a single rod may efficiently contribute to vision covers more than 4 log units.

Methods

Preparation and recording

Membrane current was recorded by means of suction electrodes (see Baylor et al., 1979) from either isolated rods of salamander (*Ambystoma tigrinum*) or rod outer segments attached to small pieces of chopped retinae of guinea pig (*Cavia cobaya*). Animals were dark adapted for more than 2 h before the experiment. The eyes were removed from guinea pig under deep anesthesia with tiopenthal (40 mg/kg of body wt.) and ketamine (150 mg/kg). The preparation was then placed in a temperature-regulated chamber and perfused with an oxygenated and buffered (pH = 7.6) solution whose composition (in mM) was: NaCl, 140; KCl, 3.6; MgCl$_2$, 2.4; CaCl$_2$, 1.2; hepes, 5; Na-ascorbate, 0.5; glucose, 10) . Both dissection and search for a light responsive cell were carried out under infrared illumination (> 900 nm) with the aid of an infrared converter. During the sensitivity measurements the infrared beam was turned off. The temperature of the bath could be set at different values ranging from room temperature (16° − 20°) to 37°C. The current recording system was essentially as described in previous papers (see for instance Cervetto et al., 1985).

Light stimuli

The light source was a tungsten halogen lamp. Light from the source was split into two independent beams both of which passed through a condenser, shutter, collimator and a system of narrowband-width interference filters and of calibrated neutral density filters. The image of a variable field aperture was focused directly on the outer segment of rods. One of the two beams was used to obtain variable intensity test flashes whose duration was 20 msec while the second beam provided the steady background illumination. The wavelength was 510 nm for the test flash and 490 nm for the constant background. The filter transmittance was measured with a silicon photodiode with a flat spectral response in the range between 450 and 960 nm (7% error). The spectral energy distribution of the source was then derived and the irradiance values converted in photons/μm^2 per flash and photons/μm^2 per second for the test flash and the background respectively.

Definitions

Absolute sensitivity

The absolute sensitivity or quantum sensitivity ($_dS_f$) was measured in darkness as the peak amplitude elicited by the absorption of a single photon which produces isomerization of a single pigment molecule (*Rh**). It is expressed in pico amperes (pA)/*Rh**. As in Baylor et al. (1979) the number of *Rh** per rod brought about by a test flash was obtained by assuming an average value for the collecting area (A) of 20 μm^2 in salamander rods and of 0.95 μm^2 in guinea pig rods. These values were obtained from the outer segment dimensions (measured during the experiment) and from a value of pigment density of 0.016 μm (Harosi, 1975) by the relation:

$$A = \frac{\pi \, d^2 L}{4} \, Q_{Rh*} f \times 2.303a \qquad (1)$$

where *d* is the diameter of the outer segment, *L* is its length, *f* a factor which expresses the imperfect absorption of unpolarized light incident normally to the long axis of the outer segment (assumed value 0.5), Q_{Rh*} the quantum efficiency of isomerization and *a* the specific axial density of the pigment. An independent way to calculate the light effectively absorbed by a rod was to estimate the average number of elementary responses elicited by single photon absorptions during a series of presentations of dim flashes of light. The collecting area is then given by the ratio of the mean number of *Rh** observed (*N*) to the flash intensity in photons per unit area (*I*). The value of *N* was calculated assuming that, with dim flashes, the probability of photon absorption is predicted by a Poisson distribution (see Baylor et al., 1984). The average value obtained by this method in guinea pig is *A* = 1.06, in excellent agreement with *A* = 0.95 obtained from Eqn. 1.

Incremental flash sensitivity

In the presence of a steady background the effect of a single Rh^* is reduced: the sensitivity measured in these conditions is called flash sensitivity (S_f). The desensitizing effect of background illumination is usually expressed in the normalized form as the incremental flash sensitivity ($S_f/{}_dS_f$). Over a certain range of intensity the relation between increment flash sensitivity and background illumination is described by the Weber-Fechner function:

$$S_f/{}_dS_f = \frac{1}{1 + I/I_h} \qquad (2)$$

where I_h is the background intensity in photons/μm^2 per second that halves the flash sensitivity.

Operative sensitivity

The absolute sensitivity and flash sensitivity are both defined for a narrow range of test flashes, when the correspondent response amplitude is linearly related to the intensity of the stimulus. In this study we shall use the term operative sensitivity in a broader sense than absolute and flash sensitivity, such as to include conditions in which linearity does not apply. For defining the operative sensitivity we consider the equation used by Lamb et al. (1981) to describe the response-intensity relation in amphibian rods:

$$\Delta J/\Delta J_{max} = 1 - e^{-KI} \qquad (3)$$

where I is the light intensity in photons/μm^2 per flash and K a constant with the dimensions of μm^2/photon. The physical meaning of the constant K corresponds to the effective collecting area of an elementary rod segment of length δ in which the dark current is completely suppressed by one photon. From Baylor et al. (1984) $\delta = L \times K/A$, where L is the total length of the outer segment and A the collecting area. Therefore, a relatively high value of the length δ corresponds to a relatively high efficiency of light in suppressing dark current. Here we define

operative sensitivity as the reciprocal of the light intensity (in photons/μm^2) necessary to produce a half saturating response. The half saturating intensity $I_{\frac{1}{2}}$ is an experimental quantity related to δ by:

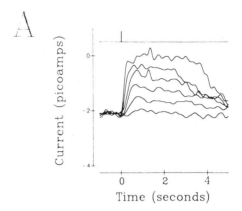

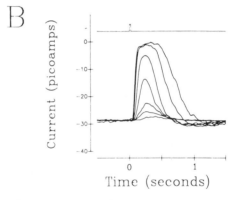

Fig. 1. *A.* Current response of a guinea-pig rod to flashes (20 msec duration; 500 nm wavelength) of increasing intensity (in photons/μm^2 per flash: 0.79; 1.95; 6.01; 9.75; 47.77; 190.19 respectively) at room temperature (17°C). Absolute sensitivity: 0.49 pA. Operative sensitivity: 0.072 photons$^{-1} \cdot \mu$m^2 per flash. Each trace is the average of 18, 36, 23, 13, 12 or 6 responses. The dim flash (1.95 photons/μm^2) failed to produce a detectable response 13 times on 36 presentations (36%), a value slightly larger than that predicted by the Poisson distribution (28%). *B.* Current response from a different rod obtained from the same retina as the rod in *A* at a temperature of 35°C. Flash intensity in photons/μm^2: 0.79; 3.72; 9.75; 47.77; 190.19; 813.16; 2643.5). Absolute sensitivity: 0.72 pA. Operative sensitivity: 0.026 photons$^{-1} \cdot \mu$m^2 per flash. The 11 failures upon 18 presentations of a dim flash (0.79 photons/μm^2) correspond to a value of 61%, again somewhat larger than that predicted by a Poisson distribution (45%). This deviation as well as that of the rod in *A* are likely due to the small sample size.

18

$$I_{\frac{1}{2}} = \frac{ln\ 2}{A \cdot \delta}\ L \qquad (4)$$

The quantity $I_{\frac{1}{2}}$ affects the position of the response-intensity function on the x-axis. Specifically, the larger the value of the half-saturating intensity the more the curve is shifted to the right. Shifts of the response-intensity curves to the right correspond to a decrease in the operative sensitivity.

Note that the dimensions of both absolute and flash sensitivity are a current per Rh^* while the dimensions of the operative sensitivity are photons$^{-1} \cdot \mu m^2$.

Results

Sensitivity: temperature dependence

Current responses to flashes of increasing intensity recorded at 17°C (A) and 35°C (B) from two distinct rods of guinea pig are illustrated in Fig. 1. At room temperature the dark current (J_D) is low and the absolute size of the transient suppression (ΔJ or photoresponse) caused by the flash is correspondingly small. When temperature is raised so as to approach the normal physiological value, the dark current increases and the time course of the photoresponse accelerates. The temperature dependence (Q_{10}) of the dark current was investigated in five rods in the interval $17° - 35°C$. The value of the Q_{10} varies from 1.8 to 2.6 which corresponds to an activation energy ranging from 10.5 to 17.2 kcal/mol.

In the rods of Fig. 1 the photoresponse produced by a single Rh^* was estimated to be 0.49 pA at 17°C and 0.72 pA at 35°C (see legend of Fig. 1 for details). Considering, however, that on average the maximal current suppression induced by a bright flash at 35°C exceeds by more than three times the maximal suppression obtained at 17°C, the fractional change of current ($\Delta J / J_D$) induced by a single Rh^* at low temperature is about two times larger than at high temperature. In addition, it is seen that the half saturating intensity of light ($I_{\frac{1}{2}}$) is more than two times larger at the highest temperature, equivalent to a two-fold decrease in the operative sensitivity.

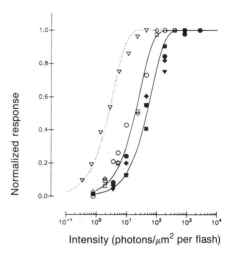

Fig. 2. Normalized amplitude of the current suppression (ΔJ) as a function of the intensity in rods of guinea-pig at room temperature (open symbols, three rods) and at body temperature (filled symbols, four rods). The amplitude was measured at fixed times after the flash presentation (150 msec for data at body temperature and 350 msec at room temperature). Data from a salamander rod at room temperature are indicated by open triangles (measured at the peak of response). The curves drawn through the experimental measures were calculated from Eqn. 2 with a K of 0.0364 at room temperature and 0.01505 at body temperature in guinea pig rods and of 0.274 μm^2/photon per flash at room temperature in the salamander rod. The average operative sensitivity (in photons$^{-1} \cdot \mu m^2$) of guinea-pig rods is 0.022 at body temperature, 0.052 at room temperature. In the salamander rod the operative sensitivity is 0.39.

In Fig. 2 the normalized amplitude of photoresponse recorded from four guinea pig rods at both room and body temperature is plotted as a function of the number of photons delivered by the test flash per μm^2. It is seen that in both temperature conditions the experimental measurements can be satisfactorily fitted by a saturating exponential function. The curve fitting the results at high temperature, however, is about 0.3 log units to the right of the curve drawn through low temperature data.

The response-intensity function of a typical salamander rod is also plotted for comparison on the same scale in Fig. 2. The extent of the shift to the left of the curve fitting the data from the salamander rod indicates a much higher operational sensitivity than in guinea pig rods. If, however, one makes an

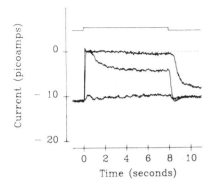

Penn and Hagins, 1972; Baylor et al., 1984; Nakatani et al., 1991). The three records presented in Fig. 3 are the responses to a 8 sec background of light of increasing intensity (in photons/μm^2 per second: 32.69, 715.26, 12544.9, respectively). Note that in the record obtained with a 715.26 photons stimulus (middle trace), the membrane current recovers up to 43% of the original dark level after a total transient suppression. This behavior, which is

Fig. 3. Responses of a guinea-pig rod to steps of light of increasing intensity (in photons/μm^2 per second: 32.69, 715.26, 12544.9, respectively). Note that the membrane current initially suppressed recovers with time, while the level of illumination remains constant. The current recovers in 5 sec by 43% of the original dark level with a saturating step of 715.26 photons/μm^2 per second.

allowance for the much larger collecting area of salamander rods (20 μm^2) compared to that of guinea pig rods (about 1 μm^2), it turns out that at room temperature the operational sensitivity in guinea-pig rods is about three times higher than that of salamander rods. At temperatures in the range between 35° and 38°C, however, the sensitivity of guinea-pig rods decreases more than two-fold, thus approaching that of salamander rods.

Light-adaptation

Absolute sensitivity is reduced by a constant background illumination. In toad rods a steady light equivalent to 6 *Rh** per second approximately halves the voltage response to a single photon (Fain, 1976; Cervetto et al., 1984). In monkey rods the absolute sensitivity is halved by a constant background equivalent to 100 *Rh**/sec (Baylor et al., 1984). This effect results from instantaneous compression exhibited by the saturating exponential function. In addition to this effect, however, constant backgrounds of sufficient duration may induce a decrease in the flash sensitivity which is usually referred to as light adaptation. There have been conflicting reports, however, on whether mammalian rods show any adaptation property (Dowling, 1967;

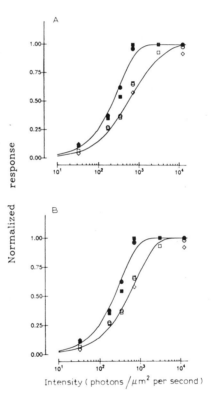

Fig. 4. Normalized amplitude of response of three guinea-pig rods plotted as a function of the log intensity of a 8 sec step of light measured at 150 sec (filled symbols) and 5 sec (open symbols) after the onset of light. Measurements at different times are fitted by different functions. In *A* the late time measures are fitted by a hyperbolic function of the type: $\Delta J / \Delta J_{max} = I / I + I_{\frac{1}{2}}$ with a $I_{\frac{1}{2}} = 605.27$ photons/μm^2 per second and a $J_{max} = 1.049$. In *B* the same data as in *A* are fitted by the function: $\Delta J / \Delta J_{max} = 1 - e^{-mKI^m}$ with a $K = 0.00299$ and $m = 0.889$. The same function also fits data measured at early times in both *A* and *B* with the same value of the K and with $m = 1$.

present to a lesser extent also in the response to intermediate levels of background illumination (not shown), is taken as an indication of the ability of rod to adapt. A large percentage of the rods investigated in this study respond to light steps in a similar way. There was, however, a fraction of rods in which the current remained constant throughout the entire duration of the light step.

The normalized amplitude of the photoresponse of three guinea pig rods is plotted as a function of the intensity of an 8 sec light step in Fig. 4. The two sets of data were obtained by measuring the amplitude of the response at 150 msec and 5 sec after the onset of the background light. It is seen that the curve fitting the response amplitude data measured at 5 sec is less steep and saturates at higher levels of light than the exponential function fitting the measurements at 150 msec. The change of the response-intensity relation during a prolonged illumination is another indication of the ability of rods to adapt to light.

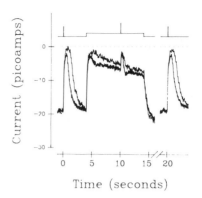

Fig. 6. Response of a guinea-pig rod to flashes and steps of bright saturating light. A bright flash was delivered 5 sec before and after the onset and after the termination of background illumination. The timing of flash and background illumination is indicated by the photocell record (uppermost trace). The other two traces are the rod responses to flashes and backgrounds of different intensity (flash intensity in photons/μm^2: 813.2 and 2643.5; background intensity in photons/μm^2 per second: 715.26 and 3051.17, respectively).

The effect of background illumination on the incremental flash sensitivity is illustrated in Fig. 5. Experimental points are well fitted by the continuous curve drawn from the Eqn. 4. The Weber-Fechner behavior of guinea pig rods, together with the other response properties described above, support the idea that the mechanism of light adaptation is well developed in mammalian rods.

Recovery from saturation

A steady light equivalent to about 10^3 Rh^* per second usually induces saturation in rods of both low vertebrates and mammals. Under these conditions, further increments in the light flux produce no detectable change in the membrane current of the rod. When the saturating light step is maintained for sufficiently long periods of time (above 5 sec) the response to a test flash superimposed on the background illumination reappears and progressively increases in amplitude. Responses to backgrounds of saturating light with superimposed flashes are illustrated in Fig. 6. In addition to the flash superimposed on background illumination, flashes of the same intensity were also delivered 5 sec before the

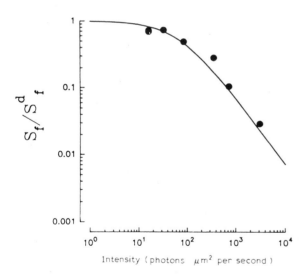

Fig. 5. Incremental flash sensitivity of a guinea-pig rod plotted on a log-log scale. Continuous curve is drawn from the Weber – Fechner relation (Eqn. 2) with a I_h = 71 photons/μm^2 per second. Eqn. 2 describes experimental data fairly well up to background illuminations of about 10^3 photons/μm^2 per second. At higher values of illumination the incremental flash sensitivity deviates significantly from the Weber – Fechner relation.

onset and after the termination of the steady illumination. Flashes of the same intensity elicited responses similar in amplitude and time course both before and after background illumination. The records shown in Fig. 6 demonstrate recovery from saturation for background illuminations of two different intensities (see legend). The extent to which the light-suppressible current reactivates in this rod is over 20% of the dark level. From the type of experiment illustrated in Fig. 6 one may estimate the range of light intensities over which a rod returns to be responsive to light after a transient period of complete saturation. On average, saturation starts to occur in rods with background lights equivalent to about 10^3 photons/μm^2 per second. By further increasing the intensity of the adapting step we have observed recovery from saturation up to more than 10^4 photons/μm^2 per second. In some case this upper limit was even higher, but could not be properly explored because of the limits of the light stimulating equipment. Recovery from saturation is likely to be caused by a severe desensitization of the transductive mechanism. The value of $I_\frac{1}{2}$ after recovery from a saturating background equivalent to 1.2×10^4 photons/μm^2 per second is about 3 log units above the control value measured in the absence of background. This corresponds to a 1000-fold drop in operative sensitivity. The flash sensitivity measured in the same conditions from the same rod is 0.5 femto amperes per Rh^*, again a value three orders of magnitude lower than the absolute sensitivity in the dark. This result rules out the possibility that a substantial component of the desensitization occurring during the recovery from saturation is due to a screening effect by the bleached pigment. Consistent with this conclusion is also the additional observation that the life time of the desensitization is of the order of 10 sec as opposed to that of the bleached pigment which is presumably of the order of tens of minutes. It seems probable that the recovery from saturation is brought about by a re-opening of a fraction of light-controlled ionic channels, perhaps reflecting an intrinsic property of the phototransductive process.

It has been reported that both amount and time course of the recovery from saturation can be suppressed in amphibian rods by procedures that limit the uphill extrusion of cytoplasmic calcium (Demontis et al., 1991) which is driven in rods by both sodium and potassium gradients (Cervetto et al., 1989). The notion that other adaptation properties in both amphibians and mammals depend on the level of the internal free calcium (Matthews et al., 1988; Matthews, 1991) raises the interesting possibility that all the aspects of the process of adaptation that we have described, eventually depend on the ability of the visual cell in regulating the internal level of free calcium. The idea that light adaptation bears a strict dependence on the energetic metabolic balance of the visual cell seems to be supported by the observations that in a variety of conditions known to depress the ionic pumps, the ability of the rod to adapt is reduced (Demontis et al., 1991).

Discussion

The efficiency by which a rod signal light changes is defined by a number of properties that include: absolute sensitivity, operative sensitivity and light adaptation. The data reported in Fig. 2 show that the operative sensitivity at body temperature is about one half of that measured at room temperature. The decrease in the operative sensitivity is paralleled by a large increase in the dark current and by an acceleration of the photoresponse. The temperature dependence of the dark current (Q_{10}) is consistent with that of the guanylate cyclase, the enzyme responsible for the synthesis of cGMP, the internal transmitter that keeps ionic channels open (Krishnan et al., 1978; Mazzoni, Demontis and Cervetto, in preparation). These observations have a special relevance in the analysis of the mechanisms responsible for controlling the rod sensitivity and adaptation. In the context of the present work, however, it is perhaps interesting to note that when we make an allowance for the different extension of the collecting area, the operative sensitivities of amphibian and mammalian rods are similar. In fact the half saturating intensity of guinea-pig rods in physiological temperature conditions (around

TABLE I

Parameters indicating sensitivity and ability to light adaptation of rods of different animals

Animal	$I_{\frac{1}{2}}$	I_{max} (flash)	I_{max} (step)	$_dS_f$	Reference
Monkey	19	120	$\simeq 2.10^3$	0.7 pA	Baylor et al. (1984)*
Cat	44	293	$\simeq 1.10^4$	1.1 pA	Tamura et al. (1989)
Rabbit	70	465	$\simeq 1.10^4$	0.8 pA	Nakatani et al. (1991)
Rat	80	531	$\simeq 1.10^4$	0.5 pA	Ratto et al. (1991)
Guinea-pig	46	306	$\simeq 1.10^4$	0.7 pA	Matthews (1991) (present report)
Toad	1	8		1.03 pA	Baylor et al. (1979)*

* Linearly polarized light.

The half saturating intensity ($I_{\frac{1}{2}}$) and the saturating flash intensity (I_{max}) are in photons/μm^2, the step saturating intensity (I_{max}) at steady state is in photons/μm^2 per second.

The tabulated values are obtained from the literature (see references in the right hand side column). The value of I_{max} (step) in monkey has been calculated from the cell no. 7 (p. 592, in Baylor et al., 1984). Data of cell no. 7 were selected for their apparent deviation from the theoretical relation $S_f/S^D_F = e^{-KI}$ predicting simple response compression, with no adaptation. For rabbit rods, both the $I_{\frac{1}{2}}$ and I_{max} (flash) have been calculated from the response-intensity data at 90 msec of fig. 2A (p. 418) of Nakatani et al. (1991).

37°C) is very close to that of salamander rods at room temperature.

Some of the parameters indicating sensitivity and ability to light adaptation of rods of different animals are reported in Table I.

The term light adaptation is generally used to indicate the process by which the visual system extends its performance over a wide range of light intensities. In the specific case of retinal rods the ability to light adaptation is recognized from: (1) the existence of a background desensitization process conforming to the Weber – Fechner function; (2) the change in the response-intensity function during exposure to steps of light; and (3) the presence of the recovery from saturation.

The notion that a significant amount of adaptation is present at the photoreceptor level is based on the observations that many investigators have made on both rods and cones of lower vertebrates (Baylor and Hodgkin, 1974; Norman and Werblin 1974; Fain, 1976; Hemilä, 1977). The fact that monkey rods are rapidly desensitized and saturated by background light (Baylor et al., 1984) has been taken for some time as an indication that the adaptation mechanism is poorly developed in rods of mammalians. Whether the absence of adaptation is a

peculiar feature of primate rods is not clear at present. There seems now little doubt, however, that rods of at least several mammalian families do show adaptation properties similar to those of amphibians (Nakatani et al., 1991). In our experiments on guinea pig rods we observe that a large number of cells do adapt, although a small fraction of investigated rods showed similar properties to those described for monkey rods.

A typical case of a light-adapting rod is illustrated in Fig. 4 where the amplitude of the response to light steps is measured at early times after the onset of the light stimulation and after several seconds when the transient component of the current suppression has reached a steady state. The two sets of data differ substantially and, clearly, the late time measurements cannot be fitted by the same type of function that describes response amplitudes measured at early times. In their analysis of the response properties to flashes and steps of light in amphibian rods Forti et al. (1989) suggest that a good fit to the late time measurements is provided by a hyperbolic function characterized by the constants $K_{\frac{1}{2}}$ and I_{max}. By this approach, however, it is difficult to identify a parameter accounting for adaptation. If one assumes that the change in the response properties occurring during adaptation eventually results from the reopening of a small fraction of ionic channels closed on a unitary segment of the rod membrane by the absorption of a single photon, a function describing this process may be:

$$\Delta J / \Delta J_{max} = 1 - e^{-mKI^m} \qquad (5)$$

were m is a constant and the other symbols are as in Eqn. 4. This type of function was firstly proposed by Weibull (1951) and later used by Green and Luce (1975) for describing responses in a system of many independent detectors. Note that for $m = 1$ Eqn. 5 reduces to Eqn. 3. As shown in Fig. 4, the curve obtained from Eqn. 5 describes well the amplitude of light-step responses at both early and late times by only changing the value of m from 1 to 0.8. The parameter m may thus be used as a measure of the state of light adaptation, dark adaptation being characterized by a m equivalent to the unity. As the rod re-adjusts its sensitivity during background illumination, m becomes smaller assuming values less than 1. A detailed discussion of the Eqn. 5 will be given in a separate paper (Demontis, Bisti and Cervetto, in preparation).

Recovery from saturation, which has also been described in amphibian rods (Cervetto et al., 1985), likely represents an extension to bright light intensities of the process of background desensitization. The membrane current activation observed during a constant background is suppressed in amphibian rods by reducing the efficiency of the ionic exchanger transporting calcium out of the cell (Demontis et al., 1991) and is enhanced by opposite procedures (Cervetto et al., 1985). Preliminary results confirm these observations also in guinea pig rods. On this basis it seems probable that the reduced effect of light observed during prolonged bright illuminations is caused by an effect of calcium ions on either one or both the enzymes that control the cytoplasmic flux of cGMP. Consistent with this hypothesis are the recent findings showing that calcium inhibits the guanylate cyclase (Koch and Stryer, 1988) and prolongs the action of phosphodiesterase, the light-activated enzyme responsible for the hydrolysis of cGMP (Kawamura and Murakami, 1991).

In principle the extent to which rods recover from saturation may have important physiological consequences. The highest level of background illumination tested in the present study is equivalent to about 2×10^4 photons/μm^2 per second, which corresponds to a retinal illumination of about 3×10^3 human scotopic trolands (with 1 mm^2 pupil area, see Wyszecki and Stiles, 1982, p. 103). Background illuminations of about the same intensity have been reported to saturate the ERG response in the monkey retina (Gouras, 1965). A process of recovery from saturation similar to that described here in isolated rods has been shown psychophysically in human subjects (Adelson, 1982). Although a causal relationship between rod and psychophysical saturation is difficult to establish, it is tempting to speculate that the limits for visual saturation in the rod system are set at the receptor level, before any significant neural interaction takes place.

Acknowledgements

We wish to thank Professor D.C. Burr and Dr. C. Morrone for helpful discussion and critical reading of the manuscript. Supported by the European Community Stimulation Action Program (contract: SC1*-0224-C) and by the Ministero della Università Ricerca Scientifica e Tecnologica (40%).

References

Adelson, E.H. (1982) Saturation and adaptation in the rod system. *Vision Res.*, 22: 1299–1312.

Aguilar, M. and Stiles, W.S. (1954) Saturation of the rod mechanism at high levels of stimulation. *Optica Acta*, 1: 59–65.

Barlow, H.B. (1972) Dark and light adaptation: psychophysics. In: D. Jameson and L.M. Hurvich (Eds.), *Handbook of Sensory Physiology, Vol. 8 (4)*, Springer, Berlin, pp. 1–28.

Baylor, D.A. and Hodgkin, A.L. (1974) Changes in time scale and sensitivity in turtle photoreceptors. *J. Physiol. (Lond.)*, 242: 729–758.

Baylor, D.A., Lamb, T.D. and Yau, K-W. (1979) Responses of retinal rods to single photons. *J. Physiol. (Lond.)*, 288: 613–634.

24

Baylor, D.A., Nunn, B.J. and Schnapf, J.L. (1984) The photocurrent, noise and spectral sensitivity of rods of the monkey *Macaca fascicularis*. *J. Physiol. (Lond.)*, 357: 575 – 607.

Cervetto, L., Torre, V., Pasino, E., Marroni, P. and Capovilla, M. (1984) Recovery from light-desensitization in toad rods. In: A. Borsellino and L. Cervetto (Eds.), *Photoreceptors*, Plenum Publishing Corporation, New York, pp. 159 – 175.

Cervetto, L., Torre, V., Rispoli, G. and Marroni, P. (1985) Mechanisms of light adaptation in toad rods. *Exp. Biol.*, 44: 147 – 157.

Cervetto, L., Lagnado, L., Perry, R.J., Robinson, D.W. and McNaughton, P.A. (1989) Extrusion of calcium from rod outer segments is driven by both sodium and potassium gradients. *Nature*, 337: 740 – 743.

Demontis, G.C., Trimarchi, C., Bisti, S. and Cervetto, L. (1991) Changes in sensitivity in retinal rods during constant illumination. *Invest. Ophthalmol.*, 32: 1168.

Dowling, J.E. (1967) The site of visual adaptation. *Science,* 155: 273 – 279.

Fain, G.L. (1976) Sensitivity of toad rods: dependence on wavelength and background illumination. *J. Physiol. (Lond.)*, 261: 71 – 101.

Forti, S., Menini, A., Rispoli, G. and Torre, V. (1989) Kinetics of phototransduction in retinal rods of the newt *Triturus cristatus*. *J. Physiol. (Lond.)*, 419: 265 – 295.

Gouras, P. (1965) Saturation of the rods in rhesus monkey. *J. Opt. Soc. Am.,* 55: 86 – 91.

Green, D.G. (1986) The search for the site of visual adaptation. *Vision Res.*, 26: 1417 – 1429.

Green, D.M. and Luce, R.D. (1975) Parallel psychometric functions from a set of independent detectors. *Psychol. Rev.*, 82: 483 – 486.

Harosi, F.I. (1975) Absorption spectra and linear dichroism of some amphibian photoreceptors. *J. Gen. Physiol.*, 66: 357 – 382.

Hemilä, S. (1977) Background adaptation in the rods of thefrog's retina. *J. Physiol. (Lond.)*, 265: 721 – 741.

Kawamura, S. and Murakami, M. (1991) Calcium-dependent regulation of cyclic GMP phosphodiesterase by a protein from frog retinal rods. *Nature*, 349: 420 – 423.

Koch, K.-W. and Stryer, L. (1988) Highly cooperative feed-back control of retinal rod guanylate cyclase by calcium ions. *Nature*, 334: 64 – 66.

Krishnan, K., Fletcher, R.T., Chader, G.J. and Krishna, G. (1978) Characterization of guanylate cyclase of rod outer segments of the bovine retina. *Biochim. Biophys. Acta,* 523: 506 – 515.

Lamb, T.D. and Pugh Jr., E.N. (1990) Physiology of transduction and adaptation in rod and cone photoreceptors. *Semin. Neurosci.,* 2: 3 – 13.

Lamb, T.D., McNaughton, P.A. and Yau, K.-W. (1981) Spatial spread of activation and background desensitization in toad rod outer segments. *J. Physiol. (Lond.)*, 319: 463 – 496.

Lasansky, A. and Marchiafava, P.L. (1974) Light-induced resistance changes in retinal rods and cones of salamander. *J. Physiol. (Lond.)*, 236: 171 – 191.

Matthews, H.R. (1991) Incorporation of chelator into guinea-pig rods shows that calcium mediates mammalian photoreceptor light adaptation. *J. Physiol. (Lond.)*, 436: 93 – 105.

Matthews, H.R., Murphy, R.L.W., Fain, G.L. and Lamb, T.D. (1988) Photoreceptor light adaptation is mediated by cytoplasmic calcium concentration. *Nature,* 334: 67 – 69.

Nakatani, K., Tamura, T. and Yau, K.-W. (1991) Light adaptation in rabbit and other mammalian rods. *J. Gen. Physiol.*, 97: 413 – 435.

Norman, R.A. and Werblin, F.S. (1974) Control of retinal sensitivity. I. Light and dark adaptation of rods and cones. *J. Gen. Physiol.*, 63: 37 – 61.

Penn, R.D. and Hagins, W.A. (1972) Kinetics of the photocurrent in retinal rods. *Biophys. J.*, 12: 1073 – 1094.

Ratto, G.M., Robinson, D.W., Yan, B. and McNaughton, P.A. (1991) Development of the light response in neonatal mammalian rods. *Nature*, 351: 654 – 657.

Shapley, R. and Enroth-Cugell, C. (1984) Visual adaptation and retinal gain control. *Prog. Retinal Res.*, 3: 263 – 346.

Tamura, T, Nakatani, K. and Yau, K.-W. (1989) Light adaptation in cat retinal rods. *Science*, 245: 755 – 758.

Weibull, W. (1951) A statistical distribution function of wide applicability. *J. Appl. Mech.*, 18: 292 – 297.

Wyszecki, G. and Stiles, W.S. (1982) *Color Science: Concepts and Methods, Quantitative Data and Formulae,* 2nd edn., Wiley, New York, 950 pp.

T.P. Hicks, S. Molotchnikoff and T. Ono (Eds.)
Progress in Brain Research, Vol. 95
© 1993 Elsevier Science Publishers B.V. All rights reserved.

CHAPTER 3

Responses of isolated cat retinal ganglion cells to injected currents during development

Leo M. Chalupa, Irini Skaliora and Robert P. Scobey

Departments of Psychology and Neurology and the Center for Neurobiology, University of California, Davis, CA 95616, U.S.A.

Introduction

Since the early 1980's anatomical experiments have provided a great deal of information about the prenatal development of the mammalian retina and retinal projections (reviewed by Chalupa and White, 1990). Research on fetal cats has yielded a particularly detailed description of some of the key events (see Fig. 1) which take place from the time that retinal ganglion cells are first generated, at about embryonic day 20, until the mature pattern of connections is attained several weeks after birth. Studies of many different mammalian species have demonstrated that early in development retinal projections are less precise and more widespread than at maturity. There is also good reason to believe that correlated activity of developing ganglion cells plays a key role in establishing the exquisite specificity of connections that characterizes the mature visual system (Kalil, 1990; Shatz, 1990).

Extracellular recordings have demonstrated that ganglion cells can generate action potentials even before photoreceptors are generated (Galli and Maffei, 1988). It has also been shown that correlated discharge patterns among neighboring retinal ganglion cells can occur before birth (Maffei and Galli-Resta, 1990; Meister et al., 1991). As yet, however, we lack information about the ontogeny of functional properties in retinal ganglion cells. For instance, it is not known when retinal ganglion cells first become capable of firing action potentials. Nor

is there any information available about the development of the different conductances that underlie spike generation. Consequently, our knowledge of the functional development of the retina has lagged far behind the morphological, histochemical and anatomical data that has been accumulated in recent years.

The whole-cell patch clamp recording technique (Hamill et al., 1981) offers a powerful tool for assessing the membrane properties of developing neurons (Hockberger et al., 1989; Nerbonne and Gurney, 1989). We have used this method to record from acutely dissociated retinal ganglion cells obtained from postnatal and prenatal cats in order to characterize the development of spiking properties in these neurons. The long-term goal of this work is to relate the functional development of retinal ganglion cells to the structural refinements that are known to occur in these neurons during ontogeny. As a first step, we have examined the response properties of dissociated ganglion cells to constant current stimulation.

Methodological considerations

The essential aspects of the procedures we employ are illustrated diagrammatically in Fig. 2. To differentiate ganglion cells from other neurons, rhodamine latex beads (RB) are injected bilaterally into the optic tract, lateral geniculate nucleus and the superior colliculus. All surgical procedures,

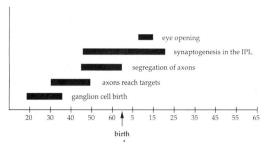

Fig. 1. Schematic of retinal development. Age is noted on the horizontal axis: the numbers before and after "birth" represent prenatal (embryonic) and postnatal days, respectively. The length of the bars represents the duration of each of the developmental events illustrated.

described in detail in previous papers (e.g., Williams and Chalupa, 1982), are performed in strict compliance with NIH guidelines. After a 2-day survival period, the retinas are removed, and dissociated enzymatically. Following brief trituration, the cells are transferred to a glass recording chamber, and viewed through an epifluorescence microscope (Zeiss IM35) using DIC and appropriate filters to detect the presence of RB. The micrographs in Fig. 3 show examples of the type of cells from which recordings are made. Typically, these neurons have translucent cell bodies of a non-granular appearance with several stumps of broken processes.

Recordings are made at room temperature with a patch-clamp amplifier (Axopatch 1-C) using the perforated variation of the whole-cell recording technique developed by Horn and Marty (1988). After formation of a high resistance (at least 1 GΩ) seal between the recording electrode and the cell membrane, Nystatin is included in the pipette solution to obtain electrical access to the cytoplasm. To assess spike generation ability, steps of depolarizing current of different intensities are injected into individual cells. The records are displayed on a computer screen and stored on disk for subsequent analysis.

Spiking patterns

All isolated retinal ganglion cells obtained from postnatal animals (1 – 6 weeks of age) manifest

spike activity in response to very small depolarizing steps of current (2 – 10 pA). Two distinctly different types of spiking patterns can be elicited. Some cells fire in a sustained manner for the duration of the stimulus, while others yield transient responses. In a given cell, one or the other response pattern is seen over a wide range of stimulus intensities, although at the highest intensities employed all cells respond in a transient fashion. Fig. 4 illustrates representative examples of both types of firing pattern. Whether a neuron responds in a sustained or a transient manner is not related to the postnatal age of the animal, nor to the salient morphological features (soma size or extent of processes) of the dissociated cells.

Retinal ganglion cells in the intact cat have also been classified into sustained or transient types based on responses to maintained light stimulation of the receptive-field center (Cleland et al., 1971). It is commonly assumed that this difference in firing patterns is due to retinal circuitry. Our observations suggest, however, that intrinsic membrane properties may play a significant role in these distinct light-mediated response patterns. Sustained and transient

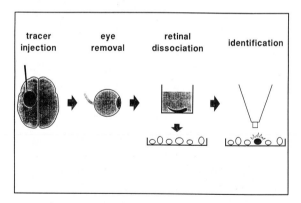

Fig. 2. Summary of the experimental procedure. A fluorescent tracer (rhodamine latex microspheres) is injected into the retinorecipient targets in order to backfill the retinal ganglion cells (RGCs). The tracer is picked up by the RGC terminals and transported retrogradely back to the cell bodies. After a survival period of 1 – 2 days (depending on the age of the animal) the eyes are removed and the retinae are enzymatically dissociated. RGCs can be identified in the recording chamber by the presence of the fluorescent microspheres.

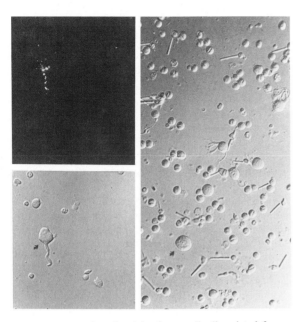

Fig. 3. The panel to the right shows cells dissociated from a postnatal day 21 (P21) cat. By this age retinal cells are already morphologically diverse (e.g., rod outer segments) but can not be unequivocally classified. The two left panels show a retinal ganglion cell at a larger magnification. This neuron can be identified as an RGC by the presence of rhodamine in its soma and main dendrite.

responses to maintained depolarizing currents have been noted previously in freshly dissociated retinal ganglion cells of the rat (Barres et al., 1988), although such functional diversity was not reported by Lipton and Tauck (1987) who studied primarily cultured rat ganglion cells. In view of our findings, it would be of interest to determine to what degree the sustained and transient response patterns could be related to the major morphological classes of cat ganglion cells. Such classes cannot be distinguished in dissociated cells since they lack extensive processes and soma size cannot be readily related to a particular region of the retina. However, given the differential projection patterns of different classes of cat retinal ganglion cells (Wässle, 1982), it would be of interest to determine whether the distinct spiking patterns we observed can be related to the retinorecipient target innervated by individual ganglion cells.

Fetal recordings

Sustained and transient responses are also manifested by fetal ganglion cells. Fig. 5 illustrates

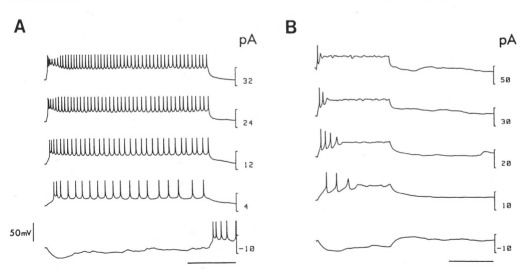

Fig. 4. Responses to current injections in postnatal cells. Sustained (*A*) and transient (*B*) spiking patterns. Each trace illustrates the cell's response to a current pulse injected through the patch electrode. The numbers on the right of each trace represent the current intensity in pA, the negative sign defining a hyperpolarizing current. Note that for the sustained pattern the frequency of the response increases with increasing stimulus intensities. As in most cells that showed this response, action potentials were of nearly constant amplitude and duration for the length of the current injection. In contrast, for the cells manifesting transient firing patterns, action potentials tend to become longer and smaller during the response. Time calibration bar: 500 msec.

examples of such firing patterns in two cells dissociated from an E55 retina. As is the case in the postnatal cells, the characteristic response pattern was obtained over a relatively broad range of cur-

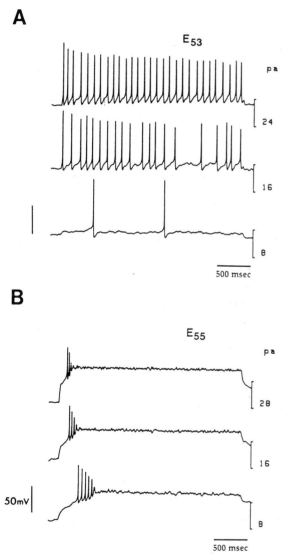

A

E$_{53}$

B

E$_{55}$

50mV

500 msec

Fig. 5. Spiking patterns in fetal RGCs. *A*. Response of an E53 neuron to injections of depolarizing current. Stimulus intensity is shown to the right of each trace in pA. A sustained firing pattern is seen, similar to the one described for the postnatal cell in Fig. 4*A*. *B*. Response of an E55 neuron to analogous stimulus parameters. This cell responded in a transient manner at all current intensities, like the postnatal neuron of Fig. 4*B*. Time calibration bar: 500 msec.

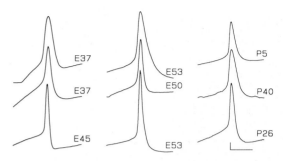

Fig. 6. Examples of action potentials generated by cells dissociated from animals of different ages in response to electrical stimulation. There was no obvious developmental trend in spike wave form in terms of duration, amplitude or rate of rise of the action potentials. Age is noted at the right of each spike in either embryonic (E) or postnatal (P) days. Calibration bars: 10 mV, 10 msec.

rent intensities. To date, the youngest fetal age from which we attempted such recording has been E37. This is at about the time the overall population of retinal ganglion cells has been generated (see Fig. 1), almost a month before birth. Even at this early stage, retinal ganglion cells capable of either sustained or transient spiking patterns are present. However, our results to date indicate that early in fetal development transient discharges are more common. Furthermore, the early fetal cells (prior to circa E40) that fire in a sustained manner, do so over a more limited range of current intensities.

It is also the case that some of the salient spike parameters (amplitude, duration and rise time) of the cells dissociated from animals of different ages appear remarkably similar. Fig. 6 illustrates typical single spikes recorded from cells at different ages. As may be seen, spikes of similar wave forms could be evoked throughout the developmental period we have investigated. The possibility remains, however, that more detailed study will reveal relatively subtle developmental changes in spike parameters. Nevertheless, our results to date indicate that retinal ganglion cells in the fetal cat attain the ability to generate spiking properties very early in development.

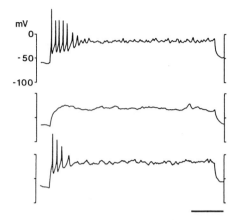

Fig. 7. Effects of TTX application on spike generation on an embryonic day 38 (E38) RGC. All traces show the cell's response to a 20 pA depolarizing current. For the middle trace 300 nM of TTX was included in the bath solution. The membrane is depolarized by the injected current but the spikes riding on the depolarization have disappeared. After TTX is washed out of the bath, the spike activity is recovered (bottom trace). Time calibration bar: 500 msec.

Effects of TTX application on spike generation

In some neural systems Ca-mediated spikes have been noted early in development, and subsequently these are replaced by Na-mediated spikes (Baccaglini and Spitzer, 1977). To determine whether the action potentials we recorded in fetal retinal ganglion cells are Na-mediated, we examined the effects of applying the voltage-gated sodium channel blocker tetrodotoxin (TTX) on spike generation. In all cases, TTX application abolished regenerative spike activity to injected currents (see Fig. 7). This was the case even in the youngest cells (E37) recorded to date. It should be noted, that these observations do not rule out the contribution of a calcium component to the action potentials obtained from either fetal or mature retinal ganglion cells. The results do indicate, however, that Na voltage-gated channels are present very early in development and that these channels are necessary for the generation of action potentials in fetal ganglion cells.

Spontaneous activity

Extracellular recordings from the intact retina have demonstrated that developing ganglion cells discharge action potentials spontaneously (Galli and Maffei, 1988; Meister et al., 1991), that is, without any external stimulation. In our recordings from dissociated cells such spontaneous activity is rarely seen. Furthermore, in the few neurons that discharged without injected current, "spontaneous" action potentials were evident only at the beginning of the recording period, when artifactual activation of the membrane by the recording pipette seemed most likely. Examples of such discharges at the beginning of the recording period are illustrated in Fig. 8. In all cases, such discharges appeared quite random, in that there was no evidence of rhythmic oscillations or synchronized bursts. These observations suggest that isolated retinal ganglion cells do not have the intrinsic capability of generating "spontaneous" actions potentials.

Discussion

Our findings indicate that developing retinal ganglion cells are capable of discharging sodium-mediated action potentials very early in develop-

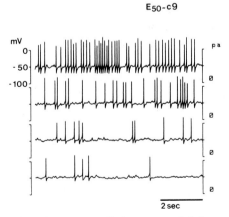

Fig. 8. Spontaneous discharges recorded from an E50 RGC. These spikes were generated in the absence of electrical stimulation. It is possible, however, that they resulted from depolarization of the cell membrane during the recording procedure.

ment. At E37, the earliest period studied to date, the overall population of retinal ganglion cells has just been generated, and the period of massive ganglion cell loss has not yet begun (Williams et al., 1986). At this age, some retinal axons are still growing towards their target nuclei, as indicated by the presence of growth cones within the optic nerve (Williams et al., 1986). This is more than a week before the first hint of segregation of retinal projections is evident within the dorsal lateral geniculate nucleus (Shatz, 1983) and the superior colliculus (Williams and Chalupa, 1982). Thus, the functional capability of individual retinal ganglion cells does not appear to be a limiting factor in delaying the establishment of ocular dominance domains within the major retinorecipient nuclei.

In other developing systems electrical activity has been shown to inhibit growth cone extension, and it has been suggested that this effect is due to an increase in intracellular calcium levels (Kater and Mills, 1991). As mentioned previously, our earliest recordings at E37 have been carried out when some ganglion cells are still growing towards their central targets, while other have already reached the main retinorecipient nuclei. It should be possible to extend these experiments to recordings from even younger neurons. In particular, recordings prior to E30 would be highly desirable since at this stage all the ganglion cells that have been generated are in the process of neurite elongation. One might even speculate that innervation of the target plays a key role in triggering the expression of excitable membrane properties.

While the voltage-gated sodium channels are present very early in development, it remains to be established whether membrane conductances are altered significantly during prenatal life. The fact that the individual spikes we have recorded prenatally appear remarkably similar to those obtained from recordings of postnatal neurons would seem to argue that at least some fetal cells possess membrane currents which are not markedly different from those present after birth. At the same time, the higher incidence of rapidly adapting cells in the younger fetuses suggests that certain membrane conductances do change with development. This issue is currently being examined by voltage-clamp recordings from fetal neurons. In particular, we are interested in assessing the contributions of calcium currents since in other developing systems calcium conductances have been reported to be prominent in developing neurons (O'Dowd et al., 1988).

The results also indicate that isolated retinal ganglion cells rarely fire spontaneous action potentials. Spontaneous discharges have been documented in recordings from the intact mammalian retina (Galli and Maffei, 1988), including that of the fetal cat (Meister et al., 1991) as early as E52. Assuming that our observations apply to the intact retina, the results indicate that voltage-gated membrane properties intrinsic to developing retinal ganglion cells are not the cause of the spontaneous discharges that have been observed in these neurons.

In this context, the results of recent studies which have demonstrated the transient expression of certain neuroactive substances in the developing retina may be of relevance. For instance, in related work from our laboratory, it has been found recently that somatostatin-containing amacrine cells and ganglion cells, which at maturity are preferentially distributed in the inferior retina (White and Chalupa, 1991), are widespread in the fetal cat retina (White and Chalupa, 1992). It is conceivable that developing ganglion cells are particularly sensitive to certain transiently expressed neuromodulators, and that this contributes to the correlated discharges that have been noted in the developing retina. From this perspective, it could prove to be informative to examine the responses of isolated developing retinal ganglion cells to somatostatin as well as other putative neuromodulators.

References

Baccaglini, P.I. and Spitzer, N.C. (1977) Developmental changes in the inward current of the action potential of Rohon-beard neurons. *J. Physiol. (Lond.)*, 271: 93 – 117.

Barres, B.A., Silverstein, B.E., Corey, D.P. and Chun, L.L.Y. (1988) Immunological, morphological, and electrophysiological variation among retinal ganglion cells purified by panning. *Neuron,* 1: 791 – 803.

Chalupa, L.M. and White, C.A. (1990) Prenatal development of visual structures. In: J.R. Coleman (Ed.), *Development of Sensory Systems in Mammals,* Wiley, New York, pp. 3 – 60.

Cleland, B.G., Dubin, M.W. and Levick, W.R. (1971) Sustained and transient neurons in the cat's retina and lateral geniculate nucleus. *J. Physiol. (Lond.),* 217: 473 – 496.

Galli, L. and Maffei, L. (1988) Spontaneous impulse activity of rat retinal ganglion cells in prenatal life. *Science,* 242: 90 – 91.

Hamill, O.P., Marty, A., Neher, E., Sakmann, B. and Sigworth, F.J. (1981) Improved patch-clamp techniques for high resolution current recordings from cells and cell-free membrane patches. *Pfluegers Arch.,* 391: 85 – 100.

Hockberger, P.E., Tseng, H.Y. and Connor, J.A. (1989) Development of rat cerebellar Purkinje cells: electrophysiological properties following acute isolation in long-term culture. *J. Neurosci.,* 9: 2258 – 2271.

Horn, R. and Marty, A. (1988) Muscarinic activation of ionic currents measured by a new whole-cell recording method. *J. Gen. Physiol.,* 92: 145 – 159.

Kalil, R.E. (1990) The influence of action potentials on the development of the central visual pathways. *J. Exp. Biol.,* 153: 1 – 16.

Kater, S.B. and Mills, L.R. (1991) Regulation of growth cone behavior by calcium. *J. Neurosci.,* 11: 891 – 899.

Lipton, S.A. and Tauck, D.L. (1987) Voltage-dependent conductances of solitary ganglion cells dissociated from the rat retina. *J. Physiol. (Lond.),* 385: 361 – 391.

Maffei, L. and Galli-Resta, L. (1990) Correlation in the discharges of neighboring rat retinal ganglion cells during prenatal life. *Proc. Natl. Acad. Sci. U.S.A.,* 87: 2861 – 2864.

Meister, M., Wong, R.O.L., Baylor, D.A. and Shatz, C.J. (1991) Synchronous bursts of action potentials in ganglion cells of the developing mammalian retina. *Science,* 252: 939 – 943.

Nerbonne, J.M. and Gurney, A.M. (1989) Development of excitable membrane properties in mammalian sympathetic neurons. *J. Neurosci.,* 9: 3272 – 3286.

O'Dowd, D.K., Ribera, A.B. and Spitzer, N.C. (1988) Development of voltage-dependent calcium, sodium, and potassium currents in *Xenopus* spinal neurons. *J. Neurosci.,* 8: 792 – 805.

Shatz, C.J. (1983) The prenatal development of the cat's retinogeniculate pathway. *J. Neurosci.,* 3: 482 – 499.

Shatz, C.J. (1990) Competitive interactions between retinal ganglion cells during prenatal development of the mammalian visual system. *J. Neurobiol.,* 21: 197 – 211.

Wässle, H. (1982) Morphological types and central projections of ganglion cells in the cat retina. In: N.N. Osborne and G. Chader (Eds.), *Progress in Retinal Research, Vol. 1,* Pergamon, London, pp. 125 – 152.

White, C.A. and Chalupa, L.M. (1991) Subgroup of alpha ganglion cells in the adult cat retina is immunoreactive for somatostatin. *J. Comp. Neurol.,* 304: 1 – 13.

White, C.A. and Chalupa, L.M. (1992) Ontogeny of somatostatin immunoreactivity in the cat retina. *J. Comp. Neurol.,* 317: 129 – 144.

Williams, R.W. and Chalupa, L.M. (1982) Prenatal development of retinocollicular projections in the cat: an anterograde tracer transport study. *J. Neurosci.,* 2: 604 – 622.

Williams, R.W., Bastiani, M.J., Lia, B. and Chalupa, L.M. (1986) Growth cones, dying axons, and developmental fluctuations in the fiber population of the cat's optic nerve. *J. Comp. Neurol.,* 246: 32 – 69.

T.P. Hicks, S. Molotchnikoff and T. Ono (Eds.)
Progress in Brain Research, Vol. 95
© 1993 Elsevier Science Publishers B.V. All rights reserved.

CHAPTER 4

Macaque ganglion cells and spatial vision

Barry B. Lee

Department of Neurobiology, Max Planck Institute for Biophysical Chemistry, D-3400 Göttingen, Germany

Introduction

Within the retino-geniculate pathway of old-world primates, including man, there exist two main cell systems. Most neurones of the parvocellular system (P-pathway) receive opponent input from two or more of the three cone types, the long- (L-), medium- (M-) and short-wavelength sensitive (S-) cones. Neurones of the magnocellular system (M-pathway) receive input from M- and L-cones to both centre and surround. These neural systems are probably already distinct at the level of the retinal bipolar cell, and they remain at least partially separate into the secondary visual areas of the cortex (see Kaplan et al., 1990, for review).

The roles of these two systems in certain psychophysical tasks have been reasonably well established. Thus, the M-pathway is likely to form the physiological substrate of heterochromatic flicker photometry (Lee et al., 1988). It is also more sensitive than the P-pathway to luminance modulation, and probably underlies detection of luminance flicker. The P-pathway probably underlies detection of chromatic modulation (Lee et al., 1989, 1990). In these contexts, the M-pathway forms the physiological basis of a psychophysically defined luminance channel, and the different cell types of the P-pathway correspond to different chromatic channels or mechanisms.

These pathways' roles in spatial vision remain more controversial. It has been proposed that cells of the P-pathway do "double-duty" and participate not only in detection of changes in colour but also in high-resolution pattern vision (Ingling and Martinez-Uriegas, 1983; Lennie, 1986; Schiller et al., 1990). According to this viewpoint, the achromatic (luminance) contrast sensitivity curve found psychophysically is an envelope of M- and P-pathway sensitivities, as sketched in Fig. 1*A*. At low spatial frequencies, the high sensitivity of the M-pathway is responsible for psychophysical detection, but at high spatial frequencies the P-pathway takes over.

I shall review here the evidence for this hypothesis. Although some types of experiment are in its support, especially those involving selective lesions of these pathways, some assumptions on which it is based are not well-founded. Physiological results suggest that the double-duty hypothesis is, at best, a major oversimplification, and that the M-pathway plays a critical role in spatial vision even in tasks requiring the highest degree of precision.

Parallel pathways in primate vision

Early psychophysical evidence suggested that a luminance channel underlay high spatial frequency vision. This proposal was derived partly from spectral sensitivity measurements under different experimental conditions. For example, when observers are required to detect coloured spots upon a white background, the resulting spectral sensitivity curve has three peaks with maxima near 470, 530 and 610 nm, as sketched in Fig. 1*B* (Sperling and Harwerth, 1971; King-Smith and Carden, 1976). These peaks are thought to represent different chromatic

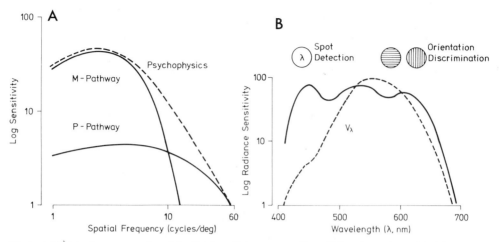

Fig. 1. *A*. Sketch of a common view of the division of labour among P- and M-pathways in spatial vision. Shown are hypothetical curves for the sensitivities of the M- and P-pathways, and for psychophysical sensitivity, as a function of spatial frequency. At low spatial frequencies, the high contrast sensitivity of the M-pathway can support psychophysical performance, but at high spatial frequencies, the P-pathway takes over. *B*. Spectral sensitivity curves for different tasks. Solid curve indicates sensitivity for detection of large, monochromatic stimuli, for example spots upon a white background. Dashed curve indicates sensitivity for detection of orientation of luminance-modulated gratings of different wavelengths.

mechanisms, which are probably related to different classes of P-pathway cells (Crook et al., 1987). On changing the experimental conditions, so that observers are required to detect the orientation of high spatial frequency, luminance-modulated gratings of different colours (either with or without background), the spectral sensitivity curve collapses to resemble the photopic luminosity function, V_λ (e.g., Pokorny et al., 1968). This spectral sensitivity was originally derived from flicker photometry and is also obtained with other methods, such as the minimally distinct border technique (Wagner and Boynton, 1972). If flicker photometry taps the activity of a luminance channel, it was thus reasonable to suppose that this channel was also involved with spatial vision close to the resolution limit.

Early descriptions of a class of phasic ganglion cells having little colour selectivity (Gouras, 1968), and of similar cells in the magnocellular layers of the lateral geniculate nucleus (LGN) (Wiesel and Hubel, 1966), suggested a physiological substrate for an achromatic channel. The description of colour- and cone-opponent, tonic ganglion cells (Gouras, 1968), and of similar neurones in the LGN (see DeValois, 1973, for review), suggested a physiological

substrate for chromatic mechanisms. However, later evidence was against this identification of cell systems with psychophysical mechanisms. It proved difficult to record from M-pathway ganglion cells near the fovea, and the short-latency antidromic potential was also weak in this region, suggesting a weak M-cell representation (Gouras, 1969). If these cells were largely absent from the fovea, they could play little role in fine spatial vision. Also, early estimates of receptive field size suggested M-pathway cells had large centre diameters (de Monasterio and Gouras, 1975) as compared with P-pathway cells. This, together with other evidence, led to a parallel being drawn with Y- and X-cells of the cat. It was therefore proposed that the cells of the P-pathway, with small receptive field centres and a high density in the fovea, were critical in analysis of high spatial frequency components of the visual image (e.g., Gouras, 1984).

It has recently become apparent that phasic ganglion cells of the M-pathway are well-represented in the fovea (Perry and Silveira, 1988), but are buried deeply in the pile of ganglion cells surrounding the foveal pit. This accounts for earlier difficulties in demonstrating their presence in this region; their rarity in microelectrode recordings and the weak antidromic potential are a consequence of their being far from the inner limiting membrane, close to the inner plexiform layer. It is likely that the proportion of M- to P-pathway cells remains constant across the retina. Also, the analogy to the X- and Y-systems of the cat is no longer thought to hold (Shapley and Perry, 1986). Lastly, the significance of any difference in receptive field diameter of M- and P-pathway cells is also unclear, and is discussed in the next section.

Visual resolution and centre size of individual primate ganglion cells

In the cat, the visual resolution displayed by individual cells is directly proportional to their centre diameter (Peichl and Wässle, 1979). It is thus surprising that, despite the suggestion that M- and P-pathway cells have different centre diameters, recent studies clearly indicate that the spatial frequencies that individual cells of these pathways can resolve are similar at a given retinal eccentricity. This is so for neurones of the LGN (Blakemore and Vital-Durand, 1986) and for retinal ganglion cells (Crook et al., 1988). This is illustrated in Fig. 2. M- and P-pathway ganglion cells were exposed to drifting, high contrast, black/white gratings at frequencies close to their resolution limit. The examples shown consist of two M-pathway (phasic) ganglion cells and two P-pathway (red- and green-on) cells recorded sequentially from parafoveal retina. The filled symbols indicate the first-harmonic response, and the open circles mean firing rates. The first-harmonic response falls steeply toward a spatial frequency which can be defined as the resolution limit of the cell (indicated by the arrows). For the two phasic cells, this criterion response corresponded to spatial frequencies of 12 and 17 cycles/degree, and for the red-on and green-on cells of 8 and 16 cycles/degree, respectively. Thus, at this retinal eccentricity, the ability of individual M- and P-pathway ganglion cells to resolve gratings is similar. The open circles represented mean firing rates, and close to the first-harmonic resolution limit they do

not differ from maintained activity (MA). This result is one way in which cells of the M-pathway differ from Y-cells of the cat. Although it is difficult both in LGN and retina to record from M-pathway cells close to the fovea, those M-pathway cells recorded responded to 30 – 40 cycles/degree, which is a similar range to that observed for P-pathway cells. Foveal acuity of the macaque also falls into this range (Cavonius and Robbins, 1973). If human resolution at different eccentricities is used to predict the analogous psychophysical function for the macaque, this correspondence holds, to a first

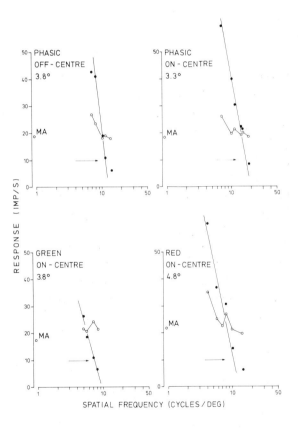

Fig. 2. Responses and resolution of M- and P-pathway cells (phasic cells, red-on and green-on cells) to high-contrast black-white gratings drifted at 10 Hz across the retina. Amplitude of first-harmonic response component is plotted against spatial frequency (filled circles); zero harmonic (maintained firing) is also shown. The resolution of the individual cell can be defined when the response falls below some criterion level, indicated by arrows. (Replotted from Crook et al., 1987, with permission.)

approximation, over the whole visual field (Crook et al., 1988).

In what follows I shall concentrate on data from the parafovea, firstly because most physiological data are available from this region, and secondly because optical factors do not play such a critical role in this region. The similarity in spatial resolution of M- and P-pathway cells is surprising, for in the cat resolution is closely related to centre size. Given certain assumptions, a cat ganglion cell gives a modulated response until approximately 2 cycles of drifting grating fit into its receptive field centre (Peichl and Wässle, 1979). If a parafoveal cell of the monkey just responds to 12 cycles/degree, this implies a centre diameter of 10 arc-minutes. This is close to reported centre diameters of phasic ganglion cells (de Monasterio and Gouras, 1975) or cells of the magnocellular layers of the LGN (Derrington and Lennie, 1984). The inconsistency between proposed centre size and visual resolution thus lies with P-pathway cells. It is thus worthwhile looking at evidence as to the centre size of these neurones in more detail.

The strongest evidence for a small centre size for these cells lies in the demonstration that midget bipolar cells connect to only one cone, and midget (P-pathway) ganglion cells connect to only one midget bipolar (see Kaplan et al., 1990, for review). The connection of individual cones to the midget system counts as one of the strongest anatomical predictions for visual physiology yet encountered. Then, the centre size of the ganglion cell should represent the sampling aperture of the cone itself. Psychophysical evidence suggests this is close to the cone diameter (e.g., Williams, 1986). The midget system is still represented in the parafovea, so one would expect a certain proportion of P-pathway ganglion cells to have centres comparable in diameter to parafoveal cones, about 2 – 3 arc-minutes. This centre diameter should allow a cell to respond to about 30 cycles/degree, much higher than the range of acuities measured physiologically.

The first physiological measurements of receptive field centre size are were carried out by de Monasterio and Gouras (1975), who reported

diameters of 6 – 8 arc-minutes for tonic, P-pathway ganglion cells. As a test, they used very tiny spots stepped across the centre. Due to the poor contrast gain of P-pathway cells (see Kaplan et al., 1990, for review), it is possible that these sizes were somewhat of an underestimate due to an "iceberg" effect. More recent measurements indicate a centre diameter of about 10 – 12 arc-minutes in the parafovea, either measured using area summation curves (Crook et al., 1988) or by fitting spatial frequency tuning curves with a difference-of-Gaussians receptive field model (Derrington and Lennie, 1984). There thus exists a serious discrepancy with the anatomical prediction.

There are several possible explanations for this discrepancy. One is that the achromatic contrast gain of P-pathway cells is so poor that their resolution is lower than expected from the model of Peichl and Wässle (1979). Another is that synaptic connections within the inner plexiform layer enlarge the centre diameter beyond that of a single cone. Lastly, it is possible that measured receptive field diameters are somewhat larger than the actual diameter due to optical blurring. This was the explanation proposed by Derrington and Lennie (1984), who for this reason based their estimate of a two-fold difference in centre size between M- and P-pathway cells on a comparison of the average M-pathway cell against the smallest P-pathway cell diameter. Against this latter argument is the fact that the optical quality of the eye is a limiting factor in the fovea, but is superior to the requirements of the parafovea. It remains to be seen which of these three factors plays the major role. In any event, in relation to psychophysical data the argument as to centre diameter of M- and P-pathway cells is something of a red herring; at a given retinal eccentricity both cell types are able to respond to spatial frequencies close to the predicted resolution limit of the macaque (Crook et al., 1988).

The above arguments suggest that some of the assumptions underlying the scheme in Fig. 1A are unjustified. In the next two sections, I shall describe physiological experiments in favour of a primary role for the M-pathway in spatial vision.

Visual performance with isoluminant patterns and cell responses

Performance on many psychophysical tasks is compromised with equal luminance patterns. Examples are perception of movement (Cavanagh et al., 1984) and fine stereopsis (Lu and Fender, 1972). The first demonstration of such impairment was with the minimally distinct border task, which is thus parent to more recent observations. In this task, two abutting, differently coloured fields are adjusted in relative radiance until the border between them is minimally distinct. It turns out that this occurs when the fields are of equal luminance, and an extensive set of observations showed that the task shares with flicker photometry all the characteristics of a photometric method (see Boynton, 1978, for review). There is now very strong physiological evidence that the M-pathway is the physiological substrate of flicker photometry (Lee et al., 1988; Lee, 1991), and it has also been shown that the M-pathway possesses characteristics which makes it very suitable as a physiological substrate for the minimally distinct border task (Kaiser et al., 1990; Valberg et al., 1992).

The hypothesis that the M-pathway underlies other tasks in which performance is impaired at equal luminance is thus attractive, but has the difficulty that many such tasks involve high-resolution vision. Visual resolution itself is minimal with equal luminance gratings (Mullen, 1985) and stereo vision requires detection of binocular disparities in the Vernier range. If the P-pathway underlies high-resolution vision, then to account for these observations some kind of signal must be derived from these predominantly chromatically responding cells which has to go through a deep minimum at equal luminance.

The type of model which has been proposed is shown in Fig. 3; a more extensive discussion of such models may be found in Ingling (1991). If a red and a green on-centre cell receive respectively L- and M-cone inputs to their centres and the opposite to their surrounds, then the activity of these two cells could be summed at a cortical level to provide a receptive field with $(+M+L)$ inputs to the centre and $(-L-M)$ inputs to the surround. This model is plausible, but is probably physiologically unrealistic. For such a model cell to deliver a "luminance" signal which becomes zero with, for example, an equal luminance red-green border, the chromatic components of the two input cells' responses must subtract to exactly balance out at equal luminance. Introduction of a small luminance imbalance should then yield a small luminance signal after the subtraction. This model implicitly assumes that the input cells' receptive field characteristics (cone balance, receptive field size, contrast gain and so on) are identical, and that up to the point of summation, their signals are transmitted with an extraordinarily high degree of linearity. Otherwise, the subtraction will not yield a veridical luminance signal. In practice, tested with actual ganglion cell responses, it is very difficult to get the model in Fig. 3 to work satisfactorily (Lee, 1991; Valberg et al., 1992). There may be several reasons for this. One may be that the receptive field characteristics of red and green on-centre cells are seldom so similar as to allow precise cancellation of the chromatic response component. Another is that at high red-green contrasts, these cells show response saturation. Subtraction of their signals is

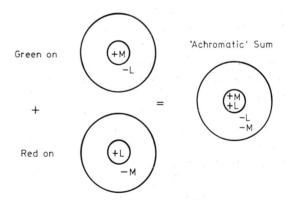

Fig. 3. Sketch of a possible model of input to an achromatic cell derived from chromatic inputs, i.e., from red and green on-centre cells with inputs from L- and M-cones to centres, and the reverse from the surrounds. Combination of these two signals yields an achromatic signal, but the assumptions of this model are implausible (see text).

then very insensitive to introduction of small luminance differences. Thirdly, recent evidence suggests that the difference in centre and surround diameters for P-pathway cells is much smaller then previously expected (Shapley et al., 1991).

Thus, the model in Fig. 3, although plausible, is very difficult to implement. Of course, it could be argued that averaging over a large number of P-pathway cells might yield a more suitable signal, but this would not seem to be consistent with high-resolution vision. It thus seems likely that the M-pathway is the predominant physiological substrate for those psychophysical tasks impaired at equal luminance.

Impairment in pattern vision at isoluminance is seldom complete. A further question of major interest is the origin of the residual performance, for it turns out that activity in the M-pathway, although minimal at equal luminance, is seldom absent. For example, with the minimally distinct border task, the residual distinctness of the edge is considerable with a red-green border, but very low with a blue-green border, when the border seems to "melt" (Boynton, 1978). It eventually became apparent that the degree of residual distinctness is directly related to the differential M- and L-cone excitations of the two colours either side of the edge. This is high with red-green (the red predominantly activates the L-cone and the green the M-cone) but low with blue-green (which lie close to the tritanopic confusion line, and can only be distinguished by the S-cones at equal luminance). M-pathway cells give a residual response at equal luminance due to some kind of non-linearity of M- and L-cone summation. This is seen as an excitatory response to passage of the edge across the receptive field, independent of the direction of movement of the edge. Examples of a M-pathway cell's response to several different equal-luminance edges are shown in Fig. 4a. The residual response is maximal with red-green and absent with blue-green, and of intermediate magnitude with white-green and white-red.

The size of the residual response in the M-pathway can be compared with psychophysical estimates of residual distinctness. It is possible to subjectively scale residual distinctness relative to an achromatic edge. When different wavelengths form a border with white, the residual distinctness is high with long wavelengths, falls to near zero at 570 nm, rises until about 480 nm and then falls again, as

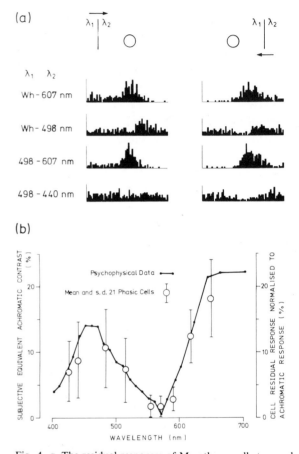

Fig. 4. a. The residual responses of M-pathway cells to equal-luminance borders for different pairs of colours. Shown are responses to two directions of movement for the combinations indicated. Speed of movement, 4°/sec. Average of ten responses, binwidth 34 msec. Residual response depends on the pairs of colours used. The response to 608/498 nm is approximately the additive sum of the residual response to 498 nm/white and 608 nm/white. The residual response to a pair of lights close to a tritanopic confusion line is very small (498/440 nm). Residual response is ultimately dependent on the differential excitations of the M- and L-cones across the edge. b. A comparison of residual distinctness estimated by a human observer after having set a border to minimal distinctness, expressed in terms of equivalent achromatic contrast (replotted from Boynton, 1978) with residual responses in the M-pathway, normalised to the cells' response to achromatic contrast, as described in the text.

shown in the solid curve plotted in Fig. 4b. It is possible to scale the residual responses of M-pathway cells with respect to their response to achromatic contrast, and means and standard deviations of 21 cells are also plotted in Fig. 4b. The size of residual responses varied substantially from cell to cell, but on average closely resembled the psychophysical data, being maximal at long wavelengths, minimal near 570 nm, then increasing and then decreasing once more. This would suggest that an M-pathway signal is large enough to account for residual distinctness with equal luminance borders. It is intriguing to speculate how far residual performance on other tasks, for example motion perception, is also mediated by this M-pathway signal; one would predict residual performance should show the same dependence on the colours used as with residual distinctness. These results also serve to illustrate how difficult it is to isolate the contributions of M- and P-pathways to performance; although the M-pathway may (under some circumstances at least) form the physiological substrate of a ''luminance channel'', this pathway does not behave as a linear, univariant mechanism, and the assumption that a ''luminance channel'' is silent at equal luminance is certainly invalid.

Vernier acuity; a high-resolution task based on the M-pathway

The ability to distinguish the relative location of two lines or edges exceeds visual resolution in precision. For human foveal vision it is typically 4 – 6 arc-seconds, as compared to a cycle length of one arc-minute for the 60 cycles/degree grating just resolved by most observers. There are a family of tasks which show this degree of precision in spatial localization, other examples being stereoacuity and the detection of small displacements. A model for Vernier performance must incorporate the activity of the array of ganglion cells providing input to some central mechanism. However, it is pertinent to ask how sensitive individual cells are to small changes in stimulus position. For example, when a single cell just responds to a grating near its resolution limit,

the phase of response is precisely defined to within a fraction of a cycle. Thus the spatial precision of the response of an individual cell, measured as response phase, substantially exceeds the cell's ability to resolve a grating (Lee et al., 1981; Shapley and Victor, 1986).

Vernier performance improves with increasing contrast. For briefly presented, flashed achromatic edges, performance rises steeply immediately above the detection threshold, reaches about 10 – 12 arc-seconds at 10% contrast, and reaches a plateau of about 6 arc-seconds at 20% contrast (Wehrhahn and Westheimer, 1990). The achromatic contrast sensitivity of the M-pathway is much higher than that of the P-pathway, most cells of which do not respond to contrasts lower than 10 – 20%. The psychophysical data thus suggest that the M-pathway may play a role in Vernier performance. To test this, we made measurements of the responses of M- and P-pathway cells to edges of different contrast flashed at various locations within their receptive fields. Knowing the amplitude and standard deviation of responses as a function of edge location, one can estimate how many stimulus presentations are necessary for a significant change in response size to occur on displacing the location of an edge within the receptive field. It should be stressed that these measurements were made with a single edge, they estimate how precisely a cell can localize an edge as a function of contrast; how the brain compares the location of *two* edges is another question.

The experiments were carried out in the parafovea, and the physiological results could be compared to psychophysical performance at the equivalent eccentricity. Table I summarizes the data obtained; a more extensive description of these results will be found elsewhere (Lee, Wehrhahn, Kremers and Westheimer, in preparation).

Separate comparisons have been made for M- and P-pathway cells. Psychophysical performance for different contrasts are shown in the first column. In the second column is the change in response amplitude (measured in a 40 msec window) for a given edge displacement, if the edge is located near

TABLE I

A comparison of psychophysical Vernier thresholds for achromatic edges presented in the parafovea with the precision of the cellular signal provided by M- and P-pathways, as a function of contrast

Contrast	Psychophysical thr., ψ min of arc	Response gradient, imp/sec/min	Response variability imp/sec	No of samples to detect ψ
M Cells ($n = 8$)				
40%	ca. 1.0	18.7	31	3.7
20%	ca. 1.1	17.6	32	3.6
10%	ca. 1.7	10.8	29	3.3
5%	ca. 2.8	5.7	27	3.8
P Cells ($n = 12$)				
40%	ca. 1.0	6.0	20	15
20%	ca. 1.1	3.4	22	45
10%	ca. 1.7	0.72	24	ca. 500
5%	ca. 2.8	No response		

the receptive field centre. The third column indicates the standard deviation of responses. The last column indicates the number of stimulus presentations required for a significant change in response amplitude (at the 5% level) for the displacements in the first column. For M-pathway cells, this is a small and constant number. For P-pathway cells, the number rises steeply as contrast is decreased; until a 5% contrast it becomes very large indeed, since response amplitude is too small to measure reliably.

These data indicate that it is the M-pathway which provides the spatial information required for Vernier tasks. Insofar as numbers of stimulus presentations are equivalent to numbers of cells required by some central mechanism, it seems unlikely that the numerical superiority of red-green P-pathway cells (about 6:1 in relation to M-pathway cells) can make up for their poor signal-to-noise ratio. Also, the large numbers required would have to be aligned along the edge, as pearls upon a necklace.

This analysis is not of course a model of Vernier acuity performance. Somehow the cortex must extract from signals arising from the matrix of ganglion cells the positional information required. The construction of such a model is not straightforward, but any model must be constrained by the information coming from the retina. It seems likely that the M-pathway carries this information. It should be stressed, however, that if the M-pathway provides the substrate for Vernier performance this does not necessarily mean it supports detection of high spatial frequencies; sampling theory limitations on performance of the ganglion cell matrix may not apply so strictly to Vernier performance as to visual resolution.

Other evidence for the role of the P-pathway in high-resolution vision

The evidence presented for an important role for the M-pathway in spatial vision has been derived from single cell recording. Objections to this hypothesis come from other kinds of evidence. An important consideration is the sampling density of different cells. Present evidence suggests that neurones of the M-pathway may make up about 10% of all retinal ganglion cells. Neurones of the P-pathway with only M- and L-cone input make up about a further 65%, P-pathway cells with S-cone input (which almost certainly play no role in fine spatial vision) make up about 15%, and the remainder project to the midbrain (Perry et al., 1984; Perry and Cowey, 1985).

At any given retinal location, the sampling density of M-pathway cells is probably about a factor of 2 – 3 lower than the Nyquist limit for visual resolution at that eccentricity, or twice that if on- and off-centre cells are considered as forming separate matrices. This provides the opportunity for aliasing in the M-pathway, since the individual neurones respond to these high spatial frequencies, and it could be argued that their ability to signal high spatial frequencies is therefore limited.

It appears that, although ganglion cells are regularly distributed across the retina, they do not form a regular (e.g., hexagonal) matrix (Wässle et al., 1981). Thus, the aliased image will consist of two-dimensional spatial noise. How far the M-pathway may extract high spatial frequency information from this noise remains unclear. One possibility is some form of spatiotemporal averaging. Temporally, for maximal spatial resolution much longer presentation times are required than the critical duration for detection (Baron and Westheimer, 1973). A more intriguing possibility is some kind of spatial averaging of the M-pathway signal, making use of the fact that gratings are elongated in space. The striate cortex would seem ideally suited to perform such averaging, since it analyses different orientations separately in different columns. Once orientation specificity has been established, perhaps by combining input from many cell types over a patch of retina, then for any local region the two-dimensional sampling matrix collapses into a one-dimensional sampling array oriented perpendicular to the optimal orientation. The density of this array for M-pathway cells could then reach or exceed the Nyquist limit for a one-dimensional image; oversampling might indeed be useful for the Vernier family of tasks. It thus may be questionable whether the two-dimensional Nyquist limit is a sharp restriction on the resolution expected of the M-pathway, if the visual system assumes stimuli to be extended in space.

Another way of assessing the functional significance of the M- and P-pathways is to search for behavioural deficits in monkeys after lesions to one or the other of the two systems. It is possible to chemically lesion the P-pathway using the drug acrylamide, which selectively destroys P-pathway ganglion cells (Merigan and Eskin, 1986). Following this lesion, form vision, as measured by spatial frequency tuning curves, is remarkably unaffected except for a mild deficit in visual acuity and lessened sensitivity at low temporal frequencies. Ability to detect changes in colour is severely impaired. These results are broadly consistent with many of the physiological findings mentioned. Alternatively, it is possible to place ibotenic acid lesions in the magnocellular or parvocellular laminae of the LGN (Schiller et al., 1990; Merigan, 1991). The monkey then has a deficit in a restricted region of the visual field corresponding to the lesion. On testing the animal with flickering stimuli, results from these experiments are consistent with physiological data which suggest that the M-pathway underlies detection of luminance modulation and the P-pathway underlies detection of chromatic modulation. However, more puzzling is the fact that after M-pathway lesions, behaviour on certain photometric tasks involving pattern vision seems to be unaffected, i.e., performance is unimpaired in comparison with control locations in the visual field, with a degradation in performance near equal luminance. It is difficult to reconcile this result with the physiological observations mentioned above, in which it was shown that it is difficult to build a model based on P-pathway activity which could serve as a basis for a photometric task.

There are certain difficulties in interpreting lesion experiments; for example it is possible that the animal may be using the visual input to the superior colliculus or other brain-stem areas under some conditions. It is also possible that the presence of input from one system may have a sustaining influence on cortical mechanisms, although the other system may be more critical for their function. Nevertheless, there seems to be a real conflict between physiological and lesion data which has yet to be resolved.

Conclusions

I have attempted here to critically examine the

evidence for the respective roles of the M- and P-pathways in spatial vision, especially as regards performance at high spatial frequencies. A widely accepted hypothesis is that the M-pathway underlies high contrast sensitivities at low spatial frequencies but that the P-pathway takes over as spatial frequency is increased above, say, 20 – 30 cycles/degree. I have attempted to show that some assumptions upon which this hypothesis is based are probably invalid. The alternative hypothesis, supported by the physiological data, is that the M-pathway can support spatial vision at high spatial frequencies as well. It is certainly parsimonious to suppose that a single mechanism is responsible for the deterioration of performance observed at equal luminance, whatever kind of tasks are involved, whether involving low (flicker photometry) or high (resolution photometry) spatial frequencies (Livingstone and Hubel, 1987).

This does not imply that the P-pathway is not implicated in spatial tasks. Detection, identification and tracking of chromatically defined objects in luminance noise, and recognition of spatial patterns by chromatic cues alone (as with the Ishihara plates used for identifying colour-defective observers) clearly must depend on the P-pathway. Although such patterns may be fairly common in the normal environment, they are less commonly studied in psychophysical experiments.

There are objections to the M-pathway being the substrate for high-resolution vision. These arise predominantly from lesion experiments. It may be that the M- and P-pathways cooperate at a cortical level in ways which have not yet been defined. Perhaps both are necessary for generation of orientation specificity in striate cortex. In any event, it is probably naive to suppose that performance can simply be parcellated between the pathways in an additive manner. In terms of the neuronal basis of visual behaviour, the partitioning of function between these pathways provides an excellent example of how physiological and behavioural investigations should be able to combine to solve these problems.

Acknowledgements

I thank P.K. Kaiser, J. Kremers, A. Valberg, C. Wehrhahn and G. Westheimer who participated in some of the experiments described, and provided much valuable discussion of the manuscript.

References

Baron, W.S. and Westheimer, G. (1973) Visual acuity as a function of exposure duration. *J. Opt. Soc. Am.,* 63: 212 – 219.

Blakemore, C. and Vital-Durand, F. (1986) Organization and post-natal development of the monkey's lateral geniculate nucleus. *J. Physiol. (Lond.),* 380: 453 – 491.

Boynton, R.M. (1978) Ten years of research with the minimally distinct border. In: J.C. Armington, J. Krauskopf and B.R. Wooten (Eds.), *Visual Psychophysics and Physiology,* Academic Press, London, pp. 193 – 208.

Cavanagh, P., Tyler, C.W. and Favreau, O.E. (1984) Perceived velocity of moving chromatic gratings. *J. Opt. Soc. Am. A,* 1: 893 – 899.

Cavonius, C.R. and Robbins, D.O. (1973) Relationship between luminance and visual acuity of the rhesus monkey. *J. Physiol. (Lond.),* 232: 501 – 511.

Crook, J.M., Lee, B.B., Tigwell, D.A. and Valberg, A. (1987) Thresholds to chromatic spots of cells in the macaque geniculate nucleus as compared to detection sensitivity in man. *J. Physiol. (Lond.),* 392: 193 – 211.

Crook, J.M., Lange-Malecki, B., Lee, B.B. and Valberg, A. (1988) Visual resolution of macaque retinal ganglion cells. *J. Physiol. (Lond.),* 396: 205 – 224.

de Monasterio, F.M. and Gouras, P. (1975) Functional properties of ganglion cells of the rhesus monkey retina. *J. Physiol. (Lond.),* 251: 167 – 195.

Derrington, A.M. and Lennie, P. (1984) Spatial and temporal contrast sensitivities of neurones in lateral geniculate nucleus of macaque. *J. Physiol. (Lond.),* 357: 219 – 240.

DeValois, R.L. (1973) Central mechanisms of colour vision. In: R. Jung (Ed.), *Central Processing of Visual Information, A: Integrative Functions and Comparative Data,* Springer-Verlag, Berlin, pp. 209 – 253.

Gouras, P. (1968) Identification of cone mechanisms in monkey ganglion cells. *J. Physiol. (Lond.),* 199: 533 – 547.

Gouras, P. (1969) Antidromic responses of orthodromically identified ganglion cells in monkey retina. *J. Physiol. (Lond.),* 204: 407 – 419.

Gouras, P. (1984) Color Vision. *Prog. Retinal Res.,* 3: 227 – 262.

Ingling, C.R. (1991) Psychophysical correlates of parvo channel function. In: A. Valberg and B.B. Lee (Eds.), *From Pigments to Perception; Advances in Understanding the Visual Process,*

Plenum, New York, pp. 413 – 424.

Ingling, C.R. and Martinez-Uriegas, E. (1983) The spatio-chromatic signal of the r-g channel. In: J. Mollon and L.T. Sharpe (Eds.), *Colour Vision; Physiology and Psychophysics,* Academic Press, London.

Kaiser, P.K., Lee, B.B., Martin, P.R. and Valberg, A. (1990) The physiological basis of the minimally distinct border demonstrated in the ganglion cells of the macaque retina. *J. Physiol. (Lond.),* 422: 153 – 183.

Kaplan, E., Lee, B.B. and Shapley, R.M. (1990) New views of primate retinal function. *Prog. Retinal Res.,* 9: 273 – 336.

King-Smith, P.E. and Carden, D. (1976) Luminance and opponent-color contributions to visual detection and adaptation and to temporal and spatial integration. *J. Opt. Soc. Am.,* 66: 709 – 717.

Lee, B.B. (1991) On the relation between cellular sensitivity and psychophysical detection. In: A. Valberg and B.B. Lee (Eds.), *From Pigments to Perception; Advances in Understanding the Visual Process,* Plenum Press, London, pp. 105 – 116.

Lee, B.B., Virsu, V. and Elepfandt, A. (1981) The phase of responses to moving gratings in cells of the cat retina and lateral geniculate nucleus. *J. Neurophysiol.,* 45: 801 – 817.

Lee, B.B., Martin, P.R. and Valberg, A. (1988) The physiological basis of heterochromatic flicker photometry demonstrated in the ganglion cells of the macaque retina. *J. Physiol. (Lond.),* 404: 323 – 347.

Lee, B.B., Martin, P.R. and Valberg, A. (1989) Sensitivity of macaque ganglion cells to luminance and chromatic flicker. *J. Physiol. (Lond.),* 414: 223 – 243.

Lee, B.B., Pokorny, J., Smith, V.C., Martin, P.R. and Valberg, A. (1990) Luminance and chromatic modulation sensitivity of macaque ganglion cells and human observers. *J. Opt. Soc. Am. A,* 7: 2223 – 2236.

Lennie, P. (1986) Recent developments in the physiology of color vision. *Trends Neurosci.,* 7: 243 – 248.

Livingstone, M.S. and Hubel, D.H. (1987) Psychophysical evidence for separate channels for the perception of form, color, motion and depth. *J. Neurosci.,* 7: 3416 – 3468.

Lu, C. and Fender, D.H. (1972) The interaction of color and luminance in stereoscopic vision. *Invest. Opthalmol.,* 11: 482 – 490.

Merigan, W.R. (1991) P- and M-pathway specialization in the macaque. In: A. Valberg and B.B. Lee (Eds.), *From Pigments to Perception; Advances in Understanding the Visual Process,* Plenum Press, London, pp. 117 – 126.

Merigan, W.R. and Eskin, T.A. (1986) Spatio-temporal vision of macaques with severe loss of Pb retinal ganglion cells. *Vision Res.,* 26: 1751 – 1761.

Mullen, K.T. (1985) The contrast sensitivity of human colour vision to red-green and blue-yellow chromatic gratings. *J.*

Physiol. (Lond.), 359: 381 – 400.

Peichl, L. and Wässle, H. (1979) Size, scatter and coverage of ganglion cell receptive field centres in the cat retina. *J. Physiol. (Lond.),* 291: 117 – 141.

Perry, V.H. and Cowey, A. (1985) Retinal ganglion cells which project to the pretectum and superior colliculus of the macaque monkey. *Neuroscience,* 12: 1125 – 1137.

Perry, V.H. and Silveira, L.C.L. (1988) Functional lamination in the ganglion cell layer of the macaque's retina. *Neuroscience,* 25: 217 – 223.

Perry, V.H., Oehler, R. and Cowey, A. (1984) Retinal ganglion cells that project to the dorsal lateral geniculate nucleus in the macaque monkey. *Neuroscience,* 12: 1110 – 1123.

Pokorny, J., Graham, C.H. and Lanson, R.N. (1968) Effect of wavelength on foveal grating acuity. *J. Opt. Soc. Am.,* 58: 1410 – 1414.

Schiller, P.H., Logothetis, N.K. and Charles, E.R. (1990) Functions of the colour-opponent and broad-band channels of the visual system. *Nature,* 343: 68 – 70.

Shapley, R.M. and Perry, V.H. (1986) Cat and monkey retinal ganglion cells and their visual functional roles. *Trends Neurosci,* 9: 229 – 235.

Shapley, R.M. and Victor, J. (1986) Hyperacuity in cat retinal ganglion cells. *Science,* 231: 999 – 1002.

Shapley, R.M., Reid, R.C. and Kaplan, E. (1991) Receptive field structure of P and M cells in the monkey retina. In: A. Valberg and B.B. Lee (Eds.), *From Pigments to Perception; Advances in Understanding the Visual Process,* Plenum, New York, pp. 95 – 104.

Sperling, H.G. and Harwerth, R.S. (1971) Red-green cone interactions in the incremental spectral sensitivity of primates. *Science,* 172: 180 – 184.

Valberg, A., Lee, B.B., Kaiser, P.K. and Kremers, J. (1992) Responses of macaque ganglion cells to movement of chromatic borders. *J. Physiol. (Lond.),* in press.

Wagner, G. and Boynton, R.M. (1972) Comparison of four methods of heterochromatic photometry. *J. Opt. Soc. Am.,* 62: 1508 – 1515.

Wässle, H., Boycott, B.B. and Illing, R.-B. (1981) Morphology and mosaic of on- and off-beta cells in the cat retina and some functional considerations. *Proc. R. Soc. Lond. (Biol.),* 212: 177 – 195.

Wehrhahn, C. and Westheimer, G. (1990) How Vernier acuity depends on contrast. *Exp. Brain Res.,* 80: 618 – 620.

Wiesel, T.N. and Hubel, D.H. (1966) Spatial and chromatic interactions in the lateral geniculate body of the rhesus monkey. *J. Neurophysiol.,* 29: 1115 – 1156.

Williams, D.R. (1986) Seeing through the photoreceptor mosaic. *Trends Neurosci.,* 9: 193.

CHAPTER 5

The neurophysiological correlates of colour induction, colour and brightness contrast

Otto D. Creutzfeldt[1]

Department of Neurobiology, Max Planck Institute for Biophysical Chemistry, D-3400 Göttingen, Germany

Introduction

The perceived colours of surfaces do not only depend on the spectral composition of the light reflected from them, but also on the spectral composition and the intensity of light reflected from the surround. These surround effects imply phenomena such as colour contrast, colour induction and coloured shadows. They have been known to psychophysicists for over 200 years and had imposed, from early on, difficulties on colour perception models based merely on the decomposition of light into various spectral domains by different wavelength sensitive filters (receptors) and linear summation of their respective outputs. Therefore, Helmholz considered them as "psychological" errors of judgement thus referring them to cortical mechanisms. But other sensory physiologists of the time such as Fechner, Hering and Mach assumed that they were of retinal origin and suggested models similar to those proposed in more recent times by, e.g., Jameson and Hurvich or Land (for review and references, see Creutzfeldt et al., 1987).

The model

A common feature to all colour contrast phenomena is that the perceived colour of a test ob-

ject (or surface) is shifted by a chromatic surround in a direction complementary to the predominant surround colour. Thus a yellow test field will look slightly greenish when surrounded by red, and slightly reddish when surrounded by green or green-blue. This is most clearly seen in the case of colour induction on a white surface which will appear as an unsaturated green when surrounded by red, as unsaturated blue when surrounded by yellow, as unsaturated red when surrounded by green and as unsaturated yellow when surrounded by blue. This type of colour induction is best seen when the test and the inducing colours are of about equal luminance.

Colour induction and colour contrast can be described by a model such as depicted in Fig. 1. Here it is assumed that the light reflected from a white surface in the centre excites the long and middle wavelength-sensitive retinal receptors and through them the red and green excited neuronal opponent channels about equally (R and G in Fig. 1A). This balanced excitation of the wide-band red- and green-sensitive neurons we may consider as the neuronal signal for white (see below). A red surround decreases, through lateral interaction, the responsiveness of the long wavelength-sensitive opponent neurons resulting in fewer red than green signals elicited by the central white surface (Fig. 1B). The green signals may be even slightly increased because of reduced opponent suppression from the red excited channels (short arrows in Fig. 1). As the

---

[1] Deceased 23 January, 1992.

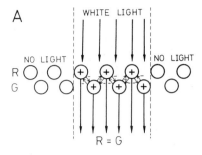

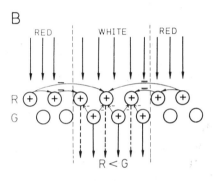

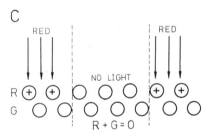

Fig. 1. Model to explain chromatic induction on white surfaces. *A*. White light excites about equally the wide band red-(R) and green (G)-sensitive opponent cells (WL- and WM-cells, L- and M-cone excited, respectively, see text) of the retino-geniculate pathway. Reciprocal opponent inhibition between the R- and G-channels is indicated by short arrows. *B*. Illumination of the surround with red light reduces the responsiveness of the R-channel (bent arrows), resulting in less R- than G-signals elicited by the white stimulus. The white surface looks therefore greenish. *C*. A red surround has no inducing effect if the central area is not illuminated. (Adapted from Creutzfeldt et al., 1990 and Kastner et al., 1992.)

excitatory responses of parvocellular neurons do not only code for the colour but, in different combinations, also for the brightness of a surface (see below), it should follow from the model of Fig. 1

that the central test field should not only look greenish but also slightly darker in the red surround. This is indeed the case. No opponent colour induction should result, if the centre is dark and only the surround is turned on (Fig. 1*C*). This also corresponds to perception.

This model can be applied to colour contrast as well. It predicts that the colour of an object should look less green in, for example, a green rather than in a red surround because the responsiveness of the green-sensitive receptor-neuron channel is reduced by the green surround. Now take a turquoise object in a blue and in a red environment: since the blue environment reflects more green and blue light than the red environment, the responsiveness of the blue- and green-sensitive chromatic channels will be reduced in the blue, but only little, if at all, enhanced in the red surround. As a consequence, the green-blue signals elicited by the turquoise test field will be reduced relative to the red-yellow signals and the test field will look more yellowish in a blue than in a red environment.

The psychophysical test

For a quantitative test of the model, we have shown to human observers two identical red, yellow or turquoise objects (test fields) with broadband reflectance but embedded in different, either red, green or blue surrounds. The whole display was illuminated by trichromatic white light except for one of the central test fields the illumination of which could be changed on demand of the observer. Subjects were asked to make the colours of the two central fields look identical by changing the spectral composition of the illumination of one of the test fields. The spectral composition of the light reflected from this field, after the match was considered satisfactory by the observer, was then measured with a spectrophotometer and compared to that of the comparison field which was surrounded by another colour. As expected, subjects had to add, e.g., more red light to the colour of the test object if it was surrounded by red light in order to match it with its colour in a green environment etc.

In a next step, we have illuminated the whole display only with monochromatic blue, green or red light, i.e., one of the primaries of our trichromatic

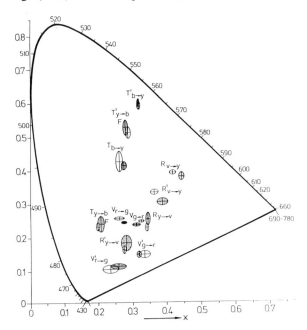

Fig. 2. CIE colour values of test fields after colour match (shaded ellipses) and monochromatic brightness match (open ellipses). Means from three observers. Test fields were coloured plates (3.15 × 3.15°; T, turquoise; V, violet; R, red) surrounded by blue (b), yellow (y), red (r), green (g) or violet (v) plates of about the same luminance. In some experiments the standard trichomatic white illuminant was changed by reducing the intensity of one of the primaries (symbols R′, T′, V′) The apparent colour of a test plate had to be compared to a matching field which was surrounded by a complementary colour. Observers were asked to match the colour of, e.g., a turquoise field surrounded by blue with that of the same turquoise comparison field but surrounded by yellow ($T_y \rightarrow b$), by changing the composition of the trichromatic illumination of the matching field. The CIE values of the light reflected from that matching field were measured with the photometer and the mean values from three observers (three measurements per observer) were drawn into a CIE chart (shaded fields, with standard deviations). Observers were then asked to match the brightness of the two testfields surrounded by different colours while they were illuminated with monochromatic blue, green or red light. The matching field was then illuminated with the three primaries as set during the monochromatic brightness match. The CIE colour values of the matching field in this illumination were also determined photometrically (open ellipses). The plots show that the colours of the matching field were about the same after the two matching procedures (for further details see text).

white. Now subjects had to match the brightness of the test fields in each monochromatic illumination by simply changing the luminance of the comparison field. If that was surrounded by green and the test field by red, the comparison field looked, of course, brighter than the test field during monochromatic red illumination and darker in monochromatic green owing to the darkness inducing effect of the brighter surround. After the brightness match was finished in the three monochromatic illumination conditions of our primaries, the matching field was illuminated with the intensities of blue, green and red as set in the monochromatic brightness match, but the rest of the display with the normal trichromatic white. The colours of the two test fields looked now nearly the same, like after the colour match, and the spectral composition of the light reflected from the comparison field was also about the same as that after the colour match (Fig. 2).

The outcome of this experiment is consistent with the hypothesis that colour contrast is, in fact, the consequence of brightness contrasts in the various spectral regions, and with what psychophysicists had suggested more or less explicitly for over 100 years. But it is not clear from these experiments where the mechanisms are located that bring about such a brightness scaling in the various spectral neuronal channels. For this one needs to look at the neuronal signals at the different levels of the visual system.

The neurophysiological data

Changes of responsiveness of spectrally sensitive opponent neurons induced by surround illumination can be found already in the parvocellular layers of the lateral geniculate body (P-LGN) and their retinal afferents (Creutzfeldt et al., 1991a). For demonstrating this we recorded from P-LGN neurons of anaesthetized trichromatic cynomolgus monkeys (*Macaca fascicularis*). The spectral response functions (SRF's) of these neurons were determined by shining $1-3°$ diameter spots of light of different dominant wavelength into the receptive

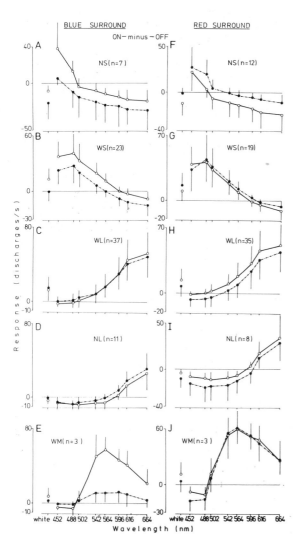

Fig. 3. Mean spectral response functions (SRF) of P-LGN cells in the various functional classes, determined without (open circles) or with surround illumination (closed circles). Stimuli were $1-3°$ spots of about 20 cd/m^2 with different maximum wavelength as indicated on the abscissa. They were shone for 3 sec into the receptive field, and a pause of 3 sec separated successive stimuli. Responses are defined as on-minus-off discharges. In each neuron measurements were repeated three times and the average and standard deviation was calculated for all neurons belong to one functional group. For names of the functional groups, see text. Open circles and continuous lines: control SRFs without surround. Closed circles and broken lines: SRFs of the same neurons when the outer surround (inner diameter 5°, outer diameter 20°) was illuminated with equiluminant blue (452 nm) $(A-E)$ or red (664 nm) $(F-J)$ light. Note that in the control situation only the W-cells are excited by white while the N-cells are inhibited (responses to white are shown at the left of each diagram). (From Creutzfeldt et al., 1991a.)

field of the cells. The stimuli were of approximately equal luminance. For every cell the average of three stimuli each lasting 3 sec was determined and the average response amplitude of all cells belonging to one of the P-LGN-opponent groups was calculated for each spectral stimulus (see Fig. $3A-J$, open circles, continuous lines). Cells were classified into narrow (N) and wide band (W) cells excited by either short (S) or long (L) wavelengths, NS-cells largely correspond to the $B+/Y-$ category of other authors and are excited by S-cones, WS-cells to the $G+/R-$ category (excited by M-cones), WL- and NL-cells to the $R+/G-$ category (excited by L-cones) and WM-cells to the $Y+/B-$ category (excited by M-cones) (Creutzfeldt et al., 1979; Lee et al., 1987). An important distinguishing criterion between W- and S-cells is that the W-cells are excited and the N-cells inhibited by white light (open circles at the left of each SRF in Fig. 3). Thus, the neuronal signal for white is a nearly equal excitation of the W-cells and inhibition of the S-cells, while that for red is a simultaneous excitation of the WL- and NL-cells etc.

Following the control, the SRF of each neuron was repeated while the outer surround was illuminated with either blue (452 nm) or red (664 nm) light at luminance equal to that of the centre stimuli. The inner diameter of the surround ring was 5°, the outer 20°, leaving a gap of $1-2°$ between the centre and the surround stimulus in order to avoid direct illumination of the receptive field. The mean SRF's in Fig. 3 clearly show that during surround illumination with blue light the responses of the S-cells (Fig. $3A$ and B, closed circles, broken lines) and during red surround illumination those of the L-cells are reduced (Fig. $3H$ and I). The effects of surround illumination with light opponent to the excitatory wavelengths of the respective cells varies between the different groups but a slight tendency for increased responses can be recognized (Fig. $3C,D,F,G$). WM-cells which constitute a small minority (4%) of the P-LGN cells, make an exception and will not be further considered here (see Creutzfeldt et al., 1991b).

The neurophysiological results are in excellent qualitative agreement with perception and with our model in that they show that chromatic surround illumination decreases responsiveness of opponent cells if the surround colour is in the excitatory spectral region of the respective cell. This is a sufficient condition for the phenomena of colour contrast, but the experiments also explain colour induction on white surfaces. As mentioned earlier, the neuronal signal for white is an about equal excitation of all W-

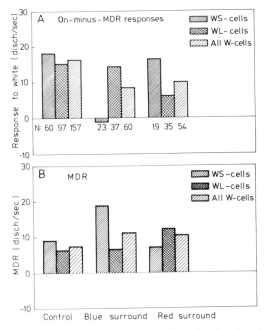

Fig. 4. Responses of W-cells to white stimuli and maintained discharge rate (MDR) during surround illumination. *A*. Responses are measured as on-minus-maintained discharge rate (MDR). Stimulation and data representation otherwise the same as in Fig. 3. N, Number of neurons in the respective groups. Mean values for WS-, WL- and all W-cells. In the control situation (left columns), the response amplitudes of the WL- and WS-cells to white stimuli were about the same, but during blue surround illumination (middle columns) the white responses of the WS-cells and during red surround illumination (right columns) those of the WL-cells were strongly reduced. The population response of all W-cells, which code for brightness, is about equally reduced by the blue and red surrounds ("All W-cells" columns). *B*. MDR of the various cell groups under the same conditions as in *A*. Note the strong increase of MDR of WS-cells during blue and of WL-cells during red surround illumination. These data show that the changes of responsiveness go largely on account of increased MDR of WS-cells during blue and of WL-cells during red surround illumination. (From Kastner et al., 1992).

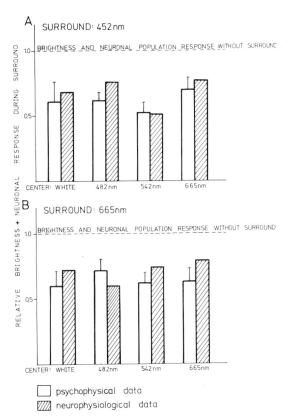

Fig. 5. Reduction of brightness (open columns) and of P-LGN responses (hatched columns) during surround illumination. Broken horizontal lines (ordinate 1.0): control values without surrounds; columns: relative values (ordinate) during illumination of the surround with blue (*A*) or red (*B*) light of about equal luminance with the centre stimulus. Measurements were done for different centre colours as indicated on the abscissa. Centre stimuli were $1-3°$ in diameter in the neurophysiological experiment and 1.5° in the psychophysical measurements. Surrounds had an inner diameter of 5° and an outer diameter of 20° in both experiments. Psychophysical data are the means from four observers (with standard deviation) and represent the luminance of a test point (without surround) after brightness adjustment to that of the comparison point with the surround. The neurophysiological data are the mean population responses (on-minus-off) of 260 P-LGN cells, obtained by adding the responses of all W-cells and subtracting those of N-cells. (From Creutzfeldt et al., 1991a).

cells (see Fig. 4, left columns). Our recordings show that during blue surround illumination (Fig. 4, middle columns) the on-minus-off responses of the WS-cells are completely suppressed and during red surround illumination (Fig. 4, right columns) the responses of the WL-cells are strongly reduced. This would mean that during blue surround illumination the white surface excites predominantly WL-cells, which code for yellow-red if excited alone or in connection with NL-cells. For perception their excitation should then indicate a yellow-reddish colour. Red surround illumination, on the other side, shifts excitation by the white surface towards the WS-cells by reducing the excitation of the red-yellow coding WL-cells thus signalling in perception an unsaturated green. Also the darkness induction of the chromatic surrounds is explained by the data as the sum of the excitations of the W-cells, which code for brightness (see Creutzfeldt et al., 1991a), is reduced about equally by both surround colours (see Fig. 4, "All W-cells" columns).

The darkness induction in perception caused by chromatic surrounds corresponds also quantitatively to the reduction of the summed population response of P-LGN unit activity. Both, brightness in perception and the P-LGN population response are reduced by about 30 – 40% during blue or red outer surround illumination if centre and surround are of about equal luminance. This is shown in Fig. 5 where the darkness induction in human observers caused by blue (Fig. 5A, white columns) or red surrounds (Fig. 5B, white columns) on different centre colours are compared with the reduction of the P-LGN unit population responses (hatched columns). In both the neurophysiological and the psychophysical experiments, intensity and spatial dimension of the centre and surround stimuli were identical. The surround had an inner diameter of 5° and an outer diameter of 20°. Fig. 5 shows that the darkness induction in perception and the reduction of the neuronal population responses of the monkey's P-LGN cells are indeed nearly identical. In the human observers, the darkness induction was even slightly stronger than the response reduction of the P-LGN cells. This may have been due to pupillary constriction in the human subjects, while an arteficial pupil of fixed diameter was located in front of the monkey's eye.

The data so far clearly indicate that the neural correlates of colour contrast, colour induction and

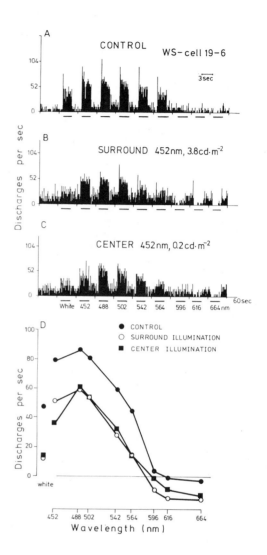

Fig. 6. Effect of surround and of centre illumination with blue light (452 nm) on the spectral response function (SRF) of a WS-cell. The SRF was determined with spots of light of different dominant wavelength (abscissa) and a diameter of 1.5°. A – C. Original histograms. D. Amplitudes of on-minus-MDR responses. A and D, closed circles: control SRF. B and D, open circles: SRF during continuous illumination of the surround (inner diameter 5°, outer diameter 20°) with blue light (452 nm) at an intensity of 3.8 cd/m². C and D, closed squares: SRF during continuous illumination of the receptive field with a 2° diameter blue light at an intensity of 0.2 cd/m². Note, that the SRFs are lowered to nearly identical values by surround illumination and by chromatic centre adaptation. In both conditions, MDR is significantly increased as compared to the control (see activity in histograms A – C at left, preceding the responses to white).

brightness contrast are already present at the level of the P-LGN. In numerous cases, we were able to record simultaneously from a P-LGN relay cell and the S-potential representing the activity of its afferent retinal optic tract fibre. In such recordings the surround-induced changes of responsiveness were identical in both units. This indicates that the mechanisms for these effects must be located in the retina. In fact, the surround effects are experimentally not distinguishable from chromatic adaptation of the receptive field centre with the same colour as the surround, but with lower intensity. We have established this for representative samples of neurons in the various functional classes and under different conditions (Creutzfeldt et al., 1991b). A typical example is shown in Fig. 6. In this WS-cell, the response amplitudes to the excitatory spectral and white stimuli were reduced about equally by continuous illumination of the surround with 3.8 cd/m^2, 452 nm light (Fig. 6B and open circles in D) as by continuous ilumination of the receptive field with the same colour but an intensity of only 0.2 cd/m^2, i.e., about 5% of that of the surround light (Fig. 6C and filled squares in D). These and other results suggest that the chromatic surround effects may in fact be due to receptor adaptation in the receptive field centre, caused by straylight scattered from the surround rather than by lateral interactions via horizontal connections in the retina. This straylight is not an experimental artefact (e.g., clowding of the eye media) as qualitatively and quantitatively the same results are obtained in healthy humans in psychophysical measurements. The horizontal arrows in Fig. 1B would then not stand for lateral connections via, e.g., horizontal cells but for intraretinal light scatter. This conclusion is consistent with a number of psychophysical, anatomical and physiological data as discussed elsewhere (Hicks et al., 1983; Creutzfeldt et al., 1991b). It is also supported by the fact that surround lights of the intensity and spatial dimensions as used in our experiments affect the maintained discharge rate (MDR) in the same direction as centre lights. Thus surround and centre illumination with light in the excitatory spectral region of a cell will increase

MDR, while surround and centre light of an opponent colour will both suppress MDR. Quantitatively, surround effects on MDR are of course much weaker than the centre effects, with about the same ratio as that for effects on responsiveness. Yet, the response changes observed during surround as well as during centre illumination go, to a large extent, on account of the altered MDR (or the off-activity), while sensitivity changes play quantitatively only a minor role. This becomes clear from Fig. 4B, where

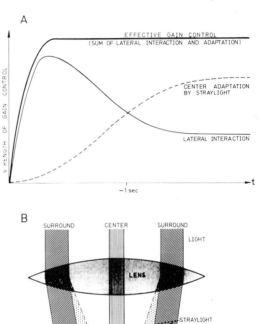

Fig. 7. Schematic sketch of the two-stage model for simultaneous colour contrast. A. Two processes are assumed, the first one (lateral interaction) starting immediately, but decaying within a second or so, while the second one (centre adaptation by straylight) develops more slowly. The sum of both is nearly constant over time. B. The lateral interaction process is assumed to act via horizontal cells changing the gain of the receptor bipolar synapse. The adaptation process exerted by straylight from the surround adapts the receptors feeding directly into the receptive field of a ganglion cell. For further explanation see text. (From Creutzfeldt et al., 1991b.)

52

the MDR of WL- and WS-cells during the various stimulus conditions is shown. It is clear from these data that the strong reduction of the on-minus-MDR responses of the WS- and the WL-cells to white centre stimuli goes essentially on account of the strong increase of MDR during blue or red surround illumination, respectively.

It is difficult to explain only with straylight the induction effects of flashing surround stimuli. These are, after a short initial period suggesting additivity of centre lights and straylight from the surround, in the same direction as the effects of continuous surrounds. A central test field thus becomes darker if light is flashed into the surround and its colour changes in a direction complementary to that of the surround flash. In order to explain this, inhibitory lateral interactions between centre and surround through horizontal connections in the retina may be assumed. This has led us to a two-stage model for surround effects such as depicted in Fig. 7.

In Fig. 7A the approximate time courses of the two mechanisms are shown. It is assumed here that the initial lateral inhibitory interaction decays within about 1 sec to a steady state level and that the centre adaptation through straylight develops with about the same time course as experimental data suggest (see Creutzfeldt et al., 1991b). In Fig. 7B, the two mechanisms are schematically presented. Lateral interaction is understood as a gain control of the transmission from the receptors to the bipolar cells, while the straylight from the surround excites and adapts directly the receptors in the receptive field centre. This model will probably have to be modified eventually, but the experimental data so far indicate that the mechanisms for colour induction, colour contrast and brightness contrast are located in the retina and maybe caused to a large extent by the eye media. This applies to the mechanisms for colour constancy as well, in as much as these are related to colour contrast and colour induction.

Summary and conclusions

Psychophysical experiments suggest that colour contrast and colour induction by surround lights can be explained as brightness contrasts (darkness induction) in the spectral region of the surround colour. It follows from this model that a chromatic surround reduces the gain of receptor-ganglion cell channels if the surround colour is in their excitatory spectral region. Thus, a green-sensitive cell (G + /R − or WS in our nomenclature) would respond less to a blue-green stimulus flashed into its receptive field when the surround (5°/20° inner/outer diameter) is illuminated with blue light. Neurophysiological experiments show that this is indeed the case and that such surround-induced response changes are present already in relay cells of the parvocellular layers of the lateral geniculate nucleus (P-LGN) and their retinal afferents. These surround-induced response changes are in qualitative and quantitative agreement with psychophysical experiments. Since the neuronal signal for white consists of a balanced excitation of the M-cone excited, green-blue-sensitive WS-cells and the L-cone excited, yellow-red-sensitive WL-cells, the findings also explain colour induction on white surfaces as well as coloured shadows: during blue surround illumination, white signals from the WS-cells, and during red surround the white signals from the WL-cells are reduced. The neurophysiological surround effects on P-LGN cells are identical but weaker than those produced by light of the same colour shone into the receptive field centres. They are therefore undistinguishable from direct adaptation of those receptors which feed directly into the receptive field of the respective cells. This suggests that they are caused by scattered light reaching the receptive field from the surround.

References

Creutzfeldt, O.D., Lee, B.B. and Elepfandt, A. (1979) A quantitative study of chromatic organisation and receptive fields of cells in the lateral geniculate body of the rhesus monkey. *Exp. Brain Res.,* 35: 527 – 545.
Creutzfeldt, O.D., Lange-Malecki, B. and Wortmann, K. (1987) Darkness induction, retinex and cooperative mechanisms in vision. *Exp. Brain Res.,* 67: 270 – 283.
Creutzfeldt, O.D., Lang-Malecki, B. and Dreyer, E. (1990)

Chromatic induction and brightness contrast: relativistic colour model. *J. Opt. Soc. Am.,* 7: 1644 – 1653.

Creutzfeldt, O.D., Crook, J.M., Kastner, S., Chao-Yi Li and Xing Pei (1991a) The neurophysiological correlates of colour and brightness contrast in lateral geniculate neurons. I. Population analysis. *Exp. Brain Res.,* 87: 3 – 21.

Creutzfeldt, O.D., Kastner, S., Xing Pei and Valberg, A. (1991b) The neurophysiological correlates of colour and brightness contrast in lateral geniculate neurons. II. Adaptation and surround effects. *Exp. Brain Res.,* 87: 22 – 45.

Hicks, T.P., Lee, B.B. and Vidyasagar, T.R. (1983) The responses of cells in macaque lateral geniculate nucleus to sinusoidal gratings. *J. Physiol. (Lond.),* 337: 183 – 200.

Kastner, S., Chao-Yi, L., Pei, X., Crook, J.M. and Creutzfeldt, O.D. (1992) Neurophysiological correlates of colour induction on white surfaces. *Eur. J. Neurosci.,* in press.

Lee, B.B., Valberg, A., Tigwell, D.A. and Tryti, J. (1987) An account of responses of spectrally opponent neurons in macaque lateral geniculate nucleus to successive contrast. *Proc. R. Soc. Lond., Ser. B,* 230: 293 – 314.

Section II

Sensory Integration in Superior Colliculus

T.P. Hicks, S. Molotchnikoff and T. Ono (Eds.)
Progress in Brain Research, Vol. 95
© 1993 Elsevier Science Publishers B.V. All rights reserved.

CHAPTER 6

Determinants of axonal and dendritic structure in the superior colliculus

Richard D. Mooney and Robert W. Rhoades

Department of Anatomy, Medical College of Ohio, Toledo, OH 43699, U.S.A.

Introduction

The constraints that govern the conformation of both the axonal arborizations and the dendritic arbors of central nervous system (CNS) neurons have been studied extensively (for reviews, see Rakic, 1975; Purves and Lichtman, 1985). The rodent superior colliculus (SC) has also been used by numerous investigators as a model for studying the development and plasticity of CNS pathways (e.g., Lund and Lund, 1971; Frost and Schneider, 1976; Land and Lund, 1979; Frost et al., 1979). This nucleus affords an excellent opportunity to address both the role of target in the determination of axonal morphology (e.g., Schneider et al., 1987; Pallas and Finlay, 1991), and also the influence of afferent input in determining the structural characteristics of postsynaptic neurons (Tokunaga et al., 1985).

The dominant input to the superficial SC laminae is that from the retina, and all of the neurons in the superficial SC laminae (the *stratum griseum superficiale* (SGS) and *stratum opticum* (SO)) are exclusively visual (e.g., Tiao and Blakemore, 1976; Chalupa and Rhoades, 1977; Finlay et al., 1978; Stein and Dixon, 1979). However, when one or both eyes are enucleated at birth, somatosensory axons that would normally terminate in the deep layers (those ventral to the SO) extend into the superficial laminae and make functional contacts with neurons in the SGS and SO (Rhoades, 1980; Rhoades et al., 1981).

Most retino-SC axons in hamster (Fig. 1*A,B*) give rise to a single dorsally directed arbor (Sachs and Schneider, 1984; Mooney and Rhoades, 1990). Contrastingly, subcortical somatosensory inputs to the deep layers in normal hamsters, in particular trigemino-SC axons (Fig. 1*C,D*), have a very different morphology. These fibers course parallel to the SC laminae in the *stratum album intermedium* (SAI) and give off multiple clusters of boutons in this layer and the ventral portion of the overlying *stratum griseum intermediale* (SGI) (Rhoades et al., 1989).

Morphology of trigemino-SC axons in the superficial SC laminae of neonatally enucleated adult hamsters

The termination of subcortical somatosensory afferents in a portion of the SC normally innervated by retinal axons raises the question addressed by the experiments in the first portion of this paper: if an axon innervates a novel target, does it retain its normal morphological characteristics or does it develop structural properties appropriate for its new termination? This question has already been addressed at the ultrastructural level by Campbell and Frost (1988). They reported that when retinal axons were induced to make permanent projections to the ventrobasal nucleus (VB) rather than the lateral geniculate nucleus (LGNd), their terminals and associated glomeruli more nearly resembled those

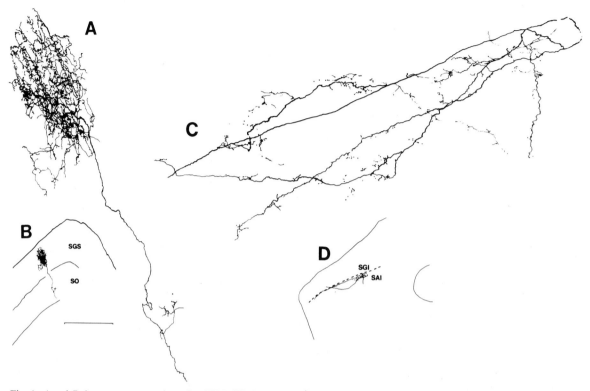

Fig. 1. *A* and *B* show a reconstruction of an HRP-filled retinotectal axon and its orientation in the SC of a normal adult hamster. *C* and *D* show a reconstruction and orientation of an HRP-filled trigemino-SC axon from a normal hamster. The calibration is 100 μm (*A* and *C*), 0.5 mm (*B*) and 1.0 mm (*D*).

normally made in the VB by somatosensory axons than retino-LGNd terminals.

We used two approaches to visualize trigemino-SC axons from subnucleus interpolaris (SpI) that were induced to innervate the superficial SC laminae by removal of both eyes on the day of birth: (1) anterograde transport of *Phaseolus vulgaris* leucoagglutinin (PHAL) (Gerfen and Sawchenko, 1984); and (2) anterograde tracing with RITC-labeled dextran (fluoro-ruby) (Schmeud et al., 1990).

Large injections of PHAL into SpI (Fig. 2*A*) resulted in numerous labeled axons in the SO and lower SGS (Fig. 2*B*) of each enucleated hamster in which successful injections were carried out. Superficial trigemino-SC axons were most dense in the lateral portion of the SGS and SO (Fig. 2*B,C*). This occurred regardless of the location of the injection

Fig. 2. *A* is a brightfield photomicrograph of a horizontal section through the brain-stem showing a PHAL injection site in SpI in an enucleate hamster. The calibration is 500 μm. *B* shows PHAL-labeled fibers entering the superficial SC laminae at its lateral border and extending medially in the SGS and SO. The inset is a lower power photomicrograph of the same section. The arrows point toward corresponding points in the two photographs. Note that the heavy labeling in the superficial laminae is restricted to the lateral SC. The calibrations are 250 μm. *C* is a photomontage of a PHAL-labeled axon that could be followed from the deep layers into the lateral portion of the SGS and SO. The arrows denote points at which the fiber gave off collaterals. The calibration is 100 μm. *D* shows another PHAL-labeled fiber in the SO. The arrows point to two distinct clusters of boutons. Note that some collaterals descend back into the SGI. The calibration is 200 μm. *E* shows two clusters (arrows) in the SGI of an enucleated animal. The calibration is 100 μm. *F* shows a fiber in the SO that gave off five distinct terminal clusters (arrows). The calibration is 200 μm.

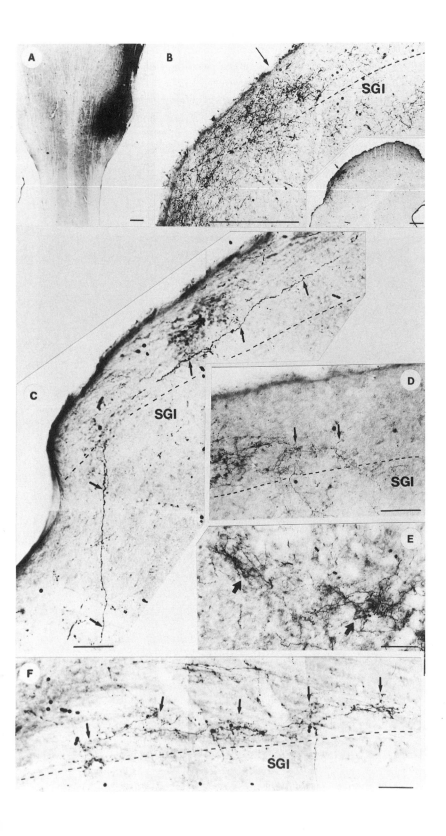

60

site within SpI. The morphology of most of the trigemino-SC axons innervating the superficial layers was similar to that of such fibers which terminated in the deep layers of normal animals. Axons generally coursed parallel to the SC surface and gave off

several distinct clusters of boutons as they traveled from the lateral boundary of the colliculus toward its medial border (Fig. 2C,D,F). Some fibers that extended into the superficial layers also sent axon collaterals back into the deep laminae (Fig. 2D). All of

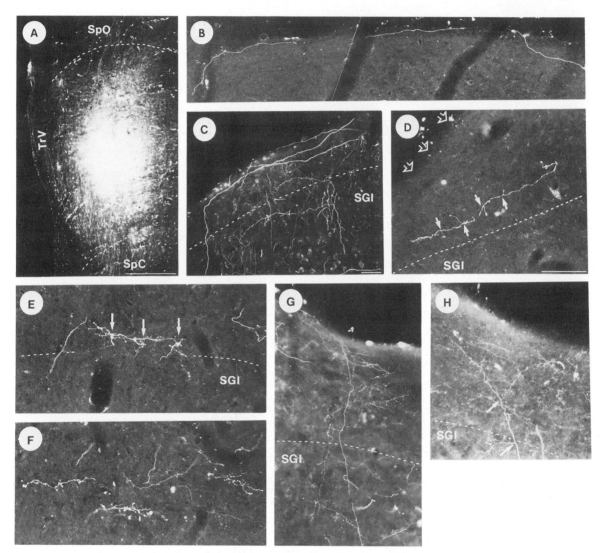

Fig. 3. *A* is an episcopic fluorescence photomicrograph of a portion of a horizontal section through SpI showing the center of a fluorruby injection site. The dashed lines denote the rostral and caudal borders of SpI. SpO, Trigeminal subnucleus oralis; SpC, trigeminal subnucleus caudalis; TrV, trigeminal spinal tract. *B* and *C* show fluoro-ruby-labeled axons ascending to the SC surface near its lateral border and turning medially. The fiber shown in *B* is unusual in that it could be followed medially for over 1 mm and never gave off any collaterals. *D* shows a portion of a labeled trigemino-SC axon in the SO that gave rise to several short collaterals (solid arrows). The open arrows denote the SC surface. *E* and *F* show portions of several horizontally oriented fibers in the lower SO. Note the three distinct clusters of boutons given off by the fiber in *E*. *G* and *H* show two fibers that arose as collaterals of trigemino-SC axons that innervated the deep laminae. Both of these collaterals ascended to the SC surface. The arrows in *H* indicate two branch points on the fiber depicted. Calibration: *A*, 250 µm; *B–H*, 100 µm.

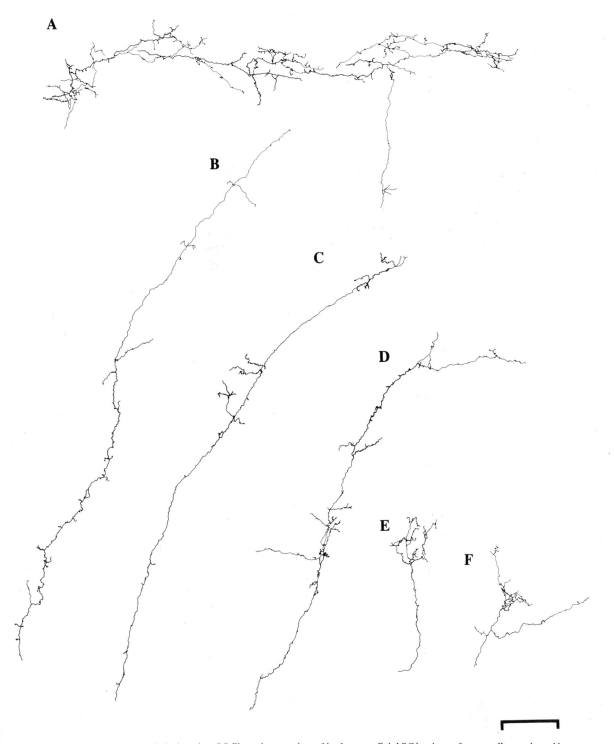

Fig. 4. Drawings of PHAL-labeled trigemino-SC fibers that terminated in the superficial SC laminae of neonatally enucleated hamsters. A – D show fibers that entered the superficial layers at the lateral border of the SC; E and F illustrate single collaterals that arose from fibers that had most of their terminal arbors in the deep layers. The calibration is 100 μm.

the enucleated animals also had a large number of labeled axons which terminated only in the deep laminae and these fibers also gave rise to clustered terminal arborizations (Fig. 2E) that did not appear significantly different from those observed in normal hamsters (Fig. 2E).

Tracing with fluoro-ruby provided the same type of results as those obtained with PHAL. Injection sites completely restricted to SpI (Fig. 3A) resulted in fairly heavy labeling in the lower SGS and SO (Fig. 3C – H) although a few fibers did extend to the SC surface (Fig. 3B,C). These axons also coursed parallel to the SC surface and generally gave off two or more distinct clusters of boutons (Fig. 3D – F).

Fig. 4 shows reconstructions of six well-labeled trigemino-SC axons from the SO and lower SGS. All of these were labeled with PHAL. Those shown in Fig. 4A – D entered the SC from its lateral border, turned medially, and gave off 3 – 5 clusters of boutons. None of these fibers appeared to be collaterals of fibers that also had substantial terminal fields in the deep layers. This latter feature was typical of most of the trigemino-SC fibers that invaded the superficial laminae. However, we did observe several instances in both the PHAL- and fluoro-ruby-labeled material in which fibers coursing through the SAI gave off a dorsally directed collateral which extended through the SGI and into the superficial laminae (Figs. 3G,H, 4E,F).

The present results demonstrate that trigemino-SC axons terminating in the superficial SC laminae of hamsters that sustained removal of both eyes on the day of birth have morphological characteristics similar to those of such axons which innervate the deep SC laminae of sighted animals (Rhoades et al., 1989). In contrast, these fibers appear very different from the retinal axons that terminate in the SGS and SO of sighted hamsters (Sachs and Schneider, 1984; Mooney and Rhoades, 1990).

The fact that trigemino-SC axons terminating in the SGS and SO of neonatally enucleated animals had morphological properties similar to those of such axons in the deep laminae in normal animals suggests a different conclusion than that prompted by the results of Campbell and Frost (1988). When

they forced retinal axons to innervate VB, the ultrastructural features of the retinal terminals more nearly resembled those of the somatosensory afferents to these nuclei than the terminals of retinogeniculate axons. However, it should be clear that the results provided by Campbell and Frost (1988), and those of the present study are *not* directly comparable. It is not unreasonable to expect that the terminal arborizations and ultrastructural features of axons may be subject to very different influences than those which shape preterminal branching.

While the present results support the conclusion that an alteration in target need not necessarily change the morphology of afferent axons, there is considerable evidence that a given fiber can have substantially different terminal arbors in different targets. For example, many large vibrissa-sensitive neurons in SpI project to multiple targets including trigeminal nucleus principalis (PrV), VB, the posterior nucleus (PO), and the deep layers of the SC (Jacquin et al., 1986). The axons of these large cells form very different terminal arbors in these targets. For example, in VB, trigeminal axons from SpI give rise to a single tightly focused terminal arbor and in PO the arbors of these axons are much more widespread (Chiaia et al., 1991). In the deep SC laminae, trigemino-SC fibers from SpI give rise to patchy terminal arbors that extend over a substantial portion of the mediolateral extent of the SGI and SAI (Rhoades et al., 1989, present results).

This apparent target dependence is not unique to axons that project rostrally from the trigeminal brain-stem complex. Retinal axons with multiple targets also have distinct morphological properties in their terminal nuclei. The terminal arbors of retinal Y-axons in the cat appear very different in the LGNd than in the SC (Bowling and Michael, 1980; Sur et al., 1987; Tamamaki et al., 1990).

The influence of afferent input upon the dendritic morphology of superficial layer SC neurons

The observation that afferents normally restricted to the deep layers retain, in large measure, their nor-

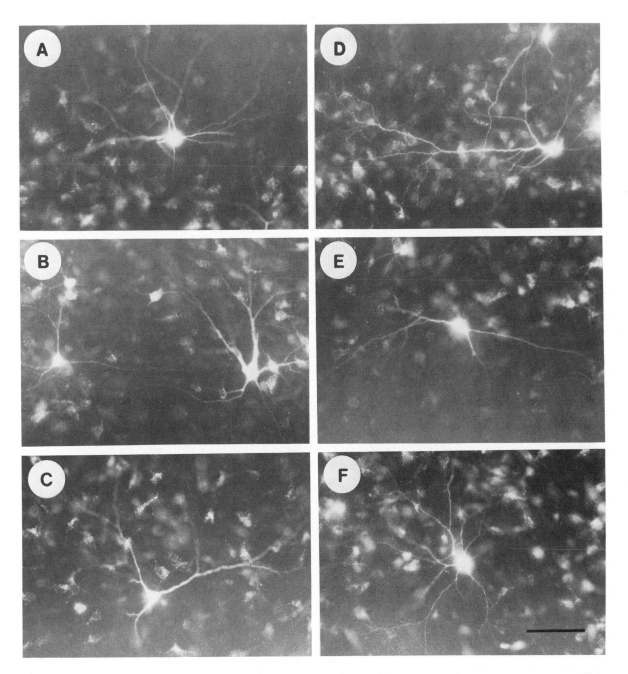

Fig. 5. *A – C* show episcopic fluorescence photomicrographs of tecto-LP cells filled with Lucifer yellow in normal adult hamsters. Note that all of these neurons have dendritic trees with a predominantly dorsal orientation. *D – F* depict Lucifer yellow-filled tecto-LP cells from neonatally enucleated adult animals. The neurons shown in *D* and *E* have dendrites that are generally horizontally oriented and that in *F* is a stellate cell. The calibration is 50 μm.

mal morphology when they extend into the superficial layers provides the substrate for the second experiment described in this paper. This study asks whether this change in the morphology of the major sensory input to the superficial SC laminae results in a corresponding alteration in the structural properties of the neurons that reside in these layers. To address this question, we examined the effects of neonatal enucleation upon a population of neurons whose dendritic arbors in normal hamsters closely match the orientation of the retinal afferents to this nucleus: the collicular cells that project to the lateral posterior nucleus (LP).

The structural properties of tecto-LP cells in normal and blinded hamsters were determined by combining retrograde transport of fluorescein-labeled microspheres (Katz and Iarovici, 1990) with injection of Lucifer yellow in a fixed slice preparation. We filled 91 retrogradely labeled tecto-LP cells in sighted animals and reconstructed 41 of them using the Eutectics Neuron Reconstruction System. We filled 87 such cells in the neonatally enucleated adult animals and reconstructed 62 of them. All cells were placed in morphological categories that have been described in detail by Mooney et al. (1992b).

Nearly 75% of the tecto-LP cells recovered from the sighted hamsters were widefield vertical neurons (Langer and Lund, 1974; Mooney et al., 1985, 1992a). Photomicrographs of several of these neurons are provided in Fig. 5A – C. These cells had somas in the lower SGS or SO and widespread dendrites that were directed toward the SC surface. The remainder of the tecto-LP cells recovered from normal hamsters were either narrow field vertical cells (15.4%), stellate cells (6.6%), or giant stellate cells (3.3%) (Fig. 6A).

The distribution of cell types labeled in blinded hamsters differed significantly from that in normal animals. Photomicrographs of several of these neurons are provided in Fig. 5D – F. In the neonatal enucleates, only 21.8% of the labeled tecto-LP neurons were widefield vertical cells, 6.9% were narrow field vertical cells, 19.5% were horizontal cells, 11.5% were stellate cells, 24.6% were giant stellate cells, and 13.8% could not be classified ac-

cording to this scheme. Most (75%) of the unclassifiable cells had dendrites that were directed only ventrally. The distribution of morphological SC cell types that projected to LP in the blinded animals (Fig. 6B) was significantly different from that in the normal hamsters $\chi^2 = 73.1$, $df = 5$, $p < 0.000001$).

It is unlikely that these results can be explained by differential transneuronal degeneration of neurons with dorsally directed dendrites. While the nearly 700% increase in the percentage of giant stellate cells in the sample from the enucleated animals might be

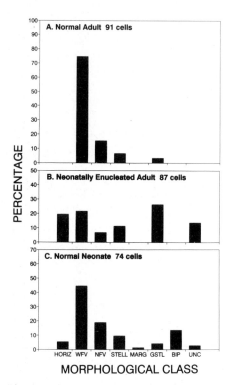

Fig. 6. A shows the categorization of tecto-LP cells in normal adult hamsters, B depicts that for neonatally enucleated adult hamsters, and C shows that for normal neonates killed on the day of birth. Note that neurons with dorsally directed dendrites (narrow field vertical cells and widefield vertical cells) predominate in the normal adults and neonates, but that this is not the case in the neonatally enucleated adult animals. HORIZ, Horizontal cells; WFV, widefield vertical cells; NFV, narrow field vertical cells; STELL, stellate cell; MARG, marginal cell; GSTL, giant stellate cell; BIP, bipolar cell (these were present only in neonates); UNC, unclassified cell.

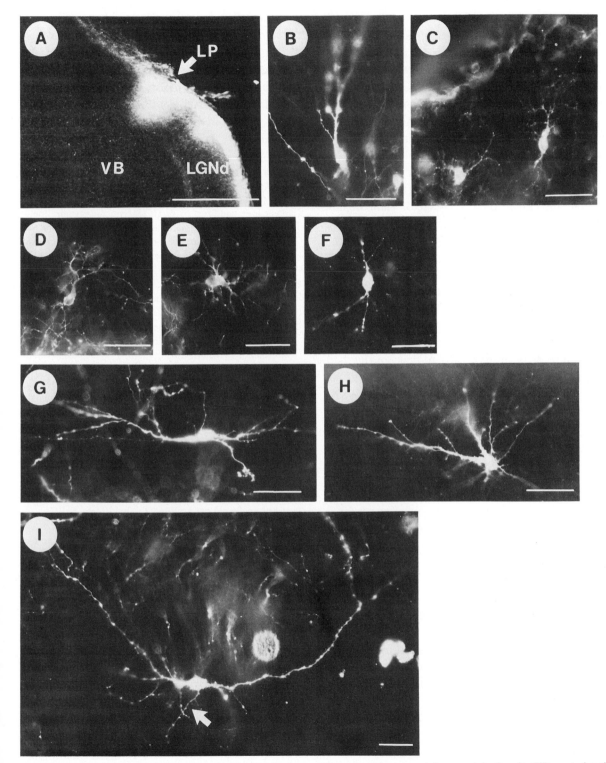

Fig. 7. Tecto-LP cells labeled by injection of Di-I into LP of a normal newborn hamster. *A* shows an injection site (VB, ventrobasal complex). In addition to the label in LP, there are labeled fibers in the optic tract and some labeled axons in the dorsal lateral geniculate nucleus (LGNd). The calibration is 200 μm. *B–D* show narrow field vertical cells; *E* shows a stellate cell; and *F* shows a bipolar cell. *G* shows a horizontal cell, and *H* and *I* show widefield vertical cells. The calibrations for *B–I* are 20 μm.

explained by differential neuron death (a loss of 85% of all tecto-LP cells, but of no giant stellate neurons within this group), it is difficult to explain the occurrence of tecto-LP neurons with horizontal and ventrally directed dendrites in this way. We observed only a few (never more than 5%) tecto-LP with horizontal dendritic arbors and no tecto-LP neurons with ventrally directed dendrites in the normal animals. Furthermore, available estimates of the SC cell loss following neonatal eye removal indicate that it is not great enough to explain the relative increase in the percentage of giant stellate cells projecting to LP. Finlay et al. (1986) have reported that there is a 30–40% cell loss in the superficial SC laminae after removal of the contralateral eye on the day of birth. While the cell loss might be somewhat greater after bilateral enucleation, it is very unlikely that it will approach 85%.

It is also unlikely that the changes we observed in the neonatally enucleated adult hamsters reflect alterations in the initial growth of neurons that had undergone little or no dendritic development at the time of enucleation (e.g., Conlee and Parks, 1983). We used retrograde labeling with the carbocyanine dye, Di-I (Godement et al., 1987), to assess the morphology of tecto-LP neurons in newborn hamsters (Fig. 7). Even at this age, nearly 70% of the tectal neurons retrogradely labeled from LP have dorsally directed dendrites (Fig. 6C).

The data presented in this paper are consistent with the conclusion that the dendrites of at least some tecto-LP cells are reoriented toward the deep laminae after removal of retinal input on the day of birth. They suggest further that retinal ganglion cell axon arbors, which are themselves dorsally directed (Sachs and Schneider, 1984; Mooney and Rhoades, 1990) and achieve this orientation early in development (Sachs et al., 1986), are required for the normal completion of dendritic development that is already underway prior to birth for many of these neurons. The reorientation of dendrites after eye removal is also consistent with the conclusion that these processes are redirected toward sources of residual afferent input.

Acknowledgements

Thanks to Dr. Carol Bennett-Clarke and to Steven Savage, Todd King, Scott Hobler, Beth Figley and Marcia Eck for their assistance. This work is supported in part by N.I.H.: EY08015 and EY04170.

References

Bowling, D.B. and Michael, C.R. (1980) Projection patterns of single physiologically characterized optic tract fibres in cat. *Nature,* 286: 899–902.

Campbell, G. and Frost, D.O. (1988) Synaptic organization of anomalous retinal projections to the somatosensory and auditory thalamus: target-controlled morphogenesis of axon terminals and synaptic glomeruli. *J. Comp. Neurol.,* 272: 383–408.

Chalupa, L.M. and Rhoades, R.W. (1977) Responses of visual, somatosensory and auditory neurons in the golden hamster's superior colliculus. *J. Physiol. (Lond.),* 270: 595–626.

Chiaia, N.L., Rhoades, R.W., Bennett-Clarke, C.A., Fish, S.E. and Killackey, H.P. (1991) Thalamic processing of vibrissal information in the rat: I. Afferent input to the medial ventral posterior and posterior nuclei. *J. Comp. Neurol.,* in press.

Conlee, J.W. and Parks, T.N. (1983) Late appearance and deprivation-sensitive growth of permanent dendrites in the avian cochlear nucleus (Nucleus Magnocellularis). *J. Comp. Neurol.,* 217: 216–226.

Finlay, B.L., Schneps, S.E., Wilson, K.G. and Schneider, G.E. (1978) Topography of visual and somatosensory projections into the superior colliculus of the golden hamster. *Brain Res.,* 142: 223–235.

Finlay, B.L., Sengelaub, D.R. and Berian, C.A. (1986) Control of cell number in the developing visual system. I. Effects of monocular enucleation. *Dev. Brain Res.,* 28: 1–10.

Frost, D.O. and Schneider, G.E. (1976) Normal and abnormal uncrossed retinal projections in Syrian hamsters as demonstrated by Fink-Heimer and autoradiographic techniques. *Soc. Neurosci. Abstr.,* 2: 812.

Frost, D.O., So, K.-F. and Schneider, G.E. (1979) Postnatal development of retinal projections in Syrian hamsters: a study using autoradiographic and anterograde degeneration techniques. *Neuroscience,* 4: 1649–1677.

Gerfen, C.R. and Sawchenko, P. (1984) An anterograde neuroanatomical tracing method that shows the detailed morphology of neurons, their axons and terminals: immunohistochemical localization of an axonally transported plant lectin *Phaseolus vulgaris* leucoagglutinin. *Brain Res.,* 290: 219–238.

Godement, P., Vanselow, J., Thanos, S. and Bonhoeffer, F. (1987) A study in the developing visual systems with a new method of staining neurons and their processes in fixed tissue. *Development,* 101: 697 – 713.

Jacquin, M.F., Mooney, R.D. and Rhoades, R.W. (1986) Morphology, response properties, and collateral projections of trigeminothalamic neurons in brainstem subnucleus interpolaris of rat. *Exp. Brain Res.,* 61: 457 – 468.

Katz, L.C. and Iarovici, D.M. (1990) Green fluorescent latex microspheres: a new retrograde tracer. *Neuroscience,* 34: 511 – 520.

Land, P.W. and Lund, R.D. (1979) Development of the rat's uncrossed retinotectal pathway and its relation to plasticity studies. *Science,* 205: 698 – 700.

Langer, T.P. and Lund, R.D. (1974) The upper layers of the superior colliculus of the rat: a Golgi study. *J. Comp. Neurol.,* 158: 405 – 436.

Lund, R.D. and Lund, J.S. (1971) Synaptic adjustment after deafferent action of the superior colliculus of the rat. *Science,* 171: 804 – 807.

Mooney, R.D. and Rhoades, R.W. (1990) Relationships between physiological and morphological properties of retinocollicular axons in the hamster. *J. Neurosci.,* 10: 3164 – 3177.

Mooney, R.D., Klein, B.G. and Rhoades, R.W. (1985) Correlations between the structural and functional characteristics of neurons in the superficial laminae of the hamster's superior colliculus. *J. Neurosci.,* 5: 2989 – 3009.

Mooney, R.D., Nikoletseas, M.M., King, T.A., Savage, S.V., Weaver, M.T. and Rhoades, R.W. (1992a) Structural and functional consequences of neonatal deafferentation in the superficial layers of the hamster's superior colliculus. *J. Comp. Neurol.,* 315: 398 – 412.

Mooney, R.D., Savage, S.V., Hobler, S., King, T.D. and Rhoades, R.W. (1992b) Normal development and effects of deafferentation upon the morphology of superior collicular neurons projecting to the lateral posterior nucleus in hamster. *J. Comp. Neurol.,* 315: 413 – 430.

Pallas, S.L. and Finlay, B.L. (1991) Compensation for population size mismatches in the hamster retinotectal system: alterations in the organization of retinal projections. *Visual Neurosci.,* 6: 271 – 281.

Purves, D. and Lichtman, J.W. (1985) *Principles of Neural Development,* Sinauer, Sunderland, MA.

Rakic, P. (1975) Role of cell interaction in development of dendritic patterns. *Adv. Neurol.,* 12: 117 – 134.

Rhoades, R.W. (1980) Effects of neonatal enucleation upon the functional organization of the superior colliculus in the golden hamster. *J. Physiol. (Lond.),* 301: 383 – 399.

Rhoades, R.W., DellaCroce, D.R. and Meadows, I. (1981) Reorganization of somatosensory input to superior colliculus in neonatally enucleated hamsters: anatomical and electrophysiological experiments. *J. Neurophysiol.,* 46: 855 – 877.

Rhoades, R.W., Fish, S.E., Chiaia, N.L., Bennett-Clarke, C.A. and Mooney, R.D. (1989) Organization of the projections from the trigeminal brainstem complex to the superior colliculus in the rat and hamster: anterograde tracing with *Phaseolus vulgaris* leucoagglutinin and intra-axonal injection. *J. Comp. Neurol.,* 289: 641 – 656.

Sachs, G.M. and Schneider, G.E. (1984) The morphology of optic tract axons arborizing in the superior colliculus of the hamster. *J. Comp. Neurol.,* 230: 155 – 167.

Sachs, G.M., Jacobson, M. and Caviness Jr., V.S. (1986) Postnatal changes in arborization patterns of murine retinocollicular axons. *J. Comp. Neurol.,* 246: 395 – 408.

Schmeud, L., Kyriakidis, K. and Heimer, L. (1990) In vivo anterograde and retrograde axonal transport of the fluorescent rhodamine-dextran-amine, fluoro-ruby, within the CNS. *Brain Res.,* 526: 127 – 134.

Schneider, G.E., Jhaveri, S. and Davis, W.F. (1987) On the development of neuronal arbors. In: C. Chagas and R. Linden (Eds.), *Working Group on Developmental Neurobiology of Mammals,* Portifical Academy of Sciences, Vatican City, pp. 31 – 64.

Stein, B.E. and Dixon, J. (1979) Properties of superior colliculus neurons in the golden hamster. *J. Comp. Neurol.,* 183: 269 – 284.

Sur, M., Esguerra, M., Garraghty, P.E., Kritzer, M.F. and Sherman, S.M. (1987) Morphology of physiologically identified retinogeniculate X- and Y-axons in the cat. *J. Neurophysiol.,* 58: 1 – 32.

Tamamaki, N., Uhlrich, D.J. and Sherman, S.M. (1990) Morphology of physiologically identified retinal axons in the cat's thalamus and midbrain as revealed by intra-axonal injection of biocytin. *Soc. Neurosci. Abstr.,* 16: 711.

Tiao, Y.C. and Blakemore, C. (1976) Functional organization in the superior colliculus of the golden hamster. *J. Comp. Neurol.,* 168: 483 – 504.

Tokunaga, A., Sugita, S., Otani, K. and Terasawa, K. (1985) Quantitative morphological changes in the superior colliculus and the parabigeminal nucleus in the bilaterally microphthalmic rat. *Dev. Brain Res.,* 23: 131 – 140.

T.P. Hicks, S. Molotchnikoff and T. Ono (Eds.)
Progress in Brain Research, Vol. 95
© 1993 Elsevier Science Publishers B.V. All rights reserved.

CHAPTER 7

Functional architecture of rodent superior colliculus: relevance of multiple output channels

P. Redgrave, G.W.M. Westby and P. Dean

Department of Psychology, University of Sheffield, Sheffield S10 2TN, U.K.

Introduction

A long-standing problem for understanding the functions of the superior colliculus has been the contrast between its anatomical and physiological complexity, and its apparently simple role in behaviour (Huerta and Harting, 1984; Dean et al., 1989). Recent developments concerning collicular mechanisms in rodents offer a possible framework for investigating this complexity, including the diversity of sensory responsiveness described for neurons in the deep layers (Drager and Hubel, 1975; Tiao and Blakemore, 1976; Chalupa and Rhoades, 1977; Rhoades et al., 1983; Larson et al., 1987). The principal idea is that anatomically distinct collicular output pathways are also functionally distinct, so that their cells of origin are likely to receive unique combinations of both sensory and non-sensory afferent input. In this way, identifying the projection to which a given collicular output contributes may offer a powerful tool for understanding how its inputs are organised.

Multiple responses and the organization of collicular efferents

Traditionally, the main function assigned to the superior colliculus has been orienting, that is saccadic redirection of the eyes and/or head towards a suddenly appearing visual or other stimulus (Sprague and Meikle, 1965). However, more recent studies of the effects of damaging or stimulating the superior colliculus in rodents have demonstrated its involvement in a wide variety of responses appropriate to novel sensory stimuli. These responses have been extensively documented elsewhere (Redgrave et al., 1981; Kilpatrick et al., 1982; McHaffie and Stein, 1982; Dean et al., 1986, 1988; Sahibzada et al., 1986; Ellard and Goodale, 1988; Northmore et al., 1988; Tehovnik, 1989) so are described only briefly here (Fig. 1).

(1) Approach movements. In addition to the familiar saccadic movements, the rodent superior colliculus appears to mediate a second type of response directed towards sensory events. Unlike saccades, where at least in primates the amplitude and velocity of movements elicited by collicular stimulation are determined primarily by the locus of the stimulation (Van Opstal et al., 1990), these movements are directly influenced by stimulation parameters. Thus, the superior colliculus could in principle control their velocity and amplitude *independently* (King et al., 1991); for this and other reasons we have suggested that they can function as pursuit movements (Dean et al., 1986).

(2) Avoidance and escape responses. Most of the movements that can be elicited from rodents by naturally threatening visual stimuli (Blanchard et al., 1986) can also be produced by appropriate electrical or pharmacological stimulation of the superior colliculus (Fig. 1), and impaired by collicular damage.

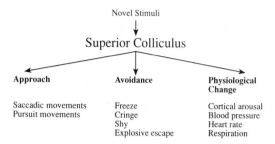

Fig. 1. A wide range of reactions appropriate to sudden novel stimuli can be elicited by direct electrical or chemical stimulation of the superior colliculus in rodents.

(3) Physiological responses. Naturally occurring approach and avoidance movements are typically accompanied by a range of physiological reactions, which can also be elicited by stimulation of the superior colliculus (Fig. 1) (Redgrave and Dean, 1985; Keay et al., 1988, 1990a; Dean et al., 1991).

How does the superior colliculus produce all these different responses? Anatomical analysis of the descending projections of the rodent superior colliculus indicates that they consist of a series of largely independent output channels to different regions of brain-stem and spinal cord. Thus, the two major ipsi- and contra-lateral descending fibre bundles arise from different populations of cells, concentrated in different collicular layers (Redgrave et al., 1986; Sahibzada et al., 1987; Bickford and Hall, 1989). Within these two principal descending pathways individual components similarly appear to originate from distinct populations of collicular neurons (Redgrave et al., 1987, 1990a), which in some cases show regional segregation. This is illustrated in Fig. 2 for the contralateral projections to the periabducens area and to caudal medulla and spinal cord. The cells projecting to the periabducens area tend to be located more medially than those projecting to caudal medulla/spinal cord, with the boundary steadily shifting from a medial position in rostral colliculus to a much more lateral one further caudally (Redgrave et al., 1990a).

The immediate inference is that these separate collicular output channels mediate different responses to novel stimuli, and current evidence supports this

view (Dean et al., 1989). For example, lesions of the contralateral descending projection at the level of the dorsal tegmental decussation impair approach but not avoidance responses, whereas interruption of the ipsilateral descending projection primarily affects defensive responding (Dean et al., 1986; Ellard and Goodale, 1986, 1988). More detailed connections between individual responses and output pathways remain to be established, but at present it

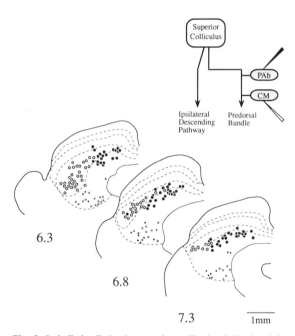

Fig. 2. Labelled cells in the superior colliculus following injections of retrogradely transported fluorescent dyes into two premotor terminal zones of the crossed descending pathway (Redgrave et al., 1990a). Small injections of Diamidino Yellow were made into the rostral dorsomedial medulla close to the abducens motor nucleus, while larger injections of either True Blue or Fast Blue were made into tectospinal/tectomedullary fibres at the level of the ventromedial caudal medulla. The three sections (numbers associated with each section = mm caudal to bregma) present quantitative plots of cells labelled by each of the two dyes in the brain of a representative animal. Filled circles indicate cells labelled by Diamidino Yellow, open circles show cells containing Fast Blue. The large circles indicate a population of large cells concentrated in the intermediate white layer of the contralateral superior colliculus, the small circles show separate populations of generally smaller cells in the lateral deep layers. In the intermediate layers, cells projecting to the caudal medulla and spinal cord were located laterally while cells with terminals in the periabducens area were concentrated in clusters more medially.

appears feasible that one aspect of collicular complexity, namely the richness of its output projections, may be related to its ability to mediate multiple responses to novel stimuli.

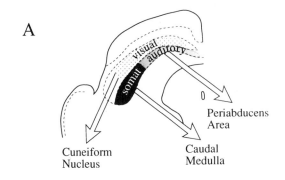

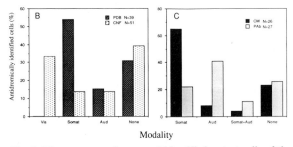

Fig. 3. The sensory preferences of identified output cells of the superior colliculus in rat. *A.* A schematic diagram identifying the sensory preferences of anatomically defined concentrations of tectal output cells to informal stimuli of different modalities. *B.* The cells of origin of the contralateral predorsal bundle and ipsilateral cuneiform nucleus show markedly different modality responsivity. Antidromic activation of visual cells was only possible from the cuneiform nucleus. In contrast, the somatosensory projection was principally to the predorsal bundle. Auditory cells projected to both pathways and about 30% of all identified cells showed no response to the extensive battery of informal stimuli employed. Modality specificity of the two pathways was significantly different ($\chi^2 = 24.92$; d$f = 3$; $P < 0.001$) (From Westby et al., 1990). *C.* In a subsequent study (Keay et al., 1990b) similar differences in sensory preference were found between tectal cells differentiated on the basis of antidromic activity induced by electrical stimulation of the periabducens area or the ventromedial caudal medulla. Cells activated by caudal medulla stimulation were preferentially sensitive to somatosensory stimuli, in particular displacement of the whiskers or light touch applied to the head. Alternatively, cells projecting to the periabducens area were most often responsive to auditory stimuli including hand clap, key jangling and whistling. Differences in the sensory preferences of antidromically identified cells were statistically significant ($\chi^2 = 11.79$; d$f = 3$; $P < 0.005$).

Sensory control of collicular outputs

The fact that the rodent superior colliculus is involved in more than one response to unexpected events raises the question of how the appropriate response is selected. One simple solution to this problem would be to have a different combination of sensory inputs for each individual output channel. This has attractive features as an explanation, because it accounts in general terms for two key features of collicular anatomy and physiology. One is the wide diversity of sensory responses recorded from collicular cells, particularly in the intermediate and deep layers where most cells of origin of the descending pathways are located (Drager and Hubel, 1975; Tiao and Blakemore, 1976; Chalupa and Rhoades, 1977; Rhoades et al., 1983; Larson et al., 1987). The other is the anatomical and histochemical evidence for a collicular mosaic, in which many of the inputs to the intermediate layers have a patchy distribution (Huerta and Harting, 1984; Illing and Graybiel, 1985, 1986; Wallace, 1986; Wallace and Fredens, 1989).

Preliminary investigation of the sensory preferences of identified output cells in rat superior colliculus directly supports this idea. In urethane-anaesthetised animals, Westby et al. (1990) found that cells antidromically identified as projecting to the ipsilateral cuneiform area typically responded to visual stimuli, whereas cells antidromically activated by stimulation of crossed descending fibres were more responsive to auditory or somatosensory stimuli (Fig. 3).

Similarly, analysis of the sensory preferences of cells projecting to different terminal zones of the crossed pathway indicates that those stimulated from the periabducens area responded mainly to auditory stimuli, in contrast to cells activated from the ventral caudal medulla which preferred somatosensory stimulation (Keay et al., 1990b).

The idea that particular sensory inputs may be preferentially directed to certain output channels of the SC has been proposed by others. Following an electrophysiological analysis of the somatosensory and nociceptive properties of cells in the rat superior colliculus, McHaffie et al. (1989) suggested that low threshold somatosensory and intense nociceptive information may be directed to different tectal output pathways associated respectively with approach and avoidance reactions.

However, differences in sensory input to at least some collicular output channels can only be part of the story. First, we have some preliminary data which suggest that the comparatively exclusive sensory preferences of tectal neurons in the urethane-anaesthetised rat can be adjusted by manipulating the chemical environment close to the recording electrode. Secondly, a substantial proportion of identified collicular output cells have no obvious functional sensory inputs. Anatomical evidence shows that the superior colliculus receives massive afferent projections from non-sensory structures in both forebrain and brain-stem (Edwards et al., 1979; Huerta and Harting, 1984a,b). Finally, functional considerations indicate the disadvantage of compulsory sensorimotor linkages, namely stereotyped and predictable behaviour patterns that cannot be influenced by context or motivation.

The question therefore arises of whether different collicular output channels also receive distinct *non-sensory* inputs. The following two sections describe (i) an anatomical study of the nigrotectal projection, and (ii) a physiological investigation of nigral and cerebellar inputs, both in relation to the medio-lateral organization of the intermediate layers illustrated in Fig. 2.

Organization of collicular afferents from substantia nigra, pars reticulata

The intermediate layers of the superior colliculus receive an extensive projection from the substantia nigra pars reticulata, a region of ventral midbrain that receives massive inputs from the caudate nucleus (Gerfen, 1985), globus pallidus (Smith and Bolam, 1990), and subthalamic nucleus (Kita and Kitai, 1987), and thereby constitutes a major output station for the basal ganglia. This projection has been the subject of numerous anatomical (Hopkins

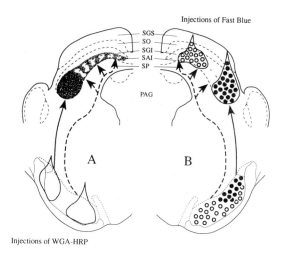

Fig. 4. A schematic representation of the topography within the connections between substantia nigra pars reticulata and the intermediate layers of the superior colliculus in rat (Redgrave et al., 1990b). *A*. Small injections (10–25 nl) of WGA-HRP (1%) were injected throughout the medio-lateral extent of rostral substantia nigra pars reticulata (*n* = 14). Laterally placed injections were associated with very dense, evenly distributed terminal label which was largely confined to the rostrolateral enlargement of the intermediate layers of the superior colliculus. In contrast, injections placed in the ventromedial pars reticulata produced dense patches of label which were largely confined to the medial and caudal intermediate layers. In the coronal section this label appeared as a lattice in which dorsal and ventral sheets of label were linked by a series of connecting bridges. In horizontal section nigral terminals in the medial intermediate layers appeared as a "matrix" within which there were unlabelled "patches". *B*. Single injections of the retrogradely transported fluorescent dye Fast Blue were made into different regions of the intermediate layers of the superior colliculus. The pattern of retrograde labelling in substantia nigra pars reticulata was entirely consistent with the anterograde tracing results (see *A*). For purposes of illustration nigral cells labelled by medial injections of Fast Blue are represented by open circles while cells labelled by lateral injections of the same tracer are indicated by filled circles. The results showed that laterally placed injections in the superior colliculus were associated with a dense concentration of retrogradely labelled cells in the entire rostrocaudal extent of dorsolateral pars reticulata. Conversely, medial and caudally placed injections produced retrograde labelling in ventral and medial regions of the rostral two thirds of pars reticulata. Taken together the anterograde and retrograde tracing data suggest that connections between pars reticulata and the intermediate layers may be divided into two major sub-components.

and Niessen, 1976; Faull and Mehler, 1978; Bentivoglio et al., 1979; Gerfen et al., 1982; Rhoades et al., 1982; May and Hall, 1986a; Williams and Faull, 1988), physiological (Hikosaka and Wurtz, 1983; Chevalier and Deniau, 1990) and behavioural studies (Redgrave et al., 1980; Imperato et al., 1981; Kilpatrick et al., 1982; Taha et al., 1982). The particular question that we were concerned with was whether the more lateral parts of the intermediate layers, which contain cells projecting to the caudal medulla and spinal cord, receive a projection distinct from that reaching medial areas containing cells projecting to the periabducens area. To answer this question a number of anatomical experiments were conducted, using both anterograde and retrograde tracing techniques. Their main findings are summarised in Fig. 4.

A series of injections of WGA-HRP placed throughout the medio-lateral extent of substantia nigra pars reticulata revealed that lateral injections produced dense terminal label in the lateral parts of the collicular intermediate layers, whereas medial injections were associated with patchy terminal label in more medial and caudal regions (Fig. 4A). Injections of fluorescent tracers into the superior colliculus produced patterns of retrograde labelling (Fig. 4B) consistent with these findings.

The spatial coincidence of cells projecting to caudal medulla and spinal cord with afferent terminals from dorsolateral substantia nigra is suggestive, but does not establish whether terminals and cells come into functional contact. However, in a series of experiments Chevalier and Deniau's group (Chevalier and Deniau, 1990) have shown that identified tectospinal cells are held under tonic inhibition by the nigrotectal projection. GABAergic inhibition of nigral cells, which are normally tonically active, produces increases in both the spontaneous firing rate and sensitivity to vibrissal stimulation of tectospinal cells (Chevalier et al., 1984). A similar investigation is required to determine the effects, if any, of the nigrotectal projection to medial intermediate layers on cells projecting to the periabducens area.

The cerebellotectal projection

The intermediate layers of the superior colliculus also receive an extensive projection from the posterior interpositus nucleus of the cerebellum (Faull and Carman, 1978; Roldan and Reinoso-Suarez, 1981; Uchida et al., 1983; Wharton, 1983; Gonzalo-Ruiz et al., 1990). The appearance of terminal label resembles that of the nigrotectal pathway and in the grey squirrel close overlap is indicated (May and Hall, 1986b). We have begun to investigate the possible functional significance of this projection, in the first instance by observing the effects of manipulating the deep cerebellar nuclei and observing any changes in collicular cells (Fig. 5). Because cells in the cerebellar nuclei fire spontaneously, the manipulation of choice was microinjection of GABA. To date, 70 spontaneously active cells have been recorded in or close to the collicular intermediate layers, 30 of which were influenced by injections of GABA into the deep cerebellar nuclei. Of these 30 cells 25 showed a decrease in activity which paralleled the suppression seen in the cerebellar nuclei themselves (Fig. 5) while 4 showed the opposite response, i.e., an increase in spontaneous activity. All 30 cells influenced by the cerebellar injections were located laterally; more medial cells that were spontaneously active were not affected by cerebellar GABA.

These data are consistent with there being functional differences between cerebellar input to that region of the intermediate layers containing cells projecting to caudal medulla and spinal cord, and to the region containing tecto-periabducens cells. However, there are two grounds for caution in accepting this conclusion. First, a more extensive sampling of medial cells is needed. Secondly, the affected cells in lateral superior colliculus have not been identified antidromically. At present there is only indirect evidence that some (8 out of 10 tested) may be tectospinal cells, since they could also be influenced (disinhibited) by microinjection of GABA into the substantia nigra (Fig. 5; Westby et al., 1991).

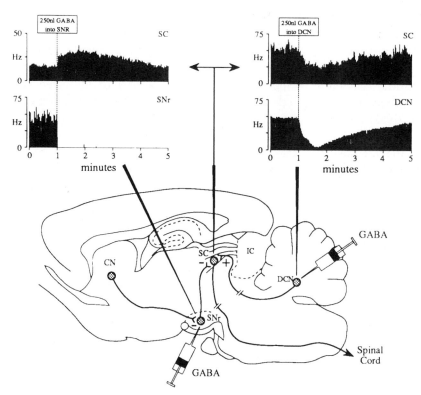

Fig. 5. Representative examples of electrophysiological recording from cells in the lateral intermediate layers of the superior colliculus, ipsilateral substantia nigra and contralateral deep cerebellar nuclei of a urethane-anaesthetised rat. The recordings are presented in sequential frequency histograms where the numbers of spikes in each 1 sec bin was plotted for a 5 min period. The lower of the two graphs on the left hand side of the diagram shows that a microinjection (200 nl) of GABA (1 M) close to the nigral recording electrode completely inhibited local spontaneous unit activity. The upper trace indicates that the spontaneous activity of a cell in the lateral intermediate layers of the ipsilateral colliculus was concurrently disinhibited. On the right side the graphs show that a similar injection of GABA into the deep cerebellar nuclei suppressed both the spontaneous activity of a local cell and a cell in the lateral intermediate layers of the contralateral colliculus.

Conclusions and implications

The argument of this chapter is that, if different collicular output channels are functionally distinct, they might be expected to have distinctive patterns of sensory and non-sensory input. If so, it should prove possible to clarify some aspects of collicular complexity by identifying input-output relations for individual output channels. The evidence reviewed above suggests that this may be a promising approach, at least for contralaterally projecting cells in the intermediate layers of the superior colliculus of the rat.

A final point concerns functional implications.

The intermediate collicular layers, and their nigrotectal afferents, have been implicated in movements *towards* a target (Hikosaka and Wurtz, 1989; Grantyn, 1988). In primates these movements are saccadic, that is discrete, essentially ballistic movements whose velocities are highly constrained for a given amplitude (Carpenter, 1988). A similar saccadic system, involving head as well as eye movements, probably exists in rodents also (Dean et al., 1989). However, as described above, there is also evidence for a non-saccadic collicular system in these animals. For example, stimulation at sites in the lateral intermediate layers of rat superior colliculus produces movements the amplitude of which increases linearly with the number of pulses in the stimulating train (McHaffie and Stein, 1982; King et al., 1991), and whose velocity varies with stimulation frequency. These results are in sharp contrast to those obtained in primates, where amplitude (and hence velocity) are determined almost entirely by the location of stimulating electrode, not by stimulation parameters (Robinson, 1972; Schiller and Stryker, 1972). This contrast has led to suggestions that in rat the rostrolateral intermediate layers and the associated tecto-medullary projection may be concerned primarily with non-saccadic head movements, whereas the tecto-periabducens projection may be more concerned with saccadic movement (Keay et al., 1990b; King et al., 1991).

References

Bentivoglio, M., van der Kooy, D. and Kuypers, H.G.J.M. (1979) The organization of the efferent projections of the substantia nigra in the rat. A retrograde fluorescent double labelling study. *Brain Res.,* 174: 1 – 17.

Bickford, M.E. and Hall, W.C. (1989) Collateral projections of predorsal bundle cells of the superior colliculus in the rat. *J. Comp. Neurol.,* 283: 86 – 106.

Blanchard, R.J., Flannelly, K.J. and Blanchard, D.C. (1986) Defensive behaviours of laboratory and wild Rattus Norvegicus. *J. Comp. Psychol.,* 100: 101 – 107.

Carpenter, R.H.S. (1988) *Movements of the Eyes,* Pion, London.

Chalupa, L.M. and Rhoades, R.W. (1977) Responses of visual, somatosensory and auditory neurones in the golden hamster's superior colliculus. *J. Physiol. (Lond.),* 270: 595 – 626.

Chevalier, G. and Deniau, J.M. (1990) Disinhibition as a basic process in the expression of striatal functions. *Trends Neurosci.,* 13: 277 – 281.

Chevalier, G., Vacher, S. and Deniau, J.M. (1984) Inhibitory nigral influence on tectospinal neurons, a possible implication of basal ganglia in orienting behaviour. *Exp. Brain Res.,* 53: 320 – 326.

Dean, P., Redgrave, P., Sahibzada, N. and Tsuji, K. (1986) Head and body movements produced by electrical stimulation of superior colliculus in rats: effects of interruption of crossed tectoreticulospinal pathway. *Neuroscience,* 19: 367 – 380.

Dean, P., Mitchell, I.J. and Redgrave, P. (1988) Responses resembling defensive behaviour produced by microinjection of glutamate into superior colliculus of rats. *Neuroscience,* 24: 501 – 510.

Dean, P., Redgrave, P. and Westby, G.W.M. (1989) Event or emergency? Two response systems in the mammalian superior colliculus. *Trends Neurosci.,* 12: 137 – 147.

Dean, P., Simkins, M., Hetherington, L., Mitchell, I.J. and Redgrave, P. (1991) Tectal induction of cortical arousal – evidence implicating multiple output pathways. *Brain Res. Bull.,* 26: 1 – 10.

Drager, U.C. and Hubel, D.H. (1975) Responses to visual stimulation and relationship between visual, auditory and somatosensory inputs in mouse superior colliculus. *J. Neurophysiol.,* 38: 690 – 713.

Edwards, S.B., Ginsburg, C.L., Henkel, C.K. and Stein, B.E. (1979) Sources of subcortical projections to the superior colliculus in the cat. *J. Comp. Neurol.,* 184: 309 – 330.

Ellard, C.G. and Goodale, M.A. (1986) The role of the predorsal bundle in head and body movements elicited by electrical stimulation of the superior colliculus in the Mongolian gerbil. *Exp. Brain Res.,* 64: 421 – 433.

Ellard, C.G. and Goodale, M.A. (1988) A functional analysis of the collicular output pathways: a dissociation of deficits following lesions of the dorsal tegmental decussation and the ipsilateral collicular efferent bundle in the Mongolian gerbil. *Exp. Brain Res.,* 71: 307 – 319.

Faull, R.L.M. and Carman, J.B. (1978) The cerebellofugal projection in the brachium conjunctivum of the rat. I. The contralateral ascending pathway. *J. Comp. Neurol.,* 178: 495 – 518.

Faull, R.L.M. and Mehler, W.R. (1978) The cells of origin of the nigrotectal nigrothalamic and nigrostriatal projections in the rat. *Neuroscience,* 3: 989 – 1002.

Gerfen, C.R. (1985) The neostriatal mosaic I. Compartmental organization of projections from the striatum to the substantia nigra in the rat. *J. Comp. Neurol.,* 236: 454 – 476.

Gerfen, C.R., Staines, W.A., Arbuthnott, G.W. and Fibiger, H.C. (1982) Crossed connections of the substantia nigra in the rat. *J. Comp. Neurol.,* 207: 283 – 303.

Gonzalo-Ruiz, A., Leichnetz, G.R. and Hardy, S.G.P. (1990) Projections of the medial cerebellar nucleus to oculomotor-related midbrain areas in the rat: an anterograde and retrograde HRP study. *J. Comp. Neurol.,* 296: 427 – 436.

Grantyn, R. (1988) Gaze control through superior colliculus: structure and function. In: J.A. Buttner-Ennever (Ed.), *Neuroanatomy of the Oculomotor System,* Elsevier, Amsterdam, pp. 273 – 333.

Hikosaka, O. and Wurtz, R.H. (1983) Visual and oculomotor function of monkey substantia nigra pars reticulata. IV. Relation of substantia nigra to superior colliculus. *J. Neurophysiol.,* 49: 1285 – 1301.

Hikosaka, O. and Wurtz, R.H. (1989) The basal ganglia. In: R.H. Wurtz and M.E. Goldberg (Eds.), *Neurobiology of Saccadic Eye Movements, Reviews of Oculomotor Research, Vol. 3,* Elsevier, Amsterdam, pp. 257 – 282.

Hopkins, D.A. and Niessen, L.W. (1976) Substantia nigra projections to the reticular formation, superior colliculus and central gray in the rat, cat and monkey. *Neurosci. Lett.,* 2:

253 – 259.

Huerta, M.F. and Harting, J.K. (1984a) Connectional organization of the superior colliculus. *Trends Neurosci.,* 7: 286 – 289.

Huerta, M.F. and Harting, J.K. (1984b) The mammalian superior colliculus: studies of its morphology and connections. In: H. Vanegas (Ed.), *Comparative Neurology of the Optic Tectum,* Plenum, New York, pp. 867 – 773.

Illing, R.B. and Graybiel, A.M. (1985) Convergence of afferents from frontal cortex and substantia nigra onto acetylcholinesterase-rich patches of the cat's superior colliculus. *Neuroscience,* 14: 455 – 482.

Illing, R.B. and Graybiel, A.M. (1986) Complementary and non-matching afferent compartments in the cat's superior colliculus: innervation of the acetylcholinesterase-poor domain of the intermediate gray layer. *Neuroscience,* 18: 373 – 394.

Imperato, A., Porceddu, M.L., Morelli, M., Faa, G. and Di Chiara, G. (1981) Role of dorsal mesencephalic reticular formation and deep layers of superior colliculus as output stations for turning behaviour elicited from the substantia nigra pars reticulata. *Brain Res.,* 216: 437 – 443.

Keay, K.A., Redgrave, P. and Dean, P. (1988) Cardiovascular and respiratory changes elicited by stimulation of rat superior colliculus. *Brain Res. Bull.,* 20: 13 – 26.

Keay, K.A., Dean, P. and Redgrave, P. (1990a) *N*-methyl-D-aspartate (NMDA) evoked changes in blood pressure and heart rate from the rat superior colliculus. *Exp. Brain Res.,* 80: 148 – 156.

Keay, K.A., Westby, G.W.M., Dean, P. and Redgrave, P. (1990b) Organization of the crossed projection from the superior colliculus to the periabducens area and caudal medulla. II. Electrophysiological evidence for separate output channels. *Neuroscience,* 37: 585 – 601.

Kilpatrick, I.C., Collingridge, G.L. and Starr, M.S. (1982) Evidence for the participation of nigrotectal gamma-aminobutyrate-containing neurones in striatal and nigral-derived circling in the rat. *Neuroscience,* 7: 207 – 222.

King, S.M., Dean, P. and Redgrave, P. (1991) Bypassing the saccadic pulse generator: possible control of head movement trajectory by rat superior colliculus. *Eur. J. Neurosci.,* 3: 790 – 801.

Kita, H. and Kitai, S.T. (1987) Efferent projections of the subthalamic nucleus in the rat: light and electron microscopic analysis with the PHA-L method. *J. Comp. Neurol.,* 260: 435 – 452.

Larson, M.A., McHaffie, J.G. and Stein, B.E. (1987) Response properties of nociceptive and low-threshold mechanoreceptive neurons in the hamster superior colliculus. *J. Neurosci.,* 7: 547 – 564.

May, P.J. and Hall, W.C. (1986a) The sources of the nigrotectal pathway. *Neuroscience,* 19: 159 – 180.

May, P.J. and Hall, W.C. (1986b) The cerebellotectal pathway in the grey squirrel. *Exp. Brain Res.,* 65: 200 – 212.

McHaffie, J.G. and Stein, B.E. (1982) Eye movements evoked by electrical stimulation in the superior colliculus of rats and hamsters. *Brain Res.,* 247: 243 – 253.

McHaffie, J.G., Kao, C.-Q. and Stein, B.E. (1989) Nociceptive neurons in rat superior colliculus: response properties, topography and functional implications. *J. Neurophysiol.,* 62: 510 – 525.

Northmore, D.P.M., Levine, E.S. and Schneider, G.E. (1988) Behaviour evoked by electrical stimulation of the hamster superior colliculus. *Exp. Brain Res.,* 73: 595 – 605.

Redgrave, P. and Dean, P. (1985) Tonic desynchronisation of cortical EEG by electrical stimulation of superior colliculus and surrounding structures in urethane-anaesthetised rats. *Neuroscience,* 16: 659 – 671.

Redgrave, P., Dean, P., Donohoe, T.P. and Pope, S.G. (1980) Superior colliculus lesions selectively attenuate apomorphine-induced oral stereotypy: a possible role for the nigrotectal pathway. *Brain Res.,* 196: 541 – 546.

Redgrave, P., Dean, P., Souki, W. and Lewis, G. (1981) Gnawing and changes in reactivity produced by microinjections of picrotoxin into the superior colliculus of rats. *Psychopharmacology,* 75: 198 – 203.

Redgrave, P., Odekunle, A. and Dean, P. (1986) Tectal cells of origin of predorsal bundle in rat: location and segregation from ipsilateral descending pathway. *Exp. Brain Res.,* 63: 279 – 293.

Redgrave, P., Mitchell, I.J. and Dean, P. (1987) Further evidence for segregated output channels from superior colliculus in rat: ipsilateral tecto-pontine and tecto-cuneiform projections have different cells of origin. *Brain Res.,* 413: 170 – 174.

Redgrave, P., Dean, P. and Westby, G.W.M. (1990a) Organization of the crossed tecto-reticulo-spinal projection in rat. 1. Anatomical evidence for separate output channels to the periabducens area and caudal medulla. *Neuroscience,* 37: 571 – 584.

Redgrave, P., Marrow, L.P. and Dean, P. (1990b) Topographical organization of the nigrotectal projection in rat: evidence for segregated channels. *Eur. J. Neurosci.,* Suppl. 3: 4253.

Rhoades, R.W., Kuo, D.C., Polcer, J.D., Fish, S.E. and Voneida, T.J. (1982) Indirect visual cortical input to the deep layers of the hamster's superior colliculus via the basal ganglia. *J. Comp. Neurol.,* 208: 239 – 254.

Rhoades, R.W., Mooney, R.D. and Jacquin, M.F. (1983) Complex somatosensory receptive fields of cells in the deep laminae of the hamster's superior colliculus. *J. Neurosci.,* 3: 1342 – 1354.

Robinson, D.A. (1972) Eye movements evoked by stimulation in the alert monkey. *Vision Res.,* 12: 1795 – 1808.

Roldan, M. and Reinoso-Suarez, F. (1981) Cerebellar projections to the superior colliculus in the cat. *J. Neurosci.,* 1: 827 – 834.

Sahibzada, N., Dean, P. and Redgrave, P. (1986) Movements resembling orientation or avoidance elicited by electrical stimulation of the superior colliculus in rats. *J. Neurosci.,* 6:

723 – 733.

Sahibzada, N., Yamasaki, D. and Rhoades, R.W. (1987) The spinal and commissural projections from the superior colliculus in rat and hamster arise from distinct neuronal populations. *Brain Res.,* 415: 242 – 256.

Schiller, P.H. and Stryker, M. (1972) Single-unit recording and stimulation in superior colliculus of the alert rhesus monkey. *J. Neurophysiol.,* 35: 915 – 924.

Smith, Y. and Bolam, J.P. (1990) The output neurones and the dopaminergic neurones of the substantia nigra receive a GABA-containing input from the globus pallidus in the rat. *J. Comp. Neurol.,* 296: 47 – 64.

Sprague, J.M. and Meikle, T.H. (1965) The role of the superior colliculus in visually guided behaviour. *Exp. Neurol.,* 11: 115 – 146.

Taha, E.B., Dean, P. and Redgrave, P. (1982) Oral behaviour induced by intranigral muscimol is unaffected by haloperidol but abolished by large lesions of superior colliculus. *Psychopharmacology,* 77: 272 – 278.

Tehovnik, E.J. (1989) Head and body movements evoked electrically from the caudal superior colliculus of rats: pulse frequency effects. *Behav. Brain Res.,* 34: 71 – 78.

Tiao, Y.C. and Blakemore, C. (1976) Functional organization in the superior colliculus of the golden hamster. *J. Comp. Neurol.,* 168: 483 – 506.

Uchida, K., Mizuno, N., Sugimoto, T., Itoh, K. and Kudo, M. (1983) Direct projections from the cerebellar nuclei to the superior colliculus in the rabbit: an HRP study. *J. Comp. Neurol.,* 216: 319 – 326.

Van Opstal, A.J., Van Gisbergen, J.A.M. and Smit, A.C. (1990) Comparison of saccades evoked by visual stimulation and collicular electrical stimulation in the alert monkey. *Exp. Brain Res.,* 79: 299 – 312.

Wallace, M.N. (1986) Spatial relationship of histochemically demonstrable patches in the mouse superior colliculus. *Exp. Brain Res.,* 62: 241.

Wallace, M.N. and Fredens, K. (1989) Relationship of afferent inputs to the lattice of high NADPH-diaphorase activity in the mouse superior colliculus. *Exp. Brain Res.,* 78: 435 – 445.

Westby, G.W.M., Keay, K.A., Redgrave, P., Dean, P. and Bannister, M. (1990) Output pathways from the rat superior colliculus mediating approach and avoidance have different sensory properties. *Exp. Brain Res.,* 81: 626 – 638.

Westby, G.W.M., Collinson, C., Redgrave, P. and Dean, P. (1991) Deep cerebellar neurons provide the tonic excitatory drive for cells in the intermediate white layer of the contralateral superior colliculus. *Eur. J. Neurosci.,* Suppl. 4: 302.

Wharton, S. (1983) Nigral and cerebellar synaptic terminals in the intermediate and deep layers of the cat superior colliculus revealed by lesioning studies. *Neuroscience,* 10: 789 – 800.

Williams, M.N. and Faull, R.L.M. (1988) The nigrotectal projection and tectospinal neurons in the rat. A light and electron microscopic study demonstrating a monosynaptic nigral input to identified tectospinal neurons. *Neuroscience,* 25: 533 – 562.

T.P. Hicks, S. Molotchnikoff and T. Ono (Eds.)
Progress in Brain Research, Vol. 95
© 1993 Elsevier Science Publishers B.V. All rights reserved.

CHAPTER 8

The visually responsive neuron and beyond: multisensory integration in cat and monkey

Barry E. Stein[1], M. Alex Meredith[2] and Mark T. Wallace[1]

Departments of [1] Physiology and [2] Anatomy, Medical College of Virginia/Virginia Commonwealth University, Richmond, VA, U.S.A.

Introduction

Vertebrates possess an impressive array of highly specialized senses for which unique peripheral organs have evolved. The eye, with its ability to orient to external stimuli in ballistic fashion and to adapt to a wide range of changes in illumination, is a marvel of bioengineering. Its sensory receptors, like those in each of the other peripheral sensory organs, have evolved to transduce only specific kinds of environmental energy into the neural code used by the brain to detect and interpret external events. By being tuned to a different form of energy, each sensory system provides the organism with a different "view" of the world. These different views extend to the sensory impressions produced by activating one receptor system or another. Once the peripheral receptors of a given sensory modality provide input signals to the nervous system, events transpiring along its sensory pathway lead ultimately to a distinct perceptual experience, and there is no way to effectively compare among the sensory experiences from different modalities. Hue, pitch and tickle, for example, are experiences unique to the visual, auditory and somatosensory systems, respectively. Each exists as an independent experience without counterpart in any other modality.

Yet, despite the presence of subjective features unique to each modality, the brain is able to integrate the information derived from different modalities into a meaningful reflection of its complex sensory environment. As one would expect of an integrative process, inputs from one sensory modality often alter the processing of information in another (see Welch and Warren, 1986, for a recent review). This can increase or decrease the effectiveness of specific sensory cues and enhance behavioral flexibility. Through the process of integration, multisensory stimulus complexes can take on meaning that their individual unimodal stimulus components do not have. Although much of what we are concerned with here pertains to higher mammals, the presence of multisensory processing per se antedates mammals, and even antedates the evolutionary invention of the nervous system. It is already present in unicellular organisms (e.g., paramecia, see Naitoh, 1968; Eckert et al., 1972) and appears to have been retained throughout multicellular speciation. It is present not only in comparatively simple organisms (e.g., flatworms, see Koopowitz et al., 1979), but also in the higher primates, and at all intervening levels of complexity. In fact, we know of no animal in which there exists a complete segregation of sensory processing.

It may seem surprising, then, that despite a voluminous literature dealing with the modality-specific properties of neurons at all levels of the nervous system in many different species, we remain largely ignorant of the processes by which simultaneous inputs from different modalities are dealt with collectively. In large part this is because investigators interested in the properties of sensory neurons study them in laboratory conditions designed to minimize the possibility that extraneous stimuli can confound results. This strategy has provided a wealth of sensory data and a good deal of insight into problems of perception and sensorimotor behavior, as evidenced by much of the work reported in this symposium concerned with "the visually responsive neuron". However, because many areas of the brain that receive visual inputs also receive converging non-visual input, the visually-responsive neuron may also be an auditory and/or somatosensory-responsive neuron. Consequently, to understand its functional properties it is necessary to examine its reponses to different sensory stimuli and to combinations of these stimuli. While multisensory convergence is especially prevalent outside the primary projection pathways, it is by no means unknown within seemingly dedicated unimodal regions such as the dorsal column nuclei, vestibular nuclei, and even striate cortex (e.g., Jabbur et al., 1971; Morrell, 1972; Fishman and Michael, 1973; Waespe et al., 1981; Noda, 1981; see also Meredith and Stein, 1986a).

Perhaps the best known site of multisensory convergence within the visual system is the superior colliculus (Stein, 1984), and its non-mammalian homologue, the optic tectum (Hartline, 1984), structures that play an integral role in attentive and orientation behaviors. Visual, auditory and somatosensory inputs project to the deep layers of the superior colliculus and do so in topographic fashion. Thus, each sensory representation is map-like and all of the maps are in spatial register with one another (see Stein and Meredith, 1990, for a brief review). In this way a sensory cue, regardless of modality, activates neurons in the same general location in the superior colliculus: the location corresponds to the position of the stimulus in sensory space. Cues positioned forward in space (or on the front of the body) activate rostral neurons, cues above the animal or on its upper body activate medial neurons, and so on. This is not only an economical way to represent sensory space, but it is also an efficient way to match incoming sensory information with outgoing "motor" information, for these sensory maps are also in register with the motor maps found in the deep layers (e.g., Stein et al., 1976; Harris, 1980; Stein and Clamann, 1981; Jay and Sparks, 1984; Sparks, 1989). Because many of the different sensory inputs converge on the same neurons, some trimodal neurons and many bimodal neurons (of all sensory combinations) are produced. A single multisensory neuron will have its two or three sensory receptive fields in spatial register with one another, and this intraneuron spatial register is likely to play a significant role in the overall alignment of the visual and non-visual maps found here (Meredith and Stein, 1990).

The typical visually-responsive superior colliculus neuron not only responds to inputs from non-visual modalities, but also integrates visual and non-visual information. The integration that occurs in response to combinations of visual and non-visual stimuli often results in a dramatic increase in the number of impulses evoked when compared with that elicited by either stimulus presented alone. This response enhancement is not merely a summation of the individual responses, but is a multiplicative increase in activity that can exceed 1200%. On the other hand, combinations of visual and non-visual cues can also evoke integrated responses that are significantly lower than those obtained from the individual stimuli. Although examples of response depression are not encountered as often as response enhancement, both forms of multisensory integration are frequently exhibited by the same neuron, as shown in Fig. 1.

The degree to which a non-visual stimulus can influence responses to visual stimuli varies not only from neuron to neuron, but can also change for a given neuron. The magnitude of these interactions is determined by a variety of factors inherent in the stimuli and the neurons themselves. The robust nature of these determinants of multisensory integration is so consistent that the determinants are referred to as "rules" for convenience.

The rules of multisensory integration

(1) *Spatial factors.* As detailed above, the different receptive fields of a given multisensory neuron show a general spatial register. This spatial registry is a key determinant of the type of interaction that will be produced. For example, when a visual and an auditory stimulus originate from the same spatial location, they fall within the excitatory receptive fields of the same multisensory neuron. This combined stimulus enhances the neuron's responses far above that to either stimulus alone. If, however, the auditory stimulus originates from a location outside its excitatory receptive field, it can no longer enhance the neuron's activity, and if it falls within an inhibitory region, it will depress the neuron's responses to the visual stimulus (Meredith and Stein, 1986b).

(2) *Temporal factors.* The temporal "window" during which multisensory integration can take place is quite long (sometimes exceeding 1500 msec). Maximal interactive effects are produced during this window by overlapping the periods of maximal unimodal influence with one another. In this way simultaneous visual and non-visual stimuli often produce dramatic interactions despite their very different input latencies (Meredith et al., 1987).

(3) *Magnitude.* Multisensory interactions are multiplicative rather than additive. In the most dramatic examples, the combination of an ineffective visual stimulus and an ineffective auditory or somatosensory stimulus reliably evokes responses (Meredith and Stein, 1986a).

(4) *Inverse effectiveness rule.* Combinations of weak unimodal stimuli produce proportionately greater response enhancements than do combinations of strong stimuli. This indicates that multisensory enhancement is most effective when unimodal stimuli are poorly effective by themselves (Meredith and Stein, 1986a).

These observations have raised several additional questions. First, can a neuron's visual receptive field properties be affected by non-visual stimuli? And if so, what are the "rules" by which this is accomplished? Second, are the rules of multisensory integration specific to the superior colliculus of the cat, or are they applicable to visually-responsive (or auditory-responsive and/or somatosensory-responsive) neurons in other structures and animals? These questions are addressed below.

Methods

All procedures were performed in compliance with the *Guide for Care and Use of Laboratory Animals* (NIH publication no. 86-23) at Virginia Commonwealth University, which is accredited by the American Association for the Accreditation of Laboratory Animal Care. The methods for many of these experiments have been described in detail elsewhere (e.g., Meredith and Stein, 1986a), and are therefore described only briefly.

Cat

Recordings were made through a resealable recording well/head-holding device (see McHaffie and Stein, 1983) implanted 1 week or more prior to experimentation. The well was implanted over either the superior colliculus, the lateral suprasylvian (LS) cortex or the anterior ectosylvian sulcus (AES). For recording, anesthesia was induced with ketamine (30 mg/kg) and maintained with either ketamine (5 – 10 mg/kg per hour) or halothane (0.5 – 2.0%). Animals were paralyzed (pancuronium bromide, 10 mg/kg; 2 – 4 mg/kg per hour) and artificially respired. The optic discs were projected and focused onto a translucent plastic hemisphere and corrective contact lenses were applied. A calibrated X-Y slide was attached to the recording well to hold and guide the recording electrode (glass insulated tungsten, > 1 MΩ impedance). The location of each successful recording penetration was marked electrolytically and, after euthanasia (barbiturate overdose) and perfusion, reconstructed from histologically prepared sections.

Responses to unimodal (visual, auditory or somatosensory) stimuli were first established to determine which stimuli would be presented during tests for multisensory interactions. All quantitative sensory tests were then conducted using reproduci-

82

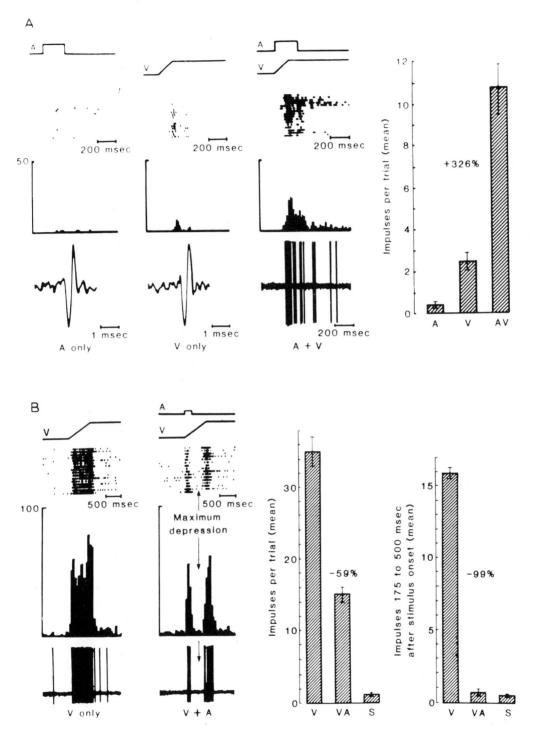

Fig. 1. *A*. Response enhancement in a bimodal (visual-auditory) neuron in cat superior colliculus. The auditory stimulus is represented by a square wave (A) and the visual stimulus by a ramp (V). The rasters below show the neuron's responses to 16 successive stimuli (each dot is one impulse). Matched peristimulus time histograms (bins = 10 msec) and oscillograms are shown below each raster. From left to right: few impulses were evoked by the auditory stimulus (200 msec, broadband noise burst) when presented alone. The visual

ble, electronically controlled stimuli initiated by a computer; the onset, duration and physical parameters of each stimulus are varied independently.

Once a neuron was isolated and its receptive field(s) mapped, multisensory tests were performed. Single-modality (e.g., visual alone, auditory alone) and multisensory (e.g., visual and auditory) stimuli were presented repeatedly (8 – 16 times) within their respective receptive fields in an interleaved manner at long interstimulus intervals (10 – 30 sec). Responses elicited by combining the stimuli were compared statistically (paired t-test) to those elicited by the single-modality presentations to determine if there was a significant ($P < 0.05$) increase (response enhancement) or decrease (response depression) in the number of impulses. By using this manner of analysis, the total product resulting from a combination of stimuli is emphasized, and arbitrary, mathematically constrained categories (i.e., inhibition, occlusion, summation, facilitation) are avoided. The magnitude of the interaction is calculated as:

$$(CM - SM_{max})/(SM_{max}) \times 100 = \% \text{ interaction}$$

where CM is the mean number of impulses evoked by the combined-modality stimulus, and SM_{max} is the mean number of impulses evoked by the most effective single-modality stimulus.

Monkey

A monkey scheduled for euthanasia was obtained for terminal experimentation. The recording and stimulation paradigms were the same as in cat, but

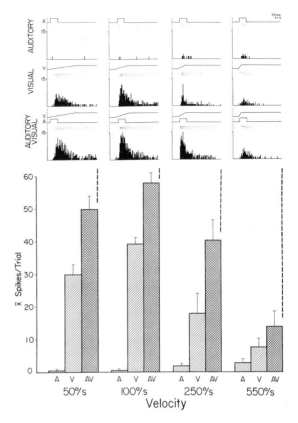

Fig. 2. Maintenance of velocity selectivity by a visual-auditory neuron in the superior colliculus during multisensory integration. As shown by the rasters and peristimulus time histograms at the top, an auditory stimulus was unreliable in activating this neuron, and generally evoked few impulses. In contrast, a moving visual stimulus was quite effective, and the neuron showed a reliable preference for movement at 100°/sec. When the auditory and visual stimuli were combined at each velocity, the auditory stimulus significantly ($P < 0.001$) enhanced responses but did not alter velocity selectivity. This is most apparent in the graph at the bottom. Note that the relative velocity preferences remained despite the response enhancement induced by the auditory stimulus.

---

stimulus (1° × 2° bar, moved at 300°/sec in the preferred direction across the receptive field) evoked impulses on 69% of the trials. When, however, the visual and auditory stimuli were presented in close temporal sequence, the combined stimulus evoked vigorous responses on every trial. Histogram on the right shows the mean response for each stimulus condition. The number of impulses evoked by the combined stimulus was significantly enhanced (paired t-test, $P < 0.001$). Vertical lines represent standard errors of the mean. B. Response depression in a bimodal (visual-auditory) neuron in cat superior colliculus. From left to right: a 2° × 4° bar of light moved at 125°/sec evoked vigorous responses. However, no response was elicited by auditory or by somatosensory stimuli when presented alone. When an auditory stimulus (200 msec, broadband noise burst) was presented during visual stimulation, it significantly inhibited responses to the visual stimulus ($P < 0.001$). The inhibitory effect was nearly complete from 175 to 500 msec after auditory onset. Peristimulus time histograms are calibrated for 100 impulses and 50 msec time bins. (Reproduced with permission from Meredith and Stein, 1983.)

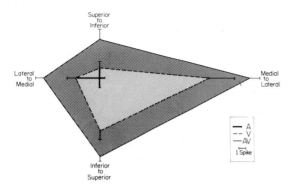

Fig. 3. Maintenance of direction selectivity by a visual-auditory neuron in the superior colliculus during multisensory integration. A polar coordinate plot illustrates the direction preferences of this neuron. The lengths of the lines reflect the mean number of impulses evoked (standard error bars are shown). The most vigorous responses were evoked when the visual stimulus moved from medial to lateral along a horizontal trajectory through the receptive field. An auditory stimulus (broadband noise burst) that was minimally effective alone produced significantly ($P < 0.001$) enhanced responses to the visual stimulus regardless of the direction of visual movement, but had no effect on the relative preference for one direction of movement over another. The crossed bars representing the mean auditory responses were obtained from four separate sets of trials with the auditory stimulus alone. Each set of auditory trials was interleaved with visual and visual-auditory trials.

the anesthetic condition was different. The animal was initially anesthetized with ketamine hydrochloride, and then maintained during surgery and recording by inhalation anesthesia using 0.5 – 2.5% halothane. A craniotomy was performed to expose the intraparietal sulcus; the wounds were infiltrated with Xylocaine and the cortex was covered with agar. Electrode penetrations were made along the intraparietal sulcus to sample neurons in both banks and the fundus. In the rostral aspect of the sulcus the electrode penetrations were extended deep to the fundus in order to sample neurons in the superior temporal sulcus.

Results

Visual receptive field properties and multisensory integration in cat superior colliculus

A number of properties characterize visually-responsive neurons in the superior colliculus, including: velocity tuning, directional selectivity, spatial summation and spatial inhibition. These properties are as common among unimodal visual neurons as among multisensory neurons (Meredith and Stein, 1986a). To determine if these properties are altered by the presence of non-visual stimuli, each property was explored by varying the parameters of the visual stimulus when it was presented alone, and then in a matching trial in which the visual stimulus was paired with a non-visual stimulus.

The neuron whose responses are documented in Fig. 2 was best activated by a visual stimulus moved across the receptive field at approximately 100°/sec. Combining the moving visual stimulus with a brief, broad-band, stationary auditory stimulus (the auditory stimulus was poorly effective on most trials when presented alone) significantly enhanced the neuron's responsiveness, but did not alter its selectivity with regard to the speed of the moving visual stimulus. Its best response was still evoked at 100°/sec. In this neuron, as well as in the others examined ($n = 4$), the presence of a non-visual stimulus did not alter its tuning for a particular velocity of moving visual stimuli.

The same effect was noted on directional selectivity ($n = 9$, an example is shown in Fig. 3), spatial summation ($n = 7$, Fig. 4, top), and spatial inhibition ($n = 7$, Fig. 4, bottom). In each case the magnitude of the response was altered significantly by the presence of a non-visual stimulus, but there was no effect on the selectivity of the visual response.

Multisensory integration in cortex

Although the characteristics of multisensory integration, including those described above, have been well established in the superior colliculus, their occurrence and general applicability for other areas of the CNS had yet to be determined. Therefore, we examined neurons in several cortical regions believed to be multisensory.

Cat. The cat's lateral suprasylvian (LS) cortex is

Spatial Summation

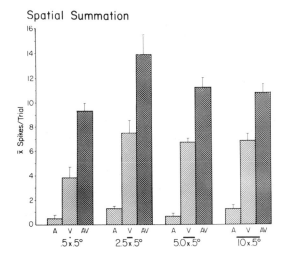

Spatial Inhibition

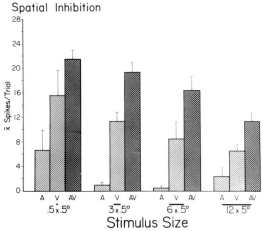

Stimulus Size

Fig. 4. Spatial summation and spatial inhibition are maintained in superior colliculus neurons during multisensory integration. The effectiveness of an auditory stimulus (A) presented alone and of visual stimuli (V) of various sizes moved across the receptive field are plotted. All stimuli were smaller than the diameter of the receptive field. Note the presence of significant ($P < 0.001$) spatial summation. The presence of a spatially coincident auditory stimulus enhanced responses to each visual stimulus (trials labeled "AV"), but did not alter the relative effectiveness of stimuli of different sizes. A similar effect is shown at the bottom for a different neuron in which smaller stimuli produced greater responses than larger stimuli despite the fact that all stimuli were confined within the borders of the excitatory receptive field (within-field spatial inhibition).

best known as a "visual" area, and has been subdivided on the basis of its multiple representations of visual space (Palmer et al., 1978). However, in the anterior LS, near the confluence of cortical areas devoted to visual, auditory and somatosensory representations, we have found scattered multisensory neurons ($n = 8$). Similarly, multisensory neurons were found in the cat's anterior ectosylvian sulcus (AES). The AES is generally characterized as an "association" cortex, but is comprised of distinct unimodal regions that include: a somatosensory area (SIV, Clemo and Stein, 1982), an auditory region (Field AES, Clarey and Irvine, 1986), and a visual area (anterior ectosylvian visual area, AEV or EVA, see Mucke et al., 1982; Olson and Graybiel, 1987). The multisensory neurons ($n = 24$) were found near the borders of these unimodal areas (Clemo et al., 1991).

Multisensory neurons in cat cortex appear to integrate sensory information in a manner virtually indistinguishable from neurons in the superior colliculus. In the example from LS depicted in Fig. 5, the neuron responded to a visual stimulus as well as to a somatosensory stimulus. Although the receptive field for each modality was rather large, they were in good spatial register, a feature commonly observed in multisensory neurons in the superior colliculus. When visual and somatosensory stimuli were presented together within their respective receptive fields, a strong enhancement of activity was produced. As with multisensory neurons in the superior colliculus, the temporal relationship between the two unimodal stimuli was an important factor in determining the level of interaction that would take place. By timing the multimodal stimuli so that the unimodal discharge trains would be overlapping, enhancement was maximized (see also Meredith et al., 1987).

The integrative properties of multisensory neurons were much the same in the AES. This is evident from the example shown in Fig. 6. The neuron responded to auditory stimuli in contralateral space and to gentle cutaneous stimulation of the contralateral body. The auditory and somatosensory receptive fields had similar spatial features: both were quite large, but excluded the most rostral and caudal areas of auditory and body space. Once again, the weak response to each unimodal stimulus

Rostral Lateral Suprasylvian Sulcus

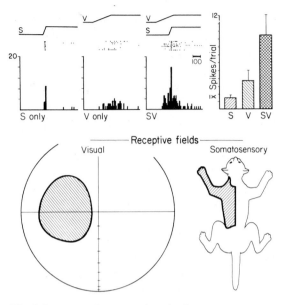

Fig. 5. Response enhancement in a visual-somatosensory neuron in cat lateral suprasylvian (LS) cortex. The visual receptive field of this neuron is depicted at bottom left, and its somatosensory receptive field at bottom right. A somatosensory stimulus (S) that indented the skin on the mid-region of the dorsal trunk elicited a brief, short latency response. A visual $2° \times 5°$ stimulus (V) moved across the visual receptive field at $100°/sec$ also produced a weak response. However, combining the two stimuli (SV), so that the tactile stimulus came on 160 msec after the visual stimulus, resulted in a significant ($P < 0.001$) enhancement of neuronal responses that exceeded the sum of the two unimodal responses.

was significantly enhanced by their combination, and this enhanced response exceeded the sum of the two unimodal responses. The same spatial rules for multisensory integration detailed in the superior colliculus were operative in this neuron. When the auditory stimulus was presented outside its receptive field, and thus out of register with the somatosensory stimulus, combining the two stimuli produced significant response depression.

Monkey. The superior temporal sulcus (STS) and portions of the intraparietal sulcus (IPS) of the rhesus monkey's cortex have been shown to be "polymodal" (e.g., Bruce et al., 1981; Duhamel et

al., 1991). Therefore, we sought to determine whether neuronal responses would be enhanced and/or degraded here by multisensory stimuli as in cat superior colliculus and cortex. Sensory driving was excellent in these regions, with the medial bank of IPS most responsive to contralateral tactile stimuli, the lateral bank most responsive to contralateral visual stimuli, and STS exhibiting excellent bilateral auditory and tactile driving. A curious feature of many somatosensory neurons in STS was the presence of "split" receptive fields. The best examples of this were neurons from which

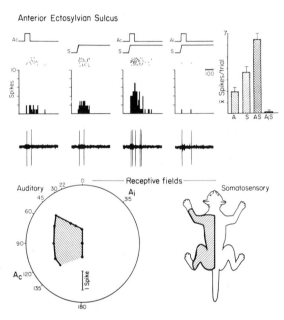

Fig. 6. Multisensory integration in a bimodal (auditory-somatosensory) neuron in cat anterior ectosylvian sulcus (AES). A broadband noise burst produced responses at each point tested (represented by closed circles) from 0° to 135° along the contralateral horizontal meridian as shown in the schematic at lower left. This is the horizontal extent of the auditory receptive field. The somatosensory receptive field encompassed the contralateral trunk and portions of the two limbs as shown on the figurine in the lower right. Presenting the contralateral auditory (Ac) or somatosensory (S) stimulus alone evoked comparatively weak responses, but the auditory-somatosensory combination produced a significantly ($P < 0.01$) more vigorous response that exceeded the sum of the two unimodal responses. When, however, the auditory stimulus was presented in ipsilateral space (Ai) it significantly ($P < 0.001$) depressed responses to the somatosensory stimulus.

vigorous driving was elicited by gentle cutaneous stimulation of either hand, but not the intervening body.

Although an exhaustive study remains to be conducted, it was interesting to note that among the neurons studied in monkey cortex ($n = 15$), those identified as responsive to only one modality (i.e., unimodal) during casual qualitative examination ($n = 9$) exhibited no response enhancements during extensive quantitative combined-modality testing. Thus, as in cat superior colliculus, qualitative tests are quite effective in identifying modality convergence patterns (though in neither case are inhibitory inputs effectively identified in this way). The sample of neurons in monkey cortex that were found to respond to more than one sensory stimulus during initial examination ($n = 6$) also showed multisensory enhancement and/or depression during quantitative evaluation. Both visual-somatosensory and auditory-somatosensory neurons were encountered.

The responses of two neurons from the TPO sub-division of the superior bank of STS (e.g., see Seltzer and Pandya, 1978) are shown here. In the auditory-somatosensory example shown at the top of Fig. 7 a somatosensory stimulus was moderately effective when presented on the lateral aspect of the face and an auditory stimulus was weakly effective when presented from the same region (i.e., 90° in contralateral space). Combining the somatosensory and auditory stimuli produced a markedly enhanced response that far exceeded the reponse to either stimulus alone. In the neuron depicted at the bottom of Fig. 7 a gentle somatosensory stimulus on the side of the face produced a reliable short-latency response, whereas visual stimuli, regardless of their location in space, were without apparent effect. However, when the visual stimulus was swept across central visual space at the same time the tactile stimulus was presented, a marked depression of the neuron's response to the somatosensory stimulus was observed. This indicated that the visual stimulus produced subthreshold (inhibitory) influences when presented alone.

Discussion

The present experiments demonstrate that despite the profound influences of multisensory integration on superior colliculus neurons, their unimodal receptive field properties are preserved during combined-modality stimulation. A visual neuron retains its directional and velocity selectivity, as well as its specificity for stimulus size, despite having its overall activity level significantly altered by a non-visual stimulus. The preservation of unimodal receptive field properties appears to be an additional "rule" of multisensory integration that may be added to the list presented in the Introduction. It ensures that a neuron's selectivity for specific stimulus features in one modality is unimpaired in the presence of stimuli from other modalities. This invariance in receptive field properties seems essential for the nervous system to maintain a constant code for stimulus features in an ever-changing sensory world.

Although the cat superior colliculus neuron is a

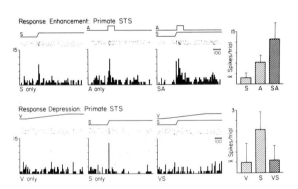

Fig. 7. Multisensory integration in bimodal neurons of monkey superior temporal sulcus (STS). Response enhancement: the neuron shown in the upper set of rasters and histograms was activated by a somatosensory (S) stimulus that indented the skin on the contralateral cheek. It was also activated by a broadband noise burst (A) originating from the same general spatial location (i.e., 90° contralateral). When the two stimuli were combined (SA), responses were significantly ($P < 0.01$) enhanced. Response depression: the neuron shown at the bottom responded to a somatosensory stimulus, but a visual stimulus was without apparent effect. When, however, the visual stimulus was combined with the somatosensory stimulus it significantly ($P < 0.01$) inhibited the neuron's responses.

major site for the convergence and integration of multisensory information (Stein, 1984; Meredith and Stein, 1986a,b; Stein and Meredith, 1990; Wallace et al., 1991), it is only one of many central nervous system sites in many species where information from several modalities converges. In the current study, single cells in cat LS and AES and in monkey IPS and STS were examined in the same fashion as were superior colliculus neurons in previous studies and found to adhere to the same set of basic integrating principles. Although the spatial, temporal and multiplicative characteristics of multisensory integration were most closely examined in cat cortex, all of the observations in monkey were consistent with those described in cat. The multisensory receptive fields of a single neuron overlapped one another in space, so that sensory stimuli that were in close spatial register fell within their excitatory receptive fields and enhanced the neuron's activity; spatially disparate stimuli produced either no interaction or depressed responses. The timing of the stimuli was a critical determinant of the interaction produced. Stimuli presented so that their unimodal discharges would overlap evoked maximal response enhancements. These interactions were multiplicative in nature and were not specific for the modality combinations examined; the same rules appeared to be operative among any combination of visual, auditory and somatosensory stimuli.

The rules of multisensory integration evident at the level of the single neuron are also consistent with studies of intact behaving animals. The attentive and orientation responses cats make to visual and auditory stimuli were predictable based on the reactions of superior colliculus neurons to these stimuli (Stein et al., 1988, 1989). When the auditory stimulus was spatially and temporally coincident with the visual stimulus, the animal's responses to the visual stimulus were enhanced in a multiplicative fashion. In contrast, when the visual and auditory stimuli were spatially disparate, responses to the visual stimulus were depressed.

It is unlikely that these complex overt behaviors depend solely on mechanisms involving the superior colliculus and/or its afferent systems. It seems far more likely that the rules of multisensory integration extend well beyond the midbrain and its afferent systems to represent a general set of principles by which multisensory neurons operate throughout the brain. Thus far the data are consistent with this postulate in cat LS and AES, as well as in the parietal and temporal cortices of the monkey. They are also consistent with behavioral and event-related potential data in human subjects (Costin et al., 1991). However, these similarities should not be taken to mean that multisensory integration in structures with different roles does not have a very different impact on behavior and perception. Surely it must, but it is likely that similar integrative processes are necessary to link immediate overt responses (e.g., mediated by the superior colliculus), cognition (mediated by cortex), and even emotive processes (e.g., mediated by the limbic system). In this way the same combinations of stimuli that enhance or degrade responses in one area of the brain will enhance or degrade responses in other areas of the brain, with the probable result being an increase or decrease in the salience of a stimulus at all levels of information processing. Yet, changes in the magnitude of the signal via multisensory integration appear to be accomplished without altering the unimodal receptive field properties that may be necessary for coding specific stimulus features.

These data indicate that the visual responses of many neurons, whether in the superior colliculus or cortex, represent only one facet of their sensory coding capabilities. Thus, the rubric "visually-responsive neuron" is particularly apt as a general designation. It is far less exclusive than the more commonly used category: "visual neuron".

Acknowledgements

We thank Nancy London for technical assistance. This work was supported by NIH grants NS 22543 and NS 08902.

References

Bruce, C., Desimone, R. and Gross, C.G. (1981) Visual properties of neurons in a polysensory area in superior temporal sulcus of the monkey. *J. Neurophysiol.,* 46: 369 – 384.

Clarey, J.C. and Irvine, D.R.F. (1986) Auditory response properties of neurons in the anterior ectosylvian sulcus of the cat. *Brain Res.,* 386: 12 – 19.

Clemo, H.R. and Stein, B.E. (1982) Somatosensory cortex: a "new" somatotopic representation. *Brain Res.,* 235: 162 – 168.

Clemo, H.R. and Stein, B.E. (1986) Effects of cooling somatosensory cortex on response properties of tactile cells in the superior colliculus. *J. Neurophysiol.,* 55: 1352 – 1368.

Clemo, H.R., Meredith, M.A., Wallace, M.T. and Stein, B.E. (1991) Is the cortex of the cat anterior ectosylvian sulcus a polysensory area? *Soc. Neurosci. Abstr.,* 17: 1585.

Costin, D., Neville, H.J., Meredith, M.A. and Stein, B.E. (1991) Rules of multisensory integration and attention: ERP and behavioral evidence in humans. *Soc. Neurosci. Abstr.,* 17: 656.

Duhamel, J.-R., Colby, C.L. and Goldberg, M.E. (1991) Congruent representations of visual and somatosensory space in single neurons of monkey ventral intraparietal cortex (area VIP). In: J. Paillard (Ed.), *Brain and Space,* Oxford University Press, Oxford, in press.

Eckert, R., Naitoh, Y. and Friedman, K. (1972) Sensory mechanisms in paramecium. I. Two components of the anterior surface. *J. Exp. Biol.,* 56: 683 – 694.

Edwards, S.B., Ginsburgh, C.L., Henkel, C.K. and Stein, B.E. (1979) Sources of subcortical projections to the superior colliculus in the cat. *J. Comp. Neurol.,* 184: 309 – 330.

Fishman, M.C. and Michael, C.R. (1973) Integration of auditory information in the cat's visual cortex. *Vision Res.,* 13: 1415 – 1419.

Harris, L.R. (1980) The superior colliculus and movements of the head and eyes in cats. *J. Physiol. (Lond.),* 300: 367 – 391.

Hartline, P.H. (1984) The optic tectum of reptiles: neurophysiological studies. In: H. Vanegas (Ed.), *Comparative Neurology of the Optic Tectum,* Plenum, New York, pp. 601 – 618.

Howard, I.P. and Templeton, W.B. (1966) *Human Spatial Orientation,* Wiley, London.

Huerta, M.F. and Harting, J.K. (1984) The mammalian superior colliculus: studies of its morphology and connections. In: H. Vanegas (Ed.), *Comparative Neurology of the Optic Tectum,* Plenum, New York, pp. 687 – 773.

Jabbur, S.J., Atweh, S.F., Tomey, G.G. and Banna, N.R. (1971) Visual and auditory inputs into cuneate nucleus. *Science,* 174: 1146 – 1147.

Jay, M.F. and Sparks, D.L. (1984) Auditory receptive fields in primate superior colliculus shift with changes in eye position. *Nature,* 309: 345 – 347.

Koopowitz, H., Bernardo, K. and Keenan, L. (1979) Primitive nervous systems: electrical activity in ventral nerve cords of the flatworm *Notoplana acticola. J. Neurobiol.,* 10: 367 – 381.

McHaffie, J.G. and Stein, B.E. (1983) A chronic head-holder minimizing facial obstructions. *Brain Res. Bull.,* 10:

859 – 860.

Meredith, M.A. and Clemo, H.R. (1989) Auditory cortical projection from the anterior ectosylvian sulcus (Field AES) to the superior colliculus in the cat: an anatomical and electrophysiological study. *J. Comp. Neurol.,* 289: 687 – 707.

Meredith, M.A. and Stein, B.E. (1983) Interactions among converging sensory inputs in the superior colliculus. *Science,* 221: 389 – 391.

Meredith, M.A. and Stein, B.E. (1985) Descending efferents from the superior colliculus relay integrated multisensory information. *Science,* 227: 657 – 659.

Meredith, M.A. and Stein, B.E. (1986a) Visual, auditory and somatosensory convergence on cells in superior colliculus results in multisensory integration. *J. Neurophysiol.,* 56: 640 – 662.

Meredith, M.A. and Stein, B.E. (1986b) Spatial factors determine the activity of multisensory neurons in cat superior colliculus. *Brain Res.,* 365: 350 – 354.

Meredith, M.A. and Stein, B.E. (1990) The visuotopic component of the multisensory map in the deep laminae of the cat superior colliculus. *J. Neurosci.,* 10: 3727 – 3742.

Meredith, M.A., Nemitz, J.W. and Stein, B.E. (1987) Determinants of multisensory integration in superior colliculus neurons. I. Temporal factors. *J. Neurosci.,* 10: 3215 – 3229.

Meredith, M.A., Wallace, M.T. and Stein, B.E. (1991) Integrating the different senses in neurons from cat association cortex (anterior ectosylvian sulcus). *Soc. Neurosci. Abstr.,* 17: 1585.

Morrell, F. (1972) Visual system's view of acoustic space. *Nature,* 238: 44 – 46.

Mucke, L., Norita, M., Benedek, G. and Creutzfeldt, O. (1982) Physiologic and anatomic investigation of a visual cortical area situated in the ventral bank of the anterior ectosylvian sulcus of the cat. *Exp. Brain Res.,* 46: 1 – 11.

Naito, Y. (1968) Ionic control of the reversal response of cilia in *Paramecium caudatum:* a calcium hypothesis. *J. Gen. Physiol.,* 51: 85 – 103.

Noda, H. (1981) Visual mossy fiber inputs to the flocculus of the monkey. In: *Vestibular and Oculomotor Physiology – Ann. N.Y. Acad. Sci.,* 374: 465 – 475.

Ogasawara, K., McHaffie, J.G. and Stein, B.E. (1984) Two visual systems in cat. *J. Neurophysiol.,* 52: 1226 – 1245.

Olson, C.R. and Graybiel, A.M. (1987) Ectosylvian visual area of the cat: location, retinotopic organization and connections. *J. Comp. Neurol.,* 261: 277 – 294.

Palmer, L.A., Rosenquist, A.C. and Tusa, R.J. (1978) The retinotopic organization of lateral suprasylvian visual areas in the cat. *J. Comp. Neurol.,* 177: 237 – 256.

Ranck, J.B. (1975) Which elements are excited in electrical stimulation of mammalian central nervous system: a review. *Brain Res.,* 98: 417 – 440.

Segal, R.L. and Beckstead, R.M. (1984) The lateral suprasylvian corticotectal projection in cats. *J. Comp. Neurol.,* 225: 259 – 275.

90

Seltzer, B. and Pandya, D.N. (1978) Afferent cortical connections and architectonics of the superior temporal sulcus and surrounding cortex in the rhesus monkey. *Brain Res.,* 149: 1 – 24.

Sparks, D.L. (1989) The neural encoding of the location of targets for saccadic eye movements. *J. Exp. Biol.,* 146: 195 – 207.

Sprague, J.M. (1966) Visual, acoustic, and somesthetic deficits in the cat after cortical and midbrain lesions. In: D.D. Purpura and M. Yahr (Eds.), *The Thalamus,* Columbia, NY, pp. 391 – 417.

Stein, B.E. (1984) Multimodal representation in the superior colliculus and optic tectum. In: H. Vanegas (Ed.), *Comparative Neurology of the Optic Tectum,* Plenum, New York, pp. 819 – 841.

Stein, B.E. and Clamann, H.P. (1981) Control of pinna movements and sensorimotor register in cat superior colliculus. *Brain Behav. Evol.,* 19: 180 – 192.

Stein, B.E. and Meredith, M.A. (1990) Multisensory integration: neural and behavioral solutions for dealing with stimuli from different sensory modalities. *Ann. N.Y. Acad. Sci.,* 608: 51 – 70.

Stein, B.E., Magalhaes-Castro, B. and Kruger, L. (1976) Relationship between visual and tactile representation in cat superior colliculus. *J. Neurophysiol.,* 39: 401 – 419.

Stein, B.E., Huneycutt, W.S. and Meredith, M.A. (1988) Neurons and behavior: the same rules of multisensory integration apply. *Brain Res.,* 448: 355 – 358.

Stein, B.E., Meredith, M.A., Huneycutt, W.S. and McDade, L. (1989) Behavioral indices of multisensory integration: orientation to visual cues is affected by auditory stimuli. *J. Cogn. Neurosci.,* 1: 12 – 24.

Waespe, W., Buttner, U. and Henn, V. (1981) Input-output activity of the primate flocculus during visual-vestibular interaction. In: *Vestibular and Oculomotor Physiology – Ann. N.Y. Acad. Sci.,* 374: 491 – 503.

Wallace, M.T., Meredith, M.A. and Stein, B.E. (1991) Cortical convergence on multisensory output neurons of cat superior colliculus. *Soc. Neurosci. Abstr.,* 17: 1379.

Welch, R.B. and Warren, D.H. (1986) Intersensory interactions. In: K.R. Boff, L. Kaufman and J.P. Thomas (Eds.), *Handbook of Perception and Human Performance, Vol. I: Sensory Process in Perception,* Wiley, New York, pp. 1 – 36.

T.P. Hicks, S. Molotchnikoff and T. Ono (Eds.)
Progress in Brain Research, Vol. 95
© 1993 Elsevier Science Publishers B.V. All rights reserved.

CHAPTER 9

Sensory integration in the deep layers of superior colliculus

Carol K. Peck, John A. Baro and Stephanie M. Warder

School of Optometry, University of Missouri, St. Louis, MO, U.S.A.

Introduction

Processing of visual information is not accomplished in isolation from the processing of sensory information in other modalities, and neurons within a number of regions of the central nervous system integrate information from visual and non-visual cues. One of the best studied of such regions is the superior colliculus of the mammalian brain and its homologue in lower vertebrates, the optic tectum. Hartline and colleagues (Hartline et al., 1978) first reported that neurons in the optic tectum of the snake integrate visual information with infrared cues from their infrared-sensing pit organs. Some of these cells respond only to simultaneous bimodal stimulation, and other cells, although responding to targets of only one of the modalities, show enhanced or depressed responses when a target in the second modality is presented simultaneously. Meredith and Stein (1986) and Meredith et al. (1987) have also studied integration of visual, auditory and somatosensory information in the superior colliculus of cats and hamsters. Integration of multimodal cues presumably enhances the ability of organisms to detect low intensity signals. The majority of multimodal cells have efferent projections to pre-motor and motor structures, and thus, collicular neurons integrating multimodal cues are likely to affect the probability of a behavioral response to those cues.

The deeper layers of the superior colliculus not only receive convergent inputs from the visual, auditory and somatosensory systems, but the ordered maps of sensory space formed by each modality are in approximate correspondence. It is possible that such alignment of sensory maps permits different sensory systems to access a common pre-motor map so that orienting eye and head movements are initiated toward targets, independent of modality. However, independent movements of the eyes, ears or body should then displace the sensory maps with respect to one another and could lead to mislocalization of targets whenever the different sense organs (e.g., eye and pinna) move independently.

Another possibility is that even "sensory" signals are coded in motor coordinates by the superior colliculus – that is, collicular neurons signal the amplitude and direction of movements necessary to look at a target (e.g., Jay and Sparks, 1987). In such a case, localization of targets would be unaffected by changes in the relative positions of sense organs. In the rhesus monkey, auditory receptive fields of collicular neurons shift with eye position, suggesting that auditory signals may have been translated into motor error coordinates. It is possible that the responses of individual collicular neurons to any sensory target (whether visual, auditory or somatosensory) would be modulated by the movement of any of the different sense organs (e.g., visual responses modulated by changes in the position of the pinnae).

Over the past 5 years, we have conducted a series of experiments designed to assess the effects of changes in eye position on the responses of collicular neurons to visual, auditory and combined modality stimulation in another well-studied visual system, that of the domestic cat. In parallel, we have examined the effects of eye position on the accuracy of saccadic localization of visual, auditory and combined modality targets. In all of the studies to be described, combined modality (visual and auditory) targets were presented simultaneously at the same location in the cat's frontal hemifield during periods where the cat's gaze was directed steadily either straight ahead or at known deviations to the left or right of primary position.

Methods

Most of the procedures used in these experiments are similar to those described in detail in previous reports (Peck, 1987, 1989, 1990) and are, therefore, described only briefly here.

Six adult cats participated in one or more of the experiments. Under deep general anesthesia with aseptic conditions, each cat first underwent surgery to implant a scleral search coil around one eye and to construct a head holder for immobilization of the head in a completely painless manner. After recovery from surgery, each cat was gradually accustomed to head restraint in order to permit training on several fixation and saccade tasks. The body was loosely restrained by placing the cat in a canvas bag and supported by a plexiglas tube centered within a magnetic coil system for monitoring the position of the eye in the orbit (Robinson, 1963). By combining brief periods of head restraint with social interaction and a highly preferred food during experimental sessions, we were easily able to accustom each cat to the experimental conditions. Visual targets were then presented at known locations in order to calibrate the voltages from the eye coil, and the cats were trained on several simple visuomotor tasks previously described in detail (Peck, 1989, 1990). These tasks encouraged the cats to direct their gaze to different positions in space, either in

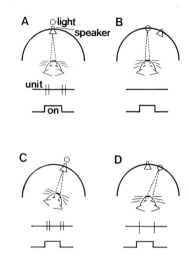

Fig. 1. Schematic of experimental situation and design. The subject was comfortably seated, with head fixed, in the center of an egocentric hoop in the plane of the interaural axis. Elevation of all targets was thus 0°. The azimuthal location of speakers and light-emitting diodes was varied from 40° left to 40° right in 10° intervals. Initial fixation was varied in 10° intervals from 20° left to 20° right by using the light-emitting diodes as fixation targets. The training tasks (see text) encouraged the subjects to voluntarily direct their gaze to different locations in head-centered space. If the superior colliculus encodes the position of auditory targets with respect to the head alone, then targets having the same location with respect to the head (e.g., A and D) should evoke the same response regardless of the position of the eyes in the orbit. (In the experiments reported in this paper, the position of the head was not changed – that is, condition C was not used.) Depending on the size of the receptive field of the neuron studied, targets at different locations (e.g., B) should produce a different response. On the other hand, if the colliculus encodes the size and amplitude of the saccade required to fixate an auditory target, the response of the cell should also vary with the position of the eyes in the orbit for a given location of the sound source with respect to the head (e.g., A vs. D).

response to visual and auditory targets, or in anticipation of visual and auditory targets. Food rewards were given for maintaining gaze position within a certain "window" (generally between ± 2° and ± 5°, depending upon the task) around the positions required by the tasks for a minimum period of time (500 msec to 3 sec, depending on the task). Breaking fixation terminated the trial and led to a time out period before the next trial. Visual targets were light-emitting diodes (LEDs) and auditory targets were bursts of white noise, produced by speakers located at the same horizontal eccentricity as each of the LEDs. As shown in Fig. 1, the targets were located on the circumference of an egocentric hoop, centered on the cat's midline. In all of the experiments reported in this paper, the hoop was oriented horizontally at the level of the cat's ear canals.

After the cat was well-trained on the behavioral tasks, a craniotomy was made over the central region of the superior colliculus and a well was constructed to permit access to the central nervous system. On each recording day, a sterile tungsten microelectrode was advanced stereotaxically into the midbrain, using conventional techniques. In most cats, each hemisphere was studied for a period of 4 – 6 weeks, with one recording session each day. Most cats would work willingly and attentively for 2 – 3 h/day. If the cat became restless, sleepy, or showed any sign of discomfort, the experiment was discontinued.

In most of the experiments, the data were digitized on-line. Discriminated spikes were fed through a Schmitt trigger and stored as timed samples with a resolution of 0.1 msec. Horizontal and vertical coordinates of eye position and the position of visual and auditory targets were digitized at 200 Hz. During the experiment, data from each trial were displayed as spike occurrences, aligned with displays of the time of onset and offset of the targets, the position of those targets, and the position of the eye in the orbit. After the experiment was complete, conventional data analyses were performed to select cells responsive to different aspects of the tasks, using displays of spike activity in the form of instantaneous frequency, dot rasters, peri-stimulus time histograms, and peri-saccade time histograms. A saccade recognition program, using a velocity criterion which was set interactively by one of the experimenters, was used to determine the beginning and end of each saccadic eye movement. Standard linear regression techniques were used to assess the effects of eye position, target position, and modality on the responses of each cell.

For the behavioral studies, accuracy of saccadic eye movements was determined by subtracting the position of the eye after the first saccade from the position of the target. This metric gives the error of estimation of target position in retinal error coordinates (e.g., retinal error is $+10°$ if the target is $10°$ to the right of the eye) and allowed us to make a direct assessment of localization accuracy as a function of the initial position of the eye in the orbit.

Results

Accuracy of saccadic localization

One of our major goals was to determine whether cats can compensate behaviorally for initial eye position in making saccadic eye movements toward auditory and visual targets. We also compared the degree of compensation for targets in the two modalities and for bimodal (visual/auditory) targets. This experiment has important implications for the neural processing of auditory information by the saccadic oculomotor system because the neural map of auditory space is constructed from cues referenced to the head (i.e., the differences in timing and intensity of the sound arriving at the two ears), not to the eyes. The location of a visual target, on the other hand, is initially encoded in terms of the retinal location of cells whose firing rates are altered by the presentation of the target, and retinotopic information is maintained in central visual pathways by point-to-point mapping. Many models of the saccadic oculomotor system have, consequently, represented the location of targets in terms of their retinal error (e.g., Scudder, 1988). Other models, however, have computed the position of targets in space by summing retinal error information with information on the position of the eye in the orbit (e.g., Robinson, 1975). If information on the location of auditory targets is maintained in a head-centered representation by the saccadic oculomotor system, then organisms (including humans) should make substantially greater errors in localizing targets with saccadic eye movements when the eye is deviated in the orbit at the time of presentation of the sound cue than when the eye is centered in the orbit. Indeed, when the eye is eccentric in the orbit, saccadic localization error should, on average, be equal but opposite to the degree of deviation of the eye, independent of the position of the auditory target. For example, when the eye is 10° to the right of primary position and a target is presented straight ahead, a head-centered oculomotor system would register zero error and no saccade should occur,

leaving the target 10° to the left of the eye — a retinal error of − 10°. Similarly, if the target were 10° to the left of primary position while the eyes were 10° right, a head-centered oculomotor system would register a target error of − 10° and, if the saccade to the target was completely accurate, the eye would move − 10°, leaving a retinal error after the saccade of − 10°. Errors in the registration of the location of auditory targets would produce scatter around these values, so that when saccadic accuracy is plotted as a function of the position of the eye in the orbit at the time the auditory target is presented, the function would have a slope of − 1.0 if there were no compensation for the position of the eye in the orbit. On the other hand, if compensation were complete, there would be no mean change in saccadic accuracy as a function of eye position, and the function would have a slope of zero. In general, the amount of compensation, c, will equal the absolute value of − 1.0 − (m), where m is the slope of the regression equation for saccadic accuracy as a function of eye position.

In most studies of saccadic accuracy, constraints are placed on saccades which are used. Typically, subjects must achieve a minimum criterion of accuracy on a given trial before that trial is included in the data set. Trials on which the saccade is in the ''wrong'' direction are almost always eliminated as well. However, for this study, exclusions could have biased the answer and therefore we analyzed *all* saccades made by each of four cats when presented with auditory targets in a task in which they voluntarily varied the position of their eyes from trial to trial. As shown in Fig. 2A, although the cats sometimes made substantial errors in localization of auditory targets, the amount of error did not change significantly as the position of the eye in the orbit varied. The positions tested encompass the cat's oculomotor range (± 23 − 25°), although there were, typically, relatively few trials when the position of the eyes was near the limit of the oculomotor range. Thus, these data support the conclusion that cats compensate for a substantial portion of oculomotor eccentricity when locating auditory targets by saccadic eye movements. Moreover, as shown in Fig. 2B and C,

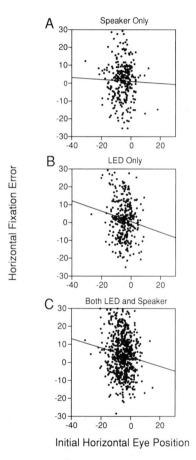

Fig. 2. Fixation errors in saccadic localization of targets as a function of the initial horizontal component of eye position in the orbit. Fixation error is the difference between the horizontal position of the stimulus and the horizontal position of the eye after the first saccade. The behavioral responses of one cat are shown when the target was a speaker alone (*A*), a LED alone (*B*), or both LED and speaker at the same location (*C*). Solid lines in *A* − *C* indicate the best fit linear regression equation for each condition. Perfect compensation for the initial position of the eye in the orbit would yield a slope of zero. Total failure of compensation would yield a slope of − 1.0.

comparable compensation for eye position was found when visual and combined modality targets were used.

Mobility of the auditory map in the superior colliculus

The behavioral data presented above imply that some portion of the saccadic oculomotor system has recoded the head-centered code of auditory space into a retinocentric code. Jay and Sparks (1987) have shown that the responses of neurons in primate superior colliculus to sounds are modulated by the position of the eyes in the orbit. In their study, the vast majority of sound-responsive neurons discharged vigorously to sounds that had an optimal deviation from the current position of the eyes in the orbit rather than to sounds having an optimal position relative to the head. However, Harris et al. (1980) had earlier reported that sound-responsive cells in cat superior colliculus discharged as a function of the position of the speaker relative to the head, independent of the position of the eyes in the orbit. These opposing results could reflect a species difference. Indeed, Harris et al. suggested that cats, unlike primates, use mostly head movements to reorient their gaze, rarely deviating the eye when the head is free to move, and thus do not need to compensate for the effects of ocular deviations. Because of the importance of this question to models of oculomotor organization, the small sample of cells examined by Harris et al., and the differences in the paradigms used in their study vs. that of Sparks and Jay, it seemed appropriate to re-examine this question.

In our first studies, we made a preliminary assessment of the speaker position(s) to which a given cell responded when the eyes were centered in the orbit and then tested its response to the same speaker positions on trials in which the cat maintained an eccentric eye position at the time of presentation of the auditory target (Peck and Wartman, 1989). Our results were very similar to those of Jay and Sparks (1987): the responses of most collicular neurons varied with the position of the eye in the orbit when sounds were presented from a fixed position with

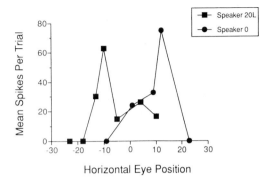

Fig. 3. Effects of eye position on the auditory response of one collicular neuron. Mean responses of one intermediate layer cell to sounds presented from a speaker at 20° to the cat's left (filled squares) or from straight ahead (0°, filled circles). Voluntary changes in the horizontal direction of gaze had similar effects on the responses of this cell to sounds from either speaker: the response was most vigorous when the eyes were about 10° to the right of the speaker and declined when the eyes were directed either further from the speaker or closer to it.

respect to the head (Fig. 3). Hartline et al. (1989) have obtained similar results.

We have now extended our results in a more quantitative study in which we also used a standard range of speaker positions for all cells. Each cell was tested with sounds presented from each of five speakers, ranging from 20° to the cat's left to 20° to its right, in 10° intervals, as the cat performed tasks which encouraged it to maintain eccentric eye positions. As shown in Fig. 4, the auditory responses of some of these cells are modulated by eye position; moreover, such modulation extends over a wide range of speaker locations in space. The neuron whose responses are illustrated was recorded in the right superior colliculus; eye position modulates its response not only to sounds in contralateral hemispace but even more dramatically in the central ipsilateral field (at 10° to the cat's right). In this cell, the predominant change with eye position is to facilitate the response to sound when the eyes are nearly centered in the orbit, while the cell illustrated in Fig. 3 responds most vigorously when the eyes are eccentric in the orbit. These two patterns imply that a change in eye position can shift the location of responsive neurons within the intermediate and

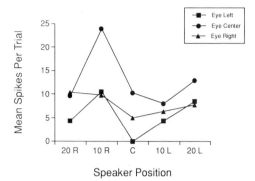

Fig. 4. Effects of eye position on the auditory response of another collicular neuron. Mean responses of a second type of intermediate layer cell to sounds presented from speakers at five different locations (20° to the right, 10° to the right, straight ahead, 10° to the left and 20° to the left) on trials with the gaze directed to the center (filled circles) or 10° to left (filled squares) or 10° to the right (filled triangles).

deep layers of the superior colliculus. The pattern illustrated in Fig. 4 implies that a larger population of neurons may respond to sounds when the eye is optimally positioned in the orbit.

Mobility of the visual map in the superior colliculus

We have previously reported that the visual responses of some collicular neurons are modulated by the position of the eye in the orbit (Peck et al., 1980). Some collicular neurons, like some neurons in other visual-oculomotor structures (e.g., Schlag et al., 1980; Andersen et al., 1990; Bruce, 1990), are modulated by eye position: visual targets produce more vigorous responses when the eyes are optimally positioned in the orbit. In the superior colliculus, the responses of individual neurons are predictable from the map of visual space. That is, cells in the medial colliculus have their receptive fields in the upper visual field, and in some of these cells visual responses are enhanced if the eye is above primary position; similarly, cells in the lateral colliculus have visual receptive fields below primary position, and for some of these cells their responses are enhanced if the eyes are deviated downward. Cells located posteriorly in the colliculus have contralateral visual

receptive fields, and some of them respond more vigorously when the eyes are deviated contralaterally. Cells with receptive fields near the visual axis do not tend to be modulated by eccentric eye position.

Because of the inherent interest of these effects, and because they have not been studied extensively, we have been routinely examining the effects of eye position on the visual responses of our cells. Receptive field location is measured by subtracting the horizontal and vertical coordinates of eye position from the horizontal and vertical coordinates of target position. When a sufficient number of trials is obtained in which visual targets are well located within the excitatory receptive field center of a given cell, we use standard regression techniques to relate the number of spikes produced in response to a given target to the position of the eye in the orbit. Figure 5 illustrates the response of one collicular cell to visual targets presented within the center of its receptive field on trials when the eye was directed in different horizontal directions. Eye position had a significant effect on the visual responses of this cell to targets within its receptive field center.

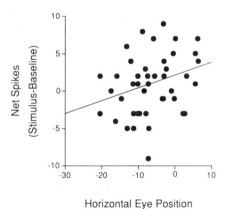

Fig. 5. Effects of eye position on the visual response in one collicular neuron. Stimulus-evoked spikes, corrected for baseline spikes on each trial, for one intermediate layer cell responding to visual targets presented within the center of its receptive field as the initial horizontal component of eye position varies. The solid line represents the best fit linear regression for these data ($y = 0.82 x - 3.89$, $F = 4.38$, $P = 0.05$).

Multisensory integration

In anesthetized, paralyzed animals, multisensory integration obeys strict spatial and temporal rules. Enhanced responses occur only when multisensory stimuli overlap in time within coincident receptive fields of a given cell; if one of the two stimuli is presented at a different spatial location than the other, or at a slightly different time, facilitation declines significantly and often switches sign, producing depression of response (Meredith and Stein, 1986; Meredith et al., 1987). Passive deviation of the eye produces the same effect on visual-auditory integration as does the misalignment of the two targets – response enhancement declines, frequently reversing into response depression (Nelson et al., 1986).

In the alert animal, changes in eye position have significant effects on the visual and auditory responses of collicular neurons. If individual multisensory neurons are mismatched for the effects of eye position, or if passive realignment of receptive fields governs multisensory interactions in the alert animal as it does in the anesthetized, paralyzed animal, then we would expect significant changes in the sign (enhancement or depression) and magnitude of interaction between visual and auditory cues when the initial position of the eye changes. However, active eye movements are accompanied by feedback to both sensory and motor areas of the central nervous system, and thus it is clearly possible that active deviations of the eye in the orbit will have different consequences for sensory integration than do passive deviations.

We have examined the effects of changes in eye position on visual-auditory interactions in the same

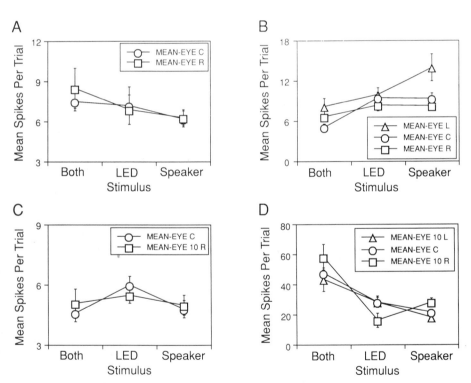

Fig. 6. Visual/auditory interactions as a function of eye position. Panels $A - D$ show the mean responses of four intermediate layer neurons to visual (LED), auditory (speaker) and combined modality (both) targets presented at the same locations when the eyes were positioned straight ahead (circles), or 10° to the left (triangles), or 10° to the right (squares). Two of these neurons (B and D) showed statistically significant visual/auditory interactions when the eye was in primary position and maintained those interactions when the gaze was directed to the left or right. Two other neurons (A and C) did not show statistically significant interactions either when the eye was in primary position or when it was 10° to the right.

animals used in the above studies, although not every cell could be successfully tested in each sensory condition and at each range of eye positions. The four cells, shown in Fig. 6, are typical of our sample in that they tended to maintain their visual-auditory interactions across changes in the position of the eye in the orbit. Cells which showed enhanced responses to combined modality cues when the eye was in primary position also showed enhanced responses when the eye was deviated 10° or more to the left or right (Fig. 6D). In some cells, the magnitude of the interaction changed slightly when the eyes were deviated in the orbit (as compared to their response in primary position) but we have yet to find a cell in which the sign of the interaction changed (e.g., from enhancement to depression); very few showed a change from significant interaction at primary position to a non-significant interaction when the eyes were deviated in the orbit (Fig. 6B). Cells which showed a depressed response to multimodal targets with the eyes at primary position also showed depressed responses to identical targets when the eyes were deviated, although the magnitude of the depression sometimes declined, as in the case of the cell illustrated in Fig. 6B. Finally, eccentric gaze did not produce significant visual-auditory interactions among those cells which did not show significant interactions when the eyes were at primary position (Fig. 6A,C).

Discussion

We have long known that the superior colliculus is involved both in vision and in the control of orienting movements toward visual targets. Our knowledge that there are multisensory inputs to the colliculus is far more recent, and it is certainly not surprising that their functions are not fully understood. In comparing the present work to previous work, it seems likely that multisensory inputs contribute to at least two aspects of behavior that are mediated, in part, through collicular mechanisms: first, the probability that the organism will respond to exteroceptive stimulation and, second, the transformation of sensory information, arriving via one of several modalities, into a code useful for motor systems. We will discuss these two issues in turn.

Multisensory influences on the probability of response

There is clear evidence, in a variety of species and preparations, that collicular neurons respond differently to simultaneously applied stimulation from retinal and non-retinal sources (e.g., infrared stimulation of the pit organ of the snake; somatosensory stimulation of the body surface in mouse, hamster, and cat; auditory stimulation in cat and primate). In addition, some saccade-related neurons in the intermediate and deep layers of the colliculus discharge more vigorously when the signal for movement is a simultaneous visual/auditory target than when a target of either modality is used in isolation (Peck, 1987). However, the superior colliculus contains a wide variety of neurons with a tremendous variety of projections to other areas of the central nervous system, and it would not be appropriate to conclude that enhancing the response of collicular elements with unknown projections would influence the probability of a particular behavioral response (e.g., orienting to a bimodal target). The recent work of Meredith and Stein (1986) and colleagues (Meredith et al., 1987) has contributed greatly in clarifying the issue of which collicular neurons show multimodal enhancement. By using antidromic activation to identify collicular neurons with descending projections to brain-stem circuits involved in motor control, they have been able to determine that cells in this population are more likely to exhibit multimodal enhancement than are other collicular neurons. These studies have helped to "close the gap" between neural response patterns and the mediation of particular behaviors. In addition, Stein et al. (1987) have shown that the probability of behavioral orienting responses is influenced by stimulus variables similar to those which influence the responses of individual collicular neurons. For example, behavioral performance is enhanced when an auditory stimulus is presented at the same location as a visual target, just as the response of most collicular neurons with descending projections is enhanced by the same manipulation. Similarly, both performance and neural response were depressed when a visual target is presented at a different location from that of an auditory target.

Nearly all previous work on multimodal interactions at the neuronal level has used animals in which the receptor/effector organs (e.g., eyes and pinnae) are aligned throughout the experiment because the animals are anesthetized and paralyzed. By recording from neurons in the alert animal, we have been able to examine an issue which can only be addressed in a behaving organism − the extent to which multimodal enhancement of neuronal response is dependent on voluntary alignment of receptor organs for the different modalities. The data presented in Fig. 6 indicate that voluntary changes in the direction of fixation do not significantly affect the visual/auditory interactions shown by individual collicular neurons. Taken together with the data presented in Figs. 3 − 5 and previous reports, the data in Fig. 6 imply that, while individual collicular neurons vary in the degree to which they are influenced by the position of the eye in the orbit, their responses to visual and auditory targets are affected similarly by eye position. This may be the way that the population as a whole is able to maintain registry between visual and auditory maps.

These studies leave many intriguing questions unanswered. We do not know whether the neurons modulated by eye position are intrinsic neurons or output neurons. Nor, if they are hypothesized to be output neurons, do we know their targets. We have not yet examined whether voluntary changes in eye position affect the probability of an orienting response to visual/auditory targets, nor do we know the effects of different stimulus conditions on the probability of generating the saccadic oculomotor component of the orienting response, although it would be interesting to address these questions.

Transformation of sensory information into a code appropriate for movements

Because the initial codes for the location of visual and auditory targets are in different coordinate systems (retinotopic and head-centered, respectively), independent movements of the eyes and external ears should create disparities between the locations of bimodal targets with respect to their receptive fields, both in the superior colliculus and at other locations in the central nervous system (cf. Bruce, 1990). If the population of sound-responsive cells within the superior colliculus maintains a head-centered map of auditory space, organisms should make substantial errors if they orient to the perceived location of auditory targets whenever the eyes are not centered in the orbit. However, the data shown in Fig. 2 indicate that there is little overall effect of eye position on the accuracy of saccadic eye movements to auditory targets. Moreover, eye position has no more effect on the accuracy of saccadic eye movements to auditory targets than to visual or bimodal targets. Cats show substantial compensation for targets of both modalities, whether presented singly or together at the same location. These data imply that the nervous system has recoded head-centered information about auditory space into a retinocentric code for the amplitude of saccadic eye movements.

In examining a possible neural substrate for such compensation among sound-responsive neurons of the superior colliculus, we assessed the effects of eye position on the sound-evoked discharge of these cells. As illustrated in Figs. 3 and 4, many collicular neurons did not respond with equal vigor to sounds from a given speaker location when their eyes were positioned in different directions, as would be expected if they responded only to the head-centered location of the speaker. Some of these cells, such as the one illustrated in Fig. 3, responded optimally to speakers at different locations when the eyes had a particular deviation from the speaker. Such cells may encode the amplitude and direction of the movement necessary to orient to the sound, as previously suggested for similar findings in primate superior colliculus (Jay and Sparks, 1987). This mechanism can be envisioned as a shift in the location of the population of responsive cells within the colliculus when the gaze is shifted to different locations in head-centered space (Fig. 7, top and middle). In

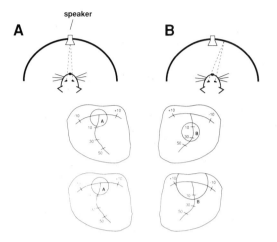

Fig. 7. The shift in the active population of auditory neurons in the superior colliculus with changes in the eye position. *A.* Cat fixating straight ahead with the speaker also straight ahead. A population of auditory cells is activated in both colliculi; the location of the population in the left colliculus is shown. *B.* When gaze is shifted to the right, a population of auditory cells such as the one shown in Fig. 3 is active in the right colliculus (middle row). Under the same conditions, a larger population of cells such as the one shown in Fig. 4 is active in the right colliculus (bottom row).

al., 1980) have shown that the visual responses of individual neurons can be modulated by eye position. The visual responses of cells in several cortical areas of primates have also been shown to be modulated by eye position (see Andersen et al., 1990; Bruce, 1990, for references). The nature of this modulation has been most extensively documented in the posterior parietal cortex of macaques (e.g., Andersen et al., 1990). Taken together, these results suggest that the modulation of visual signals by eye position is fairly common in the central nervous system of both cat and primate. The pioneering studies of Wiersma (1966) suggest that such modulation occurs in other phyla as well.

There are a number of plausible reasons for believing that the brain represents visual space in head and body coordinates. Several models of the saccadic oculomotor system specifically postulate that visual targets are recoded from retinocentric to head-centered coordinates, and thus one might well expect to find cells in some areas of the brain related to oculomotor control which respond to visual targets at certain spatial locations regardless of the position of the eyes in the orbit. Such cells have not been found, leading to wide-spread speculation that they may not exist. Zipser and Andersen (1989) have ''trained'' a neural network to locate positions in head-centered space given inputs similar to those shown by single cells in area 7 of macaque cortex; the hidden units of their model produced responses similar to those of their experimental data. Our characterization of the nature of the modulation of visual response by eye position in the cat superior colliculus is not yet as extensive as the results of Andersen et al. (1990), but the results of Fig. 5 indicate that collicular neurons of the cat may share certain characteristics with parietal neurons of the macaque – in particular, the present data are the first illustration of a significant linear component in the modulation of collicular visual responses by eye position. Differences in behavioral repertoire and oculomotor range in cat, macaque and primate have, perhaps, discouraged more detailed comparisons, but we are presently testing all of our cells on tasks which should reveal the effects of eye posi-

other cells, such as the one illustrated in Fig. 4, the magnitude of the response to sounds from a range of locations was modulated by eye position, but the optimal direction of sounds did not shift with eye position. Still other cells (not illustrated) showed both directional shifts and modulation of response amplitude with shifts in eye position. Modulation of response amplitude can be envisioned to involve recruitment of a larger population of sound-responsive neurons when the gaze is shifted to different locations in head-centered space (Fig. 7, top and bottom). Both types of response imply that auditory information is gated by the position of the eyes in the orbit, and both models propose that the representation of spatial location is distributed across a population of collicular neurons.

Not only are the spatial responses of some auditory neurons modulated by eye position but so are the responses of some visual neurons. Previous studies in cat superior colliculus (Peck et al., 1980) and intralaminar nuclei of the thalamus (Schlag et

tion. We are also planning detailed assessment of the effects of eye position on saccade-related responses in the colliculus.

The results presented in this paper, together with previous work, suggest that the superior colliculus does not encode the location of visual targets in purely retinotopic coordinates nor does it encode the location of auditory targets in purely head-centered coordinates. Moreover, because the "sensory" responses of some neurons are modulated by eye position, while the responses of other neurons are not, at the level of individual neurons, visual and auditory codes might easily be mismatched. If this were the case, changes in eye position might alter visual/auditory interactions. The results presented in Fig. 6 are representative of the sample analyzed to date in showing that the sign of visual/auditory interactions does not change with shifts in the location of fixation by the alert cat; moreover, the magnitude of these interactions is remarkably consistent with shifts in the direction of fixation within head-centered space. Thus, it appears that, while individual neurons differ in the extent of their susceptibility to changes in eye position, the visual and auditory responses of individual bimodal neurons are affected to a comparable extent. We do not know whether this similarity reflects sensory experience or non-sensory developmental events. In the barn owl, Knudsen and colleagues have shown that normal development of auditory receptive fields depends on visual experience (e.g., Knudsen and Knudsen, 1989). It is intriguing to speculate that visual experience could train individual bimodal neurons in the cat to be modulated by the position of the eyes in response to both visual and non-visual targets. The extent to which such responses contribute to a coherent perception of spatial order, independent of modality, remains one of the most intriguing questions in sensory neuroscience.

Summary and concluding remarks

The intermediate and deep layers of the superior colliculus appear to be critical parts of the neural circuits involved in the location of visual targets in ex-trapersonal space. Many neurons in these layers respond not only to visual input but also to input from other sensory systems – in particular, to auditory and somatosensory inputs – and also discharge prior to saccadic eye movements.

We have been studying neuronal responses to auditory and visual targets, presented either together or separately, in alert, trained cats. When the eyes are centered in the orbit, simultaneous visual and auditory stimulation at the same location in space produces substantial facilitation in the majority of intermediate and deep layer neurons. When the eyes are deviated in the orbit, the borders of some, but not all, auditory receptive fields shift in the direction of the deviating eye movement. Among neurons responsive to both visual and auditory input, visual receptive fields shift more substantially than do auditory receptive fields. Nonetheless, deviation of the eyes does not affect the animal's ability to locate either visual or auditory targets, and bimodal neurons continue to show stronger responses to combined modality targets than to single modality targets when the eyes are deviated. Minimally, these results imply that sensory maps are actively transformed by the movements of organisms. The results to date are also consistent with the hypothesis that the intermediate and deep layer of the superior colliculus contain a map of motor error.

References

Andersen, R.A., Bracewell, R.M., Barash, S., Gnadt, J.W. and Fogassi, L. (1990) Eye position effects of visual, memory, and saccade-related activity in areas LIP and 7a of the macaque. *J. Neurosci.*, 10: 1176–1196.

Bruce, C.J. (1990) Integration of sensory and motor signals in primate frontal eye fields. In: G.M. Edelman, W.E. Gall and W.M. Cowan (Eds.), *Signal and Sense: Local and Global Order in Perceptual Maps*, Wiley-Liss, New York, pp. 261–314.

Harris, L.R., Blakemore, C. and Donaghy, M. (1980) Integration of visual and auditory space in the mammalian superior colliculus. *Nature*, 288: 56–59.

Hartline, P.H., Kass, L. and Loop, M.S. (1978) Merging of modalities in the optic tectum: infrared and visual integration in rattlesnakes. *Science*, 199: 1225–1229.

Hartline, P.H., King, A.J., Kurylo, D.D., Northmore, D.P.M. and Vimal, R.L.P. (1989) Effects of eye position of auditory localization and auditory spatial representation in cat superior colliculus. *Invest. Ophthalmol. Vis. Sci., Abstr.,* 30: 181.

Jay, M.J. and Sparks, D.L. (1987) Sensorimotor integration in the primate superior colliculus. II. Coordinates of auditory signals. *J. Neurophysiol.,* 57: 35 – 55.

Knudsen, E.I. and Knudsen, P.F. (1989) Vision calibrates sound localization in developing barn owls. *J. Neurosci.,* 9: 3306 – 3313.

Meredith, M.A. and Stein, B.E. (1986) Visual, auditory, and somatosensory convergence on cells in superior colliculus results in multisensory integration. *J. Neurophysiol.,* 56: 640 – 662.

Meredith, M.A., Nemitz, J.W. and Stein, B.E. (1987) Determinants of multisensory integration in superior colliculus neurons. I. Temporal factors. *J. Neurosci.,* 7: 3215 – 3229.

Nelson, J.S., Meredith, M.A. and Stein, B.E. (1986) Influence of passive eye rotation on cat superior colliculus neurons. *Soc. Neurosci. Abstr.,* 12: 1538.

Peck, C.K. (1987) Visual-auditory interactions in cat superior colliculus: their role in the control of gaze. *Brain Res.,* 420: 162 – 166.

Peck, C.K. (1989) Visual responses of neurones in cat superior colliculus in relation to fixation of targets. *J. Physiol. (Lond.),* 414: 301 – 315.

Peck, C.K. (1990) Neuronal activity related to head and eye movements in cat superior colliculus. *J. Physiol. (Lond.),* 421: 79 – 104.

Peck, C.K. and Wartman III, F.S. (1989) Effects of eye position on auditory responses in cat superior colliculus. *Invest. Ophthalmol. Vis. Sci., Abstr.,* 30: 181.

Peck, C.K., Schlag-Rey, M. and Schlag, J. (1980) Visuo-oculomotor properties of cells in the superior colliculus of the alert cat. *J. Comp. Neurol.,* 194: 97 – 116.

Robinson, D.A. (1963) A method of measuring eye movement using a scleral search coil in a magnetic field. *IEEE Trans. Biomed. Eng.,* 10: 137 – 145.

Robinson, D.A. (1975) Oculomotor control signals. In: G. Lennerstrand and P. Bach-y-Rita (Eds.), *Basic Mechanisms of Ocular Motility and their Clinical Implications,* Pergamon, Oxford, pp. 337 – 374.

Schlag, J., Schlag-Rey, M., Peck, C.K. and Joseph, J.-P. (1980) Visual responses of thalamic neurons depending on the direction of gaze and the position of targets in space. *Exp. Brain Res.,* 40: 170 – 184.

Scudder, C.A. (1988) A new local feedback model of the saccadic burst generator. *J. Neurophysiol.,* 59: 1455 – 1475.

Stein, B.E., Meredith, M.A., Huneycutt, W.S. and McDade, L. (1987) Behavioral indices of multisensory integration: orientation to visual cues is affected by auditory stimuli. *J. Cognitive Neurosci.,* 1: 12 – 24.

Wiersma, C.A.G. (1966) Integration in the visual pathway of crustacea. In C.A.G. Wiersma (Ed.), *Nervous and Hormonal Mechanisms of Integration,* University of Chicago Press, Chicago, IL, pp. 151 – 177.

Zipser, D. and Andersen, R.A. (1989) A back-propagation programmed network that simulates response properties of a subset of posterior parietal neurons. *Nature,* 331: 679 – 684.

T.P. Hicks, S. Molotchnikoff and T. Ono (Eds.)
Progress in Brain Research, Vol. 95

CHAPTER 10

Early and late flash-induced field responses correspond to ON and OFF receptive field components in hamster superior colliculus

Hitoshi Sasaki, Yutaka Fukuda[1] and Yasumasa Hayashi

*Department of Physiology, Hyogo College of Medicine, Hyogo, and [1] Department of Physiology, Osaka University Medical
School, Suita, Osaka, Japan*

Introduction

While recording single unit activities of the hamster superior colliculus (SC) that was reinnervated by regenerated retinal axons through the sciatic nerve transplant (Vidal-Sanz et al., 1987; Keirstead et al., 1989) and testing their visual responses to diffuse flash stimuli, we found some correlation between latencies to diffuse flash and receptive field types (Fukuda et al., 1989). With recordings from presynaptic axons, the receptive field center was defined as either ON or OFF and we found that those with short latencies to flash stimuli were of the ON center type while those with long flash latencies were of the OFF center type. Similarly, postsynaptic cells were also segregated into those with early and late flash latencies, though receptive field properties could not be defined in most cases. Given these findings we tested in a preceding paper whether such correlation between receptive field types and flash latencies holds among SC cells in normal hamsters (Sasaki et al., 1991). As expected we observed that ON center cells showed short and OFF center cells long latencies to brief flash stimuli. Further, in the course of these experiments we realized that local field potentials from the SC elicited by a brief flash light also displayed early and long latency components, probably corresponding to short and long latency unit responses. Thus, in the present ex-

periments we searched the correlation of light-evoked field responses to single unit responses through flash stimuli in normal hamsters. Further we examined how field and single unit activities change after inactivation of the ON pathway by intravitreal injection of 2-animo-4-phosphonobutylic acid (APB) as has been done in rabbit and monkey (Massey et al., 1983; Knapp and Schiller, 1984).

General methods

Fourty seven adult golden hamsters, ranging in age from 7 to 12 weeks (body weight 90 – 110 g), were anesthetized with urethane (1.5 g/kg, i.p.). A small dose of urethane was applied further as needed. Cisternectomy was performed at the obex to reduce respiratory pulsation of the SC surface. The trachea was cannulated and the animals were immobilized with Flaxedil (35 mg/kg per hour) and were artificially ventilated. Body temperature was maintained at around 37°C with a heating pad, and the electrocardiogram was continuously monitored.

The left surface of the SC was exposed by carefully aspirating the overlying cortex. For the recording of field responses from the SC silver ball electrodes were located stereotaxically at the central part of the SC. Field responses were amplified through a filter of 0.5 – 3 kHz and averaged 20 – 50 times. Glass microelectrodes filled with 2 M NaCl (6 – 20 MΩ measured at 50 Hz) were also used for recording single unit and mass activities from the SC. Single or multi-unit activities were amplified through a filter of more than 50 Hz. Microelectrodes were stereotaxically advanced in an anterolateral to posteromedial direction so that a penetration track would be approximately perpendicular to the surface of SC. Mineral oil and agar (4% in saline) were used to prevent the SC surface from drying and to reduce its pulsation. Recording depth of the microelectrodes was estimated by reading scales of the manipulator and single unit sampling was made within the depth of 500 μm below the SC surface (Fukuda et al., 1978). In some animals recording depth was also estimated by recording characteristic field potentials evoked by electrical stimulation of the optic chiasm (Fukuda et al., 1978).

The right pupil was dilated with drops of a mixture of 0.5% tropicamide and 0.5% phenylephrine-hydrochloride (Santen Pharmaceutical, Midrin-P) and the cornea was protected from drying by a contact lens of zero power. The receptive field property of single SC cells was determined by means of a small spot of light (0.5 – 1 deg. in diameter) and small dark objects presented on a light background. Diffuse flashes were presented directly to the eye by a Xenon stroboscope (San-ei Instrument PS-101) placed at 30 – 40 cm in front of the right eye. Response latencies of units were measured on peristimulus time histograms (PSTHs) which were made by adding spike responses 20 – 100 times into a bin width of 1 or 2 msec. For localized stimulation the light spot was turned on for 50 – 500 msec on a tangent screen at 30 cm from the eye. An electric shutter was used and the light was shone on a screen by using a mirror. The intensity of light was 200 cd/cm² against the background of 3cd/cm². These light stimuli were presented usually once every 4 sec (2.4 – 10 sec).

For intravitreal injection of APB, upper rectus and oblique muscles were threaded and the sclera was punctured by a needle and a microsyringe was inserted into the eye. The DL-APB (0.5 – 5 μl, usually 2 μl) at a concentration of 250 – 500 μM (in most cases 375 μM) was injected for 1 – 2 min. The effect

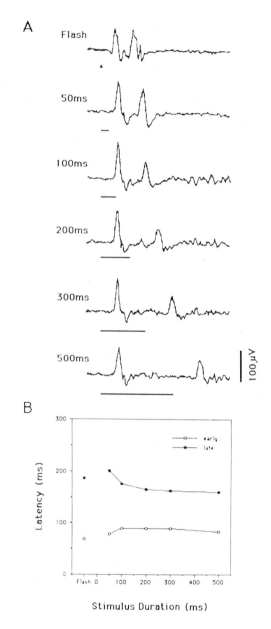

Fig. 1. *A*. Early and late components of the SC field responses to a diffuse flash (top trace) and ON and OFF responses to stationary light stimuli with various duration. As the duration of light spot becomes longer, the latency of OFF responses, measured at cessation of light, becomes shorter. *B*. Latencies of ON and OFF responses plotted as a function of duration of light. Note that latencies of OFF responses become shorter while the ON component does not change. Latencies of the early and late components induced by flash stimuli are also plotted at the extreme left.

was observed within 5 min after application of APB and it lasted up to 30 – 60 min afterwards. To monitor the effects of intravitreal injection of APB ERG was recorded with a pair of silver ball electrodes, one placed at the cornea and the other at the back of the eye ball. Recordings were made by using a filter of 0.5 – 3 kHz. ERG responses were averaged 10 – 20 times using ATAC 250 (Nihon Koden).

Early and late components of the flash-induced field response

While recording from the surface of the SC with silver ball or glass microelectrodes in response to a diffuse flash of light, two negative field responses of 100 – 500 μV were obtained as shown in the top trace of Fig. 1A. Similar negative waves were obtained by illuminating a screen with large spots of light covering responsive areas of SC cells at the recording sites. In 15 recordings the latency of the early component ranged from 39.2 to 147.1 msec with a mean of 96.3 ± 32.0 msec, whereas the latency of the late component ranged from 181.4 to 738.5 msec with a mean of 272.2 ± 137.0 msec. As shown in Fig. 1A, as the duration of a light spot was gradually elongated, the latency of the late component consistently shifted while the early one did not change.

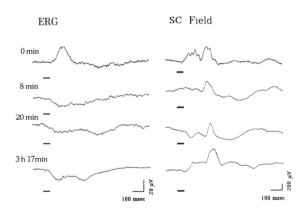

Fig. 2. Effects of APB on ERG and SC field responses to diffuse flash stimuli. After intravitreal injection of APB, the positive ERG component (b-wave) was blocked, accompanied by the disappearance of the early component of the SC field responses. For further explanations see text.

Latencies of the two components are plotted as a function of duration of light spot in Fig. 1B. Also plotted at the extreme left of the figure are latencies of the two components induced by a diffuse flash of light. We note that latencies of early and late components do not change much, though at a short duration of light the latency of OFF responses becomes longer. Although the latency of the two components varied from one experiment to the other, the border between the two components was always around 150 msec. This corresponds well with the results of the previous experiment that latencies of ON center and OFF center cells are segregated at around 150 msec. These observations suggest that early and late local field responses induced by a short duration of light as well as by brief flashing light, represent respectively summated activities of ON center and OFF center cells in the SC.

Effects of intravitreal injection of APB on early and late components of SC field responses

To provide further evidence for the suggestion that early and late field potentials represent summated activities of ON and OFF cells, respectively, we examined how the two components behave when the retinal ON pathway was blocked by intravitreal injection of APB in 11 animals. In six of these experiments ERG was also monitored to check the effects of APB in the retina. Sample responses of SC field responses induced by 50 msec light, together with ERGs, are shown in Fig. 2. Before intravitreal applications of APB the SC field response consists of oscillatory early and larger late components. Eight minutes after the APB application the positive component of the ERG, the b-wave, was replaced by a negative slow wave (Knapp and Schiller, 1984; Frishmann and Steinberg, 1989). At the same time the early component of the SC field response was completely blocked while the late component was virtually unchanged. Slight recovery of the positive ERG component, which was apparent 20 min after APB application, was accompanied by the recovery of early SC field responses. At 197 min after APB treatment recovery of the b-wave in the ERG was

106

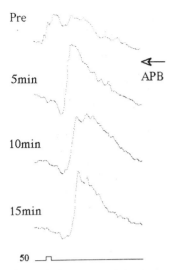

Pre

5min

10min

15min

APB

50

Fig. 3. Enlargement of the late component of the SC field response after intravitreal APB application to the contralateral eye.

not complete, and neither was the early component of the SC field potential. Similar observations were made from another animal as shown in Fig. 3. In this case the late component was rather increased in amplitude while the early component of the SC field potential was completely blocked by intravitreal injection of APB. In all ten experiments the early component was completely blocked after APB application and in one case the amplitude was reduced to about half of the control. The amplitude of the late field component was unchanged in five cases, enlarged in four cases and reduced in two cases.

Flash latencies of single SC cells

With 84 cells single unit activities were recorded from the superficial layers of the SC and their visual responses were examined. According to responses to stationary or moving small light spots or dark disks (Fukuda and Iwama, 1978), these cells were classified as either ON center (7.1%), OFF center (40.5%), ON-OFF center (41.7%), or movement-sensitive cells (10.7%). The surround components of ON, OFF and ON-OFF center cells were further examined and these cells were subclassified as

"without surround", "with antagonistic surround", "with suppressive surround", or "not identified". Fig. 4 shows sample responses of an OFF-center/ON surround cell to a centered stationary light spot as well as responses to diffuse flash. When the spot covered only the receptive field center, spike responses occurred only at the cessation of light, namely at light off (OFF responses), but when the surround component was also stimulated, ON responses appeared as well. Responding to diffuse flash light this cell showed both early and late spike discharges with latencies of 140 and 260 msec. In the case of ON-center/OFF surround cells (not illustrated) similar early and late spike responses were obtained by flash stimuli, though in this case the short latency response was much larger than the late one. ON-OFF center cells, as expected, showed brisk spike discharges at both onset and offset of the light spot and two similar sets of spike responses were obtained to diffuse flash light.

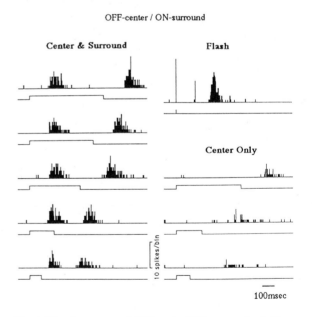

Fig. 4. Visual responses of OFF center/ON surround cell. Upon a stationary light spot covering both receptive field center and surround both ON and OFF spikes appear. With short duration of light, latencies of OFF spikes, measured from cessation of light, become longer in contrast with ON spikes with fixed latencies.

When the duration of light spot was gradually shortened as shown in Fig. 4 (left), the latency of the ON response did not change but the latency of the OFF response, measured from the cessation of light, became longer. This is exactly the same as we observed for early and late field responses (see Fig. 1). In Fig. 5 latencies of ON and OFF spike responses are plotted as a function of the duration of light spot for four representative cells of various receptive field types. In every case, latencies to diffuse flash are also plotted at the extreme left (F). Fig. 5C shows latencies of ON and OFF responses of the cell shown in Fig. 4; the latency of OFF responses changed from 160 to 270 msec upon the change of light duration from 600 to 100 msec. Similar elongation of OFF response latency towards shorter duration of light was observed in each of the other three cases. Response latencies to the diffuse flash (see plots at F on abscissae) were similar to those to a brief stationary spot. However, as shown in Fig. 5B, OFF latencies of an ON-OFF center cell to diffuse flash stimuli were exceptionally shorter than those to brief stationary light. In any case each cell revealed either early and/or late spike responses of a relatively fixed latency to diffuse flash. Regardless of the receptive field type, the latencies of the early responses to a stationary light spot ranged from 44 to 149 msec.

Fig. 6 summarizes the response latencies to diffuse flash in various types of receptive field. In 40 cells examined the early spike response to the diffuse flash was observed in cells with the receptive field of ON center with and without surround, ON-OFF center and OFF center with ON surround (Fig. 6A,C,E and G). OFF center cells having no antagonistic surround lacked this short latency response with the exception of one cell (Fig. 6B). On the contrary, the late response with latencies of

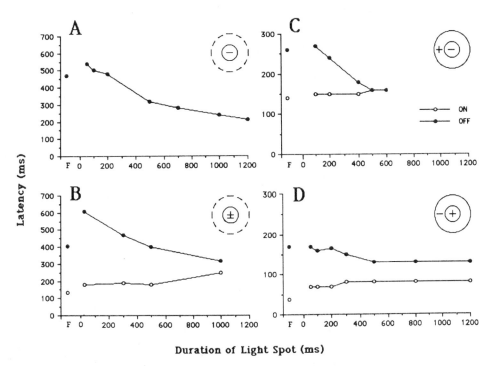

Fig. 5. Latencies of ON and OFF spike responses in four types of receptive field as a function of duration of stationary light spots. *A.* OFF center cell without surround. *B.* ON-OFF center cell without surround. *C.* OFF center ON surround cell. *D.* ON center OFF surround cell. For each cell latencies of early and late spike discharges to diffuse flash stimuli are also shown at the extreme left on F in abscissae. Longest duration of light spot varied from cell to cell, 600–1200 msec. See text for further explanations.

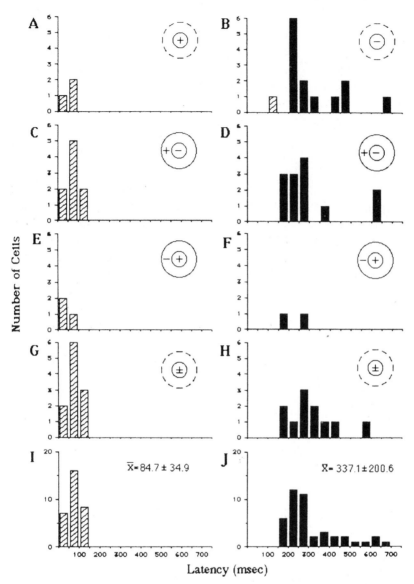

Fig. 6. Latency distributions of early and late spike responses to a diffuse flash of light. *A*. ON center cells without surround. *B*. OFF center cells without surround. *C* and *D*. OFF center ON surround cells. *E* and *F*. ON center OFF surround cells. *G* and *H*. ON-OFF center cells without surround or with suppressive surround. *I* and *J*. Summary distributions of latencies of early and late spike responses, respectively.

170 – 700 msec to the diffuse flash appeared only in receptive field types of OFF center, ON-OFF center and ON center with OFF surround, and was never observed in ON center cells having no antagonistic surround. Thus, the early and the late spike responses to diffuse flash are closely correlated to

the receptive field properties. In cells with no surround or with suppressive surround, ON center cells showed early and OFF center cells showed only late spike discharges. In the cells which have two receptive field components (ON and OFF), such as ON-OFF center cells without surround and ON or OFF center cells with antagonistic surround, both short and long latency responses are evoked by the diffuse flash. As summarized in Figs. 6*I* and *J*, latencies of short and long latency spike responses are distributed differently with respective mean latencies of $84.7 \pm 34.9 (n = 39)$ and 337 ± 200.6 msec ($n = 45$).

Effects of intravitreal application of APB on single SC cells

In some animals single or multi-unit activities were recorded from the SC and their visual responses to diffuse flash were studied before and after intravitreal application of APB. Fig. 7*A* represents three response time histograms of multi-unit activities after single flash stimuli obtained before, 1 and 6 min after APB treatment of the retina contralateral to the recorded SC. With multi-unit activities the receptive field boundary consisting of ON and OFF responses was defined on a screen and diffuse flash was applied to cover that area. Before APB application early and late spike activities appeared at latencies of 100 and 190 msec. The ERG shown at the top of Fig. 7*B* appeared normal with a dominant b-wave component preceded by a small negative wave. Within 1 min after intravitreal APB treatment early spike responses disappeared while both spontaneous and late flash responses remained unchanged or rather were enhanced slightly. In the ERG recorded at the same time the amplitude of the b-wave was largely diminished and the slow negative component became dominant. At 6 min after the APB treatment of the retina not only the early spike responses but also spontaneous activities were almost completely blocked sparing only the late spike responses which probably represent activities of OFF cells. Concomitantly the amplitude of the b-wave of the ERG was further diminished and the negative slow wave further increased in amplitude. These observations with multi-unit activities were consistent with the behavior of early and late field responses after intravitreal APB application as shown in Figs. 2 and 3.

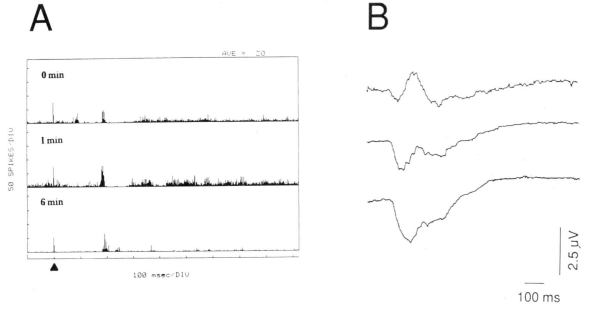

Fig. 7. Effects of intravitreal APB application on visual responses of multi-unit activities recorded from the SC and concomitantly recorded ERGs. After the APB application only early spike responses disappear, accompanied by the decrease of b-waves in the ERG. Arrow head shows artifacts of light flash.

General discussion and conclusion

From the present studies we conclude that early and late negative waves, which were induced by diffuse flash in the hamster SC, correspond respectively to summated unit activities of ON and OFF components. Observations to support this conclusion were three-fold. First, after stationary light stimuli of certain duration two negative waves that are similar to those induced by diffuse flash, appear in the SC at light ON and OFF. Second, the early negative wave disappears after blockade of the ON pathway by intravitreal APB application while the late one remains unchanged. Third, response latencies of the late negative wave of the SC field response become longer at shorter duration of light, as those of OFF discharges of OFF center cells and ON-OFF center cells.

The finding that the OFF latencies are significantly longer than ON latencies at brief light could be explained by the different time course of ON and OFF bipolar cells to brief light. ON bipolar cells in the retina depolarize to light, while OFF bipolar cells hyperpolarize to the same stimulus. ON and OFF retinal ganglion cells depolarize and hyperpolarize, respectively, with similar time courses to the bipolar cells. ON ganglion cells discharge immediately after light presentation, while OFF ganglion cells fire as the rebound of hyperpolarization. Thus, the latency of ON responses always precedes that of OFF responses to brief flash light. On the other hand, when a longer duration of light was used, it may be expected that the time course of OFF responses becomes shorter because of light adaption which will enhance and quicken OFF depolarization of receptors and as a result OFF depolarization of hyperpolarizing bipolar cells (Frumkes and Wu, 1990). In both recordings of field and unit responses the late component, i.e., the OFF component not only remained unchanged but rather increased in response amplitude after APB application. This may suggest the suppressive influence from the ON pathway onto the OFF pathway within the retina. In the cat retina such pathway has been evidenced from depolarizing rod bipolar cells to hyperpolarizing bipolar cells through inhibitory interneurons such as AII amacrine cells (Bolz et al., 1984).

References

Bolz, J., Wässle, H. and Thier, P. (1984) Pharmacological modulation of ON and OFF ganglion cells in the cat retina. *Neuroscience,* 12: 875–885.

Carter, D.A., Bray, G. and Aguayo, A.J. (1989) Regenerated retinal ganglion cell axons can form well-differentiated synapses in the superior colliculus of adult hamsters. *J. Neurosci.,* 9: 4042–4050.

Frishman, L.J. and Steinberg R.H. (1989) Intraretinal analysis of the threshold dark adapted ERG of cat retina. *J. Neurophysiol.,* 61: 1221–1232.

Frumkes, T.E. and Wu, S.M. (1990) Independent influences of rod adaptation on cone-mediated responses to light onset and offset in distal retinal neurons. *J. Neurophysiol.,* 64: 1043–1054.

Fukuda, Y. and Iwama, K. (1978) Visual receptive-field properties of single cells in the rat superior colliculus. *Jpn. J. Physiol.,* 28: 385–400.

Fukuda, Y., Suzuki, D.A. and Iwama, K. (1978) Characteristics of optic nerve innervation in the rat superior colliculus as revealed by field potential analysis. *Jpn. J. Physiol.,* 28: 347–365.

Fukuda, Y., Rasminsky, M., Keirstead, S.A., Carter, D.A., Aguayo, A.J. and Vidal-Sanz, M. (1989) Reinnervation of adult hamster superior colliculus by regenerating retinal axons. *Biomed. Res.,* 10 (Suppl. 2): 81–84.

Keirstead, S.A., Rasminsky, M., Fukuda, Y., Carter, D.A., Aguayo, A.J. and Vidal-Sanz, M. (1989) Electrophysiologic responses in hamster superior colliculus evoked by regenerating retinal axons. *Science,* 246: 255–257.

Knapp, A.G. and Schiller, P.H. (1984) The contribution of ON-bipolar cells to the electroretinogram of rabbits and monkeys. A study using 2-amino-4-phosphonobutylic acid. *Vision Res.,* 24: 1841–1846.

Massey, S.C., Redburn, D.A. and Crawford, M.L.J. (1983) The effects of 2-amino-4-phosphonobutylic acid (APB) on the ERG and ganglion cell discharge of rabbit retina. *Vision Res.,* 23: 1607–1613.

Sasaki, H., Fukuda, Y. and Hayashi, Y. (1991) ON and OFF components of the receptive fields have different latencies to diffuse flashes of light in the superior colliculus of golden hamsters. *Brain Res.,* 540: 345–348.

Vidal-Sanz, M., Bray, G.M., Villegas-Perez, M.P., Thanos, S. and Aguayo, A.J. (1978) Axonal regeneration and synapse formation in the superior colliculus by retinal ganglion cells in the adult rat. *J. Neurosci.,* 7: 2894–2909.

SECTION III

Functional and Anatomical Organization of Visual Projections

T.P. Hicks, S. Molotchnikoff and T. Ono (Eds.)
Progress in Brain Research, Vol. 95
© 1993 Elsevier Science Publishers B.V. All rights reserved.

CHAPTER 11

Functional organization of the projections from the rabbit's superior colliculus to the lateral posterior nucleus

Christian Casanova[1] and Stéphane Molotchnikoff[2]

[1] *Départements d'Ophtalmologie et de Physiologie et Biophysique, Faculté de Médecine, Université de Sherbrooke, Sherbrooke, Québec, et* [2] *Département de Sciences Biologiques, Université de Montréal, Montréal, Canada*

Introduction

If one opens a textbook on vision he will find little substantial information on the lateral posterior-pulvinar (LP-P) complex. Detailed descriptions will be given on the anatomy and physiology of the visual pathways from the retina to the lateral geniculate nucleus (LGN) and to the various areas of the visual cortex and also from the retina to the superior colliculus (SC). What appeared to be, for many years, a lack of interest on the part of visual physiologists for the LP-P complex, was mainly the result of a scarcity of details on the physiology of LP-P cells. On large part this was due to a very real difficulty in recording from cells in this part of the thalamus. Nevertheless, since the last decade or so, and thanks to continuous studies from some laboratories, our knowledge of the functional organization of this vast thalamic region has progressed considerably. The major anatomical and neurophysiological findings related to the LP-P complex are extensively reviewed in recent papers (e.g., Jones, 1985; Casanova et al., 1991b).

In all mammals, the LP-P complex does not receive any substantial direct projections from the retina (Berman and Jones, 1977; Mizuno et al., 1982; Uchida et al., 1982; Itaya and Van Hoesen, 1983; Nagakawa and Tanaka, 1984) and the few retinofugal fibers can hardly account for the overall visual responsiveness of the LP-P complex. Its main inputs come from the mesencephalon (primarily the superior colliculus) and the neocortex (almost all visual cortical areas are reciprocally connected with the LP-P complex). In rabbits, as it is for most mammals, tecto-LP cells are located in the lower half of the stratum griseum superficiale (SGSl) of the superficial layers of the colliculus (Graham and Berman, 1981). The tecto-LP units are large, multipolar cells (Graham and Berman, 1981) and their fibers terminate mainly in the upper or dorsal half of LP (Stewart et al., 1973; Holstege and Collewijn, 1982). Projections from the deep collicular layers to LP have also been demonstrated in rabbits (Holstege and Collewijn, 1982).

On the basis of its afferent and efferent connectivity, it has been proposed that LP could convey mesencephalic signals to the extrastriate cortex. Intuitively, this hypothesis necessitates that cells in the colliculus and LP must have rather similar properties and that the visual responsiveness of cells in the tecto-recipient zone of LP must depend almost entirely on signals from the superior colliculus. This chapter describes our attempt to test this hypothesis, i.e., that LP serves as a relay nucleus along an extrageniculate ascendant pathway which originates from the superior colliculus and terminates in the visual cortex.

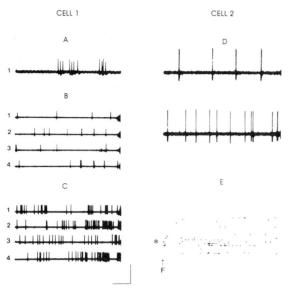

CELL 1   CELL 2

Fig. 1. Example of two LP cells whose spontaneous activity is bursty. Three superimposed traces are shown in part *A*. Note that each burst contains 3 – 4 spikes. The bursting pattern is also illustrated in part *B*; during this period the cell does not respond to visual stimulation. This pattern is changed by the brief presentation of an auditory stimulus (part *C*); the cell is then more likely to respond to light. The activity of the second LP cell is shown in parts *D* and *E*. Traces 1 and 2 represent the bursty pattern and the pattern of discharge resulting from an extravisual stimulation, respectively. When the latter stimulus is given (asterisk, part *E*), the cell becomes more responsive to a diffuse flashing light, but only for a brief period.

Properties of cells in the rabbit's LP: comparison with the superior colliculus

As a microelectrode reaches the LP and records single-spike activity, the first striking observation is that a large number (around 30%) of cells in LP have spontaneous bursting activity (Fig. 1). This discharge pattern has been reported in all mammals studied and has been related to the degree of anesthesia or the anesthetic agent itself (e.g., Godfraind et al., 1972; Mason, 1978; Gattas et al., 1979; Bender, 1982; Benedek et al., 1983; Mooney et al., 1984; Chalupa and Abramson, 1988). Inputs from the mesencephalic reticular formation could mediate the appearance and persistence of this discharge pattern (Stériade et al., 1977a,b). In any

case, when cells are bursting, they appear almost totally insensitive to any visual stimulation. Sometimes, the use of auditory or tactile stimuli which do not evoke any firing from the cell, can change the pattern of the spontaneous discharges, presumably by changing the level of arousal of the animal. Following this extra-visual stimulation, the bursting activity is greatly reduced (and even disappears) and the visual responsiveness of the cells is generally enhanced (part *E* of Fig. 1; see Gattas et al. (1979) and Bender (1982) for similar observations in primates). These periods of enhanced visual responsiveness are, however, very short and as a result, it is rather difficult, if not impossible, to fully and adequately characterize the properties of these bursting cells. One has to wonder if these units, mainly unresponsive in anesthetized and paralyzed rabbits, would exhibit strong and specific responses more easily characterizable in free behaving animals.

It is often more tedious and more demanding to define and categorize visual responses of cells in LP than it is for units in other parts of the brain involved in visual processing such as the superior colliculus, the lateral geniculate nucleus, and even the striate cortex. The spontaneous discharge level of the LP cells is fairly high (see trace 1 of Fig. 2*A*), and as mentioned above, there are oscillatory sequences of bursts. Obviously, this is not of any help when

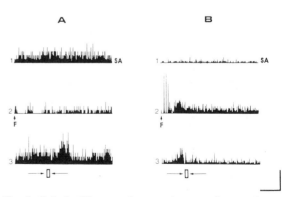

Fig. 2. Cells in LP respond to moving as well as stationary flashing stimuli. The spontaneous firing rate of the cell shown in part *A* is very high. The cell is inhibited by a diffuse flash, and responds with an increase of its discharge to a moving bar. The cell shown in part *B* responds equally to the two types of stimulation. Note that the cell is direction-selective.

someone is trying to locate and stimulate a receptive field. Also, receptive fields are very large and their precise boundaries are difficult to trace. The mean receptive field area of LP cells is 920 ± 822 deg^2 ($n = 56$). It is interesting to note that most receptive fields are located within 50° of the optic axes and their size tends to increase with eccentricity (Casanova and Molotchnikoff, 1990). Therefore, LP is likely to be involved in the perception of events occurring in the central part of the visual field. Perhaps because of the large receptive fields and their central location, we did not find any rigorous retinotopic organization within the rabbit's LP except for the fact that the position of the receptive fields tended to move slightly from the superior to the inferior portion of the visual field as the electrode descended in the LP. Detailed mapping studies are necessary to really uncover any retinotopic organization of the rabbit's LP. Such time consuming experiments showed that there are at least five major representations of the visual field in the LP-P complex of cats (Hutchins and Updyke, 1988, 1989) while most previous studies had failed to report any clear retinotopic organization (e.g., Godfraind et al., 1969, 1972; Verrart et al., 1972).

Perhaps also because cells have vast receptive fields, it is not surprising that large rather than limited stimuli are more effective in driving LP cells. The same observation has been reported previously by Stewart et al. (1973). Along this line, results from a recent study showed that two-thirds of the cells in the striate-recipient zone of the cat's LP (whose

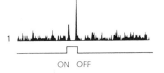

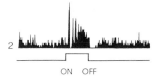

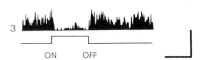

Fig. 4. Responses of three representative LP cells to localized flashing stimuli. For most cells in LP, this stimulation evoked ON and OFF responses (trace 1). See text for further explanations.

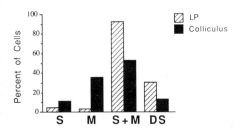

Fig. 3. Overall properties of cells in the LP and in the superior colliculus. Abbreviations: S, stationary; M, moving; DS, direction-selective. Note that most LP cells respond to flashing and moving targets. The direction-selective units shown are included in the M and S + M cell types.

receptive fields have a mean area of 152 deg^2) are tuned to low spatial frequencies (less than 0.5 c/deg) and that the remaining units are low-pass cells (Casanova et al., 1989). An additional characteristic of the rabbit's LP is that almost all units respond to both flashing and moving targets (see Fig. 2). These results are summarized in Fig. 3. Clearly, very few LP cells (less than 8%) are exclusively responsive to either flashing or moving stimuli. This large spectrum of trigger features suggests that this region of the thalamus is likely to be involved in the detection of moving as well as stationary targets. Fig. 3 also shows that many motion-sensitive units (around 30%) are direction-selective. When flashing stimuli are used to characterize LP cells, most cells (almost 60%) respond to flash onset and offset (Fig. 4, trace 1) while the majority of the remaining units respond preferentially to the onset only (trace 2). In both cases, cells responded by an increase (67%, traces 1 and 2) rather than a decrease (33%, trace 3) of their firing rate.

In contrast to LP, the superior colliculus shows a

A. TECTO-LP CELL

B TECTO-PULVINAR CELL

COLLISION TEST

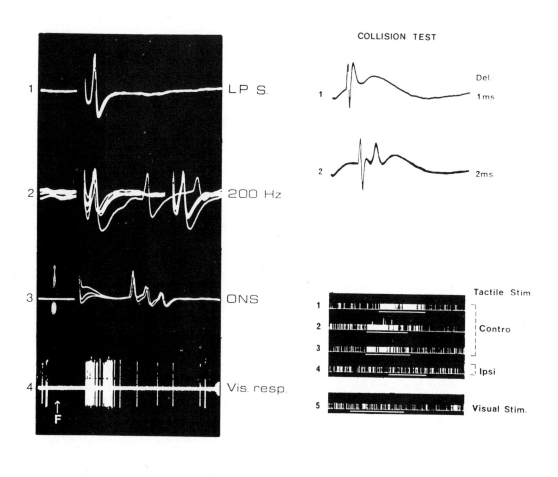

Fig. 5. *A*. Example of a tecto-LP cell identified by antidromic activation. This unit was located in the superficial layers of SC and responded preferentially to diffuse flashing light. *B*. Example of a tecto-pulvinar unit. The cell could not be visually driven, but responded to a controlateral tactile stimulation. It was located in the deep layers of the colliculus.

clear retinotopic organization and cells are relatively easy to drive (one might naively suggest, if LP is a simple relay, why it is so difficult to drive cells in LP in comparison to collicular cells). Details on the organization of the rabbit's superior colliculus can be found in the papers of Hughes (1971), Masland et al. (1971) and Graham et al. (1981). From our experiments (Casanova and Molotchnikoff, 1990), there are at least three differences between the overall cell properties in LP and SC that may somehow challenge the relay hypothesis. Firstly, the number of units exclusively sensitive to motion is higher in the SC than in LP (compare filled and hatched bars (M) of Fig. 3). For this reason, the proportion of collicular units which respond to the two stimulus types (S and M) is decreased. Secondly, direction-selective units are more frequently recorded in LP. Thirdly, the mean receptive field area of cells in LP is around three times larger than the collicular one (920 deg^2 in LP versus 296 deg^2 in SC). These differences may result from an intrinsic reorganization of the collicular input within LP, or may reflect the influence of extra-collicular signals such as those coming from the visual cortex.

The above comparison referred to the overall properties of LP and SC. Differences are also observed when comparisons are restricted to specific collicular cells. Horseradish peroxidase injections in LP have shown that tecto-LP cells are located primarily in the lower half of the SGS (Graham and Berman, 1981). According to Graham et al. (1981), most cells (75%) in the SGSl prefer moving rather than flashing stimuli, which also represents a difference from our description of LP cells properties. Finally, in some experiments we isolated tecto-LP cells by antidromic activation from LP (see Fig. 5). Because only a few cells (12 units) could be isolated, and as most of these units were not fully characterized because of time constraints, we cannot make an adequate comparison between the tecto-LP cells and the LP units. Nevertheless, some interesting observations emerged from these recordings. In agreement with anatomical studies, all tecto-LP cells identified by antidromic activation were located in the superficial layers of SC and it is interesting to note that the size of the receptive fields could vary considerably: some are small (e.g., 20 deg^2) while others are very large (e.g., 900 deg^2). Also, while most cells preferred moving stimuli (see fig. 3 of Casanova and Molotchnikoff, 1990), a few responded preferentially to flashing stimuli (Fig. 5A, trace 4).

During our investigation, we also electrically stimulated the region lying posteriorly to LP and identified as the pulvinar by Sawyer et al. (1954). The collicular cells (13 units) antidromically identified from the pulvinar were all located in the deep or multimodal layers of the colliculus and only two cells could be visually driven. Almost all tecto-pulvinar units were unresponsive to any available sensory stimulation in the laboratory. One cell was clearly responsive to tactile stimulation only and is illustrated in Fig. 5B. These electrophysiological ex-periments suggest that there are conceivably two pathways from the superior colliculus to the rabbit's LP-pulvinar complex: a first one, visually dominant, from the superficial layers to LP, and a second one, mainly non-visual, from the deep collicular layers to the region posterior to LP, referred to as the pulvinar by Sawyer et al. (1954).

Inactivation of the superficial layers of SC: effects on visual responses of cells in LP

Obviously, the comparison of cell properties between regions serially connected can be useful to determine the presence or the absence of any reorganization of the signals at the level of the recipient region. For example, comparison of receptive organization in the LGN and in the striate cortex has led Hubel and Wiesel (1959) to propose that the elongated receptive field of simple cells is likely to come from the spatial arrangement of adjacent concentric LGN receptive fields. From the results we described above, it can be suggested that the large size of the LP receptive field comes from a convergence of several tectal units on a single LP cell. But other explanations can be proposed, such as the contribution of inputs from other LP cells or from cortical neurons. The above-stated differences of properties between LP and the colliculus suggest that LP may be involved in functions which go beyond those of a simple straightforward thalamic relay, if any such exists. Additional experiments are clearly needed in order to clarify the influence of the colliculus on LP physiology. These are described below.

As we mentioned at the beginning of this chapter, the relay hypothesis requires that the visual responsiveness of cells in LP depends to some extent on the integrity of the tecto-LP neurons. In other words, LP cells should become almost, if not totally, silent when they are disconnected from their collicular afferences. The following paragraphs describe the effect of a local and temporary inactivation of the superficial layers of SC on the visual responses of cells in LP. The experimental procedure is illustrated in Fig. 6. The method used is simple,

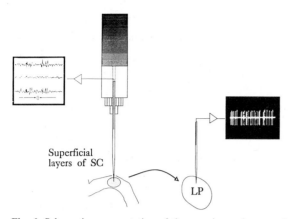

Fig. 6. Schematic representation of the experimental protocol. The superficial layers of the superior colliculus are inactivated by the nanoinjection of lidocaine. Responses in LP are recorded before, during and after the inactivation. The two electrodes are in retinotopically corresponding regions.

reliable, and has proven to be successful in other studies of cellular connectivity (e.g., Molotchnikoff et al., 1986; Casanova et al., 1991a). A micropipette with a tip aperture of 15 – 25 μm is filled with lidocaine hydrochloride (2%) dissolved in a stained solution (Chicago sky blue, 2%). The pipette is inserted in a pressure nanopump which is modified to allow simultaneous recordings. The injecting-recording pipette is placed in the superficial layers of the colliculus identified by the recording of multi-unit responses (and later confirmed histologically). The tissue surrounding the tip of the electrode is inactivated by the injection of 100 – 300 nl of lidocaine. Histological observation has indicated that the stained solution disperses no more than a distance of 500 μm from the center of injection. Control injections of a similar quantity of NaCl (0.9%) fail to change the evoked response in SC. Visual responses in LP are recorded with a glass microelectrode before, during, and after the injection in SC. Evidently, cells from which we could not obtain reliable and consistent responses before injection were not tested (e.g., the bursty cells). The results of these experiments can be summarized as follows.

Around one third of the LP cells (33 of 83 units, 40%) were not affected by the injection. Note that this does not mean that these cells do not receive any

collicular input. It is possible that the injection failed to modify the response because the region inactivated did not include the cell bodies of the tecto-LP units projecting to them.

The remaining units were affected by the temporary inactivation of the colliculus. The main effect observed during injection is an overall decrease of the visual responsiveness of the LP cells (34 of 83 units, 41%). Representative examples are shown in Fig. 7. In part A, the response of the cell to a localized flashing stimulus is totally abolished during the reduction of activity in the colliculus. In a second ex-

A

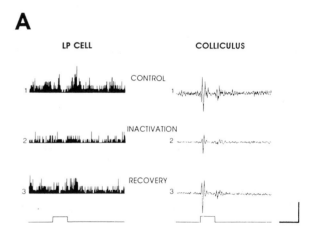

B

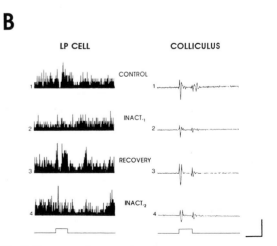

Fig. 7. Representative examples of two LP cells affected by the inactivation of the colliculus. The loss of visual responsiveness represents the primary effect of the collicular blockade.

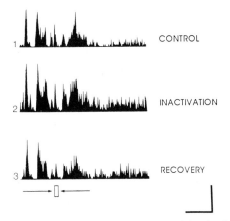

Fig. 8. Example of the enhancement of the visual response of an LP cell during the temporary inactivation of SC. This effect was rarely observed.

ample shown in Fig. 7B, two injections have been made and they are, in both cases, followed by a loss of responsiveness of the cell in LP. Note that in these two examples, the same stimulus evoked responses not only in LP but also in the colliculus. In other words the injecting-recording electrode in SC and the recording microelectrode in LP were placed in retinotopically corresponding regions. The latter observation is important because, as a general precept, responses were modified only if there was a retinotopic match of the receptive field in both structures. This, obviously, suggests that the projections from the superior colliculus to the LP nucleus are, to some extent, topographically organized.

For the last units (20%), the inactivation provoked

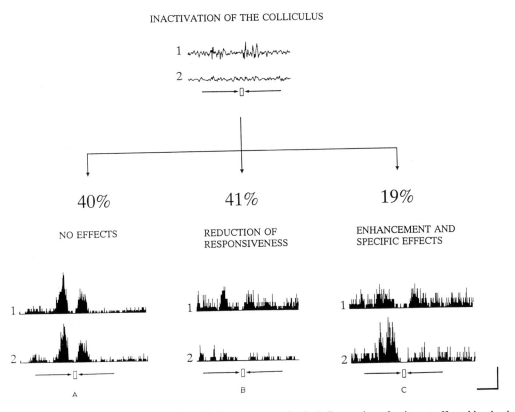

Fig. 9. Effects of the inactivation of the colliculus are summarized. *A.* Proportion of units not affected by the drug administration. *B.* For most cells affected, there was an overall decrease in responsiveness. *C.* For the remaining units, responses were enhanced or specific properties were altered such as direction selectivity.

120

either an unspecific enhancement of the response as shown in Fig. 8, or induced more specific effects such as a change of direction selectivity (see the example shown in the right part of Fig. 9).

Results are summarized in Fig. 9. Our findings indicate that the visual activation of some LP cells depends on the collicular input, representing electrophysiological evidence that, in rabbits, LP may serve as a relay along an extrageniculate pathway from the superior colliculus to the visual cortex. However, as described above, responses of some units are only modulated by the collicular input, and most are not significantly affected by the blockade of SC. Overall, these observations suggest that LP may not only convey midbrain signals to cortex, but may also be part of other pathways and perhaps may integrate its multiple inputs and be involved in functions which exceed those of thalamic relay for the colliculus.

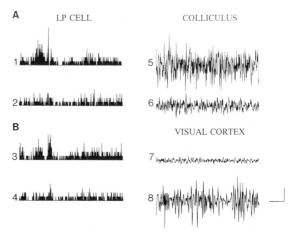

Fig. 11. Convergence of collicular and cortical inputs on a LP cell. The lidocaine inactivation of the SC (traces 5 and 6) provokes a reduction of the response to a moving bar in LP. A similar effect is reported when the activity in the visual cortex is spontaneously enhanced (traces 7 and 8).

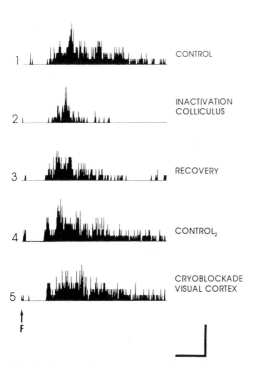

Fig. 10. Inactivation of the superior colliculus provoked a substantial decrease of activity in LP while the cryoblockade of area 17 did not modify the cell's response.

The other major input of the LP nucleus comes from the visual cortex. We did not study the effects of a cortical inactivation on the responses of all LP cells. What we did, however – and it should be pointed out that these are only preliminary results – was to study the influence of the striate cortex on cells that proved to be previously affected by the inactivation of the colliculus. The goal was to determine if there is a convergence of collicular and cortical inputs on cells in LP as has been reported in cats (Benedek et al., 1983). The cryoblockade of the striate cortex did not change the visual responses of most cells we tested, cells which were previously affected by the collicular inactivation (see Fig. 10). However, as shown in Fig. 11, we found some evidence that there are cells in the rabbit's LP that do receive inputs from the colliculus and the visual cortex. Note that the firing of the LP unit shown in Fig. 11 is reduced by the lidocaine inactivation of the colliculus as well as by the excitation of the visual cortex. Thus, this particular cell receives an excitatory and an inhibitory input from the colliculus and the cortex, respectively.

Comparison with other species

Most studies investigating the functional relationship between the superior colliculus and the LP-P complex have been realized on cats and monkeys. Chalupa and colleagues (Chalupa et al., 1983; Chalupa and Abramson, 1988) have shown that there are also significant differences between properties of cells in the superior colliculus and in the tecto-recipient zone of the cat's LP such as the size of the receptive fields (two times larger in LP) and the orientation selectivity (barely found in SC). However, in contrast to our findings, Chalupa et al. (1972) reported that inactivation of SC does not inhibit but rather facilitates the visual evoked potentials recorded in LP. Subsequent experiments have also indicated that the visual responsiveness of cells in LP depends largely on cortical inputs (Hughes and Chalupa, 1982). The simultaneous cryoblockade of almost all areas of the visual cortex abolished responses to visual stimulation of most cells in the tecto-recipient zone of LP.

In primates, Bender (1982) reported that cells in the inferior pulvinar (i.e., the main tecto-recipient zone) have properties similar to those of the striate cortex rather than those of the superior colliculus. In addition, Bender (1983, 1988) showed that collicular lesions failed to modify the visual response of pulvinar cells, whereas cortical lesions were effective. The pulvinar of monkeys is therefore more likely to convey geniculo-striate rather than collicular signals to the various extrastriate areas. According to Bender, the SC would only have a modulatory effect on the visual response of pulvinar cells.

Although there are obvious methodological differences between the present study and those described above, it seems that the impact of the colliculus on the responsiveness of LP-P cells is considerably stronger in rabbits than it is in cats and monkeys. This difference is likely related to species differences. The LP-P complex, the neocortex, and their interconnections have continuously developed during evolution and it is conceivable that, along the phylogenesis, the influence of the cortex over the thalamus has increased to the detriment of the influence of the colliculus.

Acknowledgements

We thank A. Drumheller for comments on a draft of the manuscript. This work was supported by MRC of Canada grant MT-10962 to CC and a NSERC grant to SM.

References

Bender, D.B. (1982) Receptive-field properties of neurons in the macaque inferior pulvinar. *J. Neurophysiol.,* 48: 1 – 17.

Bender, D.B. (1983) Visual activation of neurons in the primate pulvinar depends on cortex but not colliculus. *Brain Res.,* 279: 258 – 261.

Bender, D.B. (1988) Electrophysiological and behavioural experiments on the primate pulvinar. *Prog. Brain Res.,* 75: 55 – 65.

Benedek, G., Norita, M. and Creutzfeldt, O.D. (1983) Electrophysiological and anatomical demonstration of an overlapping striate and tectal projection to the lateral posterior-pulvinar complex of the cat. *Exp. Brain Res.,* 52: 157 – 169.

Berman, N. and Jones, E.G. (1977) A retino-pulvinar projection in the cat. *Brain Res.,* 134: 237 – 248.

Casanova, C. and Molotchnikoff, S. (1990) Influence of the superior colliculus on visual responses of cells in the rabbit's lateral posterior nucleus. *Exp. Brain Res.,* 80: 387 – 396.

Casanova, C., Freeman, R.D. and Nordmann, J.P. (1989) Monocular and binocular response properties of cells in the striate-recipient zone of the cat's lateral posterior-pulvinar complex. *J. Neurophysiol.,* 62: 544 – 557.

Casanova, C., McKinley, P.A. and Molotchnikoff, S. (1991a) Responsiveness of reorganized primary somatosensory (SI) cortex after local inactivation of normal SI cortex in chronic spinal cats. *Somatosens. Motor Res.,* 8: 65 – 76.

Casanova, C., Nordmann, J.P. and Molotchnikoff, S. (1991b) Le complexe noyau latéral postérieur-pulvinar des mammifères et la fonction visuelle. *J. Physiol. (Paris):* 85: 44 – 57.

Chalupa, L.M. and Abramson, B.P. (1988) Receptive-field properties in the tecto- and striate-recipient zones of the cat's lateral posterior nucleus. *Prog. Brain Res.,* 75: 85 – 94.

Chalupa, L.M., Anchel, H. and Lindsley, D.B. (1972) Visual input to the pulvinar via lateral geniculate, superior colliculus and visual cortex in the cat. *Exp. Neurol.,* 36: 449 – 462.

Chalupa, L.M., Williams, R.W. and Hughes, M.J. (1983) Visual response properties in the tectorecipient zone of the cat's lateral posterior-pulvinar complex: a comparison with the superior colliculus. *J. Neurosci.,* 3: 2587 – 2596.

Gattas, R., Oswaldo-Cruz, E. and Sousa, A.P.B. (1979) Visual receptive fields of units in the pulvinar of Cebus monkey. *Brain Res.,* 160: 413 – 430.

Godfraind, J.M., Meulders, M. and Veraart, C. (1969) Visual receptive fields in pulvinar, nucleus lateralis in posterior and nucleus suprageniculatus thalami of the cat. *Brain Res.,* 15: 552 – 555.

Godfraind, J.M., Meulders, M. and Veraart, C. (1972) Visual properties of neurons in pulvinar, nucleus lateralis posterior and nucleus suprageniculatus thalami of the cat. I. Qualitative investigation. *Brain Res.,* 44: 503 – 526.

Graham, J. and Berman, N. (1981) Origins of the projections of the superior colliculus to the dorsal lateral geniculate nucleus and the pulvinar in the rabbit. *Neurosci. Lett.,* 26: 101 – 106.

Graham, J., Pearson, H.E., Berman, N. and Murphey, E.H. (1981) Laminar organization of superior colliculus in the rabbit: a study of receptive-field properties of single units. *J. Neurophysiol.,* 45: 915 – 932.

Holstege, G. and Collewijn, H. (1982) The efferent connections of the nucleus of the optic tract and the superior colliculus in the rabbit. *J. Comp. Neurol.,* 209: 139 – 175.

Hubel, D.H. and Wiesel, T.N. (1959) Receptive fields of single neurones in the cat's striate cortex. *J. Physiol. (Lond.),* 148: 574 – 591.

Hughes, A. (1971) Topographical relationships between the anatomy and physiology of the rabbit visual system. *Doc. Ophthalmol.,* 30: 33 – 159.

Hughes, M.J. and Chalupa, L.M. (1982) Cortical cooling depressed visual neuronal responses in the tectorecipient zone of the cat's lateral posterior nucleus. *Soc. Neurosci. Abstr.,* 8: 673.

Hutchins, B. and Updyke, B.V. (1988) The lateral posterior complex of the cat: studies of the functional organization. *Prog. Brain Res.,* 75: 75 – 83.

Hutchins, B. and Updyke, B.V. (1989) Retinotopic organization within the lateral posterior complex of the cat. *J. Comp. Neurol.,* 285: 350 – 398.

Itaya, S.K. and Van Hoesen, G.W. (1983) Retinal projections to the inferior and medial pulvinar nuclei in the old-world monkey. *Brain Res.,* 269: 223 – 230.

Jones, E.G. (1985) *The Thalamus,* Plenum Press, New York, pp. 531 – 572.

Masland, R.H., Chow, K.L. and Stewart, D.L. (1971) Receptive-field characteristics of superior colliculus neurons in the rabbit. *J. Neurophysiol.,* 34: 148 – 156.

Mason, R. (1978) Functional organization in the cat's pulvinar complex. *Exp. Brain Res.,* 31: 51 – 66.

Mizuno, N., Itoh, K., Uchida, K., Uemura-Sumi, M. and Matsushima, R. (1982) A retino pulvinar projection in the macaque monkey as visualized by the use of anterograde transport of horseradish peroxidase. *Neurosci. Lett.,* 30: 199 – 203.

Molotchnikoff, S., Delaunais, D., Casanova, C. and Lachapelle, P. (1986) Influence of a local inactivation in the superior colliculus on lateral geniculate responses in rabbits. *Brain Res.,* 375: 66 – 72.

Mooney, R.D., Fish, S.E. and Rhoades, R.W. (1984) Anatomical and functional organization of pathway from superior colliculus to lateral posterior nucleus in hamster. *J. Neurophysiol.,* 51: 407 – 431.

Nakagawa, S. and Tanaka, S. (1984) Retinal projections to the pulvinar nucleus of the macaque monkey: a re-investigation using autoradiography. *Exp. Brain Res.,* 57: 151 – 157.

Sawyer, C.H., Everett, J.W. and Green, J.D. (1954) The rabbit diencephalon in stereotaxic coordinates. *J. Comp. Neurol.,* 101: 801 – 824.

Steriade, M., Oakson, G. and Diallo, A. (1977a) Reticular influences on lateralis posterior thalamic neurons. *Brain Res.,* 131: 55 – 71.

Steriade, M., Diallo, A., Oakson, G. and White-Guay, B. (1977b) Some synaptic inputs and ascending projections of lateralis posterior thalamic neurons. *Brain Res.,* 131: 39 – 53.

Stewart, D.L., Towns, L.C. and Birt, D. (1973) Visual receptive-field characteristics of posterior thalamic and pretectal neurons in the rabbit. *Brain Res.,* 57: 43 – 57.

Uchida, K., Mizuno, N., Sugimoto, T. and Itoh, K. (1982) Audioradiographic demonstration of retinal projection to the brain stem structures in the rabbit using transneuronal tracing technique with special reference to the retinal projections to the inferior olive. *Exp. Neurol.,* 78: 369 – 379.

Verrart, C., Meulders, M. and Godfraind, J.M. (1972) Visual properties of neurons in pulvinar, nucleus lateralis posterior and nucleus suprageniculatus thalami in the cat. *Brain Res.,* 44: 527 – 546.

T.P. Hicks, S. Molotchnikoff and T. Ono (Eds.)
Progress in Brain Research, Vol. 95

CHAPTER 12

Multiple visual areas in the posterior parietal cortex of primates

Carmen Cavada[1] and Patricia S. Goldman-Rakic[2]

[1] *Departamento de Morfología, Facultad de Medicina, Universidad Autónoma de Madrid, 28029 Madrid, Spain, and* [2] *Section of Neurobiology, Yale University School of Medicine, New Haven, CT 06510, U.S.A.*

Introduction

Visual perception and visuo-motor functions are characteristically altered following posterior parietal damage in man and non-human primates. Posterior parietal lesions also produce defects in other sensory and motor domains, including misperception of self body parts and inaccurate limb movements (see reviews by Lynch, 1980; Hyvä-rinen, 1982; Andersen, 1987). These disorders seem to be qualitatively comparable in humans and monkeys, although their severity is greater in man, especially after lesions of the non-dominant hemisphere. For example, ignorance or neglect to stimuli present on the side contralateral to the lesioned hemisphere is a prominent symptom of parietal damage in man (Critchley, 1953). In macaques, the deficit is less pronounced, but nonetheless similar in nature: neglect for contralateral stimuli may not be fully apparent, but when the animals are confronted with two stimuli simultaneously, they ignore the one located contralateral to the parietal ablation (Schwartz and Eidelberg, 1968; Heilman et al., 1970), a condition known as extinction. This milder form of neglect is also present, and in fact was initially described, in human patients suffering from parietal injury (Bender and Furlow, 1944; Denny-Brown et al., 1952). Thus, it is our assumption that the study of the neural organization of the posterior parietal cortex in a species, like the macaque monkey, amenable to experimental investigation

and whose symptoms after parietal damage appear comparable to those in man, may shed light on the mechanisms at function in this large expanse of primate association cortex.

The variety of disorders that follow injury to the posterior parietal cortex bespeaks a functional heterogeneity. The purpose of this chapter is to review the evidence in macaques in support of a *topographic* heterogeneity within the posterior parietal cortex involved in visual and visuo-motor functions. This extensive cortical territory appears to contain multiple areas, each characterized by its unique array of connections with other brain regions. The inference could thus be made that the anatomical parcellation of the posterior parietal region has a bearing on its functional and clinical diversity.

The parietal territory concerned with vision and eye movements encompasses most of Brodmann's area 7 (Brodmann, 1909), and is located posteriorly and medially to the somatosensory parietal cortex. Therefore, except for brief references in the architectonic survey section, we shall not cover the most anterior and lateral portions of the posterior parietal cortex, including areas 5 and 7b, whose main functional and anatomical affiliations are with the somatic sensory system (Jones and Powell, 1969; Duffy and Burchfield, 1971; Mountcastle et al., 1975; Hyvärinen and Shelepin, 1979; Leinonen et al., 1979; Robinson and Burton, 1980; Cavada and Goldman-Rakic, 1989a).

Physiological evidence for a parcellation of macaque area 7

The seminal studies carried out in the seventies on the functional properties of cells of the posterior parietal cortex of monkeys by Hyvärinen, Mountcastle, and Robinson and their colleagues (see for example, Hyvärinen and Poranen, 1974; Mountcastle et al., 1975; Robinson et al., 1978) were not aimed primarily at the elucidation of the topographical

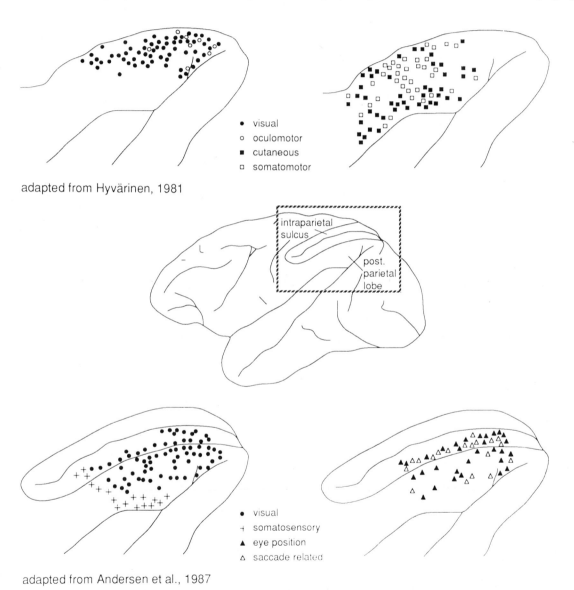

adapted from Hyvärinen, 1981

- visual
- oculomotor
- cutaneous
- somatomotor

intraparietal sulcus

post. parietal lobe

- visual
- somatosensory
- eye position
- saccade related

adapted from Andersen et al., 1987

Fig. 1. Evidence for a parcellation of the posterior parietal cortex as revealed by physiological studies. Depicted in this figure are representative examples of the topographic location of units recorded in the posterior parietal lobe and adjacent cortex of the intraparietal sulcus. The work of Hyvärinen and colleagues showed that neurons responsive to cutaneous or somatomotor stimuli are located more anteriorly and laterally in the posterior parietal lobe than those related to visual and oculomotor stimuli. The investigations of Andersen and colleagues, while confirming these previous findings, have emphasized the preferential distribution of saccade-related units within the posterior bank of the intraparietal sulcus (see also Blatt et al., 1990).

location of the different types of neurons they identified. The various groups focused on particular features of the units that were recorded. Thus, the early work of Mountcastle and colleagues emphasized the relationship of neuronal firing with movement, whereas Robinson's studies called attention to the activation of parietal neurons by visual stimuli (see for example, the review and accompanying discussion in Lynch, 1980). Hyvärinen and colleagues examined neurons responsive to both visual stimulation, and visual fixation or eye movements (Hyvärinen and Poranen, 1974; Hyvärinen, 1982). In all these studies the dependence of the recorded responses upon behavioral factors was emphasized: parietal neurons tended to fire most intensely when the stimulus had significance for the animal, suggesting strong limbic influences (Hyvärinen and Poranen, 1974; Mountcastle et al., 1975; Lynch et al., 1977; Robinson et al., 1978).

Despite the emphasis on the physiological attributes of the recorded units, crude topological indications were already given in these early investigations, and were further defined subsequently. As summarized in Fig. 1, somatosensory and visually driven neurons appeared concentrated in anterior and posterior portions, respectively, of the posterior parietal cortex; and units concerned with motor mechanisms of the eyes predominated medially (Mountcastle et al., 1975; Hyvärinen and Shelepin, 1979; Robinson and Burton, 1980; Hyvärinen, 1981; Andersen et al., 1987).

The parcellation of macaque area 7 based on architectonics

Historically, the oldest evidence for a partition of Brodmann's area 7 in monkeys was its division into two areas, 7a and 7b, by Vogt and Vogt (1919), who, like Brodmann, studied the brain of *Cercopithecus* (Fig. 2). Areas 7a and 7b, as defined by the Vogts, included practically the entire extent of the convexity of the posterior parietal lobe. Von Bonin and Bailey (1947) later adopted for the macaque monkey the lettering terminology introduced by Von Economo in his studies of the human brain. They also recognized two areas (PG and PF) on the exposed surface of the posterior parietal lobe (Fig. 2), and considered that there was a gradual transition, rather than a sharp boundary, between them. The more recent study of Pandya and Seltzer (1982) has partitioned the convexity of the posterior parietal lobe further, into five subdivisions (Fig. 2): areas PG and PF, a transitional area between them termed PFG, two areas in the parietal operculum (PGop and PFop), and area Opt, located in the most posterior part of the lobe and thus lying in the posterior portion of area 7a of Vogt and Vogt (or PG of Von Bonin and Bailey).

In Brodmann's map, area 7 extended onto the medial surface of the hemisphere to occupy the dorsal portion of the precuneate gyrus, anterior to prestriate area 19 and posterior to a medial extension of area 5 (Fig. 2). This same region was considered comparable to the cortex of the anterior parietal lobe by Von Bonin and Bailey, who therefore named it PE (area 5 in Brodmann's terminology; see Fig. 2). Pandya and Seltzer's view, however, is more in accord with Brodmann's original description: their area PGm in the precuneate gyrus lies between the prestriate cortex and the medial extension of the anterior parietal cortex (Fig. 2).

The cortex lining the banks of the intraparietal sulcus was considered by Von Bonin and Bailey (1947) analogous to the cortex of the adjacent convexities, and thus they labeled it accordingly: area PE in the medial bank, and areas PG and PF in the lateral bank. Seltzer and Pandya (1980), however, recognized a separate area in the lateral bank: POa, with internal (POa-i) and external (POa-e) divisions.

Connectional evidence for a parcellation of area 7

It seems fair to conclude from the above overview that there is little consensus on the partition of macaque area 7 relying upon architectonic criteria. In fact, in the last decade, additional subdivisions within Brodmann's area 7 have come to light, principally on the basis of connectional criteria: VIP

126

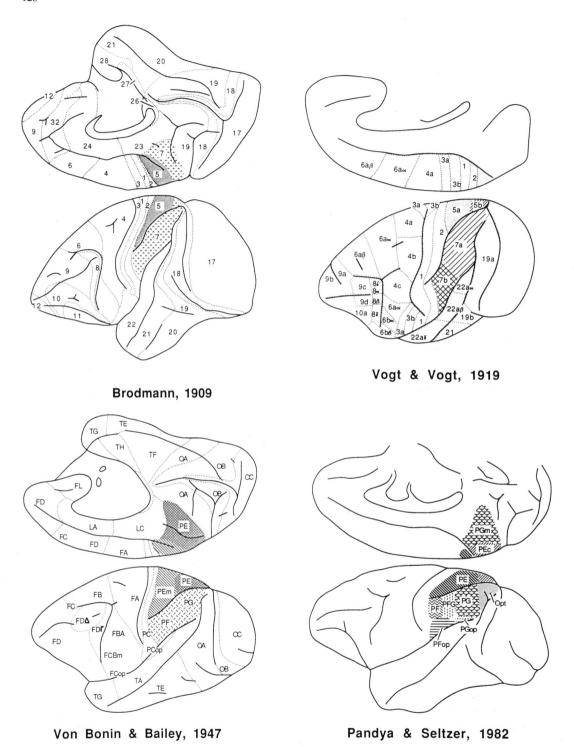

Brodmann, 1909

Vogt & Vogt, 1919

Von Bonin & Bailey, 1947

Pandya & Seltzer, 1982

Fig. 2. Cytoarchitectonic parcellations of the posterior parietal cortex in *Cercopithecus* (Brodmann, 1909; Vogt and Vogt, 1919) and macaque (Von Bonin and Bailey, 1947; Pandya and Seltzer, 1982) monkey brains. Reproduced, with permission, from Cavada and Goldman-Rakic (1989a).

(ventral intraparietal; Maunsell and Van Essen, 1983) located near the fundus of the intraparietal sulcus; LIP (lateral intraparietal; Andersen et al., 1985; Asanuma et al., 1985), which is largely coextensive with the posterior part of POa of Seltzer and Pandya (1980); MIP (medial intraparietal; Colby et al., 1988) and PIP (posterior intraparietal; Felleman et al., 1987; Colby et al., 1988), situated in the posterior end of the medial and lateral banks, respectively, of the intraparietal sulcus.

In general, these newly defined areas were characterized by their connections with other visual areas or with the prefrontal cortex. Thus, VIP was described by Maunsell and Van Essen (1983) as the intraparietal target of projections from area MT. However, in a subsequent study of MT projections, Ungerleider and Desimone (1986) observed that the area MT target cortex in the intraparietal sulcus was not restricted to the fundal region but extended further superficially in the sulcus, into a heavily myelinated zone, and they termed the new region

VIP*. LIP was defined by its prominent connections with the posterior prefrontal cortex (Andersen et al., 1985). Recently, Blatt et al. (1990) have defined ventral and dorsal subdivisions within area LIP (LIPv and LIPd, the former possibly coextensive with POa-i and VIP* of other authors). Areas MIP and PIP were described on the basis of their connections with visual prestriate areas, most notably with area PO (parieto occipital; Colby et al., 1988).

Considering that these newly defined sectors of area 7, particularly that portion of it lying in the intraparietal sulcus, were made in the context of investigations focusing on areas outside the posterior parietal cortex itself, the study of the connectional patterns of several major subdivisions of area 7, altogether encompassing a significant expanse of this cortical region, should help to clarify their identity and, in addition, their functional ascription. In the present chapter we review our studies on the complete sets of cortico-cortical connections of three area 7 subdivisions that are associated with

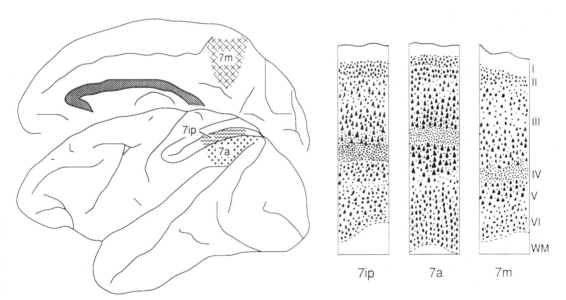

Fig. 3. Location of the subdivisions of the posterior parietal cortex addressed in the present study. Areas 7a and 7m are approximately coextensive with areas 7a of Vogt and Vogt (1919), and PGm of Pandya and Seltzer (1982), respectively. Area 7ip corresponds to area POa of Pandya and Seltzer (1982). Only the posterior part of 7ip (equivalent to area LIP of Andersen et al., 1985) was investigated here because of its selective linkage with the frontal eye field and with visual areas (see Cavada and Goldman-Rakic, 1989a,b, for additional details). The cytoarchitectonic features of areas 7ip, 7a and 7m are distinct as shown on the right half of the figure. The present study focused on the analysis of their circuitry and revealed marked differences among them, allowing inferences on their functional significance.

128

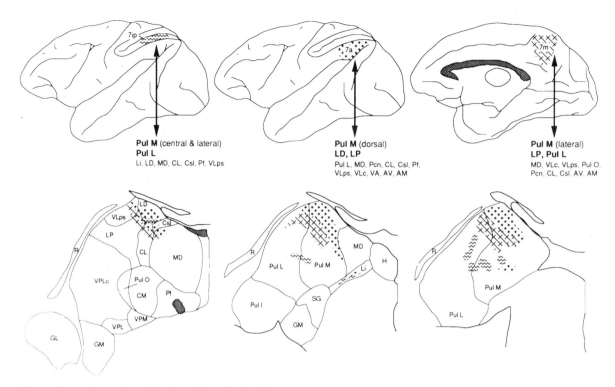

Fig. 4. Connections of areas 7ip, 7a and 7m with the thalamus. The nuclei most strongly connected with each subdivision are shown in bold type. The data used to construct this figure were taken from our own observations and the reports of Asanuma et al. (1985), Yeterian and Pandya (1985), and Schamahmann and Pandya (1990). It should be noted then, that the topographic relationships shown in the bottom diagrams of coronal thalamic sections were taken from different experimental cases, and therefore this figure does not attempt to depict the fine details on the overlap or segregation of the thalamic territories connected with each subdivision. Abbreviations: AM, anterior medial nucleus; AV, anterior ventral nucleus; CL, central lateral nucleus; CM, centromedian nucleus; Csl, central superior lateral nucleus; GL, lateral geniculate nucleus; GM, medial geniculate nucleus; H, habenula; LD, lateral dorsal nucleus; Li, limitans nucleus; LP, lateral posterior nucleus; MD, medial dorsal nucleus; Pcn, paracentral nucleus; Pf, parafascicular nucleus; Pul I, pulvinar nucleus, pars inferior; Pul L, pulvinar nucleus, pars lateralis; Pul M, pulvinar nucleus, pars medialis; Pul O, pulvinar nucleus, pars oralis; R, reticular nucleus; SG, suprageniculate nucleus; VA, ventral anterior nucleus; VLps, ventral lateral nucleus, pars postrema; VPL, ventral posterior lateral nucleus; VPLc, ventral posterior lateral nucleus, pars caudalis; VPM, ventral posterior medial nucleus.

visual processing (Cavada and Goldman-Rakic, 1989a,b). Our results lead to the conclusion that each of them participates in different distributed cortico-cortical networks formed by a constellation of visual, limbic, frontal association and motor areas. Moreover, analysis of the known physiological properties of these areas will allow some inferences about the functional role of each network. Finally, we will correlate the distinct networks of interconnected cortical areas to specific subcortical motor targets associated with each area 7 subdivi-

sion (see Cavada and Goldman-Rakic, 1991, and sections below).

We have adopted a simple and internally consistent terminology, that also respects cytoarchitectonic features and historical precedents (Fig. 3): areas 7a and 7b (after the Vogts), in the convexity of the posterior parietal lobe; area 7ip, in the posterior bank of the intraparietal sulcus (coextensive with area POa of previous studies); and 7m, on the medial surface of the parietal lobe (equivalent to PGm). Examination of the cytoarchitectonic patterns of these subdivisions reveals clear differences between them (see Fig. 3). However, the present report will focus on the analysis of axonally transported tracers placed in areas 7a, 7m and posterior 7ip (coextensive with area LIP), all of which sustain prominent connections with visual areas. The posterior sector of 7ip was chosen because, unlike anterior 7ip, it is selectively linked with the frontal cortex engaged in eye and head movements, and because in the sensory domain, it is connected to a set of visual cortices (see Cavada and Goldman-Rakic, 1989a, for additional details, and for accurate descriptions of the methods employed and of the placement of the injected tracers).

Thalamic connections of areas 7ip, 7a and 7m

The thalamic nuclei connected with areas 7ip, 7a and 7m are specified in Fig. 4. Fig. 5 shows a representative example of topographic similarities and differences in the connections of areas 7ip, 7a and 7m with the lateral and medial pulvinar nuclei, which are the main targets and sources of the thalamic connections of these area 7 subdivisions. The prominent connections of area 7m with these particular nuclei should be noted. It is this association which led us to conclude that this portion of medial parietal cortex is a genuine sector of area 7, and not of area 5. This attribution is in keeping with the cytoarchitectonic criteria of Brodmann (1909) and Pandya and Seltzer (1982), but not with the parcellation of the parietal cortex made by Von Bonin and Bailey (1947; Fig. 2). Additional support for this conclusion are the strong links between area 7m and several visual areas (see below), a characteristic of most area 7 subdivisions, but not of area 5. If we are correct, this may be still another example in which connectional criteria may prove essential in the evaluation of the organization and function of the different territories of the cerebral cortex (see also the recent review on the visual, somatosensory and motor cortices in Felleman and Van Essen, 1991).

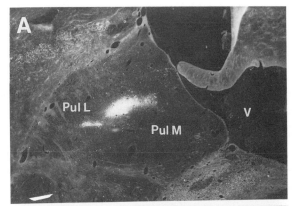
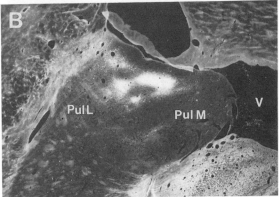
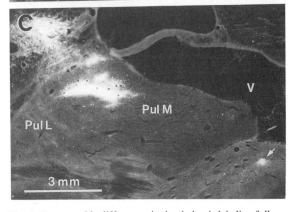

Fig. 5. Topographic differences in the thalamic labeling following HRP-WGA injections into areas 7ip (*A*), 7a (*B*) and 7m (*C*). The darkfield photomicrographs were taken from coronal sections at approximately the same posterior level of the pulvinar complex. The arrow in *C* points to a patch of labeling in the medial part of the superior colliculus. Abbreviations: Pul L, pulvinar nucleus, pars lateralis; Pul M, pulvinar nucleus, pars medialis; V, lateral ventricle. The calibration bar is the same for all three micrographs.

130

Connections with sensory areas

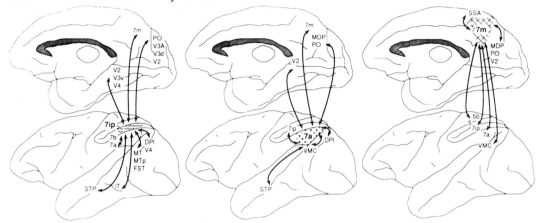

Connections with limbic and prefrontal areas

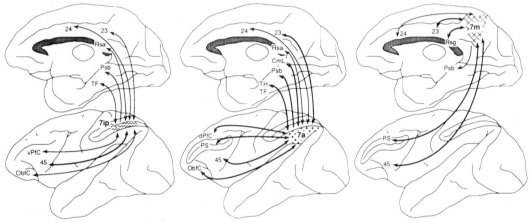

Connections with motor areas

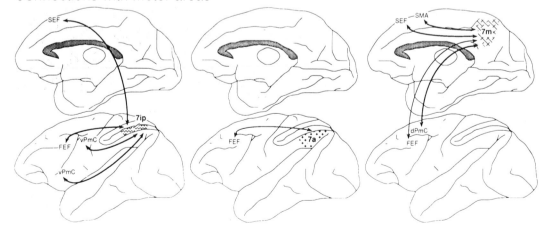

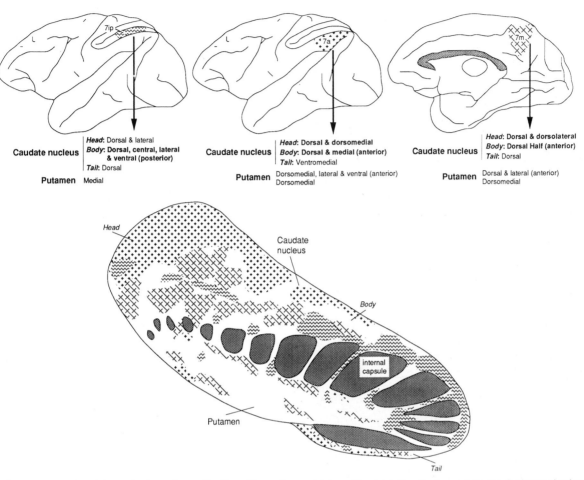

Caudate nucleus

Head: Dorsal & lateral	
Body: Dorsal, central, lateral & ventral (posterior)	
Tail: Dorsal	

Putamen   Medial

Caudate nucleus

Head: Dorsal & dorsomedial	
Body: Dorsal & medial (anterior)	
Tail: Ventromedial	

Putamen   Dorsomedial, lateral & ventral (anterior)
Dorsomedial

Caudate nucleus

Head: Dorsal & dorsolateral	
Body: Dorsal Half (anterior)	
Tail: Dorsal	

Putamen   Dorsal & lateral (anterior)
Dorsomedial

Fig. 7. Topography of the projections of areas 7ip, 7a and 7m to the neostriatum. The striatal territories receiving the densest projections from each subdivision are shown in bold type. The left caudate nucleus and putamen are viewed from above. The data used to prepare this composite figure are from Cavada and Goldman-Rakic (1991), and as in the case of Figs. 4 and 9 the connections of each subdivision were studied in different experimental animals. Therefore, this diagram is not intended to depict the fine details of the mutual relationships of the striatal territories innervated by each subdivision.

Fig. 6. Intrahemispheric cortico-cortical connections of areas 7ip, 7a and 7m. The data upon which this figure is based are from Cavada and Goldman-Rakic (1989a,b). The reader may wish to refer to these publications for more information about the nomenclature and criteria used in the identification of the various cortical areas. With the exception of the projections to the presubiculum, all cortico-cortical connections of each parietal subdivision are reciprocal. Moderate or heavy connections are shown in thick lines, whereas weak connections are in thin lines. Abbreviations: CmL, caudomedial lobule; dPfC, dorsal prefrontal convexity; DPl, dorsal prelunate area; dPmC, dorsal premotor cortex; FEF, frontal eye field; FST, fundal superior temporal area; IT, inferior temporal cortex; MDP, mediodorsal parietal area of Colby et al. (1988); MT, middle temporal area; MTp, peripheral middle temporal area; ObfC, orbitofrontal cortex; PO, parieto occipital area; PS, principal sulcus; Psb, presubiculum; Rsa, retrosplenial cortex, agranular portion; Rsg, retrosplenial cortex, granular portion; SEF, supplementary eye field; SMA, supplementary motor area; SSA, supplementary somatosensory area; STP, superior temporal polysensory area; V2, visual area 2; V3A, visual area 3, anterior portion; V3d, visual area 3, dorsal portion; V3v, visual area 3, ventral portion; V4, visual area 4; VMC, visual motion cortex of the upper bank of the superior temporal sulcus; vPfC, ventral prefrontal convexity; vPmC, ventral premotor cortex.

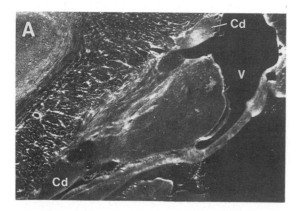

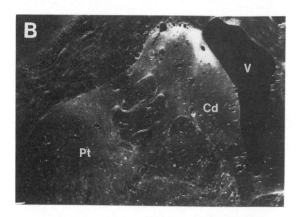

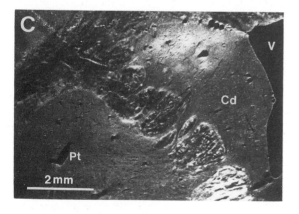

Fig. 8. Representative darkfield photomicrographs showing striatal territories heavily labeled after HRP-WGA injections into areas 7ip (*A*: at the level of the transition between body and tail of the caudate nucleus), 7a (*B*: head of the caudate nucleus), and 7m (*C*: head of the caudate nucleus). Abbreviations: Cd, caudate nucleus; Pt, putamen; V, lateral ventricle. The calibration bar is the same for all three micrographs.

Connections of areas 7ip, 7a and 7m with sensory cortices

Probably the connectivity of the area 7 subdivisions with cortices whose sensory or motor properties are known in some detail are the best aid in the analysis of the functional affiliation of those subdivisions. Fig. 6 summarizes the complete sets of intrahemispheric cortico-cortical connections of areas 7ip, 7a and 7m with sensory, limbic, prefrontal and motor areas. Only some salient features of these connections are commented upon below. For a lengthier discussion the reader may wish to refer to the original descriptions in Cavada and Goldman-Rakic (1989a,b), and to subsequent confirmations by Andersen et al. (1990), Blatt et al. (1990) and Baizer et al. (1991).

In the sensory domain, area 7ip is the most widely interconnected with visual areas. These include V2, V3, PO, MT and V4, all of which are connected with the primary visual cortex, and also areas involved in higher levels of visual information processing, like IT, STP, DP1, MTp and FST (see Felleman and Van Essen, 1991, for a recent comprehensive account of visual cortico-cortical connections). The connections of areas 7a and 7m with regions connected with the striate cortex are more restricted, and include areas V2 and PO. Both 7a and 7m are connected with the motion visual areas of the upper bank of the superior temporal sulcus (VMC), and area 7a has in addition strong connections with the STP area. The connections of each subdivision with the various visual areas are reciprocal and selective, involving particular portions of each. For example, the anterior part of area PO, containing the representation of the upper visual field, is preferentially connected with 7m and 7a, whereas posterior PO, where the lower visual field is mapped, is connected with 7ip. Area 7m departs from the other subdivisions in that it is also connected to somatosensory areas, including SSA and area 5.

Common among the sensory affiliations of all three area 7 subdivisions is their linkage with visual areas, or portions thereof, where the periphery of the visual field is mapped (V2, V3, PO), and with areas involved in the analysis of visual motion (MT,

MTp, FST, VMC). These connections are likely to make a major contribution to the analysis of movement and spatial relationships of the visual world, the latter for a long time attributed to the posterior parietal cortex (Mishkin et al., 1983; Van Essen and Maunsell, 1983), and whose impairment may underlie at least part of the visual neglect syndrome that follows parietal damage.

It is important to add, however, that the posterior parietal subdivisions, most prominently 7ip and 7a, are not exclusively connected with cortices in the "dorsal" visuospatial pathway. Both areas are strongly and selectively linked with the STP area,

and 7ip has additional connections with the IT cortex. These two temporal visual regions are within the "ventral" object recognition visual pathway, therefore suggesting that areas 7ip and 7a have access to information being processed not only in the dorsal spatial, but also in the ventral object recognition visual pathways. This anatomical concurrence of processing streams in two parietal subdivisions adds to the growing evidence of such intermingling at earlier levels of the visual cortico-cortical hierarchy (DeYoe and Van Essen, 1988; Krubitzer and Kaas, 1990; Maunsell et al., 1990; Felleman and Van Essen, 1991).

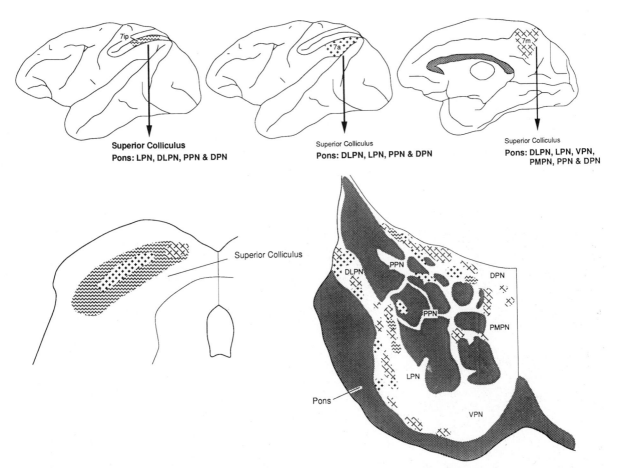

Fig. 9. Topography of the connections from areas 7ip, 7a and 7m to the superior colliculus and pons. The territories receiving the heaviest innervation from each subdivision are shown in bold type. The data used in this figure are from our own observations and the reports by Lynch et al. (1985; superior colliculus) and May and Andersen (1986; pons). Abbreviations: DPN, dorsal pontine nucleus; DLPN, dorsolateral pontine nucleus; LPN, lateral pontine nucleus; VPN, ventral pontine nucleus; PMPN, paramedian pontine nucleus; PPN, peduncular pontine nucleus.

Connections of areas 7ip, 7a and 7m with limbic and prefrontal areas

The existence of limbic influences upon the posterior parietal cortex has long been suspected on the basis of the attentional deficits subsequent to parietal damage and of the importance of the stimulus significance to drive parietal units in conscious active monkeys. All three parietal areas, but most notably 7a and 7m, have strong and selective connections with a wide set of limbic and prefrontal areas (summarized in Fig. 6, and discussed in more detail in Cavada and Goldman-Rakic, 1989a,b). The connections with several components of the hippocampal formation, including the presubiculum, caudomedial lobule and parahippocampal areas TF and TH, give the posterior parietal cortex access to the memory processing functions in which these medial temporal regions are engaged.

Perhaps one of the most revealing findings from our study is the remarkably precise circuitry connecting each of the three parietal areas with the prefrontal cortex. We found that each parietal subdivision was reciprocally connected with a distinct portion of the principal sulcus (Cavada and Goldman-Rakic, 1989b). Given the strong evidence now available that this area of prefrontal cortex is critical for visuospatial working memory, the strong connections with the visual spatial centers of the parietal cortex are likely the major source of visuospatial information to this frontal area. Moreover, these connections appear to form a major component of a wider network of areas dedicated to spatial cognition (Selemon and Goldman-Rakic, 1988). Finally, our findings imply that subareas of the principal sulcus may perform specific subfunctions related to their unique parietal inputs.

Connections of areas 7ip, 7a and 7m with motor cortices

The defects in eye movements that accompany posterior parietal damage, and the physiological properties of neurons in area 7 discussed at the beginning of this chapter strongly suggest that the posterior parietal cortex is involved in motor functions. In the anatomical domain, this suggestion is supported by the posterior parietal connections with a number of areas in the frontal lobe (see Fig. 6 and Cavada and Goldman-Rakic, 1989b), and with

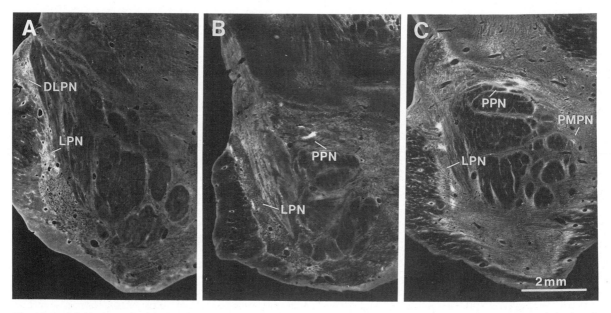

Fig. 10. Darkfield photomicrographs of coronal sections through the pons showing the nuclei labeled from HRP-WGA injections in areas 7ip (*A*), 7a (*B*) and 7m (*C*). Abbreviations as in Fig. 9. The calibration bar is the same for all three micrographs.

several subcortical motor centers. Probably the most prominent connections of the parietal subdivisions with motor areas, especially of 7ip, but also of 7a and 7m, are with the FEF and SEF cortices, which are specifically involved in the motor control of the eyes and head (Bruce and Goldberg, 1984; Van der Steen et al., 1986; Lynch, 1987; Schlag and Schlag-Rey, 1987). As is the case in relation to the connections of the parietal subdivisions with sensory, limbic and prefrontal areas, those with motor cortices are selective for each subdivision. For instance, the heaviest links of area 7ip are with the posterior part of the FEF. Only from this sector can low-threshold saccades be elicited by intracortical stimulation (Bruce et al., 1985; Huerta et al., 1986). From the rostral part of the FEF, connected with 7a and 7m, high-threshold saccades are obtained, and cortical lesions that include this region produce impairments in eye-head coordination (Robinson and Fuchs, 1969; Bruce et al., 1985; Van der Steen et al., 1986).

Connections of areas 7ip, 7a and 7m with subcortical motor centers: striatum, superior colliculus, and pons

The connections of areas 7ip, 7a and 7m with the neostriatum are summarized in Fig. 7; Fig. 8 shows representative examples of the striatal territories strongly innervated by each subdivision. Although each area projects to a large antero-posterior extent of both the putamen and the caudate nucleus, including its head, body and tail, the connections are particularly concentrated in some striatal zones. Thus, the main striatal targets of areas 7a and 7m are in the head and anterior part of the body of the caudate nucleus, with area 7a represented more medially than 7m. However, the main target zone of area 7ip in the caudate nucleus includes a sizeable part of the body, with the exclusion only of the most medial part. It is remarkable that this same zone of the caudate nucleus holds the highest concentration of neurons with activities related to saccadic eye movements (Hikosaka et al., 1989). Area 7ip is also the parietal subdivision that projects most heavily to the superior colliculus (Lynch et al., 1985; Fig. 9),

where neurons discharge before saccades (Hikosaka and Wurtz, 1983).

In addition to their output to the striatum and superior colliculus, a further pathway by which the parietal cortex may influence motor performance is via the pontine nuclei, which receive substantial projections from all three areas 7ip, 7a and 7m, specified in Fig. 9. Presumably the pontine territories specifically innervated by each subdivision have selective cerebellar, and in turn thalamic and cortical, targets. However, the precise organization of the sequence of neural connections arising from each parietal territory and impinging upon specific subcortical targets remains an open question at present.

Area 7 as a mosaic of fields integrated in diverse visual and visuo-motor networks

The selective constellations formed by the cortical and subcortical structures connected with areas 7ip, 7a and 7m support the conclusion that each subdivision participates in different distributed neural networks engaged in complex visual and visuo-motor functions. The 7ip network, in particular, includes a number of cortical and subcortical regions involved in the analysis of the visual space, visual motion and in oculo-motor functions. The functional domains of the 7a and 7m networks are less well defined, but we have shown that each engages unique sets of visual areas, in addition to specific limbic and motor structures. The connectional heterogeneity of the three area 7 subdivisions analyzed here leads to a depiction of the posterior parietal cortex, classically labeled as association cortex, as a complex mosaic of different areas with specific sensory, limbic and motor attributes. Moreover, this topographic diversity is likely the basis for the variety of disorders that follow damage to the posterior parietal cortex.

Acknowledgements

The experiments leading to this study were made

while CC was at Yale University sponsored by Fogarty International Fellowship TW03445. This work was supported by MH 38546 and MH 00298.

References

Andersen, R.A. (1987) Inferior parietal lobule function in spatial perception and visual motor integration. In: V.B. Mountcastle, F. Plum and S.R. Geiger (Eds.), *Handbook of Physiology., Sect. I: The Nervous System,* American Physiological Society, Bethesda MD, pp. 483 – 518.

Andersen, R.A., Asanuma, C. and Cowan, W.M. (1985) Callosal and prefrontal associational projecting cell populations in area 7a of the macaque monkey: a study using retrogradely transported fluorescent dyes. *J. Comp. Neurol.,* 232: 443 – 455.

Andersen, R.A., Essick, G.K. and Siegel, R.M. (1987) Neurons of area 7 activated by both visual stimuli and oculomotor behavior. *Exp. Brain Res.,* 67: 316 – 322.

Andersen, R.A., Asanuma, C., Essick, G. and Siegel, R.M. (1990) Corticocortical connections of anatomically and physiologically defined subdivisions within the inferior parietal lobule. *J. Comp. Neurol.,* 296: 65 – 113.

Asanuma, C., Andersen, R.A. and Cowan, W.M. (1985) The thalamic relations of the caudal inferior parietal lobule and the lateral prefrontal cortex in monkeys: divergent cortical projections from cell clusters in the medial pulvinar nucleus. *J. Comp. Neurol.,* 241: 357 – 381.

Baizer, J.S., Ungerleider, L.G. and Desimone, R. (1991) Organization of visual inputs to the inferior temporal and posterior parietal cortex in macaques. *J. Neurosci.,* 11: 168 – 190.

Bender, M.B. and Furlow, L.T. (1944) Phenomena of visual extinction and binocular rivalry mechanism. *Trans. Am. Neurol. Assoc.,* 70: 87 – 92.

Blatt, G.J., Andersen, R.A. and Stoner, G.R. (1990) Visual receptive field organization and cortico-cortical connections of the lateral intraparietal area (area LIP) in the macaque. *J. Comp. Neurol.,* 299: 421 – 445.

Brodmann, K. (1909) *Vergleichende Localisationslehre der Grosshirnrinde in Ihren Prinzipien Dargestellt auf Grund des Zellenbaues,* Barth, Leipzig.

Bruce, C.J. and Goldberg, M.E. (1984) Physiology of the frontal eye fields. *Trends Neurosci.,* 7: 436 – 446.

Bruce, C.J., Goldberg, M.E., Bushnell, M.C. and Stanton, G.B. (1985) Primate frontal eye field. II. Physiological and anatomical correlates of electrically evoked eye movements. *J. Neurophysiol.,* 54: 714 – 734.

Cavada, C. and Goldman-Rakic, P.S. (1989a) Posterior parietal cortex in rhesus monkey: I. Parcellation of areas based on distinctive limbic and sensory corticocortical connections. *J. Comp. Neurol.,* 287: 393 – 421.

Cavada, C. and Goldman-Rakic, P.S. (1989b) Posterior parietal cortex in rhesus monkey: II. Evidence for segregated corticocortical networks linking sensory and limbic areas with the frontal lobe. *J. Comp. Neurol.,* 287: 422 – 445.

Cavada, C. and Goldman-Rakic, P.S. (1991) Topographic segregation of corticostriatal projections from posterior parietal subdivisions in the macaque monkey. *Neuroscience,* 42: 683 – 696.

Colby, C.L., Gattass, R., Olson, C.R. and Gross, C.G. (1988) Topographical organization of cortical afferents to extrastriate visual area PO in the macaque: a dual tracer study. *J. Comp. Neurol.,* 269: 392 – 413.

Critchley, M. (1953) *The Parietal Lobes,* Arnold, London.

Denny-Brown, D., Meyer, J.S. and Horenstein, S. (1952) The significance of perceptual rivalry resulting from parietal lesion. *Brain,* 75: 433 – 471.

DeYoe, E.A. and Van Essen, D.C. (1988) Concurrent processing streams in monkey visual cortex. *Trends Neurosci.,* 11: 219 – 226.

Duffy, F.H. and Burchfield, J.L. (1971) Somatosensory system: organizational hierarchy from single units in monkey area 5. *Science,* 172: 273 – 275.

Felleman, D.J. and Van Essen, D.C. (1991) Distributed hierarchical processing in the primate cerebral cortex. *Cereb. Cortex,* 1: 1 – 47.

Felleman, D.J., Burkhalter, A. and Van Essen, D.C. (1987) Visual area PIP: an extrastriate cortical area in the posterior intraparietal sulcus of macaque monkeys. *Soc. Neurosci. Abstr.,* 13: 626.

Heilman, K.M., Pandya, D.N. and Geschwind, N. (1970) Trimodal inattention following parietal lobe ablations. *Trans. Am. Neurol. Assoc.,* 95: 259 – 261.

Hikosaka, O. and Wurtz, R.H. (1983) Visual and oculomotor functions of monkey substantia nigra pars reticulata. IV. Relation of substantia nigra to superior colliculus. *J. Neurophysiol.,* 49: 1285 – 1301.

Hikosaka, O., Sakamoto, M. and Usui, S. (1989) Functional properties of monkey caudate neurons I. Activities related to saccadic eye movements. *J. Neurophysiol.,* 61: 780 – 798.

Huerta, M.F., Krubitzer, L.A. and Kaas, J.H. (1986) Frontal eye field as defined by intracortical microstimulation in squirrel monkeys, owl monkeys, and macaque monkeys. I. Subcortical connections. *J. Comp. Neurol.,* 253: 415 – 439.

Hyvärinen, J. (1981) Regional distribution of functions in parietal association area 7 of monkey. *Brain Res.,* 206: 287 – 303.

Hyvärinen, J. (1982) Posterior parietal lobe of the primate brain. *Physiol. Rev.,* 62: 1060 – 1129.

Hyvärinen, J. and Poranen, A. (1974) Function of the parietal associative area 7 as revealed from cellular discharges in alert monkeys. *Brain,* 97: 673 – 692.

Hyvärinen, J. and Shelepin, Y. (1979) Distribution of visual and somatic functions in the parietal associative area 7 of the monkey. *Brain Res.,* 169: 561 – 564.

Jones, E.G. and Powell, T.P.S. (1969) Connexions of the

somatic sensory cortex of the rhesus monkey. I. Ipsilateral cortical connexions. *Brain,* 92: 477 – 502.

Krubitzer, L. and Kaas, J. (1990) Convergence of processing channels in the extrastriate cortex of monkeys. *Visual Neurosci.,* 5: 609 – 613.

Leinonen, L., Hyvärinen, J., Nyman, G. and Linnankoski, L. (1979) I. Functional properties of neurons in lateral part of associative area 7 in awake monkey. *Exp. Brain Res.,* 34: 299 – 320.

Lynch, J.C. (1980) The functional organization of posterior parietal association cortex. *Behav. Brain Sci.,* 3: 485 – 534.

Lynch, J.C. (1987) Frontal eye field lesions in monkeys disrupt visual pursuit. *Exp. Brain Res.,* 68: 437 – 441.

Lynch, J.C., Mountcastle, V.B., Talbot, W.H. and Yin, T.C.T. (1977) Parietal lobe mechanisms for directed visual attention. *J. Neurophysiol.,* 40: 362 – 389.

Lynch, J.C., Graybiel, A.M. and Lobeck, L.J. (1985) The differential projection of two cytoarchitectonic subregions of the inferior parietal lobule of macaque upon the deep layers of the superior colliculus. *J. Comp. Neurol.,* 235: 241 – 254.

Maunsell, J.H.R. and Van Essen, D.C. (1983) The connections of the middle temporal visual area (MT) and their relationship to a cortical hierarchy in the macaque monkey. *J. Neurosci.,* 3: 2563 – 2586.

Maunsell, J.H.R., Nealey, T.A. and DePriest, D.D. (1990) Magnocellular and parvocellular contributions to responses in the middle temporal visual area (MT) of the macaque monkey. *J. Neurosci.,* 10: 3323 – 3334.

May, J.G. and Andersen, R.A. (1986) Different patterns of corticopontine projections from separate cortical fields within the inferior parietal lobule and dorsal prelunate gyrus of the macaque. *Exp. Brain Res.,* 63: 265 – 278.

Mishkin, M., Ungerleider, L.G. and Macko, K.A. (1983) Object vision and spatial vision: two cortical pathways. *Trends Neurosci.,* 6: 414 – 417.

Mountcastle, V.B., Lynch, J.C., Georgopoulos, A., Sakata, H. and Acuña, C. (1975) Posterior parietal association cortex of the monkey: command functions for operations within extrapersonal space. *J. Neurophysiol.,* 38: 871 – 908.

Pandya, D.N. and Seltzer, B. (1982) Intrinsic connections and architectonics of posterior parietal cortex in the rhesus monkey. *J. Comp. Neurol.,* 204: 196 – 210.

Robinson, C.J. and Burton, H. (1980) Organization of somatosensory receptive fields in cortical areas 7b, retroinsula, postauditory and granular insula of *M. fascicularis. J. Comp. Neurol.,* 192: 43 – 67.

Robinson, D.A. and Fuchs, A.F. (1969) Eye movements evoked by stimulation of frontal eye fields. *J. Neurophysiol.,* 32: 637 – 648.

Robinson, D.L., Goldberg, M.E. and Stanton, G.B. (1978) Parietal association cortex in the primate: sensory mechanisms and behavioral modulations. *J. Neurophysiol.,* 41: 910 – 932.

Schlag, J. and Schlag-Rey, M. (1987) Evidence for a supplementary eye field. *J. Neurophysiol.,* 57: 179 – 200.

Schamahmann, J.D. and Pandya, D.N. (1990) Anatomical investigation of projections from thalamus to posterior parietal cortex in the rhesus monkey: a WGA-HRP and fluorescent tracer study. *J. Comp. Neurol.,* 295: 299 – 326.

Schwartz, A.S. and Eidelberg, E. (1968) ''Extinction'' to bilateral simultaneous stimulation in the monkey. *Neurology,* 18: 61 – 68.

Selemon, L.D. and Goldman-Rakic, P.S. (1988) Common cortical and subcortical target areas of the dorsolateral prefrontal and posterior parietal cortices in the rhesus monkey: a double label study of distributed neural networks. *J. Neurosci.,* 8: 4049 – 4068.

Seltzer, B. and Pandya, D.N. (1980) Converging visual and somatic sensory cortical input to the intraparietal sulcus of the rhesus monkey. *Brain Res.,* 192: 339 – 351.

Ungerleider, L.G. and Desimone, R. (1986) Cortical connections of visual area MT in the macaque. *J. Comp. Neurol.,* 248: 190 – 222.

Van der Steen, J., Russell, I.S. and James, G.O. (1986) Effects of unilateral frontal eye-field lesions in eye-head coordination in the monkey. *J. Neurophysiol.,* 55: 696 – 714.

Van Essen, D.C. and Maunsell, J.H.R. (1983) Hierarchical organization and functional streams in the visual cortex. *Trends Neurosci.,* 6: 370 – 375.

Vogt, C. and Vogt, O. (1919) Allgemeinere Ergebnisse unserer Hirnforschung. *J. Psychol. Neurol. (Leipzig),* 25: 279 – 461.

Von Bonin, G. and Bailey, P. (1947) *The Neocortex of Macaca Mulatta,* University of Illinois Press, Urbana, IL.

Yeterian, E.H. and Pandya, D.N. (1985) Corticothalamic connections of the posterior parietal cortex in the rhesus monkey. *J. Comp. Neurol.,* 237: 408 – 426.

T.P. Hicks, S. Molotchnikoff and T. Ono (Eds.)
Progress in Brain Research, Vol. 95
© 1993 Elsevier Science Publishers B.V. All rights reserved.

CHAPTER 13

Corticotectal relationships: direct and "indirect" corticotectal pathways

John G. McHaffie[1], Masao Norita[2], Daniel D. Dunning[1] and Barry E. Stein[1]

[1] *Department of Physiology, Medical College of Virginia, Richmond, VA 23298, U.S.A. and* [2] *Department of Anatomy, Niigata University School of Medicine, Asahimachi Niigata 951, Japan*

Introduction

Because the relationship between the visual cortex and superior colliculus is integral in the elaboration of visually-guided behaviors (e.g., Sprague and Meikle, 1965; Sprague, 1966a,b; Sherman, 1974, 1977; Hardy and Stein, 1988), it has long been a subject of interest. In an attempt to detail the anatomical substrate and the physiological mechanisms by which they interact, overwhelming emphasis had been placed on *direct* corticotectal projections. This idea is consistent with observations that numerous regions of visual cortex send projections to the superior colliculus (for review, see Huerta and Harting, 1984), that the action of corticofugal systems on superior colliculus neurons is excitatory (e.g., Ogasawara et al., 1984; Berson, 1985), and that corticotectal neurons probably use glutamate as their neurotransmitter (Streit, 1980; Fosse et al., 1984). Because the lateral suprasylvian (LS) cortex is known to be a primary source of *direct* visual cortical afferents to the deep laminae of the superior colliculus (SC) (e.g., Kawamura et al., 1978; Berman and Payne, 1982; Baleydier et al., 1983; Segal and Beckstead, 1984), the observation that visual neurons become unresponsive or unselec-

tive after LS removal (Ogasawara et al., 1984; Hardy and Stein, 1988) has been interpreted as being a consequence of losing direct corticotectal excitation. A similar interpretation has been proposed for the visual neglect seen in behavioral studies of LS-lesioned cats (Hardy and Stein, 1988).

However, there are anatomical data consistent with an *indirect* corticotectal route via the striatum and substantia nigra, an alternative pathway by which the visual cortical activity can access the deep laminae of the superior colliculus (Graybiel, 1978; Rhoades et al., 1982; Faull et al., 1986; May and Hall, 1986). Because the output neurons of the deep laminae are known to be modulated by the basal ganglia via the substantia nigra, pars reticulata (Hikosaka and Wurtz, 1983; Chevalier et al., 1985), the flow of visual information from LS into the striatum may be particularly important for normal deep lamina visual activity and the behaviors with which it is involved. However, the nature of striatal projections from visual cortical areas has only recently begun to be evaluated. Our recent experiments described here provide anatomical and physiological evidence to support this hypothesis and are consistent with the idea that, in addition to a direct influence on deep lamina neurons, LS may modulate tectospinal neurons indirectly via its projection to the striatum. Some of the findings described here have been presented previously (Dunning et al., 1990; McHaffie et al., 1991; Norita et al., 1991).

Abbreviations: SC, superior colliculus; ST, striatum; LS, lateral suprasylvian; SNr, substantia nigra, pars reticulata; CN, caudate nucleus; Pu, putamen.

Methods

Anatomical procedures

Eight cats anesthetized with sodium pentobarbital (35 mg/kg, i.p.) received pressure injections of various neuronal tracers into the lateral suprasylvian cortex, striatum, and/or superior colliculus. Following appropriate survival periods, animals were perfused, frozen sections (50 μm) were cut, and the tissue processed as necessary (see Norita et al., 1991, for methodological details).

Anterograde biocytin histochemistry

Biocytin (Sigma) was used as an anterograde tracer (King et al., 1989) to define the terminal distribution of efferents from the lateral suprasylvian cortex to the striatum and the superior colliculus. Sections were preincubated with Avidin D-HRP (1:500, Vector) and then reacted with DAB with 1% nickel chloride and 1% cobalt acetate. Sections were mounted and stained with neutral red.

Retrograde double-labeling fluorescent procedures

Stereotaxic injections of dextran tetramethylrhodamine and dextran fluorescein (25% aqueous solution; Molecular Probes, Eugene, OR) were made in superior colliculus, caudate, or putamen. After a 5 – 6 day survival, sections through visual cortex and injections sites were cut and mounted immediately; they were examined for the presence of single- and double-labeled neurons with a Nikon epifluorescent microscope. The positions of retrogradely labeled neurons were plotted with the aid of a drawing tube and the projections assessed quantitatively in some animals by counts of labeled neurons.

Physiological procedures

Twenty-one cats were anesthetized with ketamine hydrochloride (30 mg/kg, i.m.) and acepromazine maleate (0.3 mg/kg). A cranial opening was made over the lateral suprasylvian cortex (LS) to permit reversible deactivation with a cooling probe (see Ogasawara et al., 1984, for details), and indwelling cannulae were implanted bilaterally in the substan-

tia nigra for pharmacological deactivation with 1.0 M γ-aminobutyric acid (GABA). The area of nigra deactivated was approximately coextensive with the region where nigrotectal neurons are located (Harting et al., 1988). Neurons were evaluated for antidromic activation via electrodes implanted in the crossed descending tract caudal to its decussation (i.e., tectoreticulospinal tract) to determine their efferent status. Fig. 1 depicts the experimental preparation.

After surgery, animals were paralyzed with pancuronium bromide (1 mg/kg) and artificially respired with 0.5 – 1.5% halothane. The eyes were focused on a plexiglass hemisphere on which receptive fields were mapped. A neuron's responses to an optimal visual stimulus were evaluated quantitatively to establish a baseline (precool "control"). LS was then deactivated by placing the cooling probe directly on the overlying dura, and the tests were repeated ("cortical deactivation"). The area was then reactivated by rewarming the cortex with

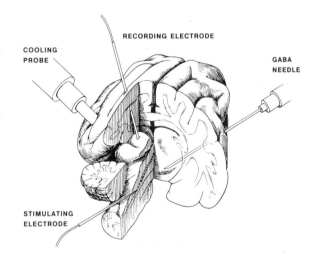

Fig. 1. A schematic depiction of the experimental preparation. Recordings were made from visual neurons in the left superior colliculus; the left lateral suprasylvian cortex was reversibly deactivated via a cooling probe, while both ipsilateral and contralateral substantia nigra (only contralateral is shown) were deactivated by GABA infused via indwelling cannulae. Stimulating electrodes, placed in the contralateral tectospinal tract of the brain-stem, were used for antidromic activation to determine the efferent status of the neuron.

mineral oil, and the tests conducted a third time (postcool/preGABA "control"). This series of tests revealed the influences of the corticotectal system(s) on that neuron but did not indicate by which route(s) these influences were exerted, since both the direct and indirect pathways were rendered inactive. Next, the functional integrity of the nigrotectal pathway was compromised by inhibiting substantia nigra activity with GABA; the neuron was again evaluated as described above ("nigra deactivation"). The area was allowed to recover by metabolic inactivation of the injected GABA, and the tests were repeated (postGABA "control"). This second series of tests revealed the influences of the presumptive indirect corticotectal system on the neuron by studying the effects of eliminating the nigrotectal link. By comparing these data to those in which both routes were inactivated by cortical cooling, the influence of the direct corticotectal projection alone was inferred.

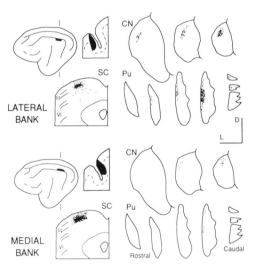

Fig. 2. The distribution of labeled fibers and terminals in the striatum and superior colliculus after injections of biocytin into the lateral (top) and medial (bottom) banks of LS. Note that the density of label in striatum is heaviest following lateral bank injections; these injections also produced labeling in the deep laminae of the superior colliculus. In contrast, medial bank injections did not produce label in the deep superior colliculus, although dense superficial labeling was present. Medial bank injections also produced less label in the striatum than did lateral bank injections. For abbreviations, see p. 139. (After Norita et al., 1991.)

Results

Anatomical experiments

Because the anatomical data about the visual corticostriatal projection are limited and, in some cases, contradictory, we first sought to establish the manner in which visual cortex projects into the striatum. We could then relate the pattern of corticofugal axon terminals seen in the striatum with the pattern of label observed in the superior colliculus from the same injection site. We chose to use the anterograde tracer biocytin, for this technique not only allows for the placement of focal injections, but also provides details concerning the morphology of terminal arborizations, thus permitting reliable distinctions between fibers-of-passage and terminal fields. Injections were made into the medial or lateral bank of LS (Fig. 2) and into areas 17/18 and 19.

Anterograde observations. Injections into the different visual areas produced markedly different patterns of labeling. Injections into area 17 resulted in dense labeling in the superficial laminae of the superior colliculus (stratum opticum and above) but produced no labeling in caudate, putamen, or deep laminae of the superior colliculus (below stratum opticum). Injections into area 19 also produced dense superficial labeling as well as some sparse labeling in the deep laminae. These injections, however, also resulted in some sparse striatal labeling, which was restricted to the tail of the caudate and the most caudal aspects of the putamen. In contrast, LS injections produced dense terminal label bilaterally in both the striatum and the superior colliculus (see Fig. 2); it was much more pronounced ipsilaterally in both structures. In the striatum, the label was restricted to the dorsolateral caudal aspect of the head of the caudate nucleus and the caudal region of the putamen. However, the relative densities and distributions of labeling in both the striatum and the superior colliculus varied according to which bank of LS was injected. Injections into the lateral bank produced dense labeling in the caudate, putamen, and both the superficial and

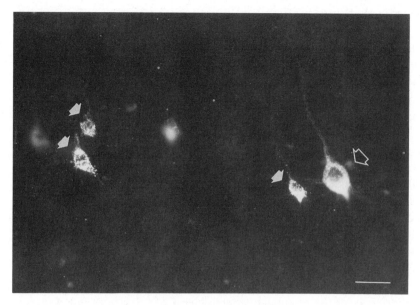

Fig. 3. Double-exposed photomicrograph of labeled pyramidal neurons in lamina V of LS following paired injections of fluorescent tracers into the caudate nucleus and superior colliculus. Solid arrows indicate corticostriatal neurons, while an open arrow marks a corticotectal neuron. Note the differences in somal sizes. With few exceptions, corticotectal and corticostriatal neurons constitute separate populations.

deep laminae of the superior colliculus; injections into the medial bank of LS produced substantially less labeling in the striatum and far less labeling in the deep superior colliculus. It appears, therefore, that the major visual input into the striatum arises *not* from primary visual cortex but from extrastriate visual areas (i.e., LS and somewhat from area 19).

Retrograde observations. Next we sought to examine the somal morphology and the laminar positions of corticostriatal and corticotectal neurons by using combined injections of retrogradely transported fluorescent dyes into the superior colliculus, caudate, and/or putamen. This strategy allowed us to determine whether corticofugal axons directed to the striatum and superior colliculus are collaterals from the same neuron or if these two pathways arise from separate populations.

Paired injections of fluorescent dyes into caudate and superior colliculus produced numerous retrogradely labeled neurons in the medial and lateral banks of LS. Corticostriatal and corticotectal neurons were intermingled in the same regions of

lamina V, indicating the topographical fidelity of the two injection sites. Some corticostriatal, but no corticotectal, neurons were found in lamina III; these neurons had a more limited distribution than those in lamina V. Within lamina V, the two populations of retrogradely labeled neurons were distributed somewhat differently, with corticotectal neurons located more ventrally than corticostriatal neurons. Soma sizes also distinguished between these neuronal populations: small to medium sized $(15-20 \ \mu m)$ pyramidal neurons proved to be corticostriatal, whereas medium to large $(20-60 \ \mu m)$ pyramidal neurons were corticotectal (see Fig. 3). Very few double-labeled neurons were observed $(0-3$ per animal); those that were found had comparatively large somas that fell within the range of sizes characteristic of corticotectal neurons. To evaluate further the segregated nature of corticostriatal neurons, we made injections into other subcortical regions targeted by corticofugal neurons. Thus, even when striatal injections were paired with injections into posterior thalamus or pontine nuclei, segregated populations of corticofugal neurons were found.

These data demonstrate that the regions of LS that give rise to the direct corticotectal projection to deep laminae of the superior colliculus also give rise to a substantial, though morphologically distinguishable, projection to the striatum. This corticostriatal component of the efferent projection from LS terminates in regions from which striatonigral projections arise (e.g., Harting et al., 1988). These, in turn, synapse on nigrotectal neurons (Rhoades et al., 1982; Williams and Faull, 1985; May and Hall 1986), which directly control the activity of descending efferents of the deep superior colliculus.

Physiological experiments

As a first step in evaluating the possible functional

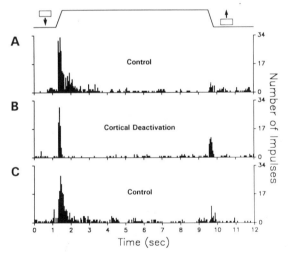

Fig. 4. Effects of cortical deactivation on the visually-evoked activity of a deep lamina superior colliculus neuron. The "control" response (*A*) to the optimal visual stimulus was moved across the receptive field in the preferred (superior → inferior) and null (inferior → superior) directions. Peristimulus time histogram bin width is 50 msec with 8 epochs. The same visual stimulus was presented beginning 1 min after initiating deactivation (cooling) of the ipsilateral LS (*B*). A statistically significant decrement (−63%, *P* < 0.02) in evoked activity was induced in the preferred direction. In this case there was also an increase in the effectiveness of the null direction (+119%, *P* < 0.05). A decrease in directional selectivity was a characteristic effect of cortical deactivation. A second "control" after LS was reactivated by warming (*C*) shows that the evoked activity returned to the "control" levels.

role of this presumptive indirect visual corticotectal pathway to deep laminae of the superior colliculus, experiments were conducted using reversible deactivation of LS alone and/or in combination with pharmacological deactivation of the last stage of the indirect (i.e., nigrotectal) pathway.

Cortical deactivation. Removing the influence of LS produced marked depression of activity in superior colliculus neurons (e.g., see also Ogasawara et al., 1984; Dunning et al., 1990). These effects were evident in 77% of the deep lamina neurons sampled (*n* = 26) as a significant (*P* < 0.05) depression in responses to a visual stimulus. Although a variety of neurons was affected, it appeared that a very high proportion (86%) of neurons that could be antidromically activated from the tectoreticulospinal tract were depressed by cortical deactivation. Thus, LS cortex exerts a significant excitatory influence on the activity of those neurons most immediately involved in overt responses, although the route(s) by which this influence is mediated cannot be determined by this method alone.

Cortical deactivation also severely degraded or eliminated directional asymmetries in most (65%) of the directionally selective neurons studied (*n* = 17). Generally, movements in the preferred direction became less effective, and in some examples there was a surprising increase in the effectiveness of movements in the least preferred (e.g., "null") direction, as shown in Fig. 4.

Nigra deactivation. Deactivation of substantia nigra produced an increase in the excitability of superior colliculus neurons in response to visual stimuli. Substantia nigra generally is considered to have inhibitory influences on the premotor responses and spontaneous activity of superior colliculus neurons (Hikosaka and Wurtz, 1983; Chevalier et al., 1984; Karabelas and Moschovakis, 1985). However, the present data, coupled with these previous observations, are consistent with a far more pervasive influence, namely that substantia nigra profoundly affects the sensory responses of

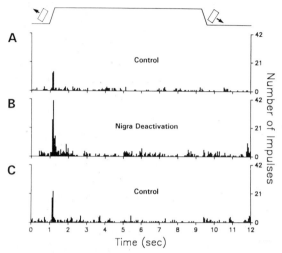

Fig. 5. The effects of bilateral substantia nigra deactivation on the visually-evoked activity of a deep lamina superior colliculus neuron. The "control" response (A) to the optimal visual stimulus was moved across the receptive field in the preferred (inferior nasal → superior temporal) and null (superior temporal → inferior nasal) directions. A statistically significant increase (+ 220%, P < 0.001) in the response to the optimal stimulus (B) occurred 3 min after initiating deactivation of substantia nigra. A second "control" after nigra was reactivated (C) shows that the evoked activity returned to the "control" levels.

superior colliculus neurons.

Typically, within 30 sec of deactivating substantia nigra by injections of GABA, the responsiveness of deep lamina neurons to the optimal visual stimulus was altered, with the effect reaching a maximum within 2 min. Usually (58% of 19 neurons tested), the effect was a statistically significant (P < 0.05) enhancement of activity as shown in a characteristic example (Fig. 5). However, in a small proportion (26%) of neurons, responses to sensory stimuli were depressed.

Although we did not attempt to determine the effects of nigra deactivation on each receptive field property (i.e., receptive field size, ocularity, velocity selectivity, etc.), direction selectivity in some deep lamina neurons became far more pronounced when the influences of nigra were removed (see Fig. 5). This enhancement of direction selectivity during nigra deactivation contrasts with the diminution of direction selectivity during LS deactivation (cf. Fig. 5 with Fig. 4). Neurons with all varieties of receptive

field properties were found to be affected by removing nigra influences. Most notably affected were those neurons that could either be identified as tectoreticulospinal (antidromically activated), or inferred to be output neurons (by virtue of their responses to multiple sensory modalities, their

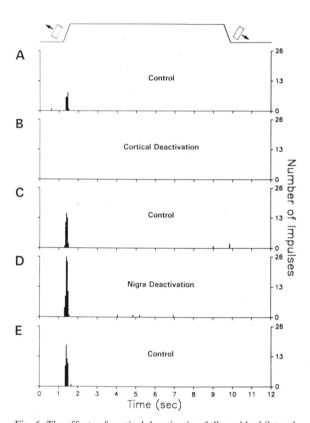

Fig. 6. The effects of cortical deactivation followed by bilateral deactivation of substantia nigra on the visually-evoked activity of a deep lamina superior colliculus neuron. The "control" response (A) to the optimal visual stimulus was moved across the receptive field in the preferred (inferior nasal → superior temporal) and null (superior temporal → inferior nasal) directions. The same visual stimulus was presented beginning 5 min after initiating deactivation (cooling) of the ipsilateral LS (B). Note that responses were eliminated. A second "control" shows that responses were reinstated after reactivating LS by warming (C). A statistically significant increase (+ 79%, P < 0.01) in the response to movement in the preferred direction occurred 3 min after initiating deactivation of substantia nigra (D). A third "control" after nigra was reactivated (E) shows that the evoked activity returned to the "control" levels. Thus, neurons that are modulated by LS cortex are also affected by substantia nigra, the last link in the indirect pathway.

binocularity and/or direction selectivity; see Meredith and Stein, 1986). Thus, the same superior colliculus neurons that are affected by deactivation of LS cortex are also affected by deactivation of substantia nigra, the last link in the indirect pathway.

The convergence of both LS and substantia nigra influences on individual deep lamina neurons was evaluated; most (78%) of those tested ($n = 18$) were affected significantly ($P < 0.05$) by both LS deactivation and nigra deactivation. The typical depression produced by LS deactivation as well as the characteristic enhancement evoked by nigra deactivation are apparent in the neuron shown in Fig. 6, which was subjected to both procedures sequentially. These data underscore the convergent nature of the direct and "indirect" corticotectal pathways in the deep laminae of the superior colliculus.

Discussion

It has been known for some time that the striatum contains visually-responsive neurons, but the source of this visual input has been in question. Widespread regions of cortex were recognized as projecting to striatum, but visual cortical inputs were thought to be sparse, because attempts to demonstrate inputs from striate cortex were largely unsuccessful (e.g., Webster, 1965; Kemp and Powell, 1970). Although these anatomical observations were essentially correct, the conclusion that visual cortex does not project to the striatum was not. Recently, it has been demonstrated in monkey that a robust corticostriatal input is derived, not from striate cortex, but from extrastriate cortical regions (Saint-Cyr et al., 1990). These visual corticostriatal projections are heaviest from an area along the medial temporal sulcus, a region considered to be the primate homologue of LS (see Van Essen et al., 1981). The present results in the cat (see also Battaglini et al., 1982; Burchinskaya et al., 1988), demonstrating a substantial corticostriatal projection from LS, are consistent with these data.

The caudal aspects of LS contain several visuotopically organized regions. Of major concern here are the regions referred to as PMLS (on the medial bank) and PLLS (on the lateral bank) by Palmer et al. (1978), which are the physiologically defined areas from which the corticostriatal projections in the present experiments were demonstrated. There are, however, significant differences between the two banks with regard to thalamic, corticotectal and intracortical connectivity. For example, PMLS receives its major thalamic input from the lateral division of the lateral posterior complex (Updyke, 1981; Raczkowski and Rosenquist, 1983), while PLLS receives its thalamic afferents from the medial division of the complex. PMLS also has far richer interconnections with areas 17, 18, 19, 20a and 21 than does PLLS (Updyke, 1981). Furthermore, the projection from PMLS to the superficial laminae of the superior colliculus is more pronounced than that from PLLS, whereas the projection to the deep laminae is denser from PLLS (Segal and Beckstead, 1984). The present experiments extend these observations by demonstrating a substantial difference between the medial and lateral banks of LS with regard to their striatal input; that is, the corticostriatal projection from the lateral bank is much more robust than that from the medial bank.

Even though LS projections to both the striatum and the superior colliculus arise from the same lamina, the fluorescent reterograde-labeling data indicate that these corticofugal projections emanate from two separate populations of neurons, each with distinct morphological features. These findings are consistent with previous reports that corticostriatal projections from primary somatosensory cortex also form a unique group of corticofugal neurons (Wise and Jones, 1977; Jones et al., 1977). The lack of significant numbers of double-labeled neurons implies that the information directed into the striatum from LS is fundamentally different from that conveyed to the superior colliculus via the direct pathway. Although the response properties of LS have been reported to be homogeneous (see Sherman and Spear, 1982, for review), there are suggestions that certain regional differences may exist (von Grünau et al., 1987); whether such distinctions exist

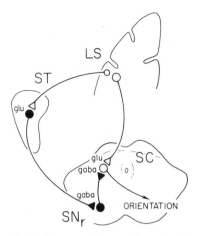

Fig. 7. Summary diagram illustrating the presumptive relationships between the direct and "indirect" corticotectal pathways. Visual areas of LS can modulate the activity of neurons in deep laminae of the superior colliculus directly via excitatory glutamatergic (glu) projections or indirectly by way of double-inhibitory GABAergic (gaba) connections through the striatum and substantia nigra. Inhibitory neurons are depicted as filled symbols; excitatory neurons as open symbols. Note that the two corticofugal pathways generally arise from morphologically distinct populations of neurons.

between the direct and indirect corticotectal pathways is not yet known. We are currently analyzing the response properties of antidromically identified LS neurons to determine what information descends via each pathway (Niida et al., 1992).

The finding of a substantial input from extrastriate visual areas into the striatum is consistent with the idea postulated by others (Graybiel, 1978; Rhoades et al., 1982; Faull et al., 1986; May and Hall, 1986) that an indirect pathway through the basal ganglia can serve as another route by which cortical visual information can affect deep lamina neurons of the superior colliculus. Although many details about the pathway remain unknown, many of the salient features exist in the literature. LS corticostriatal projections are strongly excitatory on striatal neurons (Kolomiets, 1986) and probably use glutamate as an excitatory neurotransmitter (McGeer et al., 1977; Streit, 1980; Fonnum et al., 1981). The striatum, in turn, sends a robust projection to the substantia nigra, pars reticulata (Rhoades et al., 1982; Williams and Faull, 1985;

May and Hall, 1986; Harting et al., 1988), where striatonigral axons are known to synapse directly on nigrotectal neurons (Williams and Faull, 1985). Striatonigral neurons are strongly inhibitory on nigrotectal neurons (Chevalier et al., 1984), probably using GABA as an inhibitory neurotransmitter (Feltz, 1971; Dray et al., 1976; Ribak et al., 1980; Oertel et al., 1981). Substantia nigra neurons project to deep laminae (e.g., Graybiel, 1978; Beckstead et al., 1981; Behan et al., 1987; Harting et al., 1988), where they synapse on tectospinal neurons (Chevalier et al., 1984, 1985; Williams and Faull, 1985; Karabelas and Moschovakis, 1985; May and Hall, 1986; Tokuno and Nakamura, 1987). These inputs are also strongly inhibitory (Anderson and Yoshida, 1977; Chevalier et al., 1981a, 1984; Hikosaka and Wurtz, 1983; Karabelas and Moschovakis, 1985) and also use GABA as an inhibitory neurotransmitter (Vincent et al., 1978; DiChiara et al., 1979; Araki et al., 1981; Chevalier et al., 1981b). Thus, LS cortex is "indirectly" linked to tectospinal neurons in the deep laminae of the superior colliculus via a double-inhibitory loop through the basal ganglia.

The present physiological results are consistent with the presence of this "indirect" corticotectal pathway and can be summarized as follows. First, reversible deactivation of caudal aspects of LS decreased the visual responses of deep lamina neurons, as previously observed (Ogasawara et al., 1984). Second, some of the superior colliculus neurons affected by cortical deactivation also were shown to send descending axons into the brainstem, thereby providing the first direct evidence that the LS cortex controls the activity of superior colliculus output neurons and, by inference, the visual orientation behaviors dependent on those outputs. Third, nigra deactivation dramatically enhanced the visually-evoked activity of many of these same deep lamina neurons. This suggests that the basal ganglia are involved in deep lamina *sensory processing* as well as in their well-known function of modulating premotor responses (e.g., see Hikosaka and Wurtz, 1983; Chevalier et al., 1984; Karabelas and Moschovakis, 1985). This notion is underscored by the presence of sensory responses in the striatum (e.g., Caan et al., 1984; Cherkes and Zelenskaya, 1984; Zelenskaya, 1986; Hikosaka et al., 1989; Zelenskaya and Burchinskaya, 1989) and substantia nigra (e.g., Schwarz et al., 1984; Schultz, 1986).

This cortico-striato-nigro-tectal projection not only provides an "alternate" anatomical substrate by which sensory activity in LS can modulate visual activity in the deep superior colliculus, but the neurochemistry and physiology of the constituent neurons in the indirect pathway are consistent with the experimental consequences of LS deactivation or ablation. Because LS normally *excites* striatum, its removal (as in the experiments described above) diminishes striatal activity. Since striatum tonically *inhibits* nigrotectal neurons via GABAergic inhibition, the removal of LS indirectly *disinhibits* nigrotectal neurons. Now, nigrotectal neurons, which normally *inhibit* deep lamina tectospinal neurons via GABAergic connections, increase their activity. Consequently, the predicted net effect of LS removal is the *inhibition* of tectospinal activity and the concomitant disruption of superior colliculus-mediated orientation behaviors.

Thus, the indirect pathway can provide another explanation for the profound inhibition of visual activity in deep lamina neurons following disruption of normal LS activity (Ogasawara et al., 1984; Hardy and Stein, 1988) as well as for the loss of visual orientation behaviors following LS lesions (Hardy and Stein, 1988). This circuit also suggests an explanation for the similarity in the attentive and orientation defects produced by basal ganglia and superior colliculus lesions (e.g., Adey and Lindsley, 1959; Gybels et al., 1967; Reeves and Hagamen, 1971; Marshall et al., 1974; Feeney and Wier, 1979).

The postulate of an indirect pathway also provides an attractive alternative interpretation for many puzzling consequences of cortical and midbrain lesions. For example, the inability of the superior colliculus to mediate visual orientation behaviors after cortical lesions can be viewed, at least in part, as a secondary consequence of changes in the basal ganglia induced by the loss of excitatory visual corticostriatal input. Thus, changes in striatal

activity can produce a profound depression of activity in the deep laminae via nigrotectal inhibition and, thereby, the suppression of colliculus-mediated behaviors. Recent experiments by Sprague and colleagues (Wallace et al., 1989, 1990) also have shown the importance of the nigrotectal projection in the reinstatement of visual orientation following such lesions (i.e., the "Sprague effect") by demonstrating that visual orientation capabilities induced by large cortical lesions can be reversed by lesions that eliminate the nigrotectal projection. Although the specific mechanisms underlying these effects are not completely understood, the findings do establish a complex functional interrelationship among the extrastriate visual cortex, the basal ganglia, and the superior colliculus.

By invoking this "alternative" pathway, we can also explain two perplexing behavioral observations made by Hardy and Stein (1988) regarding the functional consequences of LS lesions. First, they reported that lesions restricted to a limited portion of a visual representation in LS produced hemianopia rather than defects limited to those portions of the visual field corresponding to the topography of the lesion sites (i.e., scotomas). Because the direct corticotectal projection is topographic, one would expect a focal LS lesion to produce a scotoma that is topographically appropriate for the lesion, especially if only the direct corticotectal pathway is involved. However, the manner in which the nigrotectal component of the indirect pathway terminates in the deep laminae has much less topographical fidelity (Harting et al., 1988); thus, changes in the indirect pathway, as relayed to the superior colliculus via the nigrotectal projection, would be expected to have more widespread influences and, therefore, produce hemianopia. The second paradox relates to their observation that the visual orientation defects from LS lesions were particularly evident when an animal was required to orient and walk to a test stimulus immediately after its presentation. Deficits were often not evident when the animal simply had to move its head toward the stimulus. The presence of a complex movement-dependent deficit is a hallmark of basal ganglia-mediated sensorimotor dysfunctions and is consistent with the integral role of the indirect pathway in superior colliculus-mediated behaviors.

Acknowledgements

We wish to thank Ms. Megu Odagiri and Dr. Hideaki Shimizu for their assistance with the anatomical experiments, and Ms. Nancy London for her editorial comments. Supported in part by the Grant-in-Aid Program for Faculty of Virginia Commonwealth University (J.G.M.), a grant from the NSF International Program (J.G.M.), and NIH Grant EY06562 (B.E.S. and J.G.M.). We would also like to express our gratitude to Dr. Hiroshi Shimazu, director of the Tokyo Metropolitan Institute for Neurosciences, and the TMIN Foundation for Visiting Scientists for their generous support to J.G.M.

References

Adey, W.R. and Lindsley, D.F. (1959) On the role of the subthalamic areas in the maintenance of brain stem reticular excitability. *Exp. Neurol.,* 1: 407 – 426.

Anderson, M.E. and Yoshida, M. (1977) Electrophysiological evidence for branching nigral projections to the thalamus and the superior colliculus. *Brain Res.,* 137: 361 – 364.

Araki, M., McGeer, P.L. and McGeer, E.G. (1981) Presumptive γ-aminobutyric acid pathways from the midbrain to the superior colliculus studied by a combined horseradish peroxidase-γ-aminobutyric acid transaminase pharmacohistochemical method. *Neuroscience,* 13: 433 – 439.

Baleydier, C., Kahungu, M. and Mauguiere, F. (1983) A crossed corticotectal projection from the lateral suprasylvian area in the cat. *J. Comp. Neurol.,* 214: 344 – 351.

Battaglini, P.P., Squatrito, S., Galletti, C., Maioli, M.G. and Sanseverino, E.R. (1982) Bilateral projections from the visual cortex to the striatum in the cat. *Exp. Brain Res.,* 47: 28 – 32.

Beckstead, R.M., Edwards, S.B. and Frankfurter, A. (1981) A comparison of the intranigral distribution of nigrotectal neurons labeled with horseradish peroxidase in the monkey, cat, and rat. *J. Neurosci.,* 1: 121 – 125.

Behan, M., Lin, C-S. and Hall, W.C. (1987) The nigrotectal projection in the cat: an electron microscope autoradiographic study. *Neuroscience,* 21: 529 – 539.

Berman, N. and Payne, B.R. (1982) Contralateral corticofugal projections from the lateral suprasylvian and ectosylvian gyri in the cat. *Exp. Brain Res.,* 47: 234 – 238.

Berson, D.M. (1985) Cat lateral suprasylvian cortex: Y-cell inputs and corticotectal projection. *J. Neurophysiol.,* 53: 544 – 556.

Burchinskaya, L.F., Zelenskaya, V.S., Cherkes, V.A. and Kolomiets, B.P. (1988) Pathways for transmission of visual and auditory information to the cat caudate nucleus. *Neirofiziologiia,* 19: 385 – 393.

Caan, W., Perrett, D.I. and Rolls, E.T. (1984) Responses of striatal neurons in the behaving monkey. 2. Visual processing in the caudal neostriatum. *Brain Res.,* 290: 53 – 65.

Cherkes, V.A. and Zelenskaya, V.S. (1983) Responses of caudate nucleus neurons to different visual stimuli in the actively awake cat. *Neirofiziologiia,* 15: 370 – 376.

Cherkes, V.A. and Zelenskaya, V.S. (1984) Sensory properties of neurons of a nonspecific brain structure – the caudate nucleus. *Neirofiziologiia,* 16: 384 – 394.

Chevalier, G., Deniau, J.M., Thierry, A.M. and Feger, J. (1981a) The nigro-tectal pathway. An electrophysiological reinvestigation in the rat. *Brain Res.,* 213: 253 – 263.

Chevalier, G., Thierry, A.M., Shibazaki, T. and Feger, J. (1981b) Evidence for a GABAergic inhibitory nigrotectal pathway in the rat. *Neurosci. Lett.,* 21: 67 – 70.

Chevalier, G., Vacher, S. and Deniau, J.M. (1984) Inhibitory nigral influence on tectospinal neurons, a possible implication of basal ganglia in orienting behavior. *Exp. Brain Res.,* 53: 320 – 326.

Chevalier, G., Vacher, S., Deniau, J.M. and Desban, M. (1985) Disinhibition as a basic process in the expression of striatal functions. I. The striato-nigral influence on tectospinal/tecto-diencephalic neurons. *Brain Res.,* 334: 215 – 226.

DiChiara, G., Porceddu, M.L., Morelli, M., Mulas, M.L. and Gessa, G.L. (1979) Evidence for a GABAergic projection from the substantia nigra to the ventromedial thalamus and to the superior colliculus of the rat. *Brain Res.,* 176: 273 – 284.

Dray, A., Gonye, T.J. and Oakley, N.R. (1976) Caudate stimulation and substantia nigra activity in the rat. *J. Physiol. (Lond.),* 259: 825 – 849.

Dunning, D.D., Stein, B.E. and McHaffie, J.G. (1990) Effects of cortical and nigral deactivation on visual neurons in cat superior colliculus. *Soc. Neurosci. Abstr.,* 16: 110.

Faull, R.L.M., Nauta, W.J.H. and Domesick, V.B. (1986) The visual cortico-striato-nigral pathway in the rat. *Neuroscience,* 19: 1119 – 1132.

Feeney, D.M. and Wier, C.S. (1979) Sensory neglect after lesions of substantia nigra or lateral hypothalamus: differential severity and recovery of function. *Brain Res.,* 178: 329 – 346.

Feltz, P. (1971) Gamma aminobutyric acid and a caudato-nigral inhibition. *Can. J. Physiol. Pharmacol.,* 49: 1113 – 1115.

Fonnum, F., Storm-Mathisen, J. and Divac, I. (1981) Biochemical evidence for glutamate as neurotransmitter in the cortico-striatal and cortico-thalamic fibres in rat brain. *Neuroscience,* 6: 863 – 875.

Fosse, V.M., Heggelund, P., Iversen, E. and Fonnum, F. (1984) Effects of area 17 ablation on neurotransmitter parameters in efferents to area 18, the lateral geniculate body, pulvinar and superior colliculus in the cat. *Neurosci. Lett.,* 52: 323 – 328.

Graybiel, A.M. (1978) Organization of the nigrotectal connection: an experimental tracer study in the cat. *Brain Res.,* 143: 339 – 348.

Gybels, J.M., Meulders, M., Callens, M. and Cole, J. (1967) Disturbances of visuomotor integration in cats with small lesions of the caudate nucleus. *Arch. Int. Physiol. Biochem.,* 75: 283 – 302.

Hardy, S.C. and Stein, B.E. (1988) Small lateral suprasylvian cortex lesions produce visual neglect and decreased visual activity in the superior colliculus. *J. Comp. Neurol.,* 273: 527 – 542.

Harting, J.K., Huerta, M.F., Hashikawa, T., Weber, J.T. and Van Lieshout, D.P. (1988) Neuroanatomical studies of the nigrotectal projection in the cat. *J. Comp. Neurol.,* 278: 615 – 631.

Hikosaka, O. and Wurtz, R.H. (1983) Visual and oculomotor functions of monkey substantia nigra pars reticulata. IV. Relation of substantia nigra to superior colliculus. *J. Neurophysiol.,* 49: 1285 – 1301.

Hikosaka, O., Sakamoto, M. and Usui, S. (1989) Functional properties of monkey caudate neurons. II. *J. Neurophysiol.,* 61: 814 – 832.

Huerta, M.F. and Harting, J.K. (1984) The mammalian superior colliculus: studies of its morphology and connections. In: H. Vanegas (Ed.), *Comparative Neurology of the Optic Tectum,* Plenum, New York.

Jones, E.G., Coulter, J.D., Burton, H. and Porter, R. (1977) Cells of origin and terminal distribution of corticostriatal fibers arising from the sensory-motor cortex of monkeys. *J. Comp. Neurol.,* 173: 53 – 80.

Karabelas, A.B. and Moschovakis, A.K. (1985) Nigral inhibitory termination on efferent neurons of the superior colliculus: an intracellular horseradish peroxidase study in the cat. *J. Comp. Neurol.,* 239: 309 – 329.

Kawamura, K., Konno, T. and Chiba, M. (1978) Cells of origin of corticopontine and corticotectal fibers in the medial and lateral banks of the middle suprasylvian sulcus in the cat. An experimental study with the horseradish peroxidase method. *Neurosci. Lett.,* 9: 129 – 135.

Kemp, J.M. and Powell, T.P.S. (1970) The corticostriate projection in the monkey. *Brain,* 93: 525 – 546.

King, M.A., Louis, P.M., Hunter, B.E. and Walker, D.W. (1989) Biocytin: a versatile anterograde neuroanatomical tract-tracing alternative. *Brain Res.,* 497: 361 – 367.

Kolomiets, B.P. (1986) Involvement of visual specific and association cortex input in the shaping of neostriatal neuron response to visual stimulation in unanesthetized cats. *Neirofiziologiia,* 17: 444 – 450.

Marshall, J.F., Richardson, J.S. and Teitelbaum, P. (1974) Nigrostriatal bundle damage and the lateral hypothalamic syndrome. *J. Comp. Physiol. Psychol.,* 87: 808 – 830.

May, P.J. and Hall, W.C. (1986) The sources of the nigrotectal pathway. *Neuroscience,* 19: 159 – 180.

McGeer, P.L., McGeer, E.G., Scherer, U. and Singh, K. (1977) A glutamatergic corticostriatal path? *Brain Res.,* 128: 369 – 373.

McHaffie, J.G., Stein, B.E. and Norita, M. (1991) Corticostriatal and corticotectal projections from the cat lateral suprasylvian cortex. *Soc. Neurosci. Abstr.,* 17: 1378.

Meredith, M.A. and Stein, B.E. (1986) Visual, auditory, and somatosensory convergence on cells in superior colliculus results in multisensory integration. *J. Neurophysiol.,* 56: 640 – 660.

Niida, T., Stein, B.E. and McHaffie, J.G. (1992) Response properties of corticotectal neurons in the lateral suprasylvian cortex of cat. *Soc. Neurosci. Abstr.,* 18: 1031.

Norita, M., McHaffie, J.G., Shimizu, H. and Stein, B.E. (1991) The corticostriatal and corticotectal projections of the feline lateral suprasylvian cortex demonstrated with anterograde biocytin and retrograde fluorescent techniques. *Neurosci. Res.,* 10: 149 – 155.

Oertel, W.H., Schmechel, D.E., Brownstein, M.J., Tappaz, M.L., Ranson, D.H. and Kopin, J.J. (1981) Decrease of glutamate decarboxylase (GAD) immunoreactive nerve terminals in the substantia nigra after kainic acid lesion of the striatum. *J. Histochem. Cytochem.,* 29: 977 – 980.

Ogasawara, K., McHaffie, J.G. and Stein, B.E. (1984) Two visual corticotectal systems in cat. *J. Neurophysiol.,* 52: 1226 – 1245.

Palmer, L.A., Rosenquist, A.C. and Tusa, R.J. (1978) The retinotopic organization of the lateral suprasylvian visual areas in the cat. *J. Comp. Neurol.,* 177: 237 – 256.

Raczkowski, D. and Rosenquist, A.C. (1983) Connections of the multiple cortical areas with the lateral posterior-pulvinar complex and adjacent thalamic nuclei in the cat. *J. Neurosci.,* 3: 1912 – 1942.

Reeves, A.G. and Hagamen, W.D. (1971) Behavioral and EEG asymmetry following unilateral lesions of the forebrain and midbrain in cats. *Electroenceph. Clin. Neurophysiol.,* 30: 83 – 86.

Rhoades, R.W., Kuo, D.C., Polcer, J.D., Fish, S.E. and Voneida, T.J. (1982) Indirect visual cortical input to the deep layers of the hamster's superior colliculus via the basal ganglia. *J. Comp. Neurol.,* 208: 239 – 254.

Ribak, C.E., Vaughn, J.E., Saito, K., Barber, R. and Roberts, E. (1980) GABAergic nerve terminals decrease in the substantia nigra following hemitransections of the striatonigral and pallidonigral pathways. *Brain Res.,* 192: 413 – 420.

Saint-Cyr, J.A., Ungerleider, L.G. and DeSimone, R. (1990) Organization of visual cortical inputs to the striatum and subsequent outputs to the pallido-nigral complex in the monkey. *J. Comp. Neurol.,* 298: 129 – 156.

Schultz, W. (1986) Activity of pars reticulata neurons of monkey substantia nigra in relation to motor, sensory, and complex events. *J. Neurophysiol.,* 55: 660 – 677.

Schwarz, M., Sontag, K.-H. and Wand, P. (1984) Sensory-motor processing in substantia nigra pars reticulata in conscious cats.

J. Physiol. (Lond.), 347: 129 – 387.

Segal, R.L. and Beckstead, R.M. (1984) The lateral suprasylvian corticotectal projection in cats. *J. Comp. Neurol.,* 225: 259 – 275.

Sherman, S.M. (1974) Visual fields of cats with cortical and tectal lesions. *Science,* 185: 355 – 357.

Sherman, S.M. (1977) The effect of superior colliculus lesions upon the visual fields of cats with cortical ablations. *J. Comp. Neurol.,* 172: 211 – 223.

Sherman, S.M. and Spear, P.D. (1977) Organization of visual pathways in normal and visually deprived cats. *Physiol. Rev.,* 67: 738 – 855.

Sprague, J.M. (1966a) Interaction of cortex and the superior colliculus in mediation of visually guided behavior in the cat. *Science,* 153: 1544 – 1546.

Sprague, J.M. (1966b) Visual, acoustic, and somesthetic deficits in the cat after cortical and midbrain lesions. In: D.D. Purpura and M. Yahr (Eds.), *The Thalamus,* Columbia University Press, New York, pp. 391 – 417.

Sprague, J.M. and Meikle, T.H. (1965) The role of the superior colliculus in visually guided behavior. *Exp. Neurol.,* 11: 115 – 146.

Streit, P. (1980) Selective retrograde labeling indicating the transmitter of neuronal pathways. *J. Comp. Neurol.,* 191: 429 – 463.

Tokuno, H. and Nakamura, Y. (1987) Organization of the nigrotectospinal pathway in the cat: a light and electron microscopic study. *Brain Res.,* 436: 76 – 84.

Updyke, B.V. (1981) Projections from the visual areas of the middle suprasylvian sulcus onto the lateral posterior complex and adjacent thalamic nuclei of the cat. *J. Comp. Neurol.,* 201: 477 – 506.

Van Essen, D.C., Maunsell, J.H.R. and Bixby, J.L. (1981) The middle temporal visual area in the macaque: myeloarchitecture, connections, functional properties and topographic organization. *J. Comp. Neurol.,* 199: 293 – 326.

Vincent, S.R., Hattori, T. and McGeer, E.G. (1978) The nigrotectal projection: a biochemical and ultrastructural characterization. *Brain Res.,* 151: 159 – 164.

von Grünau, M.W., Zumbroich, T.J. and Poulin, C. (1987) Visual receptive field properties in the posterior suprasylvian cortex of the cat: a comparison between the areas PMLS and PLLS. *Vision Res.,* 27: 343 – 356.

Wallace, S.F., Rosenquist, A.C. and Sprague, J.M. (1989) Recovery from cortical blindness mediated by destruction of nontectotectal fibers in the commissure of the superior colliculus in the cat. *J. Comp. Neurol.,* 284: 429 – 450.

Wallace, S.F., Rosenquist, A.C. and Sprague, J.M. (1990) Ibotenic acid lesions of the lateral substantia nigra restore visual orientation in the hemianopic cat. *J. Comp. Neurol.,* 296: 222 – 252.

Webster, K.E. (1965) The cortico-striatal projection in the cat. *J. Anat.,* 99: 329 – 337.

Williams, M.N. and Faull, R.L.M. (1985) The striatonigral projection and nigrotectal neurons in the rat. A correlated light and electron microscopic study demonstrating a monosynaptic striatal input to identified nigrotectal neurons using a combined degeneration and horseradish peroxidase procedure. *Neuroscience,* 14: 991 – 1010.

Wise, S.P. and Jones, E.G. (1977) Cells of origin and terminal distribution of descending projections of the rat somatic sensory cortex. *J. Comp. Neurol.,* 175: 129 – 158.

Zelenskaya, V.S. (1986) Features of responses of the neurons of the caudate nucleus to various localizations of a photic stimulus in the visual field of the alert cat. *Neirofiziologiia,* 18: 241 – 250.

Zelenskaya, V.S. and Burchinskaya, L.F. (1989) Various responses of neurons of the caudate nucleus in alert cats to visual stimulation. *Neirofiziologiia,* 21: 372 – 378.

T.P. Hicks, S. Molotchnikoff and T. Ono (Eds.)
Progress in Brain Research, Vol. 95
© 1993 Elsevier Science Publishers B.V. All rights reserved.

CHAPTER 14

Abnormal visual experience and spatio-temporal properties of area 18 neurones in the cat

S. Bisti, G.P. Biral* and C. Trimarchi

Istituto di Neurofisiologia C.N.R., 56127 Pisa, Italy

Introduction

Visual information, in the cat, reaches the cortex mainly through two parallel pathways originating in the retina from the x- and y-ganglion cells. Interestingly, the two systems follow different developmental modalities. Type x ganglion cells differentiate earlier than type y and in general the x-pathway matures earlier than does the y-pathway (Walsh et al., 1983; Sur et al., 1984; Sur, 1988; Friedlander and Martin, 1989). In the process of segregation into eye-specific laminae within the LGN, the competitive interactions between axons from the two eyes are essential in promoting the right localization of the y-terminals, while the x-terminals maintain the laminar specificity even in the absence of competition (Sur, 1988; Garraghty et al., 1989). In addition, an abnormal visual experience during the first months of postnatal life interferes with the normal development of the y-system (Sherman and Spear, 1982; Sherman, 1985; Sur, 1988). The innervation of the LGN and cortical neurones by the x-fibres is first "exuberant" and then retracts, whereas the y-fibres develop by a continuous process of expansion (see Friedlander and Martin, 1989). The two systems also have a separate pattern of central projections: the geniculo-cortical

x-axons innervate only area 17, while the y-axons provide the major input to area 18 (Humphrey et al., 1985; Freund et al., 1985a,b). Consequently area 18 offers an interesting opportunity for studying the functional role of the y-system in building up the response properties of single neurones.

Visual cortical neurones are selective for several parameters of the stimulus, such as orientation, speed and direction of movement, contrast and size. Selectivity for the stimulus size represents one of the main differences between areas 17 and 18. Neurones in both areas respond to a limited range of spatial frequencies when tested with sinusoidal gratings but, when the stimulus is modulated in time, the two areas behave differently (Fig. 1). Size selectivity of each neuron in area 17 is invariant with the dynamic properties of the stimulus (Fig. 1*A*). In contrast, the size selectivity of single neurones in area 18 depends on the stimulus velocity: the higher the velocity of stimulus the larger the preferred size for any particular neuron (Fig. 1*B*). One may suppose such a size-velocity coupling to be related to a normally functioning y-input. The pattern of termination of the geniculo-cortical y-axons in area 18 supports this hypothesis. Y-fibres extend their arborization for several millimeters and often terminate in two or three separate clumps (Humphrey et al., 1985; Freund et al., 1985a,b) thus providing each neuron with inputs arising from a relatively wide retinotopic region of the LGN. This organization has been suggested to have a role in building up the spatio-

* On leave from Istituto di Fisiologia Umana , Via Campi 287, 41100 Modena, Italy.

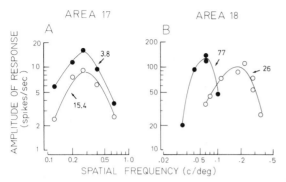

Fig. 1. Spatial-frequency tuning curves of a simple cell of area 17 (*A*) and a simple-like cell of area 18 (*B*) of normal cat. Stimulus: sinusoidal gratings drifted at constant velocity. Numbers in the figure indicate the velocities in degrees per second. Mean luminance: 7cd/m². (*A*) Contrast: 0.1. (*B*) Contrast: 0.15. (Redrawn from Bisti, 1988.)

temporal properties of area 18 neurones (Bisti, 1988).

In this study we analyzed the spatio-temporal properties of area 18 neurones by recording single unit activity in cats which had an abnormal visual experience, a condition known to interfere with the normal development of the y-system. We find that the size-velocity coupling of area 18 neurones is always abolished when the binocular convergence is altered. Two abstracts summarizing some of these results have already been presented (Bisti et al., 1989, 1990).

Methods

Experiments were performed on 10 one-year-old cats subjected, at 3 weeks of age, to surgical procedures under ketamine anaesthesia. The binocular convergence was altered in three different ways: (a) by suturing the eyelids of one eye in five kittens (monocularly deprived, MD); (b) by sectioning the optic chiasm through an oral approach in three kittens (young split-chiams cats, YSCC); and (c) by cutting the lateral rectus to induce artificial squint in two kittens. During registration, anaesthesia was induced with ketamine and maintained with a continuous infusion of sodium thiopenthal. The animal was paralyzed with pancuronium bromide. Single

unit activity has been recorded from 92 neurones in area 18 (MD, *n* = 32; YSCC, *n* = 21; strabismic *n* = 39), in correspondence with the cortical representation of the area centralis. The receptive fields of the cells were located within 10° of the area centralis (Bisti et al., 1985). On isolating a single unit we estimated the location of the receptive field in the visual space and centered the oscilloscope display (31° × 35°) on the centre of the receptive field. We evaluated the optimal orientation and direction of movement and we determined the spatial-frequency tuning curves at various velocities of drifting sinusoidal grating at fixed contrast (2 − 3 times the threshold). Cell responses were fed into a M28 Olivetti computer, which stored the raw sequence of nervous impulses and computed an on-line peristimulus time histogram (for details, see Bisti et al., 1985).

Results

Effects of monocular deprivation

We recorded single unit activity in area 18 in five cats, both ipsilaterally and contralaterally to the deprived eye. In all cells the activity was recorded during stimulation of the normal eye. Recordings obtained from the two hemispheres gave similar

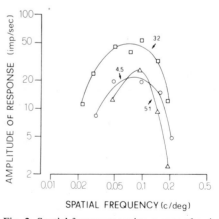

Fig. 2. Spatial-frequency tuning curves of a simple-like cell of area 18 of a monocularly deprived cat. Stimulus: sinusoidal gratings drifted at constant velocity. Numbers in the figure indicate the velocities in degrees per second. Spontaneous firing rate: 2 imp/sec. Contrast: 0.15. Mean luminance: 7 cd/m².

results. Unlike normal cats, neurones of area 18 of MD cats did not change their selectivity for spatial frequency with increasing drift velocity of the gratings.

A typical result from a simple-like cell is illustrated in Fig. 2. The amplitude of response is reported here as a function of the spatial frequency of the grating drifted at three different constant velocities. As the stimulus velocity was changed, the spatial tuning of the neuron remained largely invariant except for a scaling factor in the amplitude of response. Fig. 3 shows the spatial frequency tuning curves obtained from a binocular neuron (the only one in our sample) in response to separate stimulation of the normal eye (panel A), of the deprived eye (panel B) and to simultaneous stimulation of both eyes (panel C). In none of these three examples did velocity produce a clear shift of the tun-

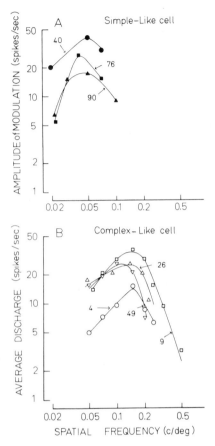

Fig. 4. Spatial-frequency tuning curves of a simple-like and a complex-like cell of area 18 of a young split-chiasm cat. Stimulus: sinusoidal gratings drifted at constant velocity. Numbers in the figure indicate the velocities in degrees per second. Contrast: 0.1. Mean luminance: 7 cd/m². Spontaneous firing rate: 3 imp/sec (A); 2.1 imp/sec (B).

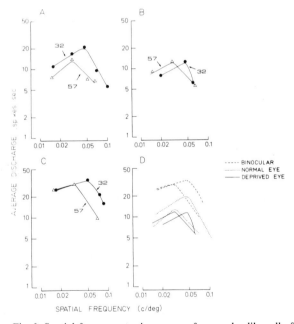

Fig. 3. Spatial-frequency tuning curves of a complex-like cell of area 18 of a monocularly deprived cat. Stimulus: sinusoidal gratings drifted at constant velocity. (A) Responses to the stimulation of the normal eye. (B) Responses to the stimulation of the deprived eye. (C) Responses to the stimulation of both eyes. (D) Curves from panels A, B, and C are superimposed. Numbers in the figure indicate the velocities in degrees per second. Spontaneous firing rate: 3.4 imp/sec. Contrast: 0.12. Mean luminance: 7 cd/m².

ing curves. This is more evident in panel D where the curves obtained by binocular stimulation envelop the curves obtained by monocular stimulation. It is interesting to note that even the few neurones with binocular input do not shift their spatial-frequency tuning curves along the spatial-frequency axis on changing the velocity of the drifting grating.

Effects of an early section of the optic chiasm

Section of the optic chiasm abolishes binocular convergence by removing the crossed projections arising from the two nasal hemiretinae. We per-

154

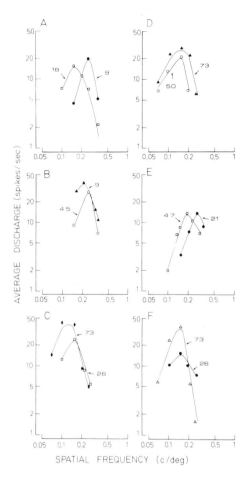

Fig. 5. Spatial-frequency tuning curves of six complex-like cells of area 18 of a strabismic cat. Stimulus: sinusoidal gratings drifted at constant velocity. Numbers in the figure indicate the velocities in degrees per second. Contrast: 0.12. Mean luminance: 7 cd/m². The six cells were recorded along a single microelectrode penetration. A. Depth: 20 μm; spontaneous firing rate: 1.2 imp/sec. B. Depth: 134 μm; spontaneous firing rate: 5.3 imp/sec. C. Depth: 236 μm; spontaneous firing rate: 3.8 imp/sec. D. Depth: 310 μm; spontaneous firing rate: 4.7 imp/sec. E. Depth: 420 μm; spontaneous firing rate: 1.6 imp/sec. F. Depth: 602 μm; spontaneous firing rate: 1.3 imp/sec.

formed the surgery at 3 weeks of age when the visual system is still endowed with a high degree of plasticity. In Fig. 4 the response amplitude recorded from single neurones in area 18 of YSCC is plotted against the spatial frequency (a simple-like cell in panel A and a complex-like cell in panel B). As with MD cats, the two cells remained tuned to the same range of

spatial frequencies at all velocities. Similar effects were observed in all neurones of our sample. These results show that the surgical suppression of binocular convergence is sufficient to induce a functional rearrangement of the spatio-temporal properties of area 18 neurones.

Effects of strabismus

The section of the lateral rectus (artificial squint) is the third experimental procedure we used to alter the cortical convergence of the binocular input. Single unit recordings in strabismic animals showed complex results. Neurones with normal and modified spatio-temporal properties were found along the same electrode penetration. Fig. 5 reports the spatial-frequency tuning curves obtained from six complex-like cells recorded along a single microelectrode penetration. The responses presented in panels A and E were recorded from neurones 400 μm apart. It is seen that the spatial frequency tuning curves shift by an amount equivalent to that described for normal animals. We must emphasize, however, that in this preparation, among size-velocity coupled cells, we also found other neurones in which the spatial frequency selectivity was invariant with velocity (panels B, C, D, F). In our sample 11 out of 34 cells (32%) maintained the normal properties. Similar behaviour was also observed in simple-like cells (Fig. 6).

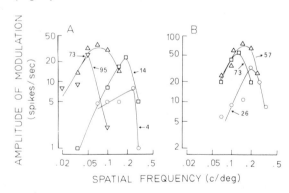

Fig. 6. Spatial-frequency tuning curves of two simple-like cells of area 18 of a strabismic cat. Stimulus: sinusoidal gratings drifted at constant velocity. Numbers in the figure indicate the velocities in degrees per second. Contrast: 0.15. Mean luminance: 7 cd/m². Spontaneous firing rate: 1.5 imp/sec (A); 3.6 imp/sec (B).

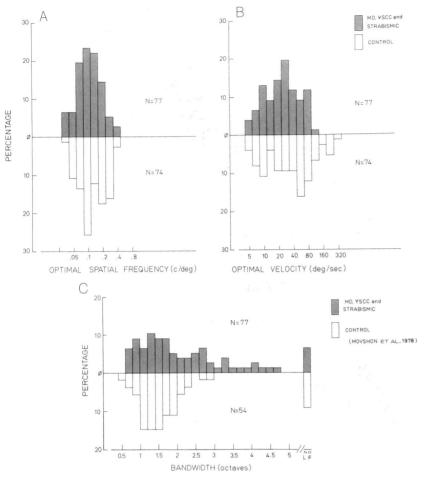

Fig. 7. Histograms of distribution of optimal spatial frequency (*A*), optimal velocity (*B*) and spatial tuning bandwidth (*C*) for neurones recorded in area 18 of monocularly deprived, strabismic and young split-chiasm cats (dashed columns) and normal animals (open columns). Data are reported as percentage of the total number of cells (MD, YSCC and strabismic cats, *n* = 77; control animals, *n* = 74 in *A* and *B*, *n* = 54 in *C*). In *C*, data obtained in experimental animals are compared with results reported by Movshon et al. (1978). The neurones which had no low spatial frequency decline in sensitivity are included as "no LF" (i.e., no low frequency cut).

Optimal spatial frequency, optimal velocity and bandwidth in MD, YSCC, strabismic and normal cats

Results reported in the previous sections show that disruption of binocular convergence early in life either abolishes or reduces the size-velocity coupling in area 18 neurons. This effect may be ascribed to an abnormal development of the y-system. One may conceive that other properties of the visual neurones are also influenced. We explored this possibility by analysing optimal spatial frequency, optimal velocity and spatial frequency tuning bandwidth for 77 cells recorded in the three groups of animals in which binocularity was altered, and by comparing

these data with those obtained in control animals. The histograms of distribution of optimal spatial frequency, optimal velocity and spatial-frequency tuning bandwidth are reported in Fig. 7 as a percentage of the total number of cells. The distributions of optimal spatial frequency (Fig. 7*A*) and optimal velocity (Fig. 7*B*) are very similar to those obtained in control animals with only a slight tendency in control animals to respond to higher velocities. The most significant difference between the two samples is in the distribution of the spatial tuning bandwidth (Fig. 7*C*) . Specifically, 15% of the investigated neurones in cats raised with abnormal binocular convergence show a much broader band tuning than control animals, but the majority maintains a nor-

156

mal size selectivity. The control data shown in Fig. 7C are replotted from Movshon et al. (1978).

Conclusions

The main finding reported in this paper is that abnormal binocular vision induced during the critical period abolishes the spatio-velocity coupling of area 18 neurones. Each cell maintains selectivity for a number of parameters of the visual stimulus, including size, but size selectivity is no longer dependent on velocity. We assume that this functional change in the response properties reflects an altered development of the y-system, which represents the major input to area 18, and is known to be particularly susceptible to an abnormal binocular experience. Unfortunately, it is impossible to separate the contribution of the geniculo-cortical y-input from that of the visual cortical area to which it projects. Certainly the spatial-frequency tuning curves of cortical neurones are much narrower than those of cells in the retina and LGN (see Derrington, 1984, for reference); consequently the observed increase in the spatial bandwidth suggests an involvement of cortical circuitry.

Several hypotheses have been advanced on the possible role of area 18 in visual perception and the general agreement is that this area plays an important role in motion perception, particularly perception of motion in depth (see for reference: Cynader and Regan, 1982; Orban et al., 1988) . The observation that a given neuron can respond to a wide range of stimuli differing in size suggests that the dynamic properties of these cells are consistent with a role in the perception of an object moving in depth, a condition in which the size of the retinal image expands or contracts. Normally the process of following an object moving in depth is associated with binocular neural convergence and vergent eye movements. In this respect it is interesting to point out that the binocular neural convergence is an important feature of area 18, and that during development the number of binocular neurones increases with time. Ocular dominance shifts from a contralateral monocular distribution at 2 weeks to an adult binocular distribution at about 10 weeks (Milleret et al., 1988; see also Friedlander and Martin, 1989), and the percentage of binocularly driven neurones of a normal adult can not be attained in the absence of visual experience (see Milleret et al., 1988, for reference). In addition, in this area, the representation of the visual field is limited to the binocular portion (Tusa et al., 1979).

In this paper we have reported data showing that animals with a disturbed binocular vision loose the spatio-velocity coupling in area 18 neurones, thus reinforcing the suggestion that spatio-temporal coupling is associated with the perception of motion in depth.

Acknowledgements

We wish to thank Dr. D.C. Burr, Dr. L. Cervetto and Dr. M.C. Morrone for helpful discussion and critical reading of the manuscript. We thank Mr. M. Antoni, Mr. A. Tacchi and Mr. P. Taccini for their excellent technical work. We are gratefully indebted to Drs. Burr and Morrone for providing the computer program. Supported by the European Community Stimulation Action Program (contract: SC1* – 0224 – C).

References

Bisti, S. (1988) Role of visual areas 17 and 18 of the cat in pattern vision. In: T.P. Hicks and G. Benedek (Eds.), *Vision within Extrageniculo-striate Systems – Progress in Brain Research, Vol. 75,* Elsevier, Amsterdam, pp. 173 – 179.

Bisti, S., Carmignoto, G., Galli, L. and Maffei, L. (1985) Spatial frequency characteristics of neurones of area 18 in the cat: dependence on the velocity of the visual stimulus. *J. Physiol. (Lond.),* 359: 259 – 268.

Bisti, S., Biral, G.P. and Trimarchi, C. (1989) Lack of binocularity changes the spatio – temporal characteristics of neurons in visual area 18 of the cat. *Soc. Neurosci. Abstr.,* 15: 793.

Bisti, S., Biral, G.P. and Trimarchi, C. (1990) Role of the visual area 18 in the perception of motion in depth. *Perception,* 19: 331.

Cynader, M. and Regan, D. (1982) Neurons in cat visual cortex tuned to the direction of motion in depth: effect of positional disparity. *Vision Res.,* 22: 967 – 982.

Derrington, A.M. (1984) Development of spatial frequency

selectivity in striate cortex of vision-deprived cats. *Exp. Brain Res.,* 55: 431 – 437.

Freund, T.F., Martin, K.A.C. and Whitteridge, D. (1985a) Innervation of cat visual areas 17 and 18 by physiologically identified X- and Y-type thalamic afferents. I. Arborization patterns and quantitative distribution of postsynaptic elements. *J. Comp. Neurol.,* 242: 263 – 274.

Freund, T.F., Martin, K.A.C., Somogyi, P. and Whitteridge, D. (1985b) Innervation of cat visual areas 17 and 18 by physiologically identified X- and Y-type thalamic afferents. II. Identification of postsynaptic targets by GABA immunocytochemistry and Golgi impregnation. *J. Comp. Neurol.,* 242: 275 – 291.

Friedlander, M.J. and Martin, K.A.C. (1989) Development of y-axon innervation of cortical area 18 in the cat. *J. Physiol. (Lond.),* 416: 183 – 213.

Garraghty, P.E., Roe, A.W., Chino, Y.M. and Sur, M. (1989) Effects of convergent strabismus on the development of physiologically identified retinogeniculate axons in cats. *J. Comp. Neurol.,* 289: 202 – 212.

Humphrey , A.L., Sur, M., Ulrich, D.J. and Sherman, S.M. (1985) Termination pattern of X- and Y-cell axons in the visual cortex of the cat: projections to area 18, to the 17/18 border region, and to both areas 17 and 18. *J. Comp. Neurol.,* 233: 190 – 212.

Milleret, C., Gary-Bobo, E. and Buisseret, P. (1988) Comparative development of cell properties in cortical area 18 of normal and dark-reared kittens. *Exp. Brain Res.,* 71: 8 – 20.

Movshon, J.A., Thompson, I.D. and Tolhurst, D.J. (1978) Spatial and temporal contrast sensitivity of neurones in area 17 and 18 of the cat's visual cortex. *J. Physiol. (Lond.),* 283: 101 – 120.

Orban, G.A., Gulyas, B. and Spileers, W. (1988) Influence of moving textured backgrounds on responses of cat area 18 cells to moving bars. In: T.P. Hicks and G. Benedek (Eds.), *Vision within Extrageniculo-striate Systems – Progress in Brain Research, Vol. 75,* Elsevier, Amsterdam, pp. 137 – 145.

Sherman, S.M. (1985) Functional organization of the W-, X-, and Y-cell pathways in the cat: a review and hypothesis. In: J.M. Sprague and A.N. Epstein (Eds.), *Progress in Psychobiology and Physiological Psychology, Vol. 11,* Academic Press, New York, pp. 233 – 313.

Sherman, S.M. and Spear, P.D. (1982) Organization of visual pathways in normal and visually deprived cats. *Physiol. Rev.,* 62: 738 – 856.

Sur, M. (1988) Development and plasticity of retinal X and Y axon terminations in the cat's lateral geniculate nucleus. *Brain Behav. Evol.,* 31: 243 – 251.

Sur, M., Weller, R.E. and Sherman, S.M. (1984) Development of X- and Y-cell retinogeniculate terminations in kittens. *Nature,* 310: 183 – 185.

Tusa, R.J., Rosenquist, A.C. and Palmer, L.A. (1979) Retinotopic organization of areas 18 and 19 in the cat. *J. Comp. Neurol.,* 185: 657 – 678.

Walsh, C., Polley, E.H., Hickey, T.L. and Guillery, R.W. (1983) Generation of cat retinal ganglion cells in relation to central pathways. *Nature,* 302: 611 – 614.

T.P. Hicks, S. Molotchnikoff and T. Ono (Eds.)
Progress in Brain Research, Vol. 95
© 1993 Elsevier Science Publishers B.V. All rights reserved.

CHAPTER 15

Visual behavior following lesion of phasic W-fibers in the cat's optic tract

C.A. Marzi, G. Tassinari and B.E. Reese[1]

Istituto di Fisiologia Umana, Universita di Verona, Verona, Italy; and [1] Department of Psychology and Neuroscience Research Institute, University of California, Santa Barbara, U.S.A.

Introduction

It is widely known that the visual system of cats, as well as that of other mammals, can be subdivided into at least three channels originating from different morphological types of retinal ganglion cells (Stone, 1983; Sherman, 1985): alpha cells are characterized by a large soma, extensive dendritic arbors and a thick axon; beta cells have a medium-sized soma and axon and a small but densely branched dendritic arbor; finally, gamma cells have a small-to-medium soma and axon and a sparsely branched dendritic tree.

There is convincing evidence that the above morphological categories correspond to the well-known physiological classification of retinal ganglion cells in terms of their transient and sustained response properties (Stanford and Sherman, 1984). A!pha cells correspond to transient or Y-cells, beta correspond to sustained or X-cells and gamma represent a rather heterogeneous population corresponding to W-cells which are characterized by a sluggish response to light (see Stone, 1983; Sherman, 1985, for reviews). Importantly, the segregation of these three main pathways continues both at the levels of the lateral geniculate nucleus (LGN) and visual cortex (Ferster, 1990).

Notwithstanding the wealth of single-cell data on the response properties to visual stimuli of the different types of ganglion cells and of their target LGN and cortical neurons, there is little direct behavioral evidence in the cat on the role of these different channels in vision. Burke et al. (1987) have studied cats following degeneration of the Y-fibers caused by pressure block. The only selective impairment which was found concerned a reduction in the ability to discriminate fast motion. Another direct attempt at testing visual behavior following selective lesioning of the Y-channel is that of Spear and coworkers (Spear et al., 1986). They found that cats that had received intraocular injections of antibodies against Y-retinal ganglion cells showed an impairment in orienting with eye and head movements to stimuli presented to the nasal hemifield of the injected eye.

On the basis of this evidence, one is led to conclude that the Y-system is mainly concerned with spatial orientation to peripheral stimuli and with perception of movement. It is interesting to mention that, in contrast to such a view, Sherman (1985) hypothesizes an important role of this system in the overall analysis of form.

No direct behavioral experiment has so far been carried out, to the best of our knowledge, to assess the role of the X- and W-channel in the cat. The retinal distribution of X-cells (with a highly dense concentration in the area centralis), their receptive fields' small size and their response properties, suggest that the sustained (X) channel is crucial for high spatial resolution (Stone, 1983; Sherman, 1985).

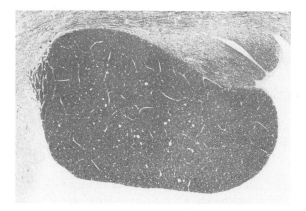

Fig. 1. Photomicrograph of a semithin section stained for myelin, cut transversely through the optic tract of a normal cat. Note that in the superficial (and middle) part of the tract the axons with the largest diameter are contained. Fine fibers are visible both in the superficial and in the deepest part of the section, while the intermediate portion contains medium-sized axons. We have recently confirmed (Reese et al., 1991) with retrograde HRP transport previous evidence (see Stone, 1983) that the largest axons correspond to retinal alphas, the medium-sized fibers arise from the betas, the fine fibers deep in the optic tract arise from the medium sized (presumably tonic) gammas, while the fine fibers superficially arise from the small-sized (presumably phasic) gamma cells.

Little can be said about the functions of W-cells other than they might be instrumental in various forms of automatic functioning of the visual system such as, possibly, the pupillary light reflexes. Finally, it is important to mention that recently Stanford (1987) has provided conjoint morphological and physiological evidence for two distinct types of W-cells: tonic and phasic.

Our general approach to the study of the role in visual behavior of the three main parallel pathways of the cat is to try and interfere selectively with each of these pathways by taking advantage of the fact that optic axons are partially segregated by their functional classes within the mammalian optic tract (OT) (Fig. 1; Guillery et al., 1982).

By using a transbuccal approach through the roof of the mouth and with the aid of an operating microscope we performed partial transections of either the superficial, subpial half of the OT immediately caudal to the optic chiasma or of the deep,

dorsal, part. The first type of transection is aimed at removing the majority of coarse (i.e., Y) fibers while leaving most of the medium-sized (i.e., X) fibers intact. Notice, however, that the small axons lying in the superficial tract are inevitably severed along with the coarse axons. We know from parallel anatomical work (Reese et al., 1991) that these small (i.e., W) axons arise from the whole contralateral retina and are likely to correspond to the above mentioned phasic W-cells (Stanford, 1987). The latter type of transection (which incidentally is much more difficult to carry out with a transbuccal approach) is instead aimed at transecting most of the fibers of the X-cells along with those of the tonic W-cells while leaving Y- and phasic W-fibers relatively intact.

In the present article we shall be concerned only with the behavioral results gathered in animals which underwent a superficial lesion of the OT, removing a vast majority of phasic W-fibers and part of the Y-fibers but almost entirely sparing X-fibers and tonic W-fibers.

We tested pattern and form discrimination learning to find out whether a total removal of the phasic W-input might interfere with higher level visual functions. An additional reason for testing pattern and form was to test Sherman's ideas on the crucial role of the Y-system for form perception (Sherman, 1985) in animals with a sizeable decrease of Y-input. Finally, given that the Y-system is widely considered to be important for temporal resolution we have tested flicker discrimination at various flicker rates and at various levels of stimulus luminance.

Methods

Surgery

In three adult cats, anesthetized with sodium pentobarbitone (40 mg/kg), the chiasmatic region was approached by a transbuccal route (Myers, 1955; Berlucchi and Rizzolatti, 1968). The superficial portion of both OTs was removed by aspiration about 1 mm caudal to the posterior end of the optic chiasm. Following completion of the lesion, the chiasmatic region was covered with gelfoam and a thin film of plastic and the soft palate was sutured and closed. The cats were administered antibiotics and allowed to recover for 2-3 weeks before retesting began. For all three animals post-operative survival time was 12 – 13 months.

Histology

Perfusions were carried out while each cat was heavily anesthetized with sodium pentobarbitone (see Reese et al., 1991, for details). The OTs caudal to the transections were dissected, osmicated and embedded in resin, and semithin sections were cut transversely through each OT and stained with *p*-phenylenediamine so as to have a qualitative estimate of the extent of anterograde axonal degeneration (See Reese et al., 1991, for details).

Behavior

Formal behavioral testing was carried out in a modified and partially automated Thompson box and included two flux-equated form discriminations and contrast sensitivity tested at two spatial frequencies in the range of the low-middle frequencies of the cat's contrast sensitivity function (see Blake, 1988, for a recent review). The stimuli were

Fig. 2. Photomicrograph of a semithin section of one optic tract of cat C1 (survival time, 13 months), cut transversely central to a superficial transection. Only fibers in the superficial part of the tract have undergone complete degeneration and have been substituted by myelin debris. The deeper fibers appear intact. Among them one can notice many large-sized axons as well as fine and middle ones. Location and extent of degeneration in the optic tract of the other side was very similar.

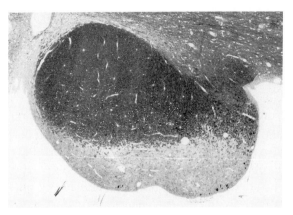

Fig. 3. Photomicrograph of a semithin section of one optic tract of cat C4 (survival time, 12 months), cut central to a transection of the superficial part of the optic tract somewhat deeper than that in Fig. 2. Again, there are various large axons spared in the middle portion of the tract and all deeper fibers are intact. A similar extent and location of the degenerated area was present in the optic tract of the other side.

back-projected onto two side-by-side translucent panels. The panel displaying the correct stimulus, if pushed open, disclosed a food container from which the cat was allowed to eat a piece of beef kidney. The panel displaying the negative stimulus was locked and could not be pushed open. Following pressing of the incorrect panel the cat was allowed to push open the other panel and eat the food. After completion of each trial the stimuli went off and the cat was trained to run back to the starting position in order to interrupt a photoelectric beam which switched on again the stimuli for the subsequent trial. Usually, each daily session consisted of 40 trials and there were 5 – 6 sessions in a week.

Finally, in the same apparatus as the one described above, we tested the animals in a discrimination of flicker using red-LEDs at various light intensity and various flicker frequencies. The animal's task was to discriminate between a flickering and a steady red light seen through the two above translucent panels. To make sure that the animals were not relying for their discrimination on possible intensity cues, we reversed the brightness of the positive and negative stimuli at the end of the flicker discrimination problem.

Prior to formal testing all the animals were trained to master the discrimination strategy by learning an easy light-dark discrimination to a criterion of 90% correct trials in two consecutive sessions.

Subjects

A total of nine adult male cats were used for this study. Two animals (C4 and C6) were tested both pre- and post-operatively (except for flicker discrimination, which was tested only post-operatively). One cat (C1) was tested only post-operatively and the remaining six animals (C8, C9, C10, C11, C12 and C13) served as normal controls. It is interesting to mention that one of the intact controls used (C8) was a Siamese cat, a strain which has been reported to have (among other abnormalities) an abnormal visual resolution (Blake and Antoinetti, 1976). However, in the present study there were no noticeable differences with respect to the other intact ordinary cats and its results will be described together with those of the other animals.

Results

Histology

The microscopic examination of semithin sec-

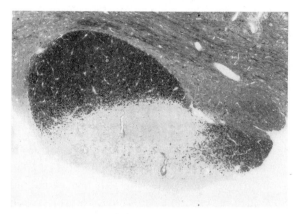

Fig. 4. Photomicrograph of a semithin section of one optic tract of cat C6 (survival time, 12 months) central to a transection of the superficial part of the optic tract. Such transection is deeper than those in Figs. 2 and 3 and leaves very few, if any, large axons spared while middle-sized and fine axons in the deep part of the tract are intact. The lesion in the optic tract of the other side was much shallower than this one and similar in extent and location to that shown in Fig. 2.

tions of both OTs in each cat showed that in all cases there was an interruption of fibers in the most superficial portion of the OT. However, the extent and depth of the transection varied from animal to animal. C1 had a bilaterally symmetric, very superficial lesion which was probably sufficient to sever

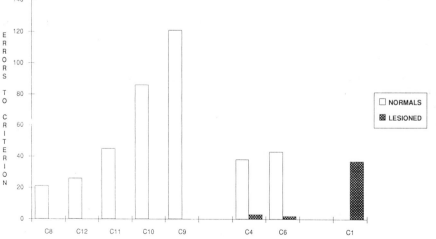

Fig. 5. Performance of normal and lesioned cats in the discrimination of an orientation discrimination. Two animals, C4 and C6, have been tested both before and after the lesion. One animal (C1) has been tested only post-operatively.

most phasic W-axons but left the vast majority of Y-fibers intact (Fig. 2). C4 had a deeper, bilaterally symmetric lesion which should remove all phasic W-fibers and interfere with a considerable proportion of Y-fibers (Fig. 3). Finally, C6 had an asymmetric lesion with the left OT being severed to a rather great depth so as to interrupt not only all phasic W-input but also the great majority of Y-fibers (Fig. 4). The right OT, on the other hand, had a very shallow lesion, still deep enough to interrupt phasic W-fibers, but insufficient for severing substantial numbers of Y-axons.

Summing up then, all three animals received lesions which we believe were deep enough to remove most phasic W-input to the visual centers. One animal (C1) had practically no additional damage to the other channels, another one (C4) had some involvement of the Y-system on both sides and finally, the third animal (C6) had one OT practically devoid of phasic W- as well as Y-fibers but the other OT was almost entirely spared except for the most superficial portion.

Behavior

Post-operative recovery in the three operated animals was uneventful and there were no obvious neurological symptoms. Binocular and monocular visual field size, as tested with a method similar to that used by Sherman and Sprague (1979) was within normal range.

Pattern and form discriminations. Figs. 5 and 6 show the results (number of errors to criterion, i.e., 90% correct in two consecutive sessions) of normal controls and operated animals (pre- and post-operative testing) on a pattern (vertical vs. horizontal black and white stripes) and a form (circle vs. plus) discrimination.

In both discrimination problems there is little doubt that the lesion did not cause any effect given that there was an almost perfect post-operative retention in the two cats (C4 and C6) tested before and after lesion. Moreover, the animal which was tested only following the OT lesion (C1) had a level of performance within the range of that of normal control animals.

Contrast sensitivity at two spatial frequencies. Fig. 7 shows the performance of six cats tested in the discrimination of vertical stripes of a

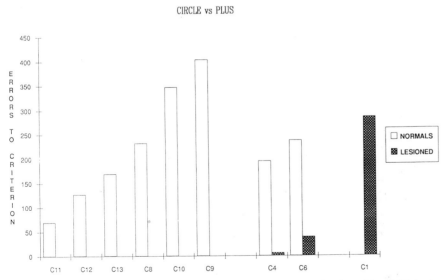

Fig. 6. Performance of normal and lesioned animals in a form discrimination. C4 and C6: both pre- and post-operative testing; C1: only post-operative testing.

164

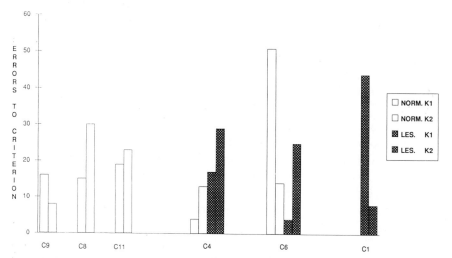

CONTRAST SENSITIVITY 0.1 c/d K1=17% K2=7.5%

Fig. 7. Performance of normal and lesioned animals in the discrimination of a sinusoidal grating of a spatial frequency of 0.1 c/d from a homogeneous grey of similar average luminance. Two contrast values (17% and 7.5%) were used. C4 and C6: both pre- and post-operative testing; C1: post-operative testing only.

spatial frequency of 0.1 c/d (cycles/degree) from a homogeneous grey of the same overall luminance as the striped pattern. Two contrast levels were tested in two separated discimination tasks: 17% and 7.5%.

One animal (C4) did not show post-operative retention of the discrimination at both contrast levels; however, the overall number of errors to re-attain criterion was very low and therefore the effect of the lesion can be considered as trivial. The same

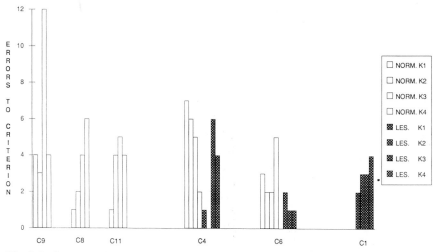

CONTRAST SENSITIVITY 0.5 c/d K1=20% K2=7.5% K3=6% K4=4.5%

Fig. 8. Performance of normal and lesioned animals in the discrimination of a sinusoidal grating of a spatial frequency of 0.5 c/d from a homogeneous grey of similar average luminance. Four contrast values were used (20%, 7.5%, 6% and 4.5%). C4 and C6: both pre- and post-operative testing; C1: post-operative testing only.

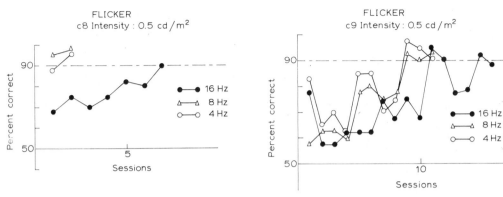

Fig. 9. Performance of two normal cats C8 (left-hand side) and C9 (right-hand side) in the discrimination of a light flickering at different rates from a steady light.

reasoning applies to the slight post-operative retention impairment of C6 at the 7.5% contrast level. Finally, the post-operative performance of C1 was within the normal range.

Fig. 8 shows the performance of the same six animals as above with gratings of a spatial frequency of 0.5 c/d tested at four contrast levels (20%, 7.5%, 6% and 4.5%) in successive discrimination tasks.

Clearly, both retention and post-operative original learning were not affected by the lesion in any animal.

Flicker discrimination. Four of the above animals were initially trained to learn to discriminate a light flickering at 4 c/sec from a steady light of similar hue and luminance (1.2 cd/m²). There were no noticeable differences among normal, control

animals and operated animals during this initial phase of original learning with stimuli of relatively high luminance. It is important to mention that the lesioned animals (C4 and C6) learned the flicker discrimination when already operated and therefore do not have a pre-post comparison for this task.

We then tested the animals at a lower intensity level (0.5 cd/m²) at three different frequencies: 4 c/sec, 8 c/sec and 16 c/sec. On each session only one frequency was tested and the different frequencies were intermingled in an unpredictable order throughout various days of testing. Figs. 9 and 10 show the performance of normal and operated animals, respectively, during several testing sessions.

In all animals it took longer to reach the level of 90% correct responses for the highest flicker fre-

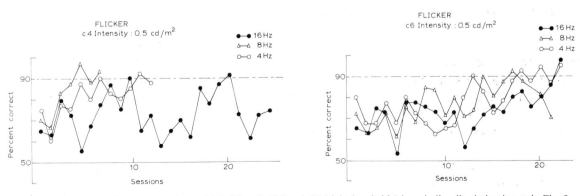

Fig. 10. Performance of two operated cats C4 (left-hand side) and C6 (right-hand side) in a similar discrimination as in Fig. 9.

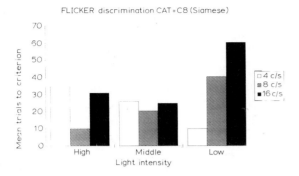

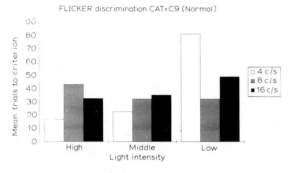

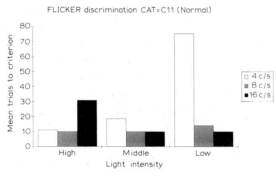

Fig. 11. Performance of three normal cats C8 (top), C9 (middle) and C11 (bottom) in a flicker discrimination at three different rates and three different luminance levels (1.2 cd/m^2; 0.5 cd/m^2; 0.3 cd/m^2).

quency than for the other two; however, performance at all frequencies was clearly worse for the two operated animals (Fig. 10). Particularly striking was the difference between the normal cat C8 on the one hand and the two operated cats C4 and C6 on the other.

Finally, we tested the above cats plus one more normal animal (C11) using a method of limits for threshold's assessment. Using a performance criterion of no more than 1 error in a total of 10 consecutive trials, testing began with the lowest frequency (4 c/d) and the highest of three decreasing levels of stimulus luminance (1.2 cd/m^2; 0.5 cd/m^2; 0.3 cd/m^2). Once criterion was reached on each of these luminance values, the animal was tested with a higher flicker frequency. If a cat did not reach criterion after three consecutive sessions on any particular combination of frequency and luminance, testing was interrupted.

Figs. 11 and 12 show the performance of normal and operated cats, respectively; all animals found the task more difficult at the lowest luminance level but only the two operated animals failed to reach criterion at one (C4) or two (C6) flicker frequencies (notice, however, the bad performance of normal cat C11 at 4 c/sec for the low luminance condition).

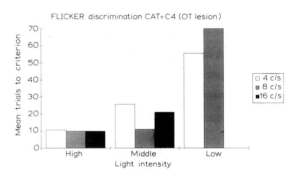

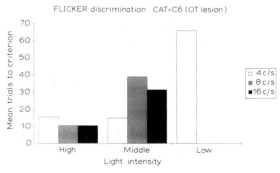

Fig. 12. Performance of two operated animals C4 (top) and C6 (bottom) in the same flicker discrimination task as in Fig. 11. C4 was not tested at low luminance level with a 16 c/sec flickering light because it did not reach criterion at the preceding flicker rate. The same applies to C6 which did not reach criterion at 4 c/sec with low luminance stimuli. Criterion: at least 10 correct consecutive responses (allowing one error) in no more than three consecutive 40-trial sessions.

Conclusions

All in all, these results show that a presumably complete removal of the phasic W-input as well as a reduced (but by no means complete) Y-input to the visual centers does not impair pattern and form discrimination. Such a result is not surprising in the light of the evidence of Galambos et al. (1967) that cats with a destruction of up to 80 – 90% of the OT can still master flux-equated form discriminations. The novel and potentially interesting finding of the present study is that flicker discrimination at a low luminance level is impaired in two animals which underwent a section of the supérficial portion of the OT. If confirmed on other animals and, perhaps more importantly, if confirmed by a study (now in progress) comparing the performance of the same animals before and after the selective OT lesion, one might tentatively argue that phasic W-fibers are important for temporal resolution at low luminance levels. It is hard to decide whether the impairment found in our two animals is related to the presumably total removal of the phasic W-input or to the largely partial interference with the Y-input. This problem can be tackled only by studying cats with complete lesions of the Y-system.

On a more general ground, our results seem to show a promising dissociation of symptoms following transection of the superficial portion of the OT, i.e., an impairment of temporal resolution and a substantial integrity of spatial discrimination functions, as witnessed by an unimpaired discrimination of bars of different contrast and spatial frequency. It would be most interesting to find an opposite dissociation, i.e., an impaired spatial resolution and an intact temporal resolution following selective lesioning of the X-fibers and tonic W-fibers running in the deeper portion of the OT.

Acknowledgements

This research was supported by an E.T.P. twinning grant from the European Science Foundation (8823) and by Contratto CMR: 89.01703.04.

References

Berlucchi, G. and Rizzolatti, G. (1968) Binocularly driven neurons in visual cortex of split-chiasm cats. *Science,* 159: 308 – 310.

Blake, R. (1988) Cat spatial vision. *Trends Neurosci.,* 11: 78 – 83.

Blake, R. and Antoinetti, D.N. (1976) Abnormal visual resolution in the Siamese cat. *Science,* 194: 109 – 110.

Burke, W., Cottee, L.J., Hamilton, K., Kerr, L., Kyriacou, C. and Milosavljevic, M. (1987) Function of the Y optic nerve fibres in the cat: do they contribute to acuity and ability to discriminate fast motion? *J. Physiol. (Lond.),* 392: 35 – 50.

Ferster, D. (1990) X- and Y-mediated synaptic potentials in neurons of areas 17 and 18 of cat visual cortex. *Visual Neurosci.,* 4: 115 – 133.

Galambos, R., Norton, T.T. and Frommer, G.P. (1967) Optic tract lesions sparing pattern vision in cats. *Exp. Neurol.,* 18: 8 – 25.

Guillery, R.W., Polley, E.H. and Torrealba, F. (1982) The arrangement of axons according to fiber diameter in the optic tract of the cat. *J. Neurosci.,* 2: 714 – 721.

Myers, R.E. (1955) Interocular transfer of pattern discrimination in cats following section of crossed optic fibers. *J. Comp. Physiol. Psychol.,* 48: 470 – 473.

Reese, B.E., Guillery, R.W., Marzi, C.A. and Tassinari, G. (1991) Position of axons in the cat's optic tract in relation to their retinal origin and chiasmatic pathway. *J. Comp. Neurol.,* 306: 539 – 553.

Sherman, S.M. (1985) Functional organization of the W-, X-, and Y-cell pathways in the cat: a review and hypothesis. In: J.M. Sprague and A.N. Epstein (Eds.), *Progress in Psychobiology and Physiological Psychology,* Academic Press, Orlando, FL, pp. 234 – 314.

Sherman, S.M. and Sprague, J.M. (1979) Effects of visual cortex lesions upon the visual fields of monocularly deprived cats. *J. Comp. Neurol.,* 188: 291 – 312.

Spear, P.D., Miller, S., Vielhuber, K. and Kornguth, S.E. (1986) Visual field defects in cats with neonatal or adult immunological loss of retinal ganglion cells. *Brain Res.,* 368: 154 – 157.

Stanford, L.R. (1987) W-cells in the cat retina: correlated morphological and physiological evidence for two distinct classes. *J. Neurophysiol.,* 57: 218 – 244.

Stanford, L.R. and Sherman, M. (1984) Structure/function relationships of retinal ganglion cells in the cat. *Brain Res.,* 297: 381 – 386.

Stone, J. (1983) *Parallel Processing in the Visual System: the Classification of Retinal Ganglion Cells and its Impact on the Neurobiology of Vision,* Plenum, New York.

T.P. Hicks, S. Molotchnikoff and T. Ono (Eds.)
Progress in Brain Research, Vol. 95
© 1993 Elsevier Science Publishers B.V. All rights reserved.

CHAPTER 16

Visuotopic organization of corticocortical connections in the visual system

Paul-Antoine Salin, Pascal Girard and Jean Bullier

Vision et Motricité INSERM U94, 69500 Bron, France

Introduction

Most structures in the visual system contain a representation of the contralateral visual hemifield and are interconnected by a dense network of connections. It is usually thought that these connections are visuotopically organized, i.e., that they link together regions of these visual structures which represent the same zone of the visual world. More specifically, such visuotopically organized connections are supposed to link neurons with overlapping receptive fields (RFs). A particularly clear example of such an organization was demonstrated between the lateral geniculate nucleus (LGN) and the striate cortex by Tanaka (1983) who identified pairs of interconnected LGN and cortical neurons by cross-correlation and showed that the RFs of the afferent LGN neurons were contained within the RF of the recipient cortical neuron. Visuotopic organization is not limited to thalamocortical connections, however, as evidenced by the results of McIlwain's studies of corticotectal connections with electrical stimulation (McIlwain, 1973, 1977) which showed a similar visuotopic organization. McIlwain, summarizing his results, gave a definition of visuotopic connections: "the cells of the striate cortex which project functionally to a collicular neuron also look collectively at the same area of visual space as that collicular cell" (McIlwain, 1973). In this report, we present evidence that some corticocortical connections do not follow this "common view" rule of

visuotopic organization and we describe a new concept of organization of corticocortical connections in the visual system.

Visuotopic organization of projections from area 18 to area 17

In the course of our studies of corticocortical connections in the visual system using retrograde tracers, we have always been surprised by the large expanse of cortex containing labeled cells in extrastriate cortical areas after small injections of retrograde tracers are placed in striate cortex. Large extrastriate regions are labeled even when the injections are small enough to mark only narrow columns of labeled cells in the LGN (Perkel et al., 1986; Salin et al., 1989). This led us to suggest that neurons belonging to extrastriate areas and projecting to a given site in area 17 may, as a population, be encoding a much larger region of visual field than that collectively represented by their target neurons in area 17, thus clearly breaking McIlwain's rule of organization. We have recently addressed this question directly by studying the visuotopic organization of connections between area 18 and area 17 in the cat with electrophysiological mapping. A small injection of a retrograde fluorescent tracer (rhodamine labeled latex microspheres, fast blue or diamidino yellow) was placed in area 17. After an appropriate survival time for the transport of the retrograde label, a fine-grain electrophysiological map was

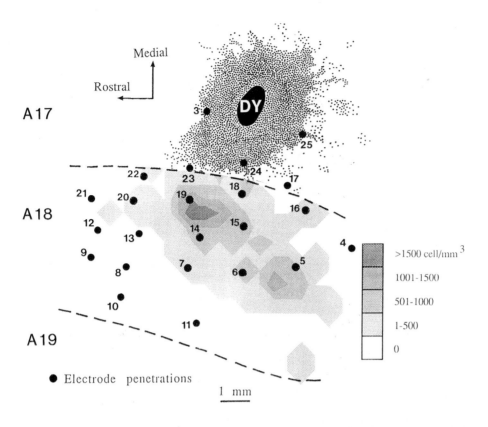

Medial

Rostral

A 17

DY

3

25

22

23

24

17

18

A 18

21

20

19

16

12

14

15

13

9

4

8

7

6

5

10

11

A 19

>1500 cell/mm^3

1001-1500

501-1000

1-500

0

● Electrode penetrations

1 mm

PAS 11   DY

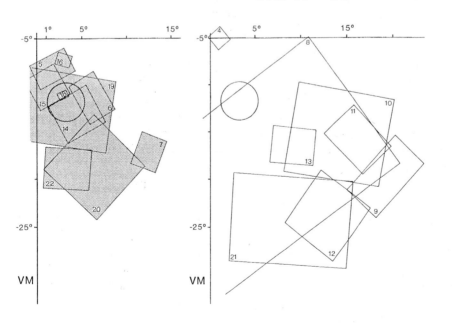

made of the surface of area 18 in order to identify the extent of visual field encoded in the region containing retrogradely labeled cells. Typical results of such an experiment are presented in Fig. 1. The upper part of the figure illustrates the mechanically flattened surface of the regions of areas 17 and 18 containing the injection site in area 17 and the labeled cells in area 18. The injection site of diamidino yellow (DY) is shown in black in area 17 and the locally labeled cells surrounding it are represented as small dots. Within area 18, the density of labeled cells was estimated by counting neurons in a grid made up of 480 μm side squares placed over the surface of the flattened cortex. In the upper part of Fig. 1, different levels of labeling densities are illustrated by different shades of grey and the points of entry of electrophysiological penetrations are illustrated by the large numbered dots. The positions of these penetrations on the cortical surface were recorded on photographs of the blood vessel pattern and by lesions made by passing current through the microelectrode. Labeled cells were observed with a fluorescence microscope and the labeling density maps and electrophysiological maps were matched using the electrolytic lesions as landmarks.

The lower part of Fig. 1 is divided in two parts; the left part presents the smallest RFs of neurons recorded in penetrations which fell within the region of area 18 containing labeled cells (RFs shaded in grey) and the right part illustrates the smallest RFs of neurons recorded in penetrations located outside the region of labeling (RFs as clear rectangles). The extent of visual field represented by the neurons contained within the uptake zone of the injection site in area 17 was estimated by computing the aggregate RF (Dow et al., 1981) using sizes and positions of

RFs recorded in penetrations located in or near the region of high color density surrounding the needle track (see Keizer et al., 1983; Bullier et al., 1984a; Kennedy and Bullier, 1985; Salin et al., 1989, for details on the methods of estimating the extent of the uptake zone of fluorescent dyes). The extent of visual field represented by neurons located in the uptake zone is illustrated by a disk in the lower part of Fig. 1.

The RF pattern of Fig. 1 illustrates the major result obtained in this and numerous other cases: the connections from area 18 to area 17 are not limited to interconnections between visuotopically corresponding regions of these two areas (Salin et al., 1992). Neither the total extents of the RFs, nor even the RF centers of neurons recorded within the zone of labeling in area 18, are contained within the representation of the uptake zone of the tracer in area 17. For example, penetration 5, which was located in a region of relatively high labeling density (501 – 1000 cells/mm^3) in area 18 yielded RFs which were located several degrees away from the aggregate RF of the uptake zone in area 17. As expected, penetrations located close to the highest peak of labeling density gave RFs which tended to overlap with the aggregate RF of the uptake zone (for example penetrations 14, 15 and 19 in Fig. 1), thus demonstrating a partial visuotopic match between strongly interconnected regions in areas 17 and 18. On the other hand, we found numerous cases of penetrations located at the outer border of the labeled zone (for example penetration 7 in Fig. 1) which returned RFs which clearly did not overlap with the representation of the uptake region. Thus, it is likely that some of the connections from area 18 to area 17 are not visuotopically organized: i.e., that

Fig. 1. Electrophysiological mapping of the region of area 18 containing labeled cells after an injection of fluorescent retrograde tracer (diamidino yellow, DY) in area 17. The region of areas 17 and 18 containing the injection site and the labeled cells has been mechanically flattened. The uptake region of the dye is illustrated by the black region labeled DY in area 17. The density of labeled cells is illustrated by shades of grey in area 18 and dots in area 17. Electrode penetrations are represented by large labeled dots. The lower part of the figure illustrates the smallest receptive fields (RFs) encountered within the penetrations in area 18. On the left and in grey are illustrated those RFs recorded in penetrations located within the labeled zone in area 18. On the right are represented as clear rectangles those RFs recorded in penetrations located outside the zone of labeling. The circular region corresponds to the aggregate RF of the uptake region of the dye in area 17 (see text). These results illustrate the presence of non-visuotopic connections from area 18 to area 17.

they link together neurons which have no regions of their RFs in common. This creates a dilemna for organizing cortical areas and transferring information among them.

Visuotopic organization of feedforward and feedback connections

Earlier results from this laboratory (Salin et al., 1989) suggested that none of the sets of cortical afferents terminating in area 17 follow the McIlwain rule of visuotopic organization. In view of the validity of this rule for subcortical and thalamocortical connections, one may wonder whether all corticocortical connections are organized in a similar fashion as afferents to area 17. We examined this question (Salin, 1988) by measuring the topography of the connection from area 17 to area 18, using similar methods as previously reported (Salin et al., 1989). The results showed that it appears to be visuotopically organized, since a column of cells in area 18 representing a zone of visual field 8 – 9° wide is innervated by a region of area 17 which encodes a similar extent of the visual field (Salin, 1988). Similar conclusions have been reached by Ferrer et al. (1988), although the extent of the visual field represented in the convergence region was much smaller in that study than in our results. Sherk and Ombrellaro (1988) also concluded that the projections from area 17 to the visual cortex of the suprasylvian sulcus are visuotopically organized.

Results obtained in the macaque monkey suggest a similar organization for the projections from area V1 to extrastriate areas. In this case, the evidence came from reversible inactivation by cooling of a limited region of area V1 situated on the operculum while recording from areas V3 or V4 (Girard et al., 1991a,b). Cooling inactivated the region of V1 situated below the cooling plate and created a functional scotoma in the visual field of the animal (Girard and Bullier, 1989). When the RFs of neurons in V3 and V4 overlapped with the border of this scotoma, we observed inactivation of the part of the RF located within the scotoma (Girard et al., 1991a,b). The interpretation of this finding is that

the connections from V1 to V3 and V4 are visuotopically organized.

It is known that connections from area 17 to extrastriate cortex have different morphological characteristics from the return projections and this difference had led authors to distinguish two types of connections, the feedforward and the feedback connections (Rockland and Pandya, 1979; Maunsell and Van Essen, 1983). Our results in cat and monkey therefore suggest that feedforward connections follow McIlwain's rule of visuotopic organization, like thalamocortical afferents. There may be some relationship between the similar visuotopic organization of feedforward and thalamocortical connections and the fact that they both terminate in layer 4. Another similarity is that inactivation of these connections leads to a silence of the target region (Schiller and Malpeli, 1977; Girard and Bullier, 1989; Girard et al., 1991a). Cortical afferents to area 17, on the other hand, which are mostly of the feedback type, avoid layer 4 and their inactivation does not silence the target area (Dreher and Cottee, 1975; Donaldson and Nash, 1975; Sherk, 1978; Sandell and Schiller, 1982). Thus feedforward and feedback connections do not differ only on morphological characteristics but also appear to be organized along very different functional principles.

Afferents to area 17 share the same convergence window

Feedback connections therefore are morphologically and functionally different from feedforward. Feedforward connections appear to follow McIlwain's rule. It is of interest to determine whether feedback connections also obey a single functional principle. Results on the afferents to area 17 in the cat suggest that this may be so. Despite their widely different topographical organizations, the different sets of cortical afferents converging to a column of cells in area 17 appear to share one functional feature: the RFs of neurons involved in these connections collectively encode the same region of visual field, whether they belong to areas 17, 18 or

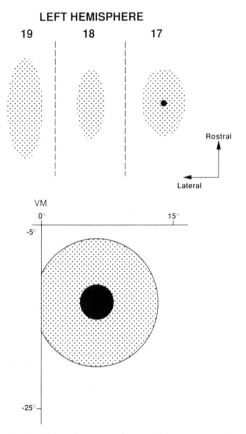

LEFT HEMISPHERE

19   18   17

Rostral

Lateral

VM

0°   15°

-5°

-25°

Fig. 2. Schematic representation of the correspondence between cortical regions involved in the connections afferent to area 17 and visual space. The upper part of the figure provides a schematic representation of areas 17, 18 and 19 of the left hemisphere of a cat after flattening. The lower part of the figure illustrates the corresponding regions in visual field (VM, vertical meridian). The large black dot in the upper part of the figure illustrates a column of cells in area 17 and its visual field representation (aggregate RF) is represented by the disk in the lower part of the figure. Neurons in areas 17, 18 and 19 which are afferent to the column in area 17 are represented as small dots in these areas. They all collectively encode a common region of visual field which is called the convergence window.

19. This was demonstrated directly by electrophysiologically mapping the zones in areas 17 and 18 containing labeled cells after an injection was placed in area 17 and with a less direct method for the afferents from area 19. Fig. 2 summarizes these results. The upper part of the figure presents a schematic representation of flattened portions of areas 17, 18 and 19 of the left hemisphere of the cat

brain, as seen from above. The lower part of the figure illustrates the lower quadrant of the right visual hemifield which is represented in those regions of areas 17 – 19. Consider a column of cells in a region of area 17 representing visual field situated approximately 10° below the horizontal meridian. This column, which is represented by a large black dot in the upper part of Fig. 2, has a broadly circular aggregate RF measuring approximately 4° in diameter (Salin et al., 1992) which is represented by the black disk in the lower part of the figure. The extent of the cortical surface of area 18 containing cells sending converging projections to this column, the region which we call convergence region (Salin et al., 1989), is illustrated by an elongated cloud of points in area 18 in the upper part of the figure. This convergence region represents a broadly circular region of visual field measuring 11° in diameter (Salin et al., 1992) which is illustrated in the lower part of the figure by the disk-like distribution of dots surrounding the black region of visual field encoded in the column of cells in area 17. By electrophysiological mapping, we found that the region of area 17 surrounding the injection site and containing cells projection to the same column appears to represent the same region of visual field as that represented by the convergence region in area 18. From our earlier results, we also know the rostro-caudal extent of the convergence region in area 19 (Salin et al., 1989). Using published data on the retinotopic organization of area 19 (Tusa et al., 1979; Albus and Beckman, 1980; Duysens et al., 1982), it is then possible to calculate the corresponding extent of visual field encoded in the labeled region in area 19. This gives a region measuring 15 – 20° across in elevation, a fair match for the extent of visual field encoded in the convergence zones of areas 17 and 18. Fig. 2 thus provides a synoptic view of the relationship between the cortical regions containing cells projecting to a column in area 17 and the visual space represented in these regions. Neurons contained in the black dot column in area 17 collectively represent a 4° wide region of visual space and are under the converging influence of a network of neurons in areas 17, 18 and 19 which col-

174

lectively encode the same large window of visual field measuring 15° across and represented by the stippled region in the lower part of Fig. 2. Let us call this region the convergence window.

Completion of the convergence window by callosal afferents

Callosal connections are known to exhibit similar convergence and divergence as ipsilateral corticocortical connections (Kennedy and Dehay, 1988) and it is therefore interesting to examine whether they also follow the same rule of connectivity. Results in the macaque monkey (Kennedy and Dehay, 1988) and more recently in the cat (Kennedy et al., 1991) demonstrate that, for a given column of cells in area 17, the convergence zones in contralateral visual areas have the same rostro-caudal extents as those in the homologous areas in the ipsilateral hemisphere. When translated in terms of visual field, this means that the population of callosal neurons projecting to a column in area 17 represents a visual field region having the same extent in elevation as that represented by ipsilateral afferent neurons and is therefore likely to be carrying information concerning the same window of visual field as that corresponding to ipsilateral afferents. This is illustrated in Fig. 3 in which we consider the case of a column of cells in area 17 which is located close to the 17 – 18 border in the left hemisphere (black dot within area 17). This column receives converging projections from regions of areas 17, 18 and 19 in the left hemisphere encoding visual field regions which extend only marginally in the left visual hemifield (fine dot region in the lower part of Fig. 3). It also receives projections from a zone of cortex situated at the 17 – 18 border of the right hemisphere representing a small crescent-shaped region in the left visual hemifield (large dot region in the lower part of the figure). Thus, afferents from the 17 – 18 border in the right hemisphere contribute to the completion of the convergence window surrounding the aggregate RF of the column of cells in area 17. In this way, every column of cells in area 17 is under the converging influence of neurons

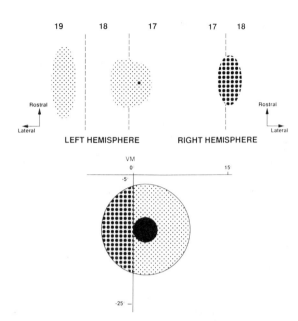

Fig. 3. Participation of callosal connections to the convergence window. The presentation of the figure is similar to that of Fig. 2 except that the column in area 17 is closer to the 17 – 18 border and that afferents from the contralateral (right) hemisphere are represented. Afferents from the ipsilateral hemisphere are illustrated as dots on the cortex and their common convergence window as the dotted region in visual field. Neurons from the right hemisphere which are afferent to the column of cells in area 17 of the left hemisphere are illustrated as large dots and their visual field representation is illustrated by the corresponding crescent-shaped region in the lower part of the figure. This figure illustrates the completion of the convergence window by callosal afferents for neurons with RFs located close to the vertical meridian (VM).

representing a broadly circular window of visual field, whether the column of cells is located in regions of area 17 representing the periphery of the visual field or whether it is located in cortex subserving regions of the visual field situated close to the vertical meridian. Such a completion role of callosal connections is in keeping with one of the functions traditionally assigned to callosal fibers of the visual system, that of providing perceptual continuity across the midline (Whitteridge, 1965). The fact that callosal connections follow the same organization principle as the ipsilateral connections suggests that the network organization of corticocortical connections includes interhemispheric as well as intrahemispheric connections.

Spatial reciprocity of corticocortical connections

So far, we have only examined the topographic organization of afferents to a column of cells in area 17 and it is not clear how this relates to that of the reciprocal projection from a column in area 17 to area 18. In the course of experiments aimed at characterizing this projection, we found that the spatial organization of corticocortical connections between areas 17 and 18 is reciprocal, i.e., that a column of cells in area 17 innervates the territory of area 18 that contains neurons projecting to it. Similarly, a column of area 18 projects to the region of area 17 which sends projections to it. This spatial reciprocity could provide a structural basis for reverberating loops between the column of cells in area 17 illustrated in Fig. 2 and the convergence regions in the various cortical areas sharing the same convergence window.

Size invariance of the convergence region

Many parameters of the organization of visual structures, such as RF size and magnification factors are known to vary with eccentricity in the visual field and one may wonder whether the convergence region and the convergence window constitute invariants across the visual field or whether their sizes depend on the eccentricity in visual field. To answer this question, we measured the convergence region in cortex subserving lower visual field and in cortex representing central visual field. The results demonstrated that the size of the convergence region for a given cortical area is constant across cortex, corresponding to an oval region measuring 5.3 mm in the rostro-caudal direction and 2.9 mm in mediolateral direction (Salin et al., 1992). This size invariance of the convergence region across cortex suggests that its dimensions are in some way constrained by morphological factors such as extent of axon collateral arborization and dendritic field, factors which do not appear to vary substantially across

cortex. In other words, the invariance of the convergence region may be another manifestation of the crystal-like morphological organization of the cortex popularized by the results of Hubel and Wiesel (Hubel, 1982). Given the size invariance of the convergence region and the well-known change in magnification factor with eccentricity, one could predict that the convergence window would be smaller for connections between regions of cortex representing central visual field than for connections between cortical regions encoding the periphery. This is indeed what we found by direct electrophysiological mapping. Instead of a 15° window, as found in peripheral visual field, we observed a convergence window measuring 5 – 7° across in cortex subserving central visual field. Thus, the convergence window appears to be scaled to the RF size and scatter of neurons which are also smaller in cortex representing more central regions of the visual field.

Functional aspects of the network organization of afferents to area 17

What could be the functional counterpart of this convergence window? The results of Mignard and Malpeli (1991) show that some area 18 neurons provide a functionally significant input to cells of the upper layers of area 17. It is clear, however, that neurons of area 18 contained in the convergence region corresponding to a column of cells within area 17 cannot possibly all provide a major excitatory drive, otherwise the RF sizes of the neurons in this column would be determined by the size of the convergence window and would be much larger than they actually are. This lack of a powerful excitatory drive from neurons situated at the periphery of the convergence region is further supported by the results of electrical stimulation of area 18 afferents to area 17, showing that neurons in area 17 can be orthodromically driven from area 18 only when their RFs are in perfect visuotopic correspondence with those of the stimulated neurons in area 18 (Bullier et al., 1988). It is not clear at the moment whether neurons providing non-visuotopic connections are mostly involved in inhibitory interactions through interneurons or whether they provide sub-threshold excitatory drive.

It is likely that at least those neurons of the convergence regions providing non-visuotopic inputs to area 17 neurons are involved in some kind of modulatory influence on the visual responses. It is well established that the RFs of visual cortical neurons possess modulatory regions beyond the so-called classical RF. Visual stimulation of these modulatory regions generate inhibitory and facilitatory effects (Nelson and Frost, 1978, 1985) which are believed to play an important role in cortical processing of visual information (Nelson, 1975; Allman et al., 1985; Orban et al., 1987; Gilbert and Wiesel, 1990). Horizontal connections within a given cortical area are usually assumed to provide the structural basis mediating modulatory interactions beyond the classical RF. However, neurons of area 17 are innervated not only by intrinsic connections but also by neurons situated in several other areas and these interarea connections correspond to the same convergence window as intrinsic connections (Fig. 2). Therefore, it appears likely that modulatory influences coming from regions beyond the classical RF arise from the converging action of the whole network reciprocally coupled to a given column in area 17 and that intrinsic connections only provide one component of these modulatory effects.

Because of the impossibility of identifying non-visuotopic connections with electrical stimulation (Bullier et al., 1988), we have recently used another technique, the temporal cross-correlation (Nelson et al., 1992). This method has been used with success in the retino-geniculo-striate pathway to identify monosynaptically connected pairs of neurons (Cleland et al., 1971; Tanaka, 1983). The signature of such a monosynaptic connection in the cross-correlation histogram (CCH) is a sharply defined peak displaced with respect to the time origin. To our surprise, we practically never isolated such a pattern in a sample of more than two hundred CCHs computed from the firing of neuron pairs with one member of the pair in area 17 and the other in area

18. The majority of the peaks observed in our CCHs were broad (10 – 50 msec) and centered on the origin of time or only slightly displaced with respect to it. The usual interpretation of such a pattern is that the two neurons under study are activated by a common set of neurons (Perkel et al., 1967). Several arguments reviewed elsewhere (Nelson et al., 1992) suggest that such generators of common input belong to the cortex and it is likely that the network organization revealed by our anatomical experiments constitutes the structural basis of these cortical generators. More specifically, we hypothesize that the numerous cortical neurons belonging to the network associated with a given convergence window (Fig. 2) could provide a common input to a pair of neurons in areas 17 and 18 through axonal bifurcation (Bullier and Kennedy, 1987), through recurrent collaterals of axons of pyramidal cells in these two areas, or through polysynaptic chains created by these collaterals. Further support for this hypothesis is provided by the fact that the temporal coupling revealed by the presence of peaks in the CCHs is observed only when the RFs of the coupled neurons are distant by no more than 8°. This value of 8° is remarkably close to the radius of the convergence window at this eccentricity, suggesting that the common input generators may belong to the cortical network collectively representing the convergence window.

Synthesizing the global relationships among perceptual elements remains an unsolved problem in perception since Gestalt theorists brought this question into prominence more than sixty years ago. Today, we see in neuroscience that a column of neurons in area 17 receives convergent input from a network of neurons situated in other cortical areas. Assuming that this convergence is also found at the level of the individual neuron, a neuron of area 17 could therefore be influenced by populations of neurons having different functional characteristics. By switching from one set of such afferents to another for its major source of functional input, a neuron in area 17 could therefore modify considerably its functional characteristics as a spatio-temporal filter.

Acknowledgements

We thank Jerry Nelson for creative discussions and comments on the manuscript, Pascal Giroud for graphic design, Françoise Girardet and Michèle Soulier for secretarial assistance. Financial support to P.A. Salin from the bourse Fouassier, Fondation de la Recherche Médicale and Fédération des Aveugles de France is gratefully acknowledged. Supported by CEE contract SC1 0329C.

References

Albus, K. and Beckmann, R. (1980) Second and third visual areas of the cat: interindividual variability in retinotopic arrangement and cortical location. *J. Physiol. (Lond.),* 299: 247 – 276.

Allman, J., Miezin, F. and McGuiness, E. (1985) Stimulus specific responses from beyond the classical receptive field: neurophysiological mechanisms for local-global comparisons in visual neurons. *Annu. Rev. Neurosci.,* 8: 407 – 429.

Bullier, J. and Kennedy, H. (1987) Axonal bifurcation in the visual system. *Trends Neurosci.,* 10: 205 – 210.

Bullier, J., Kennedy, H. and Salinger, W. (1984a) Bifurcation of subcortical afferents to visual areas 17, 18 and 19 in the cat cortex. *J. Comp. Neurol.,* 228: 309 – 328.

Bullier, J., Kennedy, H. and Salinger, W. (1984b) Branching and laminar origin of projections between visual cortical areas in the cat. *J. Comp. Neurol.,* 228: 329 – 341.

Bullier, J., McCourt, M.E. and Henry, G.H. (1988) Physiological studies on the feedback connection to the striate cortex from cortical areas 18 and 19 of the cat. *Exp. Brain Res.,* 70: 90 – 98.

Cleland, B.G., Dubin, M.W. and Levick, W.R. (1971) Simultaneous recording of input and output of lateral geniculate neurones. *Nature,* 231: 191 – 192.

Donaldson, I.M.L. and Nash, J.R.G. (1975) The effect of a chronic lesion in cortical area 17 on the visual responses of units in area 18 of the cat. *J. Physiol. (Lond.),* 245: 325 – 332.

Dow, B.M., Synder, A.Z., Vautin, R.G. and Bauer, R. (1981) Magnification factor and receptive field size in foveal striate cortex of the monkey. *Exp. Brain Res.,* 44: 213 – 228.

Dreher, B. and Cottee, L.J. (1975) Visual receptive-field properties of cells in area 18 of cat's cortex before and after acute lesions in area 17. *J. Neurophysiol.,* 381: 735 – 750.

Duysens, G., Orban, G.A., Van der Glas, H.W. and De Zegher, F.E. (1982) Functional properties of area 19 as compared to area 17 of the cat. *Brain Res.,* 231: 279 – 291.

Ferrer, J.M.R., Price, D.J. and Blakemore, C. (1988) The organization of corticocortical projections from area 17 to area 18 of the cat's visual cortex. *Proc. R. Soc. Lond. (Biol.),* 233: 77 – 98.

Gilbert, C.D. and Wiesel, T.N. (1990) The influence of contextual stimuli on the orientation selectivity of cells in primary visual cortex of the cat. *Vision Res.,* 30: 1689 – 1701.

Girard, P. and Bullier, J. (1989) Visual activity in area V2 during reversible inactivation of area 17 in the macaque monkey. *J. Neurophysiol.,* 62: 1287 – 1302.

Girard, P., Salin, P.A. and Bullier, J. (1991a) Visual activity in macaque area V4 depends on area 17 input. *Neuroreport,* 2: 81 – 84.

Girard, P., Salin, P.A. and Bullier, J. (1991b) Visual activity in areas V3A and V3 during reversible inactivation of area V1 in the macaque monkey. *J. Neurophysiol.,* 66: 1493 – 1503.

Hubel, D.H. (1982) Exploration of the primary visual cortex 1955 – 78. *Nature,* 299: 515 – 524.

Keizer, K., Kuypers, H.G.J.M., Huisman, A.M. and Dann, O. (1983) Diamidino yellow dihydrochloride (DY.2HCl), a fluorescent retrograde neuronal tracer which migrates only very slowly out of the cell and can be used in combination with TB and FB in double labelling experiments. *Exp. Brain Res.,* 51: 179 – 191.

Kennedy, H. and Bullier, J. (1985) A double-labelling investigation of the afferent connectivity to cortical areas V1 and V2 of the macaque monkey. *J. Neurosci.,* 5: 2815 – 2830.

Kennedy, H. and Dehay, C. (1988) Functional implications of the anatomical organization of the callosal projections of visual areas V1 and V2 in the macaque monkey. *Behav. Brain Res.,* 29: 225 – 236.

Kennedy, H., Meissirel, C. and Dehay, C. (1991) Callosal pathways in primates and their compliancy to general rules governing the organization of cortico-cortical connectivity. In: B. Dreher and S. Robinson (Eds.), *Neuroanatomy of the Visual Pathways and their Retinotopic Organization,* McMillan, London, pp. 324 – 359.

Maunsell, J.H.R. and Van Essen, D.C. (1983) The connections of the middle temporal visual area (MT) and their relationship to a cortical hierarchy in the macaque monkey. *J. Neurosci.,* 3: 2563 – 2586.

McIlwain, J.T. (1973) Retinotopic fidelity of striate cortex-superior colliculus interactions in the cat. *J. Neurophysiol.,* 36: 702 – 710.

McIlwain, J.T. (1977) Topographic organization and convergence in corticotectal projections from areas 17, 18 and 19 in the cat. *J. Neurophysiol.,* 40: 189 – 198.

Mignard, M. and Malpeli, J.G. (1991) Patterns of information flow through visual cortex. *Science,* 251: 1249 – 1251.

Nelson, J.I. (1975) Globality and stereoscopic fusion in binocular vision. *J. Theor. Biol.,* 49: 1 – 88.

Nelson, J.I. and Frost, B.J. (1978) Orientation selective inhibition from beyond the classic visual receptive field. *Brain Res.,* 139: 359 – 365.

Nelson, J.I. and Frost, B.J. (1985) Intracortical facilitation among co-oriented, co-axially aligned simple cells in cat striate cortex. *Exp. Brain Res.,* 61: 54 – 61.

and Fluothane (2 – 3% of total gaseous mixture), intubated with a tracheal cannula and connected to a respirator. It was trepanated and a small incision was made in the dura overlying the cortex representing the center of the visual field (areas 17 – 18: about A6 to P4 and L1 to L4; area 19: about P0 to P5 and L6 to L11). Pressure points and wounds were then infused with local anaesthetic (Xylocaine 2%). The animal was maintained on the nitrous oxide anaesthesia and Fluothane (0.5%). Gallamine triethiodide (Flaxedil: 200 mg) and D-tubocurarine (Tubarine: 20 mg) dissolved in 5% dextrose solution (30 ml) were continuously administered at the rate of 5.6 ml/h to maintain paralysis of ocular muscles. Respiratory rate was controlled by the experimenter so as to maintain constant, physiological levels of expired CO_2 (3.5 – 4.5%). Temperature, heart rate and, occasionally, EEG were also monitored during the experiment.

Recording was carried out with tungsten microelectrodes having an impedance measured at 1000 Hz of 3 – 6 MΩ. The stimulation procedure was adapted from Henry et al. (1967). A neutral contact lens having a 3 mm artificial pupil was placed on each eye to prevent dehydration and improve image resolution. This was also ensured by the use of appropriate dioptric lenses, when necessary, which focused the image on the retina. Moreover, the optic axis of one of the eyes was deviated using a risley biprism so that the RFs of the two eyes would be located on widely separated coordinates on the tangent screen, placed at 171 cm from the animal. Two projectors, placed behind the animal, allowed for the independent stimulation of each of the eyes. The two stimuli were equated for brightness, and an appropriate computer-controlled optic bench system ensured the independent and precise definition of the other parameters: stimulus velocity and directionality, bar length and width, position and orientation in space, stimulus onset and duration of sweep.

Upon isolating a cell, the best stimulus parameters were determined for the dominant eye. The RF for the unresponsive eye of a cell which appeared to be monocularly driven was estimated to be situated at the corresponding visual field location as for the responsive eye. This qualitative protocol was next followed by a quantitative one. Each eye was first stimulated separately to determine the monocular response and then the binocular responses were tested at null and disparate presentations. Disparity was created experimentally by delaying the initiation of the sweep of one of the two stimuli. Besides the zero condition, ten other conditions were tested in a pseudo-random fashion, disparity varying in 0.2° steps from − 1° to + 1°.

Results

Whenever a cell was isolated from background activity and gave a robust response to the stimuli, it was subjected first to the qualitative and then to the quantitative protocols described above. Thus, 143 cells are described on which all protocols were completed, 78 from areas 17 – 18 and 65 from area 19, respectively. A number of RF properties were examined, which are of marginal pertinence to the principal theme of this report. They are thus only briefly described.

The RF sizes obtained were generally quite small in either areas and corresponded to those obtained by Hubel and Wiesel (1965) and by others (Duysens et al., 1982a,b), including ourselves (Lepore and Guillemot, 1982). The cells were also classed according to simple, complex or end-stopped categories. In areas 17 – 18, simple cells made up the largest group whereas in area 19, no simple cells were found and complex cells predominated.

Ocular dominance was assessed for all cells. The results show that most cells were binocularly driven (85% for areas 17 – 18 and 88% for area 19) and that there was a clear preponderance of units having a balanced dominance and a slight bias in favour of the contralateral eye. Actually, the amount of binocular activation is more important than that which can be deduced from these ocular dominance data. A number of cells which were classed monocular using the method of stimulating each eye separately showed strong binocular interactions

TABLE I

Number of monocular and binocular cells sensitive to disparity in areas 17/18 and 19 in normal cat

	Areas 17/18			Area 19		
	Mono	Bino	%	Mono	Bino	%
Tuned excitatory	2	13	19%	1	4	8%
Tuned inhibitory	1	9	13%	–	3	5%
Far cell	2	15	22%	–	4	6%
Near cell	2	11	17%	–	10	15%
Insensitive	3	7	13%	4	24	43%
Unclassified	2	11	16%	3	12	23%
Total	12	66		8	57	

when the two eyes were stimulated simultaneously (see Table I).

Orientation preference was assessed with the hand-held ophthalmoscope used to determine the RF of each eye. The optimal orientation was estimated as being that orientation of a slit, varied in approximately 15° steps, which produced the best response, as determined by ear, over a number of sweeps. It appeared from the present study that no anisotropy in favour of the vertical and horizontal axes existed for either areas.

Binocular interaction and disparity tuning was evaluated in the present experiment by using two stimulating conditions: monocular viewing, where each eye was stimulated separately and binocular viewing, whereby both eyes were stimulated simultaneously. In the latter case, the timing between the initiation of the two stimuli was adjusted so as to create a pre-determined spatial disparity. If binocular interaction consisted of only linear summation, then the response to the simultaneous stimulation of the two eyes should be equivalent to the sum of the responses of either eye stimulated separately or possibly, if it is assumed that a particular cell only responds with a maximal discharge rate, to that produced by stimulation of the dominant eye. Moreover, the binocular response of apparent monocularly driven cells should equal the monocular response. Discharge rates obtained dur-

ing simultaneous stimulation which are smaller or larger than these two limits would indicate non-linear binocular interactions either of the inhibitory or of the excitatory type, respectively.

Response profiles for the disparity continuum ($-1°$ to $+1°$) were derived from the peri-stimulus time histogram obtained at each disparity. An ex-

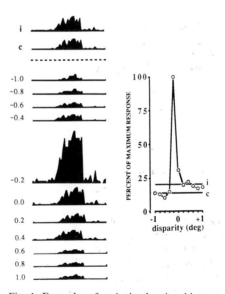

Fig. 1. Examples of peri-stimulus time histograms from which were derived the sensitivity profiles of one tuned-excitatory cell in areas 17/18 of the normal cat. Besides the response to the 11 disparities, the response to monocular ipsilateral (i) and contralateral (c) eye stimulation is also shown at the top.

182

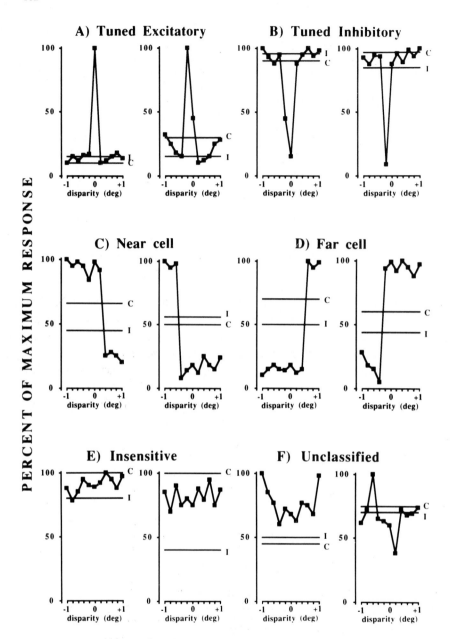

Fig. 2. Representative examples of the five subtypes of disparity-sensitive cells as well as one which did not respond differentially to stimulus disparity, the insensitive cell (*E*) in areas 17/18 of the normal cat. The different subtypes: tuned excitatory (*A*) and tuned inhibitory (*B*) cells are those which prefer stimulus on the fixation plane, the former responding with excitation and the latter with inhibition to binocular stimulation around 0 disparity. The near cell (*C*) and far cell (*D*) are those units which are excited at one set of disparities and inhibited at another set of disparities. The spatial arrangement of the two stimuli are such that one can presume that the first subtype prefers stimuli situated in front of the fixation plane, and the second, stimuli which appear behind the fixation plane. Unclassified (*F*) represents cells which show non-linear interactions but which cannot be categorized into an identifiable subtype.

ample of a tuned excitatory cell illustrating how these disparity profiles were computed is presented in Fig. 1. Thus, the response to ipsilateral and contralateral stimulation, as well as to stimulation at each disparity is used to derive a disparity-specific peri-stimulus time histogram (left of Fig. 1). The summed discharges within each histogram are used to obtain the points which are shown for each disparity on the right of Fig. 1.

Despite some variety of response profiles, it was clear that six subsets of response profiles could be derived. Cells making up the first subset, termed "insensitive", gave essentially the same response at each disparity (see Figs. 2E and 3E). Moreover, the response to simultaneous stimulation of the two eyes was neither greater than the highest response of the dominant eye nor smaller than the smallest response of each eye.

A large proportion of cells could be grouped into four classes according to their response profiles to the disparate stimulation. Examples of these are presented in Fig. 2 (areas 17 – 18) and Fig. 3 (area 19). Since these sensitivity profiles resembled in most respects those previously described by Poggio and Fisher (1977), Maunsell and Van Essen (1983), Poggio (1984, 1985), Poggio and Poggio (1984) and Poggio et al. (1985a,b; 1988) for the monkey cortex, the same terminology was employed to characterize them. Thus, one class of cells responded with strong excitation to a very narrow range of disparities. These were thus termed tuned excitatory (TE) disparity detectors (see Figs. 2A and 3A). On the other hand, some units showed a strong inhibitory response to precise spatial disparities. These were called tuned inhibitory (TI) disparity detectors (see Figs. 2B and 3B). A third type of cell gave a very strong excitatory response to one set of disparities and an inhibitory one to another set. These corresponded to the near (see Figs. 2C and 3C) and far neurons (see Figs. 2D and 3D) of Poggio (1984, 1985). The relative proportions of each of these subsets for each area are given in Table I.

Two points, irrespective of area examined, are immediately obvious upon inspection of Table I. First, a substantial number of cells in each group,

termed "unclassifiable", showed some form of binocular interaction, essentially of the excitatory type. However, no consistent repeatable response profile could be derived which would have permitted a grouping of a number of units into some identifiable class. Examples of two unclassifiable cells from each area are presented in Fig. 2F (areas 17 – 18) and Fig. 3F (area 19). Second, a subgroup of cells which were classed monocular using individual eye stimulation showed some form of binocular interaction when the eyes were stimulated simultaneously (areas 17 – 18: 7 disparity-sensitive and 2 unclassifiable; area 19: 1 tuned excitatory and 3 unclassifiable).

Comparing the results obtained for the different areas, three major differences with regards to disparity interactions are evident: first, as is clear from Table I, a substantially larger proportion of cells in areas 17 – 18 than in area 19 show one of the four clearly defined disparity profiles (71% vs. 34%, respectively). Second, the strength of the interaction, as defined by the non-linear increase in discharge rate of binocular as compared to monocular stimulation, was much weaker in area 19 than in areas 17 – 18. The only cells on which this analysis could be meaningfully carried out are the TE neurons. All 15 TE cells in areas 17 – 18 gave binocular responses at optimal disparity which were greater than the summed monocular responses. In some cases (see, among others, example in Fig. 1 and Fig. 2A), the combined response was larger by at least a factor of two. The binocular response of the 5 TE cells found in area 19 was never higher than the summed monocular responses. The third difference between areas 17 – 18 responses and those of area 19 can also be illustrated by these TE cells and from those showing suppressive responses at a particular disparity, namely, the TI cells. In general, cells in the former areas had extremely fine disparity profiles (see Fig. 2A,B), that is, they seemed to respond recisely to one disparity and not to adjacent ones. Units in area 19 (for example see Fig. 3A,B), on the other hand, had fairly wide profiles, suggesting that their degree of discrimination of disparities near the optimum was not as good.

184

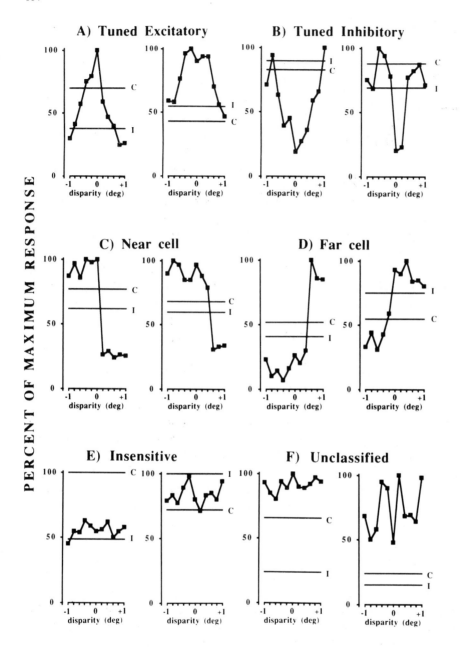

Fig. 3. Representative examples of the five subtypes of disparity-sensitive cells as well as one which did not respond differentially to stimulus disparity, the insensitive cell (*E*) in area 19 of the normal cat. The different subtypes: tuned excitatory (*A*) and tuned inhibitory (*B*) cells are those which prefer stimulus on the fixation plane, the former responding with excitation and the latter with inhibition to binocular stimulation around 0 disparity. The near cell (*C*) and far cell (*D*) are those units which are excited at one set of disparities and inhibited at another set of disparities. Unclassified (*F*) represents cells which show non-linear interactions but which cannot be categorized into an identifiable subtype.

Discussion

The objective of the present experiments was to determine whether disparity-sensitive cells are present in area 19 of the cat and whether these are as numerous and well defined as in areas 17 – 18. The results indicate that there are disparity-sensitive cells in the former area, although their proportion appears to be smaller than in areas 17 – 18, and the nature of their response profiles seems less precise.

In the cat, most cells were binocularly driven in the different areas. Moreover, many of the cells which appeared to be monocular showed binocular interaction when the two eyes were stimulated simultaneously. This indicates that most, if not all cells are sensitive to binocular stimulation, provided that the stimulation procedure is appropriate. Bilateral interaction is presumed to act as one of the possible substrates for depth discrimination based on binocular disparity. Results obtained in the monkey with respect to disparity tuned cells in areas beyond striate cortex led to the expectation that disparity tuning would be one of the dominant characteristics of cells in area 19. This was not found to be the case. Complementary to the paucity of interactive effects was the broader degree of tuning of the disparity-sensitive cells.

Given these electrophysiological results, as well as the behavioural results showing that subtotal lesions of areas 17 – 18 abolish stereoscopic discrimination based on disparity (Ptito et al., 1991) while leaving pattern perception nearly intact, it can be concluded that area 19 is only minimally involved in the analysis of disparity information in the cat. This is at the same time surprising but yet explicable. Explicable because area 19 receives its inputs not only in an hierarchical fashion from areas 17 – 18 but also in parallel from three subcortical sources: the C-lamina of the dorsal lateral geniculate nucleus (d-LGN), the medial interlaminar nucleus (MIN) and the pulvinar complex (Sherman, 1985a,b). Cells in the pulvinar complex generally have large RF and coarse tuning properties (Leventhal et al., 1980; Casanova et al., 1989), which make them inappropriate to signal the fine spatial characteristics of

disparity tuned neurons. Much less is known about the RF properties of cells in the MIN. However, cells of the C-lamina of d-LGN mainly belong to the W-class (Sherman, 1985a,b). These cells, which constitute a generally heterogeneous class, are also those which are usually termed "sluggish", "hard to drive" etc., and are not thought to be involved in the analysis of fine spatial detail (as the X-type cells of areas 17 – 18, for example). The electrophysiological results in recipient area 19 are therefore a reflection of the poorly defined properties as regards precise spatial characteristics of these lower order contributors to the activity of its component cells.

The results are at the same time surprising since, if one uses this lower to higher order argument to justify RF properties of cells in the terminal area, area 19 receives a large input from cells in areas 17 – 18, which are themselves well tuned to spatial disparity. One would have assumed that this lower order property would be maintained at the subsequent relay of the functional stream. One is also surprised since the results point to a significant difference between cat and monkey functional organization, which, however, is paralleled by differences in anatomical organization. The results might also reflect an ethological difference between primates and cats, in the sense that the latter is not really as good a visual animal, having less need for highly organized and possibly redundant pathways for discriminating fine stereoscopic details.

Acknowledgements

J.-P. Guillemot and F. Lepore are grateful to the Natural Sciences and Engineering Research Council and to the Fonds FCAR of the Ministère de l'Education de la Province de Québec for their support.

References

Barlow, H.B., Blakemore, C. and Pettigrew, J.D. (1967) The neural mechanisms of binocular depth discrimination. *J. Physiol. (Lond.),* 193: 327 – 342.

Bishop, P.O. and Henry, G.H. (1971) Spatial vision. *Annu. Rev. Psychol.,* 22: 119 – 160.

186

Bishop, P.O., Henry, G.H. and Smith, C.J. (1971) Binocular interaction fields of single units in the cat's striate cortex. *J. Physiol. (Lond.)*, 216: 39–68.

Burkhalter, A. and Van Essen, D.C. (1986) Processing of color, form and disparity information in visual areas VP and V2 of ventral extrastriate cortex in the macaque monkey. *J. Neurosci.*, 6: 2327–2351.

Casanova, C., Freeman, R.D. and Nordmann, J.P. (1989) Monocular and binocular response properties of cells in the striate-recipient zone of the cat's lateral posterior-pulvinar complex. *J. Neurophysiol.*, 62: 544–557.

Cynader, M. and Regan, D.M. (1978) Neurons in cat parastriate cortex sensitive to direction of motion in three-dimensional space. *J. Physiol. (Lond.)*, 274: 549–569.

Cynader, M. and Regan, D.M. (1982) Neurons in cat visual cortex tuned to the direction of motion in depth: effect of positional disparity. *Vision Res.*, 22: 967–982.

Duysens, J., Orban, G.A., Van der Glas, H.W. and Maes, H. (1982a) Receptive field structure of area 19 as compared to area 17 of the cat. *Brain Res.*, 231: 293–308.

Duysens, J., Orban, G.A., Van der Glas, H.W. and Zegher, F.E. (1982b) Functional properties of area 19 as compared to area 17 of the cat. *Brain Res.*, 231: 279–291.

Felleman, D.J. and Van Essen, D.C. (1987) Receptive field properties of neurons in area V3 of macaque monkey extrastriate cortex. *J. Neurophysiol.*, 57: 889–920.

Ferster, D.A. (1981) Comparison of binocular depth mechanisms in areas 17 and 18 of cat visual cortex. *J. Physiol. (Lond.)*, 311: 623–655.

Fisher, B. and Kruger, J. (1979) Disparity tuning and binocularity of single neurons in the cat visual cortex. *Exp. Brain Res.*, 35: 1–8.

Gardner, J.C. and Cynader, M. (1987) Mechanisms for binocular depth sensitivity along the vertical meridian of the visual field. *Brain Res.*, 413: 60–74.

Gardner, J.C. and Raiten, E.J. (1986) Ocular dominance and disparity sensitivity: why there are cells in the visual cortex driven unequally by the two eyes. *Exp. Brain Res.*, 64: 505–514.

Henry, G.H., Bishop, P.O. and Coombs, J.S. (1967) Inhibitory and sub-liminal excitatory receptive fields of simple units in cat striate cortex. *Vision Res.*, 9: 1289–1296.

Hubel, D.H. and Livingstone, M.S. (1987) Segregation of form, color and stereopsis in primate area 18. *J. Neurosci.*, 7: 3378–3415.

Hubel, D.H. and Wiesel, T.N. (1965) Receptive fields and functional architecture in two nonstriate visual areas (18 and 19) of the cat. *J. Neurophysiol.*, 30: 1561–1573.

Hubel, D.H. and Wiesel, T.N. (1970) Cells sensitive to binocular depth in area 18 of the macaque monkey cortex. *Nature*, 225: 41–42.

Joshua, D.E. and Bishop, P.O. (1970) Binocular single vision and depth discrimination. Receptive field disparities for central and peripheral vision and binocular interaction on

peripheral single units in cat striate cortex. *Exp. Brain Res.*, 10: 389–396.

Lepore, F. and Guillemot, J.-P. (1982) Visual receptive field properties of cells innervated through the corpus callosum. *Exp. Brain Res.*, 46: 413–424.

Lepore, F., Samson, A., Paradis, M.-C., Ptito, M. and Guillemot, J.-P. (1992) Binocular interaction and disparity coding at the 17–18 border: contribution of the corpus callosum. *Exp. Brain Res.*, 40: 129–140.

Le Vay, S. and Voigt, T. (1988) Ocular dominance and disparity coding in cat visual cortex. *Visual Neurosci.*, 1: 395–414.

Leventhal, A.G., Keens, J.S. and Tork, I. (1980) The afferent ganglion cells and cortical projections of the retinal recipient zone (RRZ) of the cat's pulvinar complex. *J. Comp. Neurol.*, 194: 535–554.

Livingstone, M.S. and Hubel, D.H. (1987a) Connections between layer 4B of area 17 and the thick cytochrome oxidase stripes of area 18 in the squirrel monkey. *J. Neurosci.*, 7: 3371–3377.

Livingstone, M.S. and Hubel, D.H. (1987b) Psychophysical evidence for separate channels for the perception of form, color, movement and depth. *J. Neurosci.*, 7: 3416–3468.

Maske, R., Yamane, S. and Bishop, P.O. (1986a) Stereoscopic mechanisms: binocular responses of the striate cells of cats to moving light and dark bars. *Proc. Roy. Soc. Lond. (Biol.)*, 229: 227–256.

Maske, R., Yamane, S. and Bishop, P.O. (1986b) End-stopped cell and binocular depth discrimination in the striate cortex of cats. *Proc. Roy. Soc. Lond. (Biol.)*, 229: 257–276.

Maunsell, J.H.R. and Van Essen, D.C. (1983) Functional properties of neurons in middle temporal visual area of the macaque monkey II. Binocular interaction and sensitivity to binocular disparity. *J. Neurophysiol.*, 49: 1148–1167.

Pettigrew, J.D., Nikara, T. and Bishop, P.O. (1968) Binocular interaction on single units in striate cortex: simultaneous stimulation by single moving slit with receptive fields in correspondence. *Exp. Brain Res.*, 6: 391–410.

Poggio, G.F. (1984) Processing of stereoscopic information in monkey visual cortex. In: G.M. Edelman, W.E. Gall and W.M. Cowans (Eds.), *Dynamic Aspects of Neocortical Function*, Wiley, New York, pp. 613–635.

Poggio, G.F. (1985) Cortical mechanisms of stereopsis. *Invest. Ophthalmol. Visual Sci.*, 26: 133.

Poggio, G.F. and Fisher, B. (1977) Binocular interaction and depth sensitivity of striate and pre-striate cortical neurons of the behaving rhesus monkey. *J. Neurophysiol.*, 40: 1392–1405.

Poggio, G.F. and Poggio, T. (1984) The analysis of stereopsis. *Annu. Rev. Neurosci.*, 7: 379–412.

Poggio, G.F., Gonzalez, F. and Krause, F. (1985a) Binocular correlation system in monkey visual cortex. *Soc. Neurosci. Abstr.*, 11: 17.

Poggio, G.F., Motter, P.C., Squatrito, S. and Trotter, Y. (1985b) Response of neurons in visual cortex (V1 and V2) of the alert macaque to dynamic random-dot stereograms. *Vision Res.,* 25: 397–406.

Poggio, G.F., Gonzalez, F. and Krause, F. (1988) Stereoscopic mechanisms in monkey visual cortex: binocular correlation and disparity selectivity. *J. Neurosci.,* 8: 4531–4550.

Ptito, M., Lepore, F. and Guillemot, J.-P. (1992) Loss of stereopsis following lesions of cortical areas 17–18 in the cat. *Exp. Brain Res.,* 89: 521–530.

Regan, D.M. and Cynader, M. (1982) Neurons in cat visual cortex tuned to the direction of motion in depth: effect of stimulus speed. *Invest. Ophthal. Visual Sci.,* 22: 535–550.

Regan, D.M., Beverley, K.I. and Cynader, M. (1979) The visual perception of motion in depth. *Sci. Am.,* 241: 136–151.

Sherman, S.M. (1985a) Functional organization of the W-, X- and Y-cell pathways in the cat: a review and hypothesis. In: J.M. Sprague and A.N. Epstein (Eds.), *Progress in Psychobiology and Physiological Psychology, Vol. II,* Academic Press, New York, pp. 233–314.

Sherman, S.M. (1985b) Parallel W-, X- and Y-cell pathways in the cat: a model for visual function. In: D. Rose and V.G. Dobson (Eds.), *Models of the Visual Cortex,* Wiley, Chichester, pp. 71–95.

Van Essen, D.C. (1985) Functional organization of primate visual cortex. In: A. Peters and G. Jones (Eds.), *Cerebral Cortex: Vol. 3, Visual Cortex,* Plenum, New York, pp. 259–329.

Van Essen, D.C. and Maunsell, J.H.R. (1983) Hierarchical organization and functional streams in the visual cortex. *Trends Neurosci.,* 6: 370–375.

Von der Heydt, R., Adorjani, C., Hanny, P. and Baumgartner, G. (1978) Disparity sensitivity and receptive field incongruity of units in the cat striate cortex. *Exp. Brain Res.,* 31: 523–545.

SECTION IV

Development and Plasticity

T.P. Hicks, S. Molotchnikoff and T. Ono (Eds.)
Progress in Brain Research, Vol. 95
© 1993 Elsevier Science Publishers B.V. All rights reserved.

CHAPTER 18

Cortical convergence of ON- and OFF-pathways and functional adaptation of receptive field organization in cat area 17

Daniel Shulz, Dominique Debanne and Yves Frégnac

Institut Alfred Fessard, C.N.R.S., 91198 Gif sur Yvette Cedex, France

Introduction

The receptive fields (RF) of sensory neurons in the primary visual cortex are classically subdivided in two categories, i.e., "simple" and "complex" (Hubel and Wiesel, 1962) on the basis of the spatial distribution of their responses to the presentation (ON) and extinction (OFF) of stationary visual stimuli. Following the initial criteria defined by Hubel and Wiesel, simple cells are characterized by separate ON- and OFF-subregions within which spatial summation occurs. In addition, an antagonistic interaction is found when the ON- and OFF-subregions are stimulated conjointly. Conversely, complex cells show a homogeneous field of mixed ON- and OFF-responses, and lack spatial summation and antagonism.

A model of extrinsic and intrinsic connectivity was proposed to account for these two classes of cortical receptive fields, which are predominant in different, distinct cortical areas (Hubel and Wiesel, 1962). The simple type, found mostly in area 17, was thought to result from the convergence of the axonal projections of a small number of principal cells in the lateral geniculate nucleus (LGN), of the same functional type and whose receptive field centers were aligned in the visual field. In this scheme the spatial envelope formed by all afferents RFs gives the target cortical RF its elongated form with

separate ON- and OFF-discharge zones. A similar scheme of cortico-cortical convergence established from several simple cortical cells with partially overlapping receptive fields was proposed to form complex receptive fields, which were found to be predominant in area 18. A specific consequence of this hierarchical model of cortical organization was that complex cells should be fed by simple cortical cells and never contacted monosynaptically by geniculate relay neurons. The transfer of information was thus considered to be purely sequential, from LGN relay cells to simple cells in the cortex and in turn from simple to complex neurons.

Since this first classification of the spatial structure of cortical receptive fields, numerous studies showed that the separation or mixing of ON- and OFF-subregions of cortical receptive fields was not so clearly distinct as initially proposed. The separation between simple and complex appeared to be largely dependent on the index used to quantify the spatial overlap of ON- and OFF-discharge zones (compare Dean and Tolhurst, 1983, with Heggelund, 1986). Moreover, some complex cortical cells were shown to receive direct geniculate contacts (Hoffman and Stone, 1971; Tanaka, 1983). These observations raised the question as to whether the traditional dichotomy simple/complex was inappropriate, and whether it would be more realistic to consider that the two classes of cortical RFs form a continuum in the degree of spatial superposition of ON- and OFF-regions. The first two parts of this chapter review different connectivity schemes proposed for the genesis of simple and complex RFs and discuss the relative degree of convergence of ON- and OFF-afferents along the retino-geniculo-cortical pathway.

Studies of development and plasticity may unexpectedly provide an additional understanding of the spatial organization of cortical receptive fields, by describing the processes which lead to their formation. In addition, these studies make it possible to test the validity of proposed connectivity models indirectly. The experimental approach presented in the final part of the present chapter is to artificially impose different activity levels in ON- and OFF-pathways, and look for possible refinements or shaping of the spatial RF structure of cortical cells. These changes can be interpreted in terms of adaptive geniculo- and cortico-cortical connections, and support specific models of RF structure (see Fig. 4). This view, where plasticity is used as a probe to reveal the adaptive capacity of a structural anlage may seem at odds with the pioneering observations of Hubel and Wiesel (1963). These authors found that visual cortical neurons recorded in very young, visually inexperienced kittens already had functional characteristics similar to those of adult cells. They concluded that the circuitry responsible for the emergence of simple and complex RFs reaches maturity very rapidly and is under strict genetic control, the role of visual experience being restricted to the "functional validation" of connections already present at the onset of visual stimulation (around the end of the first week in the kitten). Paradoxically, the same authors described a postnatal phase of development ("critical period") during which activity-dependent processes could indeed change the functional properties of visual cortical cells. However, no systematic study was attempted at that time to assess if such functional modifications could potentially alter the ON/OFF organization of RFs.

After a brief overview of data supporting activity dependence in the development of the spatial organization of cortical receptive fields, we will report recent electrophysiological experiments demonstrating that it is possible to modify the spatial structure of the receptive field during the time of recording of a single cell in the paralyzed and anesthetized animal. It will be shown that differential conditioning of ON- and OFF-responses induces long-lasting changes of spatial receptive field organization in kitten and cat visual cortex. Finally, we will discuss various models of connectivity which could subserve the selection of simple and complex RF organizations through activity-dependent processes during development.

Separation of ON- and OFF-channels along the retino-geniculo-cortical pathway

At the retinal level

Ganglion cells in the retina of cats have concentric receptive fields with antagonistic center and surround areas, which give a response of opposite sign (ON or OFF) when stimulated with light (Kuffler, 1953; see also Hartline, 1938; Cleland et al., 1971). These cells show either an activation when the center of the receptive field is illuminated or when a darker stimulus is presented to the surround (ON-center), or, conversely, an activation when a dark stimulus is presented in the RF center or when the surround is stimulated with light (OFF-center). These two types of ganglion cell are in fact part of distinct functional networks in the retina, whose connections with bipolar cells are different: ON-center ganglion cells are contacted by depolarizing bipolar cells in sublamina b of the inner plexiform layer, whereas the synapses between the hyperpolarizing bipolar cells and the OFF-center ganglion cells are restricted within sublamina a (Famiglietti et al., 1976; Nelson et al., 1978; but see Freed and Sterling, 1983, 1985). Furthermore the center-surround organization and the antagonism between the two discharge zones of the ganglion receptive field are not a mere consequence of a cross-interaction between the ON- and OFF-systems, but result from the activation of tangential pathways in the retina, i.e., the horizontal and probably also the amacrine cells (Werblin and Dowling, 1969).

The independence of ON- and OFF-pathways was confirmed in the mudpuppy (Slaughter and Miller, 1981) and in the cat retina (Bolz et al., 1984) by intraocular perfusion of 2-amino-4-phosphono-butyric acid (APB), an analogue of glutamic acid. This compound reversibly blocks the response of depolarizing bipolar cells (at the origin of the ON-pathway) leaving the response of photoreceptors, horizontal and OFF-bipolar cells unaltered. In addition, the spatial organization of OFF-center ganglion cells is unchanged during APB perfusion, which indicates that each system (ON- and OFF-) generates the center-surround antagonism separately. Further evidence for distinct parallel ON- and OFF-channels in the retina comes from the extensive anatomical work by Wässle and collaborators (1981a,b; review in Wässle, 1982) who showed a differential stratification of the dendritic trees of ON-center and OFF-center ganglion cells (for both the alpha and the beta morphological classes).

At the geniculate level

The anatomical and functional separation of the ON- and OFF-systems at the retinal level is also preserved at the geniculate level. Principal cells in the LGN have receptive fields similar to those of retinal ganglion cells, i.e., show concentric center/surround organization with spatial antagonism (Hubel and Wiesel, 1961). Despite these similarities, the geniculate receptive fields are probably not the simple expression of a one to one projection from the retina. Simultaneous recordings of a postsynaptic neuron in the LGN and one of its afferent ganglion cells demonstrate that its predominant excitatory input generally comes from a retinal cell of the same functional type (ON/OFF- and X/Y-classes, Cleland et al., 1971a,b); the degree of retino-geniculate convergence was suspected to be very small in this study using cross-correlation analysis, most of the LGN cells receiving their excitatory drive from only one single retinal ganglion cell (Cleland and Lee, 1985, but see Hamos et al., 1987) even though as many as six ganglion cells could contribute to the excitatory drive of individual LGN cells (Cleland et al., 1971a,b). Although there

is strong evidence that the center and the surround subregion in a LGN cell RF arise from projections of different retinal ganglion cells (Hubel and Wiesel, 1961; Hammond, 1972; Virsu et al., 1977), the center and the opposite surround responses originate from the same functional ON- or OFF-system: the center response is fed through direct excitatory inputs and the surround response through indirect inhibitory interneurons (Maffei and Fiorentini, 1972; Hammond, 1973).

Reversible blockade of the retinal ON-center channel by APB as shown in the monkey (Schiller, 1982), in the rabbit (Knapp and Mistler, 1983), and in the cat (Horton and Sherk, 1984) indicates that an effective suppression of the activity of ON-center cells in LGN can be produced while leaving intact both the center and the surround responses of OFF-center neurons. This functional segregation of ON- and OFF-channels in the LGN has, however, no clear anatomical counterpart in the cat (but see below) in contrast to the organization found in other species such as the ferret (Stryker and Zahs, 1983), the mink (Le Vay and McConnell, 1982), the tree shrew (Conway and Schiller, 1983) and the rhesus monkey (Schiller and Malpelli, 1978). In the ferret for instance, the large majority of cells situated in the anterior leaflet (Linden et al., 1981) of layers A and A1 present ON-center responses, while the posterior leaflets contain predominantly OFF-center cells and layer C contains mixed types of RF. Interestingly, recent evidence in the cat indicates that the relative proportions of ON-center and OFF-center cells in A layers differ at different depths within a given lamina (Bowling and Wieniawa-Narkiewicz, 1986, 1987). However, this sublamination is more graded than the separation observed in the monkey, where the more dorsal parvocellular layers contain mostly ON-center cells and the two ventral parvocellular layers contain principally OFF-center cells (Schiller and Malpelli, 1978; Malpelli et al., 1981). In summary, the segregation of ON- and OFF-channels already achieved in the inner plexiform layer of the retina could be preserved at least locally (depending on the species) at the geniculate level (Bowling and Caverhill, 1989). This separation could allow a differential modulatory action of several ascending systems and an independent control of transmission of distinct cell type populations.

At the cortical level

As mentioned in the Introduction, spatial convergence of the excitatory afferents according to their functional type, at the level of the first order simple cells in the cortex, was hypothesized by Hubel and Wiesel ("single line model", 1962) who considered that a simple cell receives inputs from a group of geniculate cells whose RFs are aligned in the visual field and which are of the same type, either ON- or OFF-center. According to this model, the antagonistic zone originated from the uniform nature of the surround of the afferent geniculate cells. A different model was proposed by Bishop et al. (1971), mostly to account for the response of cortical simple cells to moving visual stimuli, where the "inhibitory" or suppressive sidebands originated from intracortical inhibition activated through a pool of different LGN cells. Heggelund (1981a) proposed that these LGN cells driving the intracortical inhibitory input to simple cells were of the same type as the excitatory direct input. Additional support for the "single line" model was provided by Lee and collaborators (1977, 1981a,b) who compared the responses of geniculate and cortical neurons to stimulation with sinusoidal gratings. Most of the responses of simple cortical cells could be explained by a single type of afferent units at lower levels (either ON- or OFF-center).

A somewhat more elaborate description was made by Bullier and collaborators (1982) who studied first-order cortical simple cells in layer IV (determined by latency measurements following electrical stimulation of the optic chiasm and the optic radiations). These simple cells were shown to receive only one type of geniculate input (either ON- or OFF-center) when the cortical RF was exclusively restricted to one zone of discharge (respectively ON or OFF), or two types of geniculate inputs when the cortical RF exhibited two distinct antagonistic subzones of discharge. This "multiple line" model was confirmed using simultaneous extracellular recordings and correlations of activity of a suspected connected pair of geniculate and cortical cells, which showed the contribution of the center region of the geniculate RF to the response of the cortical neuron to be much higher than the contribution of the surround (Tanaka, 1983). These findings were taken as evidence that excitatory subfields of a simple cortical neuron receive direct and separate connections from different ON-center and OFF-center geniculate cells. Note that the convergence of two ON-center and three OFF-center geniculate neurons onto a single simple cortical cell (corresponding respectively to the ON- and the OFF-subregions) was clearly demonstrated using cross-correlation techniques only in one case (Tanaka, 1983).

Further evidence for a possible convergence of ON- and OFF-channels at the level of a uniform subregion of the cortical RF was obtained by the study of the effects of intraocular injection of APB, which blocks transmission of information processed by the ON-pathway (see p. 193). In monkey primary visual cortex, the response of both simple and complex neurons to the light edge of a bar moving across the RF was lost during the perfusion of APB (Schiller, 1982), while the dark edge response was maintained. This effect was accompanied in some cells by the appearance of a previously absent dark-edge response, indicating a possible inhibitory interaction between ON- and OFF-channels. A slightly more confused state of affairs has been reported in the cat, where the dominant effect induced by intraocular APB infusion was found to be a general reduction of responsiveness of cortical cells to stimulation through the injected eye (Sherk and Horton, 1984). Moreover, while for most simple cells the response to the static and dynamic presentation of a light bar is abolished, a significant level of response was retained for a light edge moving across the RF. This APB-resistant response may originate from the ON-surround of OFF-center geniculate cells.

In summary, these data taken together support the hypothesis that for a limited population of simple cells, the ON- and OFF-channels remain separated up to the cortical level: excitatory geniculate inputs exhibit the same functional type as that expressed by the considered cortical subfield. For a large proportion of simple cells as well as for most of the complex cells, it nevertheless seems probable that the convergent excitatory ON- and OFF-pathways represent the whole spatial extent of the RF. In some cases an inhibitory interaction between both afferent pathways can be observed.

Control of the spatial structure of visual cortical receptive fields by intracortical inhibition

The proposal of a putative connectivity scheme responsible for the spatial functional organization of visual RFs requires a preliminary knowledge of excitatory and inhibitory circuits of intrinsic and extrinsic origin contributing to the RF structure. There is a general agreement that simple cells are the main recipient cell type for LGN axons (see for example Bullier and Henry, 1979a,b; Ferster, 1981). Simple cells are often recorded in layers III, IV and VI, and less in layers II and V (Hubel and Wiesel, 1962; Gilbert, 1977), corresponding with the laminar distribution of LGN afferents. Complex cells are uncommon in layer IV and are more often recorded in layers II, III and V (Gilbert, 1977; Martin and Witteridge, 1984). While some of the complex cells (20 – 40%) are directly contacted by geniculate fibers, most receive additional connections from callosal fibers, from recurrent collaterals of corticofugal axons and other intrinsic cortical afferents (Singer et al., 1975; Bullier and Henry, 1979a,b). Besides the excitatory afferent geniculo-cortical connectivity described above, the convergence of ON- and OFF-channels onto simple cells in the cortex also involves local inhibitory circuits (Heggelund, 1981a,b; Palmer and Davis, 1981; Ferster and Lindström, 1983). Simultaneous recordings of connected pairs of geniculate X cells and striate simple cells (Tanaka, 1983) showed that while the early ON-phasic component of the response to a stationary stimulus was similar for both cells, the response lasted longer in the geniculate cell than in the cortical cell. This difference in the duration of

suprathreshold activity was taken as evidence for the triggering of intracortical inhibitory polysynaptic inputs which could regulate the time locking of the response evoked in striate cells.

The role of GABA-ergic inhibition in shaping the spatial organization of visual cortical RFs has been more directly assessed using global (osmotic minipumps) and local (iontophoresis) applications of the GABA-A antagonist bicuculline. The removal of GABA-ergic inhibition by iontophoresis of bicuculline induces a late response in cortical cells similar to that observed in the LGN (see fig. 1 in Wolf et al., 1986). It abolishes the functional selectivity for orientation and direction of movement. It also modifies the spatial structure of the cortical RF (Sillito, 1975), with the result that almost all layer IV simple RFs showed complex-like responses during iontophoresis of bicuculline. Similar observations have been made in the developing cortex: strong (but very heterogeneous) reorganizations of the ON- and OFF-subzones were also observed in 2 – 4-week-old kittens during iontophoresis of bicuculline (Wolf et al., 1986), and very large complex-like RFs were recorded in cortical hemispheres which had been perfused with bicuculline through osmotic minipumps (Ramoa et al., 1988). One may conclude from these observations that inhibitory processes selectively mask excitatory responses which in certain cells extend uniformly across the whole RF. The spatial specificity of this inhibitory control would result in the shaping of spatially separate ON- and OFF-profiles from an initially mixed convergence of excitatory ON- and OFF-inputs.

Shaping of the spatial organization of visual cortical receptive fields by visual experience

Normal development of RF organization

So far we have reviewed evidence for the separation of the two functionally distinct ON- and OFF-systems in the retino-geniculo-cortical pathway of the adult cat. The convergence of the excitatory ON- and OFF-afferents at the cortical level together with the involvement of inhibitory intracortical connectivity results in the stabilization of only two major types of cortical receptive fields. The rules which control the emergence of these two classes of RF are, however, poorly understood. Very few attempts have been made electrophysiologically to justify the simple/complex scheme by looking quantitatively at the development of the spatial arrangement of ON- and OFF-responses. It still remains to be clarified why only two types of receptive field, among all the possible arrangements of ON- and OFF-input, are stabilized in the adult, and whether the typology once acquired by a cell is fixed throughout life (see Lehky and Sejnowski, 1988).

Previous studies have shown that the cortical neuropil is far from being completely developed at birth. For example, the number of synapses was seen to increase considerably during an early phase of postnatal development (Cragg, 1975) and neuroanatomical and physiological evidence has been provided for the postnatal formation and regression of excitatory and inhibitory connectivity (Innocenti et al., 1977; Komatsu and Iwakiri, 1991). Moreover, the immaturity of the primary visual cortex, concerning both the afferent connectivity and the laminar organization during at least the first three postnatal weeks (Shatz and Luskin, 1986) is difficult to reconcile with the proposal that cortical receptive fields do not show any major reorganization in structure after birth, as proposed by Hubel and Wiesel (1963) and Braastad and Heggelund (1985). Even if the two types of RF (i.e., simple and complex) are indeed recorded in the very young kitten, the relative representation of several RF properties to static stimulation have been shown to evolve during a postnatal developmental period. OFF-responses were found more prominent at the time of eye opening, and this asymmetry in the relative responsiveness was reversed by the middle of the critical period (Albus and Wolf, 1984). Furthermore, the width of the discharge zone decreases gradually with age in both simple and complex RFs, as well as the latency between the onset of the stimulus and the beginning of the response (Braastad and Heggelund, 1985). These changes, together with the fact that both excitatory and inhibitory synaptic potentials (Komatsu and Iwakiri, 1991) are less efficient

in the young kitten than in the adult, suggest that there is a postnatal reorganization of the receptive field structure and of its underlying connectivity during the first weeks of age (see also Tsumoto and Suda, 1982). Whether this process is dependent on visually structured activity, or on propagated activity of retinal or non-retinal origin, is still not yet fully understood (see Archer et al., 1982, and next section).

The major problems met in studies of the development of ON/OFF-responses in cortical neurons are the extremely low level of responsiveness, rapid habituation, and high variability of the static visual response (see for example Hubel and Wiesel, 1963, and Frégnac and Imbert, 1978). Despite this difficulty in recording in the very young animal, Braastad and Heggelund (1985) reported globally adult-like RF organizations and both simple and complex cells were found at the time of eye opening. Different observations were obtained by Albus and Wolf (1984) recording from normally reared kittens at 1–4 weeks of age. After the second postnatal week the proportion of multimodal simple receptive fields with segregated ON- and OFF-subregions increased gradually with age. Interestingly, the few complex-like cells recorded in the very young kittens were found in layer IV, which is classically thought to contain unimodal and simple cells in the adult (see Hubel and Wiesel, 1962). Their presence in this layer could be considered as a transient stage in the functional development of layer IV simple RFs, which could require the gradual development of GABA-ergic inhibitory input to these neurons in order to exhibit antagonistic subfields (Komatsu and Iwakiri, 1991; see also Sillito, 1975).

Abnormal development of spatial receptive field organization

Although numerous studies have demonstrated that functional properties of cortical cells can be modified by manipulation of visual input (review in Frégnac and Imbert, 1984), there is a lack of quantitative evidence demonstrating that the spatial organization of the cortical receptive field depends on visual experience. Abnormally large receptive fields ($> 10°$) with two or more distant zones of discharge have been occasionally reported in kittens following a selective exposure to a grating stimulus of fixed orientation and spatial frequency (Spinelli et al., 1972; Singer and Tretter, 1976). In some of the cells recorded in these animals, the response histograms to a single slit of light moving across the receptive field show two or more discharge zones, separated by a distance which corresponds exactly to the spatial period of the grating experienced during the restricted exposure. These results suggest that ectopic zones of weak responses can be revealed in cortical neurons by extreme rearing conditions which locally disrupt the precision of the retinotopic map (Milleret et al., 1988). These additional subfields could be progressively masked by the late development of intracortical inhibition and the spatial extent of the RF refined by visual experience. Uncommon receptive fields were also described after selective exposure of animals to planetarium-like environments (Pettigrew and Freeman, 1973; Van Sluyters and Blakemore, 1973).

Plasticity of visual cortical receptive field organization

The data reviewed in the last section support our central proposal that a reorganization of the spatial structure of cortical RFs occurs during visual functioning. There is, however, no direct evidence of acute changes in the relative strength of ON- and OFF-responses during the recording from a single neuron. In order to demonstrate whether simple and complex RFs could be different functional expressions of the same omnipotent structure, we have recently developed an approach to induce modifications in the spatial organization of ON- and OFF-responses in restricted regions of the RF using juxtacellular current injection. The experimental protocol is adapted from a differential cellular conditioning technique which had been succesfully used in the anesthetized and paralyzed animal to modify the orientation selectivity, ocular dominance and interocular orientation disparity of cortical neurons

(see Frégnac et al., 1988; review in Frégnac and Shulz, 1992).

This conditioning procedure has been devised to implement cellular analogs of learning. The underlying theoretical assumption is that the synaptic gain of active synapses is controlled by the temporal correlation between afferent and postsynaptic activity of the recorded cell (Hebb, 1949; Sejnowski, 1977; Bienenstock et al., 1982). The experimental paradigm used to control this correlation is to impose various levels of postsynaptic activity by applying iontophoretic current pulses (usually less than $+/- 10$ nA) through the juxtacellular recording electrode ($2 - 20$ MΩ, 3 M KCl) as a function of the physical parameters of the visual stimulus presented within the RF of the recorded cell. For a given characteristic of the visual input, a positive change in the correlation between pre- and postsynaptic activity was imposed by increasing the postsynaptic firing rate, i.e., concomitantly by applying a depolarizing pulse (positive current and increase of extracellular potassium). In alternation, for a different input message, a negative change in correlation was imposed by reducing or blocking the postsynaptic response, i.e., by applying a negative current pulse (which appears to hyperpolarize the target cell through a juxtacellular field effect). Adaptation of three different properties intrinsic to visual cortical organization: ocular dominance (Frégnac et al., 1988; Shulz and Frégnac, 1992), orientation selectivity (Frégnac et al., 1988, 1992) and interocular orientation disparity (Shulz and Frégnac, 1992), were demonstrated in $30 - 40\%$ of the conditioned cells, following several tens of associative pairings, and these changes could last up to several hours. The synaptic basis of these functional modifications has been looked for, using a similar type of protocol adapted in vitro. Compound excitatory postsynaptic potentials, recorded intracellularly in layers II – IV in kitten and adult guinea pig visual cortex, can be up- and down-regulated as a function of the temporal correlation between afferent white matter stimulation and the membrane potential of the target neurone

198

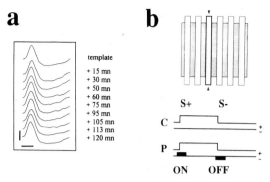

a

template
+ 15 mn
+ 30 mn
+ 50 mn
+ 60 mn
+ 75 mn
+ 95 mn
+ 105 mn
+ 113 mn
+ 120 mn

b

S+   S-

C

P

ON   OFF

Fig. 1. Experimental protocol. *a*. For each cell, the shape of the extracellular action potential was monitored on a digital oscilloscope and compared with an initial template in order to establish the identity of the recorded neuron. *b*. The spatial distribution of ON- and OFF-responses in the RF (shaded area) was explored with an optimally oriented bar flashed sequentially in several positions. During control (C) the optimal stimulus was presented 10 – 50 times without iontophoretic current (ON-duration: 3000 msec, OFF-duration: 3000 msec). During pairing (P) restricted to a given position in the RF (arrow), iontophoretic pulses of opposite polarity (+ / −) were applied through the KCl recording electrode concomitantly with the presentation (ON) and extinction (OFF) of the visual stimulus, in such a way as to impose a significant increase (S^+) or decrease (S^-) of the visual response. The RF was explored in the paired position and in the unpaired positions after pairing in the same conditions as before (C, without current).

(Friedlander et al., this volume). These synaptic changes which could underlly functional adaptation of the RF are in addition shown to be input-specific.

The protocol we developed in order to modify the RF structure was chosen to benefit from the natural asynchrony in the activation between ON- and OFF-pathways. As shown in Fig. 1, this requires the separate activation of ON- and OFF-afferents. The data reviewed in the preceding sections show clearly that these two systems remain separate from the retina to the cortex, and for a majority of simple cells and many of the complex cells in area 17, the presentation (ON) and extinction (OFF) of the stimulus within the receptive field will indeed activate separate sets of cortical synapses. The independent manipulations of the level of responses to the presentation and the extinction of a static stimulus in a fixed position of the RF are thought to

lead to a competition between converging afferents of antagonistic type.

Before the conditioning procedure, an optimally oriented static bar of light was presented repetitively in at least two non-overlapping positions of the receptive field (see Fig. 1). During the differential pairing procedure, the response of the recorded cell to either the presentation (ON-response) or the extinction (OFF-response) of the stimulus in a fixed position of the RF (position with arrows in Fig. 1) was artificially increased to a "high" firing rate (S^+). In alternation, the antagonistic response was decreased to obtain a "low" level or eventually blocked (S^-). Finally, after pairing, the relative ON- and OFF-responses in the paired and unpaired positions were studied. Additional control positions in the RF were systematically explored as a control of the spatial selectivity of the effect, and in 47% of modified cells a possible generalization of the effects was quantitatively measured across the whole width of the RF. To ensure that the receptive field position remained unchanged throughout the recording session, additional controls were performed before and after pairing by studying responses to dynamic stimulation across the RF. Any temporal shift of the peaks of discharge in the response histogram with respect to the onset of the stimulation was considered as evidence for residual movements of the eyes and the cell was discarded from further analysis. The temporal evolution of the relative ratio of complexity: $S^+/(S^+ + S^-)$, in both the paired and unpaired positions was calculated using a moving average technique on $2 - 4$ pairs of successive ON- and OFF-stimulations (Frégnac and Bienenstock, 1981), and statistically compared before, versus after pairing, using non-parametric tests (significance level of 0.05 using Kolmogorov-Smirnov and Mann-Whitney tests).

We could induce significant long-lasting modifications of the ratio of ON- and OFF-responses in about 40% of the paired cells. Such changes were never observed spontaneously and the functional reorganization in the paired position was predicted in more than 90% of the cases by the pattern of activity imposed during the pairing procedure. The relative preference between the two test stimulus characteristics (ON/OFF) was generally displaced towards that which had been paired with imposed increased visual responsiveness. The probability of inducing functional changes was comparable in the kitten from 4 to 15 weeks of age and in older kittens and adults (from 16 weeks to adulthood). However, as had been observed for the other functional properties of cortical cells, the largest effects were induced in the youngest animals at the peak of the critical period.

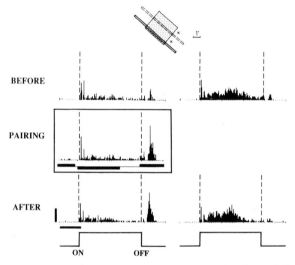

BEFORE

PAIRING

AFTER

ON   OFF

Fig. 2. Potentiation of an OFF-response of a simple cell recorded in a 5-week-old kitten. Two positions of the RF (shaded rectangle) were studied in alternation. Response histograms for the paired (solid bar) and control (dotted bar) positions are shown respectively in the left and right columns. Before pairing this cell exhibited a strong dominant ON-response in both positions. The pairing procedure consisted of 50 associations of a negative current pulse (-4 nA, 2000 msec) with the presentation of the test stimulus, and of a positive current ($+4$ nA, 2000 msec) with the extinction of the same stimulus. The onset of the current pulses preceded the ON- and OFF-transitions of the visual stimulus by 100 msec. A significant reinforcement of the OFF-response was imposed during pairing whereas the negative current was ineffective in reducing the ON-response. Ten minutes after pairing, the OFF-response in the paired position was significantly potentiated (modification of the ON/(ON + OFF) ratio, Kolmogorov-Smirnov, $P < 0.008$). This effect was selective for the paired position (compare the two histograms before and after in the right column) and lasted for at least an additional hour until the cell was lost. Calibration bars: horizontally 1 sec; vertically 10 action potentials/sec.

An example of a significant modification of the relative ON/OFF ratio in a simple cell recorded at the peak of the critical period is illustrated in Fig. 2. Initially, the cell showed a uniform dominant ON-response throughout the RF, and a sluggish and variable OFF-response. The pairing procedure (P) consisted of reinforcement of the OFF-response. The negative current applied during the presentation of the stimulus, however, had no significant effect on the level of the ON-response. After 50 pairings, a significant increase in the OFF-response similar to that imposed during pairing was observed in the absence of iontophoretic current applied through the recording electrode. Thus, in this initially simple RF, the paired position after conditioning exhibited a typical complex-like response, while the unpaired control position still retained its dominant ON-characteristic.

Modifications of the RF structure have been induced in complex cells as well, as illustrated in Fig. 3. This neuron recorded in a 6-week-old kitten initially shows a tonic ON-response and a phasic OFF-response in the two studied positions. The conditioning (not shown) consisted of a reinforcement (S^+) of the OFF-response whereas the ON-response was associated with a low level of firing (S^-). Forty minutes after pairing, the ON-response in the conditioned position had almost disappeared and the OFF-response was greatly potentiated. The complexity ratio in this position was completely reversed by the conditioning, while the unpaired control position remained unchanged.

In 56% of modified cells, the effects of the conditioning were restricted to the paired position, suggesting the presence of different ON- and OFF-synaptic sets subviewing the same RF zone. In the remaining 44%, the effects were not restricted to the paired position. In half of these cases the modification was uniform and affected the whole extent of the RF. In the other cells antagonistic effects were observed in other parts of the RF, which could suggest heterosynaptic changes induced by the pairing procedure. This interpretation does not preclude excitatory homosynaptic changes, the expression of which could be controlled by the spatial extent of in-

200

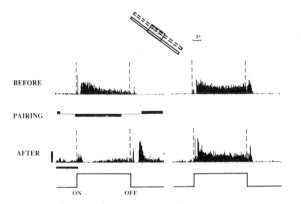

BEFORE

PAIRING

AFTER

ON   OFF

Fig. 3. Depression of an ON-response of a complex cell recorded in a 6-week-old kitten. Control response histograms for the paired position (solid bar in the upper RF diagram) are shown on the left; recordings in the unpaired position (dotted bar) are shown on the right. Before pairing a tonic ON-response and a transient OFF-response were observed uniformly across the RF. The pairing procedure (not shown) consisted of 50 associations of a negative current (-3 nA, 2120 msec) with the presentation of the light bar (preceding its onset by 100 msec), and of a depolarizing current ($+3.2$ nA, 2150 msec) following the extinction of the same stimulus with a constant delay of 500 msec. Forty minutes after pairing, the ON-response in the paired position was significantly depressed whereas a late OFF-response was significantly potentiated (modification of the ON/(ON + OFF) ratio tested with Kolmorogov-Smirnov, $P < 0.0005$). However, the ON/OFF ratio was unchanged in the unpaired position. Following the pairing procedure the spatial structure of this initially complex RF exhibited two antagonistic regions of opposite response ON-OFF dominance. Calibration bars: horizontally 1 sec; vertically 20 action potentials/sec.

hibitory processes. An illustration of this latter case was found in a few simple cells which initially showed a complete spatial separation between ON- and OFF-responses, and where the conditioning was attempted on the medial border of one of the subfields. In this chosen position (i.e., ON) an S$^-$ pairing resulted in a significant decrease of the paired dominant response, as predicted from our working hypothesis. This effect was generalized to the entire subfield. However, a significant increase in the opposite response (i.e., OFF) was apparent in the unpaired antagonistic subfield of the RF. Our interpretation of these observations in multimodal fields is that ON- and OFF-inputs overlap within the RF,

but that suprathreshold modifications are only expressed in the zones where inhibitory responses of the same functional type were not present.

In spite of occasional global excitability changes, most modifications could be interpreted in terms of competitive changes in responsiveness. These results are consistent with the hypothesis that temporal correlation between pre- and postsynaptic activities could control the efficiency of transmission of already existing synapses. The same rule of synaptic plasticity could hold both in the developing and adult cortex. The significant potential of functional plasticity in adult RFs found in our study is certainly not specific to the primary visual cortex. It is consistent with recent studies showing reordering of topographic maps in the somatosensory cortex of adult animals (Merzenich et al., 1984; Clark et al., 1988). In contrast to our artificially imposed procedures of cellular conditioning, this experiment describes adaptation of topographic mapping of the sensory input as a result of learning processes in the normal behaving animal. Although based on the comparison of sensory maps rather than on changes described at the single neuron level, a large functional reorganization has been demonstrated in the topography of cortical cutaneous receptive fields in the somatosensory cortex of the adult monkey. Dynamic changes in somatotopy could be traced following manipulation of the peripheral afferents (by amputation or fusion of digits of the monkey's hand) or following learning periods where a particular peripheral region (tip of one digit) was continuously stimulated during an attentive task (review in Jenkins et al., 1990). A similar approach was applied recently to the primary visual cortex of adult cats (Kaas et al., 1990) and monkeys (Gilbert and Wiesel, 1991; Heinen and Skavenski, 1991). Restricted lesions of the retina were shown to induce a significant reorganization of the cortical maps such that RFs in the silenced regions shifted their representation to sample portions of the visual space surrounding the retinal lesions. Taken together with the results of our own study, these changes emphasize the adaptive capacities of primary sensory cortical networks in the adult animal, which can be

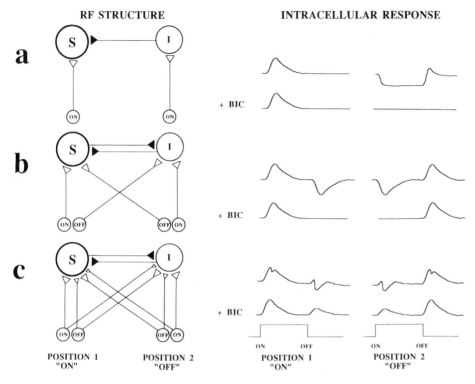

RF STRUCTURE   INTRACELLULAR RESPONSE

Fig. 4. Theoretical connectivity schemes subserving simple receptive fields. Three different models of the structure of a simple RF (S) are compared, which all involve direct excitation (open triangle) from geniculo-cortical ON- and OFF-pathways and intracortical inhibition (filled triangle, through cortical interneuron I). The right panel shows the intracellular ON- and OFF-responses of the S-cell predicted by each connectivity diagram (*a* – *c*), when stimulating each of the two antagonistic subregions of the RF (position 1, "ON", position 2, "OFF"). Three models are presented: *a* is adapted from Heggelund (1981a,b), *b* from Palmer and Davis (1981), and *c* is the "Simplex" RF model. In the right panel, the predicted intracellular responses to stimulation in each position are illustrated in the presence (upper trace) and in the absence (lower trace, + BIC) of GABA-A inhibition.

functionally expressed during selective phases of learning or in response to peripheral injury.

Conclusion: what plasticity tells about receptive field structure

The demonstration of experimentally induced transformation of a simple RF subzone into a complex one (and conversely) suggests a reunifying model of RF organization, called "Simplex" model, where cortical receptive fields are presumed to be derived from a unique type of afferent connectivity (see Fig. 4). Modifications of synaptic gains under the control of local coactivity make this RF model compatible with spatial organization plasticity revealed using our paradigm and described during epigenesis. They are also in agreement with mathematical simulations (Linsker, 1986) of the emergence of two stable final states (simple and complex) during spontaneous or evoked functioning.

This model can be compared with classical schemes of a bimodal simple RF presented in Fig. 4a, and uses the basic spatial antagonism schematized by Heggelund (1981a,b). It takes into account the demonstration by Bishop and colleagues (1971, 1973) of suppressive zones of activity, initially suggested by Hubel and Wiesel (1962) to explain the existence of inhibitory antagonism between ON- and OFF-subzones in simple RFs. Enhancement of the ongoing activity by a conditioning stimulus and the presentation of a test stimulus over the RF reveals suppressive sidebands around the excitatory region which were often asymmetric in strength. The stronger inhibitory sideband corresponds to the spatial opponent inhibition reported by Palmer and Davis (1981) using systematic and extensive static exploration of the RF. As described in Heggelund's model (Fig. 4a), the ON-presentation of the light bar elicits a direct excitatory response in position 1 and a tonic indirect inhibition in position 2. No antagonistic response is observed after the extinction of the light bar in position 1, whereas the consecutive release of inhibition in position 2 creates an excitatory rebound which is not synaptically mediated. Note that the functional type (simple/complex) of interneuron (I) does not need to be defined in this model. Bicuculline application would not affect the response in the first position but would abolish all responses in the second position.

This initial RF model was modified by Palmer and Davis (1981) and confirmed by Ferster (1988) on the basis of intracellular records. Inhibitory postsynaptics potentials were observed upon extinction of the stimulus in an ON-zone and conversely when a stimulus was presented in an OFF-region. In the model presented in Fig. 4b, each position of the bimodal RF is sustained by both types of LGN input (one direct and the other indirect through an intracortical interneuron). The interneuron (I) and the considered cell (S) in this case have antagonistic simple RFs and inhibit each other. The ON-presentation of the test stimulus gives a direct excitatory response in position 1 and an indirect inhibitory one in position 2. The extinction of the same stimulus elicits an indirect inhibitory response in position 1 and a direct excitatory response in position 2. Bicuculline application would remove inhibitory responses in each position and reveal pure excitatory responses of corresponding type in each RF subregion (i.e., ON-response in the ON "zone", and OFF-response in the OFF "zone").

The "Simplex" RF model we propose shows similar properties but assumes a more complex-like structure in each subfield: as shown in Fig. 4c, each

position feeds direct parallel ON- and OFF-inputs with different relative synaptic weights (symbolized by the size of the triangles). When the test stimulus is turned ON in position 1, the composite intracellular response remains excitatory because of a stronger efficiency in the transmission of the direct LGN ON-input compared with those of the indirect LGN ON-input. When the light bar is turned OFF, the relative synaptic weights of each input line leads to an inhibitory composite output dominated by the indirect inhibitory pathway. A similar reasoning could explain the antagonistic visual response observed in position 2. This connectivity scheme correctly predicts (using Hebbian schemes of excitatory synaptic plasticity) the functional modifications observed after our conditioning procedure, shown in Figs. 2 and 3. However, one cannot totally exclude the contribution of inhibitory synaptic plasticity since in particular in the complex RF shown in Fig. 3, the loss of the ON-response in the paired position could also be due to the depression of an excitatory ON-input or to the potentiation of an inhibitory ON-input. The "Simplex" model also adequately simulates the effects of bicuculline application (+ BIC in Fig. 4), since the predicted visual response would be "complex-like" as found by Sillito (1975) and Ramoa et al. (1988). Thus complex RFs could be simply formed from the "Simplex" model by removing (physically or virtually) inhibitory connections.

In conclusion, simple and complex RFs which are classically considered as two major functional types which coexist in the adult primary visual cortex could arise from a common omnipotent "Simplex" connectivity scheme. After a developmental stage where activity-dependent processes progressively shape the spatial structure of the cortical RFs, only a restricted part of the connections would be functionally expressed. Hebbian-like rules of synaptic plasticity are proposed to regulate spatial competition between simple and complex configurations of ON- and OFF-afferents across the RF, which would eventually result in the selective stabilization of one of these mutually exclusive final states. The connections which are not recruited by simple RFs might still be anatomically present, but would be silent or masked by inhibitory processes. It remains nevertheless plausible that later coherent changes in coactivity levels, induced by anomalous visual experience or imposed through learning, might reveal local adaptation in the complexity ratio expressed in subregions of the receptive field, even at the adult age.

Acknowledgements

The experimental work presented in this review was supported by funds from HFSP and CEE (Brain ST2J-0416-C) to Yves Frégnac. Dominique Debanne was supported by MRT and Fondation Singer-Polignac. We are grateful to Dr. Etienne Audinat and Pr. Michael J. Friedlander for their comments. We thank Dr. Kirsty Grant for help with the English and Michèle Gautier for technical assistance.

References

Albus, K. and Wolf, N. (1984) Early postnatal development of neuronal function in the kittens visual cortex: a laminar analysis. *J. Physiol. (Lond.)*, 349: 153 – 185.

Archer, S.M., Dubin, M.W. and Stark, L.A. (1982) Abnormal development of kitten retino-geniculate connectivity in the absence of action potentials. *Science*, 217: 743 – 745.

Bienenstock, E., Cooper, L.N. and Munro, P. (1982) Theory for the development of neuron selectivity: orientation specificity and binocular interaction in visual cortex. *J. Neurosci.*, 2: 23 – 48.

Bishop, P.O., Combs, J.S. and Henry, G.H. (1971) Response to visual contours: spatio temporal aspects of excitation in the receptive fields of single striate neurons. *J. Physiol. (Lond.)*, 219: 625 – 657.

Bishop, P.O., Coombs, J.S. and Henry, G.H. (1973) Receptive fields of simple cells in the cat striate cortex. *J. Physiol. (Lond.)*, 231: 31 – 60.

Bolz, J., Wässle, H. and Thier, P. (1984) Pharmacological modulation of ON and OFF ganglion cells in the cat retina. *Neuroscience*, 12: 875 – 885.

Bowling, D.B. and Caverhill, J.I. (1989) ON/OFF organization in the cat lateral geniculate nucleus: subliminae Vs columns. *J. Comp. Neurol.*, 283: 161 – 168.

Bowling, D.B. and Wieniawa-Narkiewicz, E. (1986) The distribution of ON- and OFF-centre X- and Y-like cells in the A layers of the cat's lateral geniculate nucleus. *J. Physiol. (Lond.)*, 375: 561 – 572.

Bowling, D.B. and Wieniawa-Narkiewicz, E. (1987) Differences in the amplitude of X-cell responses as a function of depth in layer A of lateral geniculate nucleus in cat. *J. Physiol. (Lond.)*, 390: 201 – 212.

Braastad, B.D. and Heggelund, P. (1985) Development of spatial receptive field organization and orientation selectivity in the kitten striate cortex. *J. Neurophysiol.*, 53: 1158 – 1178.

Bullier, J. and Henry, G.H. (1979a) Ordinal position of neurons in cat striate cortex. *J. Neurophysiol.*, 42: 1251 – 1263.

Bullier, J. and Henry, G.H. (1979b) Laminar distribution of first-order neurons and afferent terminals in cat striate cortex. *J. Neurophysiol.*, 42: 1271 – 1281.

Bullier, J., Mustari, M.J. and Henry, G.H. (1982) Receptive-field transformations between LGN neurons and S-cells of cat striate cortex. *J. Neurophysiol.*, 47: 417 – 438.

Clark, R.M., Allerd, T., Jenkins, W.M. and Merzenich, M.M. (1988) Receptive fields in the body surface map in adult cortex defined by temporally correlated inputs. *Nature*, 332: 444 – 446.

Cleland, B.G. and Lee, B.B. (1985) A comparison of visual responses of cat lateral geniculate nucleus neurones with those of ganglion cells afferent to them. *J. Physiol. (Lond.)*, 369: 249 – 268.

Cleland, B.G., Dubin, M.W. and Levick, W.R. (1971a) Sustained and transient neurones in the cats retina and LGN. *J. Neurophysiol.*, 217: 473 – 496.

Cleland, B.G., Dubin, M.W. and Levick, W.R. (1971b) Simultaneous recording of input and output of lateral geniculate neurones. *Nature*, 231: 191 – 192.

Conway, J.L. and Schiller, P.H. (1983) Laminar organization of tree shrew dorsal lateral geniculate nucleus. *J. Neurophysiol.*, 50: 1330 – 1342.

Cragg, B.G. (1975) The development of synapses in the visual system of the cat. *J. Comp. Neurol.*, 160: 147 – 166.

Dean, A.F. and Tolhurst, D.J. (1983) On the distinctness of simple and complex cells in the visual cortex of the cat. *J. Physiol. (Lond.)*, 344: 305 – 325.

Famiglietti, E.V., Kaneko, A. and Tachibana, M. (1976) Neuronal architecture of ON and OFF pathways to ganglion cells in the carp retina. *Science*, 198: 1267 – 1269.

Ferster, D. (1981) A comparison of binocular depth mechanisms in area 17 and 18 of the cat visual cortex. *J. Physiol. (Lond.)*, 331: 623 – 655.

Ferster, D. (1988) Spatially opponent excitation and inhibition in simple cells of the cat visual cortex. *J. Neurosci.*, 8: 1172 – 1180.

Ferster, D. and Lindström, S. (1983) An intracellular analysis of geniculo-cortical connectivity in area 17 of the cat. *J. Physiol. (Lond.)*, 342: 181 – 215.

Freed, M.A. and Sterling, P. (1983) Spatial distribution of input from depolarizing cone bipolars to dendritic tree of on-center alpha ganglion cell. *Soc. Neurosci. Abstr.*, 9: 806.

Freed, M.A. and Sterling, P. (1985) Microcircuitry of cone bipolar input to on-center alpha and beta ganglion cells. *Assoc. Res. Vis. Ophthal.*, 9: 194.

Frégnac, Y. and Bienenstock, E. (1981) Specific functional modifications of individual cortical neurones, triggered by vision and passive eye-movement, in immobilized kittens. In: L. Maffei (Ed.), *Pathophysiology of the Visual System*, Junk, The Hague, pp. 101–108.

Frégnac, Y. and Imbert, M. (1978) Early development of visual cells in normal and dark reared kittens: relationship between orientation selectivity and ocular dominance. *J. Physiol. (Lond.)*, 278: 27–44.

Frégnac, Y. and Imbert, M. (1984) Development of neuronal selectivity in the primary visual cortex of the cat. *Physiol. Rev.*, 64: 325–434.

Frégnac, Y. and Shulz, D. (1992) Models of synaptic plasticity and cellular analogs of learning in the developing and adult vertebrate visual cortex. In: V. Casagrande and P. Shinkman (Eds.), *Advances in Neural and Behavioral Development, Vol. 4*, Neutral Ablex, New Jersey, in press.

Frégnac, Y., Shulz, D., Thorpe, S. and Bienenstock, E. (1988) A cellular analogue of visual cortical plasticity. *Nature*, 333: 367–370.

Frégnac, Y., Shulz, D., Thorpe, S. and Bienenstock, E. (1992) Cellular analogues of visual cortical epigenesis: I. Plasticity of orientation selectivity. *J. Neurosci.*, 12: 1280–1300.

Gilbert, C. (1977) Laminar differences in receptive field properties of cells in cat primary visual cortex. *J. Physiol. (Lond.)*, 268: 391–421.

Gilbert, C. and Wiesel, T.N. (1991) Dynamic properties of visual cortical cells. *NATO Advanced Research Workshop on Physiological and Computational Aspects of Cortical Functions, Sirolo, Italy*, pp. 20–25.

Hammond, P. (1972) Chromatic sensitivity and spatial organization of LNG neurone receptive field in cat: con-rod interaction. *J. Physiol. (Lond.)*, 225: 391–413.

Hammond, P. (1973) Contrasts in spatial organization of receptive fields at geniculate and retinal levels: centre, surround and outer surround. *J. Physiol. (Lond.)*, 228: 115–137.

Hamos, J.E., Van Horn, S.C., Rackowski, D. and Sherman, S.M. (1987) Synaptic circuits involving an individual retinogeniculate axon in the cat. *J. Comp. Neurol.*, 259: 165–192.

Hartline, H.K. (1938) The responses of single optic nerve fibers of the vertebrate eye to illumination of the retina. *Am. J. Physiol.*, 212: 400–415.

Hebb, D.O. (1949) *The Organization of Behavior*, Wiley, New York.

Heggelund, P. (1981a) Receptive field organization of simple cells in cat striate cortex. *Exp. Brain Res.*, 42: 89–98.

Heggelund, P. (1981b) Receptive field organization of complex cells in cat striate cortex. *Exp. Brain Res.*, 42: 99–107.

Heggelund, P. (1986) Quantitative studies of the discharge fields of single cells in cat striate cortex. *J. Physiol. (Lond.)*, 373: 277–292.

Heinen, S.J. and Skavenski, A.A. (1991) Recovery of visual responses in foveal V1 neurons following bilateral foveal le-

sions in adult monkey. *Exp. Brain Res.*, 83: 670–674.

Hoffmann, K.P. and Stone, J. (1971) Conduction velocity of afferents to cat visual cortex: a correlation with cortical receptive field properties. *Brain Res.*, 32: 460–466.

Horton, J.C. and Sherk, H. (1984) Receptive field properties in the cat's lateral geniculate nucleus in the absence of ON-center retinal input. *J. Neurosci.*, 4: 374–380.

Hubel, D.H. and Wiesel, T.N. (1961) Integrative action in the cat's lateral geniculate body. *J. Physiol. (Lond.)*, 155: 383–398.

Hubel, D.H. and Wiesel, T.N. (1962) Receptive fields, binocular interaction and functional architecture in the cat's visual cortex. *J. Physiol. (Lond.)*, 160: 106–154.

Hubel, D.H. and Wiesel, T.N. (1963) Receptive fields of cells in striate cortex of very young, visually inexperienced kittens. *J. Neurophysiol.*, 26: 994–1002.

Innocenti, G.M., Fiore, L. and Caminiti, R. (1977) Exuberant projection into the corpus callosum from the visual cortex of newborn cats. *Neurosci. Lett.*, 4: 237–242.

Jenkins, W.M., Merzenich, M.M., Ochs, M.T., Allard, T. and Guic-Robles, E. (1990) Functional reorganization of primary somatosensory cortex in adult owl monkeys after behaviorally controlled tactile stimulation. *J. Neurophysiol.*, 63: 92–104.

Kaas, J.H., Krubitzer, L.A., Chino, Y.M., Langston, A.L., Polley, E.H. and Blair, N. (1990) Reorganization of retinotopic maps in adult mammals after lesions of the retina. *Science*, 248: 229–231.

Knapp, A.G. and Mistler, L.A. (1983) Response properties of cells in the rabbit's lateral geniculate nucleus during reversible blockade of retinal on-center channel. *J. Neurophysiol.*, 50: 1236–1245.

Komatsu, Y. and Iwakiri, M. (1991) Postnatal development of neuronal connections in cat visual cortex studied by intracellular recording slice preparation. *Brain Res.*, 540: 14–24.

Kuffler, S.W. (1953) Discharge patterns and functional organization of the mammalian retina. *J. Neurophysiol.*, 16: 37–68.

Lee, B.B., Virsu, V. and Creutzfeldt, O. (1977) Responses of cells in the cat lateral geniculate nucleus to moving stimuli at various levels of light and dark adaptation. *Exp. Brain Res.*, 27: 51–59.

Lee, B.B., Elefandt, A. and Virsu, V. (1981a) Phase of responses to moving sinusoïdal gratings in cells of cat retina and lateral geniculate nucleus. *J. Neurophysiol.*, 45: 807–817.

Lee, B.B., Elefandt, A. and Virsu, V. (1981b) Phase of responses to sinusoïdal gratings of simple cells in cat striate cortex. *J. Neurophysiol.*, 45: 818–828.

Lehky, S.R. and Sejnowski, T.J. (1988) Network model of shape-from-shading: neural function arises from both receptive and projective fields. *Nature*, 333: 452–454.

Le Vay, S. and McConnell, K.S. (1982) ON and OFF layers in the lateral geniculate nucleus of the mink. *Nature*, 300: 350–351.

Linden, D.C., Guillery, R.W. and Cucchiaro, J. (1981) The dorsal geniculate nucleus of the normal ferret and its postnatal development. *J. Comp. Neurol.*, 203: 189 – 211.

Linsker, R. (1986) From basic network principles to neural architecture: emergence of orientation selective cells. *Proc. Natl. Acad. Sci. U.S.A.*, 83: 8390 – 8394.

Maffei, L. and Fiorentini, A. (1972) Retinogeniculate convergence and analysis of contrast. *J. Neurophysiol.*, 35: 65 – 72.

Malpelli, J.G., Schiller, P.H. and Colby, C.L. (1981) Response properties of single cells in monkey striate cortex during reversible inactivation of individual lateral geniculate laminae. *J. Neurophysiol.*, 46: 1102 – 1119.

Martin, K.A.C. and Whitteridge, D. (1984) Form, function and intracortical projections of spiny neurones in the striate visual cortex of the cat. *J. Physiol. (Lond.)*, 353: 463 – 504.

Merzenich, M.M., Nelson, R.J., Stryker, M.P., Cynader, M.S., Schoppmann, A. and Zook, J.M. (1984) Somatosensory cortical map changes following digit amputation in adult monkeys. *J. Comp. Neurol.*, 224: 591 – 605.

Milleret, C., Gary-Bobo, E. and Buisseret, P. (1988) Comparative development of cell properties in cortical area 18 of normal and dark-reared kittens. *Exp. Brain Res.*, 71: 8 – 20.

Nelson, R., Famiglietti, E.V. and Kolb, H. (1978) Intracellular staining reveals different levels of stratification for ON- and OFF-center ganglion cells in the cat retina. *J. Neurophysiol.*, 41: 472 – 483.

Orban, G. (1984) *Neural Operations in the Visual Cortex*, Springer, Berlin, Heidelberg.

Palmer, L.A. and Davis, T.A. (1981) Receptive field structure in cat striate cortex. *J. Neurophysiol.*, 46: 260 – 276.

Pettigrew, J.D. and Freeman, R.D. (1973) Visual experience without lines: effect on developing cortical neurons. *Science*, 182: 599 – 601.

Ramoa, A.S., Paradiso, M.A. and Freeman, R.D. (1988) Blockade of intracortical inhibition in kitten striate cortex: effects on receptive field properties and associated loss of ocular dominance plasticity. *Exp. Brain Res.*, 73: 285 – 296.

Schiller, P.H. (1982) Central connection of the retinal ON and OFF pathways. *Nature*, 297: 580 – 583.

Schiller, P.H. and Malpelli, J.G. (1978) Functional specificity of lateral geniculate nucleus laminae of the rhesus monkey. *J. Neurophysiol.*, 41: 788 – 797.

Sejnowski, T.J. (1977) Statistical constraints on synaptic plasticity. *J. Theor. Biol.*, 69: 387 – 389.

Shatz, C.J. and Luskin, M.B. (1986) Relationship between the geniculocortical afferents and their cortical target cells during development of the cat's primary visual cortex. *J. Neurosci.*, 6: 3655 – 3668.

Sherk, H. and Horton, J.C. (1984) Receptive field properties in the cat's area 17 in the absence of ON center retinal input. *J. Neurosci.*, 4: 381 – 393.

Shulz, D. and Frégnac, Y. (1992) Cellular analogues of visual cortical epigenesis: II. Plasticity of binocular integration. *J. Neurosci.*, 12: 1301 – 1318.

Sillito, A.M. (1975) The contribution of inhibitory mechanisms to the receptive field properties of neurones in striate cortex of the cat. *J. Physiol. (Lond.)*, 250: 305 – 329.

Singer, W. and Tretter, F. (1976) Unusually large receptive fields in cats with restricted visual experience. *Exp. Brain Res.*, 26: 171 – 184.

Singer, W., Tretter, F. and Cynader, M. (1975) Organization of cat striate cortex: a correlation of receptive field properties with afferent and efferent connections. *J. Neurophysiol.*, 38: 1080 – 1098.

Slaughter, M.M. and Miller, R.F. (1981) 2-amino-4-phosphobutyric acid: a new pharmacological tool for retina research. *Science*, 211: 182 – 184.

Spinelli, D.N., Hirsch, H.V.B., Phelps, H.W. and Metzler, J. (1972) Visual experience as a determinant of the response characteristics of cortical receptive fields in cats. *Exp. Brain Res.*, 15: 289 – 304.

Stryker, M.P. and Zahs, K.R. (1983) On and off subliminae in the lateral geniculate nucleus in the ferret. *J. Neurosci.*, 3: 1943 – 1951.

Tanaka, K. (1983) Cross-correlation analysis of geniculo-striate neuronal relationships in cats. *J. Neurophysiol.*, 49: 1303 – 1318.

Tsumoto, T. and Suda, K. (1982) Laminar differences in development of afferent innervation to striate cortex neurons in kittens. *Exp. Brain Res.*, 45: 433 – 466.

Van Sluyters, R.C. and Blakemore, C. (1973) Experimental creation of unusual neuronal properties in visual cortex of kitten. *Nature*, 246: 506 – 508.

Virsu, V., Lee, B.B. and Creutzfeldt, O.D. (1977) Dark adaptation and receptive fields of cells in the cat lateral geniculate nucleus. *Exp. Brain Res.*, 27: 35 – 50.

Wässle, H. (1982) Morphological types and central projections of ganglion cells in the cat retina. In: N. Osborne and G. Chader (Eds.), *Progress in Retinal Research*, Pergamon Press, Oxford, pp. 125 – 152.

Wässle, H., Boycott, B.B. and Illing, R.B. (1981a) Morphology and mosaic of ON- and OFF-beta cells in the cat retina and some functional considerations. *Proc. R. Soc. Lond. (Biol.)*, 212: 177 – 195.

Wässle, H., Peichl, L. and Boycott, B.B. (1981b) Morphology and topography of ON- and OFF-alpha cells in the cat retina. *Proc. R. Soc. Lond. (Biol.)*, 212: 157 – 175.

Werblin, F.S. and Dowling, J.E. (1969) Organization of the retina of the mudpuppy, *"Nectorus maculosus"*. II. Intracellular recording. *J. Neurophysiol.*, 32: 339 – 355.

Wolf, N., Hicks, T.P. and Albus, K. (1986) The contribution of GABA-mediated inhibitory mechanisms to visual response properties of neurons in the kitten's striate cortex. *J. Neurosci.*, 6: 2779 – 2795.

T.P. Hicks, S. Molotchnikoff and T. Ono (Eds.)
Progress in Brain Research, Vol. 95
© 1993 Elsevier Science Publishers B.V. All rights reserved.

CHAPTER 19

Temporal covariance of postsynaptic membrane potential and synaptic input – role in synaptic efficacy in visual cortex

M.J. Friedlander, Y. Frégnac[1] and J.P. Burke

Neurobiology Research Center and Department of Physiology and Biophysics, University of Alabama at Birmingham, Birmingham, AL 35294, U.S.A.

Background

The microcircuitry of the primary visual areas of the cerebral cortex underlies a number of neurophysiological functions that contribute to visual perception and visuomotor function (Gilbert and Wiesel, 1983; Sparks, 1986; Martin, 1988). The distribution, strength and modifiability of these synaptic connections are major factors in the elaboration of emergent properties such as binocular vision (Hubel and Wiesel, 1962, 1977; Ferster, 1981; Ferster and Lindstrom, 1983; Miller et al., !989b) and orientation sensitivity (Hubel and Wiesel, 1962; Ferster, 1986, 1987; Douglas et al., 1988). For example, stereopsis (Baker et al., 1974; Ferster, 1981), depth acuity or occlusion tasks (Baitch and Levi, 1988) and appropriate motor responses such as gaze stability (Leigh et al., 1989) and eye-hand coordination (Georgopoulos and Grillner, 1989) all depend on normal binocular vision. The development of such normal binocular interaction depends on the correct parceling of the functional output domains of the axons in the visual cortex (LeVay et al., 1978; Shatz and Stryker, 1978; Sherman and Spear, 1982; Frégnac and Imbert, 1984; Tieman, 1985; Reiter

and Stryker, 1988; Friedlander and Martin, 1989; Friedlander et al., 1991). The processes that control the structural development and strength of synapses within the visual cortex depend on competitive interactions (Stent, 1973; Hubel et al., 1977; LeVay et al., 1980; Schwartz and Rothblat, 1980; Bienenstock et al., 1982; Van Essen, 1982; Wiesel, 1982; Reiter and Stryker, 1988; Bear and Cooper, 1989; Tumosa et al., 1989) that facilitate the strengthening of certain synapses and the weakening of others. These competitive processes are most in evidence during critical developmental periods. Favorable activity patterns at one group of synapses vs. another neighboring group leads to profound changes in the *structure* of the synaptic circuitry of the cortex (Shatz and Stryker, 1978; LeVay et al., 1980; Schwartz and Rothblat, 1980; Kossut et al., 1983; reviewed in Frégnac and Imbert, 1984; Tieman, 1984, 1985; Friedlander et al., 1991). However, other evidence suggests that imbalances in the synaptic competition process lead to *functional* changes of intracortical synaptic circuits and that various procedures may unmask dormant or suppressed connections (Duffy et al., 1976; Kratz et al., 1976; Burchfiel and Duffy, 1981; Mower et al., 1984; Gordon et al., 1988; Immamura and Kasamatsu, 1989). Nonetheless, the imbalanced activity leads to amblyopia (Dews and Wiesel, 1970; Loop and Sherman, 1977; Griffin and Mitchell, 1978;

---

[1] On sabbatical leave from Unit CNRS UA 1121, Laboratory of Neurobiology and Neuropharmacology of Development, University of Paris XI, 91405, Orsay Cedex, France.

Baitch and Levi, 1988). Thus, there are compelling practical reasons to understand, at the cellular and molecular level, the initial events in the processes that regulate development and maintenance of synaptic efficiency and structure. In addition, recent studies (Frégnac et al., 1988, 1990; Burke et al., 1991) suggest that the capacity to regulate synaptic efficacy in an activity-dependent fashion in the visual cortex is not completely lost in adults. Besides the practical usefulness of understanding such processes, there is a potential for understanding the basic mechanisms of synaptic plasticity. This potential may be hastened to fruition by the convergence of theoretical and experimental work (Baker et al., 1974; Sejnowski, 1977a,b; Bear et al., 1987; Cline et al., 1987; Gamble and Koch, 1987; Kleinschmidt et al., 1987; Bear and Cooper, 1989; Bonhoeffer et al., 1989; Gu et al., 1989; Miller et al., 1989b; Sejnowski et al., 1989; Sejnowski and Tesauro, 1989; Artola et al., 1990; Cline and Constantine-Paton, 1990; Constantine-Paton et al., 1990; Gally et al., 1990; Kossell et al., 1990; Hahm et al., 1991; Montague et al., 1991).

One major way that neural networks respond to the environment is by modifying synaptic function (Bliss and Lynch, 1988; Komatsu et al., 1988; Nicoll et al., 1988; Carew, 1989; Brown et al., 1990; Frégnac and Shulz, 1991) and structure (Schwartz and Rothblat, 1980; Tieman, 1985; Desmond and Levy, 1988; Bailey and Chen, 1989a; Calverly and Jones, 1990; Constantine-Paton et al., 1990; Friedlander et al., 1991) in an activity-dependent fashion (Bienenstock et al., 1982; Levy and Steward, 1983; Reiter et al., 1986; Collingridge and Bliss, 1987; Frégnac et al., 1988; Kimura et al., 1989; Bear et al., 1990; Constantine-Paton et al., 1990). A number of investigators have suggested that the activity dependence of synaptic modifiability is due to the ability of connected neural elements to detect temporal conjunctions of their activation (James, 1890; Cajal, 1911; Wood-Jones and Porteus, 1928; Konorski, 1948; Hebb, 1949; Marr, 1970; Stent 1973; Von der Malsburg, 1973). One particularly attractive hypothesis states that neural elements that successfully participate in activating other neurons (temporally correlated pre- and postsynaptic activity) have their connections strengthened (the Hebbian rule – Hebb, 1949; Stent, 1973; Bienenstock et al., 1982; Kelso et al., 1986; Bliss and Lynch, 1988; Sejnowski and Tesauro, 1989). This idea has been successfully applied to explain a number of types of synaptic plasticity including long-term potentiation (LTP) in the hippocampus (Levy and Steward, 1983; Bliss and Lynch, 1988; Bekkers and Stevens, 1990; Malinow and Tsien, 1990) and development of ocular dominance columns in the visual cortex (Stent, 1973; Reiter et al., 1986; Kleinschmidt et al., 1987; Reiter and Stryker, 1988; Gu et al., 1989; Montague et al., 1991). A complementary hypothesis is that other neural processes that are unsuccessful in activating a neuron (uncorrelated pre- and postsynaptic activity) or that are active when the neuron responds in an opposite polarity to other inputs (anti-correlated pre- and postsynaptic activity) will be weakened (Tsumoto and Suda, 1979; Bienenstock et al., 1982; Abraham and Goddard, 1983; Frégnac et al., 1988; Reiter and Stryker, 1988; Bonhoeffer et al., 1989; Sejnowski and Tesauro, 1989; Stanton and Sejnowski, 1989; Brown et al., 1990; Kossell et al., 1990; Frégnac and Shulz, 1991). Experimental evidence for this hypothesis includes the observations that (1) temporal conjunctions of pre- and postsynaptic activation are necessary and sufficient for subsequent potentiation of synaptic transmission (Baranyi and Feher, 1981b; Kelso et al., 1986; Wigstrom et al., 1986; Baranyi and Szente, 1987; Brown et al., 1990; Frégnac et al., 1990), and (2) the discovery of receptor molecules that can perform a logical AND operation such as detecting temporal correlations in pre- and postsynaptic activity. This function is performed by the class of excitatory amino acid receptors that show both voltage and ligand dependence (N-methyl-D-aspartate or NMDA receptors – Collingridge, 1987; Collingridge and Bliss, 1987; Collingridge and Singer, 1990; Nicoll et al., 1990). They do so indirectly by detecting presynaptic activity in the terminal at that site via postsynaptic transmitter binding and detecting postsynaptic activity by a dependence on depolarization from activity from neighboring synapses on the same cell. These receptors occur at a number of sites that show synaptic plasticity such as the CA1 region of the hippocampus (Collingridge, 1987; Collingridge and Bliss, 1987; Nicoll et al., 1990; Radpour and Thomson, 1991), the neocortex including visual cortex (Tsumoto et al., 1987; Komatsu and Toyama, 1988; Bode-Greuel and Singer, 1989; Colman and Bear, 1989; Fox et al., 1989; Gu et al., 1989; Kimura et al., 1989; Miller et al., 1989a; Sutor and Hablitz, 1989a,b; Bear et al., 1990; Tsumoto, 1990), and other visual areas of the CNS such as the optic tectum (Cline et al., 1987; Cline and Constantine-Paton, 1990) and dorsal lateral geniculate nucleus (LGN$_d$) (Heggelund and Hartveit, 1990; Sillito et al., 1990; Hahm et al., 1991). Moreover, blockade of the NMDA receptors in these areas during development disrupts a number of types of functional and structural synaptic plasticity (Bear et al., 1990; Cline and Constantine-Paton, 1990; Hahm et al., 1991). Of course, such experiments that use APV to block NMDA receptor activation also affect the visual responsiveness of the neurons in these visual pathways, and thus such a dual "visual deprivation" effect suggests caution in the interpretation of these results.

Although NMDA receptors are strongly implicated in the coincidence-detecting mechanism that initiates various types of synaptic plasticity, the sequence of events for modifying synaptic potency after NMDA receptor activation is poorly understood. It is known that there is a rise in intracellular postsynaptic calcium levels (Lynch et al., 1983; MacDermott et al., 1986; Mayer et al., 1987; Connor et al., 1988; Malenka et al., 1988) after NMDA receptor activation, some of which may be due to flux through the NMDA channel itself (MacDermott et al., 1986; Ascher and Nowack, 1988, but see Iino et al., 1990; Gilbertson et al., 1991; Hollman et al., 1991). Calcium acts as a second messenger to activate various biochemical cascades including protein kinases (Malenka et al., 1988, 1989; Malinow et al., 1988, 1989). Intracellular calcium levels are also regulated by the phosphoinositide pathways (Dudek and Bear, 1989;

Dudek et al., 1989; Rana and Hokin, 1990) which may modify subsequent synaptic efficacy in a number of ways. These alterations may be at the postsynaptic level including changes in postsynaptic receptors and/or ion channel function (Davies et al., 1989) or changes in structure (Levy and Desmond, 1985; Desmond and Levy, 1988; Harris and Stevens, 1989; Calverly and Jones, 1990; Halpain and Greengard, 1990). Or, the modifications may be at the presynaptic site including altered presynaptic structure (Bailey and Chen, 1988, 1989a,b; Schmidt, 1990; Friedlander et al., 1991) or neurotransmitter release (Dolphin et al., 1982; Bekkers and Stevens, 1990; Malinow and Tsien, 1990; Malinow, 1991, but see Friedlander et al., 1990, 1992; Larkman et al., 1991). It is implicit that if the initial detection of a conjunction of pre- and postsynaptic activity occurs postsynaptically (such as by NMDA receptor activation) and the subsequent modification in synaptic function or structure occurs presynaptically, there must be a mechanism for retrograde transynaptic signaling. Such a potential role has been attributed to several molecules (arachidonic acid: Williams et al., 1989; nitric oxide or NO: Garthwaite et al., 1988, 1989; Gally et al., 1990; Bohme et al., 1991; Montague et al., 1991; Shibuki and Okada, 1991; Friedlander et al., 1992).

Experimental evidence for the sufficiency of temporal contiguity between pre- and postsynaptic activation to induce synaptic strengthening is most convincing for LTP in the hippocampus (Wigstrom et al., 1986; Bliss and Lynch, 1988), although it has also been demonstrated in neocortex including visual cortex (Tsumoto and Suda, 1979; Baranyi and Feher, 1981a,b; Baranyi and Szente, 1987; Frégnac et al., 1988, 1990; Frégnac and Shulz, 1989, 1991; Burke et al., 1991). It remains uncertain whether such relatively rapid alterations in functional synaptic efficacy can ultimately trigger the types of long-term structural change observed in various neural networks such as those seen with monocular visual deprivation (MD) (Fifkova, 1970; Shatz and Stryker, 1978; Tieman, 1984; Friedlander et al., 1991) in the visual cortex, after long-term sensitization or habituation in invertebrate ganglia

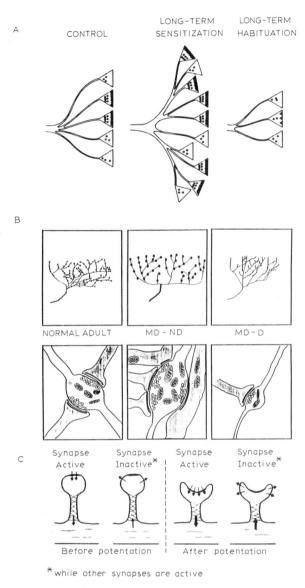

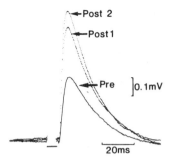

Fig. 2. Example of potentiated synaptic transmission at a synaptic contact between a single presynaptic CA3 neuron and a single target CA1 neuron after pairing of depolarization of the CA1 neuron by intracellular current injection with tetanic activation of the single CA1 neuron by intracellular current pulses. The unitary synaptic potential (EPSP elicited in a postsynaptic neuron by a single action potential in a single presynaptic neuron) was enhanced and subsequently further enhanced after two sets of sequential pairings. Averaged records of several hundred trials from the control and post-pairing epochs are shown. (Reprinted with permission from Friedlander et al., 1990, their fig. 7.)

Fig. 1. Examples of proposed structural changes that can occur at various synaptic sites in a variety of species and brain regions due to particular modulation of neural activity in an experience-dependent fashion. A. Changes in the sensory axon arborization in *Aplysia* due to long-term sensitization and habituation. (Reprinted with permission from Bailey and Chen, 1988, their fig. 3.) B. Alteration in the extent of individual geniculocortical axon arborizations and their synaptic boutons in cat visual cortex after monocular visual deprivation. (Reprinted with permission from Friedlander et al., 1991, their fig. 16.) C. Proposed structural changes in dendritic spines on rat hippocampal neurons after induction of long-term potentiation. (Reprinted with permission from Desmond and Levy, 1988, their fig. 5.)

(Bailey and Chen, 1989a,b) or after LTP in hippocampus (Chang and Greenough, 1984; Desmond and Levy, 1988) (see Fig. 1).

Recent experimental evidence from hippocampus (Malenka, 1990) and visual cortex (Frégnac et al., 1990; Hirsch and Gilbert, 1990; Burke et al., 1991) slice preparations has demonstrated that relatively short periods of temporal covariance in pre- and postsynaptic activity can regulate synaptic efficacy. In the extreme case, intracellular activation of a single presynaptic neuron with concomitant depolarization of one of its target neurons (Friedlander et al., 1990) was occasionally sufficient to potentiate subsequent synaptic transmission between these two cells (Fig. 2). In this case, the temporal conjunction consisted of tetanic bursts of activity in the single presynaptic neuron (a hippocampal CA3 cell) and a concomitant strong depolarization induced by direct intracellular current injection into a single postsynaptic neuron (a hippocampal CA1 cell) in adult guinea-pig hippocampus. This experiment could be a variant of the classic method of inducing LTP in a hippocampal CA1 neuron (Bliss and Lynch, 1988). In this case, the presynaptic element(s) is tetanically activated but the postsynaptic cell receives sufficient depolarization to induce synaptic potentiation, not by simultaneous activation of neighboring presynaptic afferent terminals, but by direct intracellular current injection. Thus, the cooperativity usually necessary for LTP induction via activation of many afferents is bypassed by using direct postsynaptic depolarization. This result implies that the cooperative effect that is able to induce synaptic potentiation results simply from an induced depolarization of the postsynaptic neuron. It does not require an extrasynaptic (to the synapse being potentiated) chemical signal such as occupation of numerous ligand binding sites at neighboring postsynaptic regions or diffusion of chemical signals between neighboring presynaptic terminals. The temporal conjunction of presynaptic activity in a single axon's arbor and postsynaptic depolarization (however induced) is thus sufficient to induce synaptic potentiation. This result from adult animals has recently been replicated using whole-cell recording (Malinow, 1991) in the hippocampus of young rats.

The question can be raised as to what degree sustained high frequency bursts of activity occur in presynaptic neurons under natural conditions. We have thus been interested in determining the minimal conditions of pre- and postsynaptic co-activation necessary to induce synaptic enhancement or depression. Therefore, we have investigated whether several repeated conjunctions of single presynaptic action potentials with successfully imposed postsynaptic depolarization can modulate subsequent synaptic efficacy. We have extended this analysis to asking whether uncorrelated or anti-correlated activity in pre- and postsynaptic elements also leads to changes in synaptic efficacy. Such mechanisms could potentially play a role in the long-term and profound changes that occur in visual cortical function after imbalanced binocular vision that lead to the weakening of drive from one eye. While such changes eventually result in major structural rearrangement of the axonal arborizations and synapses within the visual cortex over time, there is also evidence to suggest that these structural changes are not likely to be sufficient to completely

account for the drastic physiological changes (Friedlander et al., 1991) and thus further functional alterations in existing synaptic circuits are implicated. The additional observation that the physiological effects of imbalanced binocular vision on cortical cells can be rapidly reversed (Duffy et al., 1976; Kratz et al., 1976; Burchfiel and Duffy, 1981; Mower et al., 1984) suggests that processes must be at work in the amblyope's cortex that can regulate the potency of existing synapses. Thus, it is of considerable interest to evaluate how epochs of reinforced excitatory synaptic transmission (pairing of several single presynaptic pulses with postsynaptic depolarization) vs. epochs of non-reinforced excitatory synaptic transmission (pairing of several single presynaptic pulses with no additional postsynaptic depolarization or with postsynaptic hyperpolarization) affect synaptic efficacy in the visual cortex. Such conjunctive mechanisms may play a role in the early stages of a cascade that ultimately leads to structural alterations in synapses as well as rapidly affecting functional synaptic efficacy. In order to determine the capacity for short periods of temporal conjunctions or disjunctions of pre- and postsynaptic activity to rapidly modulate synaptic efficacy, we use an experimental paradigm that allows for the testing of these hypotheses in a controlled environment. Our experiments are directed at understanding the early processes of modified synaptic efficacy in visual cortex, including those that can occur rapidly in mature as well as immature animals, that may underlie experience-dependent modification in cortical function. These properties may also impart a dynamic feature to adult cortical neuron receptive field organization (Frégnac et al., 1988; Shulz et al., this volume), making the mature circuit capable of acting as an adaptive network.

Our experiments utilize the conventional brain slice preparation of visual cortex from cats and pigmented guinea-pigs. This preparation allows for stable long-term intracellular recording from cortical neurons in identified layers while selectively activating particular groups of afferent fibers. Thus, the membrane potential of a postsynaptic neuron can be directly manipulated in a temporally discrete fashion to evaluate the role of conjunctions of pre- and postsynaptic activity (covariance) on synaptic efficacy. An additional advantage of this preparation is that by selective placement of multiple sets of stimulating electrodes, the spatial specificity of the effects of pairing postsynaptic depolarization with presynaptic activation of a particular set of afferents can be evaluated. Thus, the degree to which synaptic enhancement or depression is confined to the synaptic sites on a given neuron that were conjointly activated with postsynaptic polarization can be determined. In the remainder of this chapter, we present some of our preliminary findings obtained in vitro from adult guinea pigs and kittens on the ability of synapses on visual cortical neurons to alter their efficacy dependent on temporal conjunctions of pre- and postsynaptic activity.

Methods

The methods of the experimental preparation we use are described in detail in Frégnac et al. (1991). Briefly, we used kittens and pigmented guinea-pigs of 5 postnatal weeks (weight: 400 – 600 g), and 8 – 15 weeks (300 – 700 g), respectively. Kittens were anesthetized with 2 – 3% vaporized halothane in a 1:1 $N_2O:O_2$ mixture. Guinea pigs were deeply anesthetized with ether. The occipital pole of one cerebral cortex including areas 17 and 18 was removed and blocked in the frontal plane. Slices were cut at 500 μm and maintained in an Oslo-type interface recording chamber at 33°C between ACSF and humidified gas (95% O_2:5% CO_2). The ACSF was comprised of the following in mM: NaCl, 124; KCl, 2; $MgSO_4$, 2; $CaCl_2$, 2; KH_2PO_4, 1.25; $NaHCO_3$, 26; and glucose, 11, saturated with 95% O_2:5% CO_2. Flow rate was maintained at 1 ml/min.

Recording micropipettes were back-filled either with 2 M filtered potassium methylsulfate (DC resistance from 40 to 80 MΩ) or with 0.5 M KCl and biocytin. The stimulating electrodes consisted of pairs of 25 μm insulated nichrome wires positioned in the white matter (WM) < 2 mm from the bottom of cortical layer 6 and in cortical layer 3, approx. 2

mm from the recording site. The spatial specificity of the effects of pre- and postsynaptic conjunction of activity were evaluated with the two sets of stimulating electrodes. Thus, two stimulating sites (white matter, WM; and intracortical, IC) could be independently activated in conjunction with various levels of postsynaptic polarization. In order to determine that the two sets of stimulating electrodes were indeed activating different sets of afferents to the postsynaptic neuron (either directly or indirectly via different cortical interneurons), we first used an occlusion test to evaluate the interactions of the synaptic potentials elicited from the two stimulating sites. The average EPSPs elicited from each site alone were compared and digitally summed. Then, the two sites were simultaneously stimulated and the EPSP evoked by combined stimulation was compared to the digital sum of the two independent EPSPs. The difference between the digital sum and the combined EPSP was used as an index of the ability of our spatially separated stimulating electrodes to activate different sets of synapses to the same neuron. In most cases, the stimulating electrodes activated largely separate groups of synapses.

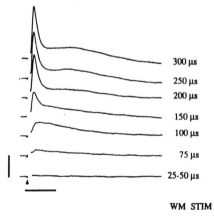

WM STIM

Fig. 3. Stimulation intensity curves established in a layer 3 cell, recorded in area 17 of a 31-day-old kitten, in response to white matter stimulations with a current pulse of various durations and constant intensity (25 μA) applied through a bipolar stimulation electrode. The resting potential was – 86 mV. Note the increasing size of the sag shown by the descending phase of the PSP for increasing durations of stimulation, which indicates the progressive recruitment of polysynaptic inhibitory pathways. Calibration bars: voltage, 5 mV; time, 20 msec.

Most recordings were obtained from cortical layer 3, and restricted in kitten to the medial bank of area 17. Acceptable criteria for resting potentials were > − 55 mV (mean, − 70 mV; S.D., 11 mV), action potential amplitude 70 − 110 mV and input resistance > 15 MΩ (mean, 44 MΩ; S.D., 25 MΩ).

Single, constant current stimuli (50 − 150 μA) were delivered to the WM or IC site at 0.2 − 1.0 Hz during a control period of 15 − 30 min, with delivery in most cases of a 100 msec, − 0.1/ − 0.2 nA constant current hyperpolarizing pulse after the evoked synaptic response in order to evaluate input resistance on a trial by trial basis. The white matter or intracortical stimulus strength was initially normalized to elicit a compound EPSP of approx. 20 − 25% of the value necessary to elicit an action potential (3 − 10 mV). These stimulus intensities were usually below threshold for evoking IPSPs that appeared to truncate the early EPSP (Fig. 3).

After this series of preliminary tests, the protocols to evaluate the effect of pairing synaptic activation with varying levels of postsynaptic polarization in response to activation of one stimulating site were run. A pulse sequencing circuit under computer control was used to activate the stimulating electrode and deliver varying levels of polarization via the intracellular recording electrode. Controls consisted of evoking the PSP with no current injection (C), pseudo-pairing (PP), and fixed delay pairing (FDP) of the intracellular polarizing pulse with stimulation (Fig. 4). For these control protocols, the membrane polarization was stepped by the same amount and polarity as the test trials but the steps were applied at various phase positions (PP), randomized with respect to the occurrence of the WM or IC stimulation or significantly later (120 msec) than the WM or IC stimulation (FDP), respectively. Intensity of intracellular current injection varied from ± 0.1 to ± 7 nA. Pairings were delivered at a low temporal frequency, ranging from 0.2 Hz to 1 Hz, over 20 − 200 trials (on average 90 trials). Generally, the PSPs were evaluated during a 15 min pre-pairing and 15 min post-pairing period. Statistical assessments of the effect on the evoked PSP peak amplitude during the various conditions were made

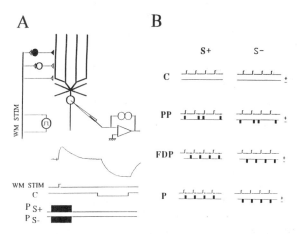

Fig. 4. Protocols of cellular conditioning. A. Schematic representation of the single stimulating site electrophysiological experiment. Upper part: intracellular recording of a visual cortical neuron, and concomitant extracellular stimulation of afferent fibers (WM STIM). Dendrites and axons are represented respectively by thick and thin lines, and somas and synapses by circles and triangles. The presynaptic input feeding the impaled target neuron is assumed to be mixed, monosynaptic, and polysynaptic through excitatory (open circles) and/or inhibitory interneurons (filled circles). Lower part, from top to bottom: postsynaptic potential recording (PSP) as a function of time, in response to white matter stimulation (WM STIM) followed by a hyperpolarizing pulse of − 0.1 to − 0.4 nA (delay 140 msec, duration 100 msec) in order to assess membrane resistance values during the control (C) trials. During pairing (P), an intracellular depolarizing (P(S⁺); upward deflection) or hyperpolarizing (P(S⁻); downward deflection) 50 msec current pulse (filled rectangle) applied in the postsynaptic neuron precedes by 10 msec WM STIM such that its action overlaps temporally with the time course of the evoked PSP. B. Temporal sequences of afferent stimulation (upper line) and current injection of a given polarity (+/−, filled rectangles on the lower line) used in the various protocols. In each condition (C: control, PP: pseudopairing, FDP: fixed delay pairing, P: pairing), the same elementary sequence is repeated 20 − 200 times (only four repetitions shown here) at low frequency (0.2 − 1.0 Hz). Left column S⁺, protocols with depolarizing current injection resulting eventually in potentiation; right column S⁻, protocols with hyperpolarizing current injection inducing mostly depression in the test PSP.

using non-parametric tests (Kolmogorov-Smirnov test with a level of $P < 0.05$ indicating significance). Similar conclusions were reached using parametric tests (t-test with a level of $P < 0.005$). In some cases, neurons were labeled by intracellular iontophoresis of 5% biocytin.

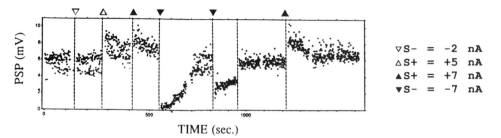

Fig. 5. Time course of synaptic potentiation and depression induced by low frequency pairing. Changes in PSPs amplitudes observed for each successive trial, following low temporal frequency (0.2 – 1 Hz) pairing in kitten visual cortical neuron. Potentiation and depression observed in a neuron from a 4-week-old kitten. Time units (in seconds) on abscissa do not correspond to a continuous scale: intermittent blocks (120) of individual trials, corresponding to the average PSPs have been put in succession. Vertical dotted lines indicate intermissions (not shown) of various test procedures. Dots represent peak amplitudes of individual EPSPs during eight epochs (a control period followed by pairings with postsynaptic current injection levels as indicated).

Results

Our preliminary results (from running complete protocols on over 25 cells) suggest that significant modulation of synaptic efficacy can occur over many minutes subsequent to relatively short periods of covariance of pre- and postsynaptic activity at relatively low frequencies (approx. 0.1 – 0.5 Hz), without massive high frequency stimulation of afferents, after a relatively few number of conjunctions and without the need to pharmacologically block synaptic inhibition. Moreover, in most cases, the rapid regulation of synaptic efficacy appears to be spatially specific in that it does not generalize to the postsynaptic neuron or to all other synapses on the neuron. Interestingly, in many cases, there are heterosynaptic effects but they generally are of opposite sign (i.e., a heterosynaptic depression when homosynaptic potentiation is induced).

The effects of pairings on the peak amplitude of the evoked PSP from one of our experiments are illustrated in Fig. 5. For this neuron, a series of pairings were performed sequentially. Fig. 5 illustrates the effects of the polarity and amplitude of the pairings on the peak amplitude of the EPSP. Note that conjunctions of strong postsynaptic depolarization paired with presynaptic activity enhanced the EPSP and conjunctions of strong postsynaptic hyperpolarization paired with presynaptic activation depressed

the EPSP. Also, note that weaker currents had no effect on the subsequent EPSP amplitudes.

The spatial specificity of the observed effects of pairing protocols are illustrated in Figs. 6 and 7. Fig. 6 shows the effects of a negative pairing (postsynaptic hyperpolarization) on the IC pathway with no pairing (no postsynaptic current injection) concomitant with activation of the WM pathway. The recording arrangement is shown in the upper panels along with the functional separability of the two pathways by using our combined stimulation occlusion protocol. The effects of the pairing are illustrated in the middle panels. Note that the paired pathway EPSP was depressed (arrowed trace indicates post-pairing averaged EPSP) and the EPSP on the same cell elicited from the unpaired pathway was unchanged. The lower four panels illustrate the effects of the protocol on the EPSP peak amplitude and the cell's resting membrane potential. The dashed line indicates the pairing epoch. Note the selective effects on the EPSP and lack of effect on V_m. Input resistance (R_{in}, not illustrated) also did not change after the pairing.

The selectivity and reversibility of the pairing protocol are illustrated for another cell in Fig. 7. This is a similar experiment to that illustrated in Fig. 6, except the pairing procedure is positive (postsynaptic depolarization in conjunction with afferent stimulation) and the paired pathway is reversed se-

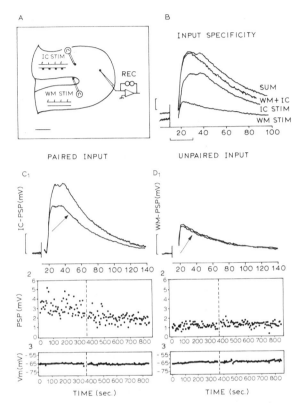

quentially so that each pathway gets to serve as a control unpaired and experimental paired pathway. The upper panels show the averaged EPSPs before and after (arrows) a weak positive pairing (+2 nA postsynaptic current injection) of the WM pathway and no pairing of the IC pathway. The paired EPSP significantly increased (homosynaptic potentiation) and the unpaired EPSP significantly decreased (heterosynaptic depression). The effects of reversing the protocol (positive pairing of the IC pathway and no pairing of the WM pathway) are illustrated in the middle panels. In this case, the IC paired pathway EPSP significantly increased while the unpaired WM pathway EPSP did not change (a nonsignificant decrease). With a subsequent stronger pairing of the IC pathway (+5 nA vs. +2 nA postsynaptic current injection), the paired EPSP slightly decreased, while the unpaired EPSP significantly decreased.

The percentage change in the amplitude of a sample of EPSPs subjected to our spatial specificity tests are summarized in Fig. 8 for the positive pairing protocols only. The top histogram summarizes the percentage change in the EPSPs for the paired pathway (all are positive pairings with postsynaptic depolarization). The dark bars represent statistically significant changes. Note that the sample as a whole tended strongly towards enhancement, even

Fig. 6. Spatial input specificity of synaptic depression in the kitten visual cortex. *A*. Schematic representation of the electrophysiological experiment: intracellular recording of a layer 3 visual cortical neuron from 27-day-old kitten visual cortex isolated brain slice preparation. Postsynaptic potentials (PSPs) were evoked by electrical stimulation at two spatially separate sites – one in the white matter (WM STIM), and one in layer 3 (IC STIM) – in an interleaved, alternating fashion at 0.2 Hz. The IC-evoked response was temporally paired with brief (80 msec) membrane hyperpolarization (−3.0 nA) over 75 trials, while the activation of the WM-evoked response of the same cell was not paired with the hyperpolarization of the target neuron. *B*. Separability of the synaptic responses evoked by electrical stimulation at two spatially separate afferent sites determined by the lack of occlusion of the synaptic responses. Simultaneous stimulation of the separate sites (WM + IC), which allows for temporal correspondence of the peaks of the individual PSPs evoked from either site (WM STIM and IC STIM), is compared to the digital summation of the individual responses. *C* and *D*. Spatial specificity of negative pairing. *C*. PSP depression following the pairing of membrane hyperpolarization with the IC-evoked PSP. C_1. Averaged intracellular responses of the paired pathway before and after (arrow) the pairing procedure. Note the statistically significant homosynaptic depression (a change in the mean peak amplitude from 2.8 ± 0.1 mV (mean ± S.E.) before pairing to 2.1 ± 0.1 mV, after pairing, a percentage change of

−23.76%, Kolmogorov-Smirnov *P*-value < 0.05). C_2. Trial-by-trial record of the peak amplitude of the IC-evoked PSP during the control (pre-) and the postpairing periods. C_3. Trial-by-trial record of the resting membrane potential during the control and postpairing periods. *D*. Lack of modification of synaptic strength in the heterosynaptic pathway following the negative pairing procedure. D_1. Averaged intracellular responses of the unpaired pathway before and after (arrow) negative pairing. Note that no significant modification of the unpaired WM-evoked PSP was observed (the mean peak amplitude before pairing was 1.2 ± 0.0 mV, and after pairing 1.2 ± 0.0 mV, a percentage change of +1.50%, Kolmogorov-Smirnov *P*-value > 0.05). D_2. Trial-by-trial record of the peak amplitude of the WM-evoked PSP during the control and the postpairing periods. D_3. Trial-by-trial record of the resting membrane potential during the control and the postpairing periods. Y-axis calibration bars are 1 mV.

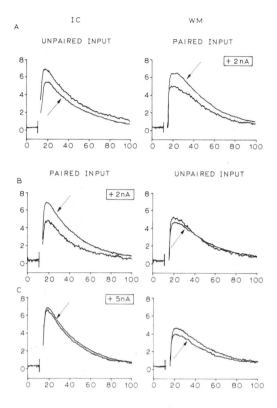

Fig. 7. Selectivity and reversibility of positive pairing in the adult guinea pig visual cortex. *A*. Homosynaptic potentiation and heterosynaptic depression following positive pairing. After a 65-trial pairing of depolarization (+ 2.0 nA, 80 msec) with the WM-evoked PSP (right panel), a statistically significant homosynaptic potentiation (mean peak amplitude change of + 31.18%) was observed (arrow). PSP peak values changed from 4.4 ± 0.2 mV to 5.8 ± 0.2 mV (Kolmogorov-Smirnov *P*-value < 0.05). The unpaired IC-evoked PSP (left panel) displayed significant heterosynaptic depression (− 19.81%) after pairing (arrow). Mean PSP peak values changed from 6.1 ± 0.1 mV to 4.9 ± 0.2 mV (Kolmogorov-Smirnov *P*-value < 0.05). *B*. Reversal of the protocol produced homosynaptic potentiation of the IC-pathway without significant heterosynaptic effects in the WM-pathway. Pairing the IC-evoked pathway with weak depolarization (+ 2.0 nA, 80 msec, 65 trials) produced significant homosynaptic potentiation of +45.5% (a change in the mean peak PSP amplitude from 4.3 ± 0.3 mV before pairing to 6.1 ± 0.1 mV after pairing, Kolmogorov-Smirnov *P*-value < 0.05). The heterosynaptic, WM-evoked PSP which was not paired with membrane depolarization was not modified by the pairing procedure (mean PSP peak amplitude values changed from 4.6 ± 0.2 mV to 4.3 ± 0.2 mV, a percentage change of − 5.6%, Kolmogorov-Smirnov *P*-value > 0.05). *C*. Heterosynaptic depression without homosynaptic potentiation produced by stronger pairing of the IC-pathway. Further pairing of the IC-

though many individual cases did not reach statistical significance. The lower histogram shows the effects on the EPSP of the unpaired pathway. Note that all significant changes were due to a decrease in the EPSP amplitude (heterosynaptic depression). The two samples of responses in the upper (paired pathways) and lower (unpaired pathways) histograms are significantly different ($P < 0.001$, χ^2 test).

Discussion

Our preliminary findings indicate that temporal covariance of pre- and postsynaptic activity can play a role in altering synaptic efficacy. This phenomenon has been demonstrated in cells of the primary visual cortex in guinea-pigs and cats and in more mature animals as well as those at the critical development age for the visual cortex. Four findings are of particular interest and merit further investigation. First, our results suggest that there is a temporal window about which the pre- and postsynaptic conjunction must occur in order to alter synaptic efficacy. This is particularly important if temporal associations are to be detected and specifically modify the connections that participated in them. Second, the effects can occur in the visual cortex beyond the classically defined critical period. To what degree these effects are equally or less likely to occur in the adult will require more detailed analyses of large samples of cells and from more animals at various ages. It is also a matter of considerable interest to determine whether such a mechanism contributes in the in vivo adult preparation (Frégnac et al., 1988; Shulz et al., this volume) to a dynamic

pathway with a stronger depolarizing pulse (+ 5.0 nA, 80 msec, 65 trials) failed to induce additional homosynaptic potentiation (the observed change in the mean PSP peak amplitude was − 3.2% from 6.1 ± 0.1 mV to 5.9 ± 0.1 mV, Kolmogorov-Smirnov *P*-value > 0.05). The unpaired WM-evoked PSP, whose PSP was not coincident with membrane depolarization during the pairing period, was significantly depressed. The observed heterosynaptic change in mean peak amplitude was − 16.4% from 4.1 ± 0.1 mV to 3.4 ± 0.1 mV (Kolmogorov-Smirnov *P*-value < 0.05).

reorganization of receptive fields that may play a role in the adult cortex in selective adaptation or attention. Third, our results suggest that a threshold mechanism operates to only allow the effects of temporal conjunction of pre- and postsynaptic activity to occur outside of a certain "dead zone" around the resting membrane potential. In vivo, cortical

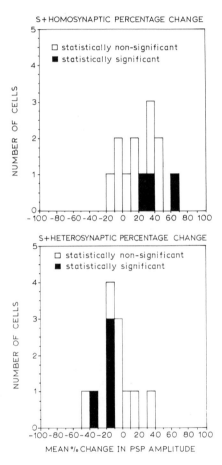

Fig. 8. Summary graph of the percentage changes in mean PSP peak amplitudes for the homosynaptic and heterosynaptic pathways as a result of positive pairing protocols. (Dark bars indicate statistically significant changes, Kolmogorov-Smirnov P-values < 0.05). Upper part: in 3 of 13 cases, significant homosynaptic potentiation of the evoked PSP was observed following the pairing procedure. Lower part: in 4 of 12 cases, significant heterosynaptic depression of the evoked PSP was observed following the pairing procedure. (A comparison of the homo- versus the heterosynaptic data points from these experiments via the Mann-Whitney U-test reveals that the data points are from two different populations; P-value < 0.05).

neurons receive a considerable amount of spontaneous synaptic activity and show considerable fluctuation in membrane potential (Ferster, 1986, 1987; Douglas et al., 1988). Thus, if a mechanism such as we have described does play a role in varying the weighting of synaptic circuits, it would require protection from trivial changes. Fourth, the effects we observed appear to be spatially specific. That is, positive pairing (conjunction of presynaptic activation and postsynaptic depolarization) only enhances the efficacy of the paired synapses, and negative pairings (conjunction of presynaptic activation and postsynaptic hyperpolarization) only reduce the efficacy of the paired synapses. In some cases, unpaired pathways onto the same cell show no effect or, in other cases, the unpaired pathway shows an opposite effect. Thus, the heterosynaptic effects are always different from the homosynaptic effects on a given cell. In addition, the general properties (such as membrane potential, input resistance and spike-generating threshold) of the postsynaptic cells are not affected by the pairing protocols even though the pairing procedures sometimes use strong levels of current injection at the soma. Thus, such a mechanism allows for very specific temporal correlation-dependent changes in the weighting of one set of synapses onto a cell. In some cases, the weighting changes can be even further enhanced by opposite heterosynaptic effects that may serve to additionally accentuate the relative strength of the signal at the paired pathway with respect to other inputs to the same cell.

These results raise a number of provocative questions. To what degree are the altered synaptic efficacies maintained? After our pairing protocols, EPSP amplitudes usually return to control levels within 5 – 20 min. The effects we observed seem different from LTP which persists for hours but usually is evoked with considerably more drastic procedures (high frequency, high strength tetanization of afferent pathways, pharmacological elimination of postsynaptic inhibition) and the changes in synaptic efficacy due to brief periods of temporal conjunctions of pre- and postsynaptic activity may, in fact, play a very different role, acting in a more continuous dynamic fashion by balancing activity in a cortical network. Further study is needed to determine if the pairing effects operate by different molecular mechanisms than does LTP. It also remains to be determined whether the altered synaptic efficacy is due to pre- or postsynaptic factors during the expression phase of the phenomenon. This will require dual intracellular recording from synaptically coupled neuronal pairs, with activation of a single afferent (Sayer et al., 1991), so that a proper quantal analysis of synaptic transmission can be applied to this question. The postsynaptic receptors that mediate the enhanced transmission are also not yet known. Pharmacological blockage of the various classes of excitatory amino acid receptors during the enhanced transmission is necessary to evaluate their respective contributions. In addition, the molecular sequelae of the induction process of this effect have not been characterized. Does the postsynaptic neuron produce and release a substance that subsequently affects presynaptic terminals? If so, the substance must recognize active terminals so that its effects will be restricted. Different factors such as nitric oxide (NO) have been proposed to act in such a manner (Williams et al., 1989; Gally et al., 1990; Bohme et al., 1991; Montague et al., 1991). The heterosynaptic effects that we occasionally observed (such as a crossed heterosynaptic depression where the homosynaptic pathway was enhanced after a positive pairing) implies that such a substance would cause opposite effects on active vs. inactive presynaptic terminals, possibly by activating a presynaptic guanylate cyclase or ADP ribosyl-transferase (Brumley et al., 1992) in the presence of high calcium if the terminals were active and inhibiting the enzymes if calcium levels are low as in inactive terminals. Moreover, NO signals are short-lived (Gally et al., 1990), so whatever effects it may have would require some sort of biochemical cascade.

Finally, it remains to be determined whether there is linkage between the rapid alterations induced by temporal covariance of pre- and postsynaptic activity and the long-term structural and functional changes in visual cortex that occur as a result of periods of imbalance in binocular activity. For example, must the types of rapid change in synaptic efficacy that we have observed precede the structural and functional changes in synapses that occur after long-term monocular visual deprivation? If so, does a period of altered efficacy (such as enhanced transmitter release from presynaptic terminals by increased probability of release or increased quantal content) cause subsequent structural changes in the synaptic boutons? These changes may induce cytoskeletal rearrangement leading to changes in bouton size, number and size of release sites or postsynaptic contacts or vesicle docking access at the active zone. Similarly, at the postsynaptic site, enhanced frequency and/or efficiency of ligand binding may lead to structural changes that further increase the postsynaptic receptor site's likelihood or efficacy of transmitter capture. The rapid covariance-induced changes in synaptic efficacy in the visual cortex have only been characterized in a preliminary fashion. However, the process appears to be a promising candidate for understanding the adaptive properties of neural networks at both the system's and molecular level.

Acknowledgements

This work was supported by NIH Grant EY05116 (M.J.F.), NIMH Grant MH10150 (J.P.B.), NATO, Foundation Philippe and HFSP (Y.F.). The technical assistance of Felicia Hester, software development of Kevin Ramer and word-processing skills of Jenelle Neville are gratefully acknowledged.

References

Abraham, W.C. and Goddard, G.V. (1983) Asymmetric relationships between homosynaptic long-term potentiation and heterosynaptic long-term depression. *Nature,* 305: 717–719.

Artola, A., Brocher, S. and Singer, W. (1990) Different voltage-dependent thresholds for inducing long-term depression and long-term potentiation in slices of rat visual cortex. *Nature,* 347: 69–72.

Ascher, P. and Nowack, L. (1988) Quisqualate- and kainate-activated channels in mouse central neurones in culture. *J. Physiol. (Lond.),* 399: 247–266.

Bailey, C.H. and Chen, M. (1988) Morphological basis of short-term habituation in *Aplysia. J. Neurosci.,* 8: 2452 – 2459.

Bailey, C.H. and Chen, M. (1989a) Structural plasticity at identified synapses during long-term memory in *Aplysia. J. Neurobiol.,* 20: 356 – 372.

Bailey, C.H. and Chen, M. (1989b) Time course of structural changes at identified sensory neuron synapses during long-term sensitization in *Aplysia. J. Neurosci.,* 9: 1774 – 1780.

Baitch, L.W. and Levi, D.M. (1988) Evidence for nonlinear binocular interactions in human visual cortex. *Vision Res.,* 28: 1139 – 1143.

Baker, F.H., Griff, P. and von Noorden, G.K. (1974) Effects of visual deprivation and strabismus on the response of neurons in the visual cortex of the monkey, including studies on the striate and prestriate cortex in the normal animal. *Brain Res.,* 66: 185.

Baranyi, A. and Feher, O. (1981a) Long-term facilitation of excitatory synaptic transmission in single motor cortical neurones produced by repetitive pairing of synaptic potentials and action potentials following intracellular stimulation. *Neurosci. Lett.,* 23: 303 – 308.

Baranyi, A. and Feher, O. (1981b) Synaptic facilitation requires paired activation of convergent pathways in the neocortex. *Nature,* 290: 413 – 415.

Baranyi, A. and Szente, M.B. (1987) Long-lasting potentiation of synaptic transmission requires postsynaptic modifications in the neocortex. *Brain Res.,* 423: 378 – 384.

Bear, M.F. and Cooper, L.N. (1989) Molecular mechanisms for synaptic modification in the visual cortex: interaction between theory and experiment. In: M.A. Gluek and D.E. Rumelhart (Eds.), *Neuroscience and Connectionist Theory,* Erlbaum, Hillsdale, NJ, pp. 65 – 93.

Bear, M.F., Cooper, L.N. and Ebner, F.F. (1987) A physiological basis for a theory of synapse modification. *Science,* 237: 42 – 48.

Bear, M.F., Kleinschmidt, A., Gu, Q. and Singer, W. (1990) Disruption of experience-dependent synaptic modifications in striate cortex by infusion of an NMDA receptor antagonist. *J. Neurosci.,* 10: 909 – 925.

Bekkers, J.M. and Stevens, C.F. (1990) Presynaptic mechanism for long-term potentiation in the hippocampus. *Nature,* 346: 724 – 729.

Bienenstock, E., Cooper, L.N. and Munro, P. (1982) Theory for the development of neuron selectivity: orientation specificity and binocular interaction in visual cortex. *J. Neurosci.,* 2: 23 – 48.

Bliss, T.V.P. and Lynch, M.A. (1988) Long-term potentiation of synaptic transmission in the hippocampus: properties and mechanisms. In: P.W. Landfield and S.A. Deadwyler (Eds.), *Long-Term Potentiation: from Biophysics to Behavior,* Liss, New York, pp. 3 – 72.

Bode-Greuel, K.M. and Singer, W. (1989) The development of *N*-methyl-D-aspartate receptors in cat visual cortex. *Dev. Brain Res.,* 46: 197 – 204.

Bohme, G.A., Bon, C., Stutzman, J.M., Doble, A. and Blan-

chard, J.-C. (1991) Possible involvement of nitric oxide in long-term potentiation. *Eur. J. Pharmacol.,* 199: 379 – 381.

Bonhoeffer, T., Staiger, V. and Aertsen, A. (1989) Synaptic plasticity in rat hippocampal slice cultures: local "Hebbian" conjunction of pre- and postsynaptic stimulation leads to distributed synaptic enhancement. *Proc. Natl. Acad. Sci. U.S.A.,* 86: 8113 – 8117.

Brown, T.H., Ganong, A.H., Kairiss, E.W. and Keenan, C.L. (1990) Hebbian synapses: biophysical mechanisms and algorithms. *Annu. Rev. Neurosci.,* 13: 475 – 511.

Brumley, L.M., Friedlander, M.J., Montague, P.R., Gancayco, C.D. and Marchase, R.B. (1992) Role of nitric oxide in NMDA receptor-mediated release of neurotransmitters and ADP-ribosylation of a 36 kDa protein. *Mol. Cell. Biol.,* 1121: 193A.

Burchfiel, J.L. and Duffy, F.H. (1981) Role of intracortical inhibition in deprivation amblyopia: reversal by microiontophoretic bicuculline. *Brain Res.,* 206: 479 – 484.

Burke, J.P., Frégnac, Y. and Friedlander, M.J. (1991) Spatial input specificity of synaptic potentiation and depression in the visual cortex. *Soc. Neurosci. Abstr.,* 17: 114.

Cajal, R. (1911) *Histologie du Système Nerveux de l'Homme et des Vertèbres. Tomes I et II,* Maloine, Paris.

Calverly, R.K.S. and Jones, D.G. (1990) Contributions of dendritic spines and perforated synapses to synaptic plasticity. *Brain Res. Rev.,* 15: 215 – 249.

Carew, T.J. (1989) Developmental assembly of learning in *Aplysia. Trends Neurosci.,* 12: 389 – 393.

Chang, F.L.F. and Greenough, W.T. (1984) Lateralized effects of monocular training on dendritic branching in adult split-brain rats. *Brain Res.,* 309: 35 – 46.

Cline, H.T. and Constantine-Paton, M. (1990) NMDA antagonists disrupt the retinotectal topographic map. *Neuron,* 3: 413 – 426.

Cline, H.T., Debski, E.A. and Constantine-Paton, M. (1987) *N*-methyl-D-aspartate receptor antagonist desegregates eye-specific stripes. *Proc. Natl. Acad. Sci. U.S.A.,* 84: 4342 – 4345.

Collingridge, G.L. (1987) The role of NMDA receptors in learning and memory (news and views). *Nature,* 330: 604 – 605.

Collingridge, G.L. and Bliss, T.V.P. (1987) NMDA receptors. Their role in long-term potentiation. *Trends Neurosci.,* 10: 288 – 293.

Collingridge, G.L. and Singer, W. (1990) Excitatory amino acid receptors and synaptic plasticity. *Trends Pharmacol. Sci.,* 11: 290 – 296.

Colman, H. and Bear, M.F. (1989) Blockade of visual cortical NMDA receptors prevents the shrinkage of lateral geniculate neurons following monocular deprivation. *Soc. Neurosci. Abstr.,* 15: 2.

Connor, J.A., Wadman, W.B., Hockberger, P.E. and Wong, R.K.S. (1988) Sustained dendritic gradients of Ca^{2+} induced by excitatory amino acids in CA1 hippocampal neurons. *Science,* 240: 649 – 653.

Constantine-Paton, M., Cline, H.T. and Debski, E. (1990) Patterned activity, synaptic convergence, and the NMDA receptor in developing visual pathways. *Annu. Rev. Neurosci.,* 13: 129 – 154.

Davies, S.N., Lester, R.A.J., Reymann, K.G. and Collingridge, G.L. (1989) Temporally distinct pre- and postsynaptic mechanisms maintain long-term potentiation. *Nature,* 338: 500 – 503.

Desmond, N.L. and Levy, W.B. (1988) Anatomy of associative long-term synaptic modification. In: P. Landfield and S.A. Deadwyler (Eds.), *Long-term Potentiation: from Biophysics to Behavior,* Liss, New York, pp. 265 – 305.

Dews, P.B. and Wiesel, T.N. (1970) Consequences of monocular deprivation on visual behavior in kittens. *J. Physiol. (Lond.),* 206: 437 – 455.

Dolphin, A.C., Errington, M.L. and Bliss, T.V.P. (1982) Long-term potentiation of the perforant path in vivo is associated with increased glutamate release. *Nature,* 297: 496 – 498.

Douglas, R.J., Martin, K.A.C. and Whitteridge, D. (1988) Selective responses of visual cortical cells do not depend on shunting inhibition. *Nature,* 332: 642 – 644.

Dudek, S.M. and Bear, M.F. (1989) A biochemical correlate of the critical period for synaptic modification in the visual cortex. *Science,* 246: 673 – 675.

Dudek, S.M., Bowen, W.D. and Bear, M.F. (1989) Postnatal changes in glutamate stimulated phosphoinositide turnover in rat neocortical synaptoneurosomes. *Dev. Brain Res.,* 47: 123 – 128.

Duffy, F.L., Snodgrass, S.R., Burchfiel, J.L. and Conway, J.L. (1976) Bicuculline reversal of deprivation on amblyopia in the cat. *Nature,* 260: 256 – 257.

Ferster, D. (1981) A comparison of binocular depth mechanisms in areas 17 and 18 of the cat visual cortex. *J. Physiol. (Lond.),* 311: 623 – 655.

Ferster, D. (1986) Orientation selectivity of synaptic potentials in neurons of cat primary visual cortex. *J. Neurosci.,* 6: 1284 – 1301.

Ferster, D. (1987) Origin of orientation-selective EPSPs in simple cells of cat visual cortex. *J. Neurosci.,* 7: 1780 – 1791.

Ferster, D. and Lindstrom, S. (1983) An intracellular analysis of geniculo-cortical connectivity in area 17 of the cat. *J. Physiol. (Lond.),* 342: 181 – 215.

Fifkova, E. (1970) Effect of unilateral deprivation on visual centers in rats. *J. Comp. Neurol.,* 140: 431 – 438.

Fox, K., Sato, H. and Daw, N. (1989) The location and function of NMDA receptors in cat and kitten visual cortex. *J. Neurosci.,* 9: 2443 – 2454.

Frégnac, Y. and Imbert, M. (1984) Development of neuronal selectivity in primary visual cortex of cat. *Physiol. Rev.,* 64: 325 – 434.

Frégnac, Y. and Shulz, D. (1989) Hebbian synapses in visual cortex. In: K.K. Kulikowski (Ed.), *Seeing Contour and Colour,* Pergamon, New York, pp. 711 – 718.

Frégnac, Y. and Shulz, D. (1991) Models of synaptic plasticity and cellular analogs of learning the developing and adult visual cortex. In: V. Casagrande and P. Shinkman (Eds.), *Advances in Neural and Behavioral Development, Vol. 4,* Neural Ablex, New Jersey, pp. 1 – 66.

Frégnac, Y., Shulz, D., Thorpe, S. and Bienenstock, E. (1988) A cellular analogue of visual cortical plasticity. *Nature,* 333: 367 – 370.

Frégnac, Y., Smith, D. and Friedlander, M.J. (1990) Postsynaptic membrane potential regulates synaptic potentiation and depression in visual cortical neurons. *Soc. Neurosci. Abstr.,* 16(1): 798.

Frégnac, Y., Burke, J.P., Smith, D. and Friedlander, M.J. (1991) Temporal covariance of presynaptic activation and postsynaptic membrane potential regulates potentiation and depression of synaptic efficacy in visual cortical neurons. (Submitted.)

Friedlander, M.J. and Martin, K.A.C. (1989) Development of Y-axon innervation of cortical area 18 in the cat. *J. Physiol. (Lond.),* 416: 183 – 213.

Friedlander, M.J., Sayer, R.J. and Redman, S.J. (1990) Evaluation of long-term potentiation of small compound and unitary EPSPs at the hippocampal CA3-CA1 synapse. *J. Neurosci.,* 10: 814 – 825.

Friedlander, M.J., Martin, K.A.C. and Wassenhove-McCarthy, D. (1991) Effects of monocular visual deprivation on geniculocortical innervation of area 18 in cat. *J. Neurosci.,* 11(10): 3268 – 3288.

Friedlander, M.J., Montague, P.R., Hester, F. and Marchase, R.B. (1992) Role of nitric oxide in NMDA receptor-mediated release of neurotransmitter in visual cortex. *Soc. Neurosci. Abstr.,* 18: 210.

Gally, J.A., Montague, P.R., Reeke Jr., G.N. and Edelman, G.M. (1990) The NO hypothesis: possible effects of a short-lived, rapidly diffusible signal in the development and function of nervous system. *Proc. Natl. Acad. Sci. U.S.A.,* 87: 3547 – 3551.

Gamble, E. and Koch, C. (1987) The dynamics of free calcium in dendritic spines in response to repetitive synaptic input. *Science,* 236: 1311 – 1315.

Garthwaite, J., Charles, S.L. and Chess-Williams, R. (1988) Endothelium-derived relaxing factor release on activation of NMDA receptors suggests role as intercellular messenger in the brain. *Nature,* 336: 385 – 388.

Garthwaite, J., Garthwaite, G., Palmer, R.M.J. and Moncada, S. (1989) NMDA receptor activation induces nitric oxide synthesis from arginine in rat brain slices. *Eur. J. Pharmacol.,* 172: 413 – 416.

Georgopoulos, A.P. and Grillner, S. (1989) Visuomotor coordination in reaching and locomotion. *Science,* 245: 1209 – 1210.

Gilbert, C.D. and Wiesel, T.N. (1983) Clustered intrinsic connections in the cat visual cortex. *J. Neurosci.,* 3: 1116 – 1133.

Gilbertson, T.A., Scobey, R. and Wilson, M. (1991) Permeation of calcium ions through non-NMDA glutamate channels in retinal bipolar cells. *Science,* 251: 1613 – 1616.

Gordon, B., Allen, E.E. and Trombley, P.Q. (1988) The role of norepinephrine in plasticity of visual cortex. *Prog. Neurobiol.,* 30: 171 – 191.

Griffin, F. and Mitchell, D.E. (1978) The rate of recovery of vision after early MD in kittens. *J. Physiol. (Lond.),* 274: 511 – 538.

Gu, Q., Bear, M.F. and Singer, W. (1989) Blockade of NMDA-receptors prevents ocularity changes in kitten visual cortex and reversed monocular deprivation. *Dev. Brain Res.,* 47: 281 – 288.

Hahm, J.O., Langdon, R.B. and Sur, M. (1991) Disruption of retinogeniculate afferent segregation by antagonists to NMDA receptors. *Nature,* 351: 568 – 570.

Halpain, S. and Greengard, P. (1990) Activation of NMDA receptors induces rapid dephosphorylation of the cytoskeletal protein MAP2. *Neuron,* 5: 237 – 246.

Harris, K.M. and Stevens, J.K. (1989) Dendritic spines of CA1 pyramidal cells in the rat hippocampus: serial electron microscopy with reference to their biophysical characteristics. *J. Neurosci.,* 9: 2982 – 2997.

Hebb, D.O. (1949) *The Organization of Behavior,* Wiley, New York.

Heggelund, P. and Hartveit, E. (1990) Neurotransmitter receptors mediating excitatory input of cells in the cat lateral geniculate nucleus. I. Lagged cells. *J. Neurophysiol.,* 63: 1347 – 1360.

Hirsch, J.A. and Gilbert, C.D. (1990) Interactions and stimulus-dependent changes of synaptic potentials evoked by activating interlaminar and horizontal pathways in the cat's striate cortex. *Soc. Neurosci. Abstr.,* 16: 1271.

Hollmann, M., Hartley, M. and Heinemann, S. (1991) Ca^{2+} permeability of KA-AMPA-gated glutamate receptor channels depends on subunit composition. *Science,* 252: 851 – 853.

Hubel, D.H. and Wiesel, T.N. (1962) Receptive fields, binocular interaction and functional architecture in the cat's visual cortex. *J. Physiol. (Lond.),* 160: 106 – 154.

Hubel, D.H. and Wiesel, T.N. (1977) Functional architecture of macaque monkey visual cortex. *Proc. Roy. Soc. Lond. (Biol.),* 198: 1 – 59.

Hubel, D.H., Wiesel, T.N. and LeVay, S. (1977) Plasticity of ocular dominance columns in monkey striate cortex. *Phil. Trans. R. Soc. Lond. (Biol.),* 278: 377 – 409.

Iino, M., Ozawa, S. and Tsuzuki, K. (1990) Permeation of calcium through excitatory amino acid receptor channels in cultured rat hippocampal neurones. *J. Physiol. (Lond.),* 424: 151 – 165.

Immamura, K. and Kasamatsu, T. (1989) Interaction of noradrenergic and cholinergic systems in regulation of ocular dominance plasticity. *Neurosci. Res.,* 6: 519 – 536.

James, W. (1890) *Psychology: Briefer Course,* Harvard University Press, Cambridge.

Kelso, S.R., Ganong, A.H. and Brown, T.H. (1986) Hebbian synapses in hippocampus. *Proc. Natl. Acad. Sci. U.S.A.,* 83: 5326 – 5330.

Kimura, F., Nishigori, A., Shirokawa, T. and Tsumoto, T. (1989) Long-term potentiation and N-methyl-D-aspartate receptors in the visual cortex of young rats. *J. Physiol. (Lond.),* 414: 125 – 144.

Kleinschmidt, A., Bear, M.F. and Singer, W. (1987) Blockade of NMDA receptors disrupts experience-dependent plasticity of kitten striate cortex. *Science,* 238: 355 – 358.

Komatsu, Y. and Toyama, K. (1988) Relevance of NMDA receptors to the long-term potentiation in kitten visual cortex. *Biomedical Res.,* 9 (Suppl. 2): 39 – 41.

Komatsu, Y., Fujii, K., Maeda, J., Sakaguchi, H. and Toyama, K. (1988) Long-term potentiation of synaptic transmission in kitten visual cortex. *J. Neurophysiol.,* 59: 124 – 141.

Konorski, J. (1948) *Conditioned Reflexes and Neuron Organization,* Cambridge University Press, London.

Kossell, A., Bonhoeffer, T. and Bolz, J. (1990) Non-Hebbian synapses in rat visual cortex. *Neuro-Report,* 1: 115 – 118.

Kossut, M., Thompson, I.D. and Blakemore, C. (1983) Ocular dominance columns in cat striate cortex and effects of monocular deprivation: a 2-deoxyglucose study. *Acta Neurol. Exp.,* 43: 273 – 282.

Kratz, K.E., Spear, P.D. and Smith, D.C. (1976) Postcritical period reversal of effects of monocular deprivation on striate cortex cells in the cat. *J. Neurophysiol.,* 39: 501 – 511.

Larkman, A., Stratford, K. and Jack, J. (1991) Quantal analysis of excitatory synaptic action and depression in hippocampal slices. *Nature,* 350: 344 – 347.

Leigh, R.J., Thurston, S.E., Tomsak, R.L., Grossman, G.E. and Lanska, D.J. (1989) Effect of monocular visual loss upon stability of gaze. *Invest. Ophthalmol. Vis. Sci.,* 30: 288 – 292.

LeVay, S., Stryker, M.P. and Shatz, C.J. (1978) Ocular dominance columns and their development in layer IV of the cat's visual cortex. *J. Comp. Neurol.,* 179: 223 – 244.

LeVay, S., Wiesel, T.N. and Hubel, D.H. (1980) The development of ocular dominance columns in normal and visually deprived monkeys. *J. Comp. Neurol.,* 191: 1 – 51.

Levy, W.B. and Desmond, N.L. (1985) The rules of elemental synaptic plasticity. In: W.B. Levy, J. Anderson and S. Lehmkuhle (Eds.), *Synaptic Modification, Neuron Selectivity and Nervous System Organization,* Erlbaum, Hillsdale, NJ, pp. 105 – 121.

Levy, W.B. and Steward, O. (1983) Temporal contiguity requirements for long-term associative potentiation/depression in the hippocampus. *Neuroscience,* 8: 791 – 797.

Loop, S.M. and Sherman, S.M. (1977) Visual discriminations during eyelid closure in the cat. *Brain Res.,* 128: 329 – 339.

Lynch, G., Larson, J., Kelso, S., Barrionuevo, G. and Schottler, F. (1983) Intracellular injections of EGTA block induction of hippocampal long-term potentiation. *Nature,* 305: 719 – 721.

MacDermott, A.B., Mayer, M.L., Westbrook, G.L., Smith, S.J. and Baker, J.L. (1986) NMDA-receptor activation increases cytoplasmic calcium concentration in cultured spinal cord neurones. *Nature,* 321: 519 – 522.

Malenka, R.C. (1990) Factors controlling the time course of

synaptic potentiation in area CA1 of the hippocampus. *Soc. Neurosci. Abstr.,* 16: 651.

Malenka, R.C., Kauer, J.A., Zucker, R.S. and Nicoll, R.A. (1988) Postsynaptic calcium is sufficient for potentiation of hippocampal synaptic transmission. *Science,* 242: 81 – 84.

Malenka, R.C., Kauer, J.A., Perkel, D.J., Mauk, M.D., Kelly, P.T., Nicoll, R.A. and Waxham, M.N. (1989) An essential role for postsynaptic calmodulin and protein kinases activity in long-term potentiation. *Nature,* 340: 554 – 557.

Malinow, R. (1991) Transmission between pairs of hippocampal slice neurons: quantal levels, oscillations, and LTP. *Science,* 252: 722 – 724.

Malinow, R. and Tsien, R.W. (1990) Presynaptic enhancement shown by whole-cell recordings of long-term potentiation in hippocampal slices. *Nature,* 346: 177 – 180.

Malinow, R., Madison, D.V. and Tsien, R.W. (1988) Persistent protein kinase activity underlying long-term potentiation. *Nature,* 335: 820 – 824.

Malinow, R., Schulman, H. and Tsien, R.W. (1989) Inhibition of postsynaptic PKC or CaMKII blocks induction but not expression of LTP. *Science,* 245: 862 – 866.

Marr, D.C. (1970) A theory for cerebral cortex. *Proc. R. Soc. Lond. (Biol.),* 176: 161 – 234.

Martin, K.A.C. (1988) From single cells to simple circuits in the cerebral cortex. *Q. J. Exp. Physiol.,* 73: 637 – 702.

Mayer, M.L., MacDermott, A.B., Westbrook, G.L., Smith, S.J. and Barker, J.L. (1987) Agonist- and voltage-gated calcium entry in cultured mouse spinal cord neurons under voltage clamp measured using arsenazo III. *J. Neurosci.,* 7: 3230 – 3244.

Miller, K.D., Chapman, B. and Stryker, M.P. (1989a) Visual responses in adult cat visual cortex depend on *N*-methyl-D-aspartate receptors. *Proc. Natl. Acad. Sci. U.S.A.,* 86: 5183 – 5187.

Miller, K.D., Keller, J.B. and Stryker, M.P. (1989b) Ocular dominance column development: analysis and simulation. *Science,* 245: 605 – 615.

Montague, P.R., Gally, J.A. and Edelman, G.M. (1991) Spatial signaling in the development and function of neural connections. *Cereb. Cortex,* 1(2): 199 – 220.

Mower, G.D., Christen, W.G., Burchfiel, J.L. and Duffy, D.H. (1984) Microiontophoretic bicuculline restores binocular responses to visual cortical neurons in strabismic cats. *Brain Res.,* 309: 168 – 172.

Nicoll, R.A., Kauer, J.A. and Malenka, R.C. (1988) The current excitement in long-term potentiation. *Neuron,* 1: 97 – 103.

Nicoll, R.A., Malenka, R.C. and Kauer, J.A. (1990) The role of calcium in long-term potentiation. *Physiol. Rev.,* 70: 513 – 566.

Radpour, S. and Thomson, A.M. (1991) Coactivation of local circuit NMDA receptor mediated EPSPs induces lasting enhancement of minimal Schaffer collateral EPSPs in slices of rat hippocampus. *Eur. J. Neurosci.,* 3: 602 – 613.

Rana, R.S. and Hokin, L.E. (1990) Role of phosphoinositides in transmembrane signaling. *Physiol. Rev.,* 70: 115 – 164.

Reiter, H.O. and Stryker, M.P. (1988) Neural plasticity without postsynaptic action potentials: less-active inputs become dominant when visual cortical cells are pharmacologically inhibited. *Proc. Natl. Acad. Sci. U.S.A.,* 85: 3623 – 3627.

Reiter, H.O., Waitzman, D.M. and Stryker, M.P. (1986) Cortical activity blockade prevents ocular dominance plasticity in the kitten visual cortex. *Exp. Brain Res.,* 65: 182 – 188.

Sayer, R.J., Friedlander, M.J. and Redman, S.J. (1991) In: H. Wheal and A. Thomson (Eds.), *Excitatory Amino Acids and Synaptic Function,* Academic Press, London, pp. 211 – 222.

Schmidt, J.T. (1990) Long-term potentiation and activity-dependent retinotopic sharpening in the regenerating retinotectal projection of goldfish: common sensitive period and sensitivity to NMDA blockers. *J. Neurosci.,* 10: 233 – 246.

Schwartz, M.L. and Rothblat, L.A. (1980) Long-lasting behavioral and dendritic spine deficits in the monocularly deprived albino rat. *Exp. Neurol.,* 68: 136 – 146.

Sejnowski, T.J. (1977a) Storing covariance with non-linearly interacting neurons. *J. Math. Biol.,* 4: 303 – 321.

Sejnowski, T.J. (1977b) Statistical constraints on synaptic plasticity. *J. Theor. Biol.,* 69: 387 – 389.

Sejnowski, T.J. and Tesauro, G. (1989) The Hebb rule for synaptic plasticity: algorithms and implementations. In: J.H. Byrne and W.O. Berry (Eds.), *Neural Models of Plasticity,* Academic Press, New York, pp. 94 – 103.

Sejnowski, T.J., Chattarji, S. and Stanton, P.K. (1989) Induction of synaptic plasticity by Hebbian covariance in the hippocampus. In: R. Durbin, C. Miall and G. Mitchison (Eds.), *The Computing Neuron,* Addison-Wesley, New York, pp. 105 – 124.

Shatz, C.J. and Stryker, M.P. (1978) Ocular dominance in layer IV of the cat's visual cortex and the effects of monocular deprivation. *J. Physiol. (Lond.),* 281: 267 – 283.

Sherman, S.M. and Spear, P.D. (1982) Organization of visual pathways in normal and visually deprived cats. *Physiol. Rev.,* 62: 738 – 855.

Shibuki, K. and Okada, D. (1991) Endogenous nitric oxide release required for long-term synaptic depression in the cerebellum. *Nature,* 349: 326 – 328.

Sillito, A.M., Murphy, P.C., Salt, T.E. and Moody, C.I. (1990) Dependence of retinogeniculate transmission in cat or NMDA receptors. *J. Neurophysiol.,* 63: 347 – 355.

Sparks, D.L. (1986) Translation of sensory signals into commands for control of saccadic eye movements: role of primate superior colliculus. *Physiol. Rev.,* 66: 118 – 171.

Stanton, P.K. and Sejnowski, T.J. (1989) Associative long-term depression in the hippocampus induced by Hebbian covariance. *Nature,* 339: 215 – 217.

Stent, G. (1973) A physiological mechanism for Hebb's postulate of learning. *Proc. Natl. Acad. Sci. U.S.A.,* 70: 997 – 1001.

Sutor, B. and Hablitz, J.J. (1989a) Long-term potentiation in frontal cortex: role of NMDA-modulated polysynaptic excitatory pathways. *Neurosci. Lett.,* 97: 111–117.

Sutor, B. and Hablitz, J.J. (1989b) EPSP's in rat neocortical neurons in vitro. II. Involvement of *N*-methyl-D-aspartate receptors in the generation of EPSPs. *J. Neurophysiol.,* 61: 621–634.

Tieman, S.B. (1984) Effects of monocular deprivation on geniculocortical synapses in the cat. *J. Comp. Neurol.,* 222: 166–176.

Tieman, S.B. (1985) The anatomy of geniculocortical connections in monocular deprived cats. *Cell. Mol. Neurobiol.,* 5: 35–45.

Tsumoto, T. (1990) Excitatory amino acid transmitters and their receptors in neural circuits of the cerebral neocortex. *Neurosci. Res., 9:* 79–102.

Tsumoto, T. and Suda, K. (1979) Cross-depression: an electrophysiological manifestation of binocular competition in the developing visual cortex. *Brain Res.,* 168: 190–194.

Tsumoto, T., Hagihara, K., Sato, H. and Hata, Y. (1987) NMDA receptors in the visual cortex of young kittens are more effective than those of adult cats. *Nature,* 327: 513–514.

Tumosa, N., Tieman, S.B. and Tieman, D.G. (1989) Binocular competition affects the pattern and intensity of ocular activation columns in the visual cortex of cats. *Vis. Neurosci.,* 2: 391–407.

Van Essen, D. (1982) Neuromuscular synapse eliminate. In: H.C. Spitzer (Ed.), *Neuronal Development,* Plenum, New York, pp. 333–376.

Von Der Malsburg, C. (1973) Self organization of orientation-sensitive cells in the striate cortex. *Kybernetik,* 14: 85–100.

Wiesel, T.N. (1982) Postnatal development of the visual cortex and the influence of environment. *Nature,* 299: 583–591.

Wigstrom, H., Gustafsson, B., Huang, Y.Y. and Abraham, W.C. (1986) Hippocampal long-lasting potentiation is induced by pairing single afferent volleys with intracellularly injected depolarizing current pulses. *Acta Physiol. Scand.,* 126: 317–318.

Williams, J.H., Errington, M.L., Lynch, M.A. and Bliss, T.V.P. (1989) Arachidonic acid induces a long-term activity-dependent enhancement of synaptic transmission in the hippocampus. *Nature,* 341: 739–743.

Wood-Jones, F. and Porteus, S.D. (1928) *The Matrix of the Mind,* Honolulu, Mercantile, Honolulu.

T.P. Hicks, S. Molotchnikoff and T. Ono (Eds.)
Progress in Brain Research, Vol. 95
© 1993 Elsevier Science Publishers B.V. All rights reserved.

CHAPTER 20

Potentiation of the extrageniculo-striate pathway: a possible role in visual pattern discrimination

Svetlana I. Shumikhina

Institute of Higher Nervous Activity and Neurophysiology, Academy of Sciences of the U.S.S.R., 117865 Moscow, U.S.S.R.

Introduction

A problem in understanding brain mechanisms that are responsible for discrimination of visual stimuli has a fairly enough history. The pioneering studies of Hubel and Wiesel (1959, 1962, 1965), which allowed to distinguish in the cat primary visual cortex neurons with simple and complex receptive fields (RFs), were a basis for intensive investigations of different authors in this direction. Though different subtypes of RFs were described owing to later studies, the classification of Hubel and Wiesel has remained valid and shall be used throughout this article. As is known, many properties distinguish complex RFs of visual cortical neurons from simple ones as well as from RFs of geniculate neurons. According to Hubel and Wiesel (1962, 1965) simple cells comprise the first stage of cortical information processing while complex cells form the second stage of this process. Complex RFs consist of overlapping on and off areas, unlike simple RFs that consist of separate on and/or off areas, and that have inhibitory flanks in their RFs, which are absent in complex RFs. The size of complex RFs is larger than the size of the simple ones. Complex cells do not respond in linear fashion to activation of different points within their RFs in contrast to simple cells. As a rule, complex cells have some level of spontaneous activity and they are less narrow tuned to the orientation of stimuli. Such cells are more responsive to high velocities of stimulus movement (Hubel and

Wiesel, 1959, 1962, 1965; Henry, 1977; Leventhal and Hirsch, 1978; Supin, 1981; Sherman and Spear, 1982; Orban, 1984). Some properties of complex cells (larger RF, overlapping on and off areas) can be explained by the convergence of afferents of simple cells, as was suggested initially by Hubel and Wiesel, while other properties (spontaneous activity, sensitivity to higher velocities) are not. On the other hand, such properties of complex cells as their spontaneous activity, the larger size of their RFs, a broader orientation tuning and sensitivity to high velocities of moving stimuli as well as to low spatial and high temporal frequencies, can be explained by their having inputs from Y-like geniculate cells (the hypothesis of parallel processing of visual information: Stone, 1972, 1983; Stone and Dreher, 1973; Maffei and Fiorentini, 1973; Sherman and Spear, 1982; Spitzer and Hochstein, 1988). A problem, however, with the above hypothesis is that it does not properly explain other properties of complex RFs, such as for example, the structure of the RFs.

Nevertheless, many data exist in conflict with both hypotheses. For example, the fact that some complex cells, like simple ones, receive monosynaptic input from the dorsal lateral geniculate nucleus (LGN) (Hoffmann and Stone, 1971; Bullier and Henry, 1979a,b,c; Tanaka, 1979), contradicts the hierarchical hypothesis of Hubel and Wiesel. The other fact that both simple and complex cells can receive inputs from X- as well as from Y-like geniculate neurons, contradicts the hypothesis of parallel processing. Data from experiments in which the antagonist of GABA receptors, bicuculline, was used (Krnjević and Schwartz, 1967; Sillito, 1984) showing an enlargement of RFs and a reduction of orientation and directional selectivity in some complex cells (Sillito, 1984; Volgushev, 1989), are not in agreement with both hypotheses, because the data propose a role of intracortical inhibition in the formation of complex RFs. These contradictions can be overcome, if we assume an involvement of an additional source of visual information into the process of the formation of complex RFs, such as input from the pulvinar-lateral posterior (Pulv-LP) complex (in the remaining part of the text, this will be referred to as the pulvinar or Pulv-LP).

Arguments in favour of an involvement of pulvinar input in the process of formation of complex receptive fields

There are strong arguments to suppose that Pulv-LP takes part in the formation of complex RFs. My hypothesis, based on the involvement of the pulvinar input in the process of the formation of complex RFs, combines elements of both the hierarchical hypothesis of Hubel and Wiesel and the hypothesis of parallel processing, proposed by other authors (e.g., see Sherman and Spear, 1982; Stone, 1983; Spitzer and Hochstein, 1988), as well as taking into account intracortical inhibition as one of the factors of this process. The hypothesis is based on the following data.

(1) The Pulv-LP complex receives direct input from the retina (Itoh et al., 1979; Kawamura et al., 1979; Guillery et al., 1980; Leventhal et al., 1980). The "geniculate wing" (Guillery et al., 1980), a site to which the retina projects is not an extension of the LGN, but it is a part of the pulvinar. This fact derives from the detailed studies of Hutchins and Updyke (1989) that the geniculate wing as well as the medial interlaminar nucleus of the LGN have their own incomplete representations of the visual field.

(2) The Pulv-LP complex receives also direct retinotopically organized inputs from other visual subcortical structures – superior colliculus and pretectum – i.e., from visual structures that receive retinal inputs as well (Kawamura and Kobayashi, 1975; Berman and Jones, 1977; Graham, 1977; Berson and Graybiel, 1978; Graham and Berman, 1981) and can transmit to the pulvinar complex information from all types (X, Y, W) of ganglion cells of the retina (Godfraind et al., 1972; Hoffmann, 1973; Magalhaes-Castro et al., 1976; Ogawa and Takahashi, 1981; Sawai et al., 1985; Hada and Hayashi, 1990; see also Shumikhina, 1981; Stone, 1983).

(3) All neurons of the Pulv-LP are spontaneously active (Mason, 1978), their RFs are larger than the RFs of geniculate neurons; directionally responsive and directionally selective neurons comprise the largest group of visually responsive cells of the Pulv-LP complex (Godfraind et al., 1969; Meulders et al., 1971; Mason, 1978, 1981; Harutiunian-Kozak et al., 1981b; Chalupa and Abramson, 1988). A majority of neurons responds especially well to fast moving stimuli (Mason, 1978). Pulv-LP neurons are revealed that have on/off responses in each point of the RF, as well as those with on or off responses, which have concentric and diffuse RFs and orientation selectivity (Godfraind et al., 1969; Mason, 1978; Harutiunian-Kozak et al., 1981a,b).

(4) Under adequate conditions, visual sensitivity can be revealed in all cytoarchitectonic subdivisions of the Pulv-LP complex, and the percentage of visually responsive neurons has been estimated to be as high as 93% (Chalupa et al., 1983; Chalupa and Abramson, 1988; Hutchins and Updyke, 1989).

(5) There is a direct input from all subdivisions of the Pulv-LP complex to the striate cortex (Albus et al., 1980; Hughes, 1980; Bullier et al., 1984; Shumikhina, 1990).

(6) The Pulv-LP complex projects to layer Ia and to the border of layers IVβ and V of area 17 (Miller and Benevento, 1979); i.e., pulvinar input can affect cells of all layers of the visual cortex. Pulvinar afferents establish contacts on thin branches and spines of dendrites and make asymmetric synapses (Adrianov, 1977; Miller and Benevento, 1979).

(7) Input from the pulvinar has its own way of cor-

tical excitation, that differs from the geniculate one (Shumikhina, 1984a).

(8) Striate input from Pulv-LP is weaker than input from the LGN (Morillo, 1961; Shumikhina, 1984a; Malpeli et al., 1986).

(9) Interaction of pulvinar and geniculate afferent inputs can be revealed in the visual cortex (Morillo, 1961; Shumikhina, 1984b, 1988).

(10) Complex cells of the striate cortex are a cortical target for input from the Pulv-LP (Shumikhina and Volgushev, 1989, 1990a,b).

(11) The visual activity, orientation and directional selectivity of complex cells are spared (although these become weaker) after the complete inactivation of all layers of the LGN and its medial interlaminar nucleus, while the visual activity of simple cells is blocked; additional inactivation of Pulv-LP results in the disappearance of the activity of complex cells (Malpeli, 1983; Malpeli et al., 1986).

(12) Changes in efficacy of Pulv-LP input results in a reduction of orientation selectivity of complex cells having both pulvinar and geniculate inputs (Shumikhina and Volgushev, 1990b).

I would now like to present in more detail our own data. It is well known that the visual activity of pulvinar neurons is unstable and depends significantly on type and depth of anaesthesia (Chalupa et al., 1983; Chalupa and Abramson, 1988; Hutchins and Updyke, 1989). Due to this factor, we conducted our experiments on awake cats. Recently, I have conducted chronic electrophysiological experiments on alert cats (Shumikhina, 1984a). I have recorded evoked potentials to stimulation of the LGN and the pulvinar, in area 17 of the visual cortex. Responses to stimulation of the pulvinar were recorded at latencies of 2.6 ± 0.6 msec and to stimulation of the LGN at latencies of 2.0 ± 0.5 msec (see Fig. 1). I did not find any significant difference between these latencies. There were differences in the shape of the evoked potentials to stimulation of these structures. The amplitude of these responses was significantly larger to geniculate stimulation under the same intensity of stimulation, and the latency of

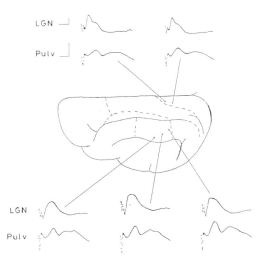

Fig. 1. Evoked potentials in the visual and association cortex to 1 Hz stimulation of the lateral geniculate nucleus (LGN, 0.3 mA) and pulvinar (Pulv, 0.6 mA) in the alert cat. Averaging from eight presentations; negativity upward. Calibration: 100 μV, 5 msec. (Adapted from Shumikhina, 1984a.)

a negative component N1 was significantly shorter to geniculate than pulvinar stimulation (7.2 ± 0.8 msec and 13.7 ± 1.2 msec). When I recorded evoked potentials to paired stimulation of the LGN or the pulvinar, I found significant differences in the way area 17 was activated by inputs from the LGN and the pulvinar (Figs. 2, 3). If there is a strong depression of the test response to paired stimulation of the LGN at short interstimulus intervals and its gradual restoration at longer intervals, the depression of the test response to paired stimulation of the pulvinar is very short, and already at short enough interstimulus intervals (20 – 40 msec) a significant (2 – 4 times) facilitation of the test response is revealed (Shumikhina, 1984a). Similar facts has been obtained by others (Malis and Kriger, 1956; Schoolman and Evarts, 1959; Demetrescu and Steriade, 1965), but I have conducted a quantitative investigation and have examined recovery cycles of evoked potentials to pulvinar stimulation in unrestrained cats. I have also obtained evidence of interaction of afferent inputs from the pulvinar and the LGN in the striate cortex of awake cats (see

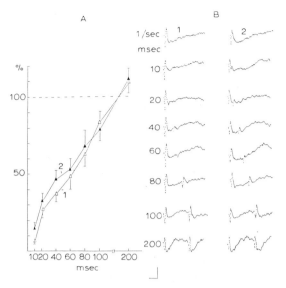

Fig. 2. Recovery of evoked potentials during paired stimulation of the lateral geniculate nucleus in the visual and association cortex in the alert cat. *A*. Recovery curves in the association (1) and visual (2) cortex to stimulation of the lateral geniculate nucleus. Abscissa, intervals between test and conditioning stimuli; ordinate, amplitude of response to test stimulation as a percentage of the amplitude of the response to conditioning stimulation. Average data (7 cats, *n* = 104 for each point). *B*. Evoked potentials in the association (1) and visual (2) cortex to 1 Hz and paired stimulation of the lateral geniculate nucleus under varied interstimulus intervals (shown at left) in one of the cats. Averaging from eight presentations; negativity upward. Calibration: 100 μV, 50 msec (for lower oscillograms: 100 μV, 5 msec). (Adapted from Shumikhina, 1984a.)

Shumikhina, 1984b, 1988). Convergence of pulvinar and geniculate inputs on single cells in area 17 has also been shown by Morillo (1961).

Shumikhina and Volgushev (1989, 1990a,b) showed that in alert cats prepared under local anaesthesia using a long-lasting anaesthetic (lidocaine hydrochloride), 33% of neurons in area 17 responded to electrical stimulation of Pulv-LP and the RFs of those neurons consist of overlapping on and off areas (Fig. 4). These cells can be classified as having complex RFs according to Hubel and Wiesel (1962, 1965). We have recorded 46 neurons from 11 cats. Animals were immobilized with D-tubocurarine and artificially respired. Light flash stimuli (rectangles with sides from 0.5 to 3 deg, 21.2

cd/m^2, 150 – 200 msec) were presented under conditions of mesopic light adaptation to one eye, while the other eye was closed. The variability of the latency served as the main criterion for orthodromic response. Additional criteria could be provided when we recorded cells in the superficial cortical layers, as it is known that corticogeniculate and corticopulvinar neurons are located in deep (V to VI) layers (Gilbert and Kelly, 1975; Abramson and Chalupa, 1985). We always verified the subcortical placement of the tips of the stimulating electrodes, as it is known that the cortico-recipient zone is located in a definite region of the Pulv-LP (Updyke, 1977; Berson and Graybiel, 1978). High-frequency stimulation was not used for this purpose because it could affect the properties of cortical neurons. Four groups of neurons in the visual cortex were defined on the basis of presence/absence of input from two

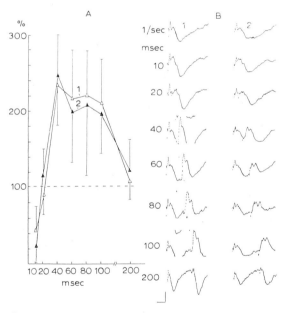

Fig. 3. Recovery of evoked potentials during paired stimulation of the pulvinar in the visual and association cortex in the alert cat. *A*. Recovery curves in the visual (2) and association (1) cortex to stimulation of the pulvinar. Average data (14 cats, *n* = 120 for each point). *B*. Evoked potentials in the visual (2) and association (1) cortex to 1 Hz and paired stimulation of the pulvinar in one of the cats. Symbols as in Fig. 2. (Adapted from Shumikhina, 1984a.)

subcortical structures: (1) cells with inputs from Pulv-LP and the LGN (13 cells, 28%); (2) cells with input only from the LGN (10 cells, 22%); (3) cells with input only from Pulv-LP (2 cells, 4%); and (4) cells non-responsive to electrical stimulation (0.2 msec, 10 − 60 V) of these structures (21 cells, 46%). Stimulation of the LGN resulted in the excitation of 50% of cells from the 46 neurons tested, at latencies of 0.8 − 10.8 msec (mean 3.7 ± 0.7 msec). Stimulation of the Pulv-LP elicited responses in 33% of the cells at latencies of 0.8 − 10.2 msec (mean 2.9 ± 0.6 msec). Pulvinar and geniculate projections are closely connected with each other: 87% of neurons with Pulv-LP input also responded to geniculate stimulation, while 62% of neurons with geniculate input also responded to pulvinar stimulation. We have tested RF properties of 8 cells with both pulvinar and geniculate inputs, 3 cells with input only from the LGN, and 1 cell with input only from the

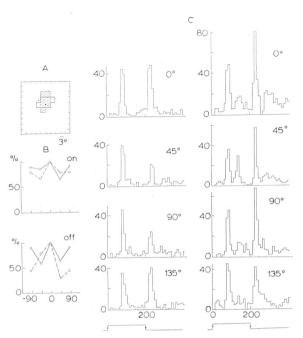

Fig. 5. Orientation selectivity of a neuron with inputs from the pulvinar and the lateral geniculate nucleus. *A*. Schematic representation of the receptive field (RF). The RF-centre is the point of the maximal neuronal discharge. Solid line, on-response zone; hatched area, off-response zone; cross, centre of gaze; open circle, on centre; black circle, off-centre. *B*. Orientation tuning curve of the neuron before (dotted line) and after (solid line) high frequency pulvinar stimulation. Abscissa, stimulus orientation in degrees from the horizontal; ordinate, number of spikes in the response as a percentage of maximal. *C*. Peristimulus time histograms (PSTH) of neuronal responses to flashes presented to the centre of the RF (light bar 3 × 0.5 deg) at different orientations before (left) and after (right) high frequency pulvinar stimulation. Figures near each histogram, orientation of the stimulus. The PSTHs are based on 20 stimulus presentations. (Combined from Shumikhina and Volgushev, 1990b.)

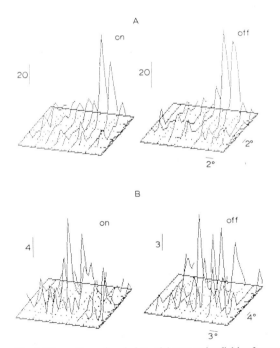

Fig. 4. Three-dimensional plots of the receptive fields of neurons. *A*. With pulvinar and geniculate inputs. *B*. With input only from the pulvinar. Vertical axis: number of spikes in response to presentation of stimuli in each of 100 (10 × 10) points of the visual field; the plane of the plot corresponds to the plane of the screen. (Adapted from Shumikhina and Volgushev, 1990b.)

pulvinar. The RF size of 9 neurons with pulvinar input varied from 2 to 54 deg², and these cells had centres that were located 2 − 17 deg from the gaze. The RF width of 8 cells with both pulvinar and geniculate inputs varied from 1.5 to 8 deg (mean 5 ± 1 deg) and their length varied from 1.5 to 12 deg (mean 7 ± 1 deg). 62% of these neurons were orientation-selective. The width of their orientation tuning curves varied from 22 to 150 deg (mean 82 ± 13 deg). These neurons preferred horizontal stimulus orientations as a rule (75%) (Fig. 5), while neurons with input only from the LGN more often preferred oblique stimulus orientations (this difference was not significant). The RF size of 3 neurons with inputs only from the LGN varied from 9 to 39 deg^2, and these cells had centres that were located 2 – 14 deg from the gaze. The RF width of these cells varied from 3 to 8 deg (mean 5 ± 1 deg) and their length varied from 3 to 10 deg (mean 7 ± 1 deg). The RF size of the neuron with input only from the pulvinar composed 24 deg^2. The RF width of this neuron composed 6 deg and its length composed 6 deg as well. To test for a possible role of pulvinar input in the formation of complex RFs, we tried to use high-frequency stimulation (200 Hz, 10 sec, 25 V) of the pulvinar before the presentation of stimuli of different orientations. The tetanization resulted in a reduction of the orientation selectivity of complex cells in the visual cortex showing inputs from

Pulv-LP and the LGN (Fig. 5). This reduction was at the expense of a three-fold increase of the response to stimuli opposite to the optimal orientation. There was also a significant intensification (more than two-fold) of responses to stimuli of other orientations. Thus, we have shown that changes in efficacy of pulvinar input result in changes in properties of complex RFs of neurons in area 17, i.e., they evoke adaptive modifications of complex RFs.

I would like to propose that pulvinar input tonically excites complex cells. Such tonic excitation is manifested as spontaneous activity in these neurons. The pulvinar input complicates the basic properties of complex RFs having inputs of simple or geniculate cells (see Fig. 6, for details). As a result, complex cells have RFs of larger size and of broader orientation tuning than simple ones and acquire sensitivity to high velocities. The phasic character of the excitation of complex cells is deter-

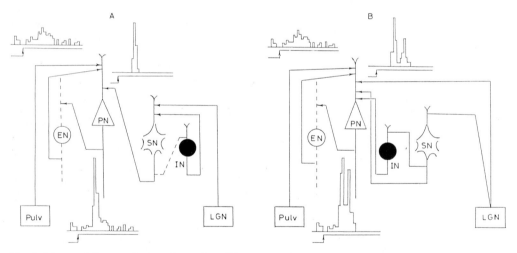

Fig. 6. Scheme of the organization of complex cell inputs that determine its receptive field properties. *A*. A pyramidal neuron (PN, complex cell) receiving a monosynaptic pulvinar input and a disynaptic geniculate input (input from simple cell). *B*. A pyramidal neuron receiving monosynaptic pulvinar and geniculate inputs. SN, a stellate cell; EN, excitatory neuron; IN, inhibitory neuron. Interrupted line, connections that determine "vague" physiological mechanisms, revealed by the method of paired stimuli. Peristimulus time histograms, supposed response of the pyramidal neuron as a result of its excitation by pulvinar and geniculate inputs to optimally oriented stimuli. Here, well-known data are used, such as: (1) the majority of simple cells are located in layer IV of the striate cortex and these are stellate cells as a rule (Kelly and Van Essen, 1974; Bullier and Henry, 1979a,b,c); (2) the majority of complex cells are located in layers II + III, V and VI of the striate cortex and these are pyramidal cells as a rule (Kelly and Van Essen, 1974; Lin et al., 1979); (3) both simple and complex cells can receive mono- as well as disynaptic geniculate inputs (Hoffmann and Stone, 1971; Toyama et al., 1974; Bullier and Henry, 1979a,b,c; Ferster and Lindström, 1983); (4) simple cells can excite and inhibit complex cells as well (Volgushev, 1987, 1988); (5) inhibition can be revealed between cells with both weakly and significantly distinctive preferred orientations (Blakemore and Tobin, 1972; Toyama et al., 1981; Volgushev, 1987).

mined by inhibitory processes at the level of simple cells, or by input from inhibitory neurons. The adaptivity of complex RFs can be achieved in this case by changes in the efficacy of pulvinar input. These considerations are stated in short by Shumikhina (1991).

Conclusions

At first sight it may seem paradoxical that the intensification of the pulvinar input can result in a reduction of the orientation selectivity of complex cells and, consequently, to a worsening of the discrimination of visual patterns. However, behavioural manifestations cannot always follow directly from physiological phenomena. As is known from studies of young animals, simple RFs are experience-insensitive, while complex RFs possess a certain adaptivity (Hirsch, 1985). Complex cells are higher-order output neurons, which transmit information to other visual cortical areas (Hubel and Wiesel, 1965; Denney et al., 1968; Toyama et al., 1974; Gilbert and Wiesel, 1983), and properties of their RFs are formed later during the course of development (Sherman and Spear, 1982; Hirsch, 1985), but these cells have worse detector characteristics (larger size of RF, broader orientation tuning, a sensitivity to low spatial frequencies) than simple cells. It is hard to believe that this is only by chance. As has been shown by different authors, the visual responses of Pulv-LP can be increased in situations of interest to visual stimuli, and the activity of Pulv-LP neurons depend on visually evoked eye movements (e.g., see Chalupa, 1977; Fabre-Thorpe et al., 1986). Experiments with lesions of Pulv-LP also have shown that this structure is involved in processes of visual discrimination and attention (Chalupa, 1977; Zihl and Von Cramon, 1979; Fabre-Thorpe et al., 1986). Consequently, it can be concluded from these data that potentiation of pulvinar input has to result in improvement of visual discrimination. I suppose, that the reduction of the orientation selectivity of complex cells after tetanization of the pulvinar input can mean that the selective attention to visual stimuli (our potentiation of pulvinar input may be con-

sidered as a model of this process) actively depresses (masks) some reactions of sign detectors and, as a result, subserves the finer discrimination of visual patterns. The involvement of pulvinar input into the process of the formation of complex RFs can be important for providing the plasticity of cortical reactions.

References

Abramson, B.P. and Chalupa, L.M. (1985) The laminar distribution of cortical connections with the tecto- and cortico-recipient zones in the cat's lateral posterior nucleus. *Neuroscience,* 15: 81 – 95.

Adrianov, O. (1977) The problem of organization of thalamo-cortical connections. *J. Hirnforsch.,* 18: 191 – 221.

Albus, K., Meyer, G. and Sanides, D. (1980) The retinotopy of cortical and subcortical areas projecting to the visual cortex (V1, V2, V3) of the cat. *Exp. Brain Res.,* 41: A18.

Berman, N. and Jones, E.G. (1977) A retino-pulvinar projection in the cat. *Brain Res.,* 134: 237 – 248.

Berson, D.M. and Graybiel, A.M. (1978) Parallel thalamic zones in the LP-pulvinar complex of the cat identified by their afferent and efferent connections. *Brain Res.,* 147: 139 – 148.

Blakemore, C. and Tobin, E.A. (1972) Lateral inhibition between orientation detectors in the cat's visual cortex. *Exp. Brain Res.,* 15: 439 – 440.

Bullier, J. and Henry, G.H. (1979a) Ordinal position of neurons in cat striate cortex. *J. Neurophysiol.,* 42: 1251 – 1263.

Bullier, J. and Henry, G.H. (1979b) Neural path taken by afferent streams in striate cortex of the cat. *J. Neurophysiol.,* 42: 1264 – 1270.

Bullier, J. and Henry, G.H. (1979c) Laminar distribution of first-order neurons and afferent terminals in cat striate cortex. *J. Neurophysiol.,* 42: 1271 – 1281.

Bullier, J., Kennedy, H. and Salinger, W. (1984) Bifurcation of subcortical afferents to visual areas 17, 18 and 19 in the cat cortex. *J. Comp. Neurol.,* 228: 309 – 328.

Chalupa, L.M. (1977) A review of cat and monkey studies implicating the pulvinar in visual function. *Behav. Biol.,* 20: 149 – 167.

Chalupa, L.M. and Abramson, B.P. (1988) Receptive-field properties in the tecto- and striate-recipient zones of the cat's lateral posterior nucleus. In: T.P. Hicks and G. Benedek (Eds.), *Vision within Extrageniculo-Striate Systems – Progress in Brain Research, Vol. 75,* Elsevier, Amsterdam, pp. 85 – 94.

Chalupa, L.M., Williams, R.W. and Hughes, M.J. (1983) Visual response properties in the tectorecipient zone of the cat's lateral posterior-pulvinar complex: a comparison with the superior colliculus. *J. Neurosci.,* 3: 2587 – 2596.

Demetrescu, M. and Steriade, M. (1965) Comparative study of the visual cortex recovery cycle by stimulation of the lateral geniculate body or by direct cortical stimulation. *Electroenceph. Clin. Neurophysiol.,* 18: 636–637.

Denney, D., Baumgartner, G. and Adorjani, C. (1968) Responses of cortical neurones to stimulation of the visual afferent radiations. *Exp. Brain Res.,* 6: 265–272.

Fabre-Thorpe, M., Vievard, A. and Buser, P. (1986) Role of the extrageniculate pathway in visual guidance. II. Effects of lesions in the pulvinar-lateral posterior thalamus complex in the cat. *Exp. Brain Res.,* 62: 596–606.

Ferster, D. and Lindström, S. (1983) An intracellular analysis of geniculo-cortical connectivity in area 17 of the cat. *J. Physiol. (Lond.),* 342: 181–215.

Gilbert, C.D. and Kelly, J.P. (1975) The projections of cells in different layers of the cat's visual cortex. *J. Comp. Neurol.,* 163: 81–106.

Gilbert, C.D. and Wiesel, T.N. (1983) Functional organization of the visual cortex. In: J.-P. Changeux, J. Glowinski, M. Imbert and F.E. Bloom (Eds.), *Molecular and Cellular Interactions Underlying Higher Brain Functions – Progress in Brain Research, Vol. 58.* Elsevier, Amsterdam, pp. 209–218.

Godfraind, J.M., Meulders, M. and Veraart, C. (1969) Visual receptive fields of neurons in pulvinar, nucleus lateralis posterior and nucleus suprageniculatus thalami of the cat. *Brain Res.,* 15: 552–555.

Godfraind, J.M., Meulders, M. and Veraart, C. (1972) Visual properties of neurons in pulvinar, nucleus lateralis posterior and nucleus suprageniculatus thalami in the cat. I. Qualitative investigation. *Brain Res.,* 44: 503–526.

Graham, J. (1977) An autoradiographic study of the efferent connections of the superior colliculus in the cat. *J. Comp. Neurol.,* 173: 629–654.

Graham, J. and Berman, N. (1981) Origins of the projections of the superior colliculus to the dorsal lateral geniculate nucleus and the pulvinar in the rabbit. *Neurosci. Lett.,* 26: 101–106.

Guillery, R.W., Geisert, E.F., Jr., Polley, E.H. and Mason, C.A. (1980) An analysis of the retinal afferents to the cat's medial interlaminar nucleus and to its rostral thalamic extension, the "geniculate wing". *J. Comp. Neurol.,* 194: 117–142.

Hada, J. and Hayashi, Y. (1990) Retinal X-afferents bifurcate to lateral geniculate X-cells and to the pretectum or superior colliculus in cats. *Brain Res.,* 515: 149–154.

Harutiunian-Kozak, B.A., Hekimian, A.A., Dec, K. and Grigorian, G.E. (1981a) The structure of visual receptive fields of cat's pulvinar neurons. *Acta Neurobiol. Exp.,* 41: 127–145.

Harutiunian-Kozak, B.A., Hekimian, A.A., Dec, K. and Grigorian, G.E. (1981b) Responses of cat's pulvinar neurons to moving visual stimuli. *Acta Neurobiol. Exp.,* 41: 147–162.

Henry, G.H. (1977) Receptive field classes of cells in the striate cortex of the cat. *Brain Res.,* 133: 1–28.

Hirsch, H.V.B. (1985) The role of visual experience in the development of cat striate cortex. *Cell. Mol. Neurobiol.,* 5: 103–121.

Hoffmann, K.-P. (1973) Conduction velocity in pathways from retina to superior colliculus in the cat: a correlation with receptive-field properties. *J. Neurophysiol.,* 36: 409–424.

Hoffmann, K.-P. and Stone, J. (1971) Conduction velocity of afferents to cat visual cortex: a correlation with cortical receptive field properties. *Brain Res.,* 32: 460–466.

Hubel, D.H. and Wiesel, T.N. (1959) Receptive fields of single neurons in the cat's striate cortex. *J. Physiol. (Lond.),* 148: 574–591.

Hubel, D.H. and Wiesel, T.N. (1962) Receptive fields, binocular interaction and functional architecture in the cat's visual cortex. *J. Physiol. (Lond.),* 160: 106–154.

Hubel, D.H. and Wiesel, T.N. (1965) Receptive fields and functional architecture in two non-striate visual areas (18 and 19) of the cat. *J. Neurophysiol.,* 28: 229–289.

Hughes, H.C. (1980) Efferent organization of the cat pulvinar complex, with a note on bilateral claustrocortical and reticulocortical connections. *J. Comp. Neurol.,* 193: 937–964.

Hutchins, B. and Updyke, B.V. (1989) Retinotopic organization within the lateral posterior complex of the cat. *J. Comp. Neurol.,* 285: 350–398.

Itoh, K., Mizuno, N., Sugimoto, T., Nomura, S., Nakamura, Y. and Konishi, A. (1979) Cerebello-pulvino-cortical and retino-pulvino-cortical pathways in the cat as revealed by the use of the anterograde and retrograde transport of horseradish peroxidase. *J.Comp. Neurol.,* 187: 349–357.

Kawamura, S. and Kobayashi, E. (1975) Identification of laminar origin of some tecto-thalamic fibers in the cat. *Brain Res.,* 91: 281–285.

Kawamura, S., Fukushita, N. and Hattori, S. (1979) Topographical origin and ganglion cell type of the retino-pulvinar projection in the cat. *Brain Res.,* 173: 419–429.

Kelly, I.P. and Van Essen, D.C. (1974) Cell structure and function in the visual cortex of the cat. *J. Physiol. (Lond.),* 238: 515–547.

Krnjević, K. and Schwartz, S. (1967) The action of τ-aminobutyric acid on cortical neurons. *Exp. Brain Res.,* 3: 320–336.

Leventhal, A.G. and Hirsch, H.V. (1978) Receptive-field properties of neurons in different laminae of the visual cortex of the cat. *J. Neurophysiol.,* 41: 948–962.

Leventhal, A.G., Keens, J. and Törk, I. (1980) The afferent ganglion cells and cortical projections of the retinal recipient zone (RRZ) of the cat's "pulvinar complex". *J. Comp. Neurol.,* 194: 535–554.

Lin, C.-S., Friedlander, M.F. and Sherman S.M. (1979) Morphology of physiologically identified neurons in the visual cortex of the cat. *Brain Res.,* 172: 344–348.

Maffei, L. and Fiorentini, A. (1973) The visual cortex as a spatial frequency analyser. *Vision Res.,* 13: 1255–1267.

Magalhaes-Castro, H.H., Murata, L.A. and Magalhaes-Castro, B. (1976) Cat retinal ganglion cells as shown by the horseradish peroxidase method. *Exp. Brain Res.,* 25: 541–549.

Malis, L.J. and Kriger, L. (1956) Multiple response and excitability of cat's visual cortex. *J. Neurophysiol.,* 19: 172–186.

Malpeli, J.G. (1983) Activity of cells in area 17 of the cat in absense of input from layer A of lateral geniculate nucleus. *J. Neurophysiol.,* 49: 595–610.

Malpeli, J.G., Lee, C., Schwark, H.D. and Weyand, T.G. (1986) Cat area 17. I. Pattern of thalamic control of cortical layers. *J. Neurophysiol.,* 56: 1062–1073.

Mason, R. (1978) Functional organization in the cat's pulvinar complex. *Exp. Brain Res.,* 31: 51–66.

Mason, R. (1981) Differential responsiveness of cells in the visual zones of the cat's LP-pulvinar complex to visual stimuli. *Exp. Brain Res.,* 43: 25–33.

Meulders, M., Veraart, C. and Godfraind, J.M. (1971) Quantitative analysis of visual receptive fields of cells in pulvinar, lateralis posterior and suprageniculatus nuclei in the cat. *Brain Res.,* 31: 372.

Miller, J.W. and Benevento, L.A. (1979) Multiple thalamic inputs to primary visual cortex in the monkey and cat. *Anat. Rec.,* 193: 623–624.

Morillo, A. (1961) Microelectrode analysis of some functional characteristics and inter-relationships of specific, association and non-specific thalamocortical systems. *Electroenceph. Clin. Neurophysiol.,* 13: 9–20.

Ogawa, T. and Takahashi, Y. (1981) Retinotectal connectivities within the superficial layers of the cat's superior colliculus. *Brain Res.,* 217: 1–11.

Orban, G.A. (1984) *Neuronal Operations in the Visual Cortex,* Springer, Berlin, 368 pp.

Sawai, H., Fukuda, Y. and Wakakuma, K. (1985) Axonal projections of X-cells to the superior colliculus nucleus of the optic tract in cats. *Brain Res.,* 341: 1–6.

Schoolman, A. and Evarts, E.V. (1959) Responses to lateral geniculate radiation stimulation in cats with implanted electrodes. *J. Neurophysiol.,* 22: 112–129.

Sherman, S.M. and Spear, P.D. (1982) Organization of visual pathways in normal and visually deprived cats. *Physiol. Rev.,* 62: 738–855.

Shumikhina, S.I. (1981) *Functional Organization of Tecto-Cortical Connections,* Nauka, Moscow, 99 pp.

Shumikhina, S.I. (1984a) Evoked potentials in the visual and association cortex of alert cats during paired uniform stimulation of the lateral geniculate body and pulvinar. *Neurophysiology,* 16: 394–400.

Shumikhina, S.I. (1984b) Monomodal convergence in the visual system of waking cats. *Zh. Vyssh. Nervn. Deyat. im. I.P.Pavlova,* 34: 1128–1134.

Shumikhina, S.I. (1988) Integration of geniculate, pulvinar, and collicular afferent inputs by visual and association cortices of alert cats. *Perception,* 17: 409.

Shumikhina, S.I. (1990) Divergence between axonal collaterals of thalamic neurons running to the cat visual and association cortex. *Neurophysiology,* 22: 384–389.

Shumikhina, S.I. (1991) Properties and adaptivity of complex receptive fields may not only be due to intracortical inhibition. *Perception,* 20: 111.

Shumikhina, S.I. and Volgushev, M.A. (1989) Receptive-field properties of cat visual cortex neurons with pulvinar input. *Perception,* 18: 511–512.

Shumikhina, S.I. and Volgushev, M.A. (1990a) Correlation between pulvinar and geniculate corticopetal projections with some receptive-field properties of cat visual cortex neurons. *Perception,* 19: 373.

Shumikhina, S.I. and Volgushev, M.A. (1990b) Receptive-field properties of cat visual cortex neurons with pulvinar input. *Sensornye Systemy,* 4: 370–378.

Sillito, A.M. (1984) Functional considerations of the operation of GABA-ergic inhibitory processes in the visual cortex. In: *Cerebral Cortex, Vol. 12,* Plenum Press, New York, London, pp. 91–117.

Spitzer, H. and Hochstein, S. (1988) Complex-cell receptive field models. *Prog. Neurobiol.,* 31: 285–309.

Stone, J. (1972) Morphology and physiology of the geniculocortical synapse in the cat. The question of parallel input to the striate cortex. *Invest. Ophthalmol.,* 11: 338–345.

Stone, J. (1983) *Parallel Processing in the Visual System,* Plenum Press, New York, 438 pp.

Stone, J. and Dreher, B. (1973) Projection of X- and Y-cells of the cat's lateral geniculate nucleus to area 17 and 18 of visual cortex. *J. Neurophysiol.,* 36: 551–567.

Supin, A.Y. (1981) *Neurophysiology of Mammalian Vision,* Nauka, Moscow, 252 pp.

Tanaka, K. (1979) Afferent connection to the visual cortical cells from X and Y cells in the lateral geniculate nucleus of the cat. *J. Physiol. Soc. Jap.,* 41: 325.

Toyama, K., Matsunami, K., Ohno, T. and Tokashiki, S. (1974) An intracellular study of neuronal organization in the visual cortex. *Exp. Brain Res.,* 21: 45–66.

Toyama, K., Kimura, M. and Tanaka, K. (1981) Organization of cat visual cortex as investigated by cross-correlation technique. *J. Neurophysiol.,* 46: 202–214.

Updyke, B.V. (1977) Topographic organization of the projections from cortical areas 17, 18 and 19 onto the thalamus, pretectum and superior colliculus in the cat. *J. Comp. Neurol.,* 173: 81–122.

Volgushev, M.A. (1987) Comparison of the properties of excitatory and inhibitory neurons in cat visual cortex. *Sensory Systems,* 1: 381–389.

Volgushev, M.A. (1988) Comparison of the properties of excitatory and inhibitory neurons in cat visual cortex. *Perception,* 17: 408.

Volgushev, M.A. (1989) Role of cortical inhibition in reorganization of receptive fields of cat visual cortex neurons under different adaptation levels. *Perception,* 18: 512.

Zihl, J. and Von Cramon, D. (1979) The contribution of the second visual system to directed visual attention in man. *Brain,* 102: 835–856.

T.P. Hicks, S. Molotchnikoff and T. Ono (Eds.)
Progress in Brain Research, Vol. 95
© 1993 Elsevier Science Publishers B.V. All rights reserved.

CHAPTER 21

Long-term changes in visual mechanisms following differential stimulation of color and luminance channels during development

Heywood M. Petry*

Departments of Psychology, Ophthalmology and Visual Sciences, University of Louisville, Louisville, KY 40292, U.S.A.

Color-opponent and luminance channels

The idea that visual information is processed through parallel channels is strongly supported by anatomical and physiological data from the mammalian visual system. Consistent correlations in the morphological and physiological characteristics of cells (e.g., soma size, dendritic spread, conduction velocity, receptive field size, response linearity, sustained or transient nature of response, ON-, OFF-, or ON-OFF center response), have resulted in investigators classifying retinal ganglion cells and thalamic neurons into functional groups, such as the W-, X-, and Y-cell classification developed in cat, and the color-opponent (parvocellular, chromatic, narrow-band) and luminance channel (magnocellular, achromatic, broad-band, brightness) distinction in monkey. The exact relationship of the activity in these channels to visual perception is far from understood. However, a clear difference in function between neurons of the color-opponent and luminance pathways in monkeys (and the basis for the nomenclature chosen for use here) is that the color-opponent channel provides the basis for color vision. This capability is due to the manner in which signals originating from different classes of cone photoreceptors feed into the cell's receptive field. Whereas luminance cells receive additive inputs from the different classes of cones, color-opponent receptive fields are formed by antagonistic signals from two or more cone types. In the trichromatic monkey, post-receptoral color mechanisms include one population of cells that show red/green antagonism and others that show blue/yellow antagonism.

Human psychophysical studies strongly support the existence of parallel visual channels. In fact, observations on human color perception prompted Ewald Hering to postulate separate red/green, blue/yellow, and white/black channels more than 100 years ago (Hering, 1878). Recent psychophysical studies have tried to relate visual performance to underlying channels by determining thresholds under highly constrained stimulus and adaptation conditions. In one classic study, King-Smith and Carden (1976) showed that visual detection could be mediated by either the color-opponent or luminance channel depending upon the physical characteristics of the test stimulus and background. When relatively small and brief narrow-band test flashes were used, the spectral sensitivity function obtained followed that of the luminance channel. Larger and longer duration test stimuli, however, produced the characteristic color-opponent func-

---

* Correspondence to: H.M. Petry, Department of Psychology, Life Sciences Building, University of Louisville, Louisville, Kentucky 40292, U.S.A.

tion, as did the use of a white background that depressed the sensitivity of the luminance channel. Sensitivity for intermediate conditions was determined by the most sensitive of the two channels, based on probability summation.

As a result of recent advances in the characterization of these channels at the neural level, there has been a corresponding resurgence of interest in how the responses of visual channels relate to visual perception (see DeYoe and Van Essen, 1988; Livingstone and Hubel, 1988; Merigan, 1989; Merigan and Maunsell, 1990; Schiller and Logothetis, 1990; Schiller et al., 1990; Merigan et al., 1991) Attempts to parcel out the functions of these channels have included a variety of approaches; e.g., neuroanatomical pathway tracing, electrophysiological recording, histochemical correspondences, selective chemical lesions, and psychophysical tests at isoluminance. Another approach to investigating structure/function relationships is through selective deprivation during development.

Visual development and binocular competition

Appropriate visual experience during early postnatal life is especially important in the development of vision. Disorders of human visual development, such as amblyopia, have been modeled by rearing animals for limited amounts of time in abnormal visual environments (e.g., produced by lid-closure, surgical deviation or optical defocus of one or both eyes) that were intended to mimic naturally occurring environmental abnormalities (e.g., ptosis, cataracts, strabismus, anisometropia). Results clearly show that abnormal visual stimulation during development has a profound detrimental effect on the functioning of visual neurons, on the structure of the visual pathways and on the visual behavior of the animal (for review, see Sherman and Spear, 1982; Boothe et al., 1985). Interestingly, simultaneous deprivation of both eyes does not result in the severe visual impairments that are produced when only one of the two eyes is selectively deprived. The mechanism underlying this result is thought to be the result of abnormal competitive

mechanisms between weakly stimulated neurons driven by the deprived eye and normally stimulated cells driven by the non-deprived eye. In this model of abnormal "binocular competition", the weakly stimulated cells are thought not to develop normally because they are at a disadvantage in the competition for synaptic sites in visual cortex, where neural input driven by the two eyes converges. Abnormal binocular competition produced by the differential stimulation of the eyes has formed the basis of models of competitive mechanisms during visual development. However, as competition appears to be a general characteristic of the central nervous system, it is likely that competitive interactions also occur among other populations of visual neurons during development (e.g., W-, X- and Y-cell channels, ON- and OFF-center channels, coloropponent and luminance channels). Unfortunately, studies of competition between functional visual channels have been limited since a prolonged differential stimulation of selected channels is a difficult condition to achieve during development.

Differential stimulation of visual channels in the tree shrew

We have been able to differentially stimulate the opponent-color and luminance channels during development by utilizing an animal model that possesses a well-developed central visual system based on a relatively simple photoreceptor organization. Tree shrews (*Tupaia belangeri*) have a highly cone-dominated retina (ca. 95% cones, Müller and Peichl, 1989) that contains only two functional classes of cones, short-wavelength-sensitive (SWS) and long-wavelength-sensitive (LWS) (Jacobs and Neitz, 1986; Petry and Hárosi, 1990). Thus they exhibit dichromatic color vision of the deutan type based on a single "blue/yellow" color-opponent channel (Polson, 1968). Since the SWS and LWS cone pigments are displaced widely on the wavelength axis (Petry and Hárosi, 1990), deep-red light effectively deprives the SWS cones of photic stimulation without affecting stimulation of the LWS cones (see Fig. 1). Furthermore, as shown in Fig. 2,

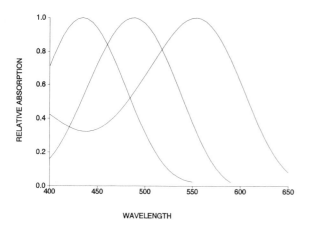

Fig. 1. Relative absorption of tree shrew visual pigments. The SWS cone pigment peaks at ca. 435 nm, the rod pigment at 490–500 nm and the LWS cone pigment at 556 nm. Kodak Safelight 1A filters, which were used for the red light rearing, do not transmit wavelengths shorter than 600 nm. Thus only the LWS cones should have been stimulated by the red light. Pigment data from Petry and Hárosi (1990).

normal activity of the color-opponent channel is dependent upon input from both types of cones, whereas the luminance channel appears to be driven only by the LWS cones.[1] Thus, deep-red light results in a differential stimulation of these visual channels. It should be noted that red light would not selectively stimulate the luminance channel in trichromats (such as the rhesus macaque) since red light would stimulate its LWS and MWS (mid-wavelength-sensitive) cones and thus provide adequate activation of the red/green color-opponent channel as well as the luminance channel. This difference may explain why red-light-rearing has not been found to produce significant effects in trichromatic monkeys (Brenner et al., 1985).

If the tree shrew eye was stimulated with nothing but red light, what would be the predicted impact on the post-receptoral color-opponent and luminance channels? First, the lack of SWS activity should pro-

duce reduced stimulation of those cells normally excited by the SWS cones, and possible overstimulation and adaptation of color-opponent cells normally inhibited by that cone type. This, in turn, should result in a profound disruption of the equilibrium of a color-opponent channel that is normally driven by fluctuations in the stimulation of the SWS and LWS cones. Cells in the luminance channel, however, would be stimulated normally by fluctuations in the excitation and inhibition of the LWS cones. The end result would be expected to produce a competitive advantage for luminance channel neurons at those levels where competition between channels would normally occur. Determination of the effects that this may have on visual mechanisms and visual behavior in these animals should add to our understanding of the interactions between functional visual channels during development.

In our laboratory we have studied the visual system of normal and red-light-reared (RLR) shrews at many levels, using a variety of methodological techniques. At the photoreceptor level, we used immunohistochemical methods and monoclonal antibodies selective for cone type to directly demonstrate the presence of SWS cones in the retinas of RLR shrews. Spectral sensitivity at the retinal level was assessed electrophysiologically by recording the electroretinogram (ERG), a fast, non-invasive measure commonly used clinically in humans to screen for retinal disfunction. Dif-

TREE SHREW VISUAL SYSTEM

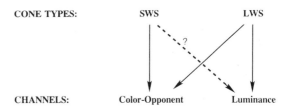

Fig. 2. Diagram showing cone inputs to color-opponent and luminance channels in the tree shrew. The dotted line indicates the possibility of a small inhibitory contribution of the SWS cones to the luminance channel.

[1] In humans, SWS cone input to the luminance channel is negligible (Eisner and MacLeod, 1980; Verdon and Adams, 1987) and possibly inhibitory (Stockman et al., 1991). Electrophysiological studies from our laboratory have indicated that this may also be the case in tree shrews (e.g., Fig. 7).

ferences in neural activity in the visual thalamus and primary visual cortex were assessed histochemically by measuring cytochrome oxidase (CO) reactivity, which has been widely used to study local differences in metabolic activity in the visual systems of normal and visually deprived animals. And our use of behavioral methods allowed us to obtain psychophysical thresholds for color discrimination and spectral sensitivity under different adaptation conditions. Overall, our results show that spectral deprivation during early post-natal visual development produced differences in cortical activity and in visual performance, but apparently had little effect at earlier levels of visual processing. We interpret these findings in terms of neural competition between the color-opponent and luminance channels.

Spectrally restricted rearing

We studied the visual systems of adult tree shrews that had been reared from birth to at least 8 weeks of age in cyclic red light that was limited to long wavelengths beyond 600 nm (Kodak 1A safelight filters). To insure that potential effects were not due to light deprivation, illumination in the red light room was adjusted to be equivalent to that in the main colony room where normal tree shrews were born, reared and housed under standard fluorescent lighting. Also, because we were interested in the long-term effects of the selective rearing (rather than short-term after-effects), RLR animals were subsequently housed under the normal white, fluorescent lighting for a considerable period of time (e.g., 1 year or longer).

As Fig. 1 shows, red light of 600 nm and beyond selectively deprives the SWS cones of photic stimulation, but not the LWS cones. Stimulation of the rod photoreceptors is also likely to be affected, but because the rod peak is approximately 50 nm longer than the SWS cones, and because rods are typically much more sensitive than cones, it is possible that the 600 nm exposure may have been sufficient to provide adequate, though reduced, rod stimulation. As noted previously (see Fig. 2), selective deprivation of the SWS cones should maximally

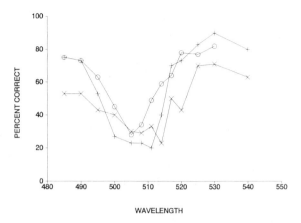

Fig. 3. Data for discrimination of narrow-band chromatic lights from equally bright achromatic lights for normal and RLR tree shrews. Circles represent mean data from 3 normal shrews. Other symbols represent individual data of 2 RLR animals. Chance level of performance is 33.3% correct. Modified from Petry and Kelly (1991).

affect the equilibrium of the tree shrew's opponent-color channel, but should have little detrimental impact on the LWS-driven luminance channel.

Chromatic/achromatic discriminations

Since any deprivation effect would be expected to be strongest at output level, we first asked whether the RLR shrews were able to discriminate chromatic lights from equally bright achromatic lights. In other words, did they have color vision? Since normal tree shrews possess only SWS and LWS cones, if the SWS cones were not functional then RLR shrews should not be able to make this discrimination. We tested color vision behaviorally using a 3-alternative forced-choice paradigm (Petry and Kelly, 1991). The animals were trained to choose the chromatic light paired with 2 achromatic lights for which they were rewarded with juice or sweetened milk. To make sure the animal's selection was not based on brightness, the intensity of the achromatic stimulus was varied about the brightness match in 11 0.1 log unit steps. Also the ambient illumination in the testing apparatus was made sufficient to saturate the rod photoreceptors. The ability of RLR and normal tree shrews to discriminate narrow-band chromatic lights from equally bright white lights is plotted in Fig. 3. The fact that the RLR shrews were able to perform above chance levels (i.e., > 33% correct) for at least some regions of the spectrum indicated that the RLR shrews have color vision. This result means that the RLR shrews must still have functional SWS cones and a functional color-opponent channel. Performance for all animals broke down at their "neutral point" (ca. 505 nm), which is characteristic for deutan-type dichromats. However, the performance of the RLR shrews was significantly poorer overall compared to normals. This suggests that the neural mechanisms underlying chromatic/achromatic discriminations were compromised by the red light rearing.

To further investigate the deficit, we asked whether the RLR animals might also perform differently on intensity discriminations. Dichromats cannot use hue to distinguish monochromatic lights at their neutral point from achromatic lights, but discriminations based on small intensity differences should be possible. Thus, we analyzed the performance of RLR and normal shrews using the data collected at all 11 intensity steps at the neutral point. A percent correct score was obtained for all trials at a particular intensity step for each animal, and the frequency of occurrence of those percent correct scores for all steps is plotted by group in Fig 4a. Whereas the RLR shrews never performed better than 60% correct at any intensity level, the normal shrews performed at 70, 80 and even 100% correct for some intensity steps. The difference in the distribution of the percent correct scores indicates that even when no wavelength coding was involved, the RLR shrews performed more poorly. This is likely because this test was conducted under relatively high adaptation conditions, and the brightness discriminations would have involved the "deprived" color-opponent channel (Schiller and Logothetis, 1990). When small wavelength cues were added to the test (i.e., the test light was varied within ± 10 nm of the neutral point), the difference between groups was accentuated, as shown in Fig. 4b. The performance of the normal animals improved markedly on this second task, but the performance of the RLR shrews improved only marginally. It occurred to us that a simple explanation for these discrimination deficits might be a loss of some SWS cones in the RLR shrews, thus weakening the color-opponent mechanism. To pursue this possibility we looked at the photoreceptor composition in RLR and normal tree shrew retinas.

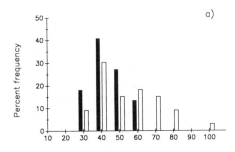

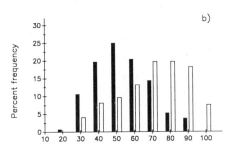

Fig. 4. Histograms of relative frequency of the percent correct scores obtained for normal and RLR tree shrews on visual discrimination tasks involving all 11 intensity values per wavelength. a. Percent correct score distribution at the neutral point for 2 RLR animals (filled bars) and 3 normals shrews (open bars) where only brightness cues are available. b. Distribution of scores for wavelengths ± 10 nm from the neutral point (i.e., 495 – 514 nm) where discriminations could be based on brightness and hue. See text for details. Modified from Petry and Kelly (1991).

Immunohistochemical studies of tree shrew retina

Fig. 5a shows a radial section of tree shrew retina. Although rod photoreceptors are discernable by the slight vitreal displacement of their nuclei relative to those of the cone photoreceptors (which are organized in a single row, see Fig. 5), the identification of cones as SWS or LWS type is not clear in a

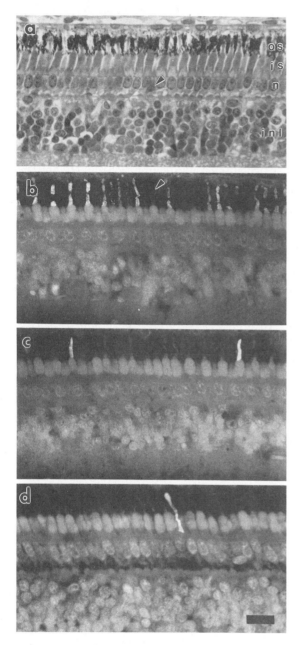

Nissl stain. To specify the spectral identity of single cone photoreceptors we used monoclonal antibodies developed by collaborators in Budapest, Hungary (Szél et al., 1988). Fig. 5*b* – *d* demonstrates the specificity of the antibodies. A fluorescent photomicrograph of a radial section reacting with COS-1, which selectively binds to LWS cones (and MWS cones if they had been present) is shown in Fig. 5*b*. As expected the majority of tree shrew cone outer segments show this specificity, however, a small population of cone outer segments (arrow) as well as the rod outer segments were unlabeled. This second cone population was labeled by an antibody specific for SWS cones (OS-2), shown in Fig. 5*c*. All cones were labeled by one or other of these antibodies. We were also able to identify rods, shown in Fig. 5*d*, by employing an anti-rhodopsin antibody (provided by H. Hamm). Immunohistochemical reaction of RLR tree shrew retinas verified the

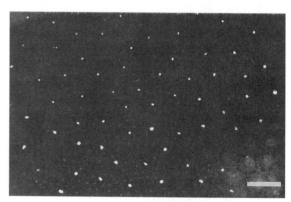

Fig. 6. Tangential section through the cone outer segments of a RLR tree shrew retina. Bright spots indicate those OSs immunoreactive for monoclonal antibody OS-2, which labels SWS cones. Scale bar: 25 μm. Data from Petry et al. (1992a).

Fig. 5. Tree shrew retina. *a*. Radial section of normal tree shrew retina stained with Stevenel's. Note that photoreceptor nuclei are arranged in a single row, except for rod nuclei which are displaced vitreally (arrow). Some photoreceptor outer segments are shrouded by the dark pigment epithelium. OS, outer segment; IS, inner segment; N, photoreceptor nuclei; INL, inner nuclear layer. *b*. Radial section showing brightly labeled outer segments immunoreactive for monoclonal antibody COS-1, which labels

the LWS cones in tree shrew. The arrow indicates a cone OS unlabeled by COS-1. *c*. Section showing two cone OSs that were immunoreactive for monoclonal antibody OS-2, which labels SWS cones. The spacing is typical for this cone type. *d*.. Rod OS labeled with anti-rhodopsin antibody. Its vitreally-displaced nucleus is out of the plane of section. Scale bar: 20 μm (*a* – *d*). Data from Petry et al. (1992a).

presence of SWS cones and rods despite their deprivation during the restricted rearing. Tangential sections at the level of the cone outer segments of normal and RLR retinas revealed similar distributions of the SWS cones. Fig. 6 shows the local distribution of OS-2 labeled cone outer segments in the retina of a RLR shrew. The hexagonal packing of the SWS cones is characteristic of normal shrews and other mammalian species (e.g., Müller and Peichl, 1989). Preliminary analysis of packing distribution revealed no evidence of SWS cones missing from the retinas of the RLR tree shrews. Thus the poorer performance of the RLR animals on the discrimination tasks does not appear to be the result of a reduced population of SWS cones. On the other hand, it is possible that the normal synaptic organization of SWS and LWS cones onto second-order neurons may have been modified in the RLR animals. For example, if fewer SWS cone contacts were made in the RLR animals, sensitivity at short wavelengths may be reduced which would affect the animals' ability to make discriminations based on wavelength. To investigate possible changes early in the visual system, spectral sensitivity was determined using the electroretinogram.

Electroretinogram spectral sensitivity

The gross retinal activity represented in the ERG provides a fast, non-invasive indicator of retinal function. Although the component waves of the ERG appear to be actually generated by Müller cells (see Dowling, 1987, for review), they reflect the activity of different populations of retinal neurons. The ERG b-wave predominately reflects the activity of ON-bipolar cells. We determined the spectral sensitivity of the b-wave in normal and RLR shrews by presenting 500 msec flashes of monochromatic light from across the spectrum and determining the intensity necessary to evoke criterion b-wave amplitudes of 100 μV. The flashes were presented with no background, and data were collected from dark-adapted animals anesthetized with ketamine and xylazine. The RLR shrews were tested immediately

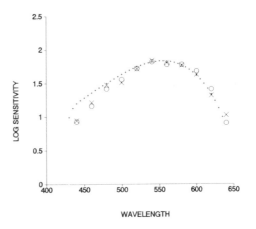

Fig. 7. Dark-adapted retinal spectral sensitivity of normal (circles) and red-light-reared (X's) tree shrews. Data were collected by varying the intensity of monochromatic 500 msec flashes of light necessary to produce a criterion 100 μV amplitude of the electroretinogram b-wave. Data points represent the mean of 2 animals per group. Small symbols show the predicted luminance channel sensitivity (i.e., LWS cone pigment absorption spectra adjusted for absorption of the lens and cornea). From Kelly, Gülük and Petry (unpublished).

upon being removed from the red light. The results, shown in Fig. 7, revealed no differences in the relative sensitivity of the normal and RLR animals, as assessed by the shape of their ERG b-wave spectral sensitivity functions. There was also no apparent difference in the shapes of the wave forms themselves. These results suggest that the RLR shrews possess normal retinal spectral sensitivity. However, the shape of the b-wave sensitivity curve could be fit with the LWS cone pigment absorption spectra alone (adjusted for absorption of the lens and cornea), which implies that color-opponent channel activity was not strongly reflected in the tree shrew ERG b-wave under our recording conditions. Hence, we cannot conclude that there are no differences in the retinal functioning of RLR and normal shrews, although we can say that the relative sensitivity of the LWS cone mechanism at this level does not appear to have been sensitized or otherwise changed by the red light rearing. However, because ERG amplitude is dependent upon electrode placement and recording conditions as well as stimulus in-

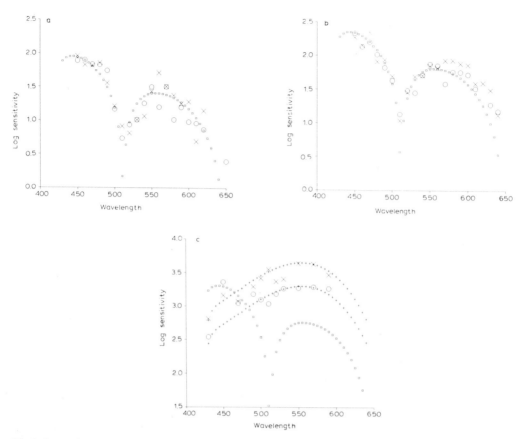

Fig. 8. Spectral sensitivity measured under 430 lux white light adaptation (*a*), 16 lux white light illumination (*b*) and in complete darkness (*c*) for normal (circles) and red-light-reared (X's) tree shrews. Small squares represent predicted sensitivity of the color opponent channel and small crosses that of the luminance channel in tree shrew. Note shifted range of ordinate in *c*. Data in *a* and *b* from Petry and Kelly (1991). Data in *c* from Petry et al. (1992b).

tensity, we cannot conclude that the overall sensitivity of the animals was indeed equivalent. To determine if such differences might exist at higher levels, we measured spectral sensitivity behaviorally, using a modification of the psychophysical paradigm previously described.

Behavioral spectral sensitivity

Behavioral spectral sensitivity was measured in normal and RLR shrews by requiring the animals to choose which of three panels was continuously illuminated (until a response was made) with narrowband chromatic light, the other two panels being dark. Thresholds were determined using a modified

method-of-limits / staircase paradigm (Petry et al., 1984) for spectral lights from 450 to 650 nm, under three different levels of achromatic adaptation (i.e., 430 lux, 16 lux, and darkness). Since background intensity is one factor that determines the relative sensitivity of the color-opponent and luminance channels (King-Smith and Carden, 1976), the three adaptation levels were chosen to reveal the different contributions of these two channels to overall spectral sensitivity. The functions shown in Fig. 8*a* were obtained under 430 lux adaptation lighting. The data showed maxima at 450 nm and at 550 – 570 nm with a minimum near 505 nm, the tree shrews' neutral point. Spectral sensitivity curves of this shape are characteristic for tree shrews (Jacobs and Neitz,

1986) and human deuteranopes (Zrenner, 1983) under conditions where the sensitivity of the color-opponent channel (rather than the luminance channel) determines sensitivity across much of the visible spectrum. The small squares show the predicted sensitivity of a color-opponent channel determined by a subtractive interaction of the SWS and LWS cone mechanisms. Since the long duration and relatively large stimulus size used in the current experiment were expected to favor the color-opponent channel (King-Smith and Carden, 1976), it is reasonable that the data in Fig. 8a represent the sensitivity of the tree shrew's single color-opponent channel. No dif-

ference was seen in the overall or relative sensitivity of RLR and normal shrews.

Under lower levels of adaptation (16 lux), the data reflected a 0.4 log unit increase in sensitivity, but could still be fit by the color-opponent function (see Fig. 8b). There was, however, a tendency for the RLR animals to be slightly more sensitive to longer wavelengths. Fig. 8c demonstrates the substantial increase in sensitivity and the differences in the shape of the curves when spectral sensitivity was measured in complete darkness (save for the stimulus light). For normal animals, the sensitivity of the LWS cone-driven luminance channel was dominant, except for 450 nm where detection appeared to be still determined by the color-opponent channel. This general result was expected, since the absence of any background would favor the luminance channel. Interestingly, very little rod contribution was apparent, except for a small increase in sensitivity at 480 nm that was found for both subjects.

Unexpected was our finding of consistently increased sensitivity of the RLR shrews at longer wavelengths. This was coupled with a small decrease in sensitivity at the blue end of the spectrum. In fact, except for a curious dip at 520 – 530 nm, the RLR data were well-fit by the predicted sensitivity of the luminance channel alone. This is an interesting result that would not be predicted from a simple loss in the sensitivity of the SWS cone mechanism alone, but would be predicted if the sensitivity of the luminance channel were enhanced relative to normal. If the luminance channel were truly enhanced in the RLR shrews, what might be the neural mechanism responsible? To pursue this issue we employed a histochemical indicator of functional activity to assess potential differences in the brains of normal and RLR shrews.

Cytochrome oxidase histochemistry

Cytochrome oxidase (CO) is a mitochondrial enzyme involved in energy metabolism that has been used extensively as an indicator of functional neural activity. Within the neuron, CO reactivity is highest

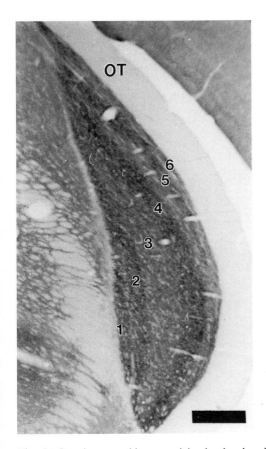

Fig. 9. Cytochrome oxidase reactivity in the dorsal lateral geniculate nucleus of a red-light-reared tree shrew. The pattern of darkly reactive layers 1, 2, 4 and 5 and lightly reactive layers 3 and 6 is also characteristic of normal shrews (Wong-Riley and Norton, 1988). Scale bar: 400 μm. OT, Optic tract. Data from Gülük et al. (1991).

in the dendrites and parallels the intensity and type of synaptic input. This marker has been used to study local differences in metabolic activity in the visual systems of normal and visually deprived animals. Specifically, differences in CO activity have been shown to correspond to functional differences between populations of neurons under study and decreases in reactivity have been found to correspond to decreases in retinal activity produced by retinal impulse blockade or monocular deprivation (for review, see Wong-Riley, 1989).

We measured the CO reactivity of the dLGN and striate cortex in normal and RLR tree shrews using a procedure slightly modified from Lachica et al. (1987). At the level of the dLGN, reactivity resembled the pattern recently described for tree shrews by Wong-Riley and Norton (1988). No differences were seen between RLR and normal shrews. Fig. 9 shows a characteristic section from the dLGN of a RLR shrew in which layers 1, 2, 4 and 5 were darkly

reactive and layers 3 and 6 (which have been postulated to contain W-like cells, Norton, 1982; Wong-Riley and Norton, 1988) were lightly reactive.

On the other hand, differences between normal and RLR shrews were seen in the CO reactivity of striate cortex. In layer IV of striate cortex, which receives the majority of geniculo-cortical afferents in tree shrews, two sub-layers separated by a cell-sparse cleft can be differentiated in Nissl-stained sections as shown in Fig. 10a. However, as described by Wong-Riley and Norton (1988), CO reactivity divides layer IV into 3 sub-layers: two darkly reactive layers (IVa and IVb) separated by a lightly reactive layer (IVm) that spans, but is much wider than, the cleft region. We also observed this pattern, shown in Fig. 10b, in 11 normally-reared animals and in 4 tree shrews that were housed for several weeks in the red light as adults. However, for all 6 tree shrews reared from birth in the red light, CO

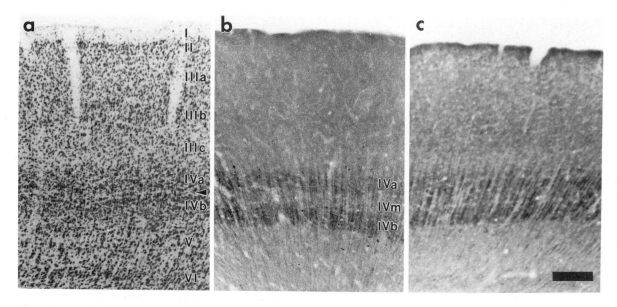

Fig. 10. Tree shrew striate cortex. *a.* Nissl-stained coronal section shows differentiation of 6 layers, with layers III and IV further subdivided. A cell-sparse cleft (arrowhead) divides layer IV. No differences were seen in Nissl-stained sections from RLR and normal tree shrews. *b.* cytochrome oxidase (CO) reacted coronal section from a normally-reared tree shrew shows the banding pattern in layer IV produced by darker CO reactivity in layers IVa, IVb and paler reactivity of IVm. *c.* Comparable section from a red-light-reared tree shrew showing the solid band of dark reactivity in layer IV caused by increased reactivity of IVm relative to IVa and IVb. Top is dorsal, left is medial. Scale = 200 μm. Data from Gülük et al. (1991).

reactivity in layer IV was much more uniform, as shown in Fig. 10c.

To quantify this observation, we measured the optical density produced by the CO reactivity relative to baseline reactivity defined by the white matter. Layer-by-layer measurements in 2 RLR shrews and 2 normal animals showed that layer IV overall, and sublayer IVm in particular, were significantly darker in the RLR animals than in the normals.[1] (The fact that no differences in reactivity were found for layer V, which does not receive geniculate projections, indicated that the results could not be attributed to the parameters of the CO reactions.) These findings are displayed in the bar graphs presented in Fig. 11, which show that the difference in the pattern within layer IV was due to an increase in CO reactivity in layer IVm relative to IVa and IVb, rather than a decrease in the reactivity of IVa and IVb. This result, that a deprivation paradigm (the spectrally-restricted rearing) resulted in increased CO reactivity, is very interesting since previous work has shown that other deprivation paradigms produce lower levels of local neural activity, not greater ones (Wong-Riley and Norton, 1988, in tree shrew; Wong-Riley, 1989, for review).

Furthermore, our finding of a different pattern of oxidative metabolism more than 1 year after the animals were removed from the red light, implies (as do the psychophysical results presented above) that mechanisms of visual development were permanently altered by the restricted spectral illumination during early post-natal development.

Proposed mechanism: competition between visual channels

What might be the mechanisms of visual development that underlie: (1) the differences in CO reac-

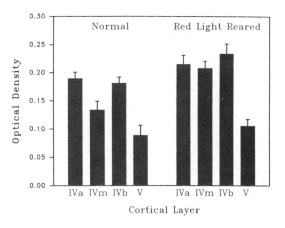

Fig. 11. Cytochrome oxidase reactivity in striate cortex of red-light-reared and normal tree shrews. Measurements of the optical density of layers IVa, IVm, IVb, V, and white matter were made on coronal sections, taking care to define sampling areas well within laminar borders and avoiding blood vessels or other artifacts that would influence the optical density value. Bar graphs show the overall increase in reactivity for RLR shrews of layer IV and the relative increase of reactivity in layer IVm. The uniform reactivity of layer V across groups shows that the difference in layer IV is not due to an overall increased reactivity of all cortical layers. Measurements were made relative to reactivity of the white matter to control for minor differences in tissue processing. Data from Gülük et al. (1991).

tivity in the visual cortex of the RLR animals; (2) the poorer performance of the RLR shrews on chromatic/achromatic discriminations and brightness discriminations; and (3) their increased dark-adapted sensitivity to selected regions of the spectrum? We propose that these differences may be based on a relative weakening of the color-opponent channel and strengthening of the luminance channel in the RLR shrews. Since deep-red light differentially stimulates the color-opponent and luminance visual channels in the tree shrew, it is quite likely that abnormal competitive interactions among the neurons comprising these channels were present during visual development. As described above, deprivation of photic stimulation of the SWS cones during development would selectively affect the color-opponent channel. This supposition is supported by recordings of spectral properties of optic nerve fibers in RLR ground squirrels immediately upon

[1] A 2 × 3 analysis-of-variance revealed a statistically significant effect of rearing condition (normal, RLR, $P < 0.01$) and of layer (IVa, IVm, IVb, $P < 0.05$). One-way analysis-of-variance for layers revealed a significant difference between RLR and normal animals for layer IVm ($P < 0.01$) and not for layers IVa, IVb, or V.

removal from the red light (McCourt and Jacobs, 1983). Results showed the RLR squirrels to possess significantly fewer fibers that displayed input from SWS cones (i.e., were color-opponent). This effect may have been a temporary one as the recordings were made before the RLR squirrels had visual experience in white light, thus allowing no time for recovery of SWS cone input to ganglion cells. But even a temporary disadvantage of color-opponent neurons during early post-natal development may be sufficient to produce long-term changes at higher levels of processing.

In RLR tree shrews, a competitive advantage of the luminance cells during development may have resulted in the formation and/or strengthening of more geniculocortical luminance cell connections in striate layer IV relative to connections from the disadvantaged color-opponent neurons. An increased number of synapses by luminance-type geniculate afferents would result in the observed overall darker CO reactivity, if luminance neurons in the tree shrew dLGN were metabolically more active than color-opponent neurons. Based on evidence from the monkey and cat, a metabolic difference between color-opponent and luminance cells is likely. For example, in the monkey dLGN, parvocellular neurons, which exhibit color-opponency, are less reactive for CO than magnocellular cells, which display broad-band spectral sensitivity (Schiller and Malpeli, 1978; Liu and Wong-Riley, 1990). In the cat dLGN, color-opponent properties have been linked to W-cells (Wilson et al., 1976), which as a class are less reactive for CO than X-cells, which in turn are less reactive than Y-cells (Kageyama and Wong-Riley, 1985). W-cell layers of the tree shrew dLGN are also the least reactive for CO (Wong-Riley and Norton, 1988), but further generalization must await anatomical and physiological distinction of color-opponent and luminance cells in the tree shrew visual system.

Color-opponent and luminance neurons have been encountered in single-unit recordings from tree shrew optic nerve (Van Dongen et al., 1976) and striate cortex (Petry and Gülük, unpublished

data). A W-, X-, and Y-like distinction has also been reported physiologically in the tree shrew dLGN (Sherman et al., 1975; Ter Laak and Thijssen, 1978). However, other than the fact that color-opponent cells showed a sustained response pattern (which makes it unlikely that they are Y-cells), no further parallels have been drawn between the two classification schemes. Unfortunately, interpretation of the lack of an RLR effect on the dLGN is dependent upon whether W- or X-like cells carry color information in the tree shrew. If W-like cells are color-opponent, then competition in the dLGN may be prevented by the laminar segregation of W-cells. In fact, a general characteristic of visual channels is that they appear to remain segregated until significant cross-talk and convergence occurs at cortical levels. However, if X-like cells are color-opponent in this species, then evidence of competitive interactions may be masked by the mixing of X- and Y-like cells in geniculate layers 1, 2, 4 and 5. (That is, increased Y-like cell activity coupled with decreased X-like cell activity may offset to provide no apparent difference in CO reactivity in these dLGN layers.)

Competitive interactions between cells of the color-opponent and luminance channels may also underlie the different pattern of reactivity in striate layer IV of the RLR animals. To see how, let us consider the functional organization of layer IV. The schematic in Fig. 12 illustrates what is known about the functional organization of layer IV of tree shrew striate cortex. (Vertically organized orientation columns have been omitted for clarity; see Lund et al., 1985, for review). Geniculate afferents are horizontally segregated by eye of origin (and lamina of LGN projection) and by the ON-, OFF- or ON/OFF response of their receptive field center (Conley et al., 1984; Norton et al., 1985; Raczkowski and Fitzpatrick, 1990). Quite possibly, color-opponent and luminance channels are also segregated at this level, but the organization of tree shrew striate cortex with respect to color processing has not been worked out. Within layer IV, sub-layer IVm is the least well-defined. For example, IVm has been described as a transition zone between the ON- and OFF-center

TREE SHREW STRIATE CORTEX

(ORGANIZATION OF LAYER IV)

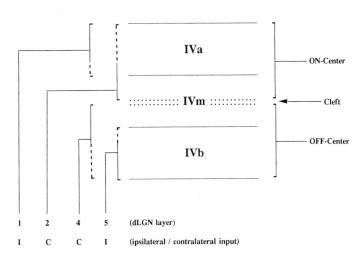

Fig. 12. Schematic drawing of functional organization of layer IV of tree shrew striate cortex emphasizing the sub-division of layer IV into IVa, IVm and IVb by cytochrome oxidase histochemistry. Projections from ipsilateral (I) and contralateral (C) layers of the dorsal lateral geniculate nucleus are summarized from Conley et al. (1984), Conley (1988) and Raczkowski and Fitzpatrick (1990). (Dotted lines indicate disputed projections.) The organization of ON- and OFF-center response properties is summarized from Norton et al. (1985). Vertically organized orientation columns have been omitted for clarity. The restricted-rearing data presented here suggest that IVm may be specialized for color coding.

dominance of sub-layers IVa and IVb (Kretz et al., 1986). It contains stellate cells with dendritic spreads that are very different from the norm for layer IV (Geisert and Guillery, 1979) and shows a projection pattern (to IIIb) that is different from that of upper IVa and lower IVb (Muly et al., 1989). Based on its lower CO reactivity compared to IVa and IVb, Wong-Riley and Norton (1988) suggested that IVm might receive W-cell projections from similarly poorly-reactive LGN layer 3, although such a projection has not been verified by tract-tracing techniques (Conley et al., 1984). These differences in cytoarchitecture, inputs, projections, CO reactivity and response properties of the cells in sub-layer IVm compared to IVa and IVb, suggest that IVm may have a different functional role, such as color vision.

Let us speculate that color-opponent dLGN neurons normally project to cortical color cells in layer IVm, which are sandwiched between the luminance-cell dominated IVa and IVb. The competitive advantage afforded to luminance cells by

red light rearing may allow them to extend their synaptic influence into IVm during early visual development. This might occur by the expansion (or lack of retraction) of geniculate luminance-cell dendrites in IVm, much like the size of ocular dominance columns corresponding to the non-deprived eye expand relative to the deprived-eye columns following monocular deprivation (see Hubel et al., 1977, for review). An increase in the relative density of luminance-cell terminals in IVm would explain the higher CO reactivity of this sub-layer relative to IVa and IVb in the RLR animals.

What might be the effect of abnormal geniculo-cortical connections on visual behavior? Abnormal input from geniculate luminance neurons to cortical color-opponent cells could be expected to produce sensory differences such as those observed psychophysically in the RLR shrews. For example, abnormal contacts of luminance cells onto cortical neurons that are normally color-opponent would serve to decrease the signal-to-noise ratio by diluting the color information carried by the color-opponent cells, much like adding white desaturates a spectral hue. Such a mechanism could account for the impaired ability of the RLR shrews to discriminate monochromatic lights from equally bright achromatic lights. Weakening of the color-opponent channel by abnormal input from luminance neurons may also underlie the poorer brightness discriminations of the RLR animals. Correspondingly, the increase in sensitivity of the RLR animals at selected regions of the spectrum is consistent with a strengthened luminance channel in the RLR shrews. Increased sensitivity was only evident in those regions of the spectrum and under those adaptation conditions that should favor the contributions of the luminance channel. If this is in fact the case, it indicates that selected deprivation during visual development not only can produce detrimental effects, but can also enhance sensory performance mediated by one visual channel at the expense of another. This is quite interesting in itself, particularly since the development of color vision in humans appears to contain a substantial post-natal component (Teller and Bornstein, 1987; Brown and Teller, 1989; Brown, 1990).

The results of this study provide an impetus for further investigations of competitive interactions between functional channels and also show that the unique visual system of the tree shrew provides an excellent model to study these interactions. Clearly, what is needed is further electrophysiological characterization of layer IV and other areas of tree shrew visual cortex with regard to color-opponency and cone inputs. These data would help clarify the mechanisms of color-coding in normal and RLR tree shrew cortex. Such investigations are presently underway in our laboratory.

Acknowledgements

The methodologically diverse studies described in this chapter could not have been performed without the contributions of my students and collaborators: Seema Agarwala, Karen Bjorn, Jonathan Erichsen, Alev Gülük, Ferenc Hárosi, John Kelly, Pál Röhlich, Ágoston Szél and Cedric Williams. I am also appreciative of excellent technical assistance provided by Danielle Morais, and by Richard Reeder, Glenn Hudson and Bob Chorley of the Social and Behavioral Sciences Electronics Shop. The work was supported by NIH Grant R29 EY07113, and by BRSG funds obtained from SUNY-Stony Brook.

References

Boothe, R., Dobson, V. and Teller, D.Y. (1985) Postnatal development in vision in human and nonhuman primates. *Annu. Rev. Neurosci.,* 8: 495 – 545.

Brenner, E., Schelvis, J. and Nuboer, J.F.W. (1985) Early colour deprivation in a monkey (*Macaca fascicularis*). *Vision Res.,* 25: 1337 – 1339.

Brown, A.M. (1990) Development of visual sensitivity to light and color vision in human infants: a critical review. *Vision Res.,* 30: 1159 – 1188.

Brown, A.M. and Teller, D.Y. (1989) Chromatic opponency in 3-month-old human infants. *Vision Res.,* 29: 37 – 45.

Conley, M. (1988) Laminar organization of geniculostriate projections: a common organizational plan based on layers rather than individual functional classes. *Brain Behav. Evol.,* 32: 187 – 192.

Conley, M., Fitzpatrick, D. and Diamond, I.T. (1984) The laminar organization of the lateral geniculate body and striate cortex in the tree shrew (*Tupaia glis*). *J. Neurosci.,* 4: 171 – 197.

DeYoe, E.A. and Van Essen, D.C. (1988) Concurrent processing streams in monkey visual cortex. *Trends Neurosci.,* 11: 219 – 226.

Dowling, J.E. (1987) *The Retina,* Harvard University Press, Cambridge, MA, 281 pp.

Eisner, A. and MacLeod, D.I.A. (1980) Blue-sensitive cones do not contribute to luminance. *J. Opt. Soc. Am.,* 70: 121 – 123.

Geisert Jr., E.E. and Guillery, R.W. (1979) The horizontal organization of stellate cell dendrites in layer IV of the visual cortex of the tree shrew. *Neuroscience,* 4: 889 – 896.

Gülük, A.E., Agarwala, S. and Petry, H.M. (1991) Patterns of cytochrome oxidase activity in the geniculostriate pathway of red-light-reared tree shrews. *Invest. Ophthalmol. Vis. Sci. (Suppl.),* 32: 1117.

Hering, E. (1878) Zur Lehre vom Lichtsinne (Principles of a new theory of the color sense). Translated by K. Butler. In: R.C. Teevan and R.C. Birney (Eds.), *Color Vision, Selected Readings,* Van Nostrand Reinhold, New York, pp. 28 – 31.

Hubel, D.H., Wiesel, T.N. and LeVay, S. (1977) Plasticity of ocular dominance columns in monkey striate cortex. *Phil. Trans. R. Soc. Lond. B.,* 278: 377 – 409.

Jacobs, G.H. and Neitz, J. (1986) Spectral mechanisms and color vision in the tree shrew (*Tupaia belangeri*). *Vision Res.,* 26: 291 – 298.

Kageyama, G.H. and Wong-Riley, M.T.T. (1985) An analysis of the cellular localization of cytochrome oxidase in the lateral geniculate nucleus of the cat. *J. Comp. Neurol.,* 242: 338 – 357.

King-Smith, P.E. and Carden, D. (1976) Luminance and opponent color contributions to visual detection and adaptation and to temporal and spatial integration. *J. Opt. Soc. Am.,* 66: 709 – 717.

Kretz, R., Ragar, G. and Norton, T.T. (1986) Laminar organization of on and off regions and ocular dominance in the striatecortex of the tree shrew (*Tupaia belangeri*). *J. Comp. Neurol.,* 251: 135 – 145.

Lachica, E.A., Condo, G.J. and Casagrande, V.A. (1987) Development of cytochrome oxidase staining in the retinal and lateral geniculate nucleus: a possible correlate of on- and off-center channel maturation. *Dev. Brain Res.,* 34: 298 – 302.

Liu, S. and Wong-Riley, M.T.T. (1990) Quantitative light- and electron-microscopic analysis of cytochrome oxidase distribution in neurons of the lateral geniculate nucleus of the adult monkey. Visual Neurosci., 4: 269 – 288.

Livingstone, M.S. and Hubel, D.H. (1988) Segregation of form, color, movement, and depth: anatomy, physiology and perception. *Science,* 240: 740 – 749.

Lund, J.S., Fitzpatrick, D. and Humphrey, A.L. (1985) The striate visual cortex of the tree shrew. In: A. Peters and E.G. Jones (Eds.), *Cerebral Cortex, Vol. 3, Visual Cortex,* Plenum Press, New York, pp. 157 – 205.

McCourt, M.E. and Jacobs, G.H. (1983) Effects of photic environment on the development of spectral response properties of optic nerve fibers in the ground squirrel. *Exp. Brain Res.,* 49: 443 – 452.

Merigan, W.H. (1989) Chromatic and achromatic vision of macaques: role of the P pathway. *J. Neurosci.,* 9: 776 – 783.

Merigan, W.H. and Maunsell, J.H.R. (1990) Macaque vision after magnocellular lateral geniculate lesions. *Visual Neurosci.,* 5: 347 – 352.

Merigan, W.H., Katz, L.M. and Maunsell, J.H.R. (1991) The effects of parvocellular lateral geniculate lesions on the acuity and contrast sensitivity of macaque monkeys. *J. Neurosci.,* 11: 994 – 1001.

Müller, B. and Peichl, L. (1989) Topography of cones and rods in the tree shrew retina. *J. Comp. Neurol.,* 282: 581 – 594.

Muly, E., Fitzpatrick, D. and Raczkowski, D. (1989) Efferent projections of layer 4 in the tree shrew striate cortex: evidence for parallel pathways to the superficial layers. *Soc. Neurosci. Abstr.,* 15: 1398.

Norton, T.T. (1982) Geniculate and extrageniculate visual systems in the tree shrew. In: A.R. Morrison and P.L. Strick (Eds.), *Changing Concepts of the Nervous System,* Academic Press, New York, pp. 377 – 409.

Norton, T.T., Rager, G. and Kretz, R. (1985) On and off regions in layer IV of striate cortex. *Brain Res.,* 327: 319 – 323.

Petry, H.M. and Hárosi, F.I. (1990) The visual pigments of tree shrew (*Tupaia belangeri*) and galago (*Galago crassicaudatus*): a microspectrophotometric investigation. *Vision Res.,* 30: 839 – 851.

Petry, H.M. and Kelly, J.P. (1991) Psychophysical measurement of spectral sensitivity and color vision in red-light-reared tree shrews *(Tupaia belangeri). Vision Res.,* 31: 1749 – 1757.

Petry, H.M., Fox, R. and Casagrande, V.A. (1984) Spatial contrast sensitivity of the tree shrew. *Vision Res.,* 24: 1037 – 1042.

Petry, H.M., Erichsen, J.T. and Szél, A. (1992a) Immunocytochemical identification of photoreceptor populations in the retinas of normal and red-light-reared tree shrews. *Neurosci. Abstr.,* 18: 838.

Petry, H.M., Williams, C.D. and Kelly, J.P. (1992b) Enhanced luminance channel sensitivity in red-light-reared tree shrews: the result of a competitive advantage during development? *Invest. Ophthalmol. Vis. Sci.* (Suppl.), 33: 714.

Polson, M.C. (1968) Spectral sensitivity and color vision in *Tupaia glis.* Doctoral dissertation, Indiana University, Bloomington, IN.

Raczkowski, D. and Fitzpatrick, D. (1990) Terminal arbors of individual, physiologically identified geniculocortical axons in the tree shrew's striate cortex. *J. Comp. Neurol.,* 302: 500 – 514.

Schiller, P.H. and Logothetis, N.K. (1990) The color-opponent and broad-band channels of the primate visual system. *Trends Neurosci.,* 13: 392 – 398.

Schiller, P.H. and Malpeli, J.G. (1978) Functional specificity of lateral geniculate laminae of the rhesus monkey. *J. Neurophysiol.,* 41: 788 – 797.

Schiller, P.H., Logothetis, N.K. and Charles, E.R. (1990) Role of the color-opponent and broad-band channels in vision. *Visual Neurosci.,* 5: 321 – 346.

Sherman, S.M. and Spear, P.D. (1982) Organization of visual pathways in normal and visually deprived cats. *Physiol. Rev.,* 62: 738 – 855.

Sherman, S.M., Norton, T.T. and Casagrande, V.A. (1975) X- and Y-cells in the dorsal lateral geniculate nucleus of the tree shrew (*Tupaia glis*). *Brain Res.,* 93: 152 – 157.

Stockman, A., MacLeod, D.I.A. and DePriest, D.D. (1991) The temporal properties of the human short-wave photoreceptors and their associated pathways. *Vision Res.,* 31: 189 – 208.

Szél, A., Diamantstein, T. and Rohlich, P. (1988) Identification of the blue-sensitive cones in the mammalian retina by anti-visual pigment antibody. *J. Comp. Neurol.,* 273: 593 – 602.

Teller, D.Y. and Bornstein, M.H. (1987) Infant color vision and color perception. In: *Handbook of Infant Perception, Vol. 1,* Academic Press, Orlando, FL, pp. 185 – 236.

Ter Laak, H.J. and Thijssen, J.M. (1978) Receptive field properties of optic tract fibres from on-center sustained and transient cells in a tree shrew (*Tupaia chinensis*). *Vision Res.,* 18: 1097 – 1109.

Van Dongen, P.A.M., Ter Laak, H.J., Thijssen, J.M. and Vendrik, A.J.H. (1976) Functional classification of cells in the op-

250

tic tract of a tree shrew (*Tupaia chinensis*). *Exp. Brain Res.*, 24: 441 – 446.

Verdon, W. and Adams, A.J. (1987) Short-wavelength-sensitive cones do not contribute to mesopic luminosity. *J. Opt. Soc. Am. A*, 4: 91 – 95.

Wilson, P.D., Rowe, M.H. and Stone, J. (1976) Properties of relay cells in the cat's lateral geniculate nucleus: a comparison of W-cells with X- and Y-cells. *J. Neurophysiol.*, 39: 1193 – 1209.

Wong-Riley, M.T.T. (1989) Cytochrome oxidase: an endogenous metabolic marker for neuronal activity. *Trends Neurosci.*, 12: 94 – 101.

Wong-Riley, M.T.T. and Norton, T.T. (1988) Histochemical localization of cytochrome oxidase activity in the visual system of the tree shrew: normal patterns and effect of retinal impulse blockage. *J. Comp. Neurol.*, 272: 562 – 578.

Zrenner, E. (1983) *Neurophysiological Aspects of Color Vision in Primates*, Springer-Verlag, Berlin, 218 pp.

T.P. Hicks, S. Molotchnikoff and T. Ono (Eds.)
Progress in Brain Research, Vol. 95
© 1993 Elsevier Science Publishers B.V. All rights reserved.

CHAPTER 22

The development of visual cortical properties depends on visuo-proprioceptive congruence

P. Buisseret

Laboratoire de Neurophysiologie, Collège de France, 75231 Paris, Cedex 05, France

Introduction

The development of functional properties in visual cortex neurons has been shown to depend on visual experience during a critical postnatal period (see Frégnac and Imbert, 1984; Hirsch, 1985). Extraretinal factors, specifying the content of the visual experience in association with retinal inputs, are required in the developmental process of orientation selectivity (Buisseret et al., 1978). We have demonstrated that one of the necessary extraretinal factors is the sensory afferent input from both eye and neck muscles during gaze movements (Buisseret and Gary-Bobo, 1979; Buisseret, 1992).

These conclusions were based on the results of several series of experiments in which the coexistence of these sensory inputs with retinal inputs was more or less severely impaired. These results indicated that both inputs have to be congruent to be effective in specifying visual cortical cells for orientation.

We will describe several experiments from which some results have already been published, but giving them a new insight.

First example

The goal of this experiment was to give to visually naive animals a visual experience in which the retinal inputs should be normal but the sensitive inputs of extraocular muscles should be biased. The procedure of giving a 6 h visual exposure to previously dark-reared 5 – 6-week-old kittens (Imbert and Buisseret, 1975; Buisseret et al., 1978) was chosen because it allowed an important restoration of orientation selectivity (80%) (see Fig. 2) and made it possible to perform surgery on the animals 1 or 2 days before their exposure to light.

Applying this method it has been shown that eye movements were necessary during visual experience and that the relevant information came from eye muscle receptors (see Gary-Bobo et al., 1986). Moreover, it was shown that the direction of eye movement during the visual experience influences the distribution of the preferred orientation of visual cortical cells (Buisseret et al., 1988a). In order to specify the relation between retinal afferents and eye muscle afferents we dissociated both parameters leaving only a single one on each side of the same animal, the other parameter being suppressed (Buisseret et al., 1988a).

On one side, normal visual inputs were maintained by keeping motor efferents intact but the eye muscles were deafferented by an intracranial section of the ophthalmic branch of the trigeminal nerve, where sensory fibers of extraocular muscles (EOMs) are known to run (Batini and Buisseret, 1974). On the other side, biased EOMs inputs were obtained by the total resection of 4 out of the 6 EOMs, leaving a couple of recti muscles, either those of the horizon-

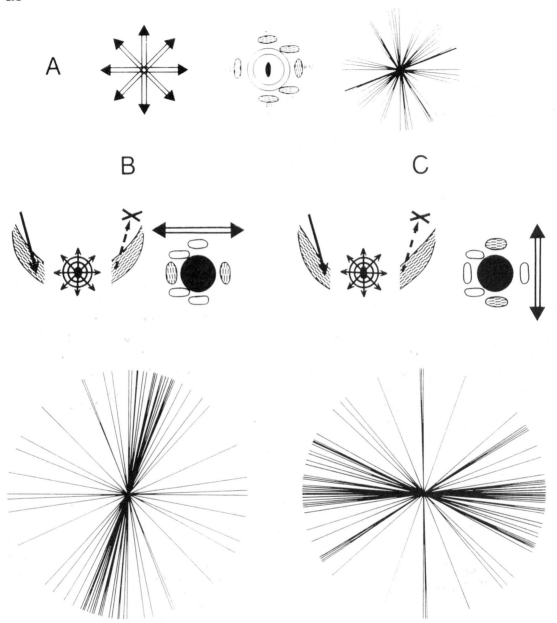

Fig. 1. Examples of the distribution of the preferred orientation in a control kitten (*A*), in a kitten with normal visual inputs associated with biased sensory inputs corresponding to horizontal eye movement (*B*) and to vertical eye movement (*C*). For each situation, the diagrammatic representation of the experiment and polar plot of the preferred orientations are shown. In *A*, control situation, an open viewing eye (center) with all eye muscles intact moved in every direction (left rosette of arrows). Each line in the polar plot (on the right) represents the preferred orientation of one of the recorded selective cells in one kitten. In *B*, the right open eye with intact motor output (continuous arrow) remained free to move in any direction (superimposed rosette of arrows) but deprived of proprioceptive inputs (dashed arrow) by section of the trigeminal ophthalmic branch (cross). The left eye was deprived of vision (black spot) and moved exclusively in the horizontal plane (large arrow). In *C*, a similar situation with vertical movement of the left eye.

tal eye movement or those of the vertical one. Abnormal vision was suppressed by an eyelid suture and a dark occluder glued over it.

After recovering from the surgery, the animals were given a visual experience of 6 h in the main animal room with congeners. They were put back in the dark for one night before the electrophysiological experiment which consisted of an analysis of the functional visual properties of a sample of cortical cells in area 17. A conventional procedure was used for the animal preparation (Gary-Bobo et al., 1986) and classical visual analysis of trigger features was performed (Buisseret et al., 1988a). Interest was focused on the distribution of the preferred orientation of the recorded visual cells.

In the present experiment, the distribution was different from that of normal intact animals. Most of the visual cells were selective for the orientation orthogonal to the direction of movements that the occluded eye had been able to perform (Fig. 1). When the recti medialis and lateralis were present exclusively, a majority of cells were selective for vertical stimuli (Fig. 1B); on the contrary, when superior and inferior recti were kept most of the cells were tuned around horizontal orientation (Fig. 1C). In the latter case, for example, cells responded to the displacement of a horizontal bar moving along a vertical axis. This is, from a retinal point of view, exactly the same as a vertical displacement of the eye in front of a horizontal edge of luminance.

From a general point of view, during a visual experience the best visual response, even of cells nonselective for orientation as those in dark-reared animals (Imbert and Buisseret, 1975), is obtained when the receptive field is crossed by (or crosses) an edge of luminance oriented orthogonally to the direction of displacement of the visual stimulus or to that of the eye. In our situation, it occurred in every direction since the seeing eye moved freely in every direction.

In the present experiment, the visual cells acquired a specificity only for horizontal stimuli (Fig. 1B) or vertical stimuli (Fig. 1C), corresponding to the best responses during vertical and horizontal

movements, respectively, and we assume this resulted from the congruence of retinal inputs from the seeing eye with the proprioceptive inputs from the moving eye which occurred exclusively when both eyes moved vertically (Fig. 1B) or horizontally (Fig. 1C).

Second example

We know from previous results that either suppression of eye movements by sections of oculomotor nerves III, IV and VI (Buisseret et al., 1978; Gary-Bobo et al., 1986) or suppression of eye muscle sensory afferents by sections of the ophthalmic branche (V1) of the trigeminal nerve (Buisseret and Gary-Bobo, 1979) prevent the large restoration of orientation selectivity normally observed after only 6 h of visual experience in intact dark-reared animals (see

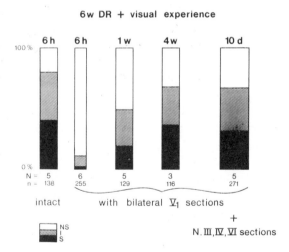

Fig. 2. Distributions of orientation selectivity of visual cortical cells in 6-week-old dark-reared (6w DR) kittens after different durations of visual experience: 6 hours (6 h), 1 week (1 w), 4 weeks (4 w) and 10 days (10 d) in different conditions: intact with bilateral sections of the ophthalmic branch (V1) of the trigeminal nerve and with the associated bilateral sections of motor nerves III, IV and VI. NS, Non-specific cells for the orientation of the stimulus; I, immature cells, orientation selective but broadly tuned; S, specific cells, selective for orientation as in adults; N, number of kittens; n, number of cells.

254

Fig. 2, 6 h). However, a more prolonged visual experience, with eye muscles deafferented but eye movements free, was shown to allow only a slow and partial restoration (Trotter et al., 1981) (Fig. 2, 1 w and 4 w). Since suppression of either extraocular proprioception or eye movements prevents a rapid restoration of orientation selectivity (Gary-Bobo et al., 1986), we tested the association of eye muscle deafferentation and eye immobilization on the level of restoration of orientation selectivity after a prolonged visual experience, expecting a reduction of the restoration of orientation selectivity. Five dark-reared kittens, 5 – 6-week-old, were operated under anesthesia. The ophthalmic branches of the trigeminal nerves (V1) and the eye motor nerves III, IV and VI were intracranially severed on both sides. The kittens were put in a normal day – night lighted animal room for 10 days. The orientation selectivity characteristics of 271 visual cells were analyzed. Unexpected results were obtained, with a majority of cells showing orientation selectivity, of which 31% were truly specific cells and 36% were immature (selective but broadly tuned) while the remaining 33% were still non-selective (Fig. 2, 10 d). The level of orientation selectivity in this distribution (67%) was actually over that observed in V1 sectioned kittens after only 1 week (19% specific + 30% immature) and the distribution was very similar to that of V1 lesioned kittens with 4 weeks duration of visual experience (36% specific, 32% immature, 32% non-specific).

We propose the following explanation for this unexpected higher level of orientation selectivity in animals with both sections than in those with only V1 sections. During the visual experience, when an animal attempts to look at something in the periphery of its visual field, if it has V1 and oculomotor nerves sectioned it ought to move the head. Consequently, there are more visual retinal inputs congruent with neck proprioceptive ones than when eye movements are possible. The addition of oculomotor nerve section to eye muscle deafferentation increases the occurrence of visual inputs congruent with neck proprioceptive ones during visual experience.

Third example

Suppression of eye movements is known to prevent the restoration of orientation selectivity during a visual experience of short duration given to previously dark-reared kittens (Gary-Bobo et al., 1986). Immobilization of the eyes makes virtually constant, or null, the afferent inputs from eye muscles, whereas the slips of images onto the retinae are still present even though they may be reduced. Correlated retinal and muscular inputs of movements are no more present.

There is an opposite situation in which slips of images onto the retinae are suppressed even when the eyes are moving: stroboscopic illumination. We have shown that kittens with visual experience in stroboscopic light have a very slow development of orientation selectivity of their visual cortical cells (Crémieux et al., 1992). After 7 days with 6 h/day of 2Hz, 0.1 msec stroboscopic flashes, the proportion of orientation-specific cells (21% and that of immature cells 35%) was less than the proportion (40% of orientation-specific and 40% of immature cells) after 6 h of normal visual experience and much less, of course, than after 1 week of normal vision (Fig. 3).

When actual durations of visual experience are compared, one can consider the total duration of

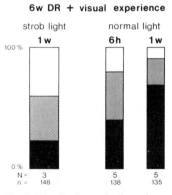

Fig. 3. Distributions of orientation selectivity of visual cortical cells in 6-week-old dark reared (6w DR) kittens, after a visual experience either in strob light or in normal light, for 1 week (1 w), 6 hours (6 h) or 1 week (1 w), respectively. N, Number of kittens; n, number of cells.

strob flashes (2 min) or the total duration of visual image persistence. If the latter duration is evaluated between 80 and 130 msec, the functional durations of visual experience would correspond to 6 – 10 h. But in the former hypothesis, one has to conclude that the 2 min of strob flashes were tremendously effective in specifying the neurons. In the second case, in contrast, the efficiency of a strob light, with a cumulative duration corrected for persistence, would be less than that of continuous light. We suggest that the low level of selectivity after strob light could be due to the lack of true congruence of retinal inputs which were suppressed, and eye muscle inputs, which remained present.

Another argument to strengthen this suggestion is the similarity of the reduction of speed and levels of orientation selectivity development between strob rearing and a continuous visual experience of similar duration with eye muscle deafferented (Buisseret et al., 1991).

Since a function of extraocular sensory inputs during visual experience has been demonstrated in the acquisition of orientation selectivity by visual cortical cells, responses of these cells to eye muscle stimulation have been searched and studied (Buisseret and Maffei, 1977; Enomoto et al., 1983; Ashton et al., 1984; Milleret et al., 1987, 1988). Interactive responses were also studied, either the effects of a continuous visual activation on the proprioceptive responses (Milleret et al., 1987; Buisseret et al., 1988b) or the effects of proprioceptive stimulation during a specific visual stimulation (Milleret et al., 1991).

Visual cells were recorded in the cortical area 17 of adult cats and their visual characteristics conventionally analyzed. By means of a computer program, the responses of each cell were analyzed during the optimal visual stimulation alone, the proprioceptive stimulation (electrical stimulation of the nerve branch of oblique inferior muscle, 3 shocks, 0.1 msec, 300 Hz) alone and during both stimulations applied together with the proprioceptive one delivered before, during, or after the visual response in an interleaved sequence of delays.

Interactive responses appeared (Fig. 4), mostly as phasic increases of the cell discharge with reduced latencies and followed by inhibitions. But interactive responses were present exclusively when the

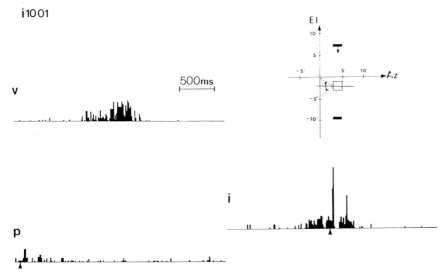

Fig. 4. Example of an interactive visuo-proprioceptive response in a visual cortical cell. Top right: diagram of the visual field, (E1) elevation, (Az) azimuth, with the receptive field of the recorded cell. V, Peristimulus time histogram of the visual response alone; P, PSTH of the proprioceptive response to electrical stimulation of the nerve branch innervating the inferior oblique muscle (3 shocks, 300 Hz; 0.1 msec); i, PSTH of an interactive response, when the proprioceptive stimulation was delivered at the time indicated by the arrow.

proprioceptive stimulation occurred either just before or during the visual response.

Conclusions

We showed that some aspects of the results which demonstrate the role of the sensitive afferents of gaze muscle (eye and neck muscles) in the processes of orientation selectivity development of visual cortical cells, also suggest that both visual retinal inputs and inputs of eye muscle receptors ought to interact in a congruent manner during visual experience.

It is assumed that proprioceptive inputs of eye muscles associated in a congruent manner with the retinal inputs may be the functional physiological correlate of the plasticity models which suggest paired activities in the associative learning for strengthening synaptic transmission (Baranyi and Feher, 1981) or of the more recent models which propose the covariance hypothesis (Frégnac and Shulz, 1989; see also Frégnac and Shulz, 1992, for a review of these models).

References

Ashton, J.A., Boddy, A. and Donaldson, I.M.L. (1984) Directional selectivity in the responses of units in cat primary visual cortex to passive eye movement. *Neuroscience*, 13: 653 – 662.

Baranyi, A. and Feher, O. (1981) Synaptic facilitation requires paired activation of convergent pathways in the neocortex. *Nature*, 290: 413 – 415.

Batini, C. and Buisseret, P. (1974) Sensory peripheral pathway from extrinsic eye muscles. *Arch. Ital. Biol.*, 112: 18 – 32.

Buisseret, P. (1992) Suppression of cervical afferents impairs visual cortical cells development. In: A. Berthoz, W. Graf and P.P. Vidal (Eds.), *The Head-Neck Sensory Motor System*, Oxford University Press, Oxford, pp. 188 – 192.

Buisseret, P. and Gary-Bobo, E. (1979) Development of visual cortical orientation specificity after dark-rearing: role of extraocular proprioception. *Neurosci. Lett.*, 13: 259 – 263.

Buisseret, P. and Maffei, L. (1977) Extraocular proprioceptive projections to the visual cortex. *Exp. Brain Res.*, 28: 421 – 425.

Buisseret, P., Gary-Bobo, E. and Imbert, M. (1978) Ocular motility and recovery of orientational properties of visual cortical neurons in dark-reared kittens. *Nature*, 272: 816 – 817.

Buisseret, P., Gary-Bobo, E. and Milleret, C. (1988a) Development of the kitten visual cortex depends on the relationship between the plane of eye movements and visual inputs. *Exp.*

Brain Res., 72: 883 – 948.

Buisseret, P., Gary-Bobo, E. and Milleret, C. (1988b) Visuoproprioceptive interactions in area 18 neurones of the anaesthetized cat. *J. Physiol. (Lond.)*, 406: 25P.

Buisseret, P., Gary-Bobo, E., Przybyslawski, J. and Cremieux, J. (1991) Development of selectivity in visual cortex of kittens deprived of motion vision. *Third IBRO World Congress of Neurosciences Abstracts*. p. 313.

Cremieux, J., Buisseret, P. and Gary-Bobo, E. (1992) Experimental evidence that rearing kittens in stroboscopic light retard maturation of the visual cortex: a new tool for studying critical periods. *Vision Res.*, 32: 41 – 45.

Enomoto, H., Matsumura, M. and Tsutsui, J. (1983) Projections of extraocular muscle afferents to the visual cortex in the cat. *Neuro-ophthalmol.*, 3: 49 – 57.

Frégnac, Y. and Imbert, M. (1984) Development of neuronal selectivity in primary visual cortex of cat. *Physiol. Rev.*, 64: 325 – 434.

Frégnac, Y. and Shulz, D. (1989) Hebbian synapses in visual cortex. In: K.K. Kulikowski (Ed.), *Seeing Contour and Colour*, Pergamon Press, Oxford, pp. 711 – 718.

Frégnac, Y. and Shulz, D. (1992) Models of synaptic plasticity and cellular analogs of learning in the developing and adult vertebrate visual cortex. In: V. Casagrande and P. Shinkman (Eds.), *Advances in Neural and Behavioral Development, Vol. 4*, Neural Ablex Publ. New Jersey, in press.

Gary-Bobo, E., Milleret, C. and Buisseret, P. (1986) Role of eye movements in developmental processes of orientation selectivity in the kitten visual cortex. *Vision Res.*, 26: 557 – 567.

Hirsch, H.V.B. (1985) The role of visual experience in the development of cat striate cortex. *Cell. Mol. Neurobiol.*, 5: 103 – 121.

Imbert, M. and Buisseret, P. (1975) Receptive field characteristics and plastic properties of visual cortical cells in kittens reared with or without visual experience. *Exp. Brain Res.*, 22: 25 – 36.

Milleret, C., Gary-Bobo, E. and Buisseret, P. (1987) Réponses des neurones du cortex visuel (aire 18) aux stimulations proprioceptives extraoculaires: évolution chez le chat normal ou élevé à l'obscurité et interactions avec l'activité visuelle. *C.R. Acad. Sci.*, 305: 531 – 536.

Milleret, C., Gary-Bobo, E. and Buisseret, P. (1988) Extraocular proprioceptive inputs to visual cortex: an electrophysiological study during development in the cat. *Soc. Neurosci. Abstr.*, 14: 189.

Milleret, C., Houzel, J.C., Gary-Bobo, J.C. and Buisseret, P. (1991) Interactions between extraocular muscle afferents and specific visual responses in A17 of the cat: a time-course analysis. *Eur. J. Neurosci.*, S4: 53.

Trotter, Y., Gary-Bobo, E. and Buisseret, P. (1981) Recovery of orientation selectivity in kitten primary visual cortex is slowed down by bilateral section of ophthalmic trigeminal afferents. *Dev. Brain Res.*, 1: 450 – 454.

T.P. Hicks, S. Molotchnikoff and T. Ono (Eds.)
Progress in Brain Research, Vol. 95
© 1993 Elsevier Science Publishers B.V. All rights reserved.

CHAPTER 23

Reorganization processes in the visual cortex also depend on visual experience in the adult cat

Chantal Milleret[1] and Pierre Buser[2]

[1] *Collège de France, Laboratoire de Neurophysiologie, 75231 Paris Cedex 05, and* [2] *Institut des Neurosciences, Département de Neurophysiologie Comparée, CNRS et Université Pierre et Marie Curie, 75230 Paris Cedex 05, France*

Introduction

Multiple evidences have now been provided showing that normal visual experience after birth is crucial for the maturation of the properties of visual cortical cells in kittens. Visual deprivations lead to both physiological and anatomical changes in the visual cortex (see Hirsch and Leventhal, 1978; Movshon and Van Sluyters, 1981; Sherman and Spear, 1982; Frégnac and Imbert, 1984; Hirsch, 1985; Hirsch and Tieman, 1987, for reviews). Thus, when animals are deprived of vision early in life, either through dark-rearing or through binocular eyelid suture, the characteristics of the visual cells do not mature according to the normal process (Imbert and Buisseret, 1975; Blakemore and Van Sluyters, 1975; Frégnac and Imbert, 1978; Milleret et al., 1988). After monocular deprivation, most cells in the cortex cannot be driven through the deprived eye and the animals are almost blind through that eye (Wiesel and Hubel, 1963).

Until recently, susceptibility to such environmental manipulations was thought to be limited to the first few postnatal months, i.e., to the critical period (Wiesel and Hubel, 1963; Riesen, 1965; Hubel and Wiesel, 1970; Blakemore and Van Sluyters, 1974; Cynader et al., 1980; Olson and Freeman, 1980). However, some of our recent findings lead to extend such a susceptibility to the adulthood.

Our experiments were prompted by a variety of data clearly showing that plasticity of the visual system could also be characterized in the adult after partial deafferentation and that a progressive functional reorganization of this system could take place in such conditions (Galambos et al., 1967; Norton et al., 1967; Chow, 1968; Jacobson et al., 1978, 1979; Eysel, 1978, 1979; Eysel et al., 1980; Yinon, 1980; Yinon and Hammer, 1985; Kaas et al., 1990; Heinen and Skavenski, 1991). With these results in mind, the question that we addressed was whether postoperative visual experience could influence this reorganization. Our procedure was to cut the optic chiasm of adult cats midsagitally, thus depriving each hemisphere of the afferents originating from the opposite nasal retina, then to either maintain the animals in the light or in the dark or to combine the section with a monocular occlusion during a postoperative period of variable duration. In all cases, the sizes of the visual cortical receptive fields of cortical cells either activated through the direct pathway or via the corpus callosum were taken as a functional index in the final exploration achieved under anesthesia and paralysis.

In a first series of experiments, we only considered the receptive field (RF) sizes of visual cortical cells recorded in area 18, activated through the direct retino-geniculo-cortical pathway. The findings show that a postoperative visual experience is necessary for a recovery to occur.

In a second series, the RF characteristics of cells

activated through the corpus callosum were analyzed after chiasmotomy. The results demonstrate that monocular occlusion can induce an asymmetrical callosal transfer between visual cortical areas.

General methodology

The experiments were performed on adult cats which had their optic chiasm sectioned midsagitally. This surgery was achieved under Saffan anesthesia (I.M. 1.2 ml/kg: 10.8 mg/kg of Alfaxolone and 3.6 mg/kg of Alfadolone acetate) via an oral approach under aseptic conditions following a standard procedure (see Myers, 1955, for details). Some of these animals were left in a normal visual environment during their postoperative period. Some others were allowed either only a monocular patterned visual experience through eyelid suture of the other eye or no visual experience at all by being left in complete darkness during this period. The postoperative period could last from 4 h to 6 weeks. Some further intact animals were used as controls (see the Results section for some more details).

For the final recording session, anesthesia was initially induced by Saffan injection. After cannulation of the radial vein and tracheotomy, the animals were placed in a stereotaxic apparatus designed to leave free the entire visual field. The skull was removed to gain access to the visual cortex. The animal was then paralyzed with an i.v. injection of Flaxedil. The closed eye of the monocularly deprived animals was reopened. The nictitating membrane of both eyes was retracted with neosynephrine and the pupils were dilated with atropine. Contact lenses were placed to prevent the cornea from drying off. All preparations were then maintained under permanent slow infusion of a mixture of Saffan (3.6 mg/kg per hour), Flaxedil (10 – 15 mg/kg per hour), Plasmagel and glucose. The heart rate and pCO_2 (4%) were monitored throughout the experiment and the body temperature was maintained at 38°C. The positions of the optic discs were determined through back-projection with a reversible ophthalmoscope on the screen that faced the animal, at 1 m in front of its eyes. This evaluation

was made at the beginning and several times during the experiment; the position of the projection of the area centralis was then determined using the classical quantitative data provided by Vakkur et al. (1963).

Extracellular recordings were achieved through a tungsten microelectrode (1 – 2 MΩ at 1000 Hz) inserted obliquely into the visual cortex (P5 to A15; L1 to L5), either into area 17 or into area 18 or at the 17/18 border (see the Results section); after placement of the electrode, agar-agar in saline (4%) was poured upon the cortex to prevent drying off.

The experimental procedure to isolate a single unit and to analyze its properties was as follows. (1) Spikes were amplified, visualized and audiomonitored in a conventional way. (2) Recordings were made along each tract at regular 100 μm distances whenever possible, in order to reduce sampling bias. (3) Slits and spots were projected by means of a hand-held stimulator. To detect visual responses and to avoid missing spontaneous silent units, the test stimulus was permanently moved across the screen. (4) The cell's RF was mapped on the screen either for only one eye or for each eye successively. Receptive field borders (length and width) were defined by moving the optimal stimulus back and forth outside the RF and gradually approaching it until an overt response occurred. Since particular emphasis was placed on the receptive field sizes, special care was taken to plot these field limits. (5) The cell's ocular dominance was also determined whenever necessary.

Each electrode penetration, usually as far as 3000 – 4000 μm, was marked by two small electrolytic lesions (DC current; 15 μA, 15 sec) at two different depths.

At the end of the experiment, the animals were perfused with formaline (4%) and the brain was removed. Chiasmotomy was controlled for each animal on Weil or Page stained sections (40 μm); electrode penetrations were identified on Nisslstained sections (100 μm) cut in the frontal plane and were reconstructed using the electrolytic lesions as references. Using the response characteristics of the cells (Hubel and Wiesel, 1965; Harvey, 1980; Orban

TABLE I

Experimental groups and postoperative conditions in the first series of experiments

Experimental group	Number of cats	Postoperative delay between chiasmotomy and exploration	Postoperative visual condition
A	5	4 h	Binocular vision
C	10	21 – 44 days	Binocular vision
CN	4	21 – 55 days	Complete darkness

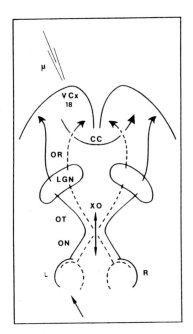

Fig. 1. Overall scheme to indicate our various experimental approaches with respect to topography of visual projections. After midsagittal section of the optic chiasm (XO), uncrossed fibers of the optic nerve (ON) remain intact, project to the visual cortex (VCx) via the optic tract (OT), the lateral geniculate nucleus (LGN) and the optic radiations (OR). In these preparations, the visual cortical cells recorded through a microelectrode (μ) on one side may be excited through either the geniculo-cortical ipsilateral pathway or the callosal route (CC), by stimulating respectively the ipsilateral (left, L) or the contralateral eye (right, R). In the first series of experiments, only the functional properties of cortical cells recorded in area 18 (18) and visually activated from the ipsilateral eye (left eye, arrow) were analyzed. In the second series, the situation was more complex (see Fig. 4).

et al., 1980; Payne, 1990; Diao et al., 1990), combined with the morphological criteria (Otsuka and Hassler, 1962; Tusa et al., 1979), we could identify the position of the areas 17 and 18 and of the 17/18 border. Each receptive field mapped through visual stimulation of each eye was then redrawn with respect to the corresponding optic disc to determine exactly its spatial location within the visual field.

Results

First part: maintaining in the dark prevents any recovery of the direct retino-geniculo-cortical pathway after section of the optic chiasm in the adult cat (Milleret and Buser, 1984)

In this first series of experiments, the 19 adult cats which underwent a midsagittal section of their optic chiasm were divided into three experimental groups: two were maintained with binocular vision but differed by their postoperative delay (A group, 4 h; C group, 21 – 44 days); the remaining one (CN group) was placed in complete darkness for 21 – 55 days before the final exploration (Table I).

Five further intact animals were placed under the same experimental conditions for electrophysiological study (see the Methodology section) and served as control (T) group.

A total of 357 recorded cells could be studied for their reactivity to visual stimulation of the eye ipsilateral to the investigated cortex (area 18; Fig. 1). Their distribution among groups was as follows: T,

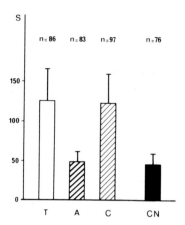

Fig. 2. Mean RF areas (S, in deg²) in the T, A, C and CN experimental groups, respectively (see text and Table I for definition of groups). Confidence limits at $P = 0.05$; n, number of cells. (Modified from Milleret and Buser, 1984.)

88; A, 84; C, 107; CN, 78. Between group comparisons were made possible since recordings were all performed in the same cortical zone, extending from the projection zone of the horizontal meridian to that of the lower part of the visual field.

The majority of these cells displayed well circumscribed receptive fields. They could be classified as simple, complex or hypercomplex, using the most commonly accepted criteria (Hubel and Wiesel, 1962, 1965).

In a first analysis, it appeared that the mean RF sizes were different in the various experimental groups (Fig. 2): (i) this mean displayed a highly significant reduction in the A group (50 deg²) with respect to the control animals (T, 125 deg²); this reduction was about equal to a factor of 3; (ii) on the other hand, the mean size was much larger in the C group, which had a long postoperative period (122 deg²), the difference between this group and the T group being no longer significant (at $P = 0.05$); thus, a complete recovery seems to occur within 6 weeks after the chiasmotomy; (iii) no such restoration took place in animals maintained in the dark during the postoperative period after partial deafferentation (CN group); their mean RF size remained at low values (46 deg²), even after postoperative periods as long as 55 days.

We then tried to establish which kind of RFs (central and/or peripheral) were relatively more affected by chiasmotomy and which ones had undergone some recovery. Fig. 3 illustrates this analysis and shows that large RFs which prevail at relatively high eccentricities in control animals (in agreement with other authors, such as Hubel and Wiesel, 1965) disappeared in the A group and were restored in the C group. Again, no such recovery could be observed in the CN animals.

In addition to these cells with circumscribed RFs, units with diffuse responses were also encountered, particularly in the C group (9% against $1 - 2.5\%$ in the other groups T, A and CN). Visual experience after chiasmotomy thus seems to favor the appearance of a few abnormal visual responses; in absence of such an experience, the development of these abnormalities is prevented.

Second part: a monocular occlusion elicits an asymmetrical callosal transfer between visual cortical areas in optic chiasm sectioned adult cats

The effects of a monocular occlusion were studied in areas 17 and 18 and at the boundary between both areas by comparing the cortical location of cells activated via the corpus callosum, as well as the spatial distribution and sizes of their RFs in several distinct experimental groups (Fig. 4, first column).

The first two groups (XO_1 and XO_2) only underwent a midsagittal section of the optic chiasm and were explored, either $2 - 3$ days (XO_1, $n = 7$) or 6 weeks (XO_2, $n = 5$) later on. The postoperative visual experience was here binocular. In the two other groups ($MOXO_1$ and $MOXO_2$), the optic chiasm section was combined with an occlusion of the right eye. Callosal transfer of visual information was then analyzed 6 weeks later on, through visual stimulation of either the eye that had remained open ($MOXO_1$, $n = 11$) or the one which had been closed ($MOXO_2$, $n = 7$) throughout the postoperative period.

In total, 1371 cells were recorded. Among these neurons, 304 could be activated through interhemispheric transfer (C+, Table II). The callosal origin of these interhemispheric activities was clear-

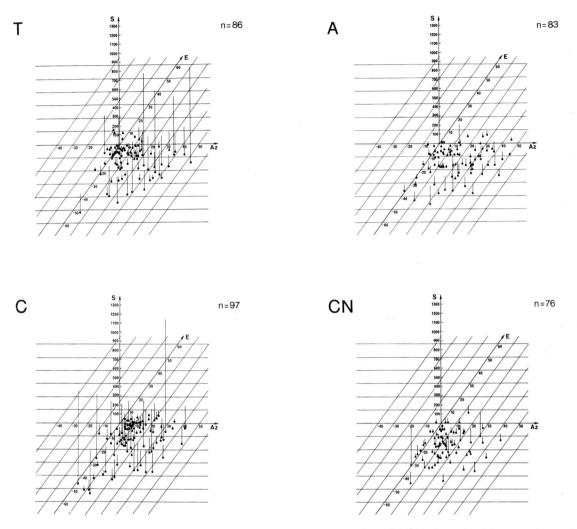

Fig. 3. Distribution of receptive field areas as a function of their location in the visual field in the T, A, C and CN groups. Az, Azimuth in degrees (x axis); E, elevation in degrees (y axis); S, receptive field area in deg^2 (z axis). Each dot in the Az-E plane indicates the geometrical center of a given visual receptive field, the area of which is plotted as S. n, Number of cells. (Modified from Milleret and Buser, 1984.)

ly established, at least in part, in the preparations (XO$_2$, 1 out of 5 animals; MOXO$_1$, 6/10; MOXO$_2$, 3/4) through local application of procaïne upon the visual cortex of origin (Fig. 5).

An analysis of the cortical location of these C+ cells in the different groups (Table II) first showed that they were mainly located at the 17/18 border. In this cortical region, their percentage was always about 50% (XO$_1$, 54%; XO$_2$, 49%; MOXO$_1$, 53%;

MOXO$_2$, 60%). A few cells (2–10%) were also located either in area 17 or in area 18. Monocular occlusion thus does not seem to alter the cortical tangential extent of the C+ cells.

As a general rule, the receptive fields of these C+ cells (mainly complex cells) were centered near or on the central vertical meridian of the visual field whatever the recording site (Fig. 4, second column). This particular feature of the cells activated through

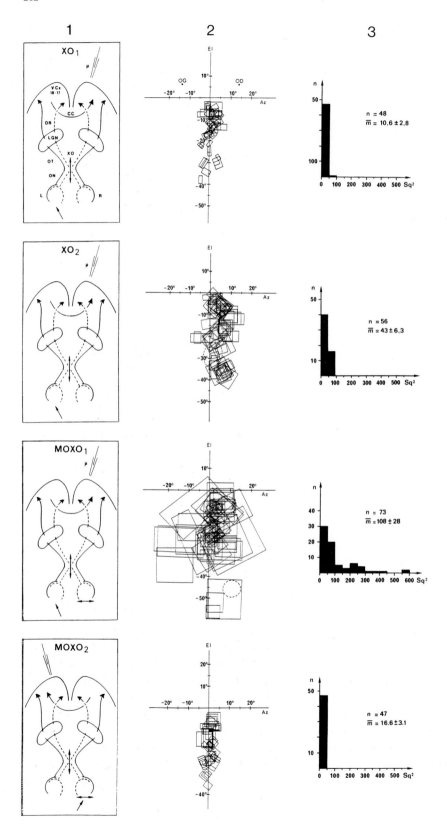

TABLE II

Number of cortical cells in the different experimental groups (XO$_1$, XO$_2$, MOXO$_1$, MOXO$_2$) in the second series of experiments as a function of the recording site

Experimental group		Area								Total
		A 17		17/18		A 18		Non loc.		number
		C+	C−	C+	C−	C+	C−	C+	C−	
XO$_1$	$n = 7$	3	126	52	44	0	64	5	65	359
XO$_2$	$n = 5$	6	0	49	50	12	217	10	35	379
MOXO$_1$	$n = 11$	4	66	77	67	9	76	27	18	344
MOXO$_2$	$n = 7$	1	52	39	25	12	154	3	3	289

A 17, area 17; 17/18, 17/18 border; A 18, area 18; Non loc., non localized cells. n, Number of cats; C+, callosal driven cells; C−, cortical cells non-activated through the corpus callosum.

the corpus callosum (Choudhury et al., 1965; Vesbaesya et al., 1967; Berlucchi and Rizzolatti, 1968; Harvey, 1980; Lepore and Guillemot, 1982; Payne et al., 1991) had thus been maintained as well, in spite of the monocular occlusion. Notice that, at least in three groups (XO$_1$, XO$_2$ and MOXO$_1$), a marked displacement toward the hemifield ipsilateral to the explored cortex clearly appeared, especially outside of the area centralis projection zone (see Fig. 4, second column).

Some marked inter-group specific differences could also be observed. Among these, the most significant and surprising one concerned the maximal lateral extent of the C+ receptive fields in the visual field, with respect to the central vertical meridian. Whereas in the XO$_1$ group the C+ receptive field extension did not exceed $7-9°$ of eccentricity on both sides of the meridian, it could reach up to $15°$ in the XO$_2$ group, especially in the hemifield ipsilateral to the explored cortex. In the MOXO$_1$ group, this extension could be as high as $25°$ while it only reached $7°$ in the MOXO$_2$ group.

Another surprising but significant difference, which is clearly and certainly closely related to the previous one, concerned the receptive field size of the C+ cells (Fig. 4, third column). Three days after optic chiasm section (XO$_1$ group), the mean receptive field size of these C+ cells was very small (10.6 ± 2.8 deg^2) but it significantly increased with the postoperative delay to reach 43 ± 6.3 deg^2 six

Fig. 4. Experimental designs and results. *First column*. Summary of the four experimental protocols. XO$_1$ and XO$_2$, adult cats with transected optic chiasm which were allowed binocular visual experience throughout the postoperative period (3 days or 6 weeks, respectively). In this series, the interhemispheric transfer was tested by stimulating the left eye (L, see arrow) and recording units from the contralateral visual cortex (VCx) in areas 17 and 18 (μ). The right eye (R), ipsilateral to the recording side, was simply masked during the exploration except to test for the ocular dominance of the recorded cells. Abbreviations ON, XO, OT, OR, CGL and CC, see Fig. 1. MOXO$_1$ and MOXO$_2$, animals with transected optic chiasm *and* monocular occlusion of the right eye during the whole postoperative period (6 weeks, double arrow); the eye was opened only on the day of the final exploration and masked when necessary. In the MOXO$_1$ group, the studied transfer was that from the left eye through the left cortex to the right one; in the MOXO$_2$, the reverse traffic was investigated, i.e., from the right eye (deprived one) through the right cortex to the left one. *Second column*. Spatial distribution of receptive fields of cortical neurons activated through the corpus callosum in the four groups XO$_1$, XO$_2$, MOXO$_1$ and MOXO$_2$, respectively. Az, Horizontal meridian; El, central vertical meridian. Each rectangle corresponds to the receptive field of one cell. OD and OG, right and left optic discs. *Third column*. Distribution of the areas (in deg^2) of the RFs drawn in column 2, for each experimental situation. n, Population of cells whose receptive fields could be determined; m, mean receptive field area with confident limits at $P = 0.05$. Bin width, 50 deg^2.

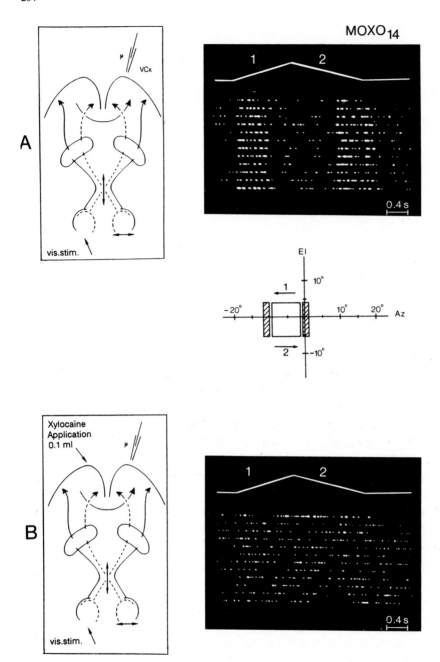

Fig. 5. Demonstration of the callosal origin of the recorded interhemispheric activities in a cat belonging to the MOXO₁ group (MOXO_1) (MOXO_{14}). *A*. On the left, general experimental protocol (see Fig. 4 for comments); on the right, 12 successive visual responses of a cortical cell activated through an interhemispheric transfer, recorded from the right cortex, represented as a dot display (control response). The visual stimulations consisted in forth and back ramp movements of a slit automatically driven across the receptive field. Both the receptive field and the extreme positions of the slit (hatched areas) are represented in the central panel: 1 corresponds to the first movement of the slit (first part of the ramp) and 2 to the second one (second part of the ramp); El, elevation; Az, azimuth. *B*. At left, experimental protocol with procaïne application on the source cortex of the callosal message topographically symmetrical to recording site (left cortex), to demonstrate the callosal origin of the visual responses recorded on the right cortex; at right, the visual response of the cell was completely suppressed 20 min after procaïne application.

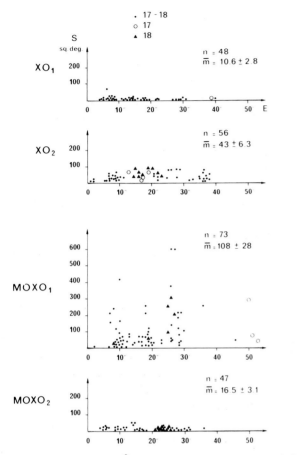

Fig. 6. Surface (S in deg²) of RFs of callosal activated cortical cells, recorded from A17 (17, open circles), A18 (18, black triangles) and at the 17/18 border (17 – 18, black points) as a function of the eccentricity (E in degrees) of their geometrical center (see text) in the different experimental groups XO₁, XO₂, MOXO₁ and MOXO₂. n, Number of cells; m, mean receptive field area with confidence limits at $P = 0.05$.

weeks after section (XO₂ group). In other words, the mean surface became about 4 times larger within a 6 week period. Whereas these last values were the same in both cortices, some asymmetry appeared in the MOXOs. In the MOXO₁ group, some receptive fields of cells recorded in the "deprived" cortex 6 weeks after the optic chiasm section were as small as in the control groups XO₁ and XO₂ (< 100 deg²); on the other hand, some others were very much larger (600 deg²). As a consequence, the mean RF size reached 108 ± 28 deg². Conversely, in the

MOXO₂ group, the RF size of the C+ cells recorded in the "non-deprived" cortex was as small as in the XO₁ group with a mean equal to 16.6 ± 3.1 deg² in spite of the 6 weeks of postoperative delay. The difference was significant between all the experimental groups compared by pair except for the XO₁ and MOXO₂ ones (Kolmogorov – Smirnov non-parametric test at 5%).

Three further interesting observations could be obtained from these last data by studying the evolution of the C+ receptive field size as a function of the distance ("eccentricity") of their geometrical center from the area centralis projection (Fig. 6). Firstly, this particular RF population did not increase their size from the center to the periphery of the visual field. In this respect, they are completely different from the whole population of visual cortical cells (Hubel and Wiesel, 1965; see also the first part of this section). Secondly, the C+ RFs increase in size with the postoperative delay (XO₂ and MOXO₁ groups compared to the XO₁ group) whatever the recording site of the corresponding cells. As a third point, it seemed that receptive fields in area 18 were somewhat larger than those in either area 17 or at the 17/18 border, particularly in the XO₂ and MOXO₁ groups.

Although the analysis of the RF size was the main aim of this study, some other characteristics of the C+ cells were also investigated such as their ocular dominance. From this analysis, it appeared that the monocular occlusion, in our experimental conditions, did not modify the distribution of this property: in all cases, most of the C+ cells (about 70%) were better activated through the direct retino-geniculo-pathway (i.e., from the ipsilateral eye to the explored cortex) than through the corpus callosum (from the contralateral eye). Other C+ cells were either binocular or dominated by the contralateral eye.

Discussion

Both series of data presented in this paper lead to the conclusion that functional reorganization in the visual cortex of the adult cat after partial deafferentation depends on visual experience. Susceptibility to at least some environmental manipulations thus extends beyond the critical period.

Discussing our data, one may first wonder whether a partial deafferentation is really compulsory to identify this susceptibility. Such a question may be asked by considering at least two different series of data. Creutzfeldt and Heggelund (1975) have described some plastic changes in the visual cortex of intact adult cats after exposure to visual stripes. These data may, however, be interpreted rather as a bias in eye movements induced by the exposure to a particular pattern than as an effect of environmental manipulation. In favor of this latter interpretation, observations exist showing that in the adult some properties of visual cortical cells can be altered through either monocular paralysis (Buchtel et al., 1972; Fiorentini and Maffei, 1974; Maffei and Fiorentini, 1976) or eye rotation (Singer et al., 1982).

The other series of data concerns the period of susceptibility to monocular occlusion which in the young animal has been so far defined on the basis of the ocular dominance (Wiesel and Hubel, 1963; Hubel and Wiesel, 1970; Blakemore and Van Sluyters, 1974; Cynader et al., 1980; Olson and Freeman, 1980). One thus ignores whether such a deprivation can act upon some other characteristics of the cortical cells such as, for instance, the size of their RFs beyond 3 months of age. In our $MOXO_1$ group (see second part of the Results section), the RFs of the callosally activated cells were larger than in the XO_2 control group. This may be interpreted in two ways: either monocular occlusion needs to be combined with chiasm section to elicit the enlargement as observed after 6 weeks, or 6 weeks of monocular occlusion are sufficient to produce this enlargement. To answer this question, we have recently separated the occlusion and the chiasmotomy, the latter being achieved 6 weeks after the occlusion and immediately followed by the exploration. The preliminary results indicate no widening of the RFs, suggesting that the two manipulations need to be combined. Exceptions do exist, however, regarding the necessity to achieve as complex

manipulations as ours to get any reorganization in the adult. Those concern local interventions on adult cortical cells, whose ocular dominance, orientation selectivity and RF size could be altered either through current injection (Frégnac et al., 1988) or after transplantation of cultured astrocytes (Müller and Best, 1989). However, considered altogether, all these data indicate that changes in visual cortical cell properties can override the classical critical period provided that some adequate manipulations be achieved.

Although our two series of experiments concerned different visual routes, the results were coherent enough to allow some general conclusions on the role of partial deafferentation and visual experience in the observed reorganizations.

(1) *Partial deafferentation decreases the RF sizes.* This reduction was particularly clear in the first series of results when comparing the T and A groups. In the second series, such reduction could only be inferred, since callosal activation cannot be directly evaluated in an intact reference group. Our next point may, however, justify extrapolation when comparing XO_1 and XO_2 groups.

(2) *A visual experience of an adequate duration (6 weeks in our case) induces some reorganization after partial deafferentation.* This appears when comparing different groups two by two: the A and C groups in the first part of the Results section; XO_1 and XO_2, XO_1 and $MOXO_1$, XO_2 and $MOXO_1$ in the second part of the Results section.

Comparing A and C groups, *recovery* occurred only after postoperative visual experience. The same type of recovery can be inferred to occur in the second pair, between XO_1 and XO_2, supposing that XO_2 became equal to intact animal. This assumption seems justified since the "callosal" RF mean area increased in approximately the same proportion as the C with respect to the A group (3 – 4 times).

Comparison of the other pairs (XO_1 and $MOXO_1$; XO_2 and $MOXO_1$) indicated that visual experience produces some *reorganization*, with the final state differing from the initial control one.

These changes, recovery or reorganization, took

place within 6 weeks after chiasmotomy. This delay is in agreement with most of the previous investigations describing such processes in the visual system of adult cats (Galambos et al., 1967; Norton et al., 1967; Eysel, 1978; Jacobson et al., 1979; Eysel et al., 1980; Yinon, 1980; Kaas et al., 1990). Recently, Yinon and Milgram (1990) could not reproduce our results on the $MOXO_1$ group, in spite of the $4-11$ months delay. The comparison is difficult, however, since they did not record any consistent interhemispheric transfer even in the control animals.

(3) *Maintaining in the dark prevents any reorganization to occur.* This point is particularly clear when comparing C and CN groups (Results section, first part): the mean RF size in the CN group remained as small as in the A group, in spite of the 6 weeks of postoperative delay. The same type of phenomenon seems to occur for the C + RFs of the $MOXO_2$ group, which were as small as those of the XO_1 group (Results section, second part). In other words, visual deprivation (through either dark-maintaining or monocular occlusion) prevented any reorganization to occur, at least within 6 weeks: the system seems to be "frozen" in the state which was present immediately after the partial deafferentation.

The persistence of visual activity thus appears to be necessary for a reorganization to occur in the visual system in the adult. This seems a more general rule since the same type of condition (persistence of functioning) for recovery or reorganization was reported to be required by Merzenich and colleagues in their study of the somatosensory system (Merzenich et al., 1988).

It should be stressed here that the changes that we could observe at the cortical level may not necessarily have been exclusively located at this upper level, but may well reflect some subcortical modifications. Actually, a few data are available so far in favor of this latter possibility, since it is known that the activity of the lateral geniculate nucleus is affected through partial deafferentation with some recovery being possible later on (Eysel, 1978, 1979; Eysel et al., 1980).

A large number of mechanisms have, at the pres-

ent time, been suggested to account for the reorganization processes in the central nervous system: sprouting and synaptogenesis, temporary loss of responsiveness (*diaschisis*), hypersensitivity of remaining synapses, switching of functional activity among residual circuitry or activation of previously existing but normally ineffective synaptic contacts. More recently, long-term potentiation or long-term depression have also been put foward, the more so since these have been described at the cortical level in the visual system of the adult (Artola and Singer, 1987; Artola et al., 1990), and are proposed as a possible mechanism for plasticity (Ben-Ari and Represa, 1990).

So far, we cannot determine which of these mechanisms are really involved. However, the present data may provide one further model for studying environmental dependence for reorganization in the adult.

References

Artola, A. and Singer, W. (1987) Long-term potentiation and NMDA receptors in rat visual cortex. *Nature*, 330: 649 – 652.

Artola, A., Bröcher, S. and Singer, W. (1990) Different voltage-dependent thresholds for inducing long-term depression and long-term potentiation in slices of rat visual cortex. *Nature*, 347: 69 – 72.

Ben-Ari, Y. and Represa, A. (1990) Brief seizure episodes induce long-term potentiation and mossy fibre sprouting in the hippocampus. *Trends Neurosci.*, 13: 312 – 317.

Berlucchi, G. and Rizzolatti, G. (1968) Binocularly driven neurons in visual cortex of split-chiasm cats. *Science*, 159: 308 – 310.

Blakemore, C. and Van Sluyters, R.C. (1974) Reversal of the physiological effects of monocular deprivation in kittens: further evidence for a sensitive period. *J. Physiol. (Lond.).*, 237: 195 – 216.

Blakemore, C. and Van Sluyters, R.C. (1975) Innate and environment factors in the development of the kitten's visual cortex. *J. Physiol. (Lond.)*, 248: 663 – 716.

Buchtel, H.A., Berlucchi, G. and Mascetti, G.G. (1972) Modification in visual perception and learning following immobilization of one eye in cats. *Brain Res.*, 37: 355 – 356.

Choudhury, B.P., Whitteridge, D. and Wilson, M.E. (1965) *Q. J. Exp. Physiol.*, 50: 214 – 219.

Chow, K. (1968) Visual discrimination after extensive ablation of optic tract and visual cortex in cats. *Brain Res.*, 9: 363 – 366.

Creutzfeldt, O.D. and Heggelund, P. (1975) Neural plasticity in visual cortex of adult cats after exposure to visual patterns.

Science, 188: 1025 – 1027.

Cynader M., Timney, B.N. and Mitchell, D.E. (1980) Period of susceptibility of kitten visual cortex to the effects of monocular deprivation extends beyond six months of age. *Brain Res.,* 191: 545 – 550.

Diao, Y.C., Jia, W.G., Swindale, N.V. and Cynader, M.S. (1990) Functional organization of the cortical 17/18 border region in the cat. *Exp. Brain Res.,* 79: 271 – 282.

Eysel, U.T. (1978) Late effects of deafferentation and signs of plasticity in the lateral geniculate nucleus of the adult cat after monocular lesions of the retina. *Arch. Ital. Biol.,* 116: 309 – 318.

Eysel, U.T. (1979) Maintained activity, excitation and inhibition of lateral geniculate neurons after monocular deafferentation in the adult cat. *Brain Res.,* 166: 259 – 271.

Eysel, U.T., Gonzales-Aguilar, F. and Mayer, U. (1980) A functional sign of reorganisation in the visual system of adult cats: lateral geniculate neurons with displaced receptive fields after lesions of the nasal retina. *Brain Res.,* 181: 285 – 301.

Fiorentini, A. and Mafféi, L. (1974) Change of binocular properties of the simple cells of the cortex in adult cats following immobilization of one eye. *Vision Res.,* 14: 217 – 218.

Frégnac, Y. and Imbert, M. (1978) Early development of visual cortical cells in normal and dark-reared kittens: relationship between orientation selectivity and ocular dominance. *J. Physiol. (Lond.),* 278: 27 – 44.

Frégnac, Y. and Imbert, M. (1984) Development of neuronal selectivity in primary visual cortex of cat. *Physiol. Rev.,* 64: 325 – 434.

Frégnac, Y., Shultz, D., Thorpe, S. and Bienenstock, E. (1988) A cellular analogue of visual cortical plasticity. *Nature,* 333: 367 – 370.

Galambos, R., Norton, T.T. and Frommer, G.P. (1967) Optic tract lesions sparing pattern vision in cats. *Exp. Neurol.,* 18: 8 – 25.

Harvey, A.R. (1980) The afferent connections and laminar distribution of cells in area 18 of the cat. *J. Physiol. (Lond.),* 302: 483 – 507.

Heinen, S.J. and Skavenski, A.A. (1991) Recovery of visual responses in foveal V1 neurons following bilateral foveal lesions in adult monkey. *Exp. Brain Res.,* 83: 670 – 674.

Hirsch, V.H.B. (1985) The tunable seer. Activity – dependent development of vision. In: E.M. Blass (Ed.), *Handbook of Behavioral Neurobiology, Vol. 8,* Plenum, New York, pp. 237 – 295.

Hirsch, V.H.B. and Leventhal, A.G. (1978) Functional modification of the developing visual system. In: M. Jacobson (Ed.), *Development of Sensory Systems,* Springer Verlag, Berlin, pp. 279 – 335.

Hirsch, V.H.B. and Tieman, S.B. (1987) Perceptual development and experience-dependent changes in cat visual cortex. In: M. Bornstein and N.J. Hillsdale (Eds.), *Sensitive Periods in Development: Interdisciplinary Perspectives,* Lawrence Erlbaum, NJ, pp. 39 – 79.

Hubel, D.H. and Wiesel, T.N. (1962) Receptive fields, binocular interaction and functional architecture in the cat's visual cortex. *J. Physiol. (Lond.),* 160: 106 – 154.

Hubel, D.H. and Wiesel, T.N. (1965) Receptive fields and functional architecture in two nonstriate visual areas (18 and 19) of the cat. *J. Neurophysiol.,* 28: 229 – 289.

Hubel, D.H. and Wiesel, T.N. (1970) The period of susceptibility to the physiological effects of unilateral eye closure in kittens. *J. Physiol. (Lond.),* 206: 419 – 436.

Imbert, M. and Buisseret, P. (1975) Receptive field characteristics and plastic properties of visual cortical cells in kittens reared with and without visual experience. *Exp. Brain Res.,* 22: 25 – 36.

Jacobson, S.G., Eames, R.A., Evans, M.J. and McDonald, W.I. (1978) Optic nerve lesions sparing spatial vision in adult cats. Presented at the Association for Research in Vision and Ophthalmology Meeting, Saragosa, FL.

Jacobson, S.G., Eames, R.A. and McDonald, W.I. (1979) Optic nerve fibre lesions in adult cats: pattern of recovery of spatial vision. *Exp. Brain Res.,* 36: 491 – 508.

Kaas, J.H., Krubitzer, L.A., Chino, Y.M., Langston, A.L., Polley, E.H. and Blair, N. (1990) Reorganization of retinotopic cortical maps in adult mammals after lesions of the retina. *Science,* 248: 229 – 231.

Lepore, F. and Guillemot, J.P. (1982) Visual receptive field properties of cells innervated through the corpus callosum in the cat. *Exp. Brain Res.,* 46: 413 – 424.

Mafféi, L. and Fiorentini, A. (1976) Asymmetry of motility of the eyes and change of binocular properties of cortical cells in adult cats. *Brain Res.,* 105: 73 – 78.

Merzenich, M.M., Recanzone, G., Jenkins, W.M., Allard, T.T. and Nudo, R.J. (1988) Cortical representational plasticity. In: P. Rakic and W. Singer (Eds.), *Neurobiology of Neocortex – S. Bernhard Dahlem Konferenzen,* Wiley, New York, pp. 41 – 67.

Milleret, C. and Buser, P. (1984) Receptive field sizes and responsiveness to light in area 18 of the adult cat after chiasmotomy. Postoperative evolution; role of visual experience. *Exp. Brain Res.,* 57: 73 – 81.

Milleret, C., Gary-Bobo, E. and Buisseret, P. (1988) Comparative development of cell properties in cortical area 18 of normal and dark-reared kittens. *Exp. Brain Res.,* 71: 8 – 20.

Movshon, J.A. and Van Sluyters, R.C. (1981) Visual neural development. *Annu. Rev. Psychol.,* 32: 477 – 522.

Müller, C.M. and Best, J. (1989) Ocular dominance plasticity in adult cat visual cortex after transplantation of cultured astrocytes. *Nature,* 342: 427 – 430.

Myers, R.E. (1955) Interocular transfer of pattern discrimination in cats following section of crossed optic fibres. *J. Comp. Physiol. Psychol.,* 48: 470 – 473.

Norton, T.T., Galambos, R. and Frommer, G.P. (1967) Optic tract lesions destroying pattern vision in cats. *Exp. Neurol.,* 18: 26 – 37.

Olson, C.R. and Freeman, R.D. (1980) Profile of the sensitive period for monocular deprivation in kittens. *Exp. Brain Res.,* 39: 17 – 21.

Orban, G.A., Kennedy, H. and Maes, H. (1980) Functional change across the 17 – 18 border in the cat. *Exp. Brain Res.,* 39: 177 – 186.

Otsuka, R. and Hassler, R. (1962) Über Aufbau und Gliederung der corticalen Sehsphäre bei der Katze. *Psychiat. Nervenkrankh.,* 203: 212 – 234.

Payne, B.R. (1990) Representation of the ipsilateral visual field in the transition zone between areas 17 and 18 of the cat's cerebral cortex. *Visual Neurosci.,* 4: 445 – 474.

Payne, B.R., Siwek, D.F. and Lomber, S.G. (1991) Complex transcallosal interactions in visual cortex. *Visual Neurosci.,* 6: 283 – 289.

Riesen, A.H. (1965) Effects of visual deprivation on perceptual function and the neural substrate. In: *Deafferentation Experimentale et Clinique – Symposium Bel Air II,* Masson, Paris, pp. 47 – 297.

Sherman, S.M. and Spear, P.D. (1982) Organization of visual pathways in normal and visually deprived cats. *Physiol. Rev.,* 62: 738 – 855.

Singer, W., Tretter, F. and Yinon, U. (1982) Evidence for long-term functional plasticity in the visual cortex of adult cats. *J. Physiol. (Lond.),* 324: 239 – 248.

Tusa, R.J., Rosenquist, A.C. and Palmer, L.A. (1979) Retinotopic organization of areas 18 and 19 in the cat. *J. Comp. Neurol.,* 185: 657 – 678.

Vakkur, G.J., Bishop, P.O. and Kozak, W. (1963) Visual optics in the cat including posterior nodal distance and retinal landmarks. *Vision Res.,* 3: 289 – 314.

Vesbaesya, C., Whitteridge, D. and Wilson, M.E. (1967) Callosal connections of the cortex representing the area centralis. *J. Physiol. (Lond.),* 191: 79 – 80.

Wiesel, T.N. and Hubel, D.H. (1963) Single-cell responses in striate cortex of kittens deprived of vision in one eye. *J. Neurophysiol.,* 26: 1003 – 1017.

Yinon, U. (1980) Monocular deafferentation effects on responsiveness of cortical cells in adult cats. *Brain Res.,* 199: 299 – 306.

Yinon, U. and Hammer, A. (1985) Optic chiasm split and binocularity diminution in cortical cells of acute and chronic operated adult cats. *Exp. Brain Res.,* 58: 552 – 558.

Yinon U. and Milgram, A. (1990) The ocular dominance and receptive field properties of visual cortex cells of cats following long-term transection of the optic chiasm and monocular deprivation during adulthood. *Behav. Brain Res.,* 38: 163 – 173.

T.P. Hicks, S. Molotchnikoff and T. Ono (Eds.)
Progress in Brain Research, Vol. 95
© 1993 Elsevier Science Publishers B.V. All rights reserved.

CHAPTER 24

Extraretinal modulation of geniculate neuronal activity by conditioning

Doris Albrecht and Helga Davidowa

Institute of Physiology, Medical School (Charité), Humboldt University of Berlin, O-1040 Berlin, Germany

Introduction

Nowadays it is well known that the dorsal part of the lateral geniculate nucleus (dLGN) does not serve as a simple "relay" station. The transmission of signals from the retina to the visual cortex is gated by the dLGN in relation to the state of the organism and to its attention to the visual environment (Singer, 1977; Burke and Cole, 1978; Sherman and Koch, 1986; Steriade et al., 1990). The dLGN serves as an integrative center, incorporating a variety of modulatory influences upon the visual signal. The intense innervation of the dLGN by non-retinal afferents, especially the ·feedback inhibition from nucleus reticularis thalami (TR), and various features of geniculate neurons are the basis of this gating process.

As seen in Fig. 1 the visually responsive neurons of the TR receive their main input from collateral axon branches of dLGN relay neurons. Thus, the TR provides a strong GABAergic input to the dLGN and is itself dependent upon input from visual cortex and various subcortical structures. For both the TR and the dLGN, it can be inferred that the influence of the visual cortex is excitatory (Molotchnikoff et al., 1984; Kayama, 1985). The dLGN is densely innervated by cholinergic fibers arising from the laterodorsal tegmental nucleus and its rostrolateral extension, the pedunculo-pontine tegmental nucleus, while the TR receives cholinergic projections from both brain-stem and basal forebrain

nuclei (Woolf and Butcher, 1986). In contrast to its nicotinic action on dLGN neurons in cats acetylcholine (Ach) induces in the rat dLGN only a slow muscarinic depolarization, whereas TR neurons are hyperpolarized by Ach via muscarinic M_2-receptors (Mc Cormick and Prince, 1987). Furthermore, dLGN and TR neurons can be influenced by a noradrenergic projection from the locus coeruleus (Lüth et al., 1978) which excites both dLGN relay neurons and TR cells (Kayama, 1985). A third projection to the dLGN and the TR arises from the dorsal raphe nucleus (Lüth and Seidel, 1987). In both structures the serotonergic influence is mainly inhibitory (Yoshida et al., 1984), although recently it has been shown in slice preparations that serotonin as well as noradrenaline can increase a hyperpolarization- activated current which reduces selectively the synaptic effectiveness of large hyperpolarizing inputs, with little effect on phasic or tonic depolarizations (Pape and Mc Cormick, 1989).

Understanding of the gating function of the dLGN is mainly brought about by experiments on slices or on anesthetized animals using electrical brain stimulation, transmitters and their blockers. Only few investigations tried to demonstrate the validity of the theory in freely moving animals on conditions which imply variation of gain of visual information beyond the sleep-waking cycle. It has been shown that dLGN neurons, e.g., of cats or pigeons change their responses to light during conditioning, i.e., by pairing light with a reward or with

272

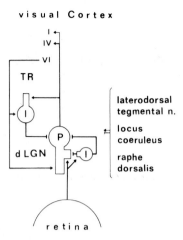

visual Cortex

Fig. 1. Schematic diagram illustrating the afferent and efferent projections to and from the dLGN. P, Relay neuron; I, inhibitory neuron; sharp arrows, excitatory influence; blunt arrows, inhibitory influences. See text for further details.

aversive stimuli (Ramos et al., 1976; Gibbs et al., 1986).

The aim of our experiments in rats was to evaluate the role of appetitive and aversive conditioned light stimuli in the determination of the response pattern of dLGN neurons. This includes an answer to the question whether a difference in the response of dLGN neurons to visual stimulation can be related to the signal value of the stimulus and therefore to associative mechanisms or to motivational, emotional or arousal processes. In addition, further investigations were aimed to clarify mechanisms leading to the observed response changes. The role of the TR and its cholinergic afferents as well as of the direct cholinergic input to the dLGN in mediation of the conditioning-related changes in single unit activity of the dLGN were of special interest. Since the persistence of response changes evoked by conditioning seems to depend as well on afferentation or properties of cells, the search of at least indirect evidence seemed to be appropriate.

Effects of an appetitive conditioned stimulus on geniculate activity

Choosing classical conditioning procedures as

model we trained water-deprived rats to react to flashes with drinking behavior (for detail, see Davidowa et al., 1982). To prevent variations in retinal illumination due to body or head movements relative to the light source a light emitting diode (LED) was attached to the animal's head. Flashes of the LED were used as conditioned stimulus (CS) in all further investigations. Response patterns of dLGN neurons to light recorded in the thirsty animal were compared with those observed after satiation. Considering size and number of relay and interneurons within the rat dLGN we assume that our spike data originate from relay neurons.

Fig. 2 demonstrates peristimulus time histograms (PSTH) of the activity of a dLGN unit recorded via chronically implanted NiCr-wire electrodes on two successive days (A,B). At the bottom of this figure a typical on-like response to flash is shown, recorded in the freely behaving rat during the satiated, relaxed state (S). The primary excitation is followed by a

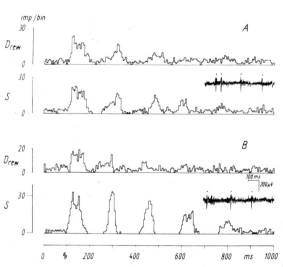

Fig. 2. Responses to flashes of a dLGN unit of a freely moving rat recorded on two successive days (A,B). D_{rew}, PSTHs recorded in the thirsty rat which reacted to the CS with drinking behavior; S, PSTHs recorded after satiation ($n = 13$ trials, intertrial interval about $20-30$ sec); arrows, onset and termination of light stimuli (LED, 7 mcd, 15 msec, 560 nm; background luminance about 0.01 cd/m^2); imp./bin, impulses per bin (binwidth 5 msec). Inserted examples of unit activity, drawn from photographs of the oscilloscope, discriminated units marked with dots.

postexcitatory inhibition with subsequent late excitations and inhibitions. A different pattern of neuronal discharges was obtained before in the thirsty, well trained rat (D_{rew}) which reacted to light with a conditioned movement to a water tube. Especially the inhibitory phases were weakened and the number of late excitatory phases reduced. In addition, the number of impulses of the excitatory phases was decreased in the thirsty animal compared with that of the satiated state. These differences in response pattern were similar in recordings at successive days (e.g., A and B), although some variations in peak amplitudes of the PSTHs and the number of late phases existed from day to day even in the satiated state (compare S in A and B) (Nicolai et al., 1982).

Such differences of response pattern in dependence of the behavioral and motivational state of the rat occurred in nearly 50% of tested dLGN neurons (compare Fig. 4). Pairs of response parameters derived from the thirsty trained and the satiated animals were compared by means of the Wilcoxon test for the whole cell group. The results

showed that responses of dLGN units to light in trained, attentive rats had a shorter peak latency, diminished inhibitory periods and reduced excitatory phases. Moreover, the number of afterdischarges was reduced in thirsty trained rats, and the variability of response phases was greater (Albrecht et al., 1980) (see also Table I, D_{rew}/S). In general, the geniculate activity is facilitated in response to the CS in thirsty trained rats.

Fig. 3 provides a better insight into the changes occurring at the neuronal level than the PSTHs. It shows several single responses of a geniculate unit to light observed in a trained thirsty animal rewarded with water (D_{rew}) and after satiation (S). In the satiated state of the quietly sitting rat the neuron discharged in bursts of relatively stable time relation to the flashes. Such a neuronal bursting pattern observed in relaxed satiated rats is comparable to discharge patterns of thalamic neurons seen in sleeping animals. It is suggested that it is able to maintain a minimum level of information. A relation exists between unit activity and evoked field potentials recorded with the same microelectrode. In correspondence with results of Creutzfeldt and Kuhnt (1973) there was a coincidence of appearance of neuronal burst discharges with the enhancement of photic afterdischarges in the EEG recordings after satiation of the animal (Albrecht, 1981). An increase of the amplitude and the number of photic afterdischarges was also obtained in other studies using reward (Hackett and Marczynski, 1969). The dispersion of spike discharges which mainly occurred during expressed attentive behavior of the trained motivated rat (Fig. 3, D_{rew}) can be regarded as a desynchronization at the neuronal level. These changes are assumed to lead to a better spatial resolution due to uncoupling of relay channels, judged by response variations between neurons, and a better temporal resolution due to the reduced inhibitory phases and afterdischarges. The change from rhythmic burst firing pattern to regular single spike activity may be responsible for the marked increase in the efficacy of transfer of information through the thalamus during periods of increased arousal and attentiveness.

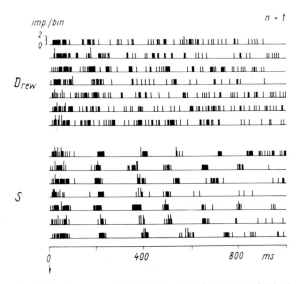

Fig. 3. Single responses of a dLGN unit to flashes recorded in the freely behaving rat. D_{rew}, Thirsty, attentive, rewarded by water; S, satiated. Arrow: termination of the light stimulus.

274

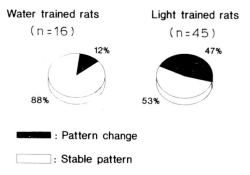

Water trained rats
(n = 16)

12%

88%

Light trained rats
(n = 45)

47%

53%

■ : Pattern change

□ : Stable pattern

Fig. 4. Percentage of response pattern changes of dLGN units in water-trained rats (controls) and in animals trained to react to light as conditioned stimulus. *n*, Number of cells.

Relation of response changes to motivation and reinforcement

The question arose whether the observed facilitation of unit activity is caused by the behavioral relevance of light stimuli or is due to arousal and/or motivational processes. Since after water intake in addition to its rewarding value and to the reduction of thirst motivation the degree of vigilance may shift from highly arousal to relaxed wakefulness, the latter could also be considered responsible for the synchronization effects of unit activity after satiation.

Experiments on two control groups of rats served to answer this question. In one group responses to light were compared in dependence of the motivational state, i.e., unit activity was recorded in the deprived thirsty rat and then after satiation. These animals were not subjected to any training procedure. A second group was submitted to a training procedure except the time-locked presentation of the light stimulus to the reinforcing one ("water-trained"). These animals were allowed to ingest the same amount of water as the light-trained animals. The flashes were applied stochastically within a period in which the rat was quietly sitting.

While in the water-trained control group few neurons changed their response pattern similar to that observed in light-trained rats as shown in Fig. 2 (Davidowa et al., 1982) (Fig. 4), there was no such pattern change in the untrained group (Albrecht et al., 1980). No significant differences between

responses were found (so called "stable" neurons in accordance with Ramos et al., 1976) although minor modulations of duration and/or amplitude of some response phases could be observed. But the sequence and the number of response phases in the PSTHs of these neurons were preserved. Such response alterations were also observed in few neurons of light-trained rats. Since the percentage of neurons which changed their response pattern is higher in rats trained to react to light stimulation than in rats being directly rewarded by water, a great part of changes has to be attributed to associational processes and the attention to light, because both trained groups showed a similar behavior and were in a similar motivated state.

Furthermore, to analyze the influence of water reward itself unit responses either to light stimuli which were delivered after reward and drinking or to stimuli given after an interstimulus interval without reward were compared in rats of the water-trained control group. For the whole group of tested neurons no significant differences could be found (Davidowa et al., 1982). Thus, it can be concluded that reward itself has a negligible influence on the dLGN responses.

The influence of motor activity seems to be more essential. When rats moved their heads or moved within the box, neuronal responses to light differed from those of motionless sitting rats (Davidowa et al., 1982; Albrecht et al., 1986). A correlation between dLGN multi-unit activity and the animal's motor behavior was already described by Schwartzbaum (1975). Therefore, trials in which movements of the animal occur have to be excluded from evaluation concerning the effect of the biological meaning of light stimulation and the motivational state.

Effects of aversive classical conditioning

Aversive conditioning is one of the most widely used paradigms for studying emotional learning. An affectively neutral CS, in our case a light stimulus, was systematically paired (interstimulus interval 900 msec) with an aversive unconditioned stimulus

(US), consisting in our experiments of cutaneous tail shock. The previously neutral CS thereby acquired aversive properties, and when subsequently presented alone evoked itself an aversive emotional reaction. In the rat the US or onset of such a CS resulted in the arrest of ongoing behavior and typically induced a characteristic crouching or "freezing" posture.

Similar to activity changes in thirsty trained rats the geniculate unit responses to the conditioned aversive light stimuli differed from those to neutral flashes (Albrecht et al., 1990). The activity was facilitated, the postexcitatory inhibitions in the PSTH were significantly reduced after pairing light with the electrical tail stimulation over 90 trials (intertrial interval on average 10 sec).

Such pairings performed in rats anesthetized with urethane (1.2 g/kg i.p.) evoked comparable changes. Although application of urethane itself (i) reduces firing frequency, (ii) increases the latency of flash-evoked responses, (iii) reduces the number of excitatory response phases and (iv) causes a prolongation of the postexcitatory inhibition of geniculate units (Albrecht and Davidowa, 1989), aversive conditioning facilitated the neuronal activity similar to that in freely moving animals (Albrecht et al., 1990). In addition, in urethane anesthetized rats the maintained activity as well as the excitatory phases in the PSTH were significantly increased by the conditioning procedure (see also Figs. 7 – 10, flash-US and Table II, flash-US). Furthermore, in accordance with general criteria of associative learning it could be shown in these experiments that (1) the response amplitude increases over the trials, (2) the response increase reaches an asymptotic level, (3) the change can occur rapidly, (4) the conditioning-related changes are a result of forward pairing and temporal contiguity of CS and US and (5) the response modulations in a part of the tested neurons appear to be of long-term nature. The ability to exhibit differential conditioning as well has been shown by Rucker et al. (1986) in rats anesthetized with urethane. The percentage of units which changed their responses to light as a function of the relevance of the aversive stimulus is comparable to that observed in freely behaving, thirsty trained animals to appetitive stimuli.

It should be emphasized that in a group of neurons the conditioning-related facilitation of activity persisted over an extinction period of at least 15 min (see also Figs. 8 – 10). Therefore, there exist not only "stable" and "plastic" dLGN neurons as postulated by Ramos et al. (1976) and demonstrated in our earlier experiments (Albrecht et al., 1980), but it is possible to divide the so called "plastic" neurons in a group of neurons with transient changes and a group with real "plastic" properties, i.e., with persistent changes. While the first only changed their activity during the CS-US paradigm, in the latter the changed discharge rate caused by forward conditioning persisted over a period up to 1 h during the extinction period (25% of the tested neurons).

Backward conditioning controls

Response changes elicited by a CS reflect either associative or non-associative learning processes. Associative learning is often distinguished from non-associative learning by using control groups in which the CS and US are randomly related (pseudoconditioning) or CS and US are applied in a reversed order (backward conditioning). In such procedures the amount and the percentage of pattern changes of dLGN neurons was smaller than in forward pairings (23% versus 46%). Moreover, in neurons in which response modulations were observed during backward pairing, these modulations of flash-evoked activity quickly extinguished, i.e., no signs of retention could be observed 10 or 15 min after termination of backward conditioning by giving flashes alone. A development of a tonic rise of activity before and around the US obtained in neurons with persistent response changes in response to forward conditioning did not occur in these neurons during backward conditioning. Interestingly, tail stimulation alone did not cause significant changes in the firing rate of most of the neurons, although the application of US caused a short desynchronization of the EEG activity of visual cortex (Albrecht et al., 1990). In contrast to dorsal LGN neurons a more pronounced facilitation of responses by backward conditioning than by forward conditioning in ventral LGN neurons point primarily to an arousal-depending activation of this structure (Davidowa and Albrecht, 1992).

Role of the TR in modulation of geniculate unit activity

It has been shown that the postexcitatory inhibitions in responses of dLGN neurons to light are caused by TR neurons (French et al., 1985). The well-expressed inhibitory phases in responses of the dLGN relay neurons to light stimuli without relevance or in satiated animals therefore may be due to a strong feedback inhibition via TR. The reduced inhibitory periods and the dispersion of light-evoked geniculate unit discharges in thirsty trained rats or during aversive conditioning can be explained by a disruption of this feedback circuit through inhibition of the TR, which leads to disinhibition of dLGN relay neurons. Such mechanisms are thought to improve the detection of visual stimuli. Moreover, disinhibition is thought to play a dominant role in gate control (Singer, 1977).

Disinhibition could be elicited by cholinergic fibers innervating the TR because of their inhibitory effects on TR neurons (Kelly et al., 1979; Mc Cormick and Prince, 1987). Recently, the inhibitory effect of cholinergic fibers on TR neurons and consequently the disinhibition model has been questioned (Kayama et al., 1986a). Therefore, the role of cholinergic afferents to the TR in mediating conditioning-related activity changes in the dLGN seemed to be of interest.

We used microinjection of atropine into the TR to block muscarinic cholinergic influences in thirsty trained animals in comparison with the satiated state. Injections of atropine were carried out after five normal trials in thirsty trained rats in order to guarantee a high level of motivation also in the drugged animal. It caused changes of geniculate unit activity in thirsty trained rats which closely resembled those obtained after satiation (Albrecht et al.,

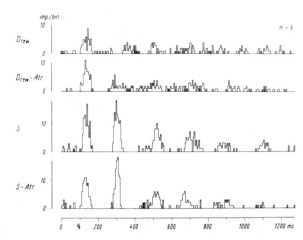

Fig. 5. Effect of atropine (Atr) injected into the ipsilateral TR (0.5 μl) over a period of 120 sec in the attentive rat ($D_{rew} - $ Atr) and in the satiated rat (S $-$ Atr) on the responses to flashes of a dLGN unit recorded by means of chronically implanted electrodes in a light-trained rat ($n = 5$ trials). Denotations as in Fig. 2.

1986). After atropine injection into the TR the postexcitatory inhibition of dLGN units was strengthened regardless of the unchanged reflex behavior of the rat (Fig. 5). Our results indicate that the difference between the flash-evoked postexcitatory inhibitory phases of dLGN unit responses in deprived and satiated rats can be attributed to cholinergic influences on the TR in thirsty trained rats. The missing effects of atropine injection in satiated animals support this view (Table I).

Injection of Ach into the TR resulted in a facilitation of responses to light of geniculate neurons. Due to the vicinity of the visual part of TR to the dLGN, an action of injected drugs on geniculate neurons by diffusion cannot be excluded, but the obtained results give no obvious hint for this. The excitatory phases of unit responses in thirsty trained rats were mostly not diminished by atropine, what could be expected by blocking the direct facilitatory cholinergic influences (see also Table I).

Atropine did not change the excitatory phases in deprived rats as much as satiation did (Table I). The enhancement of excitations after satiation, and in some neurons after atropine, could be related to a

TABLE I

Comparison of pairs of response parameters of dLGN neurons ($n = 17$)

Experimental condition, compared with flash	D_{rew}/S	D_{rew}/D_{rew} (Atr)	D_{rew} (Atr)/S	S/S(Atr)
Compared parameters				
Maintained activity	−	−	−	−
Number of impulses during first excitation	↑	−	↑	−
Number of impulses during postexcitatory inhibition	↓	↓	−	−
Number of impulses during second excitation	↑	−	↑	−
Number of impulses during second inhibition	↓	↓	−	−

The response parameters were obtained in deprived rats which were rewarded by water (D_{rew}) and in satiated rats (S) before and after injection of atropine in the TR (Atr). −, No significant changes; arrows, significant changes at the 0.01 level; ↑, increase of activity from the first to the second condition; ↓, decrease of activity from the first to the second condition (adapted from Albrecht et al., 1986).

hyperpolarization elicited from TR, which can be cause of the genesis of burst patterns (Pape and Mc Cormick, 1989). Therefore, results of these experiments point to a hyperpolarizing action of Ach on TR neurons in rats, since its application into TR reduces inhibitory periods in the dLGN unit responses to light, and atropine induces inhibitory periods in attentive rats.

In addition, in the aversive conditioning paradigm it has been shown that pairing light with tail shock leads to decrease of the activity of a lot of TR neurons, and in some of them a change from regular spiking to burst pattern has been obtained (Albrecht et al., 1992).

The results presented so far add support to an essential role of Ach action on TR neurons, and they support the disinhibition model of gating dLGN unit activity. But these experiments do not permit a statement concerning the role of direct cholinergic pathways to dLGN neurons, and do not exclude the possible participation of other transmitters in the modulation of visual information transfer in the dLGN during a learned behavior.

Location dependent changes of dLGN activity

It has been shown that the dLGN of rats consists of two portions − a dorsolateral one which includes the caudal third of the nucleus (designated as shell) and a ventromedial part in the anterior two thirds (designated as core). These regions differ concerning afferentation, synaptic arrangements and distribution of relay cell types (see in detail, Albrecht et al., 1991). Therefore it is of interest whether neurons of both regions are included to the same extent in changes of activity by conditioning. As we recorded the dLGN unit activity in these experiments by means of glass micropipettes filled with Trypan blue solution, it was possible to localize the electrode tip position exactly by iontophoretic marking. Furthermore, to study the involvement of neurons of different channels the analyses were related to on- and off-neurons, as well as "slow" and "fast" neurons. "Slow" cells probably represent W-neurons, "fast" cells mainly the Y-channel (Hale et al., 1979).

The results show that mainly responses of neurons located in the shell were changed by conditioning with aversive stimuli, whereas neurons of the core only seldom underwent response changes. Neurons with persistent changes were mainly "slow" ones and distinctly predominated as well in the shell of the dLGN (Fig. 6). "Slow" cells are mainly located in the shell region. The occurrence of response changes in geniculate neurons during conditioning seems to be related to the location of neurons within the dLGN rather than to the functionally different channels. This points to a relevance of direct control of geniculate activity by various afferents.

278

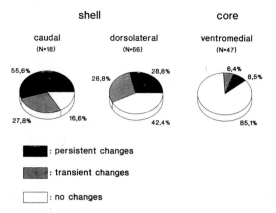

shell   core

caudal dorsolateral ventromedial
(N=18)   (N=66)   (N=47)

55,6%   28,8%   6,4%
    28,8%   8,5%

27,8% 16,6%   42,4%   85,1%

■ : persistent changes

▨ : transient changes

☐ : no changes

Fig. 6. Percentage of cells developing transient and persistent response changes in relation to their location within the dLGN.

Role of direct cholinergic afferents to the dLGN

Since the shell of the dLGN has a denser innervation of cholinergic and noradrenergic fibers than the ventromedial core (Lüth et al., 1978; Lüth and Brauer, 1983), the question arose which of these subcortical afferents are involved in the mediation of conditioning-related facilitation of the geniculate units. Gibbs et al. (1983) have shown in the pigeon that electrical stimulation of the locus coeruleus can substitute for foot shock as an effective US for associative conditioning of neurons in the avian equivalent of the mammalian dLGN. In addition, it has been found that afferents from locus coeruleus to the dLGN must be intact for associative modification in dLGN to occur (Broyles and Cohen, 1985).

As far as we are aware no one has investigated the role of cholinergic influences in the elaboration of conditioning-related changes of thalamic single unit activity. Moreover, results in relation to cholinergic influences on cortical activity are contradictory. Molnar et al. (1988) found peripheral atropine application to have no effect on evoked potential changes induced in different layers of the auditory cortex by conditioning. In contrast, Delacour et al. (1990) recently described a blocking action of iontophoretically applied atropine on changes of the activity of single units in the somatic cortex evoked by a sensory – sensory conditioning procedure.

Therefore, the present experiments were carried out to investigate the action of atropine on conditioning-related responses in geniculate units of rats anesthetized with urethane.

Iontophoretic studies

As in previous investigations (Albrecht et al., 1990, 1991) extracellular recordings were performed with glass microelectrodes (tip diameter 1 μm) filled with saturated Trypan blue solution. For iontophoretic application of drugs three-barrel micropipettes were glued to the recording electrode so that their tips were separated vertically by 20 μm. Each of the barrels contained one of the following drugs in aqueous solution: Ach 0.2 M, pH 4.0; atropine sulfate 0.1 M, pH 4.5 and sometimes L-glutamic acid monosodium 0.5 M, pH 8.0. Adjustments of pH were made with HCl or NaOH. Cationic currents were used to eject all drugs except glutamate for which anionic currents were utilized. Retaining currents (5 – 10 nA) of opposite polarity were applied to the pipettes between drug ejections. In some recordings one of the barrels was filled with NaCl and used to test the effects of applying current to the neuron under study. Occasionally, the pH of the NaCl was adjusted to equal that of one of the drugs. No significant contribution from current or pH was detected. Although the present experiments were primarily directed to establish the influence of atropine on conditioning-related changes of dLGN unit activity, we confirmed that atropine blocks the effects of Ach, at least in part.

The following schedule was applied at an intertrial interval of about 10 sec:

(1) Thirty light stimuli of 500 msec in duration were used to characterize on- and off-responses of the cell.

(2) Thirty light stimuli of 15 msec duration (flash).

(3) Thirty flashes concomitant with Ach ejection (20 – 50 nA).

(4) Thirty or 60 flashes (flash).

(5) Conditioning: in 90 trials flash stimulation was followed by tail stimulation with an in-

terstimulus interval (ISI) of 900 msec (flash-US).

(6) Extinction period: 90 flashes (flash).

(7) Thirty flashes concomitant with atropine ejection (10 – 40 nA) (Atr).

(8) Conditioning: 90 trials concomitant with atropine ejection (10 – 40 nA) (flash-US(Atr)).

(9) Extinction period: 90 flashes (flash).

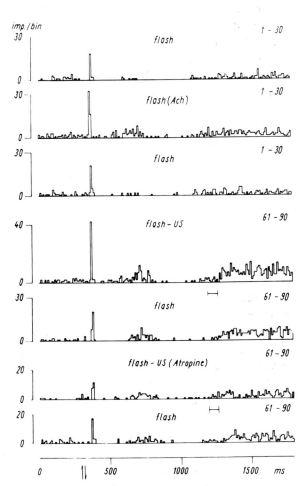

Fig. 7. Response modulations of a caudally located dLGN neuron induced by iontophoretically applied Ach (50 nA), by conditioning (flash-US) and reconditioning concomitant with atropine administration (40 nA). Ach and conditioning facilitated the flash-evoked activity. Atropine blocked the conditioning effect. The response modulations were transient. Arrows, beginning and termination of light stimulation; horizontal bar, electrical stimulation of the tail (US); binwidth, 10 msec; PSTHs are summarized from 30 trials (numbers above the PSTHs), from top to bottom: sequence of recording.

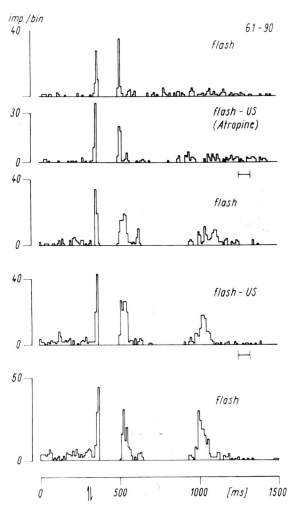

Fig. 8. Flash-evoked activity of a neuron located laterally in the dLGN. In the extinction period (third PSTH from the top) following conditioning concomitant with atropine (flash-US(Atr)), a late discharge is seen just before the moment of usual US application in conditioning trials. This pattern change is strengthened during reconditioning (flash-US) and the following extinction period. Denoted as in Fig. 7.

In general, atropine was ejected for 60 sec with interruptions of 60 sec. Sometimes the intensity of currents was reduced when necessary, or the blocker ejected continously during the last 30 trials of conditioning. Conditioning procedures with and without iontophoretic ejection of atropine were alternated in their sequence in about half of the recordings. In each rat only one neuron was tested to prevent in-

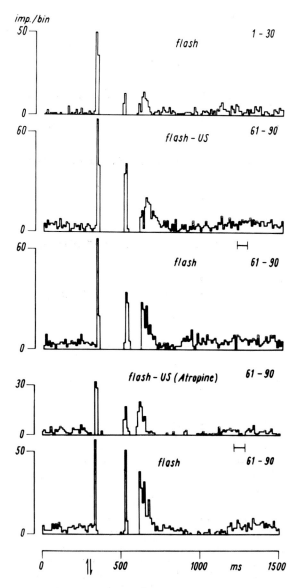

Fig. 9. Responses of an on-like neuron to flash (top), conditioning (flash-US), extinction (flash), reconditioning concomitant with atropine (flash-US(Atr)) and the second extinction period (bottom). The persistently increased excitatory phases were reduced following the atropine application during reconditioning. Denoted as in Fig. 7.

influences of preceding conditioning procedure on the investigated unit activity.

Blocking action of atropine

As in previous results (Albrecht et al. , 1990), a significant modulation of the response pattern to flashes was obtained by conditioning (19/50 cells, 38%, χ^2-test). In most neurons, iontophoretic application of the muscarinic antagonist atropine suppressed the facilitation of activity induced by conditioning (Figs. 7 – 9). However, in 5 out of the 19 "modulated" neurons the facilitatory action of conditioning could not be blocked significantly by atropine (Fig. 10). The effect of conditioning with or without atropine on different cell groups is shown in Table II. Both, on-like neurons responding to flashes with a primary excitation and off-like neurons responding with a primary inhibition, increased their discharges during the different phases of the PSTH, when light was paired with the aversive stimulus (flash-US). Significant differences in latencies were not found. Conditioning with atropine did not lead to significant changes.

Since neither amplitude nor duration of spikes were reduced during iontophoresis of atropine, it is unlikely that the blocking of conditioning-induced facilitation was due to a local anesthetic effect. Recovery from the action of atropine usually occurred within 3 – 5 min of the cessation of its application. Moreover, flash-evoked activity as well as glutamate excitation was not significantly influenced by doses of atropine sufficient to block Ach effects.

To examine whether the cholinergic input itself could induce a facilitation of flash-evoked activity, Ach was applied iontophoretically to 47 dLGN neurons. In 12 of them (26%) a significant modulation of the response to flashes was seen. As shown in Table II there was a facilitation of activity. In most cases the influence of Ach and conditioning on the same neuron was similar (Fig. 7), but often not as strong. The block by atropine and apparent correlation between the action of Ach and conditioning supports the hypothesis that cholinergic afferents play a dominant role in mediation of the potentiation elicited by conditioning. A facilitatory action of Ach, both on maintained activity and on driven discharges of dLGN units, has also been found by other investigators (Kayama et al., 1986b; Mc Cormick and Prince, 1987). These influences could be mimicked by stimulation of the mesopontine

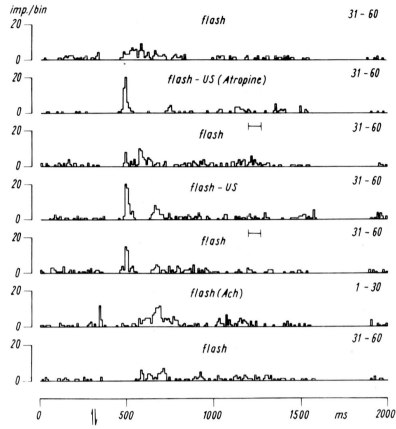

imp./bin

Fig. 10. PSTHs from the activity of a geniculate unit located laterally. In spite of atropine application the response is changed by conditioning (flash-US(Atr)). The conditioning effect was transient. Interestingly, the pattern change which reappeared during reconditioning without atropine (flash-US) persisted during the second extinction period. Remark the facilitation, especially the occurrence of an early excitation induced by Ach. During further light stimulation the response returned to the initial pattern. Denoted as in Fig. 7.

tegmentum and were blocked by the muscarinic antagonist scopolamine (Kayama et al., 1986b). In the small number of cases in which the conditioning-related facilitation was only partly blocked by atropine, a possible involvement of noradrenergic, serotonergic or cortical afferentation together with changed influences from the TR cannot be excluded.

Plasticity of dLGN neurons

It has to be underlined that the development of response changes by conditioning and their persistence could be differently influenced by atropine. In Fig. 10 an example is shown where atropine did not block the development of response changes during conditioning, but the changes were only transient and disappeared in the extinction period. However, on reconditioning without atropine the modulation persisted during extinction. Therefore, in this case atropine only blocked the development of a persistent change.

Such suppression of the persistence of response changes during conditioning by atropine occurred in 6 out of 12 "persistently modulated" neurons. In the other 6 neurons in which atropine blocked the development of changes in the response during conditioning a facilitation of flash-evoked activity was seen during the extinction period after termination of the atropine application (Fig. 8). This pattern was

TABLE II

Comparison of pairs of response parameters for groups of on- and off-like units (Wilcoxon test)

Experimental condition, compared with flash	Cell type									
	On-like (n = 26)					Off-like (n = 24)				
	flash-US (Atr)	ext.	flash-US	ext.	Ach	flash-US (Atr)	ext.	flash-US	ext.	Ach
Compared parameters										
Maintained activity	–	–	↑↑	–	–	–	–	↑	↑	–
Number of impulses during:										
first excitation	–	–	↑↑	↑↑	↑	–	–	↑↑	↑	↑↑
first inhibition										
Number of impulses during:										
postexcitatory inhibition	–	–	↑↑	–	↑	–	–	↑	–	↑
postinhibitory excitation										
Number of pulses during:										
second excitation	–	–	↑↑	–	–	–	–	↑↑	–	↑
second inhibition	–	–	↑↑	–	↑	–	–	↑↑	–	↑
Integrated activity during ISI	–	–	↑↑	–	↑	–	–	–	–	–

The response parameters were obtained during forward conditioning (flash-US) with (Atr) or without atropine, during extinction (ext.) and during iontophoresis of acetylcholine (Ach). ISI, interstimulus interval; –, no significant changes; one arrow, significant changes at the 0.05 level; two arrows, $P < 0.01$; ↑, increase of activity from the first to the second condition.

similar to that seen following conditioning in the absence of atropine (Fig. 8). As shown in Fig. 9 the response change of the geniculate unit to light persisted during the extinction period after conditioning without atropine, but was reversed by conditioning with atropine. After cessation of the action of atropine the change appeared again.

It is unlikely that the persistent increases of responsiveness were due to recovery from anesthesia, since more than 75% of the responses returned to control levels. Furthermore, the changes occurred rapidly, and those that remained enhanced were generally fixed rather than continuously increasing. These characteristics are inconsistent with gradually decreasing levels of anesthesia.

It is not possible to determine on the basis of extracellular recordings from single cells whether the recorded neuron is itself "plastic" or if the persistent enhancement of the response pattern reflects changes in groups of neurons located outside the thalamus. Our results seem to support both hypotheses, because neurons which did not change their response pattern during conditioning under atropine, expressed such changes after termination of the atropine application during the extinction period. On the other hand, there were neurons which did not change their activity at all during or after the application of atropine, although conditioning in the absence of atropine did lead to persistent modulations. In cases in which neurons developed response changes despite the action of atropine, but did not preserve them during the extinction period, Ach may be necessary for the development of long-term changes. Although neurons of the medial geniculate nucleus have been shown to undergo long-term potentiation (Gerren and Weinberger, 1983), it is not reported for dLGN neurons. Medial geniculate units expressed also plastic changes of receptive field properties during conditioning (Edeline and Weinberger, 1989).

Stimulation experiments which have shown prolonged enhancement of thalamic synaptic responsiveness when combined with Ach are cited as evidence to support the idea that cholinergic afferents increase the ability of thalamic cells to relay incoming signals toward the cortex for prolonged periods of time without disrupting the local inhibitory processes required for analytical processing (Paré et al. , 1990).

Data derived from various studies (Woody et al., 1978; Bear and Singer, 1986; Delacour et al., 1990) support the hypothesis that cholinergic mechanisms are involved in sensory plasticity, at least at the level of the cortex. Our results also support the idea that cholinergic mechanisms are involved in learning-dependent processes and that this type of action might occur at the level of the geniculate nucleus.

Conclusions

The results of our studies demonstrate that light stimuli which possess biological relevance due to pairing with appetitive or aversive stimuli evoke response patterns in single neurons of the dLGN which differ from those evoked by biologically neutral light stimuli. These response differences seem to be primarily induced by associative processes, because application of rewarding stimuli (water to thirsty rats), changes of the motivational level (satiation of thirsty rats with water), pseudo- or backward conditioning with aversive stimuli (electrical stimulation of the tail) did not lead to response differences or only to minor modulations in a small percentage of cells.

Response changes were comparable in situations of aversive and appetitive conditioning. This leads to the conclusion that associative processes elevate the selective attention of the animal to light stimulation, and that the activity changes of geniculate relay neurons reflect the facilitated transmission of signals from the retina to the visual cortex in such a situation. Although facilitation of activity by conditioning occurred even in rats anesthetized with urethane, some differences in response changes point to variations in the inducing mechanisms. In anesthetized rats mainly direct excitatory influences on geniculate cells seem to be of importance. In behaving attentive animals the nucleus reticularis thalami is additionally included in control mechanisms. Disinhibition of geniculate cells seems to be of more relevance in freely moving than in anesthetized rats.

Although we studied only the participation of cholinergic afferents in mediating response changes, acetylcholine seems to have a dominant role by means of direct action and by indirect action through the TR, because atropine blocked to a high extent conditioning-related activity changes. Application of atropine into the TR prevented mainly changes of postexcitatory inhibitions, whereas atropine iontophoretically applied to dLGN neurons mainly diminished facilitation of excitatory phases. Thus, disinhibition combined with direct excitation seems to be responsible for gating the signal processing within the dLGN. Action of acetylcholine on geniculate neurons mimicked only to a certain extent the conditioning-mediated effects, but one might consider that iontophoretically applied Ach may have a minor and shorter effect than Ach released by afferents because of the distance of the electrode to the neuron under study and the action of esterases.

The fact that only about half of the studied geniculate neurons changed their responses by appetitive as well as aversive conditioning, in freely behaving as well as in anesthetized rats, points to differences in the control of signal transmission within the dLGN. From the analysis of location and of functional type of the population of neurons in which response changes were induced it can be concluded that these differences seem to result mainly from differences in extraretinal afferentation and of synaptic connections, since mainly neurons of the caudodorsolateral part of the dLGN underwent response changes. This region has a denser innervation by cholinergic and noradrenergic fibers than the ventromedial core. Furthermore, neurons in which response changes persisted after termination of conditioning stimulus pairing were mainly located in this region, the shell. They were especially slow cells. Prolonged activity changes in this population of neurons seem to be the result of connectivity changes within the geniculate as well as of prolonged activation of cholinergic influences.

Acknowledgements

The authors would like to thank Prof. Dr. J.S. Kelly for his advice and critical comments to the last part of this chapter. They are also indebted to Mrs. U. Seider for her excellent technical assistance.

References

Albrecht, D. (1981) Die Beeinflussung der Übertragung visuell ausgelöster Erregungen im Corpus geniculatum laterale, pars dorsalis, durch zentralnervöse Aktivitätszustände bei der freibeweglichen Ratte. Thesis. Humboldt-Universität, Berlin.

Albrecht, D. and Davidowa, H. (1989) Action of urethane on dorsal lateral geniculate neurons. *Brain Res. Bull.,* 22: 923 – 927.

Albrecht, D., Davidowa, H., Gabriel, H.-J., Malikowa, A.K. and Rüdiger, W. (1980) Response variations of neurons in the lateral geniculate body of the freely moving rat. *Acta Neurobiol. Exp.,* 40: 463 – 478.

Albrecht, D., Davidowa, H. and Gabriel, H.-J. (1986) Influence of atropine microinjection into nucleus reticularis thalami on activity of lateral geniculate nucleus neurones in freely moving rats. *Behav. Brain Res.,* 19: 49 – 57.

Albrecht, D., Davidowa, H. and Gabriel, H.-J. (1990) Conditioning related changes of unit activity in the dorsal lateral geniculate nucleus of urethane-anaesthetized rats. *Brain Res. Bull.,* 25: 55 – 63.

Albrecht, D., Davidowa, H. and Gabriel, H.-J. (1991) Regional differences in the control of neuronal transmission in the lateral geniculate nucleus during conditioning in rats. *Biomed. Biochim. Acta,* 50: 61 – 70.

Albrecht, D., Uhlmann, A. and Davidowa, H. (1992) Inhibitory action of a conditioning procedure on visual responsive neurons of the nucleus reticularis thalami in rats. *Exp. Brain Res.,* 88: 199 – 203.

Bear, M.F. and Singer, W. (1986) Modulation of visual cortical plasticity by acetylcholine and noradrenaline. *Nature,* 320: 172 – 176.

Broyles, J.L. and Cohen, D.H. (1985) An input from locus coeruleus is necessary for discharge modification of avian lateral geniculate neurons during visual learning. *Soc. Neurosci. Abstr.,* 11: 1109.

Burke, W. and Cole, A.M. (1978) Extraretinal influences on the lateral geniculate nucleus. *Rev. Physiol. Biochem. Pharmacol.,* 80: 105 – 166.

Creutzfeldt, O.D. and Kuhnt, U. (1973) Electrophysiology and topographical distribution of visual evoked potentials in animals. In: R. Jung (Ed.), *Handbook of Sensory Physiology, Vol. VII/3B, Central Processing of Visual Information,*

Springer, Berlin, pp. 595 – 646.

Davidowa, H. and Albrecht, D. (1992) Modulation of visually evoked responses in units of the ventral lateral geniculate nucleus of the rat by somatic stimuli. *Behav. Brain Res.,* 50: 127 – 133.

Davidowa, H., Nicolai, A., Gabriel, H.-J. and Albrecht, D. (1982) Lateral geniculate unit activity in freely moving rats. I. Relation to behaviour and stimulus relevance. *Acta Neurobiol. Exp.,* 42: 483 – 494.

Delacour, J., Houcine, O. and Costa, J.C. (1990) Evidence for a cholinergic mechanism of ''learned'' changes in the responses of barrel field neurons of the awake and undrugged rat. *Neuroscience,* 34: 1 – 8.

Edeline, J.M. and Weinberger, N.M. (1989) Receptive field plasticity during cardiac conditioning in the dorsal medial geniculate nucleus of the guinea pig. *Soc. Neurosci. Abstr.,* 15: 81.

French, C.R., Sefton, A.J. and Mackay-Sim, A. (1985) The inhibitory role of the visually responsive region of the thalamic reticular nucleus in the rat. *Exp. Brain Res.,* 57: 471 – 479.

Gerren, R.A. and Weinberger, N.M. (1983) Long term potentiation in the magnocellular medial geniculate nucleus of the anesthetized cat. *Brain Res.,* 265: 138 – 142.

Gibbs, C.M., Broyles, J.L. and Cohen, D.H. (1983) Further studies of the involvement of locus coeruleus in plasticity of avian lateral geniculate neurons during learning. *Soc. Neurosci. Abstr.,* 9: 641.

Gibbs, C.M., Cohen, D.H. and Broyles, J.L. (1986) Modification of the discharge of lateral geniculate neurons during visual learning. *J. Neurosci.,* 6: 627 – 636.

Hackett, J.T. and Marczynski, T.J. (1969) Postreinforcement electrocortical synchronization and enhancement of cortical photic evoked potentials during instrumentally conditioned appetitive behavior in the cat. *Brain Res.,* 15: 447 – 464.

Hale, A., Sefton, J.A. and Dreher, B. (1979) A correlation of receptive field properties with conduction velocity of cells in the rat's retino-geniculo-cortical pathway. *Exp. Brain Res.,* 35: 425 – 442.

Kayama, Y. (1985) Ascending, descending and local control of neuronal activity in the rat lateral geniculate nucleus. *Vision Res.,* 25: 339 – 347.

Kayama, Y., Sumitomo, I. and Ogawa, T. (1986a) Does the ascending cholinergic projection inhibit or excite neurons in the rat thalamic reticular nucleus? *J. Neurophysiol.,* 56: 1310 – 1320.

Kayama, Y., Takagi, M. and Ogawa, T. (1986b) Cholinergic influence of the laterodorsal tegmental nucleus on neuronal activity in the rat lateral geniculate nucleus. *J. Neurophysiol.,* 56: 1297 – 1309.

Kelly, J.S., Dodd, J. and Dingledine, R. (1979) Acetylcholine as an excitatory and inhibitory transmitter in the mammalian central nervous system. *Prog. Brain Res.,* 49: 253 – 266.

Lüth, H.-J. and Brauer, K. (1983) The localization of AChE in the dorsal lateral geniculate nucleus of different mammals – a light and electron microscopical study. *Acta Histochem.,* 72: 211 – 224.

Lüth, H.-J. and Seidel, I. (1987) Immunhistochemische Charakterisierung serotoninerger Afferenzen im visuellen System der Ratte. *J. Hirnforsch.,* 28: 591 – 600.

Lüth, H.-J., Schober, W., Winkelmann, E. and Berger, U. (1978) Die catecholaminergen Verbindungen im visuellen System der Albinoratte. *Acta Histochem.,* 63: 114 – 126.

Mc Cormick, D.A. and Prince, D.A. (1987) Actions of acetylcholine in the guinea-pig and cat medial and lateral geniculate nuclei, in vitro. *J. Physiol. (Lond.),* 392: 147 – 165.

Molnar, M., Karmos, G. and Csepe, V. (1988) Effect of atropine on intracortical evoked potentials during classical aversive conditioning in cats. *Behav. Neurosci.,* 102: 872 – 880.

Molotchnikoff, S., Tremblay, F. and Lepore, F. (1984) The role of the visual cortex in response properties of lateral geniculate cells in rats. *Exp. Brain Res.,* 53: 223 – 232.

Nicolai, A., Davidowa, H. and Rüdiger, W. (1982) Lateral geniculate unit activity in freely moving rats. II. Relation to conditioning and motivation. *Acta Neurobiol. Exp.,* 42: 495 – 500.

Pape, H.-C. and Mc Cormick, D.A. (1989) Noradrenaline and serotonin selectively modulate thalamic burst firing by enhancing a hyperpolarization-activated cation current. *Nature,* 340: 715 – 718.

Paré, D., Steriade, M., Deschenes, M. and Bouhassira, D. (1990) Prolonged enhancement of anterior thalamic synaptic responsiveness by stimulation of a brain-stem cholinergic group. *J. Neurosci.,* 10: 20 – 33.

Ramos, A., Schwartz, E.L. and John, E.R. (1976) Stable and plastic unit discharges patterns during behavioral generalization. *Science,* 192: 393 – 396.

Rucker, H.K., Corbus, M.J. and Pirch, J.H. (1986) Discriminative conditioning-related slow potential and single unit responses in frontal cortex of urethane-anesthetized rats. *Brain Res.,* 376: 368 – 372.

Schwartzbaum, J.S. (1975) Interrelationship among multi-unit activity of the midbrain reticular formation and lateral geniculate nucleus, thalamocortical arousal, and behavior in rats. *J. Comp. Physiol. Psychol.,* 89: 131 – 157.

Sherman, S.M. and Koch, C. (1986) The control of retinogeniculate transmission in the mammalian lateral geniculate nucleus. *Exp. Brain Res.,* 63: 1 – 20.

Singer, W. (1977) Control of thalamic transmission by corticofugal and ascending reticular pathways in the visual system. *Physiol. Rev.,* 57: 386 – 420.

Steriade, M., Paré, D., Hu, B. nd Deschenes, M. (1990) The visual thalamocortical system and its modulation by the brain stem core. In: D. Ottoson (Ed.), *Progress in Sensory Physiology, Vol. 10,* Springer, Berlin, 122 pp.

Woody, C.D., Schwartz, B.E. and Gruen, E. (1978) Effects of acetylcholine and cyclic GMP on input resistance of cortical neurons in awake cats. *Brain Res.,* 158: 373 – 395.

Woolf, N.J. and Butcher, L.L. (1986) Cholinergic systems in the rat brain: III. Projections from the pontomesencephalic tegmentum, tectum, basal ganglia and basal forebrain. *Brain Res. Bull.,* 16: 603 – 637.

Yoshida, M., Sasa, M. and Takaori, S. (1984) Serotonin-mediated inhibition from dorsal raphe nucleus of neurons in dorsal lateral geniculate and thalamic reticular nuclei. *Brain Res.,* 290: 95 – 105.

T.P. Hicks, S. Molotchnikoff and T. Ono (Eds.)
Progress in Brain Research, Vol. 95
© 1993 Elsevier Science Publishers B.V. All rights reserved.

CHAPTER 25

The properties of the long-term potentiation (LTP) in the superior colliculus

Yasuhiro Okada

Department of Physiology, School of Medicine, Kobe University, Kobe 650, Japan

Introduction

In 1973 Bliss and Lømo (1973) discovered the phenomenon of long-term potentiation (LTP) in the hippocampus of the rabbit which was maintained for long periods after tetanic stimulation. LTP formation is interpreted to be a substantial increase in synaptic efficacy. The phenomenon has attracted great interest because of the possibility that LTP might underlie some aspect of memory storage. For this reason, research findings on the formation of LTP in the mammalian brain have mainly come from studies of the hippocampus (Teyler and Discenna, 1987; Collingridge and Bliss, 1987; Lynch et al., 1990).

On the other hand, it has been suggested that LTP might represent a general synaptic plasticity for modifying synapses throughout the brain. If that is so, it would be expected that LTP could be reliably recorded in many parts of the central and peripheral nervous systems. Besides the hippocampus, the LTP phenomenon has been observed in several areas of cerebral cortex (Komatsu et al., 1981; Voronin, 1985; Kimura et al., 1989; Artola et al., 1990), the limbic forebrain (Racine et al., 1983), the medial geniculate body (Gerren and Weinberger, 1983) and the deep cerebellar nuclei (Racine et al., 1986). LTP also has been observed in non-mammalian neural tissue such as gold fish tectum (Lewis and Teyler, 1986). However, the properties and mechanism of LTP in tissues other than the hippocampus have not been studied extensively.

We have reported LTP formation in the superficial grey layer (SGL) of the superior colliculus (SC) in in vitro (Okada, 1989; Okada and Miyamoto, 1989; Miyamoto et al., 1990) and in vivo (Shibata et al., 1990) preparations. This paper reports some properties of the LTP in the SGL of the SC.

Preparation of SC slices

To prepare SC slices from the adult guinea pig and the rat, tissue blocks of the SC were dissected out from the brain-stem and cut parasagitally into slices of between 400 and 500 μm thickness as shown schematically in Fig. 1. The postsynaptic potential (PSP) was recorded from the SGL after stimulation of the optic layer (OL). It is important that cutting must be done slightly oblique using the fibre input of the optic nerve as a guide. Cross-section cutting of SC does not result in good recording of the PSP. The electrical activity has been recorded previously from the surface of SC slices in horizontal thin sections after stimulation of the optic nerve (Kawai and Yamamoto, 1969; Okada and Saito, 1979). However, in such experiments, only two slices could be prepared from each animal. In the slice preparation used here, cutting the SC sagitally allowed us to produce ten slices from one animal. Using this preparation, recording and stimulating sites within the laminated SC were easily visualized. The potentials elicited in the SGL after stimulation of the OL

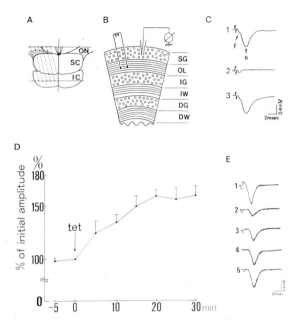

Fig. 1. Schematic drawing of the experimental arrangements using slice of the superior colliculus (SC) and the long-term potentiation evoked in the superficial grey layer (SGL) of the SC. *A.* A block of the brain-stem containing the superior and inferior colliculus. The superior colliculus was cut sagittally into half at the centre. Five to six slices were obtained from each SC. It is important that the slices must be cut at a slightly oblique angle using the fibre input of the optic nerve as a guide. Cross-section slices of the SC do not result in good recordings of the PSP. *B.* The arrangement of the recording and stimulating electrodes. *C* (1). Two kinds of negative potential in the control response. Note the earlier deflection (f) in the declining phase of the large potential (s). *C* (2). Ten minutes after removal of Ca^{2+} from the standard medium, the large potential (s) was abolished but not the earlier response (f). The early response (deflection) can now be seen clearly. *C* (3). The recovery of the later potential 10 min after reintroduction of Ca^{2+} into the perfusion medium. *D.* The time course of the LTP formation in the SGL. In the figure the adjusted amplitude of PSP as shown in *E* (2) was taken as 100%. At tet, the tetanic stimulation was applied to the optic layer (OL). Each plot is the average obtained from six slices. *E.* One of the distinct examples of the LTP formation elicited in the SGL after the tetanic stimulation to OL. *E* (1). PSP evoked by the supramaximal stimulation. *E* (2). The stimulation was adjusted to evoke PSP for the amplitude to be about 1/3 of the maximal amplitude. *E* (3) (4) and (5). PSP 10, 15 and 20 min after the tetanic stimulation. Abbreviations: ON, optic nerve; SC, superior colliculus; IC, inferior colliculus; SG, superficial grey layer; OL, optic layer; IG, intermediate grey layer; IW, intermediate white layer; DG, deep gray layer; DW, deep white layer.

or optic nerve are composed of two responses, an early potential (Fig. 1*C* − f) and a late potential (Fig. 1*C* − s). The late component was reduced by high frequency stimulation and was completely blocked in Ca^{2+}-free medium, although the early potential was not affected. These results indicate that the late negative field potential with high amplitude represents the PSP. As the intracellular recording study of the SGL neuron has not been performed, it cannot be determined whether or not the PSP represents EPSP or population spikes, but it may represent the population spikes because the repetitive extracellular unitary discharges were often superposed on the negative field potential.

The PSP recorded in SGL after OL stimulation should be retinotectal in origin. In this slice preparation, preserving the fibre running from the optic nerve, the corticotectal fibre coming into the superior colliculus from the medial side might be cut off because of the direction of the sagittal sections of the slice (Fig. 1*A*). The PSP could also be evoked by stimulation of the optic nerve as well as the OL. Slices prepared 14 days after denervation of retinotectal or corticotectal inputs to SGL of the SC indicated that the PSP of the SGL in this preparation is caused by retinotectal activation because degeneration of retinotectal fibres failed to induce the PSP of the slices whereas degeneration caused by ablation of visual cortex ipsilateral to SC did not influence the appearance of the PSP (Miyamoto et al., 1990).

Transmitter of retinotectal pathway

The excitatory transmitter in the corticotectal pathway has been thought to be glutamate (Fosse and Fonnum, 1986; Karlsen and Fonnum, 1978). On the other hand the transmitter of retinotectal input has still been under discussion (Fosse and Fonnum, 1986; Sandberg and Corazi, 1983). However, our physiological and biochemical studies (Sakurai et al., 1990; Miyamoto et al., 1990) showed that the retinotectal pathway can also be glutamatergic in nature. In slice preparations of guinea pig and rat, the PSP amplitude was reduced or blocked by application of kynurenate or quinoline dion (DNQX) to the medium. The concentration of glutamate in the right SGL was significantly reduced by 32% 14 days after left optic tract denervation compared with that in the left SGL, although the concentrations of GABA and aspartate in the SGL were not reduced (Fig. 2).

LTP formation in the SGL

Tetanic stimulation to the OL induced the long-lasting increase of the amplitude of the PSP and elicited the LTP. Fig. 1E shows one of the distinct examples of LTP formation in SGL. After obtaining the maximum response in the amplitude of the PSP, the stimulus intensity was adjusted to evoke a PSP with an amplitude of about 1/3 of the maximum amplitude, and tetanic stimulation (50 Hz frequency, 20 sec duration) was applied to the OL through the same electrode as test stimulus. In this case the PSP was increased even to 230% of the initial amplitude 20 min after tetanic stimulation. Fig. 1D shows the time course of the LTP formation in the SGL after OL stimulation. To determine the most effective parameters for inducing LTP, tetanic stimulation at 50 Hz, 100 Hz or 200 Hz for 1, 5, 10, 20 or 30 sec in duration was applied to the OL. Among these combinations of frequency and duration of the tetanus, the stimulation of 50 Hz in frequency and 20 sec in duration was found to be most effective for the induction of LTP.

LTP in SGL and the NMDA receptor

In the hippocampus, it has been reported that the NMDA receptor, a subtype of the glutamate receptors, is involved in the induction of LTP (Harris et al., 1984; Wigstrom and Gustafsson, 1984; Morris et al., 1986; Collingridge and Bliss, 1987). Actually, the removal of Mg^{2+} from the medium facilitated the formation of LTP in the SC (Miyamoto et al., 1990) and suggested, as observed in the hippocampus, the involvement of NMDA receptor channels for the LTP formation in the SC. To test this possibility in the SC slices, glutamate receptor or

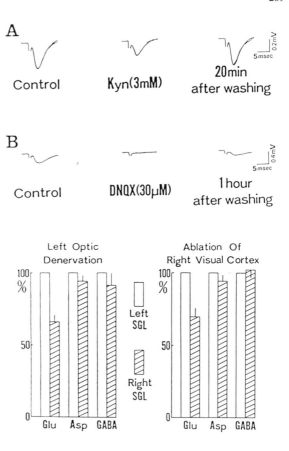

Fig. 2. Effect of kynurenic acid (Kyn) or DNQX on the PSP in the SC slice and the effect of the left optic denervation or ablation of the right visual cortex on the level of glutamate, aspartate and GABA concentrations in the left and right SGL. Upper panel: control indicates the PSP induced in the SGL by electrical stimulation to the OL. Kyn at a concentration of 3 mM (A) and DNQX at 30 μM (B) were applied to the perfusion medium. Kyn reversibly reduced the amplitude of the PSP by 50%, but DNQX completely blocked the PSP and even at 1 h after removal of the agent, only partial recovery in the amplitude was observed. Lower panel: fourteen days after the surgical operation (denervation), only the SGL fragments of the SC slices were excised under a stereomicroscope and the concentrations of the neurotransmitters were determined in the tissue. In the left panel (left optic denervation), the concentrations of Glu, Asp, and GABA in the left SGL (open histogram) were 71.1 ± 6.8, 26.5 ± 3.1, and 75.1 ± 8.5 mmol/kg protein, respectively. In the right panel (ablation of the right visual cortex), the concentrations of Glu, Asp, and GABA in the left SGL (open histogram) were 73.5 ± 5.9, 27.4 ± 3.5, and 71.5 ± 12.0 mmol/kg protein, respectively. These values are the mean concentrations of the left SGL fragments obtained from five animals. The concentrations of the neurotransmitters in the left SGL were regarded as 100%.

channel antagonists such as 2-amino-5-methyl-10,11-dihydro-5H-dibenzo a,d cyclohepten-5, 10-imine maleate (MK-801), γ-D-glutamylglycine (γ-DGG), 2-amino-4-phosphonobutyrate (APB), and glutamate diethylester (GDEE), were applied to the medium and the effect of these agents on the LTP formation was studied.

During application of 100 μM of D-APV, tetanic stimulation (50 Hz and 20 sec) to the ÓL did not increase the amplitude of the response from that of the original level before tetanic stimulation and inhibited the appearance of LTP. However, when APV was removed from the medium, the amplitude of the PSP was increased to 170% of the control value in 20 min (Fig. 3A). This masking effect of APV on the appearance of LTP was observed when APV was washed out even 80 min after the tetanic stimulation. In this case the application of D-APV even at a dose of 500 μM did not alter the amplitude of the PSP evoked by the test stimulus. The application of γ-DGG at a concentration of 1 mM also inhibited the appearance of LTP, but after the removal of the agent from the medium, the phenomenon of LTP appeared as mentioned above in the case of APV. On the other hand the MK-801 (1 μM) inhibited irreversibly the induction of LTP. GDEE or APB at a concentration of 1 mM did not eliminate the appearance of LTP, even though they reduced slightly the amplitude of PSP itself evoked by the test stimulus. The inhibition of LTP appearance by application of D-APV (100 μM), γ-DGG (1 mM) and MK-801 (1 μM) in this experiment suggests that the NMDA receptor can be involved in the process of the expression of LTP in the SGL.

Concerning the masking effect of APV and γ-DGG on the appearance of LTP, it could be speculated that even during application of D-APV, tetanic stimulation caused the modification of synaptic plasticity for the induction of LTP such as the increase of neurotransmitter release or the induction of morphological and biochemical changes at the synapse, even though the LTP phenomenon could not be observed because of the blocking of the NMDA receptor, and that removal of the inhibition by the NMDA antagonist may allow the NMDA

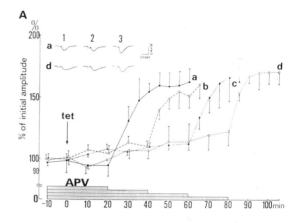

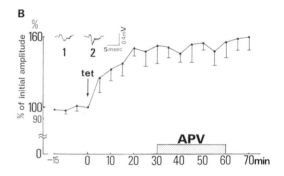

Fig. 3. Effect of D-APV (100 μM) on the LTP formation in the SC slices. In *A* tetanic stimulation was given during application of APV and in *B* APV was applied after the formation of LTP. In *A*, 10 min after the application of D-APV, tetanic stimulation was applied to the optic layer. During application of D-APV, the PSP amplitude evoked by the test stimulus was not significantly altered but tetanic stimulation failed to induce the LTP in the SGL. Insets (a-1) and (d-1) show the PSP obtained immediately before the application of tetanic stimulation in the curves (a) and (d), respectively. The perfusion period of D-APV after tetanic stimulation (tet) was fixed for 20 min (a, ●–●), 40 min (b, ○–○), 60 min (c, ▲–▲), and 80 min (d, □–□). Inset (a-2) shows the PSP obtained immediately before removal of D-APV in (a). The amplitude of the PSP was potentiated to about 160% of the initial amplitude after removal of the agent in each case (a–d) and the LTP-like phenomenon was clearly observed. Insets (a-3) and (d-3) show the potentiated PSP obtained 25 min after removal of D-APV in (a) and (d), respectively. Note that the amplitude of the PSP gradually increased in the perfusate containing D-APV following the tetanic stimulation in (b–d), and reached to about 120% of the initial amplitude immediately before removal of D-APV in (d) (inset d-2). Each plot indicates the mean amplitude (± S.E.M.) of the PSP obtained from five SC slices. In *B* D-APV (100 μM) was applied to the medium 30 min after the tetanic stimulation and after the LTP was formed.

receptor to induce LTP. It should be noted that once LTP was formed, the increase in the response was not inhibited by the application of D-APV (100 μM) (Fig. 3B). This indicates that NMDA channels may be involved in the appearance of LTP but do not seem to contribute to the primary induction and the maintenance of LTP. The same kind of masking effect for the LTP formation was also observed in the hippocampus in which γ-DGG masked the appearance of LTP in the perforant path (Dolphin, 1983). The irreversible inhibition of MK-801 for the LTP induction may be due to the possibility that this non-competitive NMDA antagonist cannot be easily washed out.

LTP in SGL and the protein kinase C

It has been proposed that in the hippocampus protein kinase C (PKC) plays a crucial role in the acquisition and the maintenance of LTP (Routtenberg, 1985; Lovinger et al., 1987; Malenka et al., 1987). In the superior colliculus slice, phorbol ester (PhEs), a PKC activator, enhanced the PSP response itself at concentrations between 0.1 μM and 0.1 nM. In this enhanced condition, the LTP could not be evoked by tetanic stimulation in the presence of PhEs. The tetanic stimulation (50 Hz, 10 sec) with which LTP could not be induced under normal conditions could evoke LTP in SGL under the application of PhEs at a concentration of 30 pM at which the PSP amplitude itself was not enhanced (Tomita et al., 1990).

On the other hand, PKC inhibitors polymixine B (0.1 μM), H-7 (100 μM) and K-252a (50 nM) eliminated the formation of LTP (Fig. 4A), but H-8, a PKA inhibitor (100 μM), did not eliminate it. The application of these agents themselves did not reduce the amplitude of PSP by the test stimulus. It is interesting that the enhanced amplitude of PSP after LTP formation reversibly decreased to the original level during the application of H-7 (Fig. 4B). These results suggest that a PKC system is involved for the maintenance of LTP in the SC. On the other hand, the NMDA receptor may relate to the earlier period of LTP formation, because the ap-

plication of APV did not influence the enhanced amplitude of PSP after tetanic stimulation (Fig. 3B).

LTP in the SGL and γ-aminobutyric acid (GABA)

It has been reported that the SC contains high amounts of GABA and especially the SGL of SC contains the highest amount of GABA (40 mmol/kg dry) and the highest GAD activity (239 mmol produced GABA/kg dry per hour) in the mammalian brain (Okada et al., 1971; Okada, 1974, 1976, 1980;

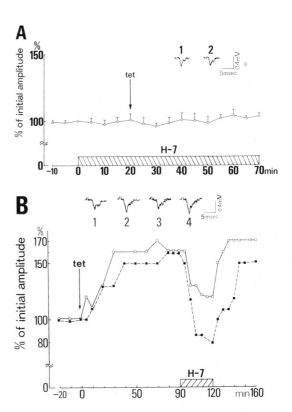

Fig. 4. Effect of H-7, a protein kinase C inhibitor on the LTP formation in the SGL of SC slices. A. During application of H-7 (100 μM) in the perfusion medium, tetanic stimulation was applied to the OL. These results were obtained from an average of five slices. B. Two examples showing the effect of H-7 (100 μM) on the PSP amplitude after the formation of LTP by tetanic stimulation. In the upper inserted figures, (1) and (2) show the PSP 10 min before and 50 min after the tetanic stimulation, (3) shows the PSP during application of H-7 and (4) after removal of H-7.

Kanno and Okada, 1988; Arakawa and Okada, 1988). GABA concentrations and GAD activity in the other layers of the SC ranged from 30 to 50% of those in the SGL.

The SC receives a substantial input from the visual cortex and retina as well as from other nuclei in the brain-stem (Lund and Lund, 1971; Sprague, 1975; Vincent et al., 1978; Wurtz and Albano, 1980; Karabelas and Moschovakis, 1985; Hikosaka and Wurz, 1985). Fibres from the retina and visual cortex terminate in the SGL and optic layers in an orderly and precise fashion. Physiological studies have revealed that both retinal and cortical projections have interactions on the SGL neurons of the superior colliculus and that retinal-evoked responses in the SGL are inhibited by the conditioning stimulus on the visual cortex. An identical inhibitory phenomenon is produced in the cortical-evoked response by optic tract stimulation and this inhibitory process can be mediated by a single mechanism, intrinsic to the colliculus and postsynaptic in nature (McIlwain and Fields, 1971). The SC on one side also exerts an inhibition on the contralateral tectum. To investigate whether the large amount of GABA in the SGL is contained in the afferent fibres terminating in the SC or originates intrinsically within interneurons, three major inputs to the SC of the rabbit were destroyed. In one group, the left visual cortex was ablated; in another group, the left optic nerve was transected just behind the eyeball; in a third group, the SC commissure was cut by knife. The GABA level and GAD activity in the SGL were determined in each animal 12 days after these surgical operations. No decrease in GABA content and GAD activity in the SGL was found by comparison with that of unoperated controls (Okada, 1974, 1992). These results indicate that the GABA concentrated in the SGL is probably intrinsic to the layer and likely contained within interneurons in the SGL.

Numerous histological and immunohistochemical studies have indicated the existence of GABAergic interneurons in the SGL (Mize et al., 1981, 1982; Mize, 1988). Cajal Ramon (1955) designated the upper SGL the "zone of horizontal cells" and the lower SGL the "zone of vertical fusiform cells". Mize showed that 45% of the SGL neurons and 30% of the intermediate grey neurons in the cat SC are GABA-immunoreactive (Mize, 1988). Electron microscopic studies have also shown that there exist many nerve terminals with flattened type vesicles in the SGL of the rat (Lund, 1969; Lund and Lund, 1971). These observations suggest that the inhibitory interaction of cortical and retinal projections on SGL neurons (McIlwain and Fields, 1971) can be mediated by intrinsic GABAergic interneurons.

On the other hand, in the slice preparation of the SC, GABA showed excitatory and inhibitory biphasic effects according to the concentrations applied (Arakawa and Okada, 1987, 1988). GABA ($5 \times 10^{-4} \sim 10^{-3}$ M) and muscimol ($10^{-6} \sim 10^{-5}$ M) enhanced the amplitude of PSP evoked in the SGL of the SC slice and they inhibited the PSP at higher concentrations. In this connection it must be worth while to investigate the effects of the GABA at different concentrations on the LTP formations in the SGL. GABA at concentrations of 3×10^{-4} M, 1×10^{-3} M and 3×10^{-3} M were applied to the perfusate. Application of GABA at the concentration of 3×10^{-4} M and 1×10^{-3} M increased the amplitude of the PSP elicited by test stimulation by $20-40\%$ and GABA at 3×10^{-3} M did not influence the amplitude evoked by test shock. Tetanic stimulation to the OL failed to induce LTP in all three cases and GABA inhibited the formation of LTP (Fig. 5B). Bicuculline methiodide (BM), a GABA$_A$ receptor antagonist, was applied to the perfusate. In the PSP of SGL, BM at concentrations greater than 10 μM elicited a long-lasting negative wave following the sharp negative wave of PSP which was recorded in the standard medium. To test the effect of BM on the LTP formation, 1 μM BM was applied because it did not influence the PSP nor did it evoke the long-lasting negative wave. Tetanic stimulation in this condition facilitated the formation of LTP, and the increase in the amplitude of PSP 15 min after tetanus was significantly higher than that of the control slices incubated in the standard medium (Fig. 5A). Thus application of GABA depressed the LTP formation whereas GABA antagonist facilitated it.

LTP in in vivo preparation

To test the LTP induction in the rat in in vivo preparation, the PSP was recorded on the surface of SGL after stimulation of the optic nerve in which tungsten electrodes were inplanted (Fig. 6A). It was extremely difficult to induce LTP in the PSP by tetanic stimulation in this in vivo preparation. However, LTP was only elicited by tetanic stimula-

tion either when the visual cortical area ipsilateral to the SGL tested was ablated (Fig. 6) or when picrotoxin, a chloride channel blocker was administered to the animal before tetanic stimulation (Shibata et al., 1990).

Concerning the involvement of GABAergic neurons for the modification of the LTP formation, application of bicuculline and picrotoxin facilitates the induction of LTP in hippocampal slices (Wigstrom and Gustafsson, 1985), and for LTP studies of slice preparation bicuculline is usually applied to the medium to simplify the induction of

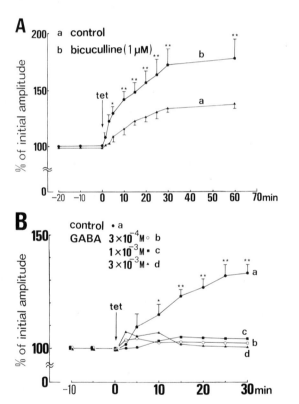

Fig. 5. Effect of GABA and bicuculline on the LTP formation of SC slices. In A, (a) shows the LTP elicited in the standard medium and (b) the LTP formation in the medium containing bicuculline (1 µM). In B, GABA was applied to the perfusion medium at concentrations of 0 (a), 3×10^{-4} M (b), 1×10^{-3} M (c), and 3×10^{-3} M (d) and tetanic stimulation was applied. In the plots of (b), (c) and (d) the S.E.M. were not shown in the figure but they were within 8% of the average value. Asterisks in the figures indicate statistically significant differences (ANOVA with Fisher's least-significant test) between (a) and (b) in A and between (a) and (b), (c) or (d) in B. (** $P < 0.01$, * $P < 0.05$).

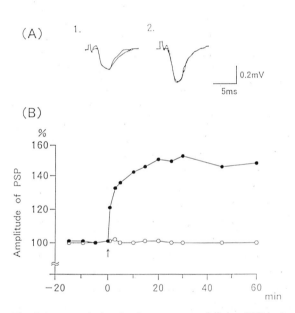

Fig. 6. An example showing the occurrence of distinct LTP in the SC after ablation of the ipsilateral visual cortex of the in vivo preparation of the rat. Before the experiment, the right visual cortical area was aspirated. The postsynaptic field potential was recorded at the surface of the right SC after stimulation of the optic nerve. Stimulus intensity was adjusted to obtain the surface negative wave whose amplitude was one-third of the maximum (evoked by the supramaximal stimulation). The line with closed circles in B shows example of LTP formation. Tetanic stimulation (100 Hz, 10 sec) was applied at the arrow. The line with the open circles represents the case in which no tetanic stimulation was applied. In the inserted figures at the top, A (1) and A (2) are the potentials just before and 20 min after tetanic stimulation. The amplitude was measured from the peak of the negativity to the baseline. In the bottom figure, the amplitude just before the addition of tetanic stimulation was taken as 100%.

LTP (Kimura et al., 1989). In slices of the visual cortex, application of low doses of bicuculline induces long-term depression by tetanic stimulation whereas bicuculline at high doses elicits LTP (Artola et al., 1990). The induction of LTP may thus be influenced by the excitability or the level of membrane potential of postsynaptic neurons which is modulated by GABAergic input.

The involvement of an extrinsic GABAergic afferent to SC such as nigro-collicular projection is not completely excluded for the modulation of the LTP formation in the SGL. However, it should be noted that the ablation of the ipsilateral visual cortical area and also the application of picrotoxin in the presence of ipsilateral visual cortex facilitated the formation of LTP in vivo preparations. The ipsilateral corticotectal pathways have been reported to exert an inhibitory action on the neural activity evoked by the retinotectal pathway (McIlwain and Fields, 1971). As discussed above, this inhibition is probably mediated by GABAergic interneurons located in the SGL because the corticotectal pathway is glutamatergic (Fosse and Fonnum, 1986; Sakurai et al., 1990) and many GABAergic interneurons located in the SGL receive corticotectal synapses (Mize, 1988). In the isolated slice preparations of the SC in which corticotectal fibres are cut as mentioned before, LTP can be easily induced by tetanic stimulation and the formation of LTP is modified by GABA agonists and antagonists. These results strongly suggest that corticotectal afferents tonically inhibit the induction of LTP elicited by tetanic stimulation of the optic nerve, probably activating GABAergic interneurons within the SGL. This ability of neurons to induce LTP in the SC may depend upon the delicate balance between excitatory and inhibitory inputs through the retinotectal, corticotectal or other extrinsic pathways.

The SC plays an important role in the integration of visual auditory and somatosensory inputs and control of eye movement. Clarification of the mechanism of synaptic plasticity within the SC would provide information on the role of LTP of the SC in visuo-motor integration. The true mechanism and function of LTP formation in the SGL of the SC in vivo and in vitro preparations remains to be investigated in further studies.

Summary and conclusions

(1) Postsynaptic potential (PSP) was recorded in the SGL of guinea pig SC slices after stimulation to the OL.

(2) Tetanic stimulation (optimum parameter: 50 Hz in frequency, 20 sec in duration) to the OL induced LTP in the PSP of SGL.

(3) NMDA-receptor antagonist MK801 inhibited the LTP occurrence but D-APV and γ-DGG masked the appearance of LTP, suggesting that the mode of involvement of the NMDA receptor for LTP formation in the SC may be different from that reported in the hippocampus.

(4) Protein kinase C inhibitors such as H-7, polymixine B and K-252a inhibited the maintenance of LTP.

(5) Application of GABA prevented the occurrence of LTP and bicuculline facilitated the formation of LTP.

(6) In in vivo preparations of the rat, the LTP in the SC was only elicited by tetanic stimulation to the optic nerve either when the visual cortical area ipsilateral to the SC tested was ablated or when picrotoxin was administered to the animal before tetanic stimulation.

References

Arakawa, T. and Okada, Y. (1987) Dual effect of γ-aminobutyric acid (GABA) on neurotransmission in the superior colliculus slices from the guinea pig. *Proc. Jpn. Acad., Ser. B,* 63: 389 – 392.

Arakawa, T. and Okada, Y. (1988) Excitatory and inhibitory action of GABA on synaptic transmission in slices of guinea pig superior colliculus. *Eur. J. Pharmacol.,* 158: 217 – 224.

Artola, A., Brocher, S. and Singer, W. (1990) Different voltage-dependent thresholds for inducing long-term depression and long-term potentiation in slices of rat visual cortex. *Nature,* 347: 69 – 72.

Bliss, T.V.P. and Lømo, T.J. (1973) Long-lasting potentiation of synaptic transmission in the dentate area of the anesthetized rabbit following stimulation of the perforant path. *J. Physiol. (Lond.),* 232: 331 – 356.

Cajal, S. Ramón, Y. (1955) *Histologie du Système Nerveux de l'Homme et des Vertèbres, Vol. 2,* Consejo, Superior de Investigaciones Cientificas, Institute Ramon Cajal, Madrid.

Collingridge, G.L. and Bliss, T.V.P. (1987) NMDA receptors – their role in long-term potentiation. *Trends Neurosci.,* 10: 288 – 293.

Dolphin, A.C. (1983) The excitatory amino acid antagonist gamma-D-glutamyl glycine masks rather than prevents long-term potentiation of the perforant path. *Neuroscience,* 10: 377 – 383.

Fosse, V.M. and Fonnum, F. (1986) Effects of kainic acid and other excitotoxins in the rat superior colliculus: relations to glutamatergic afferents. *Brain Res.,* 383: 28 – 37.

Gerren, R.A. and Weinberger, N.M. (1983) Long-term potentiation in the magnocellular medial geniculate nucleus of the anesthetized cat. *Brain Res.,* 265: 138 – 142.

Harris, E.W., Ganong, A.H. and Cotman, C.W. (1984) Long-term potentiation in the hippocampus involves activation of N-methyl-D-aspartate receptors. *Brain Res.,* 323: 132 – 137.

Hikosaka, O. and Wurtz, R.H. (1985) Modification of saccadic eye movements by GABA-related substances. I. Effect of muscimol and bicuculline in monkey superior colliculus. *J. Neurophysiol.,* 53: 266 – 291.

Kanno, S. and Okada, Y. (1988) Laminar distribution of GABA (γ-aminobutyric acid) in the dorsal lateral geniculate nucleus, area 17 and area 18 of the visual cortex, and the superior colliculus of the cat. *Brain Res.,* 451: 172 – 178.

Karabelas, A.B. and Moschovakis, A.K. (1985) Nigral inhibitory termination on efferent neurons of the superior colliculus: an intracellular horseradish peroxidase study in the cat. *J. Comp. Neurol.,* 239: 309 – 329.

Karlsen, R.L. and Fonnum, F. (1978) Evidence for glutamate as a neurotransmitter in the corticofugal fibers to the dorsal geniculate body and the superior colliculus in rats. *Brain Res.,* 151: 457 – 467.

Kawai, N. and Yamamoto, C. (1969) Effect of 5-hydroxytryptamine, LSD and related compounds on electrical activities evoked in vitro in thin slices from the superior colliculus. *Int. J. Neuropharmacol.,* 8: 437 – 449.

Kimura, F., Nishigori, A., Shirokawa, T. and Tsumoto, T. (1989) Long-term potentiation and N-methyl-D-aspartate receptors in the visual cortex of young rats. *J. Physiol. (Lond.),* 414: 125 – 144.

Komatsu, Y., Toyama, K., Maeda, J. and Sakaguchi, H. (1981) Long-term potentiation investigated in a slice preparation of striate cortex of young kittens. *Neurosci. Lett.,* 26: 269 – 274.

Lewis, D. and Teyler, T.J. (1986) Long-term potentiation in the goldfish optic tectum. *Brain Res.,* 375: 246 – 250.

Lovinger, D.M., Wong, K.L., Murakami, K. and Routtenberg, A. (1987) Protein kinase C inhibitors eliminate hippocampal long-term potentiation. *Brain Res.,* 436: 177 – 183.

Lund, R.D. (1969) Synaptic patterns of the superficial layers of the superior colliculus of the rat. *J. Comp. Neurol.,* 135: 1283 – 1285.

Lund, R.D. and Lund, J.S. (1971) Modifications of synaptic patterns in the superior colliculus of the rat during development and following deafferentation. *Vision Res.* (Suppl.), 3: 281 – 298.

Lynch, G., Markus, K., Arai, A. and Larson, J. (1990) The nature and causes of hippocampal long-term potentiation. In: J. Storm-Mathisen, J. Zimner and O.P. Ottersen (Eds.), *Progress in Brain Research, Vol. 83,* Elsevier, Amsterdam, pp. 233 – 250.

Malenka, R.C., Ayoub, G.S. and Nicoll, R.A. (1987) Phorbol esters enhance transmitter release in rat hippocampal slices. *Brain Res.,* 403: 198 – 203.

McIlwain, J.T. and Fields, H.L. (1971) Interactions of cortical and retinal projections of single neurons of the cat's superior colliculus. *J. Neurophysiol.,* 34: 763 – 772.

Miyamoto, T. and Okada, Y. (1988) Effective stimulation parameters for the LTP formation in the superior colliculus slices from the guinea pig. *Proc. Jpn. Acad., Ser. B,* 64: 256 – 259.

Miyamoto, T., Sakurai, T. and Okada, Y. (1990) Masking effect of NMDA receptor antagonists on the formation of long-term potentiation (LTP) in superior colliculus slices from the guinea pig. *Brain Res.,* 518: 166 – 172.

Mize, R.R. (1988) Immunocytochemical localization of gamma-aminobutyric acid (GABA) in the cat superior colliculus. *J. Comp. Neurol.,* 276: 169 – 187.

Mize, R.R., Spencer, R.F. and Sterling, P. (1981) Neurons and glia in cat superior colliculus accumulate [^{3}H]-gamma-aminobutyric acid (GABA). *J. Comp. Neurol.,* 202: 385 – 396.

Mize, R.R., Spencer, R.F. and Sterling, P. (1982) Two types of GABA-accumulating neurons in the superficial gray layer of the cat superior colliculus. *J. Comp. Neurol.,* 206: 180 – 192.

Morris, R.G.M., Anderson, E., Lynch, G.S. and Bandry, M. (1986) Selective impairment of learning and blockade of long-term potentiation by an N-methyl-D-aspartate receptor antagonist, AP5. *Nature,* 319: 774 – 776.

Okada, Y. (1974) Distribution of γ-aminobutyric acid (GABA) in the layers of superior colliculus of the rabbit. *Brain Res.,* 75: 362 – 365.

Okada, Y. (1976) Distribution of GABA and GAD activity in the layers of superior colliculus of the rabbit. In: E. Roberts, T.N. Chase and D.B. Tower (Eds.), *GABA in Nervous System Function,* Raven Press, New York, pp. 229 – 233.

Okada, Y. (1980) Regional distribution of GABA (γ-aminobutyric acid), GAD (glutamate decarboxylase), GABA-T (GABA-transaminase) and glutamate in the rat central nervous system. In: M. Ito (Ed.), *Integrative Control Function of Brain, III,* Kodansha, Tokyo, pp. 26 – 28.

Okada, Y. (1989) Long-term potentiation in the superior colliculus slices. In: H. Rahmann (Ed.), *Fortschritte der Zoologie. Progress in Zoology, Vol. 37 – Fundamentals of Memory Formation: Neuronal Plasticity and Brain Function,* Gustav Fischer Verlag, Stuttgart, New York, pp. 190 – 196.

Okada, Y. (1992) The distribution and function of γ-

296

aminobutyric acid (GABA) in the superior colliculus. In: R.R. Mize, R.E. Marc and A.H. Sillito (Eds.), *Mechanism of GABA in the Visual System – Progress in Brain Research, Vol. 90,* Elsevier, Amsterdam, pp. 249–262.

Okada, Y. and Miyamoto, T. (1989) Formation of long-term potentiation in superior colliculus slices from the guinea pig. *Neurosci. Lett.,* 96: 108–113.

Okada, Y. and Saito, M. (1979) Inhibitory action of adenosine, 5-HT (serotonin) and GABA (γ-aminobutyric acid) on the postsynaptic potential (PSP) of slices from olfactory cortex and superior colliculus in correlation to the level of cyclic AMP. *Brain Res.,* 160: 368–371.

Okada, Y., Nitsch-Hassler, C., Kim, J.S., Bak, I.J. and Hassler, R. (1971) Role of γ-aminobutyric acid (GABA) in the extrapyramidal motor system, I. Regional distribution of GABA in rabbit, rat, guinea pig and baboon CNS. *Exp. Brain Res.,* 13: 514–518.

Racine, R.J., Milgram, N.W. and Hafner, S. (1983) Long-term potentiation phenomena in the rat limbic forebrain. *Brain Res.,* 260: 217–231.

Racine, R.J., Wilson, D.A., Gingell, R. and Sunderland, D. (1986) Long-term potentiation in the interpositus and vestibular nuclei in the rat. *Exp. Brain Res.,* 63: 158–162.

Routtenberg, A. (1985) Protein kinase C activation leading to protein F_1 phosphorylation may regulate synaptic plasticity by presynaptic terminal growth. *Behav. Neural. Biol.,* 44: 186–200.

Sakurai, T., Miyamoto, T. and Okada, Y. (1990) Reduction of glutamate content in rat superior colliculus after retinotectal denervation. *Neurosci. Lett.,* 109: 299–303.

Sandberg, M. and Corazi, L. (1983) Release of endogenous amino acid from superior colliculus of the rabbit; in vitro studies after retinal ablation. *J. Neurochem.,* 40: 917–921.

Shibata, Y., Tomita, H. and Okada, Y. (1990) The effects of ablation of the visual cortical area on the formation of LTP in the superior colliculus of the rat. *Brain Res.,* 537: 345–348.

Sprague, J.M. (1975) Mammalian tectum: intrinsic organization, afferent inputs, and integrative mechanism. *Neurosci. Res. Prog. Bull.,* 13: 204–213.

Teyler, T.J. and Discenna, P. (1987) Long-term potentiation. *Annu. Rev. Neurosci.,* 10: 131–161.

Tomita, H., Shibata, Y., Sakurai, T. and Okada, Y. (1990) Involvement of a protein kinase C-dependent process in long-term potentiation formation in guinea pig superior colliculus slices. *Brain Res.,* 536: 146–152.

Vincent, S.R., Hattori, T. and McGeer, E.G. (1978) The nigrotectal projection: a biochemical and ultrastructural characterization. *Brain Res.,* 151: 159–164.

Voronin, L.L. (1985) Synaptic plasticity at archicortical and neocortical levels. *Neurofiziologiya,* 16: 651–665.

Wigstrom, H. and Gustafsson, B. (1984) A possible correlate of the synaptic condition for long-lasting potentiation in the guinea pig hippocampus in vitro. *Neurosci. Lett.,* 44: 327–332.

Wigstrom, H. and Gustafsson, B. (1985) Facilitation of hippocampal long-term potentiation by GABA antagonists. *Acta Physiol. Scand.,* 125: 159–172.

Wurtz, R.H. and Albano, J.E. (1980) Visual motor function of the primate superior colliculus. *Annu. Rev. Neurosci.,* 3: 189–226.

T.P. Hicks, S. Molotchnikoff and T. Ono (Eds.)
Progress in Brain Research, Vol. 95
© 1993 Elsevier Science Publishers B.V. All rights reserved.

CHAPTER 26

The nature of synaptic plasticity in the visual cortex of kittens. An electrophysiological analysis in vitro

T.P. Hicks and K.-I. Ito[1]

Departments of Biology and Psychology, 267 Bruce Eberhart Building, College of Arts and Sciences, The University of North Carolina at Greensboro, Greensboro, NC 27412 – 5001, U.S.A.

Introduction

Long-term potentiation (LTP) in the nervous system is a persistent enhancement of synaptic transmission induced by a short period of high frequency activation (known as a tetanus) of afferent fibres. Thus, the potentiated neurones exhibit a durable increased magnitude of response for periods of time on the order of hours or days, the process is localised to the set of neurones encompassing the stimulated elements, and the event displays characteristics of co-operativity and associativity: hence its close relationship with what is known about the salient features of memory and learning (Hebb, 1949; Gardner-Medwin, 1973; Andersen et al., 1977; McNaughton et al., 1978; Staubli and Lynch, 1990).

The early observations of Wiesel and Hubel (1965) in the developing visual system of cats provided the basis for subsequent investigations into such forms of synaptic plasticity in primary sensory neocortex, extending the initial investigations of LTP from hippocampus to neocortex. It is only in recent years, however (see reviews by Cynader et al., 1990; Tsumoto, 1990), that many of the molecular mechanisms underlying neocortical plasticity, and which are associated with Hebbian synaptic modification (Hebb, 1949) have begun to be understood. For example, one yet-to-be explained observation is that LTP in slices of visual cortex from kittens is considerably easier to elicit than it is in slices from mature animals (Kato et al., 1991); and this finding is in keeping with the data from deprivation studies (Wiesel and Hubel, 1965; Hubel and Wiesel, 1970).

This issue, and related other ones have been addressed in the present account, that describes experiments designed to investigate the factors leading to the expression of long-term synaptic plasticity in slices of visual cortex from kittens of various postnatal ages. We report here that low-intensity and low-frequency tetanic activation of the white matter underlying visual cortex in young animals, produces changes of certain electrophysiological measures recorded intracellularly, such as diminished EPSP amplitudes, long-lasting depolarisations of membrane potential and decreased threshold. These findings explain the rather paradoxical observation from our early studies, that post-tetanic synaptic responses measured from extracellular field potentials are *diminished* in amplitude, rather than enhanced.

Some of these data have been presented in preliminary form elsewhere (Hicks and Ito, 1991a,b).

---

[1] Present address: Department of Physiology, School of Medicine, Yamagata University, 2-2-2 Iida-Nishi, Yamagata 990-23, Japan.

Methods

The data set was collected from 16 kittens of both sexes, that ranged in age from 23 to 50 days. From these animals, recordings were obtained in 77 different slices, maintained viably in vitro for up to 20 h. Kittens were anaesthetised with pentobarbital sodium (35 mg/kg, i.p.) and a craniotomy was performed widely over the posterior pole of the skull. A block of occipital tissue about 10 × 15 mm was removed from the brain and quickly trimmed on an ice-cold, glass platform, in such a way as to preserve cortical area 17 and 18 and a significant amount of associated white matter. This block was cooled (4°C) for 5 min, the pia dissected away carefully and re-trimmed. The tissue was then placed on an agar stage and cut, in a carefully chosen plane intended to preserve if possible the columnar structure of the cortex, into 50 µm-thick slices on a Dosaka EM Co. rotory slicer (Ted Pella, Inc., Redding, CA) during submersion in 4 – 10°C, oxygenated (95% O_2, 5% CO_2) artificial cerebrospinal fluid (aCSF) of the following composition (in mM): NaCl 124, KCl 5.0, NaH_2PO_4 1.25, $MgSO_4$ 2.0, $CaCl_2$ 2.5, $NaHCO_3$ 26.0 and D-glucose 10. The slices were transferred to

an incubation chamber and kept at 30°C for at least 1 h prior to beginning the recording session to allow for tissue recovery from trauma and for ionic equilibration.

Slices were transferred to the recording chamber and placed submerged within the aCSF (ca. 100 µm below the surface), through which a constant stream of oxygenated gas was gently bubbled. Extracellular recordings of evoked cortical field potentials were made with glass micropipettes filled with aCSF having impedances of 2 – 10 MΩ, acquired with an Axoclamp (2A) device using 0.3 – 3.0 kHz signal filtration, electrodes placed approximately 150 µm below the cut surface of the submerged slices, in either layer II/III or IV. Each computer-stored wave form was a signal-averaged evoked potential generated by six successively sampled sweeps obtained at 0.1 Hz stimulating frequency. Stimulus intensity was selected on the basis of choosing the voltage necessary to elicit a potential approximately half the maximal. Bipolar, twisted platinum-iridium wires insulated except at the tips served as stimulating electrodes; these were placed at the base of the presumptive cortical columns, about 200 µm below the bottom of layer VI, in the white matter (Fig. 1).

Intracellular recordings were made with 3.0 M K^+-acetate-filled micropipettes of 60 – 110 MΩ impedance. Following suitable impalement of a neurone, resting potential was determined at periodic intervals (10 sec). To record membrane resistances, step-hyperpolarising pulses of 0.5 nA (10 msec) were delivered from the recording electrode. EPSPs were produced by the delivery of stimuli (0.2 msec duration and 80 – 200 µA intensity) to the bipolar electrode positioned in the white matter. Tetanic stimuli consisted of a 10 Hz train of pulses generated for 2 min; otherwise, each of the stimuli in the train was identical in intensity and duration to those used for generating EPSPs. Only those cells were subjected to a tetanus wherein no variance of membrane potential beyond a 1.0 mV maximum throughout a period of at least 15 min was noted. The intensity of the stimulus used for each cell was chosen on the basis of taking 80% of the intensity necessary to elicit an action potential. Signals

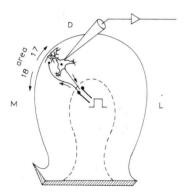

Fig. 1. Schematic depiction of the slice from visual cortex of a young kitten, showing the placements of the bipolar stimulating electrode (positioned below the white-gray matter interface) and the recording micropipette (positioned in lamina III), and indicating the afferent and efferent pathways activated by the stimulus. The parts of the cortical slice comprising areas 17 and 18 are indicated by arrows at left. D, dorsal; M, medial; L, lateral. See text for further details of the method for preparing the slices.

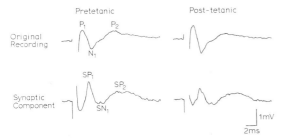

Fig. 2. The two traces of the top row illustrate samples of computer-averaged, extracellularly recorded field potentials before (left) and after (right) application of a tetanus (10 Hz, 2 min). P_1, N_1 and P_2 indicate the various peak amplitudes measured from the responses, with P representing positive-going waves and N the negative-going wave. Note the relatively larger amplitude after tetanus of the $P_1 - N_1$ component of the recording. The two traces of the bottom row illustrate computer-calculated wave forms following subtraction of the antidromic component of the original recording; this wave form represents the synaptic component of the original recording, minus contamination by Ca^{2+}-dependent non-synaptic events, with SP and SN representing synaptic positive and synaptic negative peak amplitudes, respectively.

were amplified and filtered between DC and 3.0 kHz, then were passed to a storage oscilloscope and to a 1401 A/D converter for relay to an IBM-PC 386 computer. Data were accepted only from cells displaying values of resting potential greater than 50 mV. EPSP amplitudes were assessed by measuring the voltage range between the peak value and the prestimulus level of membrane potential; manual clamping of the membrane was accomplished by hyperpolarising the cell just long enough to assess the EPSP amplitude following a single test shock.

Extracellularly recorded wave form

The potentials recorded from layers II/III and IV consisted of several identifiable components, two of which occurred within a latency of 5 msec following the shock artefact and a third one which occurred with its peak around 8.0 msec after the stimulus. The first wave (P_1 for positive 1), peaked at 1.86 ± 0.11 msec and was positive-going; the second (N_1 for negative 1), peaked at 3.26 ± 0.13 msec and was negative-going whilst the final wave, a positive-

going one (P_2), occurred at 7.90 ± 0.21 msec. Since the P_1 wave in these recordings was probably contaminated by events relating to the artefact, only N_1 and P_2 were considered in the analyses. For the extracellular data reported here, only the wave form amplitude of N_1 is plotted. As is evident from the upper traces reproduced in Fig. 2, the N_1 wave (measured from the P_1 peak to the maximal negativity) was measurably larger following tetanus than before it. On average, the increase was from a pretetanic value of 1.79 ± 0.68 mV (± 1 S.D., $n = 16$) to 2.10 ± 0.77 mV post-tetanically: an increase of over 17% measured 30 min following cessation of tetanus.

Perfusion with Ca^{2+}-free aCSF

In order to assess the degree of contribution of antidromically elicited currents to these extracellularly recorded wave forms, the aCSF was replaced following each tetanus with Ca^{2+}-free medium (Fig. 3). This change-over required about 3 or 4 min and a considerable alteration in the shape and amplitudes of the various components of the recording was evident within several minutes. The N_1 wave enlarged to 2.55 ± 0.46 mV ($n = 10$), representing a $42.5 \pm 5.8\%$ increase from the value recorded pretetanically in normal aCSF.

Isolation of the synaptic currents

Since the potential recorded in Ca^{2+}-free aCSF can be expected to represent solely, non-synaptically-induced (antidromic) currents, this wave form was computer-subtracted from each of the responses — both pre-tetanic and post-tetanic — that had been collected in normal medium. It thus became possible to compare directly the synaptic currents evoked before and after the tetanus in the absence of any contamination by antidromically-elicited currents. The resultant wave forms must be described differently than those of the direct recordings, hence the early positive-going wave (SP_1, for synaptic positive) peaks at 2.67 ± 0.19 msec (± 1 S.D.) and is relatively short-lasting. A subsequent negative-going wave (SN_1, for synaptic negative) peaks at 4.53 ± 0.23 msec and is followed by a longer-lasting SP_2 wave that peaks at 7.82 ± 0.56 msec. Comparison of these "calculated" wave forms before and after tetanus (lower traces in Fig. 2) showed the unexpected result that both SP_1 and SN_1 waves (the early responses not affected by the stimulus artefact) were diminished, rather than enhanced, after the tetanus. To clarify the mechanisms responsible for this paradoxical result — that tetanus appeared to reduce, rather than enhance the synaptic currents — it was necessary to examine the process using intracellular recording.

Effect of tetanus on the EPSP

Stable intracellular recordings from neurones of layers II/III and IV were made for periods of time of 90 – 120 min in cells having resting potentials

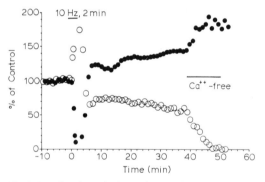

Fig. 3. Results of a typical experiment using extracellular recording and tetanic stimulation. N_1 wave amplitudes were measured from computer-averaged responses prior to and following 10 Hz, 2 min stimulation (indicated by the first horizontal bar). These amplitudes are plotted as dots. Ordinate scale is expressed in percent, with the mean control amplitude normalised as 100%. The example illustrated shows an enhancement of N_1 to about 145% of the mean control value. aCSF was switched to Ca^{2+}-free medium at the commencement of the horizontal bar at right. Note the large increase in amplitude of the N_1 wave. Open circles represent the calculated SN_1 amplitudes for each corresponding recording; these values fall to zero subsequent to perfusion with Ca^{2+}-free aCSF, as is expected from treatment with a method that blocks synaptic transmission. Abscissa scale indicates time, zero being the point of commencement of tetanic stimulation. See text for further description of the method.

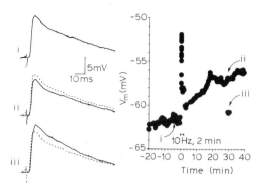

Fig. 4. Effects of a 10 Hz, 2 min tetanus on electrophysiolgical measures as recorded intracellularly. Panel at right plots Vm at regular intervals (0.1 Hz), as indicated by dots. At the time of dot (i), indicated by arrow, a stimulus applied to the white matter elicited the EPSP shown at left (top). About 30 min after tetanus, at the time of dot (ii), indicated by arrow in right panel, a second stimulus of the same intensity and duration yielded the EPSP shown at left (centre) as a continuous line, with the first EPSP replotted as the dashed trace and superimposed for ease of comparison. At the time of dot (iii), indicated by arrow in right panel, the resting membrane potential of the pretetanic condition was imposed upon the cell via manually clamping and another identical stimulus was applied, producing the EPSP (continuous trace) shown at left (bottom). The first (control) EPSP is again replotted as the dashed trace and is superimposed for ease of comparison.

ranging between − 54 and − 93 mV (mean value: − 68.6 ± 12.3 mV, ± 1 S.D., n = 9). EPSPs at the stimulus intensities tested ranged in amplitude from 2.0 to 14.0 mV (mean value: 8.1 ± 4.1) and membrane resistances ranged from 19.5 to 43.0 mΩ (mean value: 29.4 ± 7.3 MΩ). Following the tetanus, the EPSP amplitude decreased significantly ($P < 0.05$, paired t-test) to 6.0 ± 3.4 mV, a change of 26% from control levels, without a concomitant, significant change in membrane resistance. However, accompanying this decrease, and responsible for it, was a depolarisation of membrane potential that was statistically significant ($P < 0.01$), from the mean pretetanic level of − 68.6 ± 12.3 mV to − 59.7 ± 8.8 mV — a depolarisation of the membrane by an amount comprising more than 12% of the pretetanic value.

The data of Fig. 4 are illustrative of the principal findings reported above and are typical of the sample studied. This cell's resting potential was around −61 or −62 mV, prior to tetanus (points on graph at right represent individual measurements of Vm). A short time before application of the high-frequency stimulus, a sample EPSP was plotted as the control response (i, at upper left). This EPSP was evoked by a stimulus presented to the white matter: no antidromic action potential was elicited under the stimulation conditions employed.

Stimulation at 10 Hz for 2 min caused a rapidly-decaying, transient depolarisation that was complete within seconds of the tetanus offset, but the membrane potential after the tetanus never returned fully to baseline levels. Rather, there appeared a steadily growing elevation of the membrane potential over the course of the next 20 min or so. This slowly growing depolarisation asymptoted to a level of around −56 mV. At this point, another sample EPSP was collected and compared with the original (ii). In this panel (see Fig. 4), the original (pretetanic) EPSP is shown as the dashed-line trace whilst the EPSP taken post-tetanically is overlaid with the former and is shown as the continuous line. This new EPSP is noticeably diminished in amplitude from the former ("depression" by ca. 2 mV). The effect of returning the membrane's resting voltage back to its original, pretetanic level for a last test to sample the EPSP amplitude is shown in panel (iii). Here, it is clear that there had been a masking of a potentiated response (potentiation of ca. 2 or 3 mV) by the membrane depolarisation, owing to there being revealed an increase in the post-tetanic EPSP height (continuous line) compared to the control value (dashed-line trace).

The depolarised state of the membranes in all cells tested remained at their new levels for as long as the cells could be recorded; in these experiments, this recording time lasted typically up to 2 − 3 h following the tetanus.

Evidence in support of the proposition that the tetanus-induced depolarisation was responsible for the decrease in amplitude of the EPSP is provided by the data displayed in Fig. 5, where there is a significant correlation between the extent of the decrease in amplitude of the EPSP and the amount of

depolarisation produced in the membrane by the tetanus, as calculated for each cell tested. This graph indicates that the more the membrane was depolarised by the tetanus, the smaller the EPSP became. Further evidence supporting the contention that the depolarisation was responsible for the diminution of the EPSP, is the observation that when the cell's posttetanic resting potential was step-clamped manually back to its pretetanic value, the diminution of the EPSP amplitude disappeared.

Important in this context is the additional observation that the EPSP dimunition evoked at this artificially maintained level of membrane potential (i.e., at the former "control" level) not only disappeared, but in fact exhibited an enhanced amplitude. Thus, a larger EPSP could be revealed when the influences contributing to the membrane depolarisation were compensated for by clamping the membrane back to its original, pretetanic level. Accordingly, one is able to conclude that tetanus actually induced LTP, as expressed by an enlarged EPSP, but it must be kept in mind that such LTP is masked by the depolarisation of the cell's membrane. In the absence of intracellular data to reveal the mechanism depressing the apparent smaller

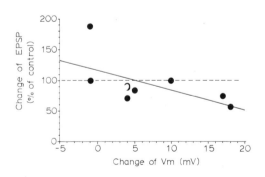

Fig. 5. Correllogramme illustrating the extent of reduction of EPSP amplitudes as a function of the magnitude of membrane depolarisation brought about by the tetanus. Ordinate: extent of change in amplitude of the EPSP following the tetanus, expressed on a normalised scale, (e.g., 100 represents no change, or 100% of control, following tetanus). Abscissa: magnitude of change in Vm, measured 20 min following application of the tetanus. Each point represents data from one cell ($n = 9$). Regression line drawn and calculated by computer shows a statistically significant correlation ($r = 0.53$; $P > 0.05$).

amplitude of the posttetanic EPSP, one might mistakenly be led to the conclusion that the tetanus produced a type of long-term depression (LTD) of synaptic transmission, rather than LTP.

A final electrophysiological observation that requires mention, is that on three of the four cells tested for their threshold level of membrane voltage that elicited an action potential, there was a pronounced shift of this value to a more hyperpolarised one. As is seen from the example provided in Fig. 6, prior to high frequency stimulation, the cell was required to be depolarised by about 14 mV before threshold was reached. Following the establishment of LTP and return of the membrane voltage back to the original, pretetanic value, the cell was required to be depolarised only by about 5 mV in order for an action potential to be elicited. Similar changes in threshold were noted for another two of three cells similarly tested. It seems therefore that for most cases not only did the tetanus effect a long-lasting depolarisation of the membrane, but it also was responsible for a decrease in the amount of depolarisation required for the cell to fire an action potential, as well as producing an enhanced

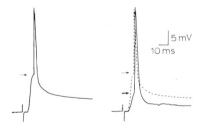

Fig. 6. Action potentials elicited from a cell from a 27-day-old kitten, before tetanus (left, and reproduced as a dashed tracing at right), and after tetanus (solid tracing at right). Thin arrows indicate threshold of the cell for elicitation of an action potential, prior to tetanus. Action potential elicited after tetanus (right) was triggered following return of Vm, via manual step-clamping of membrane voltage, back to the original value it had exhibited prior to tetanus. Thick arrow indicates the new (post-tetanic) value of threshold for the cell. Deflection at left of trace is the shock artefact delivered to the white matter.

amplitude of the EPSP consonant with what one might expect to occur in LTP. The alteration of membrane potential required for a cell to achieve threshold has not been described before for cells in studies of LTP in hippocampal slices, nor has it been reported in studies using slices of visual cortex of adult animals, irrespective of species examined (Artola et al., 1991; Keller et al., 1991).

In the visual cortex of the kitten, there is a phase of post-natal development called the critical period (Wiesel and Hubel, 1965) during which use-dependent modifications of neuronal response properties are inducible by altering the nature of, or amount of, photic experience arriving through visual inputs. Whereas it is still not known definitively to what extent thalamic and cortical response modification is involved in the processes underlying the behavioural alterations, it is certain that a major component at least of this experience-dependent developmental plasticity is cortically based (Daw et al., 1992). There are critical limits of time during which such changes can be manifested, and beyond which no modification takes place. It is interesting to note that there is a similar ontogenetic limitation for depolarisation of the membrane's resting potential and threshold changes found here, as the cortex removed from kittens older than about 46 days contained neurones that no longer appeared to have the capacity for demonstrating tetanus-induced alteration of membrane properties. Keller et al. (1991) recently also noted a lack of change in electrophysiological parameters following tetanus in the motor cortex of cats of adult ages. Whether the developmental plasticity accorded to altered visual experience noted earlier by Wiesel and Hubel (1965) is related to the membrane changes reported here, that seem also to be ontogenetically restricted, remains an intriguing question that awaits further experimental analysis.

Acknowledgements

Supported by a grant from the Human Frontiers in Science Programme and by the UNCG Research Council.

References

Andersen, P., Sundberg, S.H., Sveen, O. and Wigström, H. (1977) Specific long-lasting potentiation of synaptic transmission in hippocampal slices. *Nature*, 266: 736 – 737.

Artola, A., Bröcher, S. and Singer, W. (1991) Mechanisms of use-dependent synaptic plasticity in slices of rat visual cortex. In: B.S. Meldrum, F. Moroni, R.P. Simon and J.H. Woods (Eds.), *Excitatory Amino Acids*, Raven Press, New York, pp. 495 – 501.

Bliss, T.V.P. and Gardner-Medwin, A.R. (1973) Long-lasting potentiation of synaptic transmission in the dentate area of the unanaesthetized rabbit following stimulation of the perforant path. *J. Physiol. (Lond.)*, 232: 357 – 374.

Cynader, M., Shaw, C., Prusky, G. and Van Huizen, F. (1990) Neural mechanisms underlying modifiability of response properties in developing visual cortex. In: B. Cohen and I. Bodis-Wollner (Eds.), *Vision and the Brain*, Raven Press, New York, pp. 85 – 108.

Daw, N.W., Fox, K., Sato, H. and Czepita, D. (1992) Critical period for monocular deprivation in the cat visual cortex. *J. Neurophysiol.*, 67: 197 – 202.

Hebb, D.O. (1949) *The Organization of Behaviour*. Wiley-Interscience, New York.

Hicks, T.P. and Ito, K.-I. (1991a) Long-term enhancement in vitro appears extracellularly as apparent long-term depression via depolarization masking in kitten area 17. *J. Physiol. (Lond.)*, 446: 28P.

Hicks, T.P. and Ito, K.-I (1991b) Long-term potentiation or long-term depression: which process is established in visual cortical slices of kittens? *Can. J. Physiol. Pharmacol.*, 69: Ax.

Hubel, D.H. and Wiesel, T.N. (1970) The period of susceptibility to the physiological effects of unilateral eye closure in kittens. *J. Physiol. (Lond.)*, 206: 419 – 436.

Kato, N., Artola, A. and Singer, W. (1991) Developmental changes in the susceptibility to long-term potentiation of neurones in rat visual cortex slices. *Dev. Brain Res.*, 60: 43 – 50.

Keller, A., Miyashita, E. and Asanuma, H. (1991) Minimal stimulus parameters and the effects of hyperpolarization on the induction of long-term potentiation in the cat motor cortex. *Exp. Brain Res.*, 87: 295 – 302.

McNaughton, B.L., Douglas, R.M. and Goddard, G.V. (1978) Synaptic enhancement in fascia dentata: co-operativity among coactive afferents. *Brain Res.*, 157: 227 – 293.

Staubli, U. and Lynch, G. (1990) Stable depression of potentiated synaptic responses in the hippocampus with 1 – 5 Hz stimulation. *Brain Res.*, 513: 113 – 118.

Tsumoto, T. (1990) Long-term potentiation and depression in the cerebral neocortex. *Jpn. J. Physiol.*, 40: 573 – 593.

Wiesel, T.N. and Hubel, D.H. (1965) Comparison of the effects of unilateral and bilateral eye closure on cortical unit responses in kittens. *J. Neurophysiol.*, 28: 1029 – 1040.

SECTION V

Neural Encoding and Visually Guided Behavior

T.P. Hicks, S. Molotchnikoff and T. Ono (Eds.)
Progress in Brain Research, Vol. 95
© 1993 Elsevier Science Publishers B.V. All right reserved.

CHAPTER 27

The analysis of visual space by the lateral intraparietal area of the monkey: the role of extraretinal signals

Carol L. Colby, Jean-Réné Duhamel and Michael E. Goldberg

Laboratory of Sensorimotor Research, National Eye Institute, Bldg. 10, Room 10C–101, National Institutes of Health, Bethesda, MD 20892, U.S.A.

Introduction

Space is supramodal. It is calculated from data provided by any or all sensory modalities, calibrated only by movement. The analysis of space has long been considered to be an important role of the parietal cortex based on clinical (Critchley, 1953), behavioral (Ungerleider and Mishkin, 1982) and physiological (Mountcastle et al., 1975; Lynch et al., 1977; Robinson et al., 1978; Colby and Duhamel, 1991) grounds. The exact nature of the processing in this region has been the subject of heated discussion in the literature, perhaps because single neurons in parietal cortex discharge under a number of different circumstances, and tend to yield the answer that any given experiment is designed to produce. Thus different studies have come to the conclusion that parietal cortex is important in the generation of motor commands for operations in immediate extrapersonal space (Mountcastle, 1976), for visual attention (Robinson et al., 1978; Bushnell et al., 1981), for motor planning (Gnadt and Andersen, 1988) and for the generation of a visual map in supraretinal or head-centered coordinates (Andersen et al., 1990b).

Our view of posterior parietal cortex has evolved from a description of a single architectonically defined region (von Bonin and Bailey, 1947) to a series of different areas defined on connectional (Andersen et al., 1985; 1990a; Colby et al., 1988;

Cavada, this volume) and physiological (Goldberg et al., 1990; Colby and Duhamel, 1991; Duhamel et al., 1991b) grounds. In the experiments described in this paper, we concentrate on one subdivision of posterior parietal cortex, the lateral intraparietal area (LIP), which was originally defined on the basis of its projections from the frontal eye field (Andersen et al., 1985) and which projects to the superior colliculus (Lynch et al., 1985). This area, placed in a network concerned with orienting, eye movement, and visual attention has seemed to be ideal for a role in spatial analysis and the generation of saccades, as has been previously suggested (Andersen et al., 1990b; Barash et al., 1991).

In these experiments we attempted to understand the function of LIP by studying single neurons in this area using a large series of tasks designed to isolate various aspects of spatial analysis. In doing this we hoped to avoid the bias that any single behavioural paradigm might impose on the results. We arrived at three conclusions: (1) single LIP neurons receive several different extraretinal inputs; (2) LIP neurons signal the distance and direction of a spatial location from current or anticipated center of gaze; and (3) this signal can be instantaneously accurate.

Extraretinal inputs on LIP neurons

In order to study neurons in an awake monkey it is

308

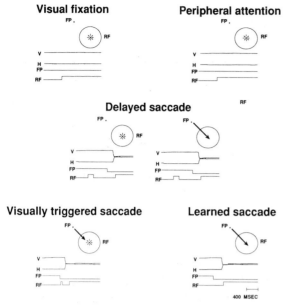

Fig. 1. Tasks used to analyze visual neurons in parietal cortex. Each panel shows a cartoon of the screen, with a fixation point (FP), receptive field (circle labeled RF), and a visual stimulus (star). A saccade is symbolized by an arrow, with the saccade destination at the arrowhead. Beneath each cartoon are lines showing horizontal (H) and vertical (V) eye positions, and two lines showing the state of FP and RF (up is on, down is off). Each task has one panel except for the delayed saccade task, which shows the stimulus appearance on the left and the saccade on the right.

necessary to use a large number of different tasks (Goldberg, 1983). In this study we began by using five tasks (Fig. 1). The basic task is the *fixation task* (Wurtz, 1969) in which the monkey initiates trial by placing its hand on a contact bar, causing a spot of light to appear on a tangent screen. The monkey looks only at the fixation point, and does not respond to a second stimulus which can be flashed anywhere on the screen. The second stimulus can be used to analyze receptive field and discharge intensity of the neuron. The monkey is rewarded for maintaining fixation until the fixation point dims, at which time it must release the bar. In the *visually triggered saccade task* the monkey looks at the fixation point, and the same stimulus appears as in the fixation task. In the version shown here the stimulus target stays on for a brief interval, as little as 50

msec, and the monkey makes a saccade to the spatial location of the stimulus. If the monkey makes a saccade of proper amplitude and direction the stimulus reappears and the monkey waits for it to dim. In this task the stimulus which was ignored in the fixation task is used by the monkey as a target for a saccade. However, this task confounds the motor processes underlying saccade generation with the attentional processes involved choosing the target. The *peripheral attention task* is used to distinguish attention from eye movement. The monkey is required to look at the fixation point, but must signal when the peripheral stimulus dims (Wurtz and Mohler, 1976). In this task, the visual events are identical to those in the fixation and saccade tasks but the behavioral situation is very different: the monkey must use the stimulus in the receptive field rather than ignore it, yet cannot make a saccade to it. Because the monkey does respond to the stimulus, it is reasonable to suggest that it has attended to the stimulus. This task, therefore, can be used to distinguish between an attentional shift accompanied by a saccadic eye movement, and a more covert attentional shift in which a saccade does not take place. In the *delayed saccade task* the monkey looks at the fixation point while a stimulus appears in the receptive field, and then disappears (Hikosaka and Wurtz, 1983). Some time later the fixation point disappears, and the monkey makes a saccade in total darkness to the location where the receptive field stimulus had been. If the saccade is accurate, usually with the combined horizontal and vertical errors of no more than 25%, the stimulus reappears and the monkey is rewarded for releasing the lever when it subsequently dims. This task has both a memory component (the monkey must remember the location of the target) and a divided attention component (the monkey must attend to both the fixation point, waiting for it to disappear, and to the target location), as well as a motor aspect. Activity which occurs immediately before a saccade in a delayed saccade task could be related to the saccade itself, or it could be a reactivation of the visual response (Fischer and Boch, 1981; Boch and Goldberg, 1989). The *learned saccade task* can distinguish between these alternatives: trials in this task are intermixed with visually triggered saccade trials. In learned saccade trials the fixation point disappears, just as in the visually triggered saccade trials, but the saccade target never appears. Instead, the monkey must make a saccade in total darkness to the same spatial location where the target appeared in the previous trials. Although this task has visual triggering information (the disappearance of the fixation point), it has no visual targeting information (Bruce and Goldberg, 1985). A simple reactivation of a visual response would not be expected to occur under these circumstances. Using these various tasks it is possible to change the behavioral significance of visual stimuli while keeping the visual events constant, and also to separate in time the appearance of a saccade target from the saccade itself.

Eye position was measured using the magnetic search coil technique (Robinson, 1963). Single unit activity was recorded using tungsten electrodes (David Haer) positioned by a Narashige microelectrode held in place using the Crist guide tube and grid technique (Crist et al., 1988). Search coil, recording cylinders, and head-holding devices were im-

planted using sterile surgical techniques under general anesthesia. All animal protocols were approved by the National Eye Institute Animal Care and Use Committee as being within the Public Health Service Guidelines for the Care and Use of Laboratory Animals.

Near the end of the series of experiments a number of small electrolytic lesions were made through the recording microelectrodes in a regular pattern to define each guide tube path. The monkey was then deeply anesthetized, perfused with normal saline and formaline-saline, and the brain frozen and sectioned. Two of the three monkeys described have been analyzed histologically. The cells described in this report were in locations histologically identified as being in the lateral intraparietal area.

We searched for cells with a detectable presaccadic burst in the delayed saccade taks, and we were able to study 28 of them in all five tasks. An example is shown in Fig. 2. The cell gives a brisk response to a visual stimulus (left panel) in the fixation task, a paradigm in which the monkey does not have to use the target for any behavior. It gives a significantly brisker on-response to the same target in the pe-

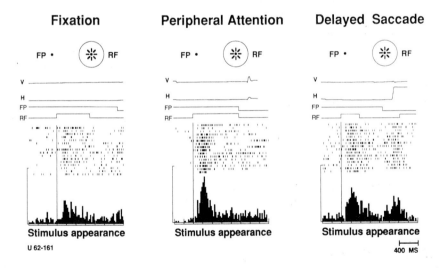

Fig. 2. Activity of LIP neuron in fixation, peripheral attention, and delayed saccade tasks. Eye movements and cartoons as in Fig. 1. Each panel consists of a raster and histogram synchronized on a particular event. In the raster diagram each vertical line represents a neuronal spike. Each horizontal line represents a trial. Successive trials are aligned on the vertical trigger line, and the event indicated by that line is described at the bottom of the panel. Histograms sum the raster above, with 4 msec bin width. In these and subsequent histograms the calibration line at the left corresponds to 100 Hz. (Data reproduced with permission from Goldberg et al., 1990.)

310

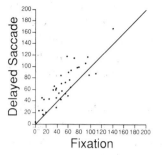

Fig. 3. Comparison of response to stimulus in delayed saccade task to response to the same stimulus in fixation task for all studied neurons. Activity is the average discharge frequency in the 100 msec epoch following the beginning of the saccade burst. Each dot represents single neuron activity averaged over 16 trials, with the abscissa representing activity in the fixation task and the ordinate representing activity in the delayed saccade task. The diagonal line has a slope of 1. Every point above the line has more activity in the saccade task.

ripheral attention task (center panel). In this task the monkey has to maintain central fixation as in the previous task, but now it must respond when the peripheral stimulus changes luminance. Because the monkey responds to the stimulus, we infer that it attends to that stimulus. The brisker on-response in the peripheral attention task is an enhancement of the visual response, and has been suggested to be associated with the process of visual attention (Robinson et al., 1978). Attention is independent of the kind of the response made to the stimulus: if we use the same stimulus in a delayed saccade task, in which the monkey, instead of releasing the lever to signal the dimming of the peripheral target, makes a saccade to it, the on-response is similarly enhanced. It is impossible to predict from the neuronal response if the monkey will make a saccade to the stimulus, or if the monkey will respond to the stimulus in some other manner that does not entail a saccade. The enhancement presumably comes from an extraretinal input that does not depend on the nature of the monkey's response to the stimulus, since in one case the monkey will make a saccade to the target, but in the other it is expressly forbidden to do so.

Enhancement is a general phenomenon in LIP. Analysis of the population of LIP neurons reveals

that the great majority of cells give an enhanced response when the stimulus is of importance to the monkey. Enhancement in the delayed saccade task is shown in Fig. 3, where the mean activity of each cell's on-response to the stimulus in the delayed saccade task is plotted against the mean activity of that cell's on-response in the fixation task. The diagonal line has a slope of 1, and if there were no differences in the responses to the stimulus in the delayed saccade and fixation tasks, an equal number of cells would be expected to lie above and below the line. Because almost all of the cells lie above the line we can assert that this enhancement of the response is a characteristic of the LIP population. The population also gives an enhanced response in the peripheral attention task. Fig. 4 shows the visual response of each neuron to the stimulus in the peripheral attention task plotted against the response of that same neuron in the fixation task. Here too most neurons lie in the enhanced range, above the equal response line.

The independence of enhancement from the monkey's response mode led to the suggestion that all of the activity in the parietal cortex during saccade tasks could be explained as an enhancement of the visual response (Bushnell et al., 1981). Gnadt and Andersen (1988), however, showed that there is activity related to the saccade in the delayed saccade task in LIP neurons. This activity can be seen as a second burst in the delayed saccade task (Fig. 2, right panel) and synchronization of the neural activity on the beginning of the saccade reveals that

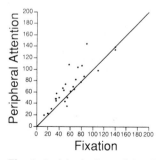

Fig. 4. Activity in the peripheral attention task plotted against activity in the fixation task.

Delayed Saccade | Visually-triggered Saccade | Learned Saccade

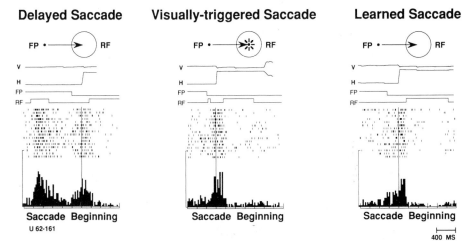

Fig. 5. Activity of same LIP neuron as in Fig. 2 in delayed saccade, visually triggered saccade and learned saccade tasks. (Data reproduced with permission from Goldberg et al., 1990.)

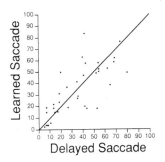

Fig. 6. Activity in the learned saccade task plotted against activity in the delayed saccade task. Presaccadic activity is average discharge in the 100 msec before the saccade begins, or if the burst starts less than 100 msec before the start of the saccade.

response to the stimulus in the visually triggered saccade task (Fig. 5, center panel), but it also discharges before the saccade in the learned saccade task, in which there is never a visual stimulus (Fig. 5, right panel). These data suggest that presaccadic activity in the learned saccade task is not dependent upon a recently present visual stimulus, and, instead, represents another form of extraretinal input to LIP.

Analysis of the population of LIP neurons reveals that the presaccadic burst in the delayed saccade task is independent of visual stimulation. We found no consistent difference in the population between

this activity begins before the saccade (Fig. 5, left panel). To determine if this activity were a reactivation of a within-fixation tonic visual response (Fischer and Boch, 1981) or independent of the visual response we studied the activity of the same neuron in the learned saccade task, in which the monkey makes a saccade without any targeting information, but instead makes the same saccade that it had been making in prior visually triggered saccade trials. Learned saccade trials are intermingled with visually triggered saccade trials. The cell gives an enhanced

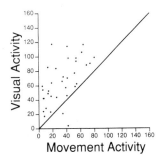

Fig. 7. Visual activity in the delayed saccade task plotted against presaccadic activity in the same task.

312

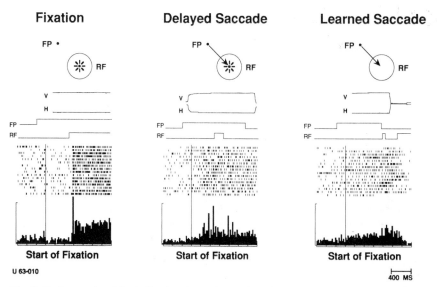

Fig. 8. Background activity in fixation, learned saccade and delayed saccade tasks. Conventions as in Fig. 2. (Some data reproduced with permission from Goldberg et al., 1990.)

the presaccadic burst in the learned saccade task, where there was no recent visual stimulus, and the presaccadic burst in the delayed saccade task, where there was a recent visual stimulus. This can be seen in Fig. 6 where the presaccadic activity in the learned saccade task is plotted against the presaccadic activity in the delayed saccade task.

Despite the presence of this presaccadic activity in LIP it is clear that visual signals predominate. We report here only those neurons that have both visual and presaccadic bursts. Even these almost inevitably had stronger visual than presaccadic signals. This can be seen in Fig. 7, which plots the visual response in the delayed saccade task, which occurs at a time

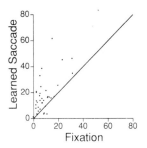

Fig. 9. Background activity in learned saccade plotted against background activity in the fixation task.

when the monkey may not break fixation, against the presaccadic burst in the same task. Note that all of the neurons except one had responses which lay above the equal response line, indicating a stronger visual response. The one exception was seen to be inhibited by the visual stimulus. These results emphasize that LIP has a strong visual mechanism which is ordinarily sufficient to drive almost every neuron, but the visual mechanism is not necessary, because a significant number of neurons have presaccadic activity which does not depend upon recent visual stimulation.

The independence from both vision and movement can be seen in a third extraretinal input which is present in most cells, an anticipatory input. When a monkey is performing a fixation task and the stimulus in the receptive field is irrelevant, there is relatively little activity during the interval between the achievement of fixation and the appearance of the target (Fig. 8, left panel). When the monkey is performing a series of delayed saccade trials, the level of activity increases (Fig. 8, center panel) before the target appears. This increased level of background activity is also seen when the monkey performs learned saccades in darkness (Fig. 8, right panel). Although the anticipatory activity is not ob-

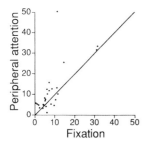

Fig. 10. Background activity in the peripheral attention task plotted against background activity in the fixation task.

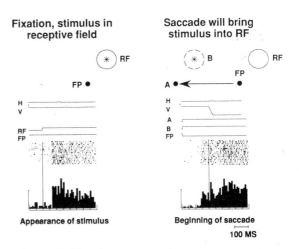

Fig. 11. Activity of LIP neuron at time of saccade that will bring stimulus in to its receptive field. Left panel: response in fixation task to appearance of stimulus in receptive field. Activity synchronized on stimulus appearance. Right panel: at beginning of saccade FP is on the fovea, stimulus is at B and no stimulus is in receptive field (RF drawn with solid line). After the saccade the fovea is at A, and the stimulus at B is in the receptive field (RF drawn with dashed line). The cell begins to discharge before the beginning of the saccade. Activity synchronized on beginning of saccade. Conventions the same as in Fig. 2. (Some data reproduced with permission from Duhamel et al., 1991a.)

vious in single trials for most cells, the population is clearly more active before the appearance of a predictable saccade target than before the predictable appearance of the same target when it is irrelevant to the animal's behavior. This can be seen in Fig. 9, which plots the background activity in the learned saccade task against background activity in the fixation task on a cell by cell basis. Anticipation can also be seen in the peripheral attention task, where 69% of the cells show higher background rates. This can be seen in Fig. 10, which plots background activity in the peripheral attention task against background activity in the fixation task.

The foregoing results illustrate the complexities of studying neurons in awake, behaving animals. For example, neurons discharge before saccades to a particular spatial location when there is no visual stimulus, even when there has been no stimulus at that spatial location for several seconds and through several fixations. It is not unreasonable to conclude that the neurons are engaged in motor planning for saccades (Gnadt and Andersen, 1988). Nonetheless, the same neurons discharge in response to an attended stimulus in the peripheral attention task when saccades to that stimulus are expressly forbidden. Without studying the neuron in a stimulus-free saccade task one could reasonably conclude that the neurons are mediating visual attention, and that activity of these neurons in visually triggered saccade tasks is more related to visual attention than to the movement itself (Bushnell, 1981). By looking at a large number of paradigms it becomes apparent that these neurons cannot be construed as signaling a specific act or stimulus.

If these neurons are carrying a univariate message they could signal that which is shared among stimulus, anticipation, attention and movement: the spatial location of the stimulus, the saccade target or the goal of the anticipated event. The intensity of the discharge may correlate with the salience of the spatial location, and the enhanced visual response may be more important in facilitating a shift of attention to the spatial location than in sustaining attention there.

The representation of visual space in LIP

Spatial locations can be coded in several ways: relative to some head, body or egocentric location, or relative to the current or anticipated center of gaze. LIP neurons use the latter coordinate system: each neuron has a receptive field at a given distance and direction from the fovea. Each time a monkey makes a saccade the representation of the visual

314

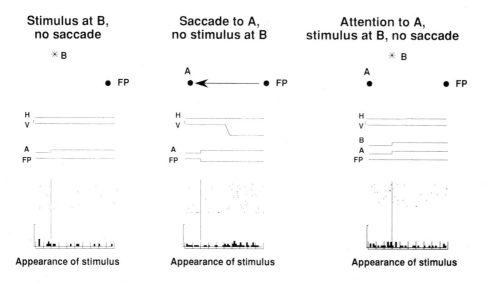

**Stimulus at B,
no saccade**

※ B

● FP

H _____
V _____

A _____
FP _____

Appearance of stimulus

**Saccade to A,
no stimulus at B**

A
● ◄———— ● FP

H _____
V _____

A _____
FP _____

Appearance of stimulus

**Attention to A,
stimulus at B, no saccade**

※ B
A
●   ● FP

H _____
V _____
B
A _____
FP _____

Appearance of stimulus

Fig. 12. Control experiments for neuron shown in Fig. 11. Left panel: no response to stimulus at B unless there is a saccade to A. Middle panel: no response to saccade from FP to A unless there is a stimulus at B. Right panel: no response to stimulus at B even if the monkey is attending to the stimulus at A in the peripheral attention task. Activity synchronized on stimulus appearance in all three panels. Conventions the same as in Fig. 2.

world in LIP is remapped: targets on the fovea at the beginning of a saccade lie in the visual periphery at the end of the saccade; other stimuli are brought into the fovea by the saccade. Although LIP neurons have been shown to vary the intensity of their discharge with orbital position, the retinal location of the receptive field does not vary with orbital position (Andersen et al., 1990b). However, these neurons do have a property which makes them uniquely suitable for spatial analysis: they can anticipate the retinal consequences of an intended saccade. Neurons in LIP can begin to respond to a stimulus even before a saccade that will bring the stimulus into the retinal receptive field. Roughly 40% of neurons in LIP (16/36) begin to discharge significantly sooner than they could be expected to if they only responded to the stimulus when it entered the receptive field. Thus the remapping of the representation of the visual world occurs earlier than it would if the response were based on reafferent visual input alone.

This phenomenon is illustrated in Fig. 11. The neuron responds to stimuli in its receptive field with a latency of 70 msec (Fig. 11, left panel). If the only

retinal locus that could drive a neuron were its receptive field (as studied in the fixation task), then its activity would begin 70 msec after the saccade has moved its the retinal receptive field to the spatial location of the target. However, the neuron begins to discharge before the beginning of the saccade. (Fig. 11, right panel). This shows that a stimulus outside the receptive field can drive the neuron when the monkey intends to make a saccade that will bring the location into the receptive field. Control experiments show that the neuron does not discharge in response to a stimulus at the new spatial location if the monkey does not make the saccade (Fig. 12, left panel), nor does it discharge in response to the saccade alone (Fig. 12, center panel). Finally, if the monkey attends to the saccade target but does not make an eye movement the stimulus does not drive the cell (Fig. 12, right). All visual neurons respond to stimuli in their retinal receptive fields. Neurons in LIP respond not only to stimuli in a retinal receptive field, but also to stimuli in the spatial location that will be brought into the receptive field by an intended saccade.

Saccades not only bring stimuli into receptive

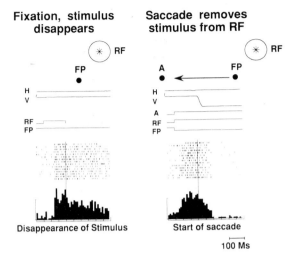

Fixation, stimulus disappears

Saccade removes stimulus from RF

Fig. 13. Truncation of tonic visual response by saccade that removes stimulus from receptive field. Left panel: tonic response of neuron after stimulus has disappeared. Activity synchronized on disappearance of saccade. Because stimulus appeared for 150 msec in each trial the on-response can be seen to the left of the trigger line. Right panel: activity synchronized on beginning of saccade. Conventions the same as in Fig. 2. (Data reproduced with permission from Duhamel et al., 1991a.)

fields, they remove stimuli from them. Neurons in LIP have a tonic visual signal that enables neurons to discharge after the stimulus has been extinguished (Gnadt and Andersen, 1988; Andersen et al., 1990b). As long as the monkey continues to fixate, such a neuron continues to describe the spatial location occupied by the now-vanished stimulus. When the monkey makes a saccade, however, the spatial location of the stimulus is no longer in the receptive field. This problem is solved by an extraretinal signal that truncates the activity of the neuron when a saccade removes the stimulus' spatial location from the neuron's receptive field. This is shown in Fig. 13, which illustrates the same neuron that was shown in Fig. 12. The neuron has a relatively tonic discharge to a stimulus flashed in its receptive field (Fig. 13, left panel). This discharge is truncated when the monkey makes a saccade that removes the stimulus from the receptive field (Fig. 13, right panel).

These results help to explain a central problem in spatial representation and oculomotor control.

Hallett and Lightstone (1976) pointed out that the correspondence between retinal and spatial location breaks down immediately after a saccade. Humans and monkeys (Mays and Sparks, 1980) can make saccades to flashed targets whose retinal location did not correspond to their spatial location because of intervening saccades. Our results show that neurons in LIP can compensate for the transient dissociation between retinal and spatial location induced by a saccade. This compensation occurs by virtue of extraretinal inputs that enable a transient shift in the retinal location that excites the cell. After the saccade retinal excitability returns to the original receptive field and visual stimuli in the original receptive field can drive the cell again.

This result has several consequences: LIP neurons signal a spatial location in relative and not in absolute terms, yet by inducing a transient shift in the retinal receptive field these neurons maintain a spatially accurate signal across saccades. Neural centers that receive projections from these neurons need not compensate for intervening eye movements: the compensation has already occurred by the time the signal is processed by LIP. By describing the visual world as it will be after the saccade, these neurons enable a continuity of processing that would be impossible if the system had to wait for retinal reafference to re-establish an accurate visual representation. This visual representation is not, however, in absolute inertial coordinates, but relative to the expected location of the fovea.

Such a representation is of prime usefulness to the oculomotor system, which must program movements not to a target in space but relative to the current center of gaze (Goldberg and Bruce, 1990). Parietal cortex, by virtue of its projection to the superior colliculus (Lynch et al., 1985), provides a major visual input to the oculomotor system. Because this visual input is always accurate even though it describes the world relative to the center of gaze, the system can rely on the parietal signal to drive the eyes to the appropriate spatial location of visual targets even when, as in the Hallett and Lightstone experiment, there is a dissonance between the retinal location of the target and the saccade necessary to acquire it.

316

References

Andersen, R.A., Asanuma, C. and Cowan, M. (1985) Callosal and prefrontal associated projecting cell populations in area 7a of the macaque monkey: a study using retrogradely transported fluorescent dyes. *J. Comp. Neurol.*, 232: 443 – 455.

Andersen, R.A., Asanuma, C., Essick, G. and Siegel, R.M. (1990a) Corticocortical connections of anatomically and physiologically defined subdivisions within the inferior parietal lobule. *J. Comp. Neurol.*, 296: 65 – 113.

Andersen, R.A., Bracewell, R.M., Barash, S., Gnadt, J.W. and Fogassi, L. (1990b) Eye position effects on visual, memory, and saccade-related activity in areas LIP and 7a of macaque. *J. Neurosci.*, 10: 1176 – 1196.

Barash, S., Bracewell, R.M., Fogassi, L., Gnadt, J.W. and Andersen, R.A. (1991) Saccade-related activity in the lateral intraparietal area II. Spatial properties. *J. Neurophysiol.*, 66: 1109 – 1124.

Boch, R.A. and Goldberg, M.E. (1989) Participation of prefrontal neurons in the preparation of visually guided eye movements in the rhesus monkey. *J. Neurophysiol.*, 61: 1064 – 1084.

Bruce, C.J. and Goldberg, M.E. (1985) Primate frontal eye fields: I. Single neurons discharging before saccades. *J. Neurophysiol.*, 53: 603 – 635.

Bushnell, M.C., Goldberg, M.E. and Robinson, D.L. (1981) Behavioral enhancement of visual responses in monkey cerebral cortex. I. Modulation in posterior parietal cortex related to selective visual attention. *J. Neurophysiol.*, 46: 755 – 772.

Colby, C.L. and Duhamel, J.-R. (1991) Heterogeneity of extrastriate visual areas and multiple parietal areas in the macaque monkey. *Neuropsychologia*, 29: 497 – 515.

Colby, C.L., Gattass, R., Olson, C.R. and Gross, C.G. (1988) Topographic organization of cortical afferents to extrastriate visual area PO in the macaque: a dual tracer study. *J. Comp. Neurol.*, 238: 1257 – 1299.

Crist, C.F., Yamasaki, D.S.G., Komatsu, H. and Wurtz, R.H. (1988) A grid system and a microsyringe for single cell recording. *J. Neurosci. Methods*, 26: 117 – 122.

Critchley, M. (1953) *The Parietal Lobes*, Edward Arnold, London.

Duhamel, J.-R., Colby, C.L. and Goldberg, M.E. (1991a) The updating of the representation of visual space in parietal cortex by intended eye movements. *Science*, in press.

Duhamel, J.R., Colby, C.L. and Goldberg, M.E. (1991b) Congruent representations of visual and somatosensory space in single neurons of monkey ventral intraparietal sulcus. In: J. Paillard (Ed.), *Brain and Space*, Oxford University Press, Oxford, in press.

Fischer, B. and Boch, R. (1981) Activity of neurons in area 19 preceding visually guided eye movements of trained rhesus monkeys. In: W.B.A. Fuchs (Ed.), *Progress in Oculomotor Research*, Elsevier North Holland, Amsterdam, pp. 211 – 214.

Gnadt, J.W. and Andersen, R.A. (1988) Memory related motor planning activity in posterior parietal cortex of macaque. *Exp. Brain Res.*, 70: 216 – 220.

Goldberg, M.E. (1983) Studying the neurophysiology of behavior: methods for recording single neurons in awake behaving monkeys. In: J.F.M.J.L. Barker (Ed.), *Methods in Cellular Neurobiology, Vol. 3*, Wiley, New York, pp. 225 – 248.

Goldberg, M.E. and Bruce, C.J. (1990) Primate frontal eye fields. III. Maintenance of a spatially accurate saccade signal. *J. Neurophysiol.*, 64: 489 – 508.

Goldberg, M.E., Colby, C.L. and Duhamel, J.-R. (1990) The representation of visuomotor space in the parietal lobe of the monkey. *Cold Spring Harbor Symp. Quant. Biol.*, 55: 729 – 739.

Hallett, P.E. and Lightstone, A.D. (1976) Saccadic eye movements to flashed targets. *Vision Res.*, 16: 107 – 114.

Hikosaka, O. and Wurtz, R.H. (1983) Visual and oculomotor functions of monkey substantia nigra pars reticulata. III. Memory-contingent visual and saccade responses. *J. Neurophysiol.*, 49: 1268 – 1284.

Lynch, J.C., Mountcastle, V.B., Talbot, W.H. and Yin, T.C.T. (1977) Parietal lobe mechanisms for directed visual attention. *J. Neurophysiol.*, 40: 362 – 389.

Lynch, J.C., Graybiel, A.M. and Lobeck, L.J. (1985) The differential projection of two cytoarchitectonic subregions of the inferior parietal lobule of macaque upon the deep layers of the superior colliculus. *J. Comp. Neurol.*, 235: 241 – 254.

Mays, L.E. and Sparks, D.L. (1980) Dissociation of visual and saccade-related responses in superior colliculus neurons. *J. Neurophysiol.*, 43: 207 – 232.

Mountcastle, V.B. (1976) The world around us: neural command functions for selective attention. The F.O. Schmitt Lecture in Neuroscience for 1975. *Neurosci. Res. Progr. Bull.* (Suppl.), 14: 2 – 47.

Mountcastle, V.B., Lynch, J.C., Georgopoulos, A., Sakata, H. and Acuña, C. (1975) Posterior parietal association cortex of the monkey: command functions for operations within extrapersonal space. *J. Neurophysiol.*, 38: 871 – 908.

Robinson, D.A. (1963) A method of measuring eye movement using a scleral search coil in a magnetic field. *IEEE Trans. Bio-Med. Eng.*, BME-10: 137 – 145.

Robinson, D.L., Goldberg, M.E. and Stanton, G.B. (1978) Parietal association cortex in the primate: sensory mechanisms and behavioral modulations. *J. Neurophysiol.*, 41: 910 – 932.

Ungerleider, L.G. and Mishkin, M. (1982) Two cortical visual systems. In: D.J. Ingle and R.J.W. Mansfield (Eds.), *Analysis of Visual Behavior*, MIT Press, Cambridge, MA, pp. 549 – 586.

von Bonin, G. and Bailey, P. (1947) *The Neocortex of Macaca mulatta*, University of Illinois Press, Urbana, IL.

Wurtz, R.H. (1969) Visual receptive fields of striate cortex neurons in awake monkeys. *J. Neurophysiol.*, 32: 727 – 742.

Wurtz, R.H. and Mohler, C.W. (1976) Organization of monkey superior colliculus: enhanced visual response of superficial layer cells. *J. Neurophysiol.*, 39: 745 – 765.

T.P. Hicks, S. Molotchnikoff and T. Ono (Eds.)
Progress in Brain Research, Vol. 95
© 1993 Elsevier Science Publishers B.V. All rights reserved.

CHAPTER 28

Visual pathways to perception and action

A. David Milner[1] and Melvyn A. Goodale[2]

[1] *Department of Psychology, University of St. Andrews, St. Andrews, Fife KY16 9JU, U.K. and* [2] *Department of Psychology, University of Western Ontario, London, Ont. N6A 5C2, Canada*

Introduction

The visual system provides the brain with a rich source of information about the structure of the world and the objects and events within it. It is perhaps understandable, therefore, that most accounts of the functional architecture of the visual system rest on an implicit assumption that its primary purpose is to deliver a unified representation of the world to the organism. Thus, even though many workers in the field have found it useful to invoke notions of "modularity" when discussing the organization of the visual system, and influential theorists such as Marr (1982) have postulated the existence of "visual primitives" which are domain-specific and relatively independent, these various inputs are thought to give rise to an integrated representation that provides the perceptual foundation for thought and action. But while this approach to vision has not prevented considerable advances at both empirical and theoretical levels, it has concentrated almost entirely on the input side of visual processing and has virtually ignored what is perhaps the most basic function of vision and the visual system, that of controlling motor output. As a consequence, it has led to what we believe may be a misleading characterization of the division of labor between the ventral and dorsal visual pathways, which emanate from the primate striate cortex to the inferotemporal cortex and to the posterior parietal cortex, respectively.

Visuomotor modules in vertebrate vision

A strong argument can be made that vision evolved in vertebrates and other organisms, not to provide perception of the world per se, but to provide distal sensory control of the movements that these organisms make in living their often precarious lives (see Goodale, 1983a, 1988). Natural selection operates at the level of overt behavior: it cares little about how well an animal "sees" the world, but a great deal about how well the animal forages for food, avoids predators, finds mates, and moves efficiently from one part of the environment to another.

A long history of work on vision in non-mammalian vertebrates has shown that many of the visual control systems for these patterns of behavior have quite independent neural substrates. In a now classic series of studies of vision in the frog (*Rana pipiens*), for example, Ingle has shown that visually elicited feeding and visually guided locomotion around barriers are separately mediated by different pathways from the retina to the motor nuclei (Ingle, 1980, 1982, 1983). Indeed, to date, at least five separate visuomotor modules, each with distinct input and output pathways, have been identified in amphibia (Ingle, 1983). While the outputs from these systems have to be coordinated, it would clearly be absurd to pretend that all these actions would be guided by a single visual representation of the world residing somewhere in the animal's brain. Indeed, one might characterize the organization not as a visual system connected to a motor system but as series of relatively independent visuomotor channels.

Similar kinds of independent visuomotor channels have been described in several mammalian species. There is evidence, for example, that the visual control of orientation to food and novel stimuli in rodents is mediated by subcortical pathways that are quite independent from those controlling avoidance of obstacles during locomotion (Goodale and Milner, 1982; Goodale, 1983b, 1988). This organization is remarkably similar to the circuitry controlling analogous behaviors in the frog. Thus, many of the different patterns of behavior exhibited by vertebrates may depend on independent pathways from visual receptors through to motor nuclei, each pathway processing a particular constellation of inputs and each evoking a particular combination of effector outputs.

Of course in mammals, particularly in the higher primates, visual processing is not always linked to specific kinds of motor output. The visual world of a monkey (and certainly the world of most humans) is more complex and unpredictable than that of a frog, and therefore more flexible information processing is required. Identifying objects and events in that world and establishing their causal relations cannot be mediated by simple input – output systems like the ones controlling visually guided feeding in amphibia. But while the formation of goals and the decision to engage in a goal-directed action can be quite independent of particular motor outputs, the *execution* of an action may nevertheless be mediated by dedicated visuomotor channels ("expert systems" in computer parlance) not dissimilar in principle from those found in amphibia. For example, much of the control of saccadic eye movements in primates has been shown to depend on sensorimotor transformations that are carried out in the superior colliculus (Sparks and May, 1990), which receives direct input from the retina. Other evidence suggests, however, that this basic tectal circuitry in the primate is modulated by a number of cortical areas which project not only to the superior colliculus itself but also directly to

motor nuclei in the brain-stem (Bruce, 1990). Thus, although the superior colliculus still plays a pivotal role in the control of saccadic eye movements, it has become a part of a cortically modulated expert system. It is our contention that this system operates alongside a series of related expert systems in cerebral cortex to support a range of skilled behaviors such as visually guided reaching and grasping, in which a high degree of coordination is required between movements of the fingers, hands, upper limbs, head and eyes. We will also argue that the visual inputs and transformations required by these visuomotor systems differ in important respects from those leading to what is generally understood as "visual perception". In short, the specific visual analyses that enable one to identify one's coffee cup and decide to pick it up, may be quite distinct from those involved in the control of the reaching and grasping movements that occur to achieve that end. We will review the evidence on visual processing in the primate cortex with these ideas in mind.

Cortical visual systems: the dorsal and ventral streams

Anatomy

The caudal half of the monkey's cerebral hemisphere is made up of a complex mosaic of interconnected visual areas (Maunsell and Newsome, 1987; Zeki and Shipp, 1988; Boussaoud et al., 1990; Felleman and Van Essen, 1991). Most, though not all (Gross, 1991) of the visual input to these areas arrives via the dorsal lateral geniculate nucleus (LGNd) and its principal efferent target the primary visual cortex (V1). Despite the high degree of interconnectivity between the different cortical visual areas, by 1982 Ungerleider and Mishkin had distinguished two broad "streams" of projections from V1: a dorsal stream ultimately projecting largely to areas within the inferior parietal lobule, and a ventral stream projecting eventually to the inferior temporal lobule (see Fig. 1). Recent anatomical studies employing retrograde fluorescent labeling techniques have confirmed that these two

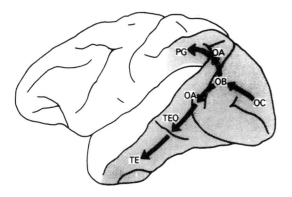

Fig. 1. Schematic diagram of the two cortical visual systems originally proposed by Ungerleider and Mishkin (1982). The dorsal stream projects from primary visual cortex (OC) to the posterior parietal lobule (PG); the ventral stream from primary visual cortex to inferotemporal cortex (TE). (Reproduced with permission from Mishkin et al., 1983).

target regions receive their inputs from largely independent sets of visual cortical areas, though to a lesser extent from separate subsets of cells within those areas (Morel and Bullier, 1990; Baizer et al., 1991).

In parallel with this growth of knowledge about visual cortical areas and their interconnections, the past decade has seen a great extension and clarification of our knowledge about the visual inputs that the cortex receives via the LGNd (De Yoe and Van Essen, 1988; Livingstone and Hubel, 1988; Schiller and Logothetis, 1990). The two main cytologically distinguishable subdivisions of ganglion cells in the primate retina are segregated in their projections to the thalamus, where they terminate selectively in the parvocellular (P) and magnocellular (M) layers of the LGNd, respectively. The M-system is essentially color-unselective but fast, with high contrast sensitivity and low spatial resolution; the P-system is color-selective and slow, with low contrast sensitivity but high spatial resolution. These P- and M-processing channels largely retain their separateness at the level of V1, and indeed in their major cortical outflows from there, e.g., in the interdigitated stripes that constitute the adjacent area V2. Nonetheless, despite the temptation to link P- and M-channels to the ventral and dorsal streams respec-

tively (e.g., Livingstone and Hubel, 1988), there is increasing evidence that both streams receive inputs from both M- and P-channels. Thus we now know that there is P-input into at least a minority of neurons in area MT in the dorsal stream (Maunsell et al., 1990), and also a large contribution from the magno pathway to neurons in V4 in the ventral stream (Ferrera et al., 1992). There is also crosstalk between V4 and MT, and indeed both V4 and MT themselves project to both posterior parietal (PP) and inferotemporal (IT) cortex (see Felleman and Van Essen, 1991). Thus although there are undoubtedly differences in emphasis between their visual inputs, it seems likely that the parietal and the temporal systems can both exploit a wide range of visual information in order to serve their respective needs.

Where versus what

The other highly influential contribution made by Ungerleider and Mishkin in their 1982 paper was to ascribe a fundamental division of labor between the two streams, on the basis of a series of electrophysiological and behavioral studies in the monkey. To summarize their conclusion in their own words: "appreciation of an object's qualities and of its spatial location depends on the processing of different kinds of visual information in the inferior temporal and posterior parietal cortex, respectively" (p. 578). This functional distinction has been thought to provide a unifying framework for theorizing about higher visual processing in the primate brain, and to encompass neatly a large body of knowledge ranging from human neuropsychology to monkey neurophysiology.

The main evidence for Ungerleider and Mishkin's position was derived from behavioral experiments in which the visual discrimination abilities of monkeys with lesions of IT or PP cortex were compared. Monkeys with inferotemporal lesions show profound impairments in visual pattern discrimination and recognition (Gross, 1973). This is not true of monkeys with PP lesions. In contrast, however, these animals show disordered reaching for food objects, which is unimpaired after IT lesions; and also

320

PP lesions, more than IT lesions, impair the monkey's ability to use a spatial "landmark" as a cue in a choice task. According to Ungerleider and Mishkin's model, then, the two lesions each disrupt circuitry respectively specialized for the perception of objects and of the spatial relations between those objects. The implicit assumption is that within the visual domain no reference need be made to the outputs of such perceptual mechanisms: they would each provide the necessary visual information for whatever purpose the animal required it.

The anatomical division proposed by Ungerleider and Mishkin has not been seriously threatened by recent advances since 1982, which have served mainly to flesh out in more detail the intermediate steps intervening between primary and higher visual cortical regions (see Fig. 2). Indeed it would be difficult to understand the undoubted differences between

the visual deficits caused by damage to the IT and PP cortex in the monkey (and comparable areas in humans) without invoking some such anatomical divergence. We shall argue here, however, that the particular functional account that Ungerleider and Mishkin offered in their 1982 paper cannot deal with a range of fresh evidence, which we believe is now converging upon a new interpretation. Our proposal is that the inferior parietal lobule, in close conjunction with areas in the premotor and prefrontal cortex, provides a specialized set of semi-independent modules for the on-line visual control of action in primates. In contrast we shall suggest that the occipitotemporal processing stream, while to some extent using similar visual information, is primarily concerned with more off-line functions, such as visual learning and recognition (see also Goodale and Milner, 1992).

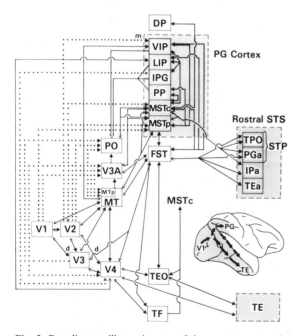

Fig. 2. Box diagram illustrating one of the most recent versions of the interconnectivity of the visual cortical areas. Despite the increasing complexity of the known interconnections, it is clear that they can still be broadly segregated into dorsal and ventral streams. There is considerable cross-talk between the two streams, however, and there may be a separate set of projections to the rostral superior temporal sulcus (STS) that is intimately connected with both streams. Thus although the two major projection streams in Ungerleider and Mishkin's (1982) model are still evident, their segregation is not nearly so clear-cut as once was thought. N.B. The label PP in this figure does not correspond to the broader usage adopted in the present text. (Reproduced with permission from Boussaoud et al., 1990).

Visual processing in the ventral stream

Physiology

There has been extensive discussion in the literature on the functions of the occipitotemporal stream of processing, thought to give rise to progressively more detailed coding of visual features, perhaps culminating in the coding of highly specific visual categories within cell networks (Desimone and Ungerleider, 1989). Neurons in the inferior temporal cortex and adjacent areas within the superior temporal sulcus (STS) typically have very large receptive fields, which furthermore frequently span both sides of the retinal midline (Gross et al., 1981). This feature would allow the cells to generalize across the visual field, and thus to code the intrinsic significance of an object irrespective of its location. At the same time, however, it is notable that many IT cells retain sufficient locational input to allow spatial gating within their receptive fields (Moran and Desimone, 1985).

It has been known for 20 years that IT cells are highly selective for the intrinsic figural and surface properties of visual stimuli. But more recent work from the laboratories of Gross (Gross et al., 1985), Rolls (Baylis et al., 1985), Perrett (Perrett et al., 1987), and others shows that many cells, especially in the adjacent areas within the STS, have a quite remarkable degree of categorical specificity: they may respond selectively to faces (real, schematic or photographed), to hands, and even to the sight of particular actions (Perrett et al., 1989). Furthermore, individual neurons may respond more strongly to one person's face than another, and some maintain their selectivity irrespective of viewpoint (Perrett et al., 1984, 1991; Hasselmo et al., 1989). Also many cells generalize their selective response over a wide range of size, color and optical transformations (see Perrett et al., 1987). Thus there is evidence for cells that code what Marr (1982) called "object-centered" visual descriptions, i.e., structural (and/or functional) information about an object independent of any particular viewpoint or viewing conditions. Of course it remains true that many cells do respond better to one viewpoint (e.g.,

the profile of a face), irrespective of the identity. Many of the properties of the object-centered cells may be derived through convergence from such cells that code more specific "viewer-centered" information (Perrett et al., 1987, 1989).

It is also relevant to our thesis that although a number of studies have been carried out using unanesthetized conscious monkeys, none have reported any dependence of IT or STS cell activity upon the animal's concurrent motor behavior in relation to the visual stimulus. However, cell responses in the ventral stream may be affected by the learning and reinforcement history of the stimuli employed (Richmond and Sato, 1987; Haenny and Schiller, 1988).

In short, it seems clear that the ventral system provides the visual analysis needed for decisions as to the significance of a stimulus with respect to previous inputs; that is, its properties make it well-suited for object recognition. This ventral stream evidently could enable the brain to arrive at a categorization of visual input as signaling a particular known object or an object of an identifiable type, irrespective of the visual conditions under which the object is currently encountered. At least in some parts of the system, viewpoint-dependent information about the input seems to be progressively discarded in favor of a more and more precise description of the intrinsic characteristics of the object. These object-centered descriptions would form the basic raw material for recognition memory and other long-term representations of the visual world. There is extensive evidence for the neuronal encoding of such visual memories in neighboring regions of the medial temporal lobe and related limbic areas (Brown, this volume; Ono, this volume).

Behavioral studies

Bilateral IT lesions in monkeys cause not only profound impairments in object and pattern discrimination and recognition (Gross, 1973; Dean, 1982), but also failures to generalize across viewing conditions. Thus such monkeys lack size constancy (Humphrey and Weiskrantz, 1969) and constancy across viewing angle (Weiskrantz and Saunders, 1984) in their visual discrimination behavior. A prediction from this loss of viewpoint constancy is that if IT-lesioned monkeys have lost the tendency to treat real objects as equivalent whether viewed from the front or from behind, they should, unlike normal monkeys, treat mirror-image stimuli as different rather than equivalent. This paradoxical prediction has been repeatedly confirmed: IT-lesioned monkeys are relatively good at visual discrimination learning between mirror-image or rotated patterns (Gross, 1978; Holmes and Gross, 1984; Gaffan et al., 1986). It should be noted that this result further implies that there is some preserved system in the IT-lesioned brain which retains the capacity to discriminate patterns, but which does not have viewpoint constancy.

In many discussions of the contrasting behavioral effects of lesions to the PP and IT areas, it has been assumed that the landmark task mentioned earlier (Pohl, 1973) is unaffected by IT lesions. However, this is not so. Although performance is not always severely affected by IT lesions (Pohl, 1973, experiment 3), neither is it always impaired by PP lesions (Ridley and Ettlinger, 1975). In the other two experiments where IT-lesioned monkeys were examined on the landmark task (Pohl, 1973, experiment 1; Ungerleider and Brody, 1977), impairments to an extent approaching those of the PP animals were reported. Thus if the landmark task is taken as diagnostic of a spatial perceptual ability, it seems that the ventral stream needs to be intact for the expression of this ability. We suggest later that the task actually requires active ocular and manual orienting abilities as much as spatial perception, and that the PP cortex may be implicated mainly in those orienting aspects. It is possible that the IT cortex might be more involved than PP in processing the relevant spatial relationships; in that case one would predict the existence of neurons in the ventral stream that code these spatial parameters within the visual field. To our knowledge such cells have never been explicitly sought.

Visual processing in the dorsal stream

The constituent areas

Current knowledge of the connectional anatomy indicates considerable complexity in the dorsal network. Fig. 2 illustrates some of the intricate connectivity between areas within the stream. In the present paper we use the term posterior parietal (PP) to refer collectively to the group of sub-areas (including LIP, VIP, MIP and PIP, as well as the shrinking 7a) that have now been distinguished in this region (e.g., Colby and Duhamel, 1991). Indeed in most lesion studies, "PP cortex" has also included variable extents of areas 5, MST, MT, 7b, DP, PO and V4. It should also be noted that there remains disagreement both on the boundaries and on the terminology for the parcelation of posterior parietal cortex (e.g., see Cavada and Goldman-Rakic, this volume).

As Andersen (1987) noted, inputs from V1 reach PP cortex along at least three major routes: one passing through area MT, a second through dorsal V3 (V3d) and area V3A, and the third via V2 and area PO. Different visual information almost certainly arrives through these routes, and this variety doubtless contributes to the heterogeneity of cell types in PP cortex that were discovered by the earliest investigators (Hyvärinen and Poranen, 1974; Mountcastle et al., 1975). Typical cells in the earlier areas such as V3d and MT respond best to moving patterns, with strong selectivity for both stimulus orientation (especially in area V3d: Felleman and Van Essen, 1987) and for the direction and speed of stimulus motion (especially in area MT). Unlike the neurons in the ventral stream, however, there is no selectivity for color in any of these areas, though color information can be exploited by them in their extraction of orientation or movement information (Saito et al., 1989). As in the ventral route, there is a general trend for receptive field size to increase as one passes along these dorsal routes; in parietal area 7a the cells may respond across the entire contralateral hemifield and span the midline to varying extents, though often excluding the fovea (Motter and Mountcastle, 1981; Andersen et al., 1990). An exception to the rule, however, is that in area LIP visual receptive fields remain relatively small and exclusively contralateral (Blatt et al., 1990).

Physiology of the dorsal stream

Visuomotor coding. Cell properties are most clearly different from those in the ventral visual areas within the parietal cortex itself, e.g., in areas MST, LIP, 7a, and 7b. Cells in these areas are virtually silent to visual stimulation under anesthesia, and their role began to be uncovered only after Hyvärinen and Poranen (1974) began monitoring their responses during simple visuomotor behavior. Mountcastle et al. (1975) identified six separate categories of visually influenced cells in area 7 (mainly in 7a: 7b is predominantly somatosensory, though it has some visual neurons, e.g., reach cells). The categories are: saccade, fixation, pursuit, reach, manipulation, and light-sensitive neurons. To illustrate when such cells would be active, one need only imagine the events that occur in a typical prehensile act. When a monkey sees an attractive object, it will typically (a) saccade toward it, (b) fixate it and (if it is moving) (c) pursue it, (d) reach out toward it, and (e) grasp it. These activities would implicate cells in the first five categories listed, respectively. And throughout the time that the stimulus was visible, (f) light-sensitive cells, the remaining category of PP cells, would also be active.

These neurons have been described in detail many times elsewhere (e.g., Lynch, 1980; Andersen, 1987) and will not be exhaustively catalogued here. It suffices to point out that their properties can not be accounted for in terms of visual stimulation alone. In all of the six categories of cells, cell activity is associated, in various ways, with a combination of visual stimulation and associated behavior. Even the light-sensitive cells fire optimally not just to a suitable stimulus but when the monkey is about to make a response (saccadic or manual) contingent upon that stimulus (Bushnell et al., 1981). There was an early controversy between those who stressed the

importance of this behavioral modulation of cell responses in PP cortex (Mountcastle et al., 1975; Lynch, 1980) and those who argued that the cells were primarily visual though modulated by the attentional significance of the stimulus (Robinson et al., 1978). The more recent attempts to separate sensory- from motor-related cell properties in posterior parietal areas, however, have all confirmed that the operation of these neurons can be fully specified only by taking both sensory- and movement-related responses into account (Andersen, 1987; Colby and Duhamel, 1991). Thus the visuomotor nature of PP cells sets them apart from cells in other visual areas: parietal visual function can be characterized as an interface between analysis of the visual world and motor action upon it. The demands of providing such an interface necessarily have important implications for the coding of visual inputs arriving at PP cortex: three aspects of this coding will now be considered.

Coding for object shape. The complex interrelated pattern of head, eye and hand movements that unfolds when a primate reaches out to pick up an object has to be guided by visual information about more than just location. Indeed there is behavioral evidence for a "distal" motor component during reaching, comprising the anticipatory finger and hand movements needed to accomplish the grasp efficiently; this is controlled, at least in part, independently from the proximal (reaching) component (Jeannerod, 1988; but see Jakobson and Goodale, 1991). Parietal cells are active in association with this distal component, just as others are with the proximal. Thus some cells (in the "manipulation" category) that fire during reaching to pick up objects are selective not for the spatially directed movement of the arm, but for the wrist, hand and finger movements made prior to and during the act of grasping the target (Hyvärinen and Poranen, 1974; Mountcastle et al., 1975). Furthermore many of these cells are now known to be visually selective (Taira et al., 1990). This subgroup of manipulation cells (found in area LIP), unlike the reach cells, are tied not to a spatial location (many indeed have no definable receptive field), but they are nonetheless visually driven, with many being selective for objects of different size and/or orientation. These manipulation neurons thus appear to be tied to object properties as well as to the distal movements that are appropriate for these properties.

The characteristics of these cells are inexplicable within a system putatively specialized for spatial perception (Ungerleider and Mishkin, 1982), but fit well within a system dedicated to the visuomotor coordination of actions. These shape- and orientation-sensitive cells in LIP may receive their visual information via orientation-selective cells in dorsal area V3 (and perhaps also from cells in V4).

Coding for motion. Visual motion information is the second major characteristic often required for active prehension. Neurons in the major relay station MT are typically selective for stimulus velocity, i.e., for both the speed and the direction of motion (Maunsell and Van Essen, 1983). Some uses to which this motion information is put become apparent when one looks at MST, the parietal area most heavily fed by MT outputs.

Firstly, one finds (especially in the lateroventral part of MST) many cells that vary in their responses to stimulus movement according to what the animal is doing; for optimal response, the animal has to be tracking the stimulus, as opposed to maintaining stationary fixation (Newsome et al., 1988). Interestingly it has recently been reported that one can track a target defined purely by color, with no luminance difference, quite accurately (presumably using one's dorsal system), despite "seeing" it illusorily as moving slowly (Lisberger and Movshon, summarized by Sejnowski, 1991). Presumably it is only the ventral system that is fooled. Secondly, one finds specificity (in MST especially, though in MT also) for relative motion, size change, and for the rotation of an object in the frontoparallel plane or in depth (Saito et al., 1986). The figural information necessary to detect changes in the orientation of objects may be provided by either area V3 or V4, both of which project to MT. Thus information traveling this dorsal stream via MT does not just concern the location of visual objects, it more generally relates to their disposition in three-dimensional space. It conveys not just where they are, but also how they are oriented with respect to the observer and how this changes from moment to moment.

Thirdly, many visual cells in the dorsomedial subregion of MST are strongly driven by large-scale optical "flow fields" such as would be created during forward or backward locomotion (Tanaka and Saito, 1989; Duffy and Wurtz, 1991). These "large-field" inputs may enable 7a, where similar "opponent-direction" receptive field properties have been found, to play a role in the visual guidance of locomotion through space (Motter and Mountcastle, 1981). Many "rotation-detecting" neurons also have large fields and may themselves contribute to the monitoring of self-motion (Tanaka and Saito, 1989).

Coding for location. Finally, it would be essential for the organization of an animal's reaching and saccadic behavior that the PP cortex be kept informed as to the direction of the animal's gaze. This information is in fact already incorporated in the firing properties of visually-responsive cells in area V3A, where activity is modulated as a function of the eye's position in the orbit (Galletti and Battaglini, 1989). Similar modulation is also found in DP and LIP (Andersen et al., 1990), as well as in 7a itself (Andersen et al., 1985b). Modulation by gaze direction is important because it permits the computation of the spatial (head-related) coordinates of the stimulus independent of retinal location. No individual cells have yet been found in PP cortex that code this information explicitly: in the above-mentioned cells, the receptive field location remains fixed across changes of orbital eye position although the response strength varies. Nevertheless, assemblies of cells within 7a could do so collectively (Zipser and Andersen, 1988; Goodman and Andersen, 1989), and indeed true visual coding of head-related location has been discovered in the premotor cortex (Gentilucci and Rizzolatti, 1990). It should be noted, however, that this kind of head-centered spatial coding would only be of value over short time spans, over which the animal's head might remain relatively stationary. Such spatial coding would be useful for guiding present action, but not for storing spatial information for future use. In the context of our hypothesis, therefore, it would not be predicted to be found in the ventral system, which would require spatial information relating to more enduring inter-item relationships, i.e., allocentric coding (cf. Milner, 1987b).

Visuomotor modules. As we have seen, a number of different cell types in the dorsal stream may be implicated in the programming and execution of a motor act such as visually guided prehension. Interestingly, the various cell types are to some extent anatomically segregated within the posterior parietal region (Hyvarinen, 1981; Andersen et al., 1985a, 1990). Although much research needs to be done, there is evidence for relative functional associations as follows: MST with pursuit cells, LIP with saccade cells (Gnadt and Andersen, 1988; Andersen et al., 1990; Blatt et al., 1990) and possibly with manipulation cells (Taira et al., 1990), and 7a with neurons coding gaze direction (Andersen et al., 1990). In order to understand fully the distribution of functions within parietal cortex, however, it will be necessary to map input – output relationships; probably there is considerable anatomical overlap between relatively independent subsystems, such that only analyses at a neuronal level will reveal the details.

It is already becoming clear, nonetheless, that there are selective links with several separate regions of the frontal cortex (Petrides and Pandya, 1984; Cavada and Goldman-Rakic, this volume). Although there are some disagreements in the literature, probably due to different conceptions of the parcelation of PP cortex, separate projections are clearly apparent to subregions of both the sulcus principalis region (area 46) and the frontal eye field region (areas 8 and 45). Each subdivision of PP cortex may project independently to its own part of each region (Cavada and Goldman-Rakic, 1989b). The frontal eye field (FEF) is closely associated with ocular control and saccade-related visual enhancement (Bruce and Goldberg, 1984). The sulcus principalis region, on the other hand, appears to have the neuronal equipment to mediate spatial short-term memory (Bruce, 1988). Some cells here code spatial *location* over a delay, while others code a delayed directional *response* which might be manual (Niki and Watanabe, 1976) or oculomotor (Funahashi et al., 1989). Similar saccade cells with mnemonic properties (though possibly with broader directional tuning) have also been discovered in parietal area LIP (Gnadt and Andersen, 1988). Finally parietal area 5 projects strongly to superior area 6 in premotor cortex, whereas area 7b projects preferentially to inferior area 6 (as well as to ventral parts of prefrontal area 46: Petrides and Pandya, 1984); reaching arm movements are associated with cells in superior area 6, and grasping actions of the hand and fingers with cells in inferior area 6 (Gentilucci and Rizzolatti, 1990).

The visual control of a manual grasping movement would probably involve the orchestration of several of these different functional interconnections between posterior parietal areas and premotor/prefrontal areas. Presumably the different functional streams operate in parallel and would interact in different ways according to the needs of the particular action that has to be programmed and controlled. The PP link with the sulcus principalis region (area 46) in prefrontal cortex is of some interest in the context of our hypothesis. This area has long been implicated in spatial short-term memory through the fact that damage to it impairs a monkey's performance on classical delayed response tasks. Thus the link is consistent with our view that the behaviors intimately associated with activity in the dorsal stream should be governed mainly by present or very recent events. That is, they should be concerned little with the history of the stimuli used, other than their very recent history (e.g., how they have moved within the field, or where they were when last seen a few seconds ago). This is the kind of information that would be of most use in programming and controlling a rapid grasping movement, for example. If this is a correct characterization of the properties of the system, it gives rise to several testable predictions.

Neurobehavioral studies of the dorsal stream

Reaching and grasping. Perhaps the most consistent and persistent disorder to follow PP lesions can be observed when a monkey attempts to retrieve small food items such as peanuts. The monkey may make errors as great as several centimeters when reaching for the object (Bates and Ettlinger, 1960). But in addition the monkey often fails to make appropriate anticipatory grasping and oriental movements of its fingers, such that even when it stumbles upon an item, it may not successfully pick it up (Haaxma and Kuypers, 1975; Faugier-Grimaud et al., 1978; Lamotte and Acuna, 1978). Importantly, as first reported by Ettlinger and Kalsbeck (1962) and confirmed several times since then, unilateral PP lesions affect the contralateral arm only, in both halves of the visual field. Occasionally there is a slightly greater degree of inaccuracy in the contralateral field, but nonetheless the ipsilateral arm, and indeed the ipsilateral hand and fingers, always remain unaffected. This output-dependent nature of the deficit speaks strongly against any interpretation of parietal misreaching in terms of a loss of "spatial perception", as recently pointed out in a critique by Ettlinger (1990).

Landmark discrimination. Bilateral PP lesions impair a monkey's ability to use a cue located between two covered foodwells to guide its choice between those foodwells (Pohl, 1973). In the standard landmark task, the cue is spatial, in that its location determines which of the two alternatives is correct on a given trial; however, it seems that this is not essential for the PP deficit to appear. It has been found that parietal lesions cause an impairment whether the discriminative cue is spatial or non-spatial, provided only that it is substantially separated from the foodwells (Bates and Ettlinger, 1960; Mendoza and Thomas, 1975; Lawler and Cowey, 1987). The cause of the deficit may thus be attentional or orientational, rather than spatial-perceptual (Lawler and Cowey, 1987). Certainly the landmark performance of both parietal and normal monkeys benefits from baiting the landmark itself (thus encouraging a manual response to it: Sayner and Davis, 1972; Milner et al., 1977). Similarly normal monkeys do best when they habitually touch the landmark prior to making their choice (Sayner and Davis, 1972). We would therefore suggest that PP lesions impair task performance mainly by reducing overt orienting by hand and eye. In contrast, the spatial element required to solve the task may come in large part via the ventral stream; certainly, as mentioned earlier, IT lesions impair landmark performance almost as much as PP lesions (Pohl, 1973; Ungerleider and Brody, 1977). If this interpretation is correct, one would predict that a non-spatial S-R separation task such as that of Lawler and Cowey should be performed better by IT than by PP lesioned animals, provided that the cues are easily discriminable.

Route learning. A deficit was reported on the learning of a stylus maze after PP lesions (Milner et al., 1977), but a control task requiring the monkeys to perform similar visually guided movements without the need for spatial choices to be made also yielded an impairment. The maze deficit itself was therefore attributed to poor visuomotor coordination. PP lesions also caused slow movement times in a test comparable to Milner et al.'s control task, in which monkeys had to extricate food along a bent wire, again consistent with impaired visuomotor coordination (Petrides and Iversen, 1979). On a larger spatial scale, it has been reported that PP lesions impair a monkey's ability to navigate back to its home cage when released in the housing room (Sugishita et al., 1978). There is also evidence that both PP and dorsolateral frontal lesions impair locomotor maze learning (Traverse and Latto, 1986). Whether these navigational deficits reflect specific sensorimotor difficulties, as opposed to putative spatial perceptual failures, is as yet unclear. One interesting possibility is that they might reflect the disruption of mechanisms for the monitoring of optic flow fields during locomotion (Motter and Mountcastle, 1981).

Visual discrimination. In general, provided there

is no gross spatial separation between discriminanda and the response or reward site, PP lesions do not cause monkeys to perform poorly on visual discriminations. Such lesions, however, do cause a disproportionate difficulty with pairs of stimuli that are oriented or mirror-image reversed with respect to one another (Ridley and Ettlinger, 1975; Eacott and Gaffan, 1992). This would be consistent with the idea of a reduced availability of viewer-centered visual representations of three-dimensional real objects. That is, the pairs of mirror-image stimuli might be coded as identical if the PP-lesioned monkey tends to rely on object-centered representations, thus making discrimination learning between them difficult. One would further predict from the physiological evidence that skills requiring the grasping or catching of moving or rotating objects would suffer after PP lesions.

Parenthetically, one would predict in contrast to this that many visuomotor skills should be *spared* following IT lesions. Pribram (1967) once remarked that his IT-lesioned monkeys retained great skill in catching gnats. What neither he nor others have ever done is to pursue this observation systematically. For example, despite their inability to scale size as a function of viewing distance in a perceptual choice task (Humphrey and Weiskrantz, 1969), we would predict that IT-lesioned monkeys would show good scaling in their finger grip aperture in the course of reaching to grasp objects at different distances. Similarly we would expect that such size constancy might be found in the visual properties of the manipulation cells of Taira et al. (1990) in area LIP; and indeed that lesions of PP cortex should impair this size constancy in reaching behavior. We would also predict that IT monkeys unable to discriminate line orientations in a choice task would nonetheless orient their hands correctly in the food retrieval task of Haaxma and Kuypers (1975).

Summary. Most of the "perceptual" impairments that have been described to follow PP lesions can be characterized as visuomotor and/or orientational. The deficits thus correspond closely to what would be expected on the basis of the observed properties of neurons recorded in posterior parietal cortex. In particular, we see no convincing evidence for a deficit in any general faculty of "spatial perception".

This in itself, however, does not speak to the frequently-associated claim that the primate parietal cortex plays a specialized role in spatial *attention*. We will now consider the evidence for this.

Spatial attention

Physiological studies

It is sometimes suggested that the neuronal "enhancement" properties of cells in area 7a uniquely qualify it as a control center for visuospatial attention (e.g., Robinson et al., 1978; Goldberg and Colby, 1989). Certainly cells in area 7a are modulated by switches of attention to different parts of the visual field (Bushnell et al., 1981). But cells in areas V4 and IT have also been shown to have attentional properties, albeit of a slightly different kind (Moran and Desimone, 1985). These neurons are selective for shape and/or color, as one would expect. However, when the monkey is attending to the place in the receptive field where this preferred stimulus is presented, the response of many cells is greater than when the animal is attending to some other location within the receptive field. In other words, this attentional modulation in the ventral stream, like the enhancement effects in PP cortex, is spatial in nature. The only difference is that an IT cell is selective for a *stimulus* in the attended place, whereas a PP cell is selective for a planned *response* to the attended place. Thus spatial attention can modulate the activity of cells in both ventral and dorsal systems; indeed it has been argued that such neuronal gating occurs in many parts of the brain (Rizzolatti et al., 1985). As we have suggested elsewhere (Goodale and Milner, 1992), independent mechanisms of spatial attention are probably needed to segregate and intensify the visual processing of particular objects in both ventral *and* dorsal streams. An object has to be selected from its background and isolated for further processing in much the same way, whether the purpose of that processing is to guide action or to subserve learning or recognition.

Neurobehavioral studies

The effects of lesions of the PP cortex on orienting and attention are consistent with the above suggestions. Disordered eye-movement control has been reported in saccade tasks and in the visual pursuit of moving targets (Lynch and McLaren, 1989). Such disorders are consistent with a central role of PP systems in ocular control, as is suggested by the single-unit physiology.

In addition, there is evidence for a mild and transient "multisensory neglect" following unilateral parietal lesions in monkeys, causing them to orient less to visual and other stimuli in the contralateral hemispace (e.g., Heilman et al., 1970; Deuel and Regan, 1985). Valenstein et al. (1982), however, have shown in the tactile modality that this is attributable to a problem in *turning* contralaterally, even when this response is made to an ipsilateral stimulus. Thus the visual orienting disorder is likewise probably a motoric "hemiakinesia" rather than a true visual neglect (Milner, 1987a). On the other hand there is clearer evidence for a more genuinely attentional disorder in the occurrence of an animal analogue of "visual extinction": animals with PP lesions tend to ignore the more contralesional of a pair of visual stimuli (Rizzolatti et al., 1985; Lynch and McLaren, 1989). For food objects presented close to the animal's face, such an extinction effect follows a lesion of area 7b and also of its projection target in premotor cortical area 6; Rizzolatti et al. (1985) take this as supporting evidence for their "premotor" theory of attention, in which the same structures are thought to control both action and attention in relation to a given spatial domain. These findings of "extinction" may mean that attentional competition by multiple visual stimuli presents special problems in the absence of PP systems designed for switching orientation between unique targets. One cannot saccade, or reach accurately, toward two separate stimuli simultaneously: thus the attentional systems in PP cortex may be more sharply focused on single targets

than those in the ventral stream. This idea would be testable physiologically.

Evidence from human neuropsychology

Spatial versus object perception

Studies of patients who have suffered damage to one putative projection system but not the other, are generally taken to support the distinction between object vision and spatial vision (e.g., Newcombe and Russell, 1969; Ungerleider and Mishkin, 1982; Newcombe et al., 1987). In extreme cases, patients with visual agnosia following brain damage including the occipito-temporal region may be unable to recognize or describe faces, common objects, pictures and abstract designs, even though they can navigate through and interact with the world, at a local level at least, with considerable skill (Humphreys and Riddoch, 1987; Farah, 1990). Conversely, patients suffering from optic ataxia, following unilateral or bilateral damage to the posterior parietal region, are often unable to reach accurately towards visual targets that they have no difficulty recognizing (Ratcliff and Davies-Jones, 1972; Perenin and Vighetto, 1988). Such observations appear to support the Ungerleider and Mishkin model, i.e., that damage to the ventral stream disturbs object vision but not spatial vision while damage to the posterior parietal region disturbs spatial vision, but leaves object vision intact. Closer examination of the behavior of these patients, however, leads to a different conclusion.

Optic ataxia and Balint's syndrome

Patients with optic ataxia not only have difficulty reaching in the right direction, they also show deficits in their ability to position their fingers or adjust the orientation of their hand when reaching toward an object, even though they have no difficulty in verbally describing the orientation of the object (Perenin and Vighetto, 1988). Similarly, parietal-damaged patients may have trouble adjusting their grasp to reflect the size of an object they are asked to pick up, as reported anecdotally by Damasio and Benton (1979). Jakobson et al. (1991) recently studied grasping movements in a patient who had recovered from Balint's syndrome, in which bilateral parietal lesions cause profound disorders of spatial attention, gaze and visually guided reaching. While the patient (VK) had no difficulty in recognizing line drawings of common objects, her ability to pick up such objects remained grossly impaired. Unlike normal subjects, for example, the size of her grasp was only weakly related to the size of the objects she was asked to pick up and she often opened her hand as wide for small objects as she did for large ones.

Fig. 3 shows examples of the grasping movements made with the index finger and thumb as the two control subjects and the patient reached out and picked up a small wooden block. The patient took much longer to initiate and execute the movement, and also had great difficulty in scaling her hand to the object, making a large number of adjustments in the aperture between her index finger and thumb as she closed in on the target. Such studies suggest that

parietal lobe damage can leave patients unable to use information about the size, shape and orientation of objects to control the posture of their hand and fingers during a grasping movement, even though they can use this same information to identify and describe these same objects. It is not only the spatial location of the object that is apparently inaccessible for controlling movement in such patients, but the intrinsic characteristics of the object as well.

Clearly, a disorder of "spatial vision" fails to capture the range of these visuomotor impairments. We suggest that a fuller description of the neuropsychological data may be achieved by postulating the existence of visuomotor modules in the human parietal lobe, much as we have proposed for the monkey. Certainly damage to superior parietal regions causes very similar patterns of visuomotor loss in optic ataxia to those seen after dorsal stream damage in the monkey: failures to reach accurately for targets, and failures to orient and shape the hand in anticipation of the object toward which the reach is directed.

Visual agnosia

If the above argument is correct, damage restricted to the human homologue of the ventral system might be predicted to spare the kinds of visuomotor guidance that are disrupted in optic ataxia, despite a possible failure to recognize the objects to which responses could be successfully made. A quite different prediction would follow from the model of Ungerleider and Mishkin, according to which the necessary object-based information should no longer be available for any purpose, including grasping movements. Such a prediction has indeed been specifically set out by Jeannerod and Decety (1990). Recently we have had an opportunity to study these differential predictions by examining the visual behavior of a patient (DF) who developed a profound visual form agnosia following carbon monoxide poisoning (cf. Benson and Greenberg, 1969). Although magnetic resonance imaging revealed a pattern of diffuse brain damage consistent with anoxia, the densest damage was evident in extrastriate areas 18 and 19, with area 17 (V1) ap-

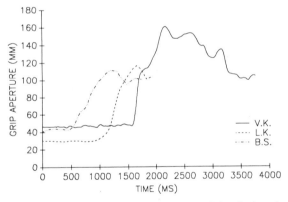

Fig. 3. Grip aperture between index finger and thumb plotted as a function of time for single grasping movements made by the patient (V.K.) with optic ataxia and two age-matched control subjects (L.K. and B.S.). The change in the grip size was measured optoelectronically from infrared light-emitting diodes attached to the finger and thumb (Watsmart, Northern Digital, Inc., Waterloo, Canada). Several differences between the performance of the patient and control subjects can be noted in these representative aperture profiles. The patient's reaction time and movement time were much longer; the patient opened her hand wider and showed many in-flight adjustments in grip aperture that were not evident in the aperture profiles of the control subjects. (Reproduced with permission from Jakobson et al., 1991).

parently largely intact. Extensive visual testing confirmed that DF's agnosia could not be reduced to a simple sensory deficit. Yet despite her profound inability to perceive the size, shape and orientation of visual objects, DF showed strikingly accurate guidance of hand and finger movements directed at the very objects whose qualities she failed to perceive (Milner et al., 1991; Goodale et al., 1991). For example, when she was presented with a pair of rectangular blocks of the same or different dimensions she was unable to indicate whether they were the same or different. Even when she was presented with a single block and was asked to indicate its width with her index finger and thumb, her matches bore no relationship to the dimensions of the object and showed considerable trial to trial variability (see

Fig. 4). Yet when she was asked simply to reach out and pick up the block, the aperture between her index finger and thumb was systematically related to the width of the object, in a manner no different from that of normal subjects. In other words, DF scaled her grip in anticipation of the dimensions of the objects she was about to pick up, even though she appeared to have no "perceptual" information about those dimensions.

A similar dissociation was seen in her responses to the orientation of stimuli. Thus, when presented with a large slot which could be placed in one of a number of different orientations, she showed great difficulty in indicating the orientation of the slot either verbally or even manually by rotating a hand-held card (see Fig. 5). In contrast, when she was asked

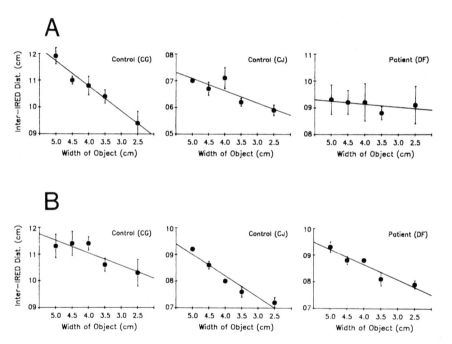

Fig. 4. The aperture between index finger and thumb plotted as a function of object width for the patient (DF) with visual form agnosia and two age-matched control subjects (CG and CJ) in two different tasks. For the task plotted in panel A, the subjects were asked to manually indicate the front-to-back extent of each of five different blocks of equal area (25 cm^2) but different dimensions (ranging from 5 × 5 cm to 2.5 × 10 cm) placed directly in front of them at a viewing distance of approximately 45 cm. The distance between the index finger and thumb was measured optoelectronically. Note that in contrast to the performance of the control subjects, DF's manual matches showed no systematic relationship to the width of the object and were much more variable from trial to trial. For the task plotted in panel B, the subjects were asked to reach out and pick up each target object. The maximum aperture of the index finger and thumb, which was achieved well before contact with the object, was again measured optoelectronically. Note that now DF's grip aperture was systematically related to the width of the object, and her performance did not differ from that of the control subjects. (Reproduced with permission from Goodale et al., 1991).

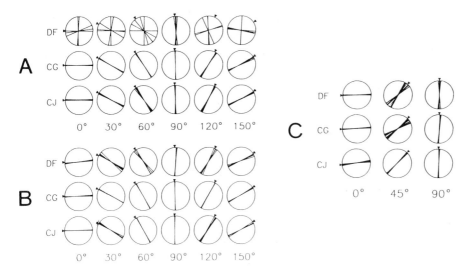

Fig. 5. The performance of the visual agnosic patient (DF) on the orientation task contrasted with that of two age-matched control subjects (CG and CJ). Performance was scored from videorecordings. Panel *A* shows polar plots that correspond to the orientation of a hand-held card that the subjects were asked to match with the orientation of slot (12.5 cm long and 3.8 cm wide) in an upright disk presented at a viewing distance of 45 cm. The triangular mark on the circumference of each circle indicates the true orientation of the slot during the depicted trials. Note that DF's performance was much less accurate and variable than that of the control subjects. Panel *B* shows polar plots that indicate the orientation of the card just before it made contact with the disk in a task in which the subjects were required to "post" the card into the slot. Note that now DF's performance is indistinguishable from that of the control subjects. Panel *C* shows polar plots that correspond to the orientation of the card in a task in which the subjects were asked to rotate the card, with eyes closed, to match an imagined slot at orientations of 0°, 45°, and 90°. The fact that DF did as well as the control subjects on this task shows that she understood what was asked of her in the matching task depicted in panel *A*. (Reproduced with permission from Goodale et al., 1991).

simply to reach out and post the card, she performed as well as normal subjects, rotating her hand in the appropriate direction as soon as she began the movement. Measurements of the orientation of the card just before it made contact with the slot showed that DF's performance was indistinguishable from the two controls (see Fig. 5).

Contrary to expectations based upon the ideas of Ungerleider and Mishkin, then, a profound loss of shape perception coexists in DF with a preserved ability to use shape in guiding action. The distinction between object vision and spatial vision is unable to do justice to the dissociations we have observed. Instead it is our belief that there are parieto-frontal systems in man that underly a variety of visuomotor skills, and that these have remained largely intact in DF. But is should be cautioned that while DF's data are consistent with the func-

tional anatomy we are proposing, her brain damage is not neatly localized within the occipitotemporal region. We hope that future investigations will explicitly compare groups of patients with known temporal and parietal lesions on the kind of tasks we have used.

Spatial perception

Nonetheless, the parietal lobe has traditionally been considered the focus for lesions that cause disorders of spatial perception and spatial orientation (broadly understood). This view has arisen because a variety of disorders come about following parietal damage, many of which can be loosely thought of as having "spatial" characteristics. Yet they can probably all be dissociated from one another. For example, neglect is "spatial" in the sense that it refers to the contralateral hemispace, and it follows parieto-temporal lesions (Heilman et al., 1983; Vallar and Perani, 1986); and optic ataxia is "spatial" insofar as patients misreach, and it follows superior parietal damage (Perenin and Vighetto, 1988). Yet although a patient with a massive parietal lesion may suffer from both disorders, the two can be clearly dissociated in many other patients (Perenin and Vighetto, 1988). Thus it is clearly not helpful to lump both disorders under the heading "spatial". A good example of a patient with "spatial" difficulties has been described by Newcombe et al. (1987). This patient provides a clear illustration of the selectivity that frequently occurs, in that although he performed poorly on a stylus maze task, he was unimpaired on the Semmes locomotor navigation task, and also on the Corsi spatial memory task. Indeed Ratcliff and Newcombe (1973) report that many of their right hemisphere-damaged patients were impaired on the stylus maze, but were unimpaired on the Semmes locomotor task. More strikingly still, De Renzi and Nichelli (1975) described two individual patients who were severely impaired on spatial short-term memory but performed normally on stylus maze learning, while another patient showed the reverse pattern.

Although it is beyond the scope of this paper to review in detail the many case reports in the neuropsychological literature, we would make certain broad predictions. We would expect that disorders specific to long-term spatial memory, deficits in the use of landmarks in topographical orientation (e.g., in a city), and in general on tasks that cannot be solved by use of egocentric cues, should tend to follow damage to the ventral system (cf. Milner, 1965, 1971; Smith and Milner, 1989). In contrast we would expect that tasks where space is defined relative to the observer (e.g., perimetric localization tasks and short-term spatial memory tasks) would tend to be impaired by dorsal system lesions. This pattern would loosely mirror that found for verbal memory losses following left-hemisphere damage (McCarthy and Warrington, 1990).

A final comment should be made about the in-triguing recent PET study by Haxby et al. (1991) on the patterns of cerebral blood flow (CBF) observed while normal subjects performed a mental rotation task and a cross-view face matching task, respectively. As compared with a control condition in which no discrimination was required but similar responses were made, it was found that CBF increased in a large area of lateral occipital cortex in both experimental conditions, but that this area extended more toward the temporal lobe during the facial task, while an additional quite separate locus of activation occurred in superior parietal cortex during the rotation task. At first sight these observations seem to provide clear support for the theory of Ungerleider and Mishkin (1982), although they do not tell directly against our view that the parietal cortex would be particularly active during visuomotor tasks, since that was not tested. However, it should be noted that both tasks involved an element of spatial perception, in that both required the integration of spatially separated pattern elements into a perceptual whole, and across a similar spatial scale. Thus, the critical difference between the tasks may not lie in their "spatial" characteristics. The crucial difference may lie in the fact that the rotation task involved the matching of spatially *identical* gestalts across 90° with respect to one another, while the facial task involved matching *different* patterns, which were different views of a given face. It may be that rotational transformations that involve no change in the intrinsic pattern tend to invoke visual representations in the parietal lobe — but these would be of little use in the face task, where access is required to a system that can construct object-centered representations. We would predict that if a PET study were carried out on subjects performing mental rotations of depicted three-dimensional objects into the fronto-parallel plane (e.g., Shepard and Metzler, 1971), then activation would be observed primarily in the occipitotemporal region. In contrast, it would be interesting to see whether or not matching of faces rotated by 90° in the picture plane would result in the parietal CBF pattern.

Conclusions

Although we have made a case for a particular division of labor between the dorsal and ventral streams, these two systems cannot function in isolation from one another. In short, there must be some form of integration which reflects the essential unity and cohesion of most of our perceptual experience and behavior. It should be noted that PP and IT themselves interconnect (Cavada and Goldman-Rakic, 1989a; Andersen et al., 1990), and both in turn connect reciprocally to areas in the superior temporal sulcus (Boussaoud et al., 1990; Morel and Bullier, 1990; Baizer et al., 1991). Thus, there appear to be important integrative areas within the superior temporal sulcus in the monkey where a great deal of the necessary interaction to ensure behavioral and perceptual unity may be achieved. Indeed there are many polysensory neurons in these areas, so that not only visual but also cross-modal perceptual integration may be enabled by these networks.

Despite the crosstalk between the dorsal and ventral streams, however, we believe that the evidence summarized in this paper indicates that each stream uses visual information in different ways. Both streams process information about orientation and shape, and probably about spatial relationships, including depth; and both are subject to the modulatory influences of an animal's shifting spatial attention. The ventral stream, however, seems able to deliver messages concerning the enduring characteristics of visual objects, while the dorsal stream is concerned with their instantaneous characteristics. The ventral stream can provide object-centered coding while the dorsal may provide entirely viewer-centered information: the former would enable a monkey to identify an object as being of an edible type, the latter to guide its actions in picking it up. Thus, although inevitably there will be differences in the ways that visual information is processed in the two systems, these differences, we believe, are not a reflection of some biologically arbitrary separation of inputs, but rather a consequence of the special transformations required for perception and action, respectively. In short, we regard it as probable that the functional modularity of the cortical visual systems, like other visuomotor systems in the brain, extends from input right through to output.

Acknowledgements

The authors would like to thank Philip Servos for his comments on an earlier version of this manuscript. Supported by grants from the Medical Research Council of Canada to M.A.G. and the William Ramsay Henderson Trust to A.D.M.

References

Andersen, R.A. (1987) Inferior parietal lobule function in spatial perception and visuomotor integration. In: V.B. Mountcastle, F. Plum and S.R. Geiger (Eds.), Handbook of Physiology, Section 1: The Nervous System, Vol. V: Higher Functions of the Brain, Part 2, Am. Physiol Assoc., Bethesda, MD, pp. 483 – 518.

Andersen, R.A., Asanuma, C. and Cowan, W.M. (1985a) Callosal and prefrontal associational projecting cell populations in area 7a of the macaque monkey: a study using retrogradely transported fluorescent dyes. J. Comp. Neurol., 232: 443 – 455.

Andersen, R.A., Essick, G.K. and Siegel, R.M. (1985b) The encoding of spatial location by posterior parietal neurons. Science, 230: 456 – 458.

Andersen, R.A., Asanuma, C., Essick, G. and Siegel, R.M. (1990) Corticocortical connections of anatomically and physiologically defined subdivisions within the inferior parietal lobule. J. Comp. Neurol., 296: 65 – 113.

Baizer, J.S., Ungerleider, L.G. and Desimone, R. (1991) Organization of visual inputs to the inferior temporal and posterior parietal cortex in macaques. J. Neurosci., 11: 168 – 190.

Bates, J.A.V. and Ettlinger, G. (1960) Posterior biparietal ablations in the monkey. Arch. Neurol., 3: 177 – 192.

Baylis, G.C., Rolls, E.T. and Leonard, C.M. (1985) Selectivity between faces in the responses of a population of neurons in the cortex of the superior temporal sulcus of the macaque monkey. Brain Res., 342: 91 – 102.

Benson, D.F. and Greenberg, J.P. (1969) Visual form agnosia. A specific defect in visual discrimination. Arch. Neurol., 20: 82 – 89.

Blatt, G.J., Andersen, R.A. and Stoner, G.R. (1990) Visual receptive field organization and cortico-cortical connections of the lateral intraparietal area (area LIP) in the macaque. J. Comp. Neurol., 299: 421 – 445.

334

Boussaoud, D., Ungerleider, L.G. and Desimone, R. (1990) Pathways for motion analysis: cortical connections of the medial superior temporal and fundus of the superior temporal visual areas in the macaque. *J. Comp. Neurol.*, 296: 462 – 495.

Bruce, C.J. (1988) Single neuron activity in the monkey's prefrontal cortex. In: P. Rakic and W. Singer (Eds.), *Neurobiology of Neocortex*, Wiley, New York, pp. 297 – 329.

Bruce, C.J. (1990) Integration of sensory and motor signals in primate frontal eye fields. In: G.M. Edelman, W.E. Gall and W.M. Cowan (Eds.), *Signal and Sense. Local and Global Order in Perceptual Maps*, Wiley-Liss, New York, pp. 261 – 314.

Bruce, C.J. and Goldberg, M.E. (1984) Physiology of the frontal eye fields. *Trends Neurosci.*, 7: 436 – 441.

Bushnell, M.C., Goldberg, M.E. and Robinson, D.L. (1981) Behavioral enhancement of visual responses in monkey cerebral cortex. I. Modulation in posterior parietal cortex related to selective attention. *J. Neurophysiol.*, 46: 755 – 772.

Cavada, C. and Goldman-Rakic, P.S. (1989a) Posterior parietal cortex in rhesus monkey: I. Parcellation of areas based on distinctive limbic and sensory corticocortical connections. *J. Comp. Neurol.*, 287: 393 – 421.

Cavada, C. and Goldman-Rakic, P.S. (1989b) Posterior parietal cortex in rhesus monkey: II. Evidence for segregated corticocortical networks linking sensory and limbic areas with the frontal lobe. *J. Comp. Neurol.*, 287: 422 – 445.

Colby, C.L. and Duhamel, J.-R. (1991) Heterogeneity of extrastriate visual areas and multiple parietal areas in the macaque monkey. *Neuropsychologia*, 29: 517 – 537.

Damasio, A.R. and Benton, A.L. (1979) Impairment of hand movements under visual guidance. *Neurology*, 29: 170 – 178.

Dean, P. (1982) Analysis of visual behavior in monkeys with inferotemporal lesions. In: D.J. Ingle, M.A. Goodale and R.J.W. Mansfield (Eds.), *Analysis of Visual Behavior*, MIT Press, Cambridge, MA, pp. 587 – 628.

De Renzi, E. and Nichelli, P. (1975) Verbal and non-verbal short-term memory impairment following hemispheric damage. *Cortex*, 11: 341 – 354.

Desimone, R. and Ungerleider, L.G. (1989) Neural mechanisms of visual processing in monkeys. In: F. Boller and J. Grafman (Eds.), *Handbook of Neuropsychology, Vol. 2*, Elsevier, Amsterdam, pp. 267 – 299.

Deuel, R.K. and Regan, D.J. (1985) Parietal hemineglect and motor deficits in the monkey. *Neuropsychologia*, 23: 305 – 314.

De Yoe, E.A. and Van Essen, D.C. (1988) Concurrent processing streams in monkey visual cortex. *Trends Neurosci.*, 11: 219 – 226.

Duffy, C.J. and Wurtz, R.H. (1991) Sensitivity of MST neurons to optic-flow stimuli, I. A continuum of response selectivity to large-field stimuli. *J. Neurophysiol.*, 65: 1329 – 1345.

Eacott, M.J. and Gaffan, D. (1992) The role of the monkey inferior parietal and inferior temporal cortex in visual discrimination of identity and orientation of shapes. *Behav.*

Brain Res., 46: 95 – 98.

Ettlinger, G. (1990) "Object vision" and "spatial vision": the neuropsychological evidence for the distinction. *Cortex*, 26: 319 – 341.

Ettlinger, G. and Kalsbeck, J.E. (1962) Changes in tactile discrimination and in visual reaching after successive and simultaneous bilateral posterior parietal ablations in the monkey. *J. Neurol. Neurosurg. Psychiat.*, 25: 256 – 268.

Farah, M. (1990) *Visual Agnosia*, MIT Press, Cambridge, MA, 184 pp.

Faugier-Grimaud, S., Frenois, C. and Stein, D.G. (1978) Effects of posterior parietal lesions on visually guided behavior in monkeys. *Neuropsychologia*, 16: 151 – 168.

Felleman, D.J. and Van Essen, D.C. (1987) Receptive field properties of neurons in area V3 of macaque monkey extrastriate cortex. *J. Neurophysiol.*, 57: 889 – 920.

Felleman, D.J. and Van Essen, D.C. (1991) Distributed hierarchical processing in the primate cerebral cortex. *Cereb. Cortex*, 1: 1 – 47.

Ferrera, V.P., Nealey, T.A. and Maunsell, J.H.R. (1992) Mixed parvocellular and magnocellular geniculate signals in visual area V4. Nature, 358: 756 – 758.

Funahashi, S., Bruce, C.J. and Goldman-Rakic, P.S. (1989) Mnemonic coding of visual space in the monkey's dorsolateral prefrontal cortex. *J. Neurophysiol.*, 61: 331 – 349.

Gaffan, D., Harrison, S. and Gaffan, E.A. (1986) Visual identification following inferotemporal ablation in the monkey. *Q. J. Exp. Psychol.*, 38B: 5 – 30.

Galletti, C. and Battaglini, P.P. (1989) Gaze-dependent visual neurons in area V3A of monkey prestriate cortex. *J. Neurosci.*, 9: 1112 – 1125.

Gentilucci, M. and Rizzolatti, G. (1990) Cortical motor control of arm and hand movements. In: M.A. Goodale (Ed.), *Vision and Action: The Control of Grasping*, Ablex, Norwood, NJ, pp. 147 – 162.

Gnadt, J.W. and Andersen, R.A. (1988) Memory related motor planning activity in posterior parietal cortex of macaque. *Exp. Brain Res.*, 70: 216 – 220.

Goldberg, M.E. and Colby, C.L. (1989) The neurophysiology of spatial vision. In: F. Boller and J. Grafman (Eds.), *Handbook of Neuropsychology, Vol. 2*, Elsevier, Amsterdam, pp. 301 – 315.

Goodale, M.A. (1983a) Vision as a sensorimotor system. In: T.E. Robinson (Ed.), *Behavioral Approaches to Brain Research*, Oxford University Press, New York, pp. 41 – 61.

Goodale, M.A. (1983b) Neural mechanisms of visual orientation in rodents: targets versus places. In: A. Hein and M. Jeannerod (Eds.), *Spatially Oriented Behavior*, Springer-Verlag, Berlin, pp. 35 – 61.

Goodale, M.A. (1988) Modularity in visuomotor control: from input to output. In: Z. Pylyshyn (Ed.), *Computational Processes in Human Vision: an Interdisciplinary Perspective*, Ablex, Norwood, NJ, pp. 262 – 285.

Goodale, M.A. and Milner, A.D. (1982) Fractionating orientation behavior in rodents. In: D.J. Ingle, M.A. Goodale and R.J.W. Mansfield (Eds.), *Analysis of Visual Behavior*, MIT Press, Cambridge, MA, pp. 549 – 586.

Goodale, M.A. and Milner, A.D. (1992) Separate visual pathways for perception and action. *Trends Neurosci.*, 15: 20 – 25.

Goodale, M.A., Milner, A.D., Jakobson, L.S. and Carey, D.P. (1991) A neurological dissociation between perceiving objects and grasping them. *Nature*, 349: 154 – 156.

Goodman, S.J. and Andersen, R.A. (1989) Microsimulation of a neural-network model for visually guided saccades. *J. Cogn. Neurosci.*, 1: 317 – 326.

Gross, C.G. (1973) Visual functions of inferotemporal cortex. In: R. Jung (Ed.), *Handbook of Sensory Physiology, Vol. 7, Part 3B*; Springer-Verlag, Berlin, pp. 451 – 482.

Gross, C.G. (1978) Inferior temporal lesions do not impair discrimination of rotated patterns in monkeys. *J. Comp. Physiol. Psychol.*, 92: 1095 – 1109.

Gross, C.G. (1991) Contribution of striate cortex and the superior colliculus to visual function in area MT, the superior temporal polysensory area and inferior temporal cortex. *Neuropsychologia*, 29: 497 – 515.

Gross, C.G., Bruce, C.J., Desimone, R., Fleming, J. and Gattass, R. (1981) Cortical visual areas of the temporal lobe: three areas in the macaque. In: C.N. Woolsey (Ed.), *Cortical Sensory Organization, Vol. 2: Multiple Visual Areas*, Humana, Clifton, NJ, pp. 187 – 216.

Gross, C.G., Desimone, R., Albright, T.D. and Schwartz, E.L. (1985) Inferior temporal cortex and pattern recognition. In: C. Chagas, R. Gattass and C.G. Gross (Eds.), *Pattern Recognition Mechanisms*, Springer-Verlag, New York, pp. 171 – 201.

Haaxma, R. and Kuypers, H.G.J.M. (1975) Intrahemispheric cortical connections and visual guidance of hand and finger movements in the rhesus monkey. *Brain*, 98: 239 – 260.

Haenny, P. and Schiller, P.H. (1988) State dependent activity in monkey visual cortex. I. Single unit activity in V1 and V4 on visual tasks. *Exp. Brain Res.*, 69: 225 – 244.

Hasselmo, M.E., Rolls, E.T., Baylis, G.C. and Nalwa, V. (1989) Object-centered encoding by face-selective neurons in the cortex in the superior temporal sulcus of the monkey. *Exp. Brain Res.*, 75: 417 – 429.

Haxby, J.V., Grady, C.L., Horwitz, B., Ungerleider, L.G., Mishkin, M., Carson, R.E., Herscovitch, P., Shapiro, M.B. and Rapoport, S.I. (1991) Dissociation of object and spatial visual processing pathways in human extrastriate cortex. *Proc. Natl. Acad. Sci. U.S.A.*, 88: 1621 – 1625.

Heilman, K.M., Pandya, D.N. and Geschwind, N. (1970) Trimodal inattention following parietal lobe ablations. *Trans. Am. Neurol. Assoc.*, 95: 259 – 261.

Heilman, K.M., Watson, R.T., Valenstein, E. and Damasio, A.T. (1983) Localization of lesions in neglect. In: A. Kertesz (Ed.), *Localization in Neuropsychology*, Academic Press, New York, pp. 471 – 492.

Holmes, E.J. and Gross, C.G. (1984) Effects of inferior tem-

poral lesions on discrimination of stimuli differing in orientation. *J. Neurosci.*, 4: 3063 – 3068.

Humphrey, N.K. and Weiskrantz, L. (1969) Size constancy in monkeys with inferotemporal lesions. *Q. J. Exp. Psychol.*, 21: 225 – 238.

Humphreys, G.W. and Riddoch, M.J. (1987) *To See but Not to See: a Case Study of Visual Agnosia*, Erlbaum, London, 124 pp.

Hyvärinen, J. and Poranen, A. (1974) Function of the parietal associative area 7 as revealed from cellular discharges in alert monkeys. *Brain*, 97: 673 – 692.

Ingle, D.J. (1980) Some effects of pretectum lesions on the frog's detection of stationary objects. *Behav. Brain. Res.*, 1: 139 – 163.

Ingle, D.J. (1982) Organization of visuomotor behaviors in vertebrates. In: D.J. Ingle, M.A. Goodale and R.J.W. Mansfield (Eds.), *Analysis of Visual Behavior*, MIT Press, Cambridge, MA, pp. 67 – 109.

Ingle, D.J. (1983) Brain mechanisms of localization in frogs and toads. In: J.P. Ewert, R.R. Capranica and D.J. Ingle (Eds.), *Advances in Vertebrate Neuroethology,*, Plenum Press, New York, pp. 177 – 226.

Jakobson, L.S. and Goodale, M.A. (1991) Factors affecting higher-order movement planning: a kinematic analysis of human prehension. *Exp. Brain Res.*, 86: 199 – 208.

Jakobson, L.S., Archibald, Y.M., Carey, D.P. and Goodale, M.A. (1991) A kinematic analysis of reaching and grasping movements in a patient recovering from optic ataxia. *Neuropsychologia*, 29: 803 – 809.

Jeannerod, M. (1988) *Neural and Behavioural Organization of Goal-directed Movements*, Oxford University Press, Oxford, 283 pp.

Jeannerod, M. and Decety, J. (1990) The accuracy of visuomotor transformation: an investigation into the mechanisms of visual recognition of objects. In: M.A. Goodale (Ed.), *Vision and Action: the Control of Grasping*, Ablex, Norwood, NJ, pp. 33 – 48.

Lamotte, R.H. and Acuna, C. (1978) Defects in accuracy of reaching after removal of posterior parietal cortex in monkeys. *Brain Res.*, 139: 319 – 326.

Lawler, K.A. and Cowey, A. (1987) On the role of posterior parietal and prefrontal cortex in visuo-spatial perception and attention. *Exp. Brain Res.*, 65: 695 – 698.

Livingstone, M. and Hubel, D. (1988) Segregation of form, color, movement, and depth: anatomy, physiology, and perception. *Science*, 240: 740 – 749.

Lynch, J.C. (1980) The functional organization of posterior parietal association cortex. *Behav. Brain Sci.*, 3: 485 – 534.

Lynch, J.C. and McLaren, J.W. (1989) Deficits of visual attention and saccadic eye movements after lesions of parieto-occipital cortex in monkeys. *J. Neurophysiol.*, 69: 460 – 468.

Marr, D. (1982) *Vision*, Freeman, San Francisco, CA, 397 pp.

Maunsell, J.H.R. and Newsome, W.T. (1987) Visual processing in monkey extrastriate cortex. *Annu. Rev. Neurosci.*, 10:

336

363 – 401.

Maunsell, J.H.R. and Van Essen, D.C. (1983) Functional properties of neurons in middle temporal visual area of the macaque monkey. I. Selectivity for stimulus direction, speed, and orientation. *J. Neurophysiol.*, 49: 1127 – 1147.

Maunsell, J.H.R., Nealy, T.A. and De Priest, D.D. (1990) Magnocellular and parvocellular contributions to responses in the middle temporal visual area (MT) of the macaque monkey. *J. Neurosci.*, 10: 3323 – 3334.

McCarthy, R.A. and Warrington, E.K. (1990) *Cognitive Neuropsychology*, Academic Press, New York, 428 pp.

Mendoza, J.E. and Thomas, R.K. (1975) Effects of posterior parietal and frontal neocortical lesions in squirrel monkeys. *J. Comp. Physiol. Psychol.*, 89: 170 – 182.

Milner, A.D. (1987a) Animal models for the syndrome of spatial neglect. In: M. Jeannerod (Ed.), *Neurophysiological and Neuropsychological Aspects of Spatial Neglect*, Elsevier, Amsterdam, pp. 259 – 288.

Milner, A.D. (1987b) Different spatial frameworks. *Behav. Brain Sci.*, 10: 128 – 129.

Milner, A.D., Ockleford, E.M. and Dewar, W. (1977) Visuospatial performance following posterior parietal and lateral frontal lesions in stumptail macaques. *Cortex*, 13: 350 – 360.

Milner, A.D., Perrett, D.I., Johnston, R.S., Benson, P.J., Jordan, T.R., Heeley, D.W., Bettucci, D., Mortara, F., Mutani, R., Terazzi, E. and Davidson, D.L.W. (1991) Perception and action in visual form agnosia. *Brain*, 114: 405 – 428.

Milner, B. (1965) Visually-guided maze-learning in man; effects of bilateral hippocampal, bilateral frontal, and unilateral cerebral lesions. *Neuropsychologia*, 3: 317 – 338.

Milner, B. (1971) Interhemispheric differences and psychological processes. *Brit. Med. Bull.*, 27: 272 – 277.

Mishkin, M., Ungerleider, L.G. and Macko, K.A. (1983) Object vision and spatial vision: two cortical pathways. *Trends Neurosci.*, 6: 414 – 417.

Moran, J. and Desimone, R. (1985) Selective attention gates visual processing in the extrastriate cortex. *Science*, 229: 782 – 784.

Morel, A. and Bullier, J. (1990) Anatomical segregation of two cortical visual pathways in the macaque monkey. *Vis. Neurosci.*, 4: 555 – 578.

Motter, B.C. and Mountcastle, V.B. (1981) The functional properties of the light-sensitive neurons of the posterior parietal cortex studied in waking monkeys: foveal sparing and opponent vector organization. *J. Neurosci.*, 1: 3 – 26.

Mountcastle, V.B., Lynch, J.C., Georgopoulos, A., Sakata, H. and Acuna, C. (1975) Posterior parietal association cortex of the monkey: command functions for operations within extrapersonal space. *J. Neurophysiol.*, 38: 871 – 908.

Newcombe, F. and Russell, W.R. (1969) Dissociated visual perceptual and spatial deficits in focal lesions of the right hemisphere. *J. Neurol. Neurosurg. Psychiat.*, 32: 73 – 81.

Newcombe, F., Ratcliff, G. and Damasio, H. (1987) Dissociable visual and spatial impairments following right posterior cerebral lesions: clinical, neuropsychological and anatomical evidence. *Neuropsychologia*, 25: 149 – 161.

Newsome, W.T., Wurtz, R.H. and Komatsu, H. (1988) Relation of cortical areas MT and MST to pursuit eye movements. II. Differentiation of retinal from extraretinal inputs. *J. Neurophysiol.*, 60: 604 – 620.

Niki, H. and Watanabe, M. (1976) Prefrontal unit activity and delayed response: relation to cue location versus direction of response. *Brain Res.*, 105: 79 – 88.

Perenin, M.-T. and Vighetto, A. (1988) Optic ataxia: a specific disruption in visuomotor mechanisms. I. Different aspects of the deficit in reaching for objects. *Brain*, 111: 643 – 674.

Perrett, D.I., Smith, P.A.J., Potter, D.D., Mistlin, A.J., Head, A.S., Milner, A.D. and Jeeves, M. (1984) Neurones responsive to faces in the temporal cortex: studies of functional organization, sensitivity to identity and relation to perception. *Hum. Neurobiol.*, 3: 197 – 208.

Perrett, D.I., Mistlin, A.J. and Chitty, A.J. (1987) Visual neurones responsive to faces. *Trends Neurosci.*, 10: 358 – 364.

Perrett, D.I., Harries, M.H., Bevan, R., Thomas, S., Benson, P.J., Mistlin, A.J., Chitty, A.J., Hietanen, J.K. and Ortega, J.E. (1989) Frameworks of analysis for the neural representation of animate objects and actions. *J. Exp. Biol.*, 146: 87 – 113.

Perrett, D.I., Mistlin, A.J., Harries, M.H. and Chitty, A.J. (1990) Understanding the visual appearance and consequence of hand actions. In: M.A. Goodale (Ed.), *Vision and Action: The Control of Grasping*, Ablex, Norwood, NJ, pp. 163 – 180.

Perrett, D.I., Oram, M.W., Harries, M.H., Bevan, R., Hietanen, J.K., Benson, P.J. and Thomas, S. (1991) Viewer-centred and object-centred coding of heads in the macaque temporal cortex. *Exp. Brain Res.*, 86: 159 – 173.

Petrides, M. and Iversen, S.D. (1979) Restricted posterior parietal lesions in the rhesus monkey and performance on visuospatial tasks. *Brain Res.*, 161: 63 – 77.

Petrides, M. and Pandya, D.N. (1984) Projections to the frontal cortex from the posterior parietal region in the rhesus monkey. *J. Comp. Neurol.*, 228: 105 – 116.

Pohl, W. (1973) Dissociation of spatial discrimination deficits following frontal and parietal lesions in monkeys. *J. Comp. Physiol. Psychol.*, 82: 227 – 239.

Pribram, K.H. (1967) In: D.B. Lindsley and A.A. Lumsdaine (Eds.), *Brain Function and Learning*, University of California Press, pp. 79 – 122.

Ratcliff, G. and Davies-Jones, G.A.B. (1972) Defective visual localization in focal brain wounds. *Brain*, 95: 49 – 60.

Ratcliff, G. and Newcombe, F. (1973) Spatial orientation in man: effects of left, right, and bilateral posterior cerebral lesions. *J. Neurol. Neurosurg. Psychiat.*, 36: 448 – 454.

Richmond, B.J. and Sato, T. (1987) Enhancement of inferior temporal neurons during visual discrimination. *J. Neurophysiol.*, 58: 1292 – 1306.

Ridley, R. and Ettlinger, G. (1975) Tactile and visuo-spatial discrimination performance in the monkey: the effects of total and partial posterior parietal removals. *Neuropsychologia*, 13: 191 – 206.

Rizzolatti, G., Gentilucci, M. and Matelli, M. (1985) Selective spatial attention: one center, one circuit, or many circuits? In: M.I. Posner and O.S.M. Marin (Eds.), *Attention and Performance XI*, Erlbaum, Hillsdale, NJ, pp. 251 – 265.

Robinson, D.L., Goldberg, M.E. and Stanton, G.B. (1978) Parietal association cortex in the primate: sensory mechanisms and behavioral modulations. *J. Neurophysiol.*, 41: 910 – 932.

Saito, H., Yukie, M., Tanaka, K., Hikosaka, D., Fukada, Y. and Iwai, E. (1986) Integration of direction signals of image motion in the superior temporal sulcus of the macaque monkey. *J. Neurosci.*, 6: 145 – 157.

Saito, H., Tanaka, K., Isono, H., Yasuda, M. and Mikami, A. (1989) Directionally selective response of cells in the middle temporal area (MT) of the macaque monkey to the movement of equiluminous opponent colour stimuli. *Exp. Brain Res.*, 75: 1 – 14.

Sayner, R.B. and Davis, R.T. (1972) Significance of sign in an S-R separation problem. *Percept. Motor Skills*, 34: 671 – 676.

Schiller, P.H. and Logothetis, N.K. (1990) The color-opponent and broad-band channels of the primate visual system. *Trends Neurosci.*, 13: 392 – 398.

Sejnowski, T.J. (1991) Back together again. *Nature*, 352: 669 – 670.

Shepard, R.N. and Metzler, J. (1971) Mental rotation of three-dimensional objects. *Science*, 171: 701 – 703.

Smith, M.L. and Milner, B. (1989) Right hippocampal impairment in the recall of spatial location: encoding deficit or rapid forgetting? *Neuropsychologia*, 27: 71 – 81.

Sparks, D.L. and May, L.E. (1990) Signal transformations required for the generation of saccadic eye movements. *Annu. Rev. Neurosci.*, 13: 309 – 336.

Sugishita, M., Ettlinger, G. and Ridley, R.M. (1978) Disturbance of cage-finding in the monkey. *Cortex*, 14: 431 – 438.

Taira, M., Mine, S., Georgopoulos, A.P., Murata, A. and Sakata, H. (1990) Parietal cortex neurons of the monkey related to the visual guidance of hand movement. *Exp. Brain Res.*, 83: 29 – 36.

Tanaka, K. and Saito, H. (1989) Analysis of motion of the visual field by direction, expansion/contraction, and rotation cells clustered in the dorsal part of the medial superior temporal area of the macaque monkey. *J. Neurophysiol.*, 62: 626 – 641.

Traverse, J. and Latto, R. (1986) Impairments in route navigation through a maze after dorsolateral frontal, inferior parietal or pre-motor lesions in cynomolgous monkeys. *Behav. Brain Res.*, 20: 203 – 215.

Ungerleider, L.G. and Brody, B.A. (1977) Extrapersonal spatial orientation: the role of posterior parietal, anterior frontal, and inferotemporal cortex. *Exp. Neurol.*, 56: 265 – 280.

Ungerleider, L.G. and Mishkin, M. (1982) Two cortical visual systems. In: D.J. Ingle, M.A. Goodale and R.J.W. Mansfield (Eds.), *Analysis of Visual Behavior*, MIT Press, Cambridge, MA, pp. 549 – 586.

Valenstein, E., Heilman, K.M., Watson, R.T. and Van Den Abell, T. (1982) Nonsensory neglect from parietotemporal lesions in monkeys. *Neurology*, 32: 1198 – 1202.

Vallar, G. and Perani, D. (1986) The anatomy of unilateral neglect after right-hemisphere stroke lesions. A clinical/CT-scan correlation study in man. *Neuropsychologia*, 24: 609 – 622.

Weiskrantz, L. and Saunders, R.C. (1984) Impairments of visual object transforms in monkeys. *Brain*, 107: 1033 – 1072.

Zeki, S. and Shipp, S. (1988) The functional logic of cortical connections. *Nature*, 335: 311 – 317.

Zipser, D. and Andersen, R.A. (1988) A back-propagation programmed network that simulates response properties of a subset of posterior parietal neurons. *Nature*, 331: 679 – 684.

T.P. Hicks, S. Molotchnikoff and T. Ono (Eds.)
Progress in Brain Research, Vol. 95
© 1993 Elsevier Science Publishers B.V. All rights reserved.

CHAPTER 29

Amygdalar and hippocampal neuron responses related to recognition and memory in monkey

Hisao Nishijo, Taketoshi Ono, Ryoi Tamura and Kiyomi Nakamura

Department of Physiology, Faculty of Medicine, Toyama Medical and Pharmaceutical University, Sugitani 2630, Toyama 930 – 01, Japan

Introduction

The medial temporal lobe, including the amygdala and hippocampal formation, has been implicated in a variety of mnemonic and cognitive processes. In monkey and human, bilateral damage to the medial temporal lobes induces global amnesia, i.e., memory deficits extending to all sensory modalities (Scoville and Milner, 1957; Mishkin, 1978, 1982; Zola-Morgan et al., 1982; Murray and Mishkin, 1983; Duyckaerts et al., 1985). Anatomical evidence suggests that all sensory information converges on the medial temporal lobe, and mnemonic and cognitive functions of the medial temporal lobe depend on such connections (Ross, 1980). It has been suggested that sequential processing of sensory information occurs in the neocortex (Turner et al., 1980; Pons et al., 1987). The amygdala receives highly integrated sensory information from all modalities in a late stage of this sequential processing (Gloor, 1960; Aggleton et al., 1980; Turner et al., 1980; Iwai and Yukie, 1987). The entorhinal cortex, which receives similar information mainly from parahippocampal gyrus and perirhinal cortices, and the amygdala also project to the hippocampal formation (Van Hoesen, 1982; Insausti et al., 1987).

The neural circuit containing the amygdala, and that containing the hippocampal formation, may function in parallel (Mishkin, 1982). However, differences in intrinsic and extrinsic anatomical connections between the amygdala and the hippocampal formation suggest functional differences. The amygdala projects not only to the hypothalamus (Oomura et al., 1970; Krettek and Price, 1978; Price and Amaral, 1981; Amaral et al., 1982; Ono et al., 1985), but also directly to the brain-stem autonomic area (Price and Amaral, 1981; Schwaber et al., 1982; Veening et al., 1984). This evidence has led some investigators to speculate that sensory inputs to emotional and autonomic processes may be relayed through the amygdala (Turner et al., 1980; LeDoux, 1990). In this information flow from the sensory cortex to the hypothalamus and lower brain-stem, the amygdala might be involved in processes through which sensory stimuli achieve motivational and emotional significance as a result of interaction between the higher sensory cortex and the limbic system, i.e., stimulus-affective association (Weiskrantz, 1956; Jones and Mishkin, 1972; Spiegler and Mishkin, 1981; Murray and Mishkin, 1985; Gaffan et al., 1988). Thus, bilateral lesions of the monkey amygdala and/or temporal cortex which produce visual-limbic disconnections (Geschwind, 1965) might cause sensory-affective dissociation (Jones and Mishkin, 1972). These assumptions imply that amygdalar neurons should respond to the affective significance of sensory stimuli (Mishkin and Aggleton, 1981).

On the other hand, the hippocampal formation has widespread connections with supramodal and polysensory association cortices such as the prefrontal, parietal and entorhinal cortices (Van Hoesen, 1982; Insausti et al., 1987). Based on these connections, it is suggested that the hippocampal formation is involved in representational memory (Goldman-Rakic, 1987), declarative memory (Squire, 1987), working memory (Olton et al., 1979), episodic memory (Tulving, 1983), cognitive mapping (O'Keefe and Nadel, 1978), relational processing (Eichenbaum et al., 1990), and configural association (Sutherland and Rudy, 1989). Unlike the amygdala, spatial cues are important determinants of hippocampal function, as shown by recording (O'Keefe and Conway, 1978; Muller and Kubie, 1987; Eichenbaum et al., 1989) and lesion studies (Morris et al., 1982; Corkin, 1984; Parkinson et al., 1988; Gaffan and Harrison, 1989). This is probably due to dense connections with the parietal cortex through the entorhinal cortex (McNaughton et al., 1989). These postulated functions of the medial temporal lobe suggest that neurons in the medial temporal cortex should respond to some, or possibly to all forms of sensory stimulation to form memories of ongoing sensory experiences and to recognize the biologically significant objects.

In this chapter, we first characterize, in several ways, the responses of amygdalar and hippocampal neurons to affective sensory stimuli. Amygdalar and hippocampal neuronal responses to stimuli that were considered to be biologically significant (Weiskrantz, 1956; Horel et al., 1975; Perrett et al., 1982) were studied in various behavioral tasks that involved the discrimination of different rewarding and aversive stimuli. Some neurons were also tested by changing the affective significance of the stimuli presented. Comparison of amygdalar and hippocampal neuronal responsiveness to affective sensory stimuli may elucidate differences in the functions of these two structures. Functional connections between the association cortex and medial temporal lobe (and the hypothalamus), which may underlie amygdalar and hippocampal responsiveness to complex sensory stimuli, were investigated by analyzing neuronal response changes

during reversible disconnection of the inferotemporal cortex from the amygdala, or disconnection of the amygdala from the hypothalamus, by cooling the inferotemporal cortex or the amygdala. We next analyzed hippocampal neurons in more detail by introducing a spatial factor. In another set of experiments, monkey hippocampal neurons were recorded during performance of a spatial moving task.

Neuronal responses to biologically significant objects in the amygdala and hippocampal formation

Experimental design for presentation of biologically significant complex sensory stimuli

Macaca fuscata monkeys were restrained painlessly in a stereotaxic apparatus by a previously prepared, surgically fixed head holder designed in our laboratory (Ono et al., 1980, 1981a, 1988). They sat in a chair facing a panel that had two shutters (one opaque and one transparent), and a bar for operant responding. Liquid was accessible to the monkey through a small spout controlled by an electromagnetic valve (Fig. 1A). Aversive stimulation was administered as a weak electric shock applied between the earlobes. The program included visual discrimination (feeding, drinking, and active avoidance), and auditory discrimination tasks (Fig. 1B,C; Nishijo et al., 1988a,b). During a recording session behavior and eye movement were monitored by TV camaras or electro-oculography, or both, as well as by direct observation by the experimenter.

Two task situations, an original and a modified one, were used. In the original version of feeding task an opaque shutter (W1) was opened at random intervals. The monkeys could see an object through a transparent shutter (W2) in front of the turntable. The animal could then obtain the object if it wanted to, by pressing the bar a predetermined number of times (fixed ratio, FR 10 – 30). The last bar press opened W2 and the animal could then take the object, and ingest it if it was desirable food (Fig. 1B, solid line). Similarly, when the FR criterion was met in drinking tasks, W1 was automatically closed and

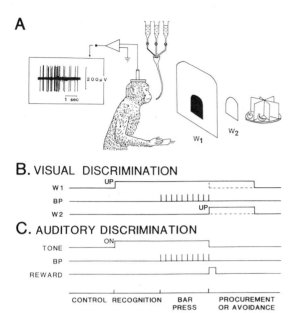

A

B. VISUAL DISCRIMINATION

W1
BP
W2

C. AUDITORY DISCRIMINATION

TONE
BP
REWARD

CONTROL RECOGNITION BAR PRESS PROCUREMENT OR AVOIDANCE

Fig. 1. Schema of an experimental setup (A) and time sequences of two operant tasks (B,C). A. Monkey sat in a chair facing a panel with a bar, and a window covered by two shutters (W1, an opaque shutter; W2, a transparent shutter in front of a turntable). Liquid delivered from a spout near monkey's mouth. B. Time sequence of visual discrimination tasks that involved feeding (solid line), drinking (dashed line), and avoidance (dashed line). C. Time sequence of auditory discrimination task. Shutters opened at Up (B). BP: indications of individual bar presses and time during which they occurred (B,C). Liquid dispensed from spout after last bar press if a particular object was presented. Tone indicated availability of reward in auditory discrimination test (C). Reward: drop of juice dispensed from spout after last bar press, or cookie or raisin on turntable became available by simultaneous opening of W1 and W2 after last bar press.

a drop of potable liquid (juice or water) portended by some symbolic object (column, cube, etc.) could be licked from a small spout (Fig. 1B, dashed line). A white and a red cylinder were usually associated, respectively, with juice and water, for example. In active avoidance tasks, a brown cylinder, for example, was associated with a weak electric shock. If the animal saw the brown cylinder and heard the 1200 Hz tone, it had to complete a FR schedule within 4–6 sec to avoid electric shock. The last bar press closed W1 (Fig. 1B, dashed line). In the auditory discrimination task a buzzer noise was associated with food (cookie or raisin), and a fundamental frequency of 800 Hz tone with a drop of juice. When the animal heard the buzzer or the 800 Hz tone, it had to complete a FR schedule to obtain the corresponding food or juice, as in the feeding task (Fig. 1C). Two pure tones (2800 or 4300 Hz) were introduced as neutral stimuli, not associated with either reward or electric shock.

In the modification of the task described above, the monkey could see an object on a stage through a one-way mirror (S1) in front of the stage when a light was turned on. However, another shutter (S2) prevented access to the bar. After a delay of at least 2 sec, S2 was opened automatically. The S1 shutter was opened by the last bar press. The monkey's behavior and the neuronal responses were essentially the same in this and the previously described situation. The task was divided into three phases: (1) visual discrimination of an object (recognition); (2) operant responding (bar pressing); and (3) ingestion or avoidance (procurement or avoidance).

Based on our behavioral tests and earlier studies (Weiskrantz, 1956; Horel et al., 1975; Perrett et al., 1982), the affective significance of these stimuli was classified into four groups: unfamiliar, familiar positive (rewarding), familiar negative (aversive), and familiar neutral. After these tests, the affective significance of some of these stimuli was altered or discontinued in reversal or extinction trials. In one example of a reversal test, salt was carefully put in, or on, the back of food so both salted and normal food appeared similar, or in another example, saline was associated with either the red or white cylinder that was previously associated with water or juice. In extinction tests, the sight of food or a cue signal was presented, but the reward remained unavailable. In some cases weak electric shock was predicted by some objects that previously indicated reward.

To evaluate the effects of disconnection, cooling probes were chronically implanted bilaterally over the dura of the anterior inferotemporal cortex in one monkey, and in the lateral amygdala in two monkeys. The temperature in the inferotemporal cortex ranged from 18° to 23°C, and around the cooling probes in the amygdala, the temperature fell

342

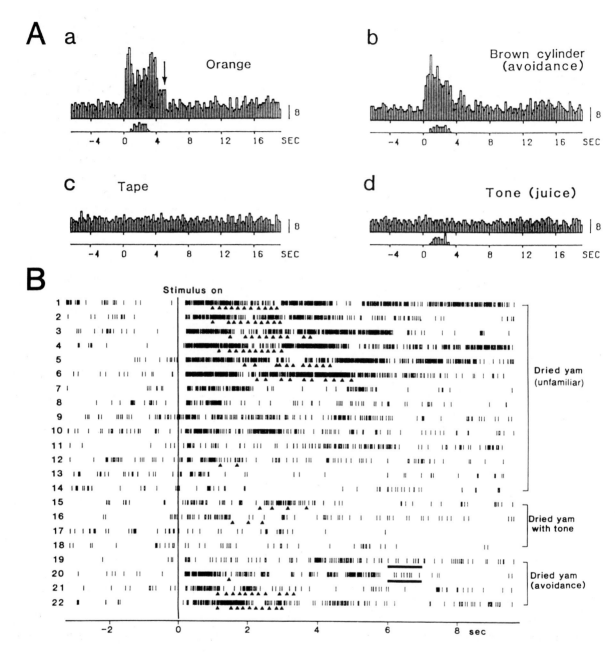

Fig. 2. Responses of Vis-I amygdalar neuron. *A*. Activity increased at the sight of positive (*a*) and negative (*b*) affect-related stimuli, but not to neutral objects (*c*). However, neuron did not respond to positive affect-related auditory stimuli (fundamental frequency of 800 Hz tone) (*d*). Note absence of neuronal response after animal put orange into mouth (*a*, indicated by arrow). Bar presses shown by histograms on time scales. Abscissae: time (sec); W1 opened at time 0. Ordinates: summed responses from four trials. Calibration at right of each histogram: number of spikes in each bin. *B*. Raster display of other responses of neuron exemplified in Fig. 2*A*. The dried yam, which was handled and smelled but never tasted, was not accepted by the monkey as food. In trials 1 – 14 the response gradually habituated. In trials 15 – 18 the dried yam was presented with the 1200 Hz tone that was used in the active avoidance task. In trials 19 – 22 the response appeared again after association with electric shock (underbars in trials 19 and 20). Shock was avoided in trials 21 and 22. Abscissae: time (sec); W1 opened at time 0. Each filled triangle below a raster display indicates one bar press.

below 20°C. This temperature depression was sufficient to suppress synaptic transmission (Jasper et al., 1970), and the effects were reversible upon restoration of normal temperature.

Amygdalar neuronal responses to affective objects or sounds

Responsiveness of amygdalar neurons. A total of 710 amygdalar neurons were tested by recording the activity changes in response to various objects, or stimulation of various sensory modalities that did or did not have affective significance. Of these 710 neurons, half responded in some phase(s) of the operant tasks. Based on their responsiveness to sensory modalities, these responsive neurons fell into five major categories; vision-related, audition-related, ingestion-related, multimodal, and selective. The multimodal categories included neurons that responded to visual, auditory, and somesthetic stimuli, as well as, when tested, to forced injection of liquid into the mouth. The selective neurons responded to repeated presentation of only one among various objects or sensory stimuli. Depending on responsiveness to other stimuli, the ingestion-related group was subdivided into three subgroups: oral sensory, oral sensory plus vision, and oral sensory plus audition. Oral sensory could mean responsive to touch, temperature, taste or odor; the modality was not determined.

Substantial numbers of amygdalar neurons responded to rewarding and/or aversive objects or sounds (biologically significant objects), but not to neutral objects or sounds. Of the amygdalar neurons, 6.8% responded (all excited) to the sight of some objects, but not to auditory, oral sensory or somesthetic stimuli (vision-related neurons). These neurons responded strongly to the sight of unfamiliar objects regardless of whether they were food or non-food, and to the sight of some familiar non-food objects. Among the vision-related neurons, more than half responded consistently to rewarding objects such as familiar food and the red or white cylinders associated with water or juice, as well as to certain non-food objects such as the brown

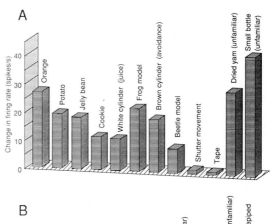

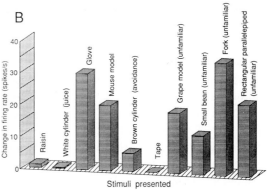

Fig. 3. Comparison of vision-related amygdalar neuron responses to various objects. *A.* Responses of Vis-I neuron. Each column shows response magnitude after the indicated objects were revealed, i.e., the mean discharge rate (spikes/sec) of four 5 sec firing rates minus spontaneous rate. Rearranged here to compare among different foods (left 5 columns), various non-food objects (midleft 3 columns), neutral (midright 2 columns), and unfamiliar objects (right 2 columns). Unfamiliar stimuli evoked the greatest responses. Neuronal responses to object shown here (and to other objects not shown) correlated with magnitude of behavioral response. *B.* Responses of Vis-II neurons. Note pronounced responses to unfamiliar objects and no response to familiar positive food and neutral object. Response magnitudes: means of mean discharge rates of three trials.

cylinder that was associated with electric shock, a syringe, a glove, etc., but not to neutral non-food objects (tape) (Vis-I type). Fig. 2 illustrates responses of a typical Vis-I neuron. This neuron responded strongly to both familiar positive (*Aa*, orange) and negative (*Ab*, brown cylinder) objects, but not to familiar neutral tape (*Ac*, tape). In contrast to its responses to visual stimuli, this neuron did not respond to familiar positive auditory stimuli (*Ad*). Those stimuli did, however, elicit various overt reactions, such as bar pressing. Fig. 2*Aa* shows no response after putting orange into the mouth (indicated by arrow), so this neuron did not respond to oral sensory stimuli. Responses of this particular neuron to various food and non-food objects are compared in Fig. 3*A*. The response magnitude was significantly different in response to different objects in that the neuron responded more strongly to more preferred food than to less preferred food. Of the 6.8% of neurons that responded to the sight of objects, almost half responded similarly to unfamiliar objects and to certain familiar negative objects. However, these neurons did not respond to familiar reward-related objects, such as food or red and white cylinders associated with water and juice (Vis-II type) (Fig. 3*B*). Among the amygdalar neurons, 13.2% responded tonically to all of the sensory modality stimuli (vision, audition, oral sensory and somesthesis) that were biologically significant or potentially significant, but not to stimuli that were known to be neutral stimuli. The response pattern of these neurons was similar to those of Vis-I neurons, but their responses were multimodal.

Another 2.4% of amygdalar neurons were highly selective for only particular familiar biologically significant objects or sounds (selective neurons): 1.0% responded for one specific food item or for a cylinder associated with a potable; 0.9% responded for one specific non-food item; and 0.5% responded for one specific sound. Examples of responses that indicated selectivity for one specific food item are shown in Fig. 4. This neuron was tested with 16 objects and seven somesthetic and auditory stimuli (not all shown), and the magnitude of its response to the sight of watermelon was great enough to make its responses to any other stimulus relatively insignificant (Fig. 4*A*). An example of a neuron that responded to a specific non-food item is shown in Fig. 4*B*. This neuron was tested with 16 objects and eight somesthetic and auditory stimuli, and responded only to the sight of a spider model.

The analysis of relation between neuronal and behavioral responses indicates one important

characteristic of amygdalar neurons. There was not always direct correlation between rate or amount of bar pressing and neuronal activity, and no direct correlation between individual bar presses and neuronal activity in the amygdala (direct, one-to-one motor-coupled response) was ever observed. Although spontaneous bar pressing during intertrial intervals was rare, when such spontaneous pressing did occur no concomitant neuronal activity change was ever observed. In high FR (FR 30) trials the responses of Vis-I neurons returned to the control level during bar pressing and then reappeared when the shutter was opened after the last bar press. Even when there was no bar pressing, Vis-I type neurons would respond to the sight of biologically significant objects. Both of these results are consistent

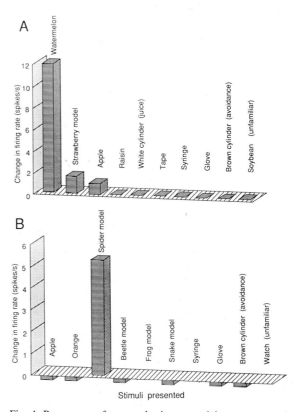

Fig. 4. Responses of two selective amygdalar neurons. *A*. Responses of neuron selective to watermelon. *B*. Responses of neuron selective to spider model. Neither neuron responded at sight of other objects presented. Other descriptions as for Fig. 3*B*.

with a previous study (Ono et al., 1980). In the bar press phase, the animal usually looked at the window, and Vis-I type neuron responses in that phase depended on the affective nature of the objects. During the bar press phase, responses of some neurons to the most preferred food were significantly stronger than responses of the same neurons to less preferred food. Nevertheless, differences in the duration of the bar press phase, which was inversely related to the rapidity of bar pressing, were not statistically significant, except in reversal tests when some confusion might be expected. Vis-II neurons seldom responded to familiar positive objects, although the animal responded behaviorally. However, there was some apparent tendency toward indirect relations between neuronal and behavioral responses. For instance, stronger neuronal responses accompanied normal bar pressing, but the same neurons responded less vigorously when bar pressing was delayed or absent (Figs. 2B, 5) as in extinction or reversal trials (see next section). Similar relations have been reported for the lateral hypothalamic area (Fukuda et al., 1986). Our present results imply that neuronal activity in the amygdala is not directly related to sensory inputs nor to overt acts of the animals. Neuronal activity may, however, reflect motivational aspects of an animal's behavioral responses (Ono et al., 1980; Nishijo et al., 1986). Consequently it may reflect an animal's attention to a biologically significant object among various exteroceptive stimuli, since some responses of those neurons were suppressed by extinction or by changing the affective significance of an object (see next section).

The present results, which indicate that many amygdalar neurons respond to biologically significant objects, are consistent with previous recording studies in cats (Sawa and Delgado, 1963; O'Keefe and Bouma, 1969) and monkeys (Sanghera et al., 1979; Ono et al., 1980, 1983). The present results along with those in previous recording studies, suggest that complex sensory stimuli, such as a biologically significant real object, are adequate stimuli for amygdalar neurons.

Effects of reversal and extinction on visual responses, and their relations to operant responding. Response change during extinction trials support a previous inference. Although Vis-I neurons responded similarly to both rewarding and aversive objects, the change in response that occurred when the affective significance of an object was altered indicates that this factor was also important in addition to the physical characteristics of the object. The neuron characterized in Fig. 2A was also studied in a gradually changing situation (Fig. 2B). Responses to unfamiliar objects (dried yam, which the monkey apparently rejected as food) habituated gradually in trials 1 – 14 as the object became familiar and the monkey learned that the object was biologically meaningless. When the dried yam plus the 1200 Hz tone was presented instead of the brown cylinder plus the 1200 Hz tone (avoidance task) without electric shock, the initial response was slight, and quickly habituated in trials 15 – 18 as the monkey learned that the dried yam was meaningless. When the dried yam plus the tone preceded electric shock (broad line below raster display in trials 19 and 20), bar pressing and neuronal responses were quickly elicited (trials 19 – 22). In trial 20 the neuronal response was elicited without bar pressing for avoidance, and in trials 20 – 22 the neural responses were time-locked to the sight of dried yam. This observation reveals that the neuronal responses were not related directly to the avoidance situation, but to the dried yam associated with electric shock. Thus, the neuronal response to the sight of dried yam was modified when associated with other stimuli (1200 Hz tone and electric shock) and evinced a relation to overt avoidance behavior.

Eight neurons that responded to the sight of reward-related objects (four oral sensory plus vision, and four selective neurons) were tested with alteration of affective significance (reversal test). Not only the visual-, but also the ingestion-related responses of all eight neurons were attenuated by salting the food. Fig. 5A shows modulation of responses of an oral sensory plus vision neuron. In the visual and ingestion phases, this neuron

346

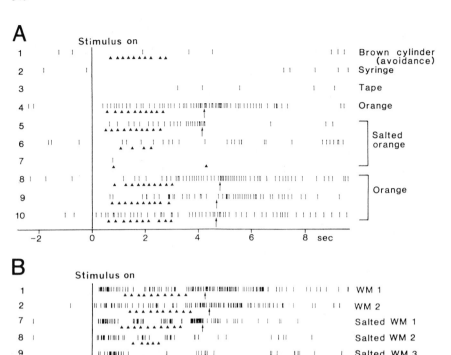

Fig. 5. Modulation of amygdalar neuron responses by reversal tests. *A.* Raster display of responses of oral sensory plus vision neuron. Neuron did not respond to avoidance task (trial 1), nor to syringe and tape (trials 2,3), but responded to ingestion and sight of orange (trial 4). Trials 5 – 10 show reversal associated with salted food. Neuronal response disappeared at the moment when animal put a salted orange into its mouth (arrow in trial 5). Other details as for Fig. 2*B*. *B.* Raster display of responses of neuron selective to watermelon. Neuron responded to sight and ingestion of normal watermelon in trials 1 and 2. After intervening 4 trials (not shown), neuronal responses decreased at the moment the animal put salted watermelon into its mouth (arrow in trial 7). In trials 8 – 11 the neuronal and bar pressing responses gradually decreased and finally disappeared. Other details as for Fig. 2*B*.

responded to orange in trials 4 and 8 – 10. However, this neuron did not respond to any known aversive or neutral object such as the brown cylinder that was associated with electric shock, a syringe (aversive), tape (neutral), or salted orange (aversive) (trials 1 – 3, 4, and others not shown). Trials 4 – 10 show the effects of salting orange. The attenuation was apparent during both the visual inspection and ingestion phases of the task. In the first salted orange trial (trail 5), the response disappeared immediately after putting salted orange into the animal's mouth.

Salting of orange was always done in such a way that the salt could not be seen, so it was first detected by the animal upon ingestion. The response to the sight of orange diminished in subsequent salted orange trials (trials 6 and 7), as well as in the first two unsalted orange trials that followed (trials 8 and 9). After the experimenter gave a piece of unsalted orange to the animal by hand, bar pressing to obtain orange began again in trials 8 – 10, and neuronal responses to the sight and ingestion of orange quickly recovered.

Fig. 5*B* shows the modulation of activity of a neuron that responded selectively to watermelon as shown in Fig. 3*A*. The neuron responded consistently at the sight and ingestion of watermelon in trials 1 and 2. In trials 7 – 11 after four intervening trials, salted watermelon reversibly modified the activity that occurred during both the sight and ingestion of that stimulus. Salted watermelon was visually indistinguishable from unsalted watermelon, and in trial 7 the neuron responded as previously until the salted watermelon was ingested (indicated by arrow), at which point the activity suddenly decreased. In trials 8 – 11 the response to the sight of watermelon rapidly decreased and finally disappeared. After the experimenter gave a piece of unsalted watermelon to the animal by hand, neuronal and bar pressing responses resumed in trials 12 and 13.

The results indicate that responses of rewarding object-related amygdalar neurons (some oral sensory plus vision and some selective to a specific food) and behavioral responses were both suppressed in reversal tests. During the test neuronal and behavioral responses were well correlated. The responses of both types of neurons were first suppressed during the initial ingestion of salted food, then suppression of visual responses followed although visual appearance of food was the same. This dependence of visual responses on oral sensory stimulation suggests that these neurons had cross-modal responsiveness based on visual-oral sensory (possibly gustatory) association suggested in part by a lesion study (Murray and Mishkin, 1985). Geschwind (1965) also suggested function of the limbic system in visual-gustatory association, which is essential for stimulus-reward association. This rapid and plastic change could be the neurophysiological basis for a role of the amygdala in learning of stimulus-affect association such as in single trials of unique object-reward association (Spiegler and Mishkin, 1981) and acquisition of fear-potentiated startle (Miserendino et al., 1990).

Locations of the neuron types. Localization of each neuron type is shown in Fig. 6. Vision-related neurons were located in the anterior laterodorsal part of the amygdala including the lateral nucleus (Fig. 6*A*, filled triangles). Vis-I neurons were more

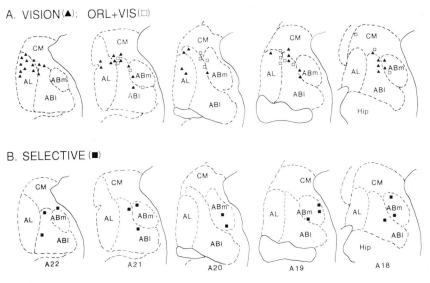

Fig. 6. Recording sites of three amygdalar neuron types. *A*. Vision-related, filled triangles; oral sensory plus vision (ORL + VIS), open squares. *B*. Selective, filled squares. CM, Corticomedial group of amygdala; AL, lateral nucleus; ABl, basolateral nucleus; ABm, basomedial nucleus. Number below each section indicates distance (mm) anterior from interaural line.

medial than Vis-II, that is, in the border area between the basolateral nucleus and the other nuclei. The audition-related neurons were located in the posterolateral part of the amygdala (mainly in the lateral and basolateral nuclei) (not shown). Ingestion-related neurons were located in the corticomedial group and the medial site of the lateral nucleus, or along the border zone between the lateral and basolateral nuclei. Among ingestion-related neurons, most oral sensory plus vision type were found along the dorsal edge of the basolateral nuclei (Fig. 6A, open squares). The multimodal type was widely distributed in the amygdala except the lateral part (not shown). The selective type was located in the basolateral and basomedial nuclei (Fig. 6B, filled squares). Patterns of distribution of sensory responsive neurons in the amygdala were largely consistent with anatomical studies which indicated topograph-

ic projections from the temporal cortex to the amygdala (Turner et al., 1980; Iwai et al., 1987). It has been reported that some inferotemporal neurons each respond to some specific figure, symbolic shape, or color (Perrett et al., 1982; Fuster and Jervey, 1982; Miyashita and Chang, 1988; Fuster, 1990). Projection from these inferotemporal cortical neurons may contribute to amygdalar neuronal responses to complex stimuli. In the next section, the functional significance of this pathway, based on investigation by reversible cooling, is described.

Amygdalar and lateral hypothalamic neuronal responses during reversible cooling of the inferotemporal cortex or the amygdala

A total of 43 amygdalar and 55 lateral hypothalamic neurons were tested by cooling the in-

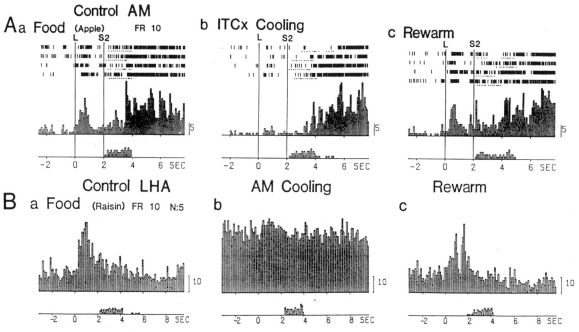

Fig. 7. Effects of cooling inferotemporal cortex (*A*) and amygdala (*B*) in a modified feeding task. *A*. Raster displays and histograms (80 msec bins, 10.24 sec) of food-responsive amygdalar neuron activity changes during control (*a*), inferotemporal cooling (*b*), and rewarmed states (*c*). Only responses to sight of food selectively suppressed, but ingestion response remained during cooling of inferotemporal cortex (*b*). *B*. Histograms (100 msec bins, 12.8 sec) of food-responsive lateral hypothalamic neuron responses for five trials during control (*a*), amygdalar cooling (*b*), and rewarmed states (*c*). There were no significant visual responses to sight of food during amygdalar cooling, although spontaneous firing rate increased remarkably (*c*). Dots under each raster line: individual bar presses. Time 0 and L, light on; S2, shutter in front of bar opened. Other descriptions as for Fig. 2*A*.

ferotemporal cortex or the amygdala to investigate functional pathways from the inferotemporal cortex to the hypothalamus through the amygdala (Fukuda et al., 1987). Of the amygdalar neurons that responded differentially to the sight of food or non-food, half became non-responsive or non-discriminative during cooling of the inferotemporal cortex. Fig. 7A shows one example of such modulation by cooling of inferotemporal cortex. Before cooling, the neuron activity increased at the sight of food and during ingestion in all trials (Fig. 7Aa). About 3 min after the start of cooling of the inferotemporal cortex, the visual responses to the sight of food disappeared in each of the four trials (Fig. 7Ab). Cooling of the inferotemporal cortex did not change responses of this particular neuron during ingestion (Fig. 7Ab). Thus deficits in the inferotemporal cortex mainly depressed visually related neuronal responses in the amygdala. This evidence suggests that the inferotemporal cortex is in one of the paths of object-related information passing from the visual cortex to the amygdala.

Cooling of the amygdala changed (weakened or depressed) responses of 40% of the food-responsive neurons in the lateral hypothalamus, and affected spontaneous firing rates of 40% of the visually responsive neurons (Fig. 7B). During cooling of the amygdala, no excitatory visual response was significantly greater than the background activity, since spontaneous firing in the lateral hypothalamus was greatly increased by bilateral cooling of the amygdala (Fig. 7Bb). In contrast to the effects of cooling the inferotemporal cortex, which did not affect amygdalar responses in the ingestion phase, amygdalar cooling depressed the responses of 25% of the lateral hypothalamic neurons that responded in the ingestion phase (not shown). Thus, deficits in the amygdala mainly depressed responses (excitatory or inhibitory) in the lateral hypothalamus that were related to visual and ingestion signals. This is consistent with our previous studies in which the effects of amygdalar stimulation on lateral hypothalamic neurons were generally either inhibitory or disinhibitory (Oomura et al., 1970; Ono et al., 1981b).

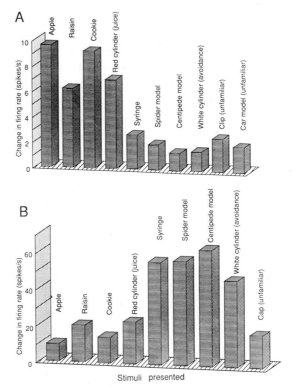

Fig. 8. Responses of rewarding-object-dominant (A) and aversive-object-dominant (B) hippocampal neurons in the hippocampal formation to various food and non-food objects. Each column indicates response magnitude (mean of 1.0 sec firing rate after visual stimulation minus 1.0 sec firing rate before visual stimulation).

Hippocampal neuron responses

Responsiveness of hippocampal neurons. A total of 864 hippocampal neurons were recorded during performance of operant tasks coupled to the presentation of rewarding, aversive or unfamiliar objects (Tamura et al., 1991). Of these, 18.5% responded to the sight of certain object(s). Of the visually responsive neurons, about half responded to virtually all objects with no significant difference in response magnitude (non-differential neurons). The remaining half of visual neurons responded differentially to different objects with significant differences in response magnitude or direction (differential neurons). The 25% of differential neurons were differentiated, responding more to rewarding objects than to aversive objects or to unfamiliar objects (rewarding-object-dominant). An example of this type of neuron is shown in Fig. 8A. Responses to rewarding objects (apple, raisin, cookie and a red cylinder associated with juice) were stronger than those to aversive objects (syringe, spider model, centipede model, white cylinder associated with shock) or those to unfamiliar objects (car model, clip). However, the order of magnitude of responses to rewarding objects did not necessarily correspond to the order of the animal's preference for the objects.

Of the differential neurons, 15% responded more to aversive objects than to rewarding objects or unfamiliar objects (aversive-object-dominant neurons). Fig. 8B shows an example of aversive-object-dominant neuron responses. The response

magnitudes to aversive objects (syringe, spider model, centipede model and white cylinder associated with shock) were significantly larger than those to objects in the rewarding or unfamiliar groups. Each 11% of the differential neurons responded strongly to only one specific object (Fig. 9A). The neuron shown in Fig. 9A responded most strongly to a shaver box. The remaining 8.0% of differential neurons responded more to unfamiliar than to familiar objects (unfamiliar-object-dominant neurons). Representative data from unfamiliar-object-dominant neurons are shown in Fig. 9B. The response magnitudes to unfamiliar objects (pineapple model, eraser, and pudding model) in the first presentation were stronger than those to any other familiar objects. This figure shows the mean response magnitudes in the first three trials of these neurons to indicated objects. The response magnitudes tended to decrease in repeated trials as the objects became more familiar.

Visual cue (or sample) responsive neurons were reported previously in monkey (Miyashita et al., 1989; Cahusac et al., 1989; Vidyasagar et al., 1991; Riches et al., 1991) and in human (Heit et al., 1988). Some of these responses were highly task- or situation-dependent. According to the reversal test in the present study (see next section), affective significance of an object is not crucial, nor is it necessarily the only determinant of responsiveness of hippocampal neurons. Although some hippocampal neurons responded differentially to biologically significant objects, it should be emphasized that these neurons did not respond to those objects in some different situations such as in clinical tests (Tamura et al., unpublished observation). Our result, along with a previous study (Miyashita et al., 1989) imply that not only an object itself, including its affective significance, but also the situation in which the object is presented, can influence the responsiveness of hippocampal neurons.

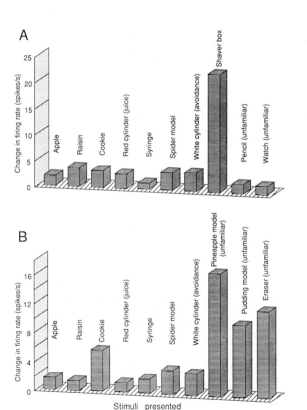

Fig. 9. Responses of selective (A) and unfamiliar-object-dominant (B) neurons in the hippocampal formation to various foods and non-food objects. Other descriptions as for Fig. 7.

Effects of reversal and extinction on hippocampal neuronal responses to the sight of objects. Nine rewarding-object-dominant and five aversive-object-dominant neurons were tested in extinction or reversal tests. Responses of seven (four rewarding-object-dominant and three aversive object-dominant) neurons to the same test object did not change in extinction or reversal tests. Although responses of the other seven (five rewarding-object-dominant and two aversive-object-dominant) neurons decreased in extinction or reversal tests, the response magnitude of five of these seven was still greater than response magnitudes to objects in other groups.

The results indicate that the differential responses of hippocampal neurons were not modulated by reversal or extinction. This is consistent with lesion studies in which hippocampal lesions did not affect the performance of monkeys in stimulus-reward association tasks (Jones and Mishkin, 1972; Spiegler and Mishkin, 1981). The present and previous results suggest that activity of these neurons might not be directly related to on-line recognition of an object (Squire et al., 1990). Human studies indicate that lesion of ventromedial parts of temporal cortex and the hippocampal formation resulted in retrograde amnesia of episodic events for a few years (Squire, 1983). This part of memory stored in the hippocampus might be related to a kind of temporary buffer memory (Rawlins, 1985) before being encoded into long-term memory. Recently, this time-limited storage in the hippocampal formation was confirmed in hippocampectomized monkeys that lost memory for about 4 weeks before surgery (Zola-Morgan and Squire, 1990). Activity of hippocampal neurons in the present study might reflect temporarily stored memory of affective objects including the previous *situation* in which the stimulus was presented, since activity was not modulated by the reversal test, and it was situation-dependent.

We speculate that a place or spatial factor might be one of the most important factors in a situation, encoding it as part of episodic memory in the hippocampal formation. This is partially consistent with reports that suggest hippocampal relations to spatial recognition and memory of place or space (O'Keefe and Nadel, 1978). In the next section we in-

troduce spatial factors to the analysis of hippocampal neurons.

Neuronal responses to spatial movement in the monkey hippocampal formation

Experimental design for introduction of a spatial factor

The monkeys were restrained painlessly in a stereotaxic apparatus and sat in a chair in a rotatable half-mirrored cab (Ono et al., 1991). They actively controlled the cab and could change its location by pressing bars (spatial moving task). The cab was driven horizontally by electric motors and could also be rotated ± 180° by the experimenter. The monkey, usually facing in the + Y direction (in Fig. 10, + Y direction is toward the right), could see various objects such as a desk, refrigerator, and experimental rack and panel set-up, etc., through the

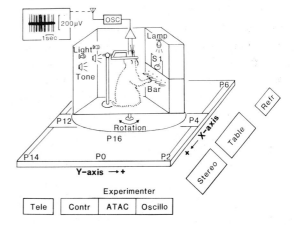

Fig. 10. Schema of experimental set-up for rotatable monkey cab. The monkey, painlessly restrained in a stereotaxic apparatus by a previously prepared, surgically fixed head holder, sat in a chair in the cab. Front, left and right walls of the cab were made of half-mirror. Rear wall was made of steel and equipped with two speakers. Five bars were mounted on lower half of cab front. Double half-mirrored shutter in upper half of cab front wall was opened pneumatically to expose food. Lamp in food bay showed object in bay. Cab on turntable was rotatable ± 180°. The monkey usually faced in + Y direction in the spatial moving task. OSC, Oscillator; Tele, telemeter; Contr, controller for spatial moving task; ATAC, minicomputer ATAC 3700; Oscillo, oscilloscope; Stereo, stereotaxic apparatus; Refr, refrigerator.

half-mirrored left, front and right walls of the cab if the room light was on, and it could see nothing in the room if the room light was off. In a set-up similarly to that described in the previous section, a double half-mirrored shutter could be opened to obtain food by pressing a bar. There were five bars across the panel of the cab in front of the monkey. The middle, near left and near right bars controlled, respectively, forward, left and right movements of the cab. The far right bar controlled backward movement. In the spatial navigation task, each of four different 0.5 sec cue tones from rear wall speakers, and indicator lamps directed the appropriate one of the four bars to be pressed. After 1.0 sec delay, the stimulus platform was illuminated so the monkey could see food or a white cylinder associated with juice. If the appropriate bar was then continuously pressed, the cab moved at a speed of 5 cm/sec for one quarter of the X or Y axis, after which the shutter opened and the monkey took the food or a drop of juice through a spout in front of its mouth. To identify directional characteristics of hippocampal neurons to visual stimuli, different food and non-food objects including human hands, arms, faces, etc. were presented from several directions to the monkey during inter-trial intervals. Neurons were further tested by rotating the monkey while the cab was in one of 3 – 5 different locations.

Mean and S.D. of firing ratio during inter-trial intervals were calculated in 25 different locations of the monkey in a spatial moving task session. Increase or decrease of activity in each location was considered to be significant if it exceeded 2.0 S.D. from the mean activity in 25 different locations.

Hippocampal neuron responses in the spatial moving task

A sample of about 170 neurons was recorded from the hippocampal formation (Ono et al., 1991). Of these, 11.5% were directionally selective with no place-related activity. These neurons were classified into two types according to the coding of stimulus direction in reference to monkey's own coordinates (egocentric) or coding of stimulus position in reference to external absolute coordinates (allocen-

tric). Of these directionally selective neurons, 75% were egocentric and these responded only to stimuli presented at a particular angle from forward of the monkey. The remaining 25% of the neurons responded only to stimuli presented from particular room locations, regardless of the monkey's location or orientation.

Of 174 hippocampal neurons, 44% showed place-related activity (place-related neurons). These neurons responded maximally when the monkey was situated at a specific location. Of these place-related neurons, 27% also exhibited directionally selective responses to stimuli presented around the monkey. Of the directionally selective and place-related responses, half of the neurons were either egocentric or allocentric. The remaining half of the directionally selective and place-related neurons

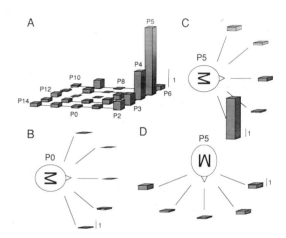

Fig. 11. Example of a hippocampal neuron with place- and direction-selective response. *A*. Increase of neuronal activity in and around P4 and P5 in inter-trial intervals during a block of spatial moving trials. Each column: mean spontaneous rate in corresponding P0 – P24 location during inter-trial interval. *B*. No response to human action from any direction, when the monkey faced + Y in position P0. *C*. Right anterior direction-selective responses to human action at almost 60° from the front when the monkey faced + Y in P5. *D*. No response to human action from any direction, when monkey was rotated + 90° (clockwise) while at P5. In *B* – *D*, stimuli were presented from several directions around the monkey during inter-trial intervals of blocks of spatial moving task different from that shown in *A*. Each column: neuronal activity in response to presentation of stimuli from several directions around monkey.

responded to a stimulus when the monkey was in a particular room location, and their directionally selective responses disappeared when the monkey was not in one specific orientation in that particular location. Fig. 11 shows an example of responses of such a directionally selective and place-related neuron. Activity of this neuron increased in and around the locations P4 and P5 during inter-trial intervals (Fig. 11*A*). The directionally selective response to a stimulus (human action) occurred in only one place P5 (or P4), in the field (Fig. 11*B*), and disappeared when the monkey was either moved from that place to P0 (Fig. 11*C*), or rotated in that location (P5) (Fig. 11*D*).

Of the place-related neurons, 42% also responded in one or more phase(s) of the spatial moving task (task-related). A typical example of a neuron which showed both task- and place-related activity follows. The spontaneous activity of this neuron increased at P8 – P10 with the room light on (not shown). This neuron also responded to the sight of food (apple) at P6 – P10, where the spontaneous activity during inter-trial intervals was also high. The responsiveness of this neuron to the sight of apple was not just visual responses. When the monkey performed the spatial moving task with the room light off, both the increment of activity at P10 – P8 and the responses to sight of apple were suppressed (not shown).

Concomitant analysis of neuronal responses and electro-oculogram indicated that the direction-selective responses were not organized retinotopically (not shown). The hippocampal formation receives massive inputs via the entorhinal cortex, or via entorhinal cortex through parahippocampal gyrus and perirhinal cortex, from the frontal eye field and the posterior region of the inferior parietal cortex (Amaral, 1987). Lesion studies in monkey and human suggest relations of the posterior part of the inferior parietal cortex and frontal eye field to, respectively, spatial allocentric and egocentric perception (Teuber, 1964; Pohl, 1973). These projections may contribute to spatial direction-selective and/or place-related responses in the hippocampal formation. The hippocampal formation also receives highly integrated visual information regarding the characteristics of an object from the inferotemporal cortex through the entorhinal cortex (Amaral, 1987). The hippocampal formation is suggested to be one focal region of integration of spatial (direction and place) and visual (object) information (McNaughton et al., 1989). The complex responsiveness of hippocampal neurons to both place and direction (Fig. 11), and to both place and task (not shown) may support this hypothesis.

Conclusions

Our results suggest functional differences between the amygdala and the hippocampal formation. Neuronal activity in the amygdala is directly related to neither simple sensory inputs nor individual overt acts of the organism, although some neurons responded exclusively to one sensory modality. The physical appearance of an object is not only a crucial determinant of responsiveness of amygdalar neurons although selective amygdalar neurons responded only to a particular object, since selective neurons would continue to respond to a particular food even if it was cut into various shapes when presented (Nishijo et al., 1988a,b). The affective contingency of the object is also the one salient determinant for responsiveness of some amygdalar neurons since in reversal tests visual responses were readily suppressed although the physical appearance remained the same. These findings suggest a role of amygdala in stimulus-affect association. These responses to the object with affective significance might reflect motivational aspects of the object. In addition, amygdalar neuron responses to an object did not change with direction, position, or its profile in clinical tests (Nishijo et al., unpublished observation). Based on these findings, we suggest that the amygdala might be part of a system for object-centered associative recognition based on affective significance, and might consequently be important for emotional reaction to an object through a pathway to the hypothalamus and lower brain-stem.

On the other hand, reward contingency was apparently not a crucial determinant for responsiveness of hippocampal neurons. Responses of hippocampal neurons were, however, situation-dependent. Another characteristic of hippocampal neurons was responsiveness to spatial cues such as direction from which an object was presented, or the location of the animal. Those responses were not merely sensory (visual), since some neurons responded only when the monkey saw an object from a particular direction and in a particular place (Fig. 11), or when the object was seen in a particular situation. We define situation here as the relation among two or more factors such as time, space and rules that regulate behavioral responses. Among situational factors, the spatial factor (place and direction) could be a very important one by which the monkey identifies a situation requiring certain behavior. We suggest that hippocampal formation may associatively encode information regarding both an object and a situation. Previous recordings and behavioral studies support this idea. Rat hippocampal neurons respond to patterns or relations of multiple stimuli (Sharp et al., 1990). Lesion studies suggest that the hippocampal formation is crucial in learning associative relations among multiple cues or factors such as configural association (Sutherland and McDonald, 1990), relational representation (Eichenbaum et al., 1990), snapshot memory (Gaffan and Harrison, 1989), and object-place association (Parkinson et al., 1988). These findings might be a neurophysiological basis for episodic memory encoded by the hippocampal formation (Tulving, 1983; Zola-Morgan et al., 1986).

On the basis of different functions of the amygdala and the hippocampal formation, these structures might function complementary. A recent anatomical study indicated interconnections in both directions between these two structures. These pathways would help coordination between the amygdala and the hippocampal formation. In fact, the animals could react differently or display different emotions toward an object in different situations (Hebb, 1972). Affective significance of an object encoded in the amygdala may be transferred to the hippocampal formation and encoded into memory. These characteristics of amygdalar and hippocampal neurons might be the neurophysiological bases of clinical symptoms in neuropathology of the medial temporal lobe, such as Alzheimer's disease (Hyman et al., 1990), schizophrenia (Stevens, 1973; Roberts, 1990; Gray et al., 1991), panic disorder (Gray, 1982), and autism (Bachevalier, 1991).

Acknowledgements

We thank Dr. A. Simpson, Showa University, for help with the manuscript, and Ms. M. Yamazaki and Ms. A. Tabuchi for typing. This study was supported partly by the Japanese Ministry of Education, Science and Culture Grants-in-Aid for Scientific Research 04246105 and 04836006, and by the Human Frontier Science Program for the third fiscal year.

References

Aggleton, J.P., Burton, M.J. and Passingham, R.E. (1980) Cortical and subcortical afferents to the amygdala of the rhesus monkey (*Macaca mulatta*). *Brain Res.*, 190: 347–368.

Amaral, D.G. (1987) Memory: anatomical organization of candidate brain regions. In: F. Plum and V.B. Mountcastle (Eds.), *Handbook of Physiology, Vol. 5*, American Physiological Society, Bethesda, MD, pp. 211–294.

Amaral, D.G., Veazey, R.B. and Cowan, W.M. (1982) Some observations on hypothalamo-amygdaloid connections in the monkey. *Brain Res.*, 252: 13–27.

Bachevalier, J. (1991) An animal model for childhood autism. In: C.A. Tamminga and S.C. Schulz (Eds.), *Advances in Neuropsychiatry and Psychopharmacology, Vol. 1*, Raven Press, New York, pp. 129–140.

Cahusac, P.M.B., Miyashita, Y. and Rolls, E.T. (1989) Responses of hippocampal formation neurons in the monkey related to delayed spatial responses and object-place memory tasks. *Behav. Brain Res.*, 33: 229–240.

Corkin, S. (1984) Lasting consequences of bilateral medial temporal lobectomy: clinical course and experimental findings in H.M. *Semin. Neurol.*, 4: 249–259.

Duyckaerts, C., Derouesne, C., Signoret, J.L., Gray, F., Escourolle, R. and Castaigne, P. (1985) Bilateral and limited amygdalohippocampal lesions causing a pure amnesic syndrome. *Ann. Neurol.*, 18: 314–319.

Eichenbaum, H., Wiener, S.I., Shapiro, M.L. and Cohen, N.J.

(1989) The organization of spatial coding in the hippocampus: a study of neural ensemble activity. *J. Neurosci.*, 9: 2764 – 2775.

Eichenbaum, H., Stewart, C. and Morris, R.G.M. (1990) Hippocampal representation in place learning. *J. Neurosci.*, 10: 3531 – 3542.

Fukuda, M., Ono, T., Nishino, H. and Sasaki, K. (1986) Visual responses related to food discrimination in monkey lateral hypothalamus during operant feeding behavior. *Brain Res.*, 374: 249 – 259.

Fukuda, M., Ono, T. and Nakamura, K. (1987) Functional relations among inferotemporal cortex, amygdala, and lateral hypothalamus in monkey operant feeding behavior. *J. Neurophysiol.*, 57: 1060 – 1077.

Fuster, J.M. (1990) Inferotemporal units in selective visual attention and short-term memory. *J. Neurophysiol.*, 64: 681 – 697.

Fuster, J.M. and Jervey, J.P. (1982) Neuronal firing in the inferotemporal cortex of the monkey in a visual memory task. *J. Neurosci.*, 2: 361 – 375.

Gaffan, D. and Harrison, S. (1989) Place memory and scene memory: effects of fornix transection in the monkey. *Exp. Brain Res.*, 74: 202 – 212.

Gaffan, E.A., Gaffan, D. and Harrison, S. (1988) Disconnection of the amygdala from visual association cortex impairs visual reward association learning in monkeys. *J. Neurosci.*, 8: 3144 – 3150.

Geschwind, N. (1965) Disconnection syndromes in animals and man. *Brain*, 88: 237 – 294.

Gloor, P. (1960) Amygdala. In: J. Field (Ed.), *Handbook of Physiology: Neurophysiology, Vol. 2*, American Physiological Society, Washington, pp. 1395 – 1420.

Goldman-Rakic, P.S. (1987) Circuitry of primate prefrontal cortex and regulation of behavior by representational memory. In: F. Plum and V.B. Mountcastle (Eds.), *Handbook of Physiology, Vol. 5*, American Physiological Society, Bethesda, MD, pp. 373 – 417.

Gray, J.A. (1982) *The Neuropsychology of Anxiety*, Clarendon Press, Oxford.

Gray, J.A., Feldon, J., Rawlins, J.N.P., Hemsley, D.R. and Smith, A.D. (1981) The neuropsychology of schizophrenia. *Behav. Brain Sci.*, 14: 1 – 84.

Hebb, D.O. (1972) *A Textbook of Psychology,* 3rd edition, Saunders, Philadelphia, PA.

Heit, G., Smith, M.E. and Halgren, E. (1988) Neural encoding of individual words and faces by the human hippocampus and amygdala. *Nature*, 333: 773 – 775.

Horel, J.A., Keating, E.G. and Misantone, L.J. (1975) Partial Klüver-Bucy syndrome produced by destroying temporal neocortex of amygdala. *Brain Res.*, 94: 347 – 359.

Hyman, B.T., Van Hoesen, G.W. and Damasio, A.R. (1990) Memory-related neural systems in Alzheimer's disease: an anatomic study. *Neurology*, 40: 1721 – 1730.

Insausti, R., Amaral, D.G. and Cowan, W.M. (1987) The entorhinal cortex of the monkey: III. Subcortical afferents. *J. Comp. Neurol.*, 264: 396 – 408.

Iwai, E. and Yukie, M. (1987) Amygdalofugal and amygdalopetal connections with modality-specific visual cortical areas in Macaques (*Macaca fuscata, M. mulatta,* and *M. fascicularis*). *J. Comp. Neurol.*, 261: 362 – 387.

Jasper, H., Shacter, D.G. and Montplaisir, J. (1970) The effects of local cooling upon spontaneous and evoked electrical activity of cerebral cortex. *Can. J. Physiol. Pharmacol.*, 48: 640 – 652.

Jones, B. and Mishkin, M. (1972) Limbic lesions and the problem of stimulus-reinforcement associations. *Exp. Neurol.*, 36: 362 – 377.

Krettek, J.E. and Price, J.L. (1978) Amygdaloid projections to subcortical structures within the basal forebrain and brainstem in the rat and cat. *J. Comp. Neurol.*, 178: 225 – 254.

LeDoux, J.E. (1990) Representation of affect in neural circuits. In: L.R. Squire, M. Mishkin and A. Shimamura (Eds.), *Learning and Memory, Discussion in Neuroscience, Vol. 6*, Elsevier: Amsterdam, Netherland, pp. 64 – 68.

McNaughton, B.L., Leonard, B. and Chen, L. (1989) Cortical-hippocampal interactions and cognitive mapping: a hypothesis based on reintegration of the parietal and inferotemporal pathways for visual processing. *Psychobiology*, 17: 230 – 235.

Miserendino, M.D.J., Sananes, C.B., Melia, K.R. and Davis, M. (1990) Blocking of acquisition but not expression of conditioned fear-potentiated startle by NMDA antagonists in the amygdala. *Nature*, 345: 716 – 718.

Mishkin, M. (1978) Memory in monkeys severely impaired by combined but not by separate removal of amygdala and hippocampus. *Nature*, 273: 297 – 298.

Mishkin, M. (1982) A memory system in the monkey. *Phil. Trans. R. Soc. London (Biol.)*, 298: 85 – 95.

Mishkin, M. and Aggleton, J. (1981) Multiple functional contributions of the amygdala in the monkey. In: Y. Ben Ari (Ed.), *The Amygdaloid Complex*, Elsevier/North-Holland Biomedical Press, Amsterdam, pp. 409 – 420.

Miyashita, Y. and Chang, H.S. (1988) Neuronal correlate of pictorial short-term memory in the primate temporal cortex. *Nature*, 331: 68 – 70.

Miyashita, Y., Rolls, E.T., Cahusac, P.M.B., Niki, H. and Feigenbaum, J.D. (1989) Activity of hippocampal formation neurons in the monkey related to a conditional spatial response task. *J. Neurophysiol.*, 61: 669 – 678.

Morris, R.G.M., Garrud, P., Rawlins, J.N.P. and O'Keefe, J. (1982) Place navigation impaired in rats with hippocampal lesions. *Nature*, 297: 681 – 683.

Muller, R.U. and Kubie, J.L. (1987) The effects of changes in the environment on the spatial firing of hippocampal complex-spike cells. *J. Neurosci.*, 7: 1951 – 1968.

Murray, E.A. and Mishkin, M. (1983) Severe tactual memory deficits in monkeys after combined removal of the amygdala and hippocampus. *Brain Res.*, 270: 340 – 344.

Murray, E.A. and Mishkin, M. (1985) Amygdalectomy impairs

356

crossmodal association in monkeys. *Science*, 228: 604 – 606.

Nishijo, H., Ono, T., Nakamura, K., Kawabata, M. and Yamatani, K. (1986) Neuron activity in and adjacent to the dorsal amygdala of monkey during operant feeding behavior. *Brain Res. Bull.*, 17: 847 – 854.

Nishijo, H., Ono, T. and Nishino, H. (1988a) Single neuron responses in amygdala of alert monkey during complex sensory stimulation with affective significance. *J. Neurosci.*, 8: 3570 – 3583.

Nishijo, H., Ono, T. and Nishino, H. (1988b) Topographic distribution of modality-specific amygdalar neurons in alert monkey. *J. Neurosci.*, 8: 3556 – 3569.

O'Keefe, J. and Bouma, H. (1969) Complex sensory properties of certain amygdala units in the freely moving cat. *Exp. Neurol.*, 23: 384 – 398.

O'Keefe, J. and Conway, D.H. (1978) Hippocampal place units in the freely moving rat: why they fire where they fire. *Exp. Brain Res.*, 31: 573 – 590.

O'Keefe, J. and Nadel, L. (1978) *The Hippocampus as a Cognitive Map*, Clarendon Press, Oxford.

Olton, D.S., Becker, J.T. and Handelmann, G.E. (1979) Hippocampus, space, and memory. *Behav. Brain Sci.*, 2: 313 – 365.

Ono, T., Nishino, H., Sasaki, K., Fukuda, M. and Muramoto, K. (1980) Role of the lateral hypothalamus and the amygdala in feeding behavior. *Brain Res. Bull.* (Suppl. 4), 5: 143 – 149.

Ono, T., Nishino, H., Sasaki, K., Fukuda, M. and Muramoto, K. (1981a) Monkey lateral hypothalamic neuron response to sight of food, and during bar press and ingestion. *Neurosci. Lett.*, 21: 99 – 104.

Ono, T., Oomura, Y., Nishino, H., Sasaki, K., Fukuda, M. and Muramoto, K. (1981b) Neural mechanisms of feeding behavior. In: K. Katsuki, R. Norgren and M. Sato (Eds.), *Brain Mechanisms of Sensation*, Wiley, New York, pp. 271 – 286.

Ono, T., Fukuda, M., Nishino, H., Sasaki, K. and Muramoto, K. (1983) Amygdaloid neuronal responses to complex visual stimuli in an operant feeding situation in the monkey. *Brain Res. Bull.*, 11: 515 – 518.

Ono, T., Luiten, P.G.M., Nishijo, H., Fukuda, M. and Nishino, H. (1985) Topographic organization of projections from the amygdala to the hypothalamus of the rat. *Neursci. Res.*, 21: 221 – 239.

Ono, T., Nishijo, H., Nakamura, K., Tamura, R. and Tabuchi, E. (1988) Role of amygdala and hypothalamic neurons in emotion and behavior. In: H. Takagi, Y. Oomura, M. Ito and M. Otsuka (Eds.), *Biowarning System in The Brain*, University of Tokyo Press, Tokyo, pp. 309 – 331.

Ono, T., Nakamura, K., Fukuda, M. and Tamura, R. (1991) Place recognition responses of neurons in monkey hippocampus. *Neurosci. Lett.*, 121: 194 – 198.

Oomura, Y., Ono, T. and Ooyama, H. (1970) Inhibitory action of the amygdala on the lateral hypothalamic area in rats. *Nature*, 228: 1108 – 1110.

Parkinson, J.K., Murray, E.A. and Mishkin, M. (1988) A selective mnemonic role for the hippocampus in monkeys: memory for the location of objects. *J. Neurosci.*, 8: 4159 – 4167.

Perrett, D.I., Rolls, E.T. and Caan, W. (1982) Visual neurons responsive to faces in the monkey temporal cortex. *Exp. Brain Res.*, 47: 329 – 342.

Pohl, W. (1973) Dissociation of spatial discrimination deficits following frontal and parietal lesions in monkeys. *J. Comp. Physiol. Psychol.*, 82: 227 – 239.

Pons, T.P., Garraghty, P.E., Friedman, D.P. and Mishkin, M. (1987): Physiological evidence for serial processing in somatosensory cortex. *Science*, 237: 417 – 420.

Price, J.L. and Amaral, D.G. (1981) An autoradiographic study of the projections of the central nucleus of the monkey amygdala. *J. Neurosci.*, 1: 1242 – 1259.

Rawlins, J.N.P. (1985) Associations across time: the hippocampus as a temporary memory store. *Behav. Brain Sci.*, 8: 479 – 496.

Riches, I.P., Wilson, F.A.W. and Brown, M.W. (1991) The effects of visual stimulation and memory on neurons of the hippocampal formation and the neighboring parahippocampal gyrus and inferior temporal cortex of the primate. *J. Neurosci.*, 11: 1763 – 1779.

Roberts, G.W. (1990) Schizophrenia: the cellular biology of a functional psychosis. *Trends Neurosci.*, 13: 207 – 211.

Ross, E.D. (1980) Sensory-specific and fractional disorders of recent memory in man. *Arch. Neurol.*, 37: 193 – 200.

Sanghera, M.K., Rolls, E.T. and Roper-Hall, A. (1979) Visual responses of neurons in the dorsolateral amygdala of the alert monkey. *Exp. Neurol.*, 63: 610 – 626.

Sawa, M. and Delgado, J.M.R. (1963) Amygdala unitary activity in the unrestrained cat. *Electroenceph. Clin. Neurophysiol.*, 15: 637 – 650.

Schwaber, J.S., Kapp, B.S., Higgins, G.A. and Rapp, P.R. (1982) Amygdaloid and basal forebrain direct connections with the nucleus of the solitary tract and the dorsal motor nucleus. *J. Neurosci.*, 2: 1424 – 1438.

Scoville, W.B. and Milner, B. (1957) Loss of recent memory after bilateral hippocampal lesions. *J. Neurol. Neurosurg. Psychiat.*, 20: 11 – 21.

Sharp, P.E., Kubie, J.L. and Muller, R.U. (1990) Firing properties of hippocampal neurons in a visually symmetrical environment: contributions of multiple sensory cues and mnemonic processes. *J. Neurosci.*, 10: 3093 – 3105.

Spiegler, B.J. and Mishkin, M. (1981) Evidence for the sequential participation of inferior temporal cortex and amygdala in the acquisition of stimulus-reward associations. *Behav. Brain Res.*, 3: 307 – 317.

Squire, L.R. (1983) The hippocampus and the neuropsychology of memory. In: W. Seifert (Ed.), *Neurobiology of the Hippocampus*, Academic Press, London, pp. 491 – 511.

Squire, L.R. (1987) *Memory and Brain*, Oxford University Press, New York.

Squire, L.R., Amaral, D.G., Zola-Morgan, S., Kritchevsky, M.

and Press, G. (1989) Description of brain injury in the amnesic patient N.A. based on magnetic resonance imaging. *Exp. Neurol.*, 105: 23 – 35.

Squire, L.R., Mishkin, M. and Shimamura, A. (Eds.) (1990) *Learning and Memory, Discussions in Neuroscience, Vol. 6*, Elsevier, Amsterdam.

Stevens, J.R. (1973) An anatomy of schizophrenia? *Arch. Gen. Psychiatry*, 29: 177 – 189.

Sutherland, R.J. and McDonald, R.J. (1990) Hippocampus, amygdala, and memory deficits in rats. *Behav. Brain Res.*, 37: 57 – 79.

Sutherland, R.J. and Rudy, J.W. (1989) Configural association theory: the role of the hippocampal formation in learning, memory, and amnesia. *Psychobiology*, 17: 129 – 144.

Tamura, R., Ono, T., Fukuda, M. and Nishijo, H. (1991) Role of monkey hippocampus in recognition of food and nonfood. *Brain Res. Bull.*, 27: 457 – 461.

Teuber, H.-L. (1964) The riddle of frontal lobe function in man. In: *The Frontal Granular Cortex and Behavior*, McGraw-Hill, New York, pp. 410 – 444.

Tulving, E. (1983) *Elements of Episodic Memory*, Clarendon, Oxford.

Turner, B.H., Mishkin, M. and Knapp, M. (1980) Organization of the amygdalopetal projections from modality-specific cortical association areas in the monkey. *J. Comp. Neurol.*, 191: 515 – 543.

Van Hoesen, G.W. (1982) The parahippocampal gyrus. New observations regarding its cortical connections in the monkey. *Trends Neurosci.*, 5: 345 – 350.

Veening, J.G., Swanson, L.W. and Sawchenko, P.E. (1984) The organization of projections from the central nucleus of the amygdala to brainstem sites involved in central autonomic regulation: a combined retrograde transport-immunohistochemical study. *Brain Res.*, 303: 337 – 357.

Vidyasagar, T.R., Salzman, E. and Creutzfeldt, O.D. (1991) Unit activity in the hippocampus and the parahippocampal temporobasal association cortex related to memory and complex behaviour in the awake monkey. *Brain Res.*, 544: 269 – 278.

Weiskrantz, L. (1956) Behavioral changes associated with ablation of the amygdaloid complex in monkeys. *J. Comp. Physiol. Psychol.*, 49: 381 – 391.

Zola-Morgan, S., Squire, L.R. and Mishkin, M. (1982) The neuroanatomy of amnesia: amygdala-hippocampus versus temporal stem. *Science*, 218: 1337 – 1339.

Zola-Morgan, S. and Squire, L.R. (1990) The primate hippocampal formation: evidence for a time-limited role in memory storage. *Science*, 250: 288 – 289.

Zola-Morgan, S., Squire, L.R. and Amaral, D.G. (1986) Human amnesia and the medial temporal region: enduring memory impairment following a bilateral lesion limited to field CA1 of the hippocampus. *J. Neurosci.*, 6: 2950 – 2967.

T.P. Hicks, S. Molotchnikoff and T. Ono (Eds.)
Progress in Brain Research, Vol. 95
© 1993 Elsevier Science Publishers B.V. All rights reserved.

CHAPTER 30

Responses of monkey basal forebrain neurons during visual discrimination task

Masaji Fukuda, Ryoichi Masuda, Taketoshi Ono and Eiichi Tabuchi

*Department of Physiology, Faculty of Medicine, Toyama Medical and Pharmaceutical University, Sugitani, Toyama 930-01,
Japan*

Introduction

It has been reported that the brain tissue of patients with Alzheimer's disease, which is characterized by severe memory disturbance, includes degeneration of the basal forebrain involving the nucleus basalis of Meynert (Whitehouse et al., 1982; Candy et al., 1983; Coyle et al., 1983). Monkeys with basal forebrain deficits had impairment of some kind of learning and memory, such as new visual object learning, relearning object discrimination, and serial reversal learning (Ridley et al., 1985, 1986). In rat experiments lesions in the nucleus basalis magnocellularis caused impairment of memory in spatial discrimination learning (Hepler et al., 1985; Kesner et al., 1990). These results suggest that the basal forebrain might contribute to learning and memory related to visual information about the external environment.

In electrophysiological experiments, monkey basal forebrain neurons responded frequently in the choice phase of a go/no-go task (Richardson and DeLong, 1990), and discriminated novelty, familiarity or recency of presentation of visual stimuli (Wilson and Rolls, 1990a,b,c). We reported that some monkey substantia innominata and lateral hypothalamic neurons responded preferentially to the sight of some objects that had contingent biological meaning, such as reward (Ono et al., 1981; Fukuda et al., 1986). The neuronal activity in

these responses changed plastically during extinction and reversal learning (Fukuda et al., 1986).

The basal forebrain receives neuronal inputs from many areas including the inferotemporal and entorhinal cortices, amygdala, hippocampus and lateral hypothalamic area (Mesulam et al., 1983; Mesulam and Mufson, 1984; Van Hoesen, 1985, 1990) which are key stations in learning and memory (Amaral, 1987; Squire, 1987). Discrimination of certain objects from others, and novelty-familiarity relations, may be important memory functions in learning stimulus-reinforcement association. We report here results of a study of organization in the monkey basal forebrain of visual information concerning real objects. We found that basal forebrain neurons selectively code information about reinforcement and novelty-familiarity relations, and have strong plastic neuronal responses that are related to learning.

Experimental design

Two monkeys (*Macaca fuscata*, 5 – 8 kg) were used. Detailed experimental procedures are described elsewhere (Ono et al., 1981, 1983; Fukuda et al., 1986, 1987). Briefly, a monkey sat in a primate chair facing a panel, 24 cm distant, that had two shutters and two bars. One shutter was a 9×12 cm one-way mirror, Sl, in front of a table on which objects were presented, at the level of the monkey's eyes, and the

360

other was a 4 × 5 cm opaque cover, S2, that prevented access to the operant bar. A second bar, fixed about 10 cm below S1, was the starting point for each trial. An experimental trial was started when the monkey held the bar fixed below S1. Usually the monkey could not see any object on the table through the one-way mirror because the space above the table was dark compared to the monkey's space. When the light on the table was turned on after a random interval, the monkey could see the object through the one-way mirror. The object was either familiar food (a piece of apple, a cookie, a raisin, etc.), familiar non-food (a wooden block, a syringe, a bolt, etc.), or a novel object from a stock of such objects maintained in the experimental room. After a delay of at least 2.0 sec, S2 was opened automatically and the animal could press the bar behind it to obtain the object on the table, if it was food that the monkey wanted. The bar had to be pressed a predetermined number of times (fixed ratio, FR, 10 – 20), and the monkey usually pressed rapidly for food, because it was deprived for at least 12 h before an experimental session. S1 was opened automatically by the last bar press, and the monkey could extend its right arm, take the food and ingest it. If necessary, symbolic objects were also used as visual stimuli to indicate reward or aversion. For example, a red steel column, 3.5 cm in diameter and 10 cm high, was associated with a piece of apple; a white steel column, of the same dimensions as the red column, indicated a drop of juice to be delivered at the last bar press from a small spout near the monkey's mouth. A black steel column was associated with weak electric shock. If a black cylinder was revealed when the light went on, the monkey had to complete a FR schedule within 4 sec to avoid the electric shock. If the test criterion was met, the last bar press turned off the light and prevented the electric shock. If the criterion was not met, a 120 msec shock was applied before the light was turned off. The electric shock was a train of capacitor-coupled square pulses (0.2 mA, 50 Hz, 10 msec), administered between the earlobes. The program included feeding, drinking and active avoidance tasks that required the monkey to dif-

ferentiate stimuli and relate them to operant bar pressing to obtain the food or potables, or avoid the electric shock. Electro-oculograms (EOG) were recorded in some, but not all sessions to monitor eye movement. The animal's behavior was also monitored by the experimenter, who was positioned behind the apparatus in the animal's blind spot.

A glass-covered tungsten microelectrode was stereotaxically inserted by a manipulator driven by a pulse motor. Single unit activity was recorded and processed conventionally. All data were analyzed by a minicomputer. The data were statistically analyzed by Student's t-test.

The task was divided into four phases: (1) control phase, prior to the light on; (2) visual discrimination

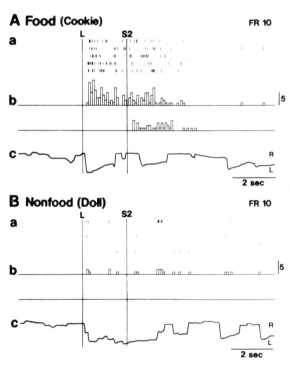

Fig. 1. Neuronal responses at the sight of familiar food (A) and non-food (B). Aa. Raster display of neuronal activity in each trial in response to the sight of food. Ab. Cumulative histogram of neuronal activity over five trials (upper, neuronal activity in 80 msec bin size; lower, bar pressing). Ac. EOG record of horizontal eye movement for first trial. B. Responses of the same neuron to the sight of non-food. The neuron responded preferentially to the sight of food. Abscissa, time (sec); L, light on; S2, shutter opened.

phase, from the time of light on until S2 was opened; (3) bar press (operant response) phase, from the time of opening S2 until the last bar press or the time limit; and (4) ingestion phase, after opening of S1 or presentation of liquid reward by the last bar press.

Patterns of response to visual stimuli

Unit activity in the basal forebrain was recorded from 491 neurons during the visual discrimination task, and analyzed for the presentation of more than four objects. Of these, 88 (17.9%) responded significantly during the visual phase, 19 during the bar press phase, and 31 during the ingestion phase including overlap for those that responded in more than one phase. The frequency of the spontaneous activity ranged from 0.0 to 67.3 spikes/sec (8.9 $\pm$ 10.1, mean $\pm$ S.D., $n = 66$). In this paper, characteristics of vision-related neurons are analyzed in detail.

Fig. 1 shows a specimen record of vision-related responses. The neuron responded to the sight of a cookie (Fig. 1A) with a latency of 280 msec, but not to the sight of a doll (Fig. 1B). The EOG records in Fig. 1Ac and 1Bc are for the first trial of a food or non-food presentation. The records indicate that the monkey's eyes were fixed equally on the object on the table when the light was turned on. Thus the neuronal response was not due to eye movement. The arm movement was controlled by the requirement to hold the fixed holding bar during the visual phase for 2.0 sec before S2 was opened.

Table I shows the number of neurons that responded to various proportions of the number of objects presented. Thirty-five neurons responded non-selectively to the sight of all objects presented, and 53 responded preferentially to the sight of some objects. Ten of these were highly selective in that they responded to the sight of only one object, although the number of objects presented to each of these neurons was limited.

The latency of visual responses ranged from 100 to 400 msec (192 $\pm$ 78, $n = 66$). The recording sites were in the nucleus of the diagonal band of Broca (Ch3), and the anterior medial and lateral sectors of the nucleus basalis of Meynert (Ch4am, Ch4al) as defined by Mesulam et al. (1983).

TABLE I

Numbers of neurons that responded to various proportions of presented objects

Number of objects evoking responses	Number of objects presented									
	4	5	6	7	8	9	10	11	12	Total
1	3	2	1	2	2	0	0	0	0	10
2	1	0	3	2	0	0	0	0	0	6
3	0	1	2	5	1	2	0	1	0	12
4	–	2	1	6	0	1	0	0	0	10
5	–	–	3	1	1	0	1	0	0	6
6	–	–	–	1	0	1	1	0	0	3
7	–	–	–	–	2	0	0	1	0	3
8	–	–	–	–	–	1	0	1	0	2
9	–	–	–	–	–	–	0	0	0	0
10	–	–	–	–	–	–	–	0	0	0
11	–	–	–	–	–	–	–	–	1	1
All	6	5	9	7	6	0	1	1	0	35
Total	10	10	19	24	12	5	3	4	1	88
No response	316	64	17	2	4	0	0	0	0	
Tested	326	74	36	26	16	5	3	4	1	491

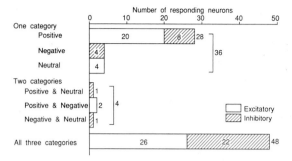

Fig. 2. Distribution of visual response patterns categorized into positive (rewarding), negative (aversive) and neutral. Most selective neurons responded to positive contingency.

Reinforcement characteristics

Every object presented here could be categorized by the nature of its expected reinforcement contingency or the animal's behavior preceding bar pressing. All foods, white column associated with juice and red column associated with apple, were identified as positive (rewarding) stimuli; the black column associated with weak electric shock was identified as a negative (aversive) stimulus; all other items were considered neutral since none of them induced bar pressing. Fig. 2 shows the distribution of neurons into the three contingency categories, positive, negative and neutral. Of 88 vision-related neurons, 36 responded to stimuli in only one contingency category, 4 responded to stimuli in two categories, and the remaining 48 neurons responded to stimuli in all categories. Of the 36 neurons that responded to stimuli in a single category, 28 were related to positive contingency although they responded to more than one object that predicted the same reinforcement. Fig. 3A shows the firing rates of a neuron that responded to the sight of several positive contingency stimuli. The neuronal activity increased at the sight of three positive related objects, apple, cookie and red column predicting apple, but did not increase at the sight of three neutral objects such as wooden block, crow model, or plastic column, nor at the sight of the black column associated with weak electric shock. Fig. 3B shows responses of a negative contingency neuron. This

neuron responded preferentially to the sight of the black column associated with weak electric shock, but not to six other rewarding or neutral objects. Fig. 3C shows the firing rate of a neuron that responded preferentially to neutral objects. This neuron responded to the sight of neutral items, but not to food, the white column predicting juice, nor to the black column associated with weak electric shock.

Of 88 vision-related neurons, 10 responded selectively to only one object among others in the same

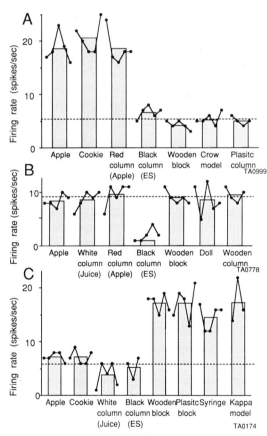

Fig. 3. Histograms of visual responses of three different neurons to three contingency categories, positive (A), negative (B) and neutral (C). Each histogram shows mean firing rate in 3 – 5 trials during 1.0 sec after the light was turned on. Broken line, spontaneous firing rate; abscissa, kinds of objects presented; ordinate, mean firing rates, spikes per second; ES, electric shock. These neurons responded preferentially to the sight of objects according to their contingency.

category. Fig. 4 shows examples of selective responsive neurons. The neuron activity in Fig. 4A increased
only at the sight of a piece of apple. The activity of
the neuron in Fig. 4B increased at the sight of a
wooden block, but did not respond to all other objects presented, positive, negative or neutral.

Novel-familiar differentiation

Ability to distinguish between novel and familiar
objects is another criterion in learning and memory
in the basal forebrain. More than 500 items were used
as visual stimuli. Each item was considered to be
novel until the animal had seen it in the first trial.
Novel objects did not normally elicit bar pressing
behavior. Of 88 vision-related neurons, 28 were
tested by the presentation of novel objects. Of these,
18 responded to the sight of both novel and familiar
non-foods. Two neurons responded preferentially
to the sight of novel objects, but not to familiar food
or non-food when presented in the first trial. Fig. 5A

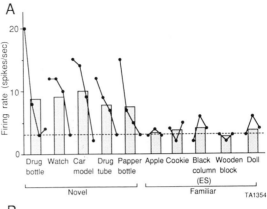

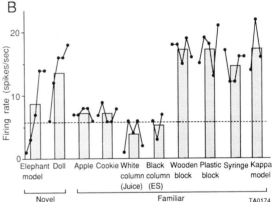

Fig. 5. Visual responses to the sight of novel and familiar objects. Filled circles connected by lines are firing rates for 1.0 sec
in each trial during the visual phase in 3 (A,B) or 4 (A) or 5 (B)
successive trials. Broken lines show spontaneous firing rates.
Stimuli presented in random order, but rearranged here to compare different categories. A. Preferential novel responses. B.
Preferential familiar non-food responses. Note in A how successive responses increased for novel non-food items to eventually match familiar non-food items.

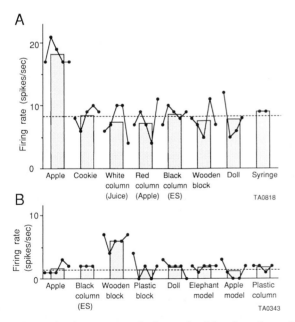

Fig. 4. Visual responses, selective to the sight of one item. A.
Visual responses to only one object (apple) or eight presented. B.
Visual responses to only one object (wood block) of eight
presented. Other descriptions as for Fig. 3.

shows an example of visual responses to the sight of
novel objects. This neuron did not respond to
familiar objects, a piece of apple nor a cookie, as
food, nor to a black column as aversive, nor to a
wooden block and doll as neutral objects. It
responded preferentially to five novel objects at the
first or second trial, but its response decreased sequentially and disappeared within three or four
trials as the presentation was repeated.

Fig. 5B shows the activity of a neuron that
responded to the sight of familiar neutral objects

such as wooden block, plastic block, syringe and kappa model; but not to familiar rewarding objects such as apple, cookie and white column (juice), or black column (electric shock). To novel objects (elephant model and doll), the neuron did not respond at the first presentation, but its activity sequentially increased as the presentation was repeated and its responsiveness in the third and fourth trial reached the same level as for familiar neutral objects. Of 28 neurons tested, 5 showed this type of responses.

Plastic changes in neuronal responses

Reinforcement contingency may be confirmed by extinction, or relearning. Fig. 6 shows two examples of such tests. The neuron depicted in Fig. 6A responded preferentially to the sight of food

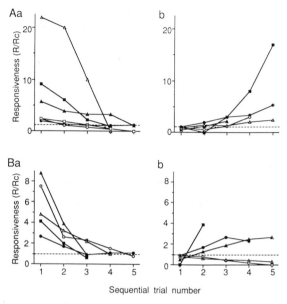

Fig. 7. Plastic changes of visual responses to familiar food during extinction (Aa) and relearning (Ab), and two types of changes (inhibition in Ba and facilitation in Bb) in response to novel objects in successive presentations. Vertical, responsiveness (R/Rc) during visual phase, defined as ratio of mean firing rate (R) for 1.0 sec during visual phase to the mean.

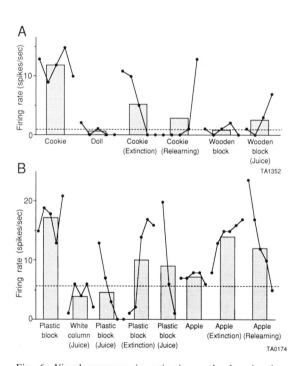

Fig. 6. Visual responses in extinction and relearning by a positive contingent neuron (A) and a neutral contingent neuron (B) in successive trials. In extinction, S2 did not open for the desired food though the FR criterion was met. Relearning constituted release of extinction and return to normal conditions. Note that the visual responses to the sight of food disappeared in extinction tests in A and after relearning in B.

(cookie), but not to neutral objects (doll or wooden block). When food was not available even if the bar was pressed, the positive related response disappeared in successive trials (third session). When the stimulus-reward relation was relearned (fourth session), the response recovered to the pre-test level. A similar phenomenon occurred in an association test with non-food (wooden block). Of 15 neurons tested for positive relations, 11 revealed similar plasticity.

A typical example of neuronal activity during association and extinction with neutral objects is shown in Fig. 6B. The third, fifth and eighth sessions in Fig. 6B show association, and the fourth and seventh sessions show extinction. The neuron responded preferentially to the sight of non-food (plastic block), and not to positive contingent objects (apple, white column (juice)). These excitatory responses became weaker in successive trials and returned to the control level when juice was again associated with this object (third and fifth sessions).

In extinction tests, the visual responses reappeared and returned to the pre-test level (fourth and seventh sessions). The plastic changes in neuronal responses could also be produced by manual delivery of a juice reward (not shown). Of four tested neurons that did not respond to positive related objects, all showed plastic changes in neuronal activity.

Repeated presentation might change contingency meaning of objects from novel to familiar. The activity that was present in an initial response decreased in successive trials and approached the familiar level as shown in Fig. 5A. Fig. 7 summarizes changes of responsiveness in extinction (Fig. 7Aa) and association (Fig. 7Ab) tests of several familiar positive reinforcement neurons, and the repeated presentation of initially novel objects that elicited two different kinds of responsiveness, initial responding (Fig. 7Ba) and final responding (Fig. 7Bb) in progressing from novel to familiar. Responsiveness (R/Rc) is defined as the ratio of mean firing rate (R) during the visual phase to the mean pre-trial control rate (Rc). The speed of learning in novel-familiar relations tended to be faster than in extinction of responsiveness to familiar objects.

Visual information in the basal forebrain

The basal forebrain receives neuronal inputs from the orbitofrontal, medial temporal and entorhinal cortices, amygdala, hippocampus and lateral hypothalamic area (Mesulam and Mufson, 1984; Aggleton et al., 1987; Van Hoesen, 1990). Visual responses in these areas of the monkey brain to the sight of various objects have been reported (Rolls et al., 1977; Ono et al., 1981, 1983; Thorpe et al., 1983; Fukuda et al., 1986; Nishijo et al., 1988a; Tamura et al., 1991). Some important factors in considering neuronal mechanisms of learning and memory of objects may be response selectivity and contingency related to visual stimulation. We reported that amygdalar, hippocampal, substantia innominata and lateral hypothalamic neurons distributed over wide areas responded preferentially to the sight of particular objects that had contingent biological meanings such as reward or aversion (Fukuda et al.,

1986; Nishijo et al., 1988a; Tamura et al., 1991). In some cases neurons in these areas responded to the sight of only one item among more than ten, suggesting that these areas might code something contingent on the object per se or some memory related to the object, but not physically characteristic of the object, such as shape, color or texture. It is not proper to consider that neurons in the basal forebrain might integrate such visual information about objects from individual physical parameters of shape, color and so on, because lesion of the basal forebrain did not induce visual agnosia. Rather, such highly organized information might be sent from the temporal cortex, amygdala, or other areas to the basal forebrain. The basal forebrain might recode stimulus-reinforcement associations using such integrated visual information about objects.

Contribution of basal forebrain to learning and memory

Lesion studies have indicated contributions of the basal forebrain to ingestive behavior such as feeding or drinking (Oomura, 1980; Ono et al., 1984). Our results, indicating that responsive neurons selectively code positive reinforcement, may support this idea. Positive contingent neurons are related to stimulus-reinforcement association, and hence to initiation of ongoing behavior such as feeding. However, this visual information may not be related to the initiation of direct movement of, for instance, an arm, since temporal separation between a visual response and initiation of arm movement is possible in our operant task.

These positive related responses showed plastic change in neuronal activity during extinction or relearning, as shown in Fig. 6, characteristics that are common in the rat basal forebrain (Ono et al., 1986). The basal forebrain receives neuronal inputs from the brain-stem that involve gustatory pathways (Jones et al., 1976; Norgren, 1976; Jones and Cuello, 1989; Martinez-Murillo et al., 1990). The gustatory information after reward acquisition may contribute to evaluation of reinforcement contingency and then to plastic changes in the basal forebrain neurons. Similar plastic changes have been reported in monkey amygdalar neurons in extinction and relearning (Nishijo et al., 1988b). The amygdala is thought to be a site of stimulus-affective association (Jones and Mishkin, 1972; Ono et al., 1983). The mutual connections between the amygdala and the basal forebrain might be among the effective factors that produce such plastic changes in neuronal activity (Nagai et al., 1982; Aggleton et al., 1987; Fukuda et al., 1987; Kordower et al., 1989).

Many non-selective responsive neurons were recorded in the monkey basal forebrain (Table I). The basal forebrain is a source of cholinergic innervation to the neocortex (Mesulam et al., 1983). The electrophysiological evidence that ACh acts as an excitatory transmitter in the neocortex (Krnjevic et al., 1971; McCormick and Prince, 1985) suggests that cortical neurons might integrate such non-selective visual inputs related to various objects. In fact, this type of neuron has been reported in the prefrontal cortex (Yamatani et al., 1990). Buzsaki et al. (1988) destroyed small and circumscribed parts of the nucleus basalis with ibotenic acid and mapped the neocortical activity quantitatively over the entire hemisphere. This gave rise to a prominent focus of EEG activity in the neocortical area where acetylcholinesterase-positive fiber density was mostly reduced. These data suggest that other functions of the basal forebrain might be control of cortical arousal or attention.

Involvement of the basal forebrain in Alzheimer's disease.

There may be more than one basis of Alzheimer's disease since damage to different brain sites can include severe memory deficits, or the same damage might cause different progress of the disease. Some have reported, variously, that the temporal cortex, the hippocampus or the amygdala are major critical sites affecting Alzheimer's disease (Kromer et al., 1990; Vogt et al., 1990; Hof and Bouras, 1991). Damasio et al. (1985a,b) reported a case of basal forebrain dementia in which the patient was not able

to properly integrate different learned components, that is, failed to integrate relation and co-occurrence of stimuli. However, the patient was able to learn separate modal stimuli, such as the name or the face of a person. Monkey with damage in the basal forebrain had deficits in new visual object learning, relearning object discrimination (reversal), and serial reversal learning (Ridley et al., 1985, 1986). These results suggest that integration of relations is an important function in the basal forebrain. This integration could be considered a kind of learning.

This idea might be supported by two items of electrophysiological evidence. (1) Reinforcement contingent neurons have response plasticity, as shown in extinction or association tests (Fig. 6). The plasticity suggests the ability to learn stimulus-reinforcement association. (2) Some neurons in the monkey basal forebrain responded to the novelty or familiarity of objects presented (Fig. 5). These neurons may also contribute to new stimulus-reinforcement association of a new object.

In general, neurons in the basal forebrain show pathological changes in Alzheimer's disease and several other types of dementia. In these patients activity of cholinesterase enzymes in the cortex decreases (Rossor et al., 1982). The medial septum, nucleus of the diagonal band of Broca (dbB), and nucleus basalis of Meynert (nbM) in primates show high levels of choline acetyltransferase (ChAT) activity (McKinney et al., 1982). The origin of cholinergic fibers to the cortex is in the basal forebrain, mainly from the nucleus basalis of Meynert (Ch4) to the prefrontal and temporal cortices, and from the medial septum (Ch2) subarea to the hippocampus (Mesulam et al., 1983, 1986). Scopolamine, a muscarinic receptor blocking agent, induces dementia-like syndromes in monkey and human, and inversely physostigmine, an anticholinesterase, improves such deficits (Bartus, 1979; Aigner et al., 1987; Rupniak et al., 1991). These conditions indicate the importance of the cholinergic system in Alzheimer's disease (Davies, 1985).

In some lesion experiments, impairment of non-matching to sample could not be demonstrated in trials of a unique object task, but scopolamine did impair this performance in lesioned monkeys (Aigner et al., 1987). Recently, functional differences between the amygdala and the hippocampus were demonstrated by several tasks (Mishkin, 1982; Squire, 1989; Zola-Morgan et al., 1991). Anatomical data indicate that neurons projecting to the hippocampus are mainly septal-dbB, while nbM neurons project to the amygdala and neocortex (Aggleton et al., 1987). The ChAT enzyme activity is highest in the temporal and motor cortices, intermediate in the prefrontal cortex, and lowest in the occipital cortex. Thus the cholinergic system from the basal forebrain may not be uniform. This suggests that the size of a lesion in the basal forebrain may be an important factor, and combined with damage in the septal and nbM may be necessary to induce memory impairment.

Conclusions

Single unit activity from the monkey basal forebrain including the nucleus basalis of Meynert and the diagonal band of Broca was recorded during a visual discrimination task to study the contribution of the basal forebrain to visual learning and memory related to novel and familiar objects. The task included discrimination of rewarding or aversive objects, novel and familiar objects, and association or dissociation with stimulus-reinforcement relations. Of 491 neurons recorded, 88 (17.9%) responded to the sight of various familiar objects. These were classified, according to their responsiveness, into four groups: attention related, positive (reward) related, negative (aversion) related and neutral. About half of the responsive neurons were nonselective. Of the neurons that responded preferentially to the sight of certain objects, most coded positive (reward) reinforcement. Responses of these neurons were plastic in extinction or relearning of stimulus-reinforcement relations. Some neurons responded preferentially to the sight of novel objects and these responses changed in successive trials to the level of responsiveness for familiar objects. Some formed new responses to categorize familiari-

ty. These results suggest that basal forebrain neurons may participate in coding novel-familiar learning, as well as stimulus-reinforcement association and arousal.

Acknowledgements

We thank Dr. A. Simpson, Showa University, for help and comments in preparing this manuscript, and Ms. M. Yamazaki and Ms. A. Tabuchi for typing. This research was partly supported by the Japanese Ministry for Education, Science and Culture Grants-in Aid for Scientific Research, 02255106 and 02NP0101.

References

Aggleton, J.P., Friedman, D.P. and Mishkin, M. (1987) A comparison between the connections of the amygdala and hippocampus with the basal forebrain in the macaque. *Exp. Brain Res.,* 67: 556 – 568.

Aigner, T.G., Mitchell, S.J., Aggleton, J.P., DeLong, M.R., Struble, R.G., Price, D.L., Wenk, G.L. and Mishkin, M. (1987) Effects of scopolamine and physostigmine on recognition memory in monkeys with ibotenic-acid lesions of the nucleus basalis of Meynert. *Psychopharmacology,* 92: 292 – 300.

Amaral, D.G. (1987) Memory: anatomical organization of candidate brain regions. In: V.B. Mountcastle, F. Plum and S.R. Geiger (Eds.), *Handbook of Physiology, Section 1. The Nervous System, Higher Functions of the Brain, Part 1, Vol. 5,* American Physiological Society, Bethesda, MD, pp. 211 – 294.

Bartus, R.T. (1979) Physostigmine and recent memory: effects in young and aged non-human primates. *Science,* 206: 1087 – 1089.

Buzsaki, G., Bickford, R.G., Ponomareff, G., Thai, L.J., Mandel, R. and Gage, F.H. (1988) Nucleus basalis and thalamic control of neocortical activity in the freely moving rat. *J. Neurosci.,* 8: 4007 – 4026.

Candy, J.M., Perry, R.H., Perry, E.K., Irving, D., Blessed, G., Fairbairn, A.F. and Tomlinson, B.E. (1983) Pathological changes in the nucleus of Meynert in Alzheimer's and Parkinson's diseases. *J. Neurol. Sci.,* 59: 277 – 289.

Coyle, J.T., Price, D.L. and DeLong, M.R. (1983) Alzheimer's disease: a disorder of cortical cholinergic innervation. *Science,* 219: 1184 – 1190.

Damasio, A.R., Eslinger, P.J., Damasio, H., Van Hoesen, G.W. and Cornell, S. (1985a) Multimodal amnesic syndrome following bilateral temporal and basal forebrain damage. *Arch. Neurol.,* 42: 252 – 259.

Damasio, A.R., Graff-Radford, N.R., Eslinger, P.J., Damasio, H. and Kassell, N. (1985b) Amnesia following basal forebrain lesions. *Arch. Neurol.*, 42: 263 – 271.

Davies, P. (1985) A critical review of the role of the cholinergic system in human memory and cognition. *Ann. N.Y. Acad. Sci.*, 444: 212 – 217.

Fukuda, M., Ono, T., Nishino, H. and Sasaki, K. (1986) Visual responses related to food discrimination in monkey lateral hypothalamus during operant feeding behavior. *Brain Res.*, 374: 249 – 259.

Fukuda, M., Ono, T. and Nakamura, K. (1987) Functional relations among inferotemporal cortex, amygdala, and lateral hypothalamus in monkey operant feeding behavior. *J. Neurophysiol.*, 57: 1060 – 1077.

Hepler, D.J., Olton, D.S., Wenk, G.L. and Coyle, J.T. (1985) Lesions in nucleus basalis magnocellularis and medial septal area of rats produce qualitatively similar memory impairments. *J. Neurosci.*, 5: 866 – 873.

Hof, P.R. and Bouras, C. (1991) Object recognition deficit in Alzheimer's disease: possible disconnection of the occipito-temporal component of the visual system. *Neurosci. Lett.*, 122: 53 – 56.

Jones, B. and Mishkin, M. (1972) Limbic lesions and the problem of stimulus-reinforcement associations. *Exp. Neurol.*, 36: 362 – 377.

Jones, B.E. and Cuello, A.C. (1989) Afferents to the basal forebrain cholinergic cell area from pontomesencephalic-catecholamine, serotonin, and acetylcholine-neurons. *Neuroscience*, 31: 37 – 61.

Jones, E.G., Burton, H., Saper, C.B. and Swanson, L.W. (1976) Midbrain, diencephalic and cortical relationships of the basal nucleus of Meynert and associated structures in primates. *J. Comp. Neurol.*, 167: 385 – 420.

Kesner, R.P., Crutcher, K.A. and Omana, H. (1990) Memory deficits following nucleus basalis magnocellularis lesions may be mediated through limbic, but not neocortial, targets. *Neuroscience*, 38: 93 – 102.

Kordower, J.H., Bartus, R.T., Marciano, F.F. and Gash, D.M. (1989) Telencephalic cholinergic system of the new world monkey (*cebus apella*): morphological and cytoarchitectonic assessment and analysis of the projection to the amygdala. *J. Comp. Neurol.*, 279: 528 – 545.

Krnjevic, K., Pumain, R. and Renaud, L. (1971) The mechanism of excitation by acetylcholine in the cerebral cortex. *J. Physiol. (Lond.)*, 215: 247 – 268.

Kromer, L., Hyman, B.T., Van Hoesen, G.W. and Damasio, A.R. (1990) Pathological alterations in the amygdala in Alzheimer's disease. *Neuroscience*, 37: 377 – 385.

Martinez-Murillo, R., Villalba, R.M. and Rodrigo, J. (1990) Immunocytochemical localization of cholinergic terminals in the region of the nucleus basalis magnocellularis of the rat: a cor-related light and electron microscopic study. *Neuroscience*, 36: 361 – 376.

McCormick, D.A. and Prince, D.A. (1985) Two types of

muscarinic response to acetylcholine in mammalian cortical neurons. *Proc. Natl. Acad. Sci. U.S.A.*, 82: 6344 – 6348.

McKinney, M., Struble, R.G., Price, D.L. and Coyle, J.T. (1982) Monkey nucleus basalis is enriched with choline acetyltransferase. *Neuroscience*, 7: 2363 – 2368.

Mesulam, M.-M. and Mufson, E.J. (1984) Neural inputs into the nucleus basalis of the substantia innominata (Ch4) in the rhesus monkey. *Brain*, 107: 253 – 274.

Mesulam, M.-M., Mufson, E.J., Levey, A.I. and Wainer, B.H. (1983) Cholinergic innervation of cortex by the basal forebrain: cytochemistry and cortical connections of the septal area, diagonal band nuclei, nucleus basalis (substantia innominata), and hypothalamus in the rhesus monkey. *J. Comp. Neurol.*, 214: 170 – 197.

Mesulam, M.-M., Volicer, L., Marquis, J.K., Mufson, E.J. and Green, R.C. (1986) Systematic regional differences in the cholinergic innervation of the primate cerebral cortex: distribution of enzyme activities and some behavioral implications. *Ann. Neurol.*, 19: 144 – 151.

Mishkin, M. (1982) A memory system in the monkey. *Phil. Trans. R. Soc. Lond. Ser. B*, 298: 89 – 95.

Nagai, T., Kimura, H., Maeda, T., McGeer, P.L., Peng, F. and McGeer, E.G. (1982) Cholinergic projections from the basal forebrain of rat to the amygdala. *J. Neurosci.*, 2: 513 – 520.

Nishijo, H., Ono, T. and Nishino, H. (1988a) Topographic distribution of modality-specific amygdalar neurons in alert monkey. *J. Neurosci.*, 8: 3556 – 3569.

Nishijo, H., Ono, T. and Nishino, H. (1988b) Single neuron response in amygdala of alert monkey during complex sensory stimulation with affective significance. *J. Neurosci.*, 8: 3570 – 3580.

Norgren, R. (1976) Taste pathways to hypothalamus and amygdala. *J. Comp. Neurol.*, 166: 17 – 30.

Ono, T., Nishino, H., Sasaki, K., Fukuda, M. and Muramoto, K. (1981) Monkey lateral hypothalamic neuron response to sight of food, and during bar press and ingestion. *Neurosci. Lett.*, 21: 99 – 104.

Ono, T., Fukuda, M., Nishino, H., Sasaki, K. and Muramoto, K. (1983) Amygdaloid neuronal responses to complex visual stimuli in an operant feeding situation in the monkey. *Brain Res. Bull.*, 11: 515 – 518.

Ono, R., Nishino, H., Fukuda, M. and Sasaki, K. (1984) Monkey amygdala, lateral hypothalamus and prefrontal cortex roles in food discrimination, motivation to bar press, and ingestion reward. In: R. Bandler (Ed.), *Modulation of Sensorimotor Activity during Alterations in Behavioral States*, Alan R. Liss, New York, pp. 251 – 268.

Ono, T., Nakamura, K., Nishijo, H. and Fukuda, M. (1986) Hypothalamic neuron involvement in integration of reward, aversion, and cue signals. *J. Neurophysiol.*, 56: 63 – 79.

Oomura, Y. (1980) Input – output organization in the hypothalamus relating to food intake behavior. In: P.J. Morgane and J. Panksepp (Eds.), *Handbook of the Hypothalamus: Physiology of the Hypothalamus, Vol. 2,*

Marcel Dekker, New York, pp. 557–620.

Richardson, R.T. and DeLong, M.R. (1990) Context-dependent responses of primate nucleus basalis neurons in a go/no-go task. *J. Neurosci.,* 10: 2528–2540.

Ridley, R.M., Baker, H.F., Drewett, B. and Johnson, J.A. (1985) Effects of ibotenic acid lesions of the basal forebrain on serial reversal learning in marmosets. *Psychopharmacology,* 86: 438–443.

Ridley, R.M., Murray, T.K., Johnson, J.A. and Baker, H.F. (1986) Learning impairment following lesion of the basal nucleus of Meynert in the marmoset: modification by cholinergic drugs. *Brain Res.,* 376: 108–116.

Rolls, E.T., Judge, S.J. and Sanghera, M.K. (1977) Activity of neurons in the inferotemporal cortex of the alert monkey. *Brain Res.,* 130: 229–238.

Rossor, M.N., Garrett, N.J., Johnson, A.L., Mountjoy, C.Q., Roth, M. and Ivesen, L.L. (1982) A post-mortem study of the cholinergic and GABA systems in senile dementia. *Brain,* 105: 313–330.

Rupniak, N.M.J., Samson, N.A., Tye, S.J., Field, M.J. and Iversen, S.D. (1991) Evidence against a specific effect of cholinergic drugs on spatial memory in primates. *Behav. Brain Res.,* 43: 1–6.

Squire, L.R. (1987) *Memory and Brain,* Oxford University Press, Oxford.

Tamura, R., Ono, T., Fukuda, M. and Nishijo, H. (1991) Role of monkey hippocampus in recognition of food and non-food. *Brain Res. Bull.,* 27: 457–461.

Thorpe, S.J., Rolls, E.T. and Maddison, S. (1983) The orbitofrontal cortex: neuronal activity in the behaving monkey. *Exp. Brain Res.,* 49: 93–115.

Van Hoesen, G.W. (1985) Neural systems of the non-human primate forebrain implicated in memory. *Ann. N.Y. Acad. Sci.,* 444: 97–112.

Van Hoesen, G.W. (1990) The dissection by Alzheimer's disease of cortical and limbic neural systems relevant to memory. In: J.L. McGaugh, N.M. Weinberger and G. Lynch (Eds.), *Brain Organization and Memory: Cells, Systems and Circuits,* Oxford University Press, New York, pp. 234–261.

Vogt, L.J.K., Hyman, B.T., Van Hoesen, G.W. and Damasio, A.R. (1990) Pathological alterations in the amygdala in Alzheimer's disease. *Neuroscience,* 37: 377–385.

Whitehouse, P.J., Price, D.L., Struble, R.G., Clark, A.W., Coyle, J.T. and DeLong, M.R. (1982) Alzheimer's disease and senile dementia: loss of neurons in the basal forebrain. *Science,* 215: 1237–1239.

Wilson, F.A.W. and Rolls, E.T. (1990a) Learning and memory is reflected in the responses of reinforcement-related neurons in the primate basal forebrain. *J. Neurosci.,* 10: 1254–1267.

Wilson, F.A.W. and Rolls, E.T. (1990b) Neuronal responses related to reinforcement in the primate basal forebrain. *Brain Res.,* 509: 213–231.

Wilson, F.A.W. and Rolls, E.T. (1990c) Neuronal responses related to the novelty and familiarity of visual stimuli in the substantia innominata, diagonal band of Broca and periventricular region of the primate basal forebrain. *Exp. Brain Res.,* 80: 104–120.

Yamatani, K., Ono, T., Nishijo, H. and Takaku, A. (1990) Activity and distribution of learning-related neurons in monkey (*Macaca fuscata*) prefrontal cortex. *Behav. Neurosci.,* 104: 503–531.

Zola-Morgan, S., Squire, L.R., Alvarez-Royo, P. and Clower, R.P. (1991) Independence of memory functions and emotional behavior: separate contributions of the hippocampal formation and the amygdala. *Hippocampus,* 1: 207–220.

T.P. Hicks, S. Molotchnikoff and T. Ono (Eds.)
Progress in Brain Research, Vol. 95
© 1993 Elsevier Science Publishers B.V. All rights reserved.

CHAPTER 31

Functional contributions of the primate pulvinar

David Lee Robinson

*Section on Visual Behavior, Laboratory of Sensorimotor Research, National Eye Institute, National Institutes of Health,
Bethesda, MD 20892, U.S.A.*

Introduction

With the development of the brain during the course of evolution, there has been an increase in the proportional size of the thalamus and association cortices (Chalupa, 1991). The nuclei of the pulvinar have been some of the leading thalamic regions in this encephalization. In spite of its size and phylogenetic enlargement, little has been known of the function of this thalamic mass.

Many studies have suggested a visual role for this part of the brain based on its anatomical connections and visually responsive cells (Robinson and McClurkin, 1989). Although it is appropriate to place the pulvinar within the visual system, there has been minimal direction to indicate an exact visual function. Within the last six years, there have been a variety of studies of the pulvinar of the primate, and from a synthesis of this work has developed the present proposal that the pulvinar contributes to the generation of visual salience (Robinson and Petersen, 1985; Petersen et al., 1985, 1987; Robinson et al., 1986, 1990, 1991; Rafal and Posner, 1987; LaBerge and Buchsbaum, 1990; Desimone et al., 1991). The pulvinar works to generate salience by opposing functional mechanisms. First, it appears to suppress information which is irrelevant. Second, it facilitates those visual data which arise in important behavioral contexts. Thus the net output of the pulvinar are signals which would be useful for perceptual as well as effector systems.

There are two qualifications to this hypothesis.

First, this function is not performed by the pulvinar alone. Many other parts of the brain, most notably the parietal cortex, have comparable functional properties and behavioral effects (Robinson et al., 1978; Bushnell et al., 1981; Posner et al., 1984; Petersen et al., 1989). Second, there will be other functions which are performed by the pulvinar; many subdivisions remain to be explored (Trojanowski and Jacobson, 1976; Baleydier and Mauguiére, 1977; Asanuma et al., 1985; Goldman-Rakic and Porrino, 1985; Giguere and Goldman-Rakic, 1987).

Within the anterior portion of the pulvinar there are at least three functional regions (Fig. 1). The first, termed the inferior map (PI), is contained entirely within the cytoarchitectural inferior pulvinar and forms a complete map of the contralateral visual field (Bender, 1981; Petersen et al., 1985). This region receives projections from both the superior colliculus and visual cortex (see Robinson and McClurkin, 1989, for detailed references). The second area, labeled the lateral map (PL), is located in the cytoarchitectural lateral pulvinar adjacent to PI, contains another complete map of the visual field, and also receives collicular and visual cortical afferents. A third region, which we termed Pdm (Petersen et al., 1985), is also located within the cytoarchitecturally defined lateral pulvinar but has poor, if any, topography. It is interconnected with cortical areas 7, MT and PO (Trojanowski and Jacobson, 1976; Baleydier and Mauguiére, 1977; Ungerleider et al., 1983, 1984; Colby et al., 1988).

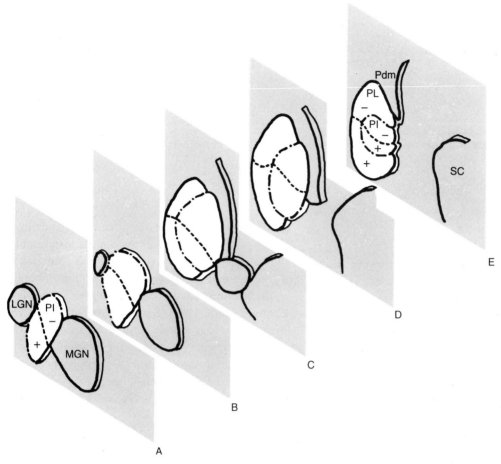

Fig. 1. Functional organization of the pulvinar. The unshaded regions show schematically the location and organization of the inferior (PI) and lateral (PL) maps. Medial and dorsal to these is area Pdm. + and − refer to the upper and lower visual field representations with the dashed line indicating the horizontal meridian. LGN, Lateral geniculate nucleus; MGN, medial geniculate nucleus; SC, superior colliculus. (Reproduced with permission from Robinson and McClurkin, 1989).

Creating salience by suppression of noise

If the pulvinar functions in the generation of visual salience, then it must have access to some form of visual information. Numerous studies have demonstrated that neurons throughout the pulvinar are visually responsive (Allman et al., 1972; Mathers and Rapisardi, 1973; Gattass et al., 1979; Benevento and Miller, 1981; Bender, 1982; Petersen et al., 1985). Although there are cells with various types of stimulus selectivity (orientation, direction or color), the dominant character of pulvinar activity is its non-selectivity. Even those neurons which are selec-

tive for a property, are not as sharply tuned as cortical cells (Bender, 1982; Petersen et al., 1985). Most cells do not discriminate for stimulus orientation, direction of movement, color, nor disparity. These weak visual properties are contrasted by a rich array of behavioral afferents modulating the visual responsivity.

The majority of pulvinar neurons respond clearly and over a wide range of speeds to stimulus movement during periods of fixation. However, when a monkey makes a series of saccadic eye movements which sweep a visual receptive field over an identical stimulus, some pulvinar neurons do not respond

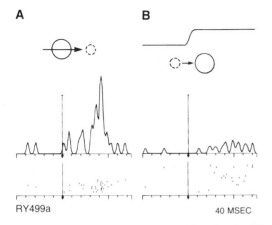

Fig. 2. Activity of pulvinar neuron with real and self-induced stimulus movement. Data on the left in *A* show the response of neuron to rapid movement of a stimulus through the receptive field during periods of fixation. *B* shows the activity of the same neuron when comparable stimulus movement is generated by a saccadic eye movement. The solid circle depicts the visual stimulus, dashed circle the visual receptive field, and the trace in *B* is for eye movements. Vertical tick marks in the rasters correspond to action potentials of the neuron. Histograms sum the data in the adjacent raster dot display.

(Fig. 2; Robinson and Petersen, 1985; Robinson et al., 1991). These cells are not activated by visual stimuli during eye movements which readily activate them during periods of fixation. Comparable effects can be demonstrated with pursuit eye movements. We have found clear examples of these types of effect in both PI and PL although there appears to be a greater concentration of them in PL (Fig. 3).

It is important to understand the physiological mechanisms which underlie this differential responding in pulvinar cells. With each eye movement the entire visual scene moves on the retina. Thus it is possible that such global visual stimulation produces a reduced excitability of neurons in the pulvinar. In order to account for such peripheral visual factors, we studied many of these same neurons while the animals performed the task in a darkened environment. In these conditions the results were the same; pulvinar cells still did not respond to visual stimuli which crossed their receptive fields during eye movements. These observations

suggest that a non-visual, extra-retinal signal suppresses these neurons with eye movements. Such a mechanism is supported by the observation that many of these same cells have a suppression of their discharge rates with saccadic eye movements made in total darkness. These data show that visually responsive neurons in the pulvinar receive an extra-retinal input which reduces their activity with each eye movement. We hypothesize that it is this signal which prevents these neurons from being activated by visual stimuli during eye movements. Comparable effects are present in neurons in the superficial layers of the superior colliculus (Robinson and Wurtz, 1976). Since neurons within this part of the colliculus project to the pulvinar (Benevento and Fallon, 1975; Partlow et al., 1977; Raczkowski and Diamond, 1978; Harting et al., 1980; Marrocco et al., 1981; Benevento and Standage, 1983), it is likely that the behavioral aspects of these properties are mediated by the tecto-pulvinar pathway. The visual

Difference index vs. number of cells

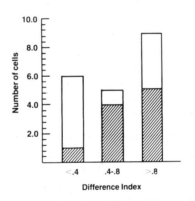

Fig. 3. Distribution of differential responding between cells in PI and PL. The difference index is a relationship of the responses in the stimulus movement conditions: DI = 1 – (EMs – EMns/F), where DI is the difference index, EMs is the response to an eye movement with a stimulus present, EMns the response with an eye movement with no stimulus present, and F the response to stimulus movement during fixation. Cells in the column to the right (> 0.8) responded much better to image motion during fixation than to the motion caused by an eye movement. Cells in the left column (< 0.4) responded well in both movement conditions. Those cells in the center column had intermediate levels of responses. The open bars represent cells recorded from PI, and the striped bars are for cells from PL.

properties of these pulvinar neurons appear to depend on striate afferents and not the superior colliculus (Bender, 1983). These physiological studies provide a clear demonstration of the pulvinar containing a suppressive process which eliminates visual responses in certain situations. Since visual excitation during eye movements is irrelevant, this mechanism is most likely part of a process for generating salience by eliminating unnecessary signals.

Many of the neurons within PI and PL have another process which removes visual signals when the eye is in certain positions. When we tested the visual excitability of pulvinar neurons around the time of eye movements, we discovered that some visually responsive cells were not driven by an identical, retinotopically positioned stimulus when the eye was in certain positions (Robinson et al., 1990). Since these observations were replicated with the animal in a darkened environment, it appears that it is the position of the eye within the orbit which gates the visual excitability rather than peripheral visual factors. Here again is a suppressive process used by the pulvinar to eliminate certain types of visual signals. We interpret these mechanisms as being used to generate visual salience. Effective stimuli become more salient by elimination of other signals when the eye is in a non-optimal position.

Experiments by Desimone et al. (1991) suggest another way in which the pulvinar uses suppression to engender salience. Rhesus monkeys were required to make form and color discriminations in two different contexts. In one situation, the stimulus to be discriminated was the only one present in the visual field; in another condition the same discriminations were required, but they were performed in the presence of other visually distracting stimuli. In the control conditions, animals could perform both tasks with a high level of accuracy. However, when the pulvinar was temporarily inactivated the animals were significantly impaired but only when distracting stimuli were present (Fig. 4). These behavioral studies suggest that in the normal condition the pulvinar has processes which can eliminate the effectiveness of irrelevant visual events. When

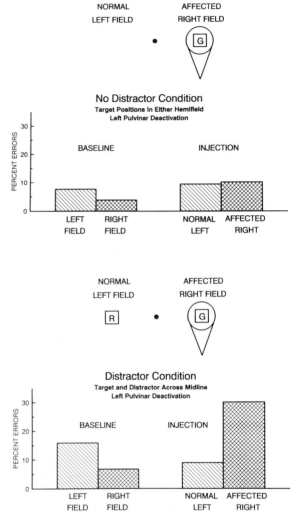

Fig. 4. Effects of pulvinar inactivation on the effectiveness of visual distractors. Data on the top show the proportion of erroneous discriminations in an uncluttered visual field with and without pulvinar inactivation. Data on the bottom show performance with the same discriminations when additional stimuli are present in the visual field. In this condition, pulvinar inactivation leads to poorer performance (right). (Reproduced with permission from Desimone et al., 1991.)

the pulvinar is not functional then the distractors become effective and performance declines. This is another suppressive mechanism in the pulvinar which functions in perception just as the processes described above function with eye movements.

These sets of studies demonstrate that the

FIXATION

SACCADE

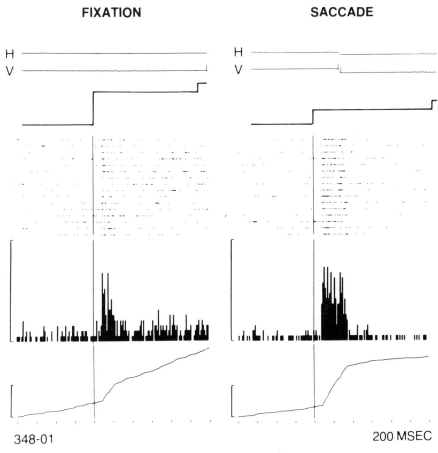

348-01

200 MSEC

Fig. 5. Enhancement of visual response for a neuron in the pulvinar. Data on the left show the response of the cell to a stimulus flashed in the receptive field during fixations. Data on the right illustrate the increased discharge of the same neuron to the identical stimulus when the animal is going to make an eye movement to fixate it. The top two traces show the horizontal (H) and vertical (V) eye position. The two tick marks on the vertical trace signify a computer identification of the appropriate eye movement. The solid traces beneath indicate the time of onset of the visual stimulus (left) and eye movement target (right). The bottom trace is a cumulative histogram which sums the number of discharges over time.

pulvinar most likely highlights important, salient visual events by removing stimulation which is unimportant. Some pulvinar cells do not respond to the visual stimulation caused by eye movements, that which occurs in certain eye positions, and that which is irrelevant to attentional tasks. Taken together these studies show that the pulvinar has processes which reduce or eliminate visual stimulation which is unnecessary or detrimental to visual perception or performance.

Generating salience by facilitation

Other studies of the pulvinar show that some visual activity is augmented in certain behavioral conditions, and these data are consistent with the hypothesis that the modulations generate salience. Neurons located within the Pdm region of the pulvinar have many physiological properties which distinguish them from those in PI and PL (Petersen et al., 1985). Their visual receptive fields are larger and their discharge latencies are longer. Cells which discharge after saccadic eye movements are more common in Pdm (Robinson et al., 1986). The cells in Pdm will respond to a visual stimulus flashed in their receptive field during periods of fixation. When the same stimulus is flashed in the identical location just prior to an eye movement to fixate it, then the discharge is dramatically enhanced (Fig. 5; Petersen et al., 1985). Since the visual stimulation is the same, the differential responding of the cells is related to some contextual differences in the two tasks. At some point prior to the eye movement, there must be some active selection of the visual target, and so this augmentation may be related to the newly acquired salience of the stimulus. When we tested these same neurons under conditions where the monkeys had to attend to the stimulus but not make an eye movement to it, the enhancement was still demonstrable. Here the behavioral state is common to both tasks, but the motor response is

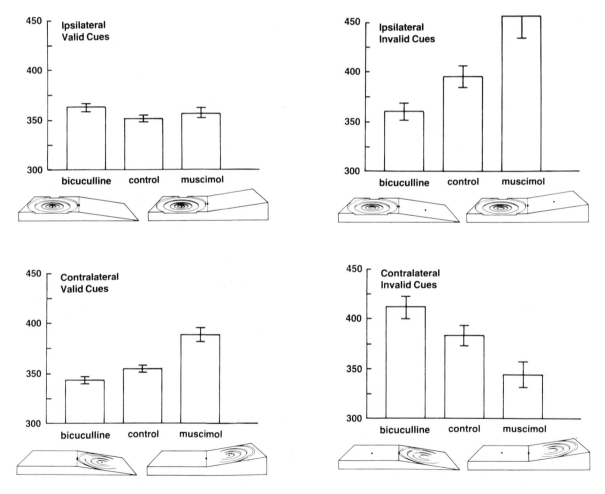

Fig. 6. Effects of modulation of the pulvinar on attentional performance. The schematics beneath each graph represent a view of the tangent screen; the depressions and elevations of the right side are used to schematically represent the speeding and impeding effects on attentional shifts of bicuculline and muscimol, respectively. Data on the left come from trials where targets were validly cued. At the top, the cue (sculpted pit) and target (dot) were in the left (ipsilateral) visual field; at the bottom, cues and targets were in the right (contralateral) field. Data on the right come from invalidly cued trials where cues and targets were in opposite hemifields. The vertical axis in each graph is the monkey's reaction time to respond to the target onset.

different. These studies demonstrate that the enhanced discharge is independent of the motor response. This combination of properties suggests that the active selection of the stimulus is the modulating condition, not eye movement or level of alertness. In other tests we demonstrated that this enhancement is present when attention is directed to the stimulus in the receptive field; it is not present for attention to other points. Taken together these studies show that in Pdm, the modulation is independent of the motor response and is selective for spatial location. Comparable properties have been described for the cells in cortical area 7, a region of the brain long associated with attentional processes (Robinson et al., 1978; Bushnell et al., 1981; Posner et al., 1984; Petersen et al., 1989).

These physiological properties of cells in Pdm suggested that this part of the brain might be involved in spatial attention; it might participate in selection for and generation of visual salience. If this is the case, then one might expect that altering the functioning of this area would alter attentional performance. To test this hypothesis, we used a cued reaction time task (Posner, 1980) and micro-injected GABA-related drugs into Pdm. Monkeys were trained to fixate a spot of light and release a bar when a visual target appeared in the periphery. Reaction times were faster for targets which were preceded by visual cues at the same location (validly cued) than for targets which were preceded by cues in the opposite hemifield (invalidly cued). It has been hypothesized that the cue controls the direction of attention. When a target appears where attention has been drawn then reaction times are fast. When we micro-injected muscimol (a GABA agonist) into Pdm, reaction times changed, as if the animal was having more difficulty shifting its attention into the contralateral visual field (Petersen et al., 1987). This was true for both validly and invalidly cued targets (Fig. 6). When we injected bicuculline (a GABA antagonist) into Pdm, the animal's performance changed in a way suggesting that it was facilitated in shifting its attention to the contralateral visual field. These data suggest that the drugs are modulating an attentional process, not some simple sensory or motor mechanisms. The electrophysiological enhancement effect, taken together with the effect of drug injections, support the hypothesis that the pulvinar participates in the generation of and selection for salience. In these studies, active selection of a target increased the discharge of pulvinar cells; augmentation or diminution of transmitter-related activity altered the animal's performance as if the salience of the attention-controlling cue changed.

Comparable data have been produced with patients who have suffered thalamic damage which most likely includes the pulvinar (Rafal and Posner, 1987). Using the same type of task which was just described for the monkey experiments, patients were tested who had neither neglect nor visual field defects. Although the patients were significantly slower for all targets in the visual field contralateral

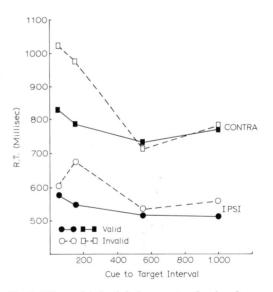

Fig. 7. Effects of thalamic lesions on attentional performance in humans. Data represented by the top two lines show the overall slowing in these patients for any targets in the visual field contralateral to the lesion (contra). The two lower lines are for targets in the visual field ipsilateral to the lesion. The solid symbols with solid lines represent trials when cue and target were in the same visual field (valid). The open symbols with dashed lines are for invalidly cued targets (cue and target in opposite field). The vertical axis is the subjects' reaction time in milliseconds, and the horizontal axis is the time between the cue and target in milliseconds. (Reproduced with permission from Rafal and Posner, 1987.)

to the lesion, they were especially slow for invalidly cued targets in that field (Fig. 7). This slowing was for the shortest cue-target intervals whereas patients with parietal lesions were slowed over most intervals (Posner et al., 1984). It is easy to propose that these humans, like the monkeys with muscimol injections, were impaired in utilizing the behavioral salience of the cue. Rafal and Posner (1987) hypothesized that the defect is in the engagement of attention at the locus of the cue.

More direct evidence for facilitation in the pulvinar comes from PET scanning in humans (LaBerge and Buchsbaum, 1990). In subjects who are making identification discriminations in the presence of varying attentional demands, there are increases in PET activity under the conditions of greatest attentional demand. There is no comparable change in the thalamus opposite the unattended side. These data suggest that when normal humans require additional salience of images there is an augmentation of activity within the pulvinar.

Monkeys trained to make discriminations using visual stimuli which are tachistoscopically presented can perform such tasks quite well (Chalupa et al., 1976). Their performance degenerates after damage to the pulvinar. Their defect may be the loss of a fast mechanism for directing attention to salient visual information; in the absence of this process, they are unable to make fast attentional scans. Similar functional defects are most likely involved in monkeys trained to scan visual arrays (Ungerleider and Christensen, 1977, 1979). After damage to the pulvinar these animals had significantly prolonged periods of fixation. With a reduced ability to generate and evaluate salience, they had no impetus to shift their attention nor to make eye movements.

Summary and conclusions

One of the major tasks facing the central nervous system is choosing which sensory events to use for perception and directed behavior. All organisms live in a rich sensory environment, and it is impossible to attend and respond to everything. Certain brain regions and systems must evaluate sensory signals and then determine which are salient. Based on recent data derived from diverse studies of the pulvinar of primates, it is the hypothesis of this paper that a major role of the pulvinar is to participate in the generation of visual salience, those processes which precede perception and action.

This process of salience generation makes use of two broad mechanisms, the suppression of noise and the enhancement of significant signals. Outlined above are experiments which show that the visual activity which might be caused by eye movements is filtered from some pulvinar cells. Visual responses associated with certain directions of gaze are removed. Finally the ability to suppress the activity of distracting visual stimuli is dependent on the integrity of the pulvinar. Conversely, there are neurons within the pulvinar which respond best when animals actively select and thus engender certain stimuli with salience. Modulation of pulvinar functioning with transmitter-related drugs changes performance as if salience is being modulated. Humans and monkeys with destruction of the pulvinar behave as if they too cannot create or evaluate salience. Finally, when salience is demanded of humans by making their visual tasks more demanding, there is an increase in PET activity.

The hypothesis here is that the pulvinar functions as an early center for the generation of visual salience. This is similar to the view of striate cortex as an early integration stage for the basic elements of visual processing (Hubel and Wiesel, 1968; Zeki, 1976; Allman et al., 1981). Vision does not take place within the complex microstructure of striate neurons, but all of the essential components are present there, and these are distributed to other cortical areas which construct specific aspects of visual perception. Similarly, regions of the pulvinar contain building blocks for visual/behavioral/oculomotor integration which they distribute to various cortical sites for shifts of attention and other types of response specification. When an organism must determine external visual salience, there are neurons within the pulvinar which signal this. Since the major efferents of these thalamic regions are the visual cortices (Benevento and Rezak, 1976; Lin and Kaas,

1979; Kennedy and Bullier, 1985), our present hypothesis is that these signals are used for the construction of visuomotor and visuoperceptual states. The pulvinar has signals related to some visual parameters, and these are modulated by several oculomotor and behavioral afferents. Such integrated signals could be transmitted to the multiple visual cortical areas for use in perception and action.

There is obviously still a lot of pulvinar to be explored. There are visually responsive neurons in more caudal regions of the pulvinar (Benevento and Miller, 1981), and there may be separate subnuclei there and elsewhere in the pulvinar. It is actually the medial pulvinar which is most strongly connected with parietal cortex (and frontal cortex), and this region remains to be explored for visual-behavioral function (Trojanowski and Jacobson, 1976; Baleydier and Mauguiére, 1977; Asanuma et al., 1985; Goldman-Rakic and Porrino, 1985; Giguere and Goldman-Rakic, 1987). Nonetheless, considering the pulvinar in relation to visual salience should provide a useful framework for future research.

References

Allman, J.M., Kaas, J.H., Lane, R.H. and Miezin, F.M. (1972) A representation of the visual field in the inferior nucleus of the pulvinar in the owl monkey. *Brain Res.,* 40: 291 – 302.

Allman, J.M., Baker, J.F., Newsome, W.T. and Petersen, S.E. (1981) Visual topography and function in cortical visual areas in the owl monkey. In: C.N. Woolsey (Ed.), *Cortical Sensory Organization, Vol 2: Multiple Visual Areas,* Humana Press, NJ, pp. 171 – 185.

Asanuma, C., Andersen, R.A. and Cowan, W.M. (1985) The thalamic relations of the caudal inferior parietal lobule and the lateral prefrontal cortex in monkeys: divergent cortical projections from cell clusters in the medial pulvinar nucleus. *J. Comp. Neurol.,* 241: 357 – 381.

Baleydier, C. and Mauguiére, F. (1977) Pulvinar-latero posterior afferents to cortical area 7 in monkeys demonstrated by horseradish peroxidase tracing technique. *Exp. Brain Res.,* 27: 501 – 507.

Bender, D.B. (1981) Retinotopic organization of the macaque pulvinar. *J. Neurophysiol.,* 46: 672 – 693.

Bender, D.B. (1982) Receptive field properties of neurons in the macaque inferior pulvinar. *J. Neurophysiol.,* 48: 1 – 17.

Bender, D.B. (1983) Visual activation of neurons in the primate pulvinar depends on cortex but not colliculus. *Brain Res.,* 279: 258 – 261.

Benevento, L.A. and Fallon, J.H. (1975) The ascending projections of the superior colliculus in the rhesus monkey *(Macaca mulatta). J. Comp. Neurol.,* 160: 339 – 362.

Benevento, L.A. and Miller, J. (1981) Visual responses of single neurons in the caudal lateral pulvinar of the macaque monkey. *J. Neurosci.,* 11: 1268 – 1278.

Benevento, L.A. and Rezak, M. (1976) The cortical projections of the inferior pulvinar and adjacent lateral pulvinar in the rhesus monkey (*Macaca mulatta*): an autoradiographic study. *Brain Res.,* 108: 1 – 24.

Benevento, L.A. and Standage, G.P. (1983) The organization of projections of the retino-recipient and nonretino-recipient nuclei of the pretectal complex and layers of the superior colliculus to the lateral pulvinar and medial pulvinar in the macaque monkey. *J. Comp. Neurol.,* 218: 307 – 336.

Bushnell, M.C., Goldberg, M.E. and Robinson, D.L. (1981) Behavioral enhancement of visual responses in monkey cerebral cortex: I. Modulation in posterior parietal cortex related to selective visual attention. *J. Neurophysiol.,* 46: 755 – 772.

Chalupa, L.M. (1991) The visual function of the pulvinar. In: A.G. Leventhal (Ed.), *The Neural Basis of Visual Function,* Macmillan, London, pp. 140 – 159.

Chalupa, L.M., Coyle, R.S. and Lindsley, D.B. (1976) Effect of pulvinar lesions on visual pattern discrimination in monkeys. *J. Neurophysiol.,* 39: 354 – 369.

Colby, C.L., Gattass, R., Olson, C.R. and Gross, C.G. (1988) Topographic organization of cortical afferents to extrastriate visual area PO in the macaque: a dual tracer study. *J. Comp. Neurol.,* 238: 1257 – 1299.

Desimone, R., Wessinger, M., Thomas, L. and Schneider, W. (1991) Attentional control of visual perception: cortical and subcortical mechanisms. *Cold Spring Harbor Symposium on Quantitative Biology,* 60: 963 – 971.

Gattass, R., Oswaldo-Cruz, E. and Sousa, A.P.B. (1979) Visual receptive fields of units in the pulvinar of cebus monkey. *Brain Res.,* 160: 413 – 430.

Giguere, M. and Goldman-Rakic, P.S. (1987) The primate medial pulvinar (MP) and its connections with the frontal lobes and other cortical areas. *Soc. Neurosci. Abstr.,* 13: 1098.

Goldman-Rakic, P.S. and Porrino, L.J. (1985) The primate mediodorsal (MD) nucleus and its projection to the frontal lobe. *J. Comp. Neurol.,* 242: 535 – 560.

Harting, J.K., Huerta, M.F., Frankfurter, A.J., Strominger, N.L. and Royce, G.J. (1980) Ascending pathways from the monkey superior colliculus: an autoradiographic analysis. *J. Comp. Neurol.,* 192: 853 – 882.

Hubel, D.H. and Wiesel, T.N. (1968) Receptive fields and functional architecture of monkey striate cortex. *J. Physiol. (Lond.),* 195: 215 – 243.

Kennedy, H. and Bullier, J. (1985) A double-labeling investigation of the afferent connectivity to cortical areas V1 and V2 of the macaque monkey. *J. Neurosci.,* 5: 2815 – 2830.

LaBerge, D. and Buchsbaum, M.S. (1990) Positron emission

380

tomographic measurements of pulvinar activity during an attention task. *J. Neurosci.,* 10: 613 – 619.

Lin, C.-S. and Kaas, J.H. (1979) The inferior pulvinar complex in owl monkeys: architectonic subdivisions and patterns of input from the superior colliculus and subdivisions of the visual cortex. *J. Comp. Neurol.,* 187: 655 – 677.

Marrocco, R.T., McClurkin, J.W. and Young, R.A. (1981) Spatial properties of superior colliculus cells projecting to the inferior pulvinar and parabigeminal nucleus of the monkey. *Brain Res.,* 222: 150 – 154.

Mathers, L.H. and Rapisardi, S.C. (1973) Visual and somatosensory receptive fields of neurons in the squirrel monkey pulvinar. *Brain Res.,* 64: 65 – 83.

Partlow, G.D., Colonnier, M. and Szabo, J. (1977) Thalamic projections of the superior colliculus in the rhesus monkey, *Macaca mulatta.* A light and electron microscopic study. *J. Comp. Neurol.,* 171: 285 – 318.

Petersen, S.E., Robinson, D.L. and Keys, W. (1985) Pulvinar nuclei of the behaving rhesus monkey: visual responses and their modulations. *J. Neurophysiol.,* 54: 867 – 886.

Petersen, S.E., Robinson, D.L. and Morris, J.D. (1987) The contribution of the pulvinar to visual spatial attention. *Neuropsychologia,* 25: 97 – 105.

Petersen, S.E., Robinson, D.L. and Currie, J.N. (1989) Influences of lesions of parietal cortex on visual spatial attention in humans. *Exp. Brain Res.,* 76: 267 – 280.

Posner, M.I. (1980) Orienting of attention. *Q.J. Exp. Psychol.,* 32: 3 – 25.

Posner, M.I., Walker, J.A., Friedrich, F.J. and Rafal, R.D. (1984) Effects of parietal injury on covert orienting of visual attention. *J. Neurosci.,* 4: 1863 – 1874.

Raczkowski, D. and Diamond, I.T. (1978) Cells of origin of several efferent pathways from the superior colliculus in *Galago senegalensis. Brain Res.,* 146: 351 – 357.

Rafal, R.D. and Posner, M.I. (1987) Deficits in human visual spatial attention following thalamic lesions. *Proc. Natl. Acad. Sci. U.S.A.,* 84: 7349 – 7353.

Robinson, D.L. and McClurkin, J.W. (1989) The visual superior colliculus and pulvinar. In: R.H. Wurtz and M.E. Goldberg (Eds.), *The Neurobiology of Saccadic Eye Movements, Reviews of Oculomotor Research, Vol. III,* Elsevier, Amsterdam, pp. 337 – 360.

Robinson, D.L. and Petersen, S.E. (1985) Response of pulvinar neurons to real and self-induced stimulus movement. *Brain Res.,* 338: 392 – 394.

Robinson, D.L. and Wurtz, R.H. (1976) Use of an extraretinal signal by monkey superior colliculus neurons to distinguish real from self-induced stimulus movements. *J. Neurophysiol.,* 39: 852 – 870.

Robinson, D.L., Goldberg, M.E. and Stanton, G.B. (1978) Parietal association cortex in the primate: sensory mechanisms and behavioral modulations. *J. Neurophysiol.,* 41: 910 – 932.

Robinson, D.L., Petersen, S.E. and Keys, W. (1986) Saccade-related activity in the pulvinar nuclei of the behaving rhesus monkey. *Exp. Brain Res.,* 62: 625 – 634.

Robinson, D.L., McClurkin, J.W. and Kertzman, C. (1990) Orbital position and eye movement influences on visual responses in the pulvinar nuclei of the behaving macaque. *Exp. Brain Res.,* 82: 235 – 246.

Robinson, D.L. McClurkin, J.W., Kertzman, C. and Petersen, S.E. (1991) Visual responses of pulvinar and collicular neurons during eye movements of awake, trained macaques. *J. Neurophysiol.,* 66: 485 – 496.

Trojanowski, J.Q. and Jacobson, S. (1976) Areal and laminar distribution of some pulvinar cortical efferents in rhesus monkey. *J. Comp. Neurol.,* 169: 371 – 392.

Ungerleider, L.G. and Christensen, C.A. (1977) Pulvinar lesions in monkeys produce abnormal eye movements during visual discrimination training. *Brain Res.,* 136: 189 – 196.

Ungerleider, L.G. and Christensen, C.A. (1979) Pulvinar lesions in monkeys produce abnormal scanning of a complex visual array. *Neuropsychologia,* 17: 493 – 501.

Ungerleider, L.G., Galkin, T.W. and Mishkin, M. (1983) Visuotopic organization of projections from striate cortex to inferior and lateral pulvinar in rhesus monkey. *J. Comp. Neurol.,* 217: 137 – 157.

Ungerleider, L.G., Desimone, R., Galkin, T.W. and Mishkin, M. (1984) Subcortical projections of area MT in the macaque. *J. Comp. Neurol.,* 223: 368 – 386.

Zeki, S.M. (1976) The functional organization of projections from striate to prestriate visual cortex in the rhesus monkey. *Cold Spring Harbor Symposium on Quantitative Biology,* 40: 591 – 600.

T.P. Hicks, S. Molotchnikoff and T. Ono (Eds.)
Progress in Brain Research, Vol. 95
© 1993 Elsevier Science Publishers B.V. All rights reserved.

CHAPTER 32

Orientation discrimination in the cat and its cortical loci

James M. Sprague[1], Peter De Weerd[2], Erik Vandenbussche[2] and Guy A. Orban[2]

[1] *Department of Anatomy, School of Medicine, University of Pennsylvania, Philadephia, PA 19104-6058, U.S.A., and*
[2] *Laboratory of Neuro- and Psychophysiology, School of Medicine, Catholic University Louvain, B-3000 Louvain, Belgium*

Introduction

The visual system of carnivores and primates is one of considerable complexity: in the domestic cat there are at least 15 separate retinotopic representations of the visual field in each hemisphere (see Rosenquist, 1985). Each of these visual areas has reciprocal connections with the thalamus and with several other visual cortical areas and many have efferent projections to the superior colliculus, the pretectum, the striatum and the pons. The anatomy and physiology of the visual system are better known in the cat than in any other species. A problem of prime importance in systems neuroscience is to delineate the neuronal streams and understand the mechanisms in the brain which give rise to detection, perception and discrimination of visual stimuli. Clearly the evolution of the brain has resulted in cell assemblies sensitive to a multiplicity of cues, all of which serve to perceive, differentiate and discriminate essential parts of the complex visual scene. One approach to begin to understand the elements of such a complex process is to use simplifying experimental strategies (Berkley and Sprague, 1979, 1982; Orban et al., 1990). One such strategy is to measure thresholds for discriminating very simple stimuli differing only in a single dimension (cue), the encoding of which is known to be present at a single cell level in certain anatomically and physiologically defined visual areas. Knowledge of these areas allows the planning of selective lesions and comparison of pre- and postoperative performance.

A generally accepted scheme in computational vision is that the visual system first performs a local analysis of the image (filtering), followed by a number of more complex operations, which to a certain extent work in parallel, and which lead to segregation, the representation of 3D surfaces, and finally object recognition. This idea has received support from a large number of anatomical and lesion studies in the monkey (for review, see Desimone and Ungerleider, 1989). In the present chapter, we have investigated whether a processing hierarchy exists in the cat, similar to the one described in monkeys.

Since the use of anatomical criteria has proved insufficient to distinguish a detailed hierarchy between areas in the cat (Rosenquist, 1985), we decided to make a rather coarse division between lower order areas (Tier I areas) and higher order areas (Tier II areas). As Tier I areas, we chose those two areas which receive the strongest input from the LGNd, i.e., areas 17 and 18. Tier II areas included all those areas which receive direct input from areas 17 and 18, i.e., areas 19, 20a, 21a and 21b, AMLS and PMLS (Rosenquist, 1985). Although it must be kept in mind that all cortico-cortical connections are reciprocal (Rosenquist, 1985), we hypothesized that the connections between Tier I and Tier II areas could be the basis of serial processing between the two groups of cortical areas. In particular, local filtering operations would be performed by Tier I areas (for a review of physiological evidence, see Orban, 1984), and second order operations would be carried out in Tier II areas using the input from Tier I areas.

To test this model, we have performed experiments in which the behavioral effects of bilateral anatomical lesions of Tier I and Tier II areas were assessed. The ablation of Tier I areas will be referred to as Tier I ablations (lesions), and similarly, the ablation of Tier II areas will be referred to as Tier II ablations. In a typical experiment, the cats were taught a visual discrimination (in our case a contour orientation discrimination task), after which a lesion was made and the animal retested. The decrease in performance after the lesion served as a measure of the lesion deficit, and as an estimation of the contribution of the removed areas to the visual discrimination being studied.

A major precondition for a clear interpretation of lesion results is the use of well-chosen stimuli. Since Hubel and Wiesel's (1959) discovery that visual cortical neurons respond to optimally oriented bars, it has become clear that contour orientation coding is a key feature of visual analysis. The use of contour stimuli in behavioral orientation discrimination tasks has two considerable advantages. Firstly, when using the same stimuli as used in physiological studies, data available from the study of single cortical neurons can be used in interpreting the discriminatory behavior of the animal before and after a lesion. Secondly, in well-controlled experiments, it is possible to show that the behavior of the animal in a contour orientation discrimination task is controlled only by the orientation of the stimulus, and not by other stimulus parameters (or only to a small extent). In this way, the loss of discriminative behavior can be linked to a single stimulus parameter: contour orientation. The use of simplified stimuli has proven a successful strategy in the understanding of visual processing in the highly complex brains of higher mammals (Berkley and Sprague, 1979, 1982; Orban et al., 1990).

The ability to discriminate contour orientation was assessed by determining the just noticeable difference (JND) in orientation using a staircase procedure (see Methods section). The JNDs used corresponded to the 73.5% correct point on the psychometric distribution. The use of JNDs offers a sensitive measure of performance, and the choice of the moderate 73.5% correct criterion guarantees that, unless the deficits are extremely large, reliable postoperative JNDs can be determined using the same method.

In our experiments, two types of contour stimuli were used. On the one hand, we used bar stimuli, i.e., the contour is defined by a luminance difference. This type of stimulus has been one of the favored tools of neurophysiologists in exploring the functioning of the visual cortex (see Orban 1984, for review). Quite recently, in 1984, von der Heydt and co-workers introduced a new type of contour stimulus in neurophysiology, namely the illusory contour. The existence of stimulus patterns giving rise to illusory contours was known long before (see Schumann, 1900), but von der Heydt et al. (1984) were the first to study neuronal activity in response to that type of contours. They used illusory contour patterns in which the contour was not defined linearly, i.e., the contour was not given in the Fourier spectrum of the stimulus, as opposed to the case of luminance-defined contours. In an impressive series of papers, von der Heydt and Peterhans demonstrated that whereas monkey V1 cells encode bar orientation and not illusory contour orientation, a large proportion of V2 cells are capable of encoding the orientation of both types of contours. This was explained by a two-stage model, in which local features (inducing elements) are encoded by some sort of local filtering (by end-stopped units in their model), followed by a global analysis in which the distribution of local features is organized into a contour of a particular orientation.

The above findings are particularly relevant for our hierarchical model of visual processing in the cat. Whereas there is convincing neurophysiological evidence suggesting that areas 17 and 18 intervene in the local filtering of the orientation of luminance-defined edges (Palmer et al., 1991; Orban, 1991), the evidence is less convincing with regard to illusory contours (see Redies et al., 1986). This could mean that, whereas bar orientation can be encoded at the level of areas 17 and 18, this might not be true for illusory contours. We hypothesized that the local analysis of elements inducing illusory contours might take place in areas 17 and 18, but that second order processing − leading to illusory contour construction − takes place in Tier II areas. The following report summarizes our evidence related to these issues.

Primary or ''early'' visual cortical areas contain neurons which are selectively sensitive to changes in certain properties of the stimuli, i.e., they code differences in orientation, size or spatial frequency, stereopsis and directions and velocity of movements. Marr (1982) distinguished the goal of early

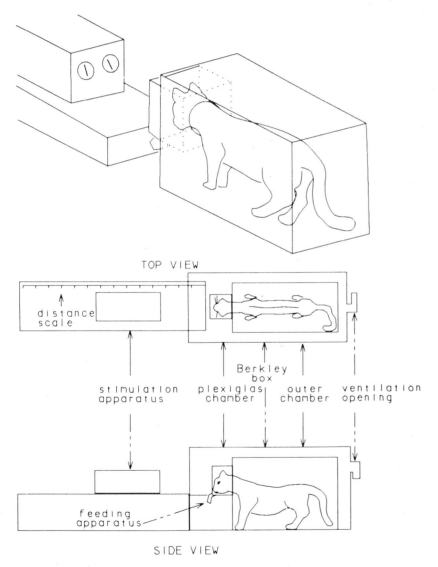

TOP VIEW

SIDE VIEW

Fig. 1. Schematic views of the training apparatus, modified from the original design of Berkley (1970). Not shown are the two glass windows through which the cat views the two stimuli; nose pushing the window in front of S + triggers termination of the trial and a food reward. Push of the other window simply terminates the trial.

vision – to form a description of the 3D surfaces of the visual scene – from that of later vision which is to identify and recognize objects. There is broad agreement that this early visual description is dependent on the registration of a set of simple primitives or functional features (Treisman and Gormican, 1988). The primitives contained in a description are not, however, represented by single cells, as envisaged in the theory of feature analysis, but rather in a distributed pattern of activity in a population of cells. The idea of population coding can be applied to all levels of visual analysis, and such a model has been proposed to represent orientation (Vogels, 1990) and object coding as well (Desimone and Ungerleider, 1989).

Methods

We have used a conditioning apparatus designed after Berkley (1970) (Fig. 1). The use of such a testing chamber with an automatic food dispenser restricts the behavior of the cat but allows the administration of a large number of daily trials. The efficiency of this apparatus in visual discrimination learning resides in the close temporal and spatial contiguity of stimulus presentation and reinforcement. Additional advantages are the closer control of viewing distance, and lack of experimenter intervention.

In our experiments, the stimuli were always

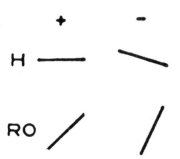

Fig. 2. Positive (+) and negative (−) stimuli used in contour orientation discrimination tasks at the horizontal (H) and the right oblique (RD) reference orientation.

presented on a screen positioned at 28.5 cm from the cat's eyes. Positive (S +) and negative (S −) stimuli (Fig. 2) were presented simultaneously, each stimulus behind a response key. An occluder not shown in Figure 1 prevented the animals from seeing the stimuli simultaneously together. The goal of this occluder was to prevent the animals from using the global, configurational cues which are available when two differently oriented contours are inspected simultaneously.

Discrimination and detection tasks

Contour orientation processing was measured in a contour orientation discrimination task. The contour was either a luminance defined bar, or one of two types of illusory contour. In the discrimination task, the cat had to distinguish between two contours of different orientation. The orientation of one of the two discriminanda remained fixed throughout the task, and is referred to as the reference orientation, which served as the positive stimulus (S +). The second stimulus deviated in orientation from the reference orientation and served as S −. To ensure the generality of our observations, the orientation discriminations were taught around two reference orientations, the horizontal (H) and the right oblique (RO). When the reference orientation was H, the S deviated clockwise, and anticlockwise when the reference orientation was RO (Fig. 2). The order in which the animals were trained for each reference orientation was randomized among animals.

For the bar stimulus, we also used a detection task. In this task, the animal was only presented with the reference orientation and no stimulus was present at the other side of the screen. Here, the animal's task was merely to push the response key behind which the reference orientation was presented.

A discrimination or detection trial started upon stimulus onset. During the first 350 msec of stimulus presentation the animal had to delay its response (response delay period: RDP) to enforce attention. Since responses during the RDP were never rewarded, they extinguished as the animals became more experienced. After the RDP, the animal was rewarded for pushing the nose key behind which the S+ was presented. Upon the animal's response, the stimuli disappeared, and a 7 sec inter-trial interval (ITI) was started during which only a dark background was visible.

The S+ was presented behind the left and right key in a balanced pseudorandom order, to avoid any associations of S+ with one of the two response keys. We balanced the random sequence in such a way that the S+ was never presented more than three times behind the same response key. In addition, within each group of six successive trials, the S+ was presented three times behind the left key and three times behind the right key. Within these limitations, all possible successions of left/right presentations were administered. We defined response bias as the occurrence of six consecutive responses with the same key, which is twice the number of times the S+ could be presented behind the same key. If this occurred, the S+ was presented behind the non-preferred key until the numbers of left and right key responses were again equalized.

Stimulus device

In the set-up used for orientation discrimination, the stimuli were back-projected onto a transparent, circular screen 75° in diameter, which was positioned 28.5 cm from the cat's eyes. Illusory contour stimuli were presented from slides, and bar stimuli were administered by means of slitmakers which allowed close control of bar width and length. The orientation of each contour was manipulated by rotating a dove prism mounted in front of the holder. A variable neutral density filter mounted in front of the dove prism permitted luminance variations from 0.50 to 200.00 cd/m². The adjustment of orientation and luminance of the stimuli was done by step motors, controlled by a PDP-11 computer. The resolution of orientation settings was 0.05°, and the resolution of luminance settings was in order of 0.001 cd/m² for luminances below 2.50 cd/m². Resolution of luminance settings near 10 and 100 cd/m² decreased by a factor of 10 and 100, respectively. Background luminance was maintained at 0.50 cd/m². Background and stimulus luminances

were measured at the start and at the end of each testing session. Continual control measurements of the luminances of bar and background over an entire session (1 h) showed that contrast (log ($\Delta I/I$)) fluctuations never exceeded 2% of the contrast set at the beginning of a session.

Bar stimuli (luminance-defined contours)

Standard length and width of the bar stimulus were 12.0° and 0.2°, respectively. Standard luminance was 15.8 cd/m², and in view of the 0.50 cd/m² background used this corresponded to a 1.49 contrast (log ($\Delta I/I$)). Two types of parametric variations have been carried out using the bar stimulus: manipulations of length and contrast. Length experiments have been used to investigate whether the cats used alternative cues to solve the discrimination task in addition to orientation (DeWeerd et al., 1990c). The issue of alternative cues will not be dealt with in this chapter.

Illusory contours

The two types of illusory contours used were similar to those devised by Vogels and Orban (1987). The first stimulus (Fig. 3) consisted of a number of inducing semicircles, separated by a gap (gap illusory contour, GIC). In the other stimulus (Fig. 3), the illusory contour was induced by shifting each inducing semicircle along the contour (phase-shifted illusory contour, PSIC). Inducing semicircles were

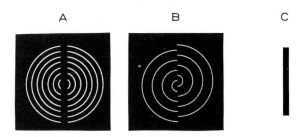

Fig. 3. Gap illusory contour (GIC, *A*), phase shifted illusory contour (PSIC, *B*) and a black bar of dimensions equal to the dimensions of the gap in the GIC (*C*).

white, on a dark background. Standard luminances for the semicircles and background were 15.81 and 0.50 cd/m² , respectively. Standard contour length was 12°. Width of the inducing semicircles was 0.2°. Variations of the width of the inducing semicircles in a 0.15 – 0.35° range did not affect thresholds in orientation discrimination. We used a 1.2° wide gap in our GIC, which is optimal for a large range of contrasts.

The choice of circular inducing elements excludes the possibility that the orientation of inducing elements is used as a cue to solve the discriminations. However, the cats could simply use an alternative cue instead of orientation, such as the position of a single local endpoint. Direct evidence that the animals do use contour orientation as a cue in the discrimination task was obtained by manipulating the strength of the contour, through variations of contour length and variations in the density of semicircles. Although cats probably do use contour orientation to solve the discrimination task, it is impossible to know directly whether the subjective percept cats have when inspecting illusory contour patterns is similar to the percept of humans. Showing that cats discriminate orientation of contours induced in a complex way, and in which humans perceive illusory contours, strongly increases the possibility that this is the case. For our purposes, however, it is sufficient that through the use of the contour patterns shown in Fig. 3, orientation discrimination is mediated by more complex processes than when using bars.

Testing procedures

Staircase procedure. In the contour orientation *discrimination* task, we wished to determine the smallest difference in orientation the animal could reliably distinguish. In the bar *detection* task on the other hand, we aimed at determining the lowest contrast at which the bar could be reliably detected. The latter task is a measure of a very basic visual capacity, and the way in which performance in this task is affected can be helpful in the interpretation of lesion effects.

When using a staircase procedure (see DeWeerd et al., 1990b), the parameter under investigation is continually adapted to performance. In the contour orientation discrimination task, the orientation difference was decreased after three consecutive correct responses, or after two correct responses followed by an incorrect and a correct response. The orientation difference was increased after a single incorrect response, a correct response followed by an incorrect response, or after two correct responses followed by two incorrect responses. The orientation difference was decreased or increased by respectively multiplying or dividing the orientation difference by a factor 1.2. In the bar detection task, bar contrast was made dependent upon performance in an analogous way as just described for the contour orientation discrimination task. Here, the contrast (log ($\Delta I/I$)) was adapted to performance by adding or subtracting a value of 0.1 to the current contrast.

When implementing the staircase in this way, one estimates the 73.5% correct point on the psychometric distribution (Wetherill and Levitt, 1965). The use of this moderate criterion enhances the possibility that it can be achieved even by severely lesioned animals.

Following the rules of a 73.5% correct staircase procedure (Wetherill and Levitt, 1965), the orientation difference was decreased after three consecutive correct responses or after two correct responses followed by an incorrect and a correct response. The orientation difference was increased after a single incorrect response, a correct response followed by an incorrect response, or after two correct responses followed by two incorrect responses. In the contour orientation discrimination tasks, the orientation difference was decreased or increased by respectively multiplying or dividing the orientation difference by a factor 1.2.

The method of constant stimuli. The staircase procedure is an adaptive procedure in which the magnitude of the orientation difference is continually adapted to performance. In the method of constant stimuli on the other hand, orientation differences are pre-defined and fixed during the test. The method of constant stimuli has been used only with the contour orientation discrimination task and not with the illusory contours.

To determine the constant stimuli thresholds, five orientation differences were selected for each reference orientation. In most cats, these orientation differences were placed slightly asymmetrically around the expected threshold. The orientation differences were selected in such a way that, given the expected threshold and a normal ogive distribution, they would lead to proportions of correct responses of 0.57, 0.70, 0.78, 0.87 and 0.93. In our experience, a strictly symmetrical distribution around the expected threshold leads to uncooperative animals, probably because of the presentation of too many orientation differences below threshold. Each orientation difference was presented to the animal during a 30-trial block of discrimination trials. Since five orientation differences were used to assess the JND in orientation for each reference, and since JNDs were measured daily at the two reference orientations, one testing session consisted of ten 30-trial blocks. From session to session, the order of the 10 orientation differences was interleaved following the rules of a Latin square, regardless of reference orientation. After Z-transformation of the proportions of correct responses, a 73.5% correct JND was calculated for each reference orientation.

Surgery

Anesthesia was induced by injection of ketamine (0.5 ml i.m.) followed by 1.0 ml atropine intramuscularly, after which the femoral vein was cannulated, and nembutal was given intravenously until respiration was stabilized at 12 – 16/min and no reflexes were evoked. Surgery was carried out using sterile technique throughout. Cortex was removed by subpial aspiration. Antibiotic was administered intramuscularly.

The animals were awake the next day, and in most cases were eating and could be returned to their home cages. Neurological examinations were given at weekly intervals until behavior was normal or un-

til deficits were stabilized before discrimination testing was resumed (2 – 3 weeks). The neurological tasks have been described in detail elsewhere (Sprague et al., 1977). The tests include visual fixation and following, localization and reaching for stationary and moving targets, jumping across gaps, eye movements with head held, pupillary response to light, blink to threat, visual placing and a food perimetry test described by Sprague and Meikle (1965), Sherman (1973) and Wallace et al. (1989).

Physiology and anatomy

After discriminative training and testing was completed, the animals were prepared for single unit recording using standard techniques (Orban et al., 1981a,b). Penetrations were made into the cortex surrounding the lesions and visual responsiveness of the units was assessed, as well as the receptive field location of the visually driven units. In order to evaluate single cells' contribution to orientation discrimination one needs to determine three characteristics: orientation bandwidth, response level and variability (Vogels and Orban, 1990). Penetrations in which cells were recorded were marked with small, electrolytic lesions for histological identification.

At the end of the physiological recording sessions, the animals were sacrificed under deep nembutal anesthesia by intracardiac perfusion of physiological saline, followed by 10% formol-saline. Embedding was in parlodion; sections were cut at 40 μ and alternately stained with cresyl violet for cell bodies and Mahon for fibers. The lesions of the cortical areas were reconstructed by using the anatomical criteria of Otsuka and Hassler (1961) and Sanides and Hoffmann (1969). The extent of the lesions in terms of visual fields was extrapolated from the data of Tusa et al. (1978, 1979, 1981) and then matched to the retinotopic positions of the RFs actually recorded in the physiological study. The physiological study was also important to assess whether the cortical tissue which appeared anatomically spared was actually functional. There was often a fringe of abnormal tissue within 1 – 2 mm of the lesion in which cells were spiking but could not be visually driven. Since the physiological assessment was done many months after the lesion it provides data about tissue which was stabilized and was no longer in a recovery period. The retinotopic limits of degeneration in the different laminae of LGN were approximated by using the physiological maps of Sanderson (1971).

Results

The visual primitives are likely to be encoded at an early stage of cortical processing in order to segregate their surface properties from background, and to locate them in the retinotopic map of cortical representation of visual space. Because of the prevalence of units with orientation selectivity in areas 17 and 18, located in the finest grain of the retinotopic maps (see Orban, 1984; Tusa et al., 1978, 1979, 1981) a logical first lesion was to remove these two areas (Tier I lesion). Areas 17 and 18 are activated in parallel by afferent fibers from the lateral geniculate nucleus and laminae A and A_1 project exclusively to them.

We will first deal with the effects of cortical lesions on the discrimination of bar stimuli, followed by an account of lesion effects on illusory contour discrimination. In the description of our results, we have divided the postoperative observation period into two parts. Short-term postoperative measurements correspond to measurements obtained in the first four months after the surgery (i.e., a maximum of 80 testing sessions). Measurements obtained in a later stage will be referred to as long-term measurements.

Tier I lesions (bar stimuli)

This part of the study has been published previously and described in detail and will only be summarized in this paper (see Orban et al., 1990, Vandenbussche et al., 1991). The Tier I lesions were of three types: (a) large lesions involving most of areas 17 and 18 ($n = 4$); (b) lesions in area 17 and only restricted extension into 18 across the vertical

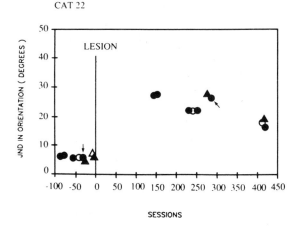

CAT 22

Fig. 4. JNDs in orientation determined at the horizontal reference measured as a function of session number before and after removal of areas 17 and 18 in cat 22. Each data point is the average of ten constant stimuli JNDs of 150 trials. Postoperatively, there was no retention of discrimination and the time before the first threshold measurements (0 – 150) was required for retraining. The thresholds were consistently elevated compared to normal performance. This animal was taken off testing for 150 days (some 107 testing sessions), and when retested on wide bars and low contrast or narrow bars and high contrast with both reference orientation interleaved in each daily session, JNDs were improved. Open symbols, narrow bars (0.2°); solid symbols, wide bars (0.6° or 1.2°); triangles, low contrast (0.33); circles, high contrast (1.25 or 2.25) (modified from Vandenbussche et al., 1991). Arrows indicate the time at which the data were taken, shown in Fig. 10.

meridian ($n = 2$); and (c) lesions limited to areas 18 and 19 ($n = 3$).

To illustrate the effects of these lesions, we will briefly describe the pre- and postoperative performance of one of the cats of our previous study with an almost complete destruction of areas 17 and 18 (cat 22) and cat 55 with a large 17 lesion which extends over the vertical meridian into area 18 from 2° to 5°.

Orientation discrimination for standard bar parameters after complete Tier I lesions. Fig. 4 (method of constant stimuli) shows the effect of the ablation of areas 17 and 18 on bar orientation discrimination measured at the horizontal reference

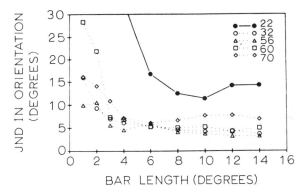

Fig. 5. JNDs in orientation as a function of bar length in cat 22 (filled symbols) compared to JNDs in four normal control cats (cats 32, 56, 60 and 70, open symbols). The staircase JNDs were averaged over the horizontal and right oblique reference orientations. The average JND of cat 22 at the 4.0° length was 32.77. Each data point corresponds to eight 75-trial staircase JNDs (two sessions).

orientation in cat 22. Performance was measured using a 0.2° wide, 12.0° long, high contrast bar (but see figure legend for additional information). The JNDs corresponding to negative session numbers were obtained before the lesion, and JNDs associated with positive numbers were determined postoperatively. Each point in the graph corresponds to the average of ten 150-trial constant stimuli JNDs. Preoperative JNDs in cat 22 were in the normal range (5.65°). After the Tier I lesion which included most of areas 17 and 18, bar orientation discrimination was severely affected. During the short-term postoperative period, performance was random at an orientation difference as large as 35°. Hence, the animal showed a complete retention deficit. Extensive retraining allowed the measurement of JNDs in orientation. In cat 22 the first threshold assessments started 150 sessions after the surgery. The effect of the lesion using the right oblique reference (not shown) was as large as at the horizontal reference.

Two years after the lesion, we assessed residual orientation discrimination abilities in cat 22. Fig. 5 shows the effect of *bar length* on orientation discrimination. Staircase JNDs were measured at the horizontal and right oblique reference orienta-

tion, using standard bar contrast and bar width. In the same figure, we plotted the JNDs of four normal control animals (cats 32, 56, 60 and 70), which show that the results of cat 22 fall completely out of the range of normal performance. The deficit in cat 22 is two-fold. On the one hand, JNDs in orientation determined with long lines were significantly elevated compared to JNDs in normal control animals. For example, at the standard length of 12.0°, the JNDs in normal cats ranged between 3.28° and 7.72° (average 4.84°) whereas in cat 22 the average JND was 14.13° (averaged over reference orientations). Hence, a very significant deficit remained (188%) even 2 years after the lesion. Furthermore, JNDs started increasing at lengths smaller than 8.0°, and this cat was not capable of discriminating bar orientation at lengths of 3.0° or shorter. This contrasts with the four control animals, in which JNDs on average increased only at lengths less than 3.0°.

We also assessed the effect of *contrast* upon bar orientation discrimination in cat 22 after the stabilization of postoperative thresholds (Fig. 6). The JNDs were obtained at the horizontal and right oblique reference orientations, and measured with the staircase procedure. The results strongly resemble

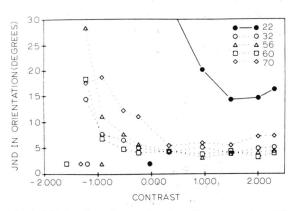

Fig. 6. JNDs in orientation as a function of bar contrast in cat 22 (filled symbols). Open symbols correspond to the JNDs in four normal cats. JNDs are averaged over reference orientations. Each data point corresponds to eight staircase JNDs of 75 trials measured during two testing sessions. Symbols just above the abscissa indicate bar contrast detection thresholds.

those presented in Fig. 5, in which the data of cat 22 fall far outside the range of normal performance. Again the deficit includes two aspects. On the one hand, JNDs in cat 22 increased for contrasts smaller than 1.49, whereas in the normal animal in which JNDs were most influenced (cat 70), JNDs remained unaffected for contrast reductions to 0.33. On the other hand, JNDs in cat 22 remained significantly elevated compared with normal performance even at the highest contrasts. For example, in the 1.49 standard contrast, the JNDs in orientation in normals ranged between 3.83° and 5.47° (average 4.39°), but in cat 22 the JND was as large as 14.25° (averaged over reference orientations).

Finally, attention must be drawn to the isolated symbols just above the abscissa in Fig. 6, which indicate the magnitude of the *contrast detection thresholds* determined in normal and lesioned cats. The deficit in cat 22 is illustrated by the rightward shift of its detection threshold relative to that of the normal controls. Detection thresholds in normal animals ranged between −1.57 and −0.93 (average −1.26), whereas the detection threshold in cat 22 was increased to a value of −0.03. Taking into account the relatively large standard deviation in the detection thresholds in individual cats (in the order of 0.19), the detection thresholds closely matched the contrasts at which orientation discrimination became difficult, but not impossible. Thus, it seems that the contrast allowing detection of the line also allows coarse orientation discrimination, not only for the normal cats, but also for the lesioned animal.

The effect of incomplete Tier I lesions. In the present section, we will present the case of an incomplete Tier I lesion which was largely restricted to area 17 (cat 55), but extended across the vertical meridian for 2 − 5°. The preoperative JND in orientation of cat 55, measured with the standard bar at the horizontal reference orientation, was 5.0°. This threshold was calculated on five 150-trial constant stimuli thresholds. After the lesion, there was a slight but significant increase of the JNDs during short-term testing at standard bar parameters (first two solid triangles in Fig. 7). The average of five

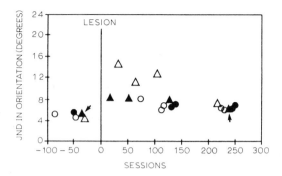

Fig. 7. The JNDs in orientation for the horizontal reference orientation measured as a function of session number before and after the ablation of area 17 for cat 55. For the open symbols, bar width was 0.2° and 0.6° or 1.2° for solid symbols. Contrast was 0.33 for the triangles and 1.25 or 2.25 for the circles. Other conventions as in Fig. 4 (modified from Vandenbussche et al., 1991). Arrows indicate the time at which the data were taken, shown in Fig. 10.

JNDs obtained during postoperative sessions 63 − 68 reached a value of 7.90°, corresponding to a 58% lesion deficit. Preoperative JNDs ranged between 3.95° and 6.14°, whereas postoperative JNDs fell in a 7.07 − 8.36° range. Notice the much larger initial deficit at the 0.33 contrast (open triangles) compared to the initial deficit observed at the standard 1.49 contrast. JNDs in orientation measured at the right oblique reference orientation are not shown in Fig. 7.

The short-term lesion effect observed in cat 55 was much smaller than the one observed in cat 22. In spite of the small deficit in cat 55, recovery during long-term constant stimuli testing was slow. Interestingly, at the time that orientation discrimination at the standard condition was fully recovered, recovery was also complete at lower contrasts.

Half a year after complete recovery, we assessed the effects of length and contrast on bar orientation discrimination, to make a final comparison with normal performance. Fig. 8 compares the effect of length in cat 55 with the effect obtained in the four normal control animals (cats 32, 56, 60 and 70). The figure shows average staircase JNDs obtained at the horizontal and right oblique reference orientations.

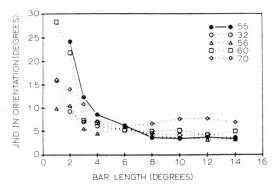

Fig. 8. JNDs in orientation as a function of bar length of cat 55 (filled symbols). Open symbols represent JNDs in four normal control cats (cats 32, 56, 60 and 70). The staircase JNDs were averaged over the horizontal and right oblique reference orientations. Each data point corresponds to eight 75-trial staircase JNDs (two sessions).

Performance of the lesioned animal fell largely within the normal range. When comparing the effect of contrast (Fig. 9) on orientation discrimination in the lesioned cat with normal controls, one reaches a similar conclusion: performance of cat 55 fell within the normal range.

Finally, the symbols just above the abscissa of Fig. 9 give the magnitude of the contrast detection threshold of cat 55 compared to those in normal cats. The contrast detection threshold of cat 55 (-0.25) lies outside the normal range of detection thresholds. This deficit is at odds with the normal effect of contrast on orientation discrimination. At a -0.92 contrast, a JND in orientation of 15.30° was observed, which falls within the limits of normal performance ($6.79-18.64°$). The -0.92 contrast at which orientation discrimination was measured is significantly lower than the -0.25 bar detection contrast, in light of the reliability of the detection threshold in cat 55 (standard deviation 0.12, $n = 8$). We have no good explanation for this finding.

Our data also show that the bar contrast detection threshold of cat 55 (-0.34) is quite close to the detection threshold obtained in cat 22 (-0.03), which had received a much larger lesion compared to cat 55. This leads to the surprising conclusion that

area 17 might be more important for the detection of a bar than for the discrimination of its orientation. It is worth mentioning that the detection thresholds of cats 22 and 55 are significantly elevated ($F(1,4) = 28.59$, $P < 0.0007$) compared to the detection thresholds in a group of four normal controls (cats 32, 56, 60 and 70). These controls had average detection thresholds of -1.26.

The differences in postoperative performance between cat 22 with a large 17 and 18 lesion and cat 55 with limited involvement of area 18 are well shown in the psychometric curves (Fig. 10). These data indicate a rather limited effect of incomplete Tier I lesions upon bar orientation discrimination. The small effect of the area 17 lesion in cat 55 contrasts strongly with the dramatic effect of a complete Tier I (17 + 18) lesion in cat 22. Other animals with lesions involving areas 18 and 19 also show very limited effect on bar orientation discrimination (Vandenbussche et al., 1991). For the 1.49 bar contrast, no short-term deficits were observed, and only at lower contrasts there was some evidence for a deficit. Thus, considerable sparing of either area 17 or area 18 results in limited deficits in bar orientation discrimination.

Conclusions. Lesions involving area 17 and large parts of area 18 produced a marked deficit in orien-

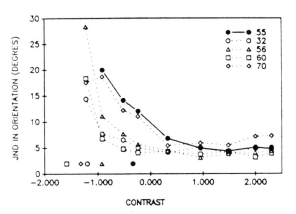

Fig. 9. JNDs in orientation as a function of bar contrast in cat 55 (filled symbols), compared to the JNDs in four normal control cats (open symbols). JNDs are averaged over reference orientations. Each data point corresponds to eight staircase JNDs of 75 trials measured during two testing sessions.

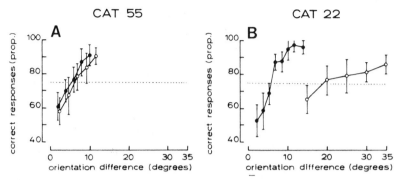

Fig. 10. Psychometric curves for the horizontal reference orientation measured pre- (solid symbols) and postoperatively (open symbols) for cats 55 (*A*) and 22 (*B*). Each data point is based on 300 trials. JNDs were measured at optimal bar width (1.2°) and contrast (2.25) for cat 22, and at 0.2° width and contrast 2.25 for cat 55. Horizontal dotted line indicates the 75% correct line used to define the JNDs. Data for these curves were taken at the points indicated by arrows in Figs. 4 and 7.

tation discrimination which included a loss in retention, and after retraining a substantial increase in thresholds for up to 3 years when tested with long bars. There was no recovery of discrimination with short bars. Lesions which involved area 17 plus small parts of 18 near the vertical meridian, or lesions limited to areas 18 and 19, produced no retention deficit and resulted in an increase in thresholds only at low contrast and narrow width of the oriented bars.

These results indicate that the visual primitive of line orientation is not only encoded by early processing in cortical areas 17 and 18, but that threshold discrimination between differently oriented, luminance-defined bars is also dependent on these areas. However, discrimination at elevated thresholds remain after removal of 17 and 18, and this finding raises the question of essential participation of other cortical areas.

This study has clearly demonstrated that removal of area 19, with adjoining parts of 18, did not result in a deficit in the discrimination other than an increase in thresholds at low contrast and narrow width of the oriented bars. Hence the next step was to remove all of the cortical areas to which areas 17 and 18 project (see Rosenquist, 1985, for summary). The intent of this part of the study was to remove as completely as possible areas 19, 20a, 21a, 21b, PMLS, AMLS, a lesion which also includes area 7 for technical reasons, and to leave areas 17 and 18

intact with a minimal amount of undercutting. This lesion we called a Tier II lesion.

Tier II lesions (bar stimuli)

Orientation discrimination for standard bar parameters. Results were obtained from four cats (12, 33, 66 and 69). For reasons of brevity, we will present only detailed results of cats 12 and 33. In some instances, statistical comparisons were carried out with a group of four normal controls (cats 32, 56, 60 and 70). In these cases, the F-tests refer to a comparison between all four experimental animals and the four controls. Preliminary results were published in Vandenbussche et al. (1989). Fig. 11 shows the limited, short-term effects of Tier II lesions on bar orientation discrimination at standard bar parameters in two cats (12, 33). JNDs are shown separately for the horizontal (H) and right oblique (RO) reference orientations before (negative numbers) and after lesions. Each point in the graph corresponds to the average of two 75-trial staircase JNDs.

JNDs before the operation of the four cats ranged between 4.53° and 5.97° when averaged over the 20 JNDs obtained during the last five sessions of the preoperative baseline. After surgical intervention, the animals were allowed a 10-session resting period, after which testing was resumed. In two cats (cats 12 and 69), JNDs returned to the preoperative

CAT 12 JOKE

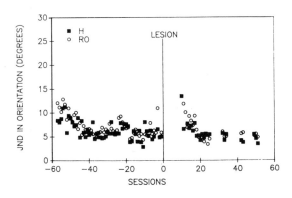

CAT 33 JUPITER

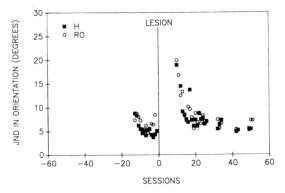

Fig. 11. JNDs in orientation plotted as a function of session number before the Tier II lesion (negative session numbers) and after that lesion (positive sessions numbers). Data are shown separately for cats 12 and 33 (upper and lower panel, respectively) for the horizontal (H) and right oblique (RO) reference orientations. In each graph, a single point corresponds to the average of two 75-trial staircase measurements.

level after as little as 10 sessions. In cats 33 and 66, the recovery was somewhat slower, and in the last animal a slight deficit remained after 60 sessions of postoperative testing (results not shown). A final assessment of the deficit was made by comparing the average JND of the last five sessions of the preoperative baseline to the average JND of the last five sessions of the postoperative baseline. After 3 months of postoperative testing (50−60 testing sessions), there was no deficit in cats 12, 33 and 69, whereas a small but statistically significant deficit

of 38% remained in cat 66 ($F(1,27) = 27.95$, $P < 0.0005$).

Clearly, the effects of large Tier II lesions on bar orientation are very different from those of Tier I lesions. Large Tier II lesions hardly affect performance at all, whereas large Tier I lesions result in a considerable retention deficit, accompanied by incomplete recovery.

Orientation discrimination as a function of length and contrast. The effects of length and contrast upon orientation discrimination in 2 cats (12, 69) were assessed immediately after the end of the short-term, postoperative measurements. Fig. 12 shows the effect of the length manipulation upon bar orientation discrimination. JNDs in orientation were averaged over reference orientations. We have plotted the results of each cat separately, to allow a straight forward comparison of the range of normal performance with that obtained in the lesion group. In Fig. 12, the range of performance of the lesioned animals falls well within the range of normal performance ($F(1,6) = 0.68$).

JNDs in orientation were also determined as a function of contrast and compared with the results

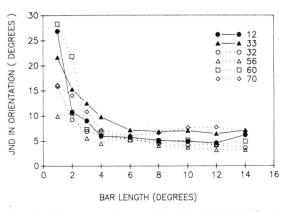

Fig. 12. JNDs in orientation as a function of bar length in two cats of Tier II-lesioned animals (cats 12, 33, solid symbols) as compared to JNDs in four normal control cats (cats 32, 56, 60 and 70, open symbols). The staircase JNDs were averaged over the horizontal and right oblique reference orientations. Each data point corresponds to eight 75-trial staircase JNDs (2 sessions).

of four normal cats (Fig. 13). JNDs in orientation were assessed with the 12.0° long and 0.2° wide bar at the horizontal and right oblique reference orientations, except for cat 69 which was tested only at the right oblique reference orientation. Average JNDs were calculated for each contrast condition, for each cat separately. This figure again shows that the effect of the Tier II lesion is very small. At most contrasts, JNDs obtained in the lesioned group largely overlap with the JNDs obtained in the control group. Statistical analysis revealed, however, that there was no significant difference in performance between the normal group ($n = 4$) and the lesion group ($n = 4$) ($F(1,6) = 2.96$). Just above the abscissa in Fig. 13, we have plotted the contrast detection thresholds of the four normal (N) control animals, together with the contrast detection thresholds of the two Tier II lesioned cats (12, 33). Just as there was no significant difference between contrast dependency of orientation discrimination between lesioned and control groups, there was also no significant difference between the detection thresholds of the two groups ($F(1,4) = 2.09$). Indeed, bar detection thresholds were -1.04 and -0.91 in cats 12 and 66 respectively, and these values fall well within the range of normal performance (bar detection thresholds in cats 33 and 69 were not assessed). Hence, in both normal and lesioned animals, detection contrast allowed coarse orientation discrimination.

Conclusions. This study has not revealed any significant deficit in discrimination beyond the early period of testing of luminance-defined, oriented bars after removal of the visual cortices to which areas 17 and 18 project. The extent of undercutting 17 and 18 which ranged from minimal in cat 66 to moderate in cats 33 and 69 was not related to postoperative performance and suggests this was not an important variable. A variable which may be important, however, is the fact that although the lesions of all four animals were large, in each case a small amount of cortex was spared (parts of PMLS, or 19, or 20a, or 21b and in all four cats most of AMLS). This factor may modify the conclusion that these cortices are not involved, in the same sense as the findings reported by Ungerleider and Mishkin (1982). They found that to achieve a disconnection between striate cortex and inferotemporal cortex in the monkey, total removal of the prestriate sector was necessary. Any remnant spared by the lesion was sufficient to leave function intact; all parts appeared to have a high degree of equipotentiality.

Illusory contours

Bravo et al. (1988) were the first to claim that cats perceive illusory contours. In the task they used, the cats were required to detect a Kanisza square, when it was available in a pattern of rotating inducing elements. The two cats which participated in this experiment only reached a performance level in the order of 70% correct, which is extremely low for a detection task. The difficulties of these cats to detect illusory contours raised questions related to the ability of the feline species to process the orientation of illusory contours. In the present section, evidence will be presented that cats actually discriminate the orientation of illusory contours quite well (De Weerd et al., 1990a; see also Berlucchi, 1988). As already mentioned in the Methods section, we will not elaborate whether this observation increases the

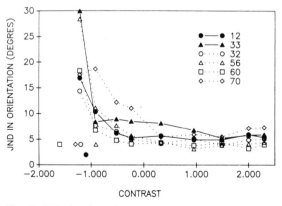

Fig. 13. JNDs in orientation as a function of bar contrast in two cats of Tier II-lesioned animals (cat 12, 33, solid symbols) compared to JNDs in four normal control cats (cats 32, 56, 60 and 70, open symbols). Conventions as in Fig. 12. Symbols above the abscissa indicate bar contrast detection thresholds of four normal cats and cat 12.

possibility that cats have a subjective percept of illusory contour generating patterns which is similar to the percept humans have (in our opinion, it does). For our present purposes, illusory contours are especially interesting because they cannot (PSIC), or only to a limited extent (GIC) be extracted by linear filtering (Vogels and Orban, 1987). Instead, the inducing endpoints have to be detected first, after which second order processes are necessary to construct the contour from the distribution of endpoints. The need for second order processing in illusory contour processing increases the possibility that Tier II areas are involved.

The study of the effects of Tier I and Tier II lesions upon orientation discrimination of illusory contours is still in progress. Five cats are included in this study. Cats 52 and 54 were subjected to a Tier II lesion; they are sacrificed but no histology is available yet. Cats 32, 56 and 60 underwent a Tier I lesion, and are still being tested. All cats were trained in orientation discrimination with the bar, GIC and PSIC. Preoperative results were very similar in all five animals. The average JNDs obtained for bar, GIC and PSIC were 4.78 (S.D. = 0.96), 9.90

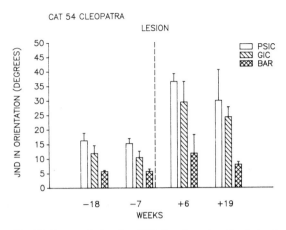

Fig. 15. Bar graph showing JNDs in orientation discrimination, in cat 54, of real bar, and two illusory contours (GIC, PSIC). Preoperative thresholds (negative numbers) and postoperative thresholds (positive numbers), showing early and late measurements. Postoperative values do not include results of session in which the cat performed randomly. Thus, the effect of the Tier II lesion on the PSIC is underestimated.

(S.D. = 1.15) and 17.18 (S.D. = 2.86), respectively (Fig. 14). These data confirm our earlier report (DeWeerd et al., 1990a), and show that cats discriminate the orientation of bars more easily than the orientation of GICs, and PSIC orientation discriminations in turn are more difficult than GIC orientation discriminations. Notice however, that a 17 – 18° difference in orientation corresponds to less than a 3 min change by the minute-pointer of an old-fashioned clock, which still corresponds to a relatively small orientation difference. With respect to the lesion results, we will restrict ourselves to data obtained during short-term postoperative testing with standard stimulus parameters. Since there were no noticeable differences between the results obtained at the horizontal and oblique reference orientations, we will make abstraction of the reference orientation.

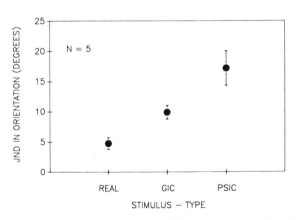

Fig. 14. Just noticeable differences (JNDs) in orientation plotted as a function of stimulus type in five normal cats for real bar, gap illusory contour (GIC), and phase shifted illusory contour (PSIC). GIC- and PSIC-JNDs are averages of the mean results obtained at both references with a GIC of five inducing circles and a PSIC of three inducing circles. Contrast of the inducing circles (log (ΔI/I)) was 1.49. Error bars represent standard deviations (from De Weerd et al., 1990c).

Tier I lesions. It has been our intention to make a smaller lesion in cat 60 (only including area 17 and a limited part of 18), and lesions as complete as possible in cats 32 and 56. Although there must be considerable variation in the size of the lesions (final conclusions must await the histology), the effect of this lesion on both GIC and PSIC orientation discriminations was very similar in all three animals. Indeed, the ability to discriminate the orientation of both the GIC and the PSIC was completely abolished during the complete short-term postoperative testing period. Even at orientation differences near 45°, the animals performed at chance level. On the other hand, there was considerable residual performance with elevated thresholds in the bar orientation discrimination task during postoperative short-term testing. The relatively small deficits in bar orientation suggest that the Tier I lesions are incomplete in all three cats used. If this is confirmed, this would indicate a clear dissociation after Tier I lesion between orientation discrimination with bars and illusory contours.

Tier II lesions. In the two animals with Tier II lesions (52, 54), we have attempted to remove all areas to which areas 17 and 18 project (Tier II lesion as defined in the Introduction). Fig. 15 shows the results in cat 54. Preoperative performance is shown during early and late periods. Similarly, the short-term postoperative testing period has been divided in two periods, to capture changes of thresholds over time. All discriminations made during the early period were affected by the lesion, the PSIC orientation discriminations being nearly abolished, JNDs in orientation obtained with the GIC being tripled, and those with the bar almost doubled. In the second part of short-term testing (Fig. 15), severe deficits remained for GIC and PSIC, whereas the deficit observed in bar orientation discrimination was small (though statistically significant). The second animal (cat 52, not illustrated) nicely replicated the results reported in cat 54. The present observations suggest that Tier II areas are far more important for illusory contour orientation discrimination than for bar orientation discrimination. Hence, our hypothesis that Tier II areas might be involved in more complex operations (i.e., if the contour is defined in a more complex way than just by a luminance difference) is supported.

Discussion

This study has utilized an experimental plan in which cats were trained to discriminate between differently oriented contours. There is general agreement between physiologists and psychophysicists that the encoding of contour orientation is one of the cornerstones of visual processing. We have presented the orientation primitive in two forms: as a bar and as an illusory contour. A bar is a simple stimulus defined by luminance contrast against a homogeneous background. The illusory contours were defined by surrounding line elements and are more complex stimuli. The stimuli were chosen as to approximate those used in neurophysiological studies of orientation processing. In view of the abundance of units in areas 17 and 18 which are selective for bar orientation (see Orban, 1984), and considering the absence of convincing evidence that single cells in these areas encode illusory contour orientation, we hypothesized that cortical visual analysis of luminance-defined contours might be restricted to areas 17 and 18, whereas the areas to which areas 17 and 18 project (Tier II areas) might intervene in the encoding of illusory contour orientation. Thus areas 17 and 18 would be of prime importance for the processing of bar and illusory contour orientations, whereas Tier II areas would contribute much more to illusory contour orientation processing than to the encoding of bar orientation. This is exactly what we found in our lesion experiments. In the remainder of the discussion, we will first consider the results obtained with the bar, and devote the final part to the processing of illusory contour orientation.

One of the main conclusions of our study is that the representation of bar orientation used for discrimination is distributed within and across both areas 17 and 18; more unexpected is that each area appears to contribute almost equally. When area 17 was removed with minimal invasion of 18, or when 18 and 19 were removed with minimal involvement of 17, there was in either case no retention deficit and JNDs in orientation were almost normal in the standard conditions. Only after contrast was reduced by a factor of 4 did an elevation of threshold appear and only for bars of narrow width, and this deficit also recovered in time.

Thus in the standard condition using long, narrow, high-contrast bars, lesions restricted to either of the components of the $17-18$ complex have a minimal effect. However, as soon as the lesions significantly involve both components, deficits appear and their severity is directly related to the amount of area 18 involved in the lesions in addition to area 17. In addition, the more of area 18 that is involved in the lesion the more the deficit spreads from narrower to include wider bars. The strength of the relationship between lesions and discriminatory behavior is further demonstrated by the fact that lesions restricted to one component of the $17-18$ complex have little effect in the standard conditions but induce a modest deficit either when contrast is reduced ten-fold or more, or when length is reduced below $4°$.

The minimal effects on orientation discrimination following removal of area 17 allows us to draw two further conclusions. Since area 17 is the only cortical area receiving input from the X-cell system (see Sherman, 1987), it would appear that afferent activity in the X-cell system is not necessary and that afferent activity in the Y-cell system is sufficient for fine orientation discrimination. Because of the near equal contribution of areas 17 and 18 to this function, and the independence of each area in sustaining threshold performance, it appears that the afferent substrate is organized in two parallel geniculo-cortical pathways carrying Y-fiber input from the lateral geniculate (chiefly laminae A, A1 and C). Furthermore, area 17 contains the population of cells which is most finely tuned to bar orientation (S-cells in the central $5°$ of the visual field; see Orban, 1984). Hence, tuning width cannot be the sole determining factor of the magnitude of JNDs in orientation. Tuning alone seems not to determine orientation thresholds. Instead, Vogels (1990) and Devos and Orban (1990) have proposed models in which orientation differences are signaled by the relative activity of overlapping orientation-selective units or filters (i.e., ratio between outputs of different units). These studies show that the number of units required to achieve a particular performance are determined by several properties such as maximal response amplitude, tuning width and response variability which determine encoding at the neuronal level (Vogels and Orban, 1990).

These results indicate that the visual primitive of line orientation is not only encoded by early processing in cortical areas 17 and 18, but that threshold discrimination between differently oriented, luminance-defined bars is also dependent on these areas. However, discrimination albeit at elevated thresholds remains after removal of $17-18$, and this finding raises the question of essential participation of other cortical areas. The first study has clearly demonstrated that removal of area 19, with significant, adjoining parts of 18, did not result in a deficit in the discrimination other than an increase in thresholds at low contrast and narrow width of the oriented bars. Our next step was to remove all of the cortical areas to which areas 17 and 18 project (see Rosenquist, 1985, for summary). The almost complete absence of any deficits observed after Tier II lesions in the bar orientation discrimination task is in sharp contrast with the pronounced deficits after complete Tier I lesions. This result not only suggests that Tier II areas are of limited importance in the processing of bar orientation, it also suggests that visual analysis in areas 17 and 18 is both necessary and sufficient to support bar orientation discrimination at threshold level. Furthermore, the absence of deficits after Tier II lesions shows that the effect of Tier I lesions is not merely the consequence of disconnecting Tier II from Tier I areas. However, these conclusions must be qualified. First, histological analysis of the Tier II lesions has shown that in almost all instances small islands of tissue remained intact (see Results section). Assuming that all Tier II areas are equipotential for orientation discrimination with a simple stimulus such as a bar, one island could be sufficient to leave the performance intact. The only final statement we can derive from our data is that none of the removed Tier II areas on its own is critical in bar orientation discrimination. We are currently making more complete Tier II lesions in animals trained in bar orientation discrimination to demonstrate that the "island-hypothesis" is not tenable. A second qualification is that other visual cortical areas (outside Tier II) may be required for the system to access the representation of orientation built-up in areas 17 and 18.

The effects of Tier I and Tier II lesions on bar orientation discrimination were quite different from those observed in illusory contour orientation discrimination tasks. In those animals which received a Tier I lesion, a limited effect was observed on bar orientation discrimination, which indicates that the Tier I lesions were incomplete. The devastating effect of these limited Tier I lesions on orientation discrimination of illusory contours thus becomes even more striking. Hence, areas 17 and 18 are clearly involved in the processing of illusory contours. We have hypothesized that units in Tier I areas might be involved in the encoding of the local endpoints which induced the illusory contours (see Peterhans and von der Heydt, 1989). Whether or not this is correct, our lesion results certainly suggest that, somehow, Tier I areas are allocated in a more extensive way when illusory contour patterns are filtered than when bar stimuli are encoded. In other words, the filtering of illusory contour patterns may be more demanding and depend upon more specific requirements than the filtering of bar stimuli.

In contrast to bar orientation discrimination, the discrimination of illusory contour orientation is almost abolished after Tier II lesions. Even when assuming that islands of intact tissue remain in the Tier II areas, it cannot be denied that Tier II areas are far more important in the processing of illusory contours than in the processing of bars. We have hypothesized that Tier II areas intervene in more complex aspects of illusory contour processing, i.e., the assembly of the contour on the basis of the distribution of endpoints encoded at the level of Tier II areas. Whether or not this detailed hypothesis is correct, the large deficit in illusory contour processing after Tier I lesions clearly shows that the input to Tier II areas must come from Tier I areas. This is in agreement with a serial model of information processing in the cat, in the same way as has been described in monkeys (see Desimone and Ungerleider, 1989, for review). A number of questions remain unanswered, however. One such question is whether the deficit in illusory contour processing is a disconnection effect, resulting from separating areas such as EVA or the insula, or areas in the lateral bank of the suprasylvian sulcus (see Rosenquist, 1985) from input coming from areas 17 and 18. Another question is whether there is not one critical Tier II area for illusory contour orientation processing. An additional question is how normal is the performance after the very pronounced long-term recovery in the Tier II-lesioned cats working with illusory contours. These and related issues are the subject of further studies.

Acknowledgements

The technical assistance of G. Vanparrijs, P. Kayenbergh, G. Meulemans, C. Huygens, W. Algeo, B. Tyrcha and K. Gallagher is kindly acknowledged. As is the assistance of B. Gulyas, L. Lagae, S. Raiguel and D. Xiao, in the electrophysiological experiments. This work was supported by grants from the Belgian National Research Council to G.A.O. and E.V. and from the Belgian Ministry of Science (GOA 84/88) to G.A.O. J.M.S. was supported in part by the University of Pennsylvania Research Foundation and by U.S. Public Health Service Grant EY02654. The authors are indebted to D. Matthews (Veterinary school, RUG) and E. Putseys for the veterinary care of the animals.

References

Berkley, M.A. (1970) Visual discriminations in the cat. In: W. Stebbins (Ed.), *Animal Psychophysics: the Design and Conduct of Sensory Experiments,* Appleton Century-Crofts, New York, pp. 231 – 247.

Berkley, M.A. and Sprague, J.M. (1979) Striate cortex and visual acuity functions in the cat. *J. Comp. Neurol.,* 187: 679 – 702.

Berkley, M.A. and Sprague, J.M. (1982) The role of the geniculocortical system in spatial vision. In: D.J. Ingle, R.J.W. Mansfield and M.A. Goodale (Eds.), *Advances in the*

Analysis of Visual Behavior, MIT Press, Cambridge, MA, pp. 525 – 547.

Berlucchi, G. (1988) New approaches to the analysis of the function of visual cortical areas in the cat with the lesion method. *E.B.B.S. Workshop: Visual Processing of Form and Motion, Tübingen.*

Berlucchi, G. and Sprague, J.M. (1981) The cerebral cortex in visual learning and memory, and in interhemispheric transfer in the cat. In: F.O. Schmitt, F.Q. Worden, Q. Adelman and S.G. Dean (Eds.), *The Organization of the Cerebral Cortex.* MIT Press, Cambridge, MA, pp. 415 – 440.

Bravo, M., Blake, R. and Morrison, S. (1988) Cats see subjective contours. *Vision Res.,* 28: 861 – 865.

Desimone, R. and Ungerleider, L.G. (1989) Neuronal mechanisms of visual processing in monkeys. In: F. Boller and J. Grafman (Eds.), *Handbook of Neuropsychology, Vol. 2,* Elsevier, New York, pp. 267 – 299.

Devos, M. and Orban, G.A. (1990) Modelling orientation discrimination at multiple reference orientations with a neural network. *Neural Comput.,* 2: 148 – 157.

De Weerd, P. (1991) Visual orientation processing in the cat: a behavior study. Thesis submitted for Ph.D. in Psychology, Katholieke Universiteit Leuven, pp. 1 – 231.

De Weerd, P., Vandenbussche, E., De Bruyn, B. and Orban, G.A. (1990a) Illusory contour orientation discrimination in the cat. *Behav. Brain Res.,* 39: 1 – 17.

De Weerd, P., Vandenbussche, E. and Orban, G.A. (1990b) Staircase procedure and contrast stimuli method in cat psychophysics. *Behav. Brain Res.,* 40: 201 – 204.

De Weerd, P., Vandenbussche, E. and Orban, G.A. (1990c) Bar orientation discrimination in the cat. *Visual Neurosci.,* 4: 257 – 268.

Doty, R.W. (1971) Survival of pattern vision after removal of striate cortex in the adult cat. *J. Comp. Neurol.,* 143: 341 – 370.

Hubel, D.H. and Wiesel, T.N. (1959) Receptive fields of single neurons in the cat's striate cortex. *J. Physiol. (Lond.),* 148: 574 – 591.

Marr, D. (1982) *Vision,* Freeman, New York.

Orban, G.A. (1984) Neuronal operations in the visual cortex. In: H.B. Barlow, T.H. Bullock, E. Florey, O.J. Grüsser and A. Peters (Eds.), *Studies of Brain Function, Vol. II,* Springer, Berlin, 367 pp.

Orban, G.A. (1991) Quantitative electrophysiology of visual cortical neurones. In: J. Cronly-Dillon (Ed.), *Vision and Visual Dysfunction, Vol. 4, The Neuronal Basis of Visual Function,* Macmillan, London, pp. 173 – 222.

Orban, G.A., Kennedy, H. and Maes, H. (1981a) Response to movement of neurons in areas 17 and 18 of the cat: velocity sensitivity. *J. Neurophysiol.,* 45: 1043 – 1058.

Orban, G.A., Kennedy, H. and Maes, H. (1981b) Response to movement of neurons in areas 17 and 18 of the cat: direction selectivity. *J. Neurophysiol.,* 45: 1059 – 1073.

Orban, G.A., Vandenbussche, E., Sprague, J.M. and De Weerd, P. (1990) Orientation discrimination in the cat: a distributed function. *Proc. Natl. Acad. Sci. U.S.A.,* 87: 1134 – 1138.

Otsuka, R. and Hassler, R. (1961) Uber Aufbau und Gliederung der corticalen Sehsphäre bei der Katze. *Arch. Psychiat. Z. Ges. Neurol.,* 203: 212 – 234.

Palmer, L.A., Jones, J.P. and Stepnoski, R.A. (1991) Striate receptive fields as linear filters: characterization in two dimensions of space. In: J. Cronly-Dillon and A.G. Leventhal, (Eds.), *Vision and Visual Dysfunction,* MacMillan, London.

Peterhans, E. and von der Heydt, R. (1989) Mechanisms of contour perception in monkey visual cortex. II. Contours bridging gaps. *J. Neurosci.,* 9: 1749 – 1763.

Redies, C., Crook, J.M. and Creutzfeldt, O.D. (1986) Neuronal responses to borders with and without luminance gradient in cat visual cortex and dorsal lateral geniculate nucleus. *Exp. Brain Res.,* 61: 469 – 481.

Rosenquist, A.C. (1985) Connections of visual cortical areas in the cat. In: A. Peters and E.G. Jones (Eds.), *Cerebral Cortex, Vol. 3,* Plenum, New York, pp. 81 – 117.

Sanderson, K.J. (1971) The projection of the visual field to the lateral geniculate and medial interlaminar nuclei in the cat. *J. Comp. Neurol.,* 143: 101 – 118.

Sanides, F. and Hoffmann, J. (1969) Cyto- and myeloarchitecture of the visual cortex of the cat and the surrounding integration cortices. *J. Hirnforsch.,* 11: 79 – 104.

Schumann, F. (1900) Beitrage sur Analyse der Gesichtswahrnehmungen. *Z. Psychol.,* 23: 1 – 32.

Sherman, S.M. (1973) Visual field defects in monocularly and binocularly deprived cats. *Brain Res.,* 49: 25 – 45.

Sherman, S.M. (1987) Functional organization of the W-, X- and Y-cell pathways in the cat: a review and hypothesis. In: J.M. Sprague and A.N. Epstein (Eds.), *Prog. Psychobiol. Physiol. Psychol., 11,* Academic Press, New York, pp. 234 – 314.

Sprague, J.M. and Meikle, T.H. (1965) The role of the superior colliculus in visually guided behavior. *Exp. Neurol.,* 11: 115 – 146.

Sprague, J.M., Levy, J., DiBerardino, A. and Berlucchi, G. (1977) Visual cortical areas mediating form discrimination in the cat. *J. Comp. Neurol.,* 172: 441 – 488.

Sprague, J.M., Berlucchi, G. and Antonini, A. (1985) Immediate postoperative retention of visual discriminations following selective cortical lesions in the cat. *Behav. Brain Res.,* 17: 145 – 162.

Treisman, A. and Gormican, S. (1988) Feature analysis in early vision: evidence from search asymmetries. *Psychol. Rev.,* 95: 15 – 48.

Tusa, R.J., Palmer, L.A. and Rosenquist, A.C. (1978) The retinotopic organization of area 17 (striate cortex) in the cat. *J. Comp. Neurol.,* 177: 213 – 236.

Tusa, R.J., Rosenquist, A.C. and Palmer, L.A. (1979) Retinotopic organization of areas 18 and 19 in the cat. *J. Comp. Neurol.,* 185: 657 – 678.

Tusa, R.J., Palmer, L.A. and Rosenquist, A.C. (1981) Multiple cortical visual areas. Visual field topography in the cat. In:

400

C.N. Woolsey (Ed.), *Cortical Sensory Organization, Vol. 2,* Humana Press, NJ, pp. 1 – 31.

Ungerleider, L.G. and Mishkin, M. (1982) Two cortical visual systems. In: D.J. Ingle, M.A. Goodale and R.J.W. Mansfield (Eds.), *Analysis of Visual Behavior,* MIT Press, Cambridge, MA, pp. 549 – 586.

Vandenbussche, E., Sprague, J.M., De Weerd, P. and Orban, G.A. (1989) Effect of higher cortical ablations on cat orientation discrimination. *Soc. Neurosci. Abstr.,* 15: 1255.

Vandenbussche, E., Sprague, J.M., De Weerd, M. and Orban, G.A. (1991) Orientation discrimination in the cat: its cortical locus. I. Areas 17 and 18. *J. Comp. Neurol.,* 305: 632 – 658.

Vogels, R. (1990) Population coding of stimulus orientation by striate cortical cells. *Biol. Cybern.,* 64: 25 – 31.

Vogels, R. and Orban, G.A. (1987) Illusory contour orientation discrimination. *Vision Res.,* 27: 453 – 467.

Vogels, R. and Orban, G.A. (1990) How well do response changes of striate neurons signal differences in orientation: a study in the discriminating monkey. *J. Neurosci.,* 10: 3543 – 3558.

Vogels, R., Orban, G.A., Eeckhout, H. and Spileers, W. (1988) Visual orientation discrimination in the primate. *Arch. Int. Physiol. Biochim.,* 96: P31.

Von der Heydt, R., Peterhans, E. and Baumgartner, G. (1984) Illusory contours and cortical neuron responses. *Science,* 224: 1260 – 1262.

Wallace, S.F., Rosenquist, A.C. and Sprague, J.M. (1989) Recovery from cortical blindness mediated by destruction of nontectotectal fibers in the commissure of the superior colliculus in the cat. *J. Comp. Neurol.,* 284: 429 – 450.

Wetherill, G.B. and Levitt, H. (1965) Sequential estimation of points on a psychometric function. *Brit. J. Math. Stat. Psychol.,* 18: 1 – 10.

T.P. Hicks, S. Molotchnikoff and T. Ono (Eds.)
Progress in Brain Research, Vol. 95
© 1993 Elsevier Science Publishers B.V. All rights reserved.

CHAPTER 33

Neuronal signals of importance to the performance of visual recognition memory tasks: evidence from recordings of single neurones in the medial thalamus of primates

F.L. Fahy, I.P. Riches and M.W. Brown

Department of Anatomy, University of Bristol, Bristol, BS8 1TD, U.K.

Introduction

Damage to the medial temporal lobes or medial diencephalon in humans results in amnesia (Scoville and Milner, 1957; Parkin, 1987; Squire, 1987; Weiskrantz, 1987; Mayes, 1988). The amnesia is particularly characterised by a loss of long-term memory for events in the subjects' lives. It has been termed "post-distractional amnesia" since a new event, including the sight of individual stimulus items, cannot consciously be recalled once the patient's attention has been distracted. The loss encompasses recognition as well as recall.

Within the medial diencephalon, such amnesia has been found to follow damage to the medial thalamus and/or mamillary bodies (Mair et al., 1979; Squire and Moore, 1979; Winocur et al., 1984; Parkin, 1987; Squire, 1987; Mayes, 1988; McEntee and Mair, 1990). Within the medial thalamus damage has been reported both to the mediodorsal (MD) and to midline (MID) nuclei of amnesic patients. Lesions of the medial thalamus in monkeys also result in difficulties in the performance of delayed nonmatching to sample, an analogue of one type of task used to test recognition memory in humans (Aggleton and Mishkin, 1983a,b; Zola-Morgan and Squire, 1985a).

Thus lesion data have shown the importance of

medial thalamus for the performance of recognition memory tasks by primates. However, the types of information relating to recognition memory that the neurones of the medial thalamus signal are unknown. The present experiments therefore investigated the activity of single neurones recorded within the medial thalamus of monkeys during their performance of recognition memory tasks with the objective of discovering what information relating to recognition memory neurones of the MD and MID nuclei might signal. A further objective was to compare the responses of such thalamic neurones with those found in the medial temporal lobes (Brown et al., 1987; Rolls et al., 1989; Riches et al., 1991a,b; Wilson and Rolls, 1991). A brief report of this work has already appeared (Fahy et al., 1991).

Materials and methods

Subjects and behavioral tasks

Two monkeys (*Macaca mulatta*) weighing 2.5 – 4.5 kg were trained to perform visual discrimination and serial recognition memory tasks before being prepared for the recording of the activity of single neurones. Both tasks required the monkey to make either a left or a right reach dependent on the stimulus that appeared on a video screen. Each trial of each of the behavioural tasks started with a cueing stimulus provided by the illumination for 0.5 sec of a dim red neon light situated centrally at the bottom of the screen. After an interval of 0.5 sec, a single stimulus was displayed on the video monitor for 2 sec. Only reaches to the correct side made between 0.1 sec and 5.0 sec after the offset of the stimulus were rewarded with fruit juice (approximately 0.5 ml). Other responses resulted in the lights being dimmed for a few seconds in the light-proof, sound-attenuating cubicle within which the animal was trained. Such trials were designated error trials and were analysed separately. Successive trials were separated by a variable interval of $1 - 3$ sec.

Each animal was successively trained on a series of visual discriminations in which one of a pair of stimuli required a left and the other a right reach to be correct. The animal was then taught the serial visual recognition memory task (based on Gaffan, 1974) in which the first and repeat presentations of infrequently seen stimuli occurred in a balanced, pseudo-random series with varying numbers of intervening trials between the first and the subsequent appearances of each stimulus. The monkey was rewarded for making left reaches for first and right reaches for subsequent presentations of the stimuli. Several pseudo-random series were employed so that the series as well as the stimuli within it changed from day to day. The stimuli were complex pictures selected from those recorded on commercially available videodisks. The stimuli used in any given series were preselected for salience by the experimenters from the many thousands available. After a picture had been used on one day it was not repeated for at least 2 weeks; some pictures had been seen very rarely if at all by the animal. A videodisk player (Sony, Lasermax LDP1500) was under the command of the computer (Acorn, BBC Model B) that controlled all the other features of the behavioural tasks. The picture synchronisation pulses of the various video signals were all locked (Masterlock) to the computer. Further, the stimuli on the colour videomonitor (Microvitec, Cub 653) were gated on and off by a videoswitch so that they were presented as complete frames starting at a known time.

During training and recording sessions the monkey was seated in a primate chair. The videomonitor was positioned 22 cm in front of the animal; the screen was 20 cm high and 27 cm wide. The animal's reaches were detected by a touch screen (Microvitec) placed in front of the monitor and modified to give an enhanced speed of detection of the response. Touches at any height to the left or right 8 cm of the screen were registered as behavioural responses. The animal's hand and eye movements were separately monitored by two cameras and eye movements were videorecorded together with the stimulus presentations using a videomixer (Videomat VM2E). Trials on which the monkey failed to fixate the stimuli or made errors were excluded from analysis. The monkeys were highly practised at both behavioural tasks before recordings began.

At times when the monkey was not performing either behavioural task, the videomonitor and touch screen were removed and three-dimensional objects or two-dimensional pictures were shown to the animal through the resultant hole and against a white background. This procedure was used when each new neurone was encountered as a means of screening both for visual responsiveness and for activity changes based upon stimulus repetition or familiarity. Some thousands of objects and pictures of widely varying colours, sizes and shapes were used in the experiments. A set of over 50 of these stimuli were shown to the animal frequently so that they were highly familiar to the animal. Other objects were seen infrequently, with at least 4 weeks elapsing before they were used again. Between presentations of the objects the animal was shown and then fed either pieces of fruit or fruit juice in a syringe. The order of presentation was pseudo-random so that the animal could not predict what would appear on any given trial. The animal's fixation was monitored, but no behavioural response was required. Control trials for this procedure were also conducted; on these trials objects were displayed in front of a colour camera (Sanyo, VCC3950) and appeared on the videomonitor in the same way as for the videodisk pictures.

Neuronal recording

Once a monkey was able to perform the behavioural tasks at > 90% correct, it was prepared under anaesthesia using aseptic techniques for the recording of single neurones by fixing a chamber made of titanium to the skull. A skin-compatible interface was furnished by surrounding the chamber with sheets of woven carbon-fibre fabric. After 2 weeks to allow recovery from the operation, recordings were made using moveable tungsten microelectrodes (Horn, 1969). Neuronal potentials were conventionally amplified, monitored, and displayed before being recorded on an FM tape recorder and a polygraph. Potentials from simultaneously recorded neurones were separated using a pulse-shape discriminator (Brown and Leendertz, 1979). The times of occurrence (to the nearest millisecond) of potentials of well-isolated single neurones were computer-processed (Acorn, BBC Model B) on- and off-line, and raster displays, peristimulus-time histograms and counts of action potentials generated.

Data analysis

The major objective of these experiments was to find neurones with activity possibly related to recognition memory. The criteria for determining neuronal responsiveness were chosen accordingly. A neurone was considered not visually responsive if no audible change in firing rate occurred in response to at least one of the first four objects shown to the monkey. To be considered visually responsive such changes in firing rate had either to occur for repeated presentations of at least one object or for the first presentations of at least four different objects. Similar criteria were used for neurones that were recorded in the serial recognition task. To determine whether the activity of visually responsive neurones was related to stimulus familiarity or recency of occurrence, counts of spikes were made for 1 sec after stimulus onset in the serial recognition

task and for 2 sec after stimulus onset when objects were shown. Spike counts to first and second (or subsequent) presentations of stimuli were compared by means of paired t-tests. Spike counts for familiar and unfamiliar stimuli were compared by two-sample t-tests. All tests were two-tailed and used a significance level of $P = 0.05$.

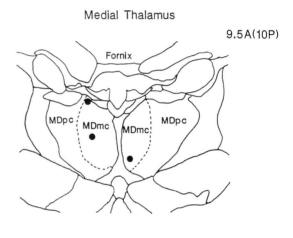

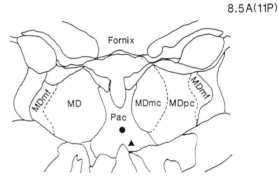

Fig. 1. The locations of neurones for which responses to first presentations of stimuli were significantly greater than those to subsequent presentations (dots). The triangle indicates a neurone that also so responded but, additionally, whose activity during the serial recognition task was significantly greater than during other tasks. The locations are plotted on the reconstructions of sections through the diencephalon at 9.5 mm and 8.5 mm anterior (A) to the interaural line (i.e., 10 mm and 11 mm posterior (P) to the outline of the sphenoid bone as seen on lateral radiographs of the skull (Aggleton and Passingham, 1981)). MDpc, Nucleus medialis dorsalis pars parvocellularis; MDmc, nucleus medialis dorsalis pars magnocellularis; MDmf, nucleus medialis dorsalis pars multiformis; Pac, nucleus paraventricularis caudalis.

Histological localisation

Note was made of the depth of each neurone at the time of recording. At the end of each electrode penetration anterior-posterior and lateral X-ray photographs were taken to show the position of the electrode in situ in relation to skull land marks and fixed, reference electrodes. Microlesions were also made at known positions near responsive cells during the recordings. From the above information the positions of the recorded neurones were plotted on to large scale tracings of magnified, cresyl violet-stained coronal sections of the brain; corrections were made for X-ray expansion and tissue shrinkage. The boundaries of the various nuclei were entered on tracings made every 1 mm through the thalamus (Olszewski, 1952).

Results

The activity of 322 neurones was recorded from MD, 168 from MID and 134 from elsewhere, in both right and left hemispheres of two monkeys. Both

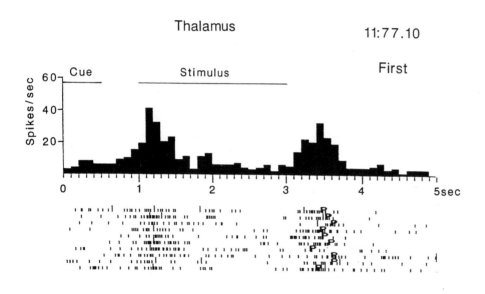

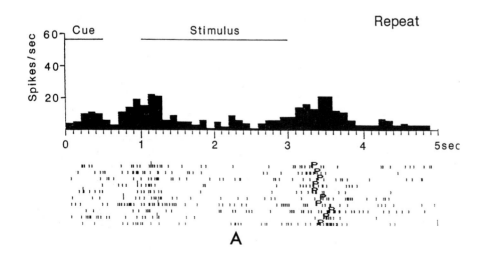

A

Thalamus   11:77.10

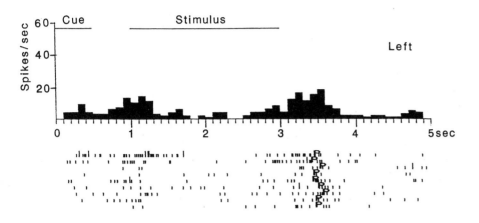

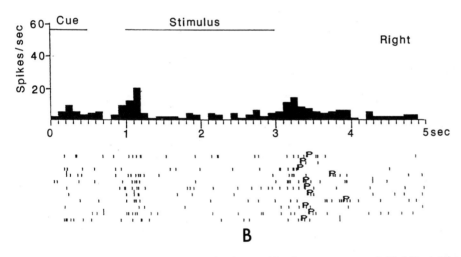

B

Fig. 2. Example of response decrement with stimulus repetition for a neurone recorded in MD. *A*. Histograms and rasters of the activity during the serial recognition task. Illustrated are responses to the *first* (upper histogram and rasters) and *repeat* (lower histogram and rasters) presentations of ten different unfamiliar stimuli. In the rasters each line is a single trial with dots representing the times of occurrence of action potentials. For each trial the time the monkey touched the screen is marked by a P. For first presentations the touch was to the left of the screen and for repeat presentations it was to the right. Note the significantly smaller responses on trials with the second (*repeat*) presentations of the stimuli, both when the stimuli were shown and when the animal made its behavioural responses. There is a slight increase in activity anticipating the onset of the stimulus for both first and repeat trials. *B*. Histograms and rasters of the activity of the same neurone during the visual discrimination task. Illustrated is activity for trials upon which were shown the stimulus requiring a touch to the left of the screen (upper histogram and rasters) and that requiring a touch to the right of the screen (lower histogram and rasters). These trials provide control data indicating that the direction of the behavioural response required of the monkey does not account for the difference in activity between *first* and *repeat* trials in *A*. The stimulus requiring a touch to the left of the screen had last been seen some days previously. Note the response on the first trial (first raster line below upper histogram) and the greatly reduced response on the trials with the second and subsequent appearances of the stimulus (remaining raster lines below upper histogram).

monkeys used both right and left paws and no obvious difference in neuronal responsiveness was noted between the right and left hemispheres. Results from the two sides have therefore been pooled (see Table I).

As described by others (e.g., Fuster and Alexander, 1973), 119/278 (43%) neurones recorded in MD fired in bursts (i.e., groups of 2–10 action potentials separated by intervals of less than 10 msec); 29/100 (29%) neurones recorded in MID showed similar activity. For certain neurones there were marked increases or decreases in activity related to gross changes in the animal's level of alertness.

General visual responsiveness

Overall, 14% (44/322) of MD and 13% (21/168) of MID neurones were visually responsive either to the sight of objects or to pictures presented in the serial recognition task. Of the 134 neurones not located in MD or MID, 25 (19%) were visually responsive. The majority of the visually responsive neurones responded to some but not all the visual stimuli presented. In this sense these neurones were selectively responsive. Both increases and decreases in firing rate were encountered. Also some neurones responded at the offset rather than the onset of stimulus presentations. A few neurones only responded to moving stimuli. No neurones with activity that was closely related to eye movements in the absence of stimulus presentation were encountered in the medial thalamus (although neurones located in the red nucleus and the oculomotor nucleus did show such activity).

Recognition-related activity

For five neurones responses were found to be maximal to the first presentations of unfamiliar stimuli that had not been seen recently, and significantly (paired t-tests, $P < 0.05$) less strong to subsequent presentations. The locations of the five neurones are shown in Fig. 1. An example is shown in Fig. 2. For this neurone the activity on trials with the first presentations of stimuli was significantly greater than that on trials with their second presen-

tations both when the stimulus was presented and at the time of the monkey's behavioural response (a touch on the left or the right of the monitor screen). The neurone's activity during the visual discrimination task indicated that these differences in response between first and repeat trials of the serial recognition task were not explicable as a simple consequence of the left or right touches made by the monkey (see Fig. 2B for further details). As for the other neurones demonstrating a significant response decrement with stimulus repetition, this neurone did not respond equally to all the stimuli presented. Accordingly, it signalled information concerning the physical characteristics of stimuli as well as about their possible prior occurrence.

The first and second presentations of the stimuli in the serial recognition task were separated by varying numbers of trials on which other stimuli were shown. Thus it was possible to ascertain whether the response to repeat presentations remained significantly smaller even after the distraction provided by these other trials. For the neurone illustrated in Fig. 2, the mean response to second presentations was still significantly smaller than that to first presentations even after ten intervening trials with other stimuli. Because this neurone did not respond to all the stimuli presented, it was not possible to establish statistically whether the response decrement persisted over an even greater number of intervening trials.

Three of the neurones with responses showing decrement on stimulus repetition were located in the magnocellular subdivision of MD. They formed 0.9% of the total recorded sample and 6.8% of the visually responsive neurones recorded in MD. For two of these neurones the stimuli evoked an increase in activity that was significantly greater for first than for repeat presentations; for the third neurone, stimuli evoked a *decrease* in activity that was significantly greater for first than for repeat presentations. In all three cases the response decrement persisted across intervening trials of other stimuli; the "memory spans" exceeded 20, 10 and 5 trials for the three individual neurones. Moreover, when the magnitude of the decrement was related to the number of intervening stimuli, none of the regression coefficients were significant, i.e., the memory spans were longer than could be established.

Responses to the sight of objects were also investigated for the neurone illustrated in Fig. 2; responses to first presentations were significantly (paired t-test, $P < 0.05$) greater than to second presentations (see Fig. 3). For this neurone the mean response to third presentations was significantly below that for first presentations and non-significantly below that to second presentations; the first and second presentations occurred before performance of the serial recognition and visual discrimination tasks, while the third presentations were given afterwards, more than 15 min after the second presentations. Thus the responses to objects for this neurone did not recover after a filled interval of over 15 min.

Two neurones exhibiting significant response decrement with stimulus repetition were found in the nucleus paraventricularis caudalis of MID. They formed 1.2% of the total and 9.5% of the visually responsive MID neurones that were recorded. As for the MD neurones, both of these MID neurones responded selectively to some and not to other

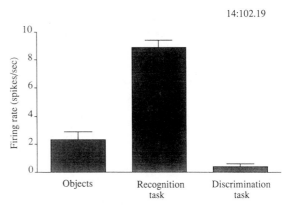

14:102.19

Fig. 4. Significant increase in mean ± S.E.M. on-going ("spontaneous") activity for a neurone recorded in nucleus paraventricularis caudalis during performance of the serial recognition task compared to that during performance of the visual discrimination task and that during the showing of objects. Objects were shown both before and after the performance of the other two tasks, the spontaneous activity level being significantly less than that during the recognition task on each occasion. During the recognition task the neurone demonstrated a significant decline in response when stimuli were repeated, even when there were intervening presentations of other stimuli. Indeed, the magnitude of the decrement was not correlated with the number of intervening presentations, i.e., the memory span of the neurone was too long (> 40) to be established here.

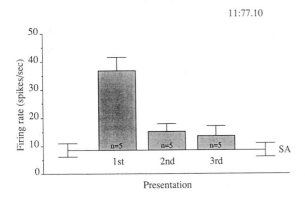

11:77.10

Fig. 3. Response decrement to repeated presentations of objects. Same MD neurone as Fig. 2. The mean (± S.E.M.) response to first presentations of unfamiliar objects was significantly greater than that to their second or third presentations. Note that the response did not recover even though performance of the serial recognition and visual discrimination tasks, i.e., a filled interval of over 15 min, intervened between the second and third presentations of the stimuli. SA, Mean ± S.E.M. spontaneous activity.

stimuli. One of the neurones was recorded during performance of the serial recognition and visual discrimination tasks as well as during the showing of objects. However, responses (increases in activity that were significantly greater for first than repeat presentations) were only found for stimuli presented during the serial recognition task. As may be seen in Fig. 4, not only the responses to stimuli but also the background activity of this neurone was very low except during the performance of the serial recognition task. Indeed, the background activity was significantly higher during the serial recognition task than during the visual discrimination task, or during the showing of objects before, or after performance of these tasks. For the second neurone data were only obtained for responses to the sight of objects (see Fig. 5). For this neurone responses were significantly greater to the first than to second presentations of unfamiliar stimuli that had not been seen for at least a few weeks. Additionally, the mean response to the first presentations of unfamiliar objects was significantly greater than that to the first presentations of highly familiar objects, even though the familiar objects had not been seen during the previous 5 min (two-sample *t*-test, $P < 0.05$). Thus this neurone signalled information concerning the prior occurrence of stimuli over at least 5 min and may also have signalled information concerning the relative familiarity of stimuli.

None of the 25 visually responsive neurones located outside MD and MID showed activity that could be related to visual recognition memory.

Eye movements

Fig. 6 illustrates the mean direction of the monkey's gaze during performance of the serial recognition memory task. There is no significant difference (anova) between first and repeat trials in either the mean direction or in the variance of gaze during the first 600 msec after stimulus onset. The activity on first trials of the neurone illustrated in Fig. 2, for example, starts to diverge from that on repeat trials at 250 msec.; there is a significant difference in mean neuronal activity before 400 msec, which is well before there is a significant difference in eye movements.

Discussion

The medial thalamus

Neurones have been found that responded maximally to the first presentations of unfamiliar stimuli that had not been seen recently and significantly less strongly when the stimuli were repeated. Such activity has not previously been reported in the medial thalamus. These neurones formed 7.7% of the visually responsive neurones encountered, a proportion not dissimilar to that found in other areas implicated in recognition memory (see Table I). Although such neurones formed but a small proportion of the visually responsive neurones, the response decrement was significant at $P < 0.005$ for four of them; the probability of such findings being due to chance

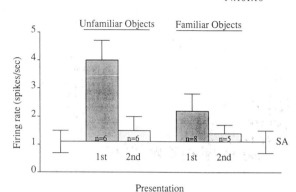

14:101.16

Fig. 5. Difference in response to unfamiliar and highly familiar objects for neurone recorded in nucleus paraventricularis caudalis. The mean ($\pm$ S.E.M.) response to first presentations of unfamiliar objects was significantly greater than that to first presentations of highly familiar objects. For both familiar and unfamiliar objects the response was significantly greater to first than to second presentations. SA, Mean $\pm$ S.E.M. spontaneous activity.

is less than 0.0005 (binomial test). In these experiments neurones with decremental responses were found in both the magnocellular division of MD and in MID (in the nucleus paraventricularis caudalis). One neurone that responded more strongly to first presentations of unfamiliar than of familiar objects was found in MID.

The presence in the medial thalamus of such neurones, whose responses signal information about the previous occurrence of stimuli, does not of itself establish either that these neurones or that that region is essential for recognition memory. Contrastingly, the fact that lesions of the medial thalamus impair performance of recognition memory tasks (Aggleton and Mishkin, 1983a,b; Zola-Morgan and Squire, 1985a) establishes the necessity of the integrity of the region for these tasks, but does not indicate that the region processes information related to recognition memory (see for example the results of removal of the heart); it is not possible to deduce from lesion experiments what individual neurones contribute. It is the combination of data from lesion and recording experiments that can begin to reveal the precise importance of the region to the operation of recognition memory.

TABLE 1

Neurones signalling information likely to be of importance to recognition memory

	Area	No. recorded	No. visual	No. declining	% Declining (of visual)	Memory span (maximum)
(a)	Medial thalamus					
	(i) Mediodorsal	322	44	3	1% (7%)	> 20
	(ii) Midline	168	21	2	1% (10%)	> 20
(b)	Lateral inferior	600	264	64	11% (24%)	≤ 2
(c)	temporal cortex	247	104	5	2% (6%)	≤ 10
(d)	Medial temporal cortex	2328	1250	150	6% (12%)	> 20
(e)	Amygdala	659	165	10	2% (6%)	≤ 10
(f)	Hippocampal formation	994	249	4	1% (5%)	≤ 8
(g)		328	151	0	0% (0%)	–
(h)	Basal forebrain					
	(i) Substantia innominata	1058	190	16	2% (8%)	> 16
	(ii) Diagonal band	489	102	14	3% (14%)	> 16
	(iii) Periventricular	572	171	5	1% (3%)	> 16

Listed are the number of neurones recorded, the number visually responsive (though the criteria are not constant from study to study) and the number of neurones with responses that decremented upon stimulus repetition ("declining") in absolute and percentage terms. The figures include three neurones in the periventricular region of the basal forebrain with incrementing rather than decrementing responses. In the last column is given the maximum "memory span" discovered. The "medial temporal cortex" includes perirhinal and entorhinal cortex plus areas TG and TE1 and TE2; "lateral inferior temporal cortex" includes all other parts of area TE. Studies quoted: (a) this report; (b) Baylis and Rolls (1987); (c) and (d) Riches et al. (1991a) and Fahy, Riches and Brown (in preparation); (e) Wilson and Rolls (1991); (f) Rolls et al. (1989); (g) Riches et al. (1991b); (h) Wilson and Rolls (1990).

The response decrements are not readily explicable as simple reflections: (i) of changes in the gross level of arousal or motivation, or (ii) of failures of the animal to look at the stimuli or of differences in eye movements, or (iii) of the left or right touches required as behavioural responses. The decrements were found during on-going performance of the serial recognition task in which every correct trial was rewarded; there was no difference in reward or effort required between trials in which stimuli were first presented and those in which they were repeated. Sometimes, towards the end of a recording session, a drop in the animal's general level of attentiveness was evidenced by an increase in the number of errors produced and in the latency of the behavioural responses. However, such changes could not explain the reported decrements in neuronal responses since first and repeat trials were interspersed throughout the whole series of trials and gross changes in arousal did not occur repeatedly from one trial to the next. Trials during which the monkey failed to look at the stimulus or made an error were excluded from analysis. Furthermore, the direction of mean gaze and variability of eye movements did not differ significantly between first and repeat trials until after changes were evident in the neuronal responses. In support of this result, F.A.W. Wilson and P.S. Goldman-Rakic (personal communication) found no difference in eye movements during the first second of presentation of stimuli between their first and repeat appearances, using the subscleral search-coil technique. Differences in neuronal activity were present during the serial recognition task but not during the visual discrimination task, so that the neuronal activity was not a direct reflection of the behavioural

410

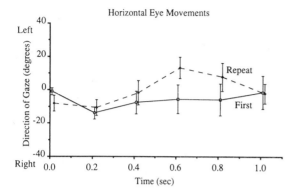

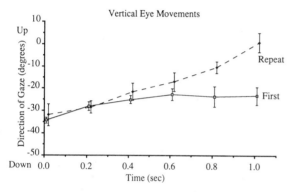

Fig. 6. Mean ± S.E.M. horizontal (upper panel) and vertical (lower panel) eye position for ten first and the corresponding ten repeat trials of the serial recognition task. Stimulus onset is at time zero. There are no significant differences in mean eye position or its variance between first and repeat trials in the 600 msec following stimulus onset.

response required on each trial. Additionally, no decremental responses were found for other visually responsive neurones (including those recorded outside MD and MID): such changes would have been expected if peripheral changes at the eye or gross changes in arousal were responsible for the decremental responses.

Decremental responses were found to the sight of objects as well as to the two-dimensional pictures used in the serial recognition task. Thus such decremental responses occur in the medial thalamus to more than one type of stimulus. Further, the animal had not been behaviourally trained to respond in any particular way to the objects. Accordingly, it is unlikely that such responses were induced by the animal's training and probable that such

decremental responses are endogenous to the region.

Two types of task-related activity found in the medial thalamus have not been described previously in similar studies of the medial temporal lobe and basal forebrain. Firstly, for one MD neurone there was significantly greater activity associated with the time of the animal's behavioural response on first than on repeat trials of the serial recognition task (in addition to such a change during presentation of the stimuli). Control trials indicated that this difference was not ascribable to the making of left or right touches per se. Such differential activity associated with the behavioural response suggests an involvement with information retrieval or performance-related aspects of the recognition task, i.e., the organisation or selection of behavioural output in contrast to the categorisation and processing of sensory input. Secondly, one of the MID neurones was almost inactive except during performance of the serial recognition task, when its activity increased markedly and responses to first presentations of stimuli were evident. Such generalised changes in activity suggest the neurone might have been part of a gating or enabling system, so possibly having a role in selective attentiveness.

Responses in other areas

Neurones with responses showing decrement on stimulus repetition have been described in the basal forebrain — substantia innominata, diagonal band of Broca, and a periventricular region just rostral to the thalamus — and in the medial temporal lobe — inferior temporal cortex, cortex around the rhinal sulcus, temporal polar cortex, the amygdala, and hippocampal formation (Rolls et al., 1982, 1989; Baylis and Rolls, 1987; Brown et al., 1987; Wilson and Rolls, 1990, 1991; Riches et al., 1991a,b). The incidence of such neurones in these areas is given in Table I. In most of the areas such neurones form about 1 – 5% of the total number recorded, and about 3 – 15% of the visually responsive neurones. The incidence found in one study (Baylis and Rolls, 1987) of lateral inferior temporal cortex was somewhat higher. Although such neurones were not found in the hippocampal formation by Riches et al. (1991b), they have been reported by Rolls et al. (1989).

Most neurones with decremental responses within the "medial temporal cortex" (i.e., the anterior and medial inferior and temporal polar cortex plus cortex around the rhinal sulcus) and medial thalamus are selectively responsive to visual stimuli, responding best to certain stimuli and not at all to others (Riches et al., 1991b). These neurones signal information about the physical characteristics of the stimuli as well as about whether stimuli have been seen before. Some neurones respond to such a small subset of the available stimuli that the significance of any response decrement cannot be established. Accordingly, the quoted figures may underestimate the incidence of decremental responses. For medial temporal cortex, Riches et al. (1991b) found a significant tendency to response decrement upon stimulus repetition for the whole population of recorded visually responsive neurones; statistically significant decrements in response were established for only 18% of these neurones. Such a tendency was not found for hippocampal neurones. Reports suggest that neurones recorded in the basal forebrain and amygdala are less selective, responding to most of the stimuli tested (Wilson and Rolls, 1990, 1991). However, differences in selectivity of the neurones of the various regions remain to be measured quantitatively. A lack of stimulus selectivity, as possibly shown by neurones of the basal forebrain, would suggest a less stimulus-bound, more global function (perhaps arousal, orienting or attentiveness) for such neurones in recognition memory (Wilson and Rolls, 1990).

Attempts have been made to determine the "memory spans" of the neurones with decrementing responses, i.e., the number of trials using other stimuli that may intervene before the response to second presentations is no longer significantly less than that to first presentations. For lateral inferior temporal cortex memory spans are typically brief. Baylis and Rolls (1987) described no neurones with a span greater than two intervening stimuli (i.e., a filled interval that is short compared to 1 min),

although F.L. Fahy, I.P. Riches and M.W. Brown (unpublished observations) have found memory spans of up to ten intervening stimuli in this region. Spans of amygdalar and hippocampal neurones also appear limited: 2 – 10 intervening stimuli (Rolls et al., 1989; Wilson and Rolls, 1991). However, in other areas (basal forebrain, medial thalamus, and medial temporal cortex) the responses of certain neurones had still not recovered even after the greatest number of intervening items tested (see Table I). The available evidence suggests that in these latter areas the maximum memory spans may considerably exceed this lower limit. For example, responses to the sight of objects did not recover for one MD neurone even after a filled interval of over 15 min. Riches et al. (1991a) have found responses evidencing memory for the previous occurrence of stimuli that had not been seen for periods of more than 24 h in medial temporal cortex. For certain neurones recorded in the basal forebrain, responses showed no sign of recovery up to the maximum number (16) of intervening stimuli tested (Wilson and Rolls, 1990).

The latencies at which responses to first presentations diverge from those to subsequent presentations have only been published for the amygdala and basal forebrain areas (Wilson and Rolls, 1990, 1991). In each instance these differential latencies range upwards from 140 msec, with means (averaging across neurones with decremental responses) of 204 – 212 msec for the different areas. These figures do not give a clear indication of whether the activity in one region occurs earlier than or, alternatively, is but a passive reflection of that in one of the other areas. Areas in which neurones with these decrementing responses have been found (medial temporal lobe, medial thalamus and basal forebrain) are all closely anatomically interconnected (Van Hoesen and Pandya, 1975; Aggleton et al., 1980, 1986; Russchen et al., 1985, 1987; Rosene and Van Hoesen, 1987; Yeterian and Pandya, 1988; Gower, 1989; Wilson and Rolls, 1990), though it remains to be established that neurones with decremental responses in the different regions have direct anatomical links to each other.

Although broadly similar response decrements upon stimulus repetition have been found across the various areas studied, certain other types of task-related activity have been recorded in only some of these areas. Background activity changes and activity differences dependent upon stimulus repetition but occurring at the time of the animal's behavioural response in the medial thalamus have already received mention. Within the hippocampal formation there are neurones that signal whether a stimulus has been seen before in a particular position (Rolls et al., 1989). Such responses could be interpreted as encoding the context of stimulus occurrence (Brown, 1982, 1990). Decrements in *reductions,* rather than increases, in activity have been found in medial temporal cortex and the periventricular region of the basal forebrain as well as in MD. Within the periventricular region of the basal forebrain three neurones that respond significantly more strongly to repeat than to first presentations have been described. The reason that increments rather than decrements in responses appear to be uncommon may be because most of the stimuli that an individual encounters in a normal environment will be seen repeatedly. Accordingly, less neuronal activity will be generated (with a consequent increase in economy) if responses decrement rather than increment when stimuli are seen again.

In addition to encoding the recency of presentation of stimuli, certain neurones are sensitive to the relative familiarity of stimuli; they respond significantly more strongly to unfamiliar than to highly familiar stimuli (Riches et al., 1991a,b). One such neurone was found in MID in these experiments. Most such neurones in the medial temporal cortex, like that found in MID, signal a mixture of recency and familiarity information (Riches et al., 1991a,b). However, the medial temporal cortex contains neurones that signal information concerning recency but not familiarity, and neurones that signal familiarity but not recency information (Riches et al., 1991a). From the activity of the ensemble of neurones signalling recency and/or familiarity information there is sufficient variability from one neurone to the next to compute the past history of encounters with stimuli, determining both when a given stimulus was last seen and whether it is familiar or not.

Functional considerations

There are a number of uses that might be made of the information encoded in the decremental responses described: behavioural habituation or attentive mechanisms, short-term memory or long-term memory, priming memory, or recognition memory (judgement of the recency of occurrence and familiarity of stimulus items). Moreover, these functions are not necessarily mutually exclusive.

Decremental responses upon stimulus repetition linked to behavioural habituation have been described in many systems from whole vertebrates (the orienting response) through sensory pathways to reduced invertebrate preparations (Thompson and Spencer, 1966; Kandel and Spencer, 1968; Kandel, 1981). The neuronal responses described above could indeed play a role in the reduction of the behavioural reaction to repeated stimuli. However, if so, the particular characteristics of these responses argue for a specific role in such a process. Firstly, the decline in response of these neurones is very rapid: the response decrement from the first to only the second presentation is often more than 50% of the full response. Secondly, the stimulus repetition need not be monotonous: the decrement may occur even when many presentations of other stimuli have intervened between the first and second occurrence of a stimulus. Thirdly, the decrement occurs to stimuli that the animal is using to obtain reward, i.e., at a time when behavioural habituation to these stimuli would be maladaptive whereas judging whether the stimuli have occurred before is essential to task performance. In addition, it has yet to be established that the mechanism responsible for the response decrement in these neurones is the same as the self-generated synaptic depression that produces habituation in simple systems (Kandel, 1981). Nevertheless, the response change must arise centrally rather than at the periphery because changes in eye movements do not provide a general explanation for it and, moreover, the change is seen in some but not all visually responsive neurones. The occurrence of similar decremental responses at early stages of the visual pathway cannot be excluded since these regions have not been explored using the same experimental techniques. Thus it remains possible that the observed decremental responses could be transmitted from earlier stages in the processing of visual input. However, the memory spans found for certain neurones in the medial temporal cortex are longer than those described for neurones in the lateral inferior temporal cortex (Baylis and Rolls, 1987; Riches et al., 1991a,b). Accordingly, the responses of the more anteriorly and medially located neurones seem unlikely to be mere passive reflections of activity in lateral inferior temporal cortex.

Similar arguments to those of the previous paragraph may be applied concerning any putative relationship between the responses of these neurones and attentive mechanisms. Because all correct trials were equally rewarded, there is no reason to expect, and no behavioural evidence to suggest, that the monkey's attention fluctuated greatly from trial to trial. Any trials for which the animal failed to look at the stimuli were excluded from analysis. If the response decrements are passive reflections of more subtle, but generalised attentive changes, why do all visually responsive neurones not so react? The decrements occur in responses to individual stimuli, and the animal could not pre-set its attention before each stimulus appeared because it was not possible to predict whether the next presentation would or would not be of a stimulus that had been seen recently. Further, when a particular stimulus was repeated it may not have been seen for many trials previously and therefore could not be regarded as being within the animal's attention span. There are changes in neuronal activity earlier than changes in eye movements, so that if there are changes due to fluctuations in attention they must alter activity in the recorded neurones before changes become evident in eye movements. Where then could any such changes in attentiveness be generated? Such changes can only be dependent upon the recognition of stimulus repetition: but that is just what is signalled

by the described decremental neuronal responses. Accordingly, either these *are* the neurones that carry that signal, or it will be necessary to find other neurones that signal the same information at a latency at least as short: such neurones might exist, but they have not yet been found. Moreover, there is at least one hint that neurones with decremental responses may indeed be involved in attentive mechanisms: the general activity of one MID neurone recorded in these experiments increased during performance of the serial recognition task in a way suggesting that it might well form part of a system mediating selective attention or enhanced activation of pathways mediating the performance of visual recognition.

Such decremental responses could contribute to priming memory (i.e., the facilitation of performance by a prior related event). However, patients suffering from the classical amnesic syndrome with damage to either the medial diencephalon or the medial temporal lobes demonstrate essentially normal priming (Shimamura, 1986; Schacter, 1987; Tulving and Schacter, 1990). This indicates that the damaged regions are not necessary for priming. It is not clear whether neurones with decremental responses found outside the lesioned areas possess memory spans sufficiently long to account for priming memory (Baylis and Rolls, 1987, and unpublished observations of the authors). If such neurones do assist with priming, then their decreased response to repeated stimuli must elsewhere be converted to the enhanced behavioural output required: very few neurones with enhanced responses to repeat presentations have been discovered.

Not all the memory spans of the described neurones are long, although most decremental responses do not recover immediately when the animal's attention is distracted by other stimulus presentations (Riches et al., 1991a,b). Thus any usefulness to recognition or other memory processes of some of the decremental responses must be limited to determining the recency of the previous occurrence of stimuli in the short-term, i.e., seconds to a minute or so. However, other neurones signal the prior occurrence of stimuli that have been seen for many minutes or, in the case of familiarity information, for days previously (Riches et al., 1991a). Such neurones clearly have access to information stored in long-term memory.

Neurones signalling information of such importance for recognition memory occur in those regions – medial thalamus, medial temporal lobe and basal forebrain – where lesions have such devastating consequences for the performance of recognition memory tasks (Mishkin, 1982; Aggleton and Mishkin, 1983a,b; Zola-Morgan and Squire, 1985a,b; Aigner et al., 1987; Zola-Morgan et al., 1989); this conjunction provides the most persuasive argument that these neurones do indeed form part of the recognition memory system. The argument is further supported by the fact that extensive recordings in the critical regions of the medial temporal lobe have not uncovered neuronal activity that could provide an alternative means of carrying out the required functions of recency and familiarity discrimination.

Conclusions

These experiments have demonstrated the presence of neuronal activity that encodes information about the previous occurrence of stimuli in the magnocellular division of the mediodorsal nucleus and the caudal part of the paraventricular midline nucleus of the medial thalamus. The conjunction of these results with the findings of lesion studies demonstrates the importance of these parts of the medial thalamus for processes necessary for recognition memory.

The findings for the medial thalamus have been considered in relation to those in other areas, particularly the medial temporal lobe and basal forebrain, areas that lesion experiments have indicated are necessary for performance of recognition memory tasks. It is concluded that these interconnected areas form part of the system allowing the discrimination of the recency of occurrence and familiarity of stimuli.

Experiments are needed to establish the directions of information flow relating to recognition memory

between these areas. Further, recency and familiarity are not the only types of information used in recognition memory: there is as yet little information concerning the encoding of absolute novelty as opposed to unfamiliarity, of the frequency of occurrence of stimuli, or of the context of occurrence of stimulus items (though see Brown, 1982, 1990; Rolls et al., 1989). Moreover, it is not known how neuronal response decrements to stimulus repetition are transformed into appropriate behavioural output, although one neurone in the mediodorsal nucleus has provided suggestive information. Recordings from those parts of the medial prefrontal cortex to which the mediodorsal nucleus projects (Giguere and Goldman-Rakic, 1988) should assist in the provision of such information.

Acknowledgements

This work was supported by grants from the Wellcome Trust and the Anatomical Society of Great Britain and Ireland. The authors wish to thank Mr. R. Chambers, Mr. J.A. Leendertz and Mrs. A.M. Somerset for their assistance with these experiments.

References

Aggleton, J.P. and Mishkin, M. (1983a) Memory impairments following restricted medial thalamic lesions in monkeys. *Exp. Brain Res.,* 52: 199 – 209.

Aggleton, J.P. and Mishkin, M. (1983b) Visual recognition impairment following medial thalamic lesions in monkeys. *Neuropsychologia,* 21: 189 – 197.

Aggleton, J.P. and Passingham, R.E. (1981) Stereotaxic surgery under X-ray guidance in the rhesus monkey, with special reference to the amygdala. *Exp. Brain Res.,* 44: 271 – 276.

Aggleton, J.P., Burton, M.J. and Passingham, R.E. (1980) Cortical and subcortical afferents to the amygdala of the rhesus monkey *(Macaca mulatta). Brain Res.,* 190: 347 – 368.

Aggleton, J.P., Desimone, R. and Mishkin, M. (1986) The origin, course and termination of the hippocampothalamic projections in the macaque. *J. Comp. Neurol.,* 243: 409 – 421.

Aigner, T.G., Mitchell, S.J., Aggleton, J.P., DeLong, M.R., Struble, R.G., Price, D.L., Wenk, G.L. and Mishkin, M. (1987) Effects of scopolamine and physostigmine on recognition memory in monkeys with ibotenic-acid lesions of the nucleus basalis of Meynert. *Psychopharmacology,* 92:

292–300.

Baylis, G.C. and Rolls, E.T. (1987) Responses of neurons in the inferior temporal cortex in short term and serial recognition memory tasks. *Exp. Brain Res.,* 65: 614–622.

Brown, M.W. (1982) Effect of context on the responses of single units recorded from the hippocampal region of behaviourally trained monkeys. In: C. Ajmone-Marsan and H. Matthies (Eds.), *Neuronal Plasticity and Memory Formation. IBRO Monograph Series Vol. 9,* Raven Press, New York, pp. 557–573.

Brown, M.W. (1990) Why does the cortex have a hippocampus? In: M. Gabriel and J. Moore (Eds.), *Learning and Computational Neuroscience: Foundations of Adaptive Networks,* M.I.T. Press, New York, pp. 233–282.

Brown, M.W. and Leendertz, J.A. (1979) A pulse-shape discriminator for action potentials. *J. Physiol. (Lond.),* 298: 17–18P.

Brown, M.W., Wilson, F.A.W. and Riches, I.P. (1987) Neuronal evidence that inferomedial temporal cortex is more important than hippocampus in certain processes underlying recognition memory. *Brain Res.,* 409: 158–162.

Fahy, F.L., Riches, I.P. and Brown, M.W. (1991) Neuronal evidence of the involvement of the primate medial thalamus in recognition memory. *Eur. J. Neurosci.* (Suppl.), 4: 88.

Fuster, J.M. and Alexander, G.E. (1973) Firing changes in cells of the nucleus medialis dorsalis associated with delayed response behavior. *Brain Res.,* 61: 79–91.

Gaffan, D. (1974) Recognition impaired and association intact in the memory of monkeys after transection of the fornix. *J. Comp. Physiol. Psychol.,* 80: 1100–1109.

Giguere, M. and Goldman-Rakic, P.S. (1988) Mediodorsal nucleus: areal, laminar, and tangential distribution of afferents and efferents in the frontal lobe of rhesus monkeys. *J. Comp. Neurol.,* 277: 195–213.

Gower, E.C. (1989) Efferent projections from limbic cortex of the temporal pole to the magnocellular medial dorsal nucleus in the rhesus monkey. *J. Comp. Neurol.,* 280: 343–358.

Horn, G. (1969) A simple device for making tungsten microelectrodes in bulk. *J. Physiol. (Lond.),* 204: 6–7P.

Kandel, E.R. (1981) Calcium and the control of synaptic strength by learning. *Nature,* 293: 697–700.

Kandel, E.R. and Spencer, W.A. (1968) Cellular and neurophysiological approaches to the study of learning. *Physiol. Rev.,* 48: 66–134.

Mair, W.G.P., Warrington, E.K. and Weiskrantz, L. (1979) Memory disorder in Korsakoff's psychosis. *Brain,* 102: 749–783.

Mayes, A.R. (1988) *Human Organic Memory Disorders,* C.U.P., Cambridge.

McEntee, W.J. and Mair, R.G. (1990) The Korsakoff syndrome: a neurochemical perspective. *Trends Neurosci.,* 13: 340–344.

Mishkin, M. (1982) A memory system in the monkey. *Phil. Trans. R. Soc. Lond. B.,* 298: 85–95.

Olszewski, J. (1952) *The Thalamus of Macaca Mulatta,* Karger, Basel.

Parkin, A.J. (1987) *Memory and Amnesia: an Introduction,* Basil Blackwell, Oxford.

Riches, I.P., Fahy, F.L. and Brown, M.W. (1991a) Involvement of the primate medial temporal lobe in recognition memory: neuronal evidence of long-term retention and discrimination of familiarity and recency. *Eur. J. Neurosci.* (Suppl.), 4: 89.

Riches, I.P., Wilson, F.A.W. and Brown, M.W. (1991b) The effects of visual stimulation and memory on neurons of the hippocampal formation and the neighboring parahippocampal gyrus and inferior temporal cortex of the primate. *J. Neurosci.,* 11: 1763–1779.

Rolls, E.T., Perrett, D.I., Caan, A.W. and Wilson, F.A.W. (1982) Neuronal responses related to visual recognition. *Brain,* 105: 611–646.

Rolls, E.T., Miyashita, Y., Cahusac, P.M.B., Kesner, R.P., Niki, H., Feigenbaum, J.D. and Bach, L. (1989) Hippocampal neurons in the monkey with activity related to the place in which a stimulus is shown. *J. Neurosci.,* 9: 1835–1845.

Rosene, D.L. and Van Hoesen, G.W. (1987) The hippocampal formation of the primate brain. In: E.G. Jones and A. Peters, (Eds.), *Cerebral Cortex, Vol. 6,* Plenum, New York, pp. 345–456.

Russchen, F.T., Amaral, D.G. and Price, J.L. (1985) The afferent connections of the substantia innominata in the monkey, *Macaca fascicularis. J. Comp. Neurol.,* 242: 1–27.

Russchen, F.T., Amaral, D.G. and Price, J.L. (1987) The afferent input to the magnocellular division of the mediodorsal thalamic nucleus in the monkey, *Macaca fascicularis. J. Comp. Neurol.,* 256: 175–210.

Schacter, D.L. (1987) Implicit memory: history and current status. *J. Exp. Psychol. Learn. Mem. Cogn.,* 13: 501–518.

Scoville, W.B. and Milner, B. (1957) Loss of recent memory after bilateral hippocampal lesions. *J. Neurol. Neurosurg. Psychiatry,* 20: 11–21.

Shimamura, A.P. (1986) Priming effects in amnesia: evidence for a dissociable memory function. *Q. J. Exp. Psychol. B,* 38A: 619–644.

Squire, L.R. (1987) *Memory and Brain,* Oxford University Press, New York.

Squire, L.R. and Moore, R.Y. (1979) Dorsal thalamic lesion in a noted case of chronic memory dysfunction. *Ann. Neurol.,* 6: 503–506.

Thompson, R.F. and Spencer, W.A. (1966) Habituation: a model phenomenon for the study of neuronal substrates of behaviour. *Psychol. Rev.,* 73: 16–43.

Tulving, E. and Schacter, D.L. (1990) Priming and human memory systems. *Science,* 247: 301–306.

Van Hoesen, G.W. and Pandya, D.N. (1975) Some connections of the entorhinal (area 28) and perirhinal (area 35) cortices of the rhesus monkey. 1. Temporal lobe afferents. *Brain Res.,* 95: 1–24.

Weiskrantz, L. (1987) Neuroanatomy of memory and amnesia: a case for multiple memory systems. *Hum. Neurobiol.,* 6:

416

93 – 105.

Wilson, F.A.W. and Rolls, E.T. (1990) Neuronal responses related to the novelty and familiarity of visual stimuli in the substantia innominata, diagonal band of Broca and periventricular region of the primate basal forebrain. *Exp. Brain Res.,* 80: 104 – 120.

Wilson, F.A.W. and Rolls, E.T. (1991) The effects of stimulus novelty and familiarity on neuronal activity in the amygdala of monkeys performing recognition memory tasks. *Exp. Brain Res.,* in press.

Winocur, G., Oxbury, S., Roberts, R., Agnetti, A. and Davis, C. (1984) Amnesia in a patient with bilateral lesions to the thalamus. *Neuropsychologia,* 22: 123 – 143.

Yeterian, E.H. and Pandya, D.N. (1988) Corticothalamic connections of paralimbic regions in the rhesus monkey. *J. Comp. Neurol.,* 269: 130 – 146.

Zola-Morgan, S. and Squire, L.R. (1985a) Amnesia in monkeys after lesions of the mediodorsal nucleus of the thalamus. *Ann. Neurol.,* 17: 558 – 564.

Zola-Morgan, S. and Squire, L.R. (1985b) Medial temporal lesions in monkeys impair memory on a variety of tasks sensitive to human amnesia. *Behav. Neurosci.,* 99: 22 – 34.

Zola-Morgan, S., Squire, L.R., Amaral, D.G. and Suzuki, W.A. (1989) Lesions of perirhinal and parahippocampal cortex that spare the amygdala and hippocampal formation produce severe memory impairment. *J. Neurosci.,* 9: 4355 – 4370.

T.P. Hicks, S. Molotchnikoff and T. Ono (Eds.)
Progress in Brain Research, Vol. 95

CHAPTER 34

Colour vision: isolating mechanisms in overlapping streams

J.J. Kulikowski and V. Walsh

Visual Sciences Laboratory, UMIST, Manchester, U.K.

Introduction

Psychophysical studies have established that colour vision is based on chromatic opponent mechanisms, that basic, perceptual colour categories are derived from the opponent mechanisms (Mullen and Kulikowski, 1990; cf. also Vautin and Dow, 1985), and that colour vision has lower temporal and spatial resolution limits than achromatic vision (De Lange 1958; Mullen, 1985, 1987).

The anatomical substrates underlying chromatic and achromatic mechanisms have been the focus of much recent research (Livingstone and Hubel, 1987; De Yoe and Van Essen, 1988; Tootell et al., 1988; Zeki and Shipp, 1988). Achromatic information can be analyzed in both the P and M streams whereas information about colour is conveyed only in the P pathway (see Zrenner, 1983; De Valois and De Valois, 1988; Kulikowski et al., 1989b, 1991; Gouras, 1991; Valberg and Lee, 1991, for full discussions).

With the exception of the spectral sensitivity function (Sperling and Harwerth, 1971; King-Smith and Carden, 1976; Crook et al., 1987) recordings from retinal and LGN cells (Lee, 1991) are poor predictors of psychophysical performance (Kulikowski, 1991a).

The data presented in this chapter demonstrate electrophysiologically the basis of colour vision and show that cortical visual evoked potentials (VEPs) correlate with the known spatio-temporal limits of colour vision.

First, the extent of overlap of the spatio-temporal properties of achromatic and chromatic-opponent cells is demonstrated. Second, an assessment of the relationship between local and global electrophysiological measures of colour vision is made, and field potential recordings are compared with single-unit and multi-unit recordings made in the same cortical site. Third, it is shown that the use of low-contrast, low-spatial frequency gratings presented at a low temporal rate dichotomize the global responses measured as VEPs: achromatic gratings elicit transient on-off responses, consistent with the responses of most transient M-cells, which are dependent on a step change in contrast, whereas chromatic gratings generate sustained responses that are different for onset and offset presentations and thus similar to the responses of chromatic-opponent cells. Fourth, chromatic VEPs are shown to be selectively diminished by administration of NMDA antagonists, consistent with the notion that NMDA receptors facilitate sustained responses. Finally, chromatic VEPs recorded from subjects with lesions of cortical visual area V4 are seen to be unchanged in shape, and little different in magnitude, relative to normals. This suggests that colour detection and categorization are mediated by mechanisms operating not later than V2 in the chromatic processing stream.

General methodology

Microelectrode recordings

Single-unit recordings were made at about 4 – 5° eccentricity in the lower visual field representation of the striate cortex of macaque monkeys prepared for acute procedures. Full details of the preparation and procedures have been given elsewhere (Kulikowski and Vidyasagar, 1986). Briefly, animals were anaesthetized with nitrous oxide and Nembutal, and paralysed with Flaxedil and Tubarine. A tungsten microelectrode was used to record the activity of single units, multi-units and field potentials (filter: 1 – 30 Hz). The cells were tested first with bars and edges in order to map the receptive field profiles. The responses of cells to chromatic stimuli were tested by projecting the stimuli through coloured filters. After receptive field mapping cells were stimulated with vertical sine-wave gratings generated on a 608 Tektroniks display monitor and presented either drifting, ON/OFF or in reversal mode. The step change in contrast of the onset and reversal presentations was equated by making the reversing grating half the contrast of the onset grating. The spatial and temporal sensitivities of chromatic cells were determined by using bars, edges or luminance-modulated gratings of the cell's preferred colour.

Visual evoked potentials

For VEP recordings the monkey was seated in a primate chair. Responses were recorded from electrodes placed on the occipital lobe 10 – 15% of inion-nasion distance either side of the midline, with a mid-frontal or linked ears reference. Signals were filtered (usually band-pass 0.3 – 30 Hz for onset/reversal and 10 – 30 Hz for 12.5 Hz reversal VEP) and averaged by a Medelec ER94 averager. Either 64, 128, or 256 sweeps of the averager were used and a typical averaged output took between 1 and 4 min to obtain. For full details of VEP recording procedures, see Kulikowski and Carden (1989). Chromatic and achromatic vertical gratings were presented in either ON/OFF or contrast reversal mode. The colour components of the chromatic gratings were defined by the luminance ratio RED/(RED + GREEN) between the values of zero for a green/dark green grating and one for a red/dark red grating. Isoluminance was determined for each monkey by recording fast reversal VEPs and finding the RED/(RED + GREEN) ratio at which the response is reduced to a residual level. The results of this procedure compare well with the isoluminant point for human observers, obtained by heterochromatic flicker photometry, that finds isoluminance at the RED/(RED + GREEN) ratio 0.5. Achromatic gratings were produced by luminance-modulated red and green gratings superimposed in phase to give a luminance-modulated yellow grating. Mean luminance (usually 50 cd/m^2) and mean hue were kept constant throughout the experiments. The displays subtended approximately 15° of visual angle at the retina, therefore accurate fixation and accommodation were not essential. To control for changes in the animal's state of adaptation or anaesthesia during the recording of the VEPs the chromatic and achromatic gratings were presented in alternation and separated by an offset presentation of a uniform yellow. Details of stimulus generation are described in Murray et al. (1987) and Kulikowski et al. (1989a). The ketamine regimes also are detailed in previous publications (Kulikowski and Carden, 1989).

Results

Properties of single units recorded in the striate cortex

Recordings were made from 116 units, some of which have been reported previously (Kulikowski and Vidyasagar, 1986). The criteria of orientation selectivity and linearity were applied to select simple cells (including end-stopped), which may contribute to linear analysis of contrast. Concentric (chromatic and achromatic) cells gave similar responses at orthogonal orientations but occasionally intermediate arrangements were observed (see ellipsoid symbols in Fig. 1). Both these groups have a low nonlinearity index (< 0.3) unlike complex or hyper-

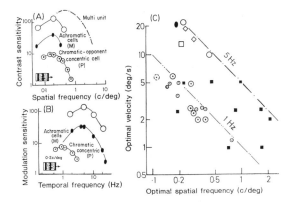

Fig. 1. *A*. Examples of spatial frequency tuning curves expressed as contrast sensitivity and modulation sensitivity, respectively. Top: the dash-dotted line shows the envelope of contrast sensitivity functions obtained by reducing contrast until the drifting grating does not elicit a modulated discharge (see Enroth-Cugell and Robson, 1966) when monitoring the multi-unit activity. All three cells have similar optimal spatial frequency ($F_{xopt} \sim 0.2$ c/deg), i.e., spatial frequency at which minimal contrast produces threshold response of a cell. Drifting luminance-modulated gratings produced modulated discharges; the chromatic opponent cell was tested with a red grating matching its red-on centre. The optimal spatial frequency can also be estimated from the Fourier transform of the spatial response profile (see Kulikowski and Vidyasagar, 1986). *B*. Temporal frequency tuning curves for the cells in *A*. Cells differ in their optimal temporal frequencies (F_{topt}). The extreme cases are illustrated: achromatic cells of the phasic type respond optimally at around 5 Hz, whereas the colour-opponent cells do so around 1 Hz. Achromatic cells have generally higher sensitivity than chromatic (tonic) cells. However, some achromatic cells not shown here (see *C*), may be of slow tonic type, like chromatic opponent cells ($F_{topt} \sim 1$ Hz); other cells (mainly of the simple type) have intermediate optimal velocities and optimal temporal frequencies. However, these slow cells have generally lower contrast/modulation sensitivities that phasic type cells. *C*. Optimal velocities for various types of visual cortical cells tuned to different optimal spatial frequencies (macaque V1) with the emphasis on chromatic sensitive cells. The optimal velocity is defined as the velocity eliciting the maximal peak responses to drifting bars (or similar response profiles in both directions). Optimal spatial frequency is determined by a combined method of computing Fourier transform and contrast sensitivity (see Kulikowski and Vidyasagar, 1986). The data for only a few simple cells (squares) are shown to avoid crowding; note the cells outlining the borders of the velocity-spatial frequency range (for the full data on simple cells, see Kulikowski, 1991a). The large diamonds show the data for two fast simple cells with a high degree of non-linearity. A large circle indicates properties of a concentric achromatic cell with a preference for high velocities. All these three cells have an optimal temporal frequency of about

complex (Hubel and Wiesel, 1968), or B-type cells (Kulikowski and Vidyasagar, 1984, 1986) which will not be considered here. The emphasis of the present study is on the spatio-temporal properties of chromatic-sensitive cells in contrast to those of achromatic cells (simple and concentric) which respond to fast motion, or flicker.

Cells defined unambiguously as chromatic opponent were those which responded much less to white spots flashed on their receptive field centres than to spots whose colour was optimally adjusted (see large circles with dots in Fig. 1) and where spontaneous activity was reduced by presenting a colour from the complementary part of the spectrum. Otherwise the cells showing some preference to chromatic stimuli were classified as chromatic-sensitive (small circles with dots). Some of these chromatic-sensitive cells were comparable to the "modified type II" cells described by Ts'o and Gilbert (1988) but, unlike them, responded to long gratings and could be activated from the surround (cf. De Valois et al., 1966; Wiesel and Hubel, 1966; Dreher et al., 1976). Cells not showing specific spectral biases were classified as achromatic.

Recordings from fibres in lamina 4 were also obtained and the characteristics of these responses

5 Hz and all have high contrast sensitivity > 100). One cell with poor orientation sensitivity marked by the ellipsoid also preferred high velocities but had the lowest contrast sensitivity (40) in this group (for details of responses see fig. 1 in Kulikowski, 1991a). Large circles with dots indicate properties of concentric cells with prominent chromatic opponency (some are double opponent showing clearly antagonistic discharges in the annulus, see Kulikowski et al., 1989). A dashed circle with a dot corresponds to a cell with very broad spatial frequency tuning – indicating the virtual absence of a surround of the kind found in type II LGN cells (Wiesel and Hubel, 1966). Cells of modified type II (T'so and Gilbert, 1988), with a suppressive surround were not identified in this sample, presumably because long bars, to which modified type II cells respond poorly, were used as stimuli. Small circles with dots describe concentric cells with weak opponency which respond slightly better to coloured than to white stimuli. All these concentric cells have very broad temporal frequency tuning with peaks around 1 Hz and low luminance contrast sensitivity, but are sensitive to a red-green chromatic border, i.e., they have high chromatic contrast sensitivity. Cells with blue-yellow opponency are not included here.

resembled those of LGN cells (Kaplan and Shapley, 1982; Hicks et al., 1983). In previous studies (Kulikowski and Vidyasagar, 1984; Thorell et al., 1984) chromatic cells have been found to have lower mean spatial resolution than achromatic cells and high susceptibility to anaesthesia. Conversely, ketamine administration (5 – 10 mg/kg) had only minimal effects on achromatic cells which responded transiently and were tuned to low spatial frequencies.

Comparison of spatio-temporal properties of linear cortical cells

Fig. 1A,B illustrates spatial and temporal frequency properties of units located between lower layer 3 and layer 4Cβ and representing the visual field 4 – 5° below the visual axis.

The examples in Fig. 1A show contrast sensitivity curves of cells selected for the similarity of their receptive field sizes and optimal spatial frequency. For reference, the top curve shows the upper range (envelope) of multi-unit contrast sensitivities of several recordings sites, thereby representing best performance of all cells responding in a modulated manner to the drifting grating. For this eccentricity maximal resolution is just below 10 c/deg and the maximal contrast sensitivity exceeds 100. Both achromatic cells behaved like phasic retinal or M-LGN cells. Conversely, the chromatic opponent cells in the striate cortex responded better to much lower spatial frequencies than P-LGN neurons, probably due to extensive spatial summation since several LGN afferents may contribute to the receptive field centre of a cortical unit (see also Livingstone and Hubel, 1987; Ts'o and Gilbert, 1988; Lennie et al., 1990).

Fig. 1B shows modulation sensitivity as a function of temporal frequency of drifting luminance-modulated gratings for the units shown in Fig. 1A. The characteristic of the chromatic opponent cell contrasts with the temporal frequency tuning curves of the two achromatic cells by having lower optimal temporal frequency and consequently lower temporal resolution. Comparing data in Fig. 1A and B illustrates the general finding that the achromatic

cells have higher luminance contrast and modulation sensitivity than chromatic cells, even when the colour of the luminance modulated grating used is of the chromatic cell's preferred colour. Notably, other concentric cells with P-inputs which seem to be achromatic have been shown to have low contrast sensitivity (e.g., Hawken and Parker, 1987).

Some simple cells also show a preference for slow movement and have low luminance contrast sensitivity similar to that found in chromatic sensitive cells. An example can be seen in Fig. 1C (parameters: $F_{xopt} = 0.2$ c/deg; $V_{opt} = 2.5$ deg/sec, hence $F_{topt} = 0.5$ Hz; for other examples see fig. 2 of Kulikowski, 1991a). However, some overlap exists: sensitivity of slow, simple cells may reach about 50 (see fig. 1.4A in Kulikowski et al., 1989c) which is similar to sensitivity of the phasic cell in Fig. 1A (see below). Thus achromatic, simple cells cover a broad range of spatial frequencies and velocities consistent with the concept of multiple channels in spatial analysis. The slowest among them are slower than the chromatic opponent cells (cf. Fig. 1C around the 1 Hz line), and the fastest give phasic responses (cf. Fig. 1C around the 5 Hz line). There are also simple cells of intermediate spatio-temporal preferences of which only a few examples are shown in Fig. 1C to avoid crowding (for further details of the range of data see Kulikowski and Vidyasagar, 1986; Kulikowski, 1991a).

The scatter diagram of the optimal velocities as a function of optimal spatial frequencies (Fig. 1C) also shows that the broadest range of parameters is covered by simple cells. The strength of response of fast and slow cells tuned to low spatial frequencies is another matter: at low contrasts slow cells are hardly stimulated by luminance-modulated gratings, unlike the phasic-type cells. Only the chromatic opponent units among slow cells in this spatial frequency range can substantially increase their responses when a chromatic component is introduced to stimuli of low contrasts (see below Fig. 3). It should be noted that the high sensitivity of phasic-type cells is not maintained over all spatial frequencies. For optimal spatial frequencies above 1 c/deg it is the tonic type of achromatic cells which are most sensitive (for psychophysical correlates, see also Kulikowski and Tolhurst, 1973; Kulikowski, 1978; Kulikowski et al., 1989a; Valberg and Lee, 1991).

Group responses of neurons: multi-unit histograms and slow field potentials

Fig. 2 illustrates the responses obtained from three cortical sites, two dominated by achromatic and one by chromatic units. The main achromatic cell (simple) in Fig. 2A (as well as the other cells which contribute to the multi-unit response), show purely transient responses, i.e., similar responses are obtained to onset and reversal for the same step change in contrast. Conversely, an achromatic cell in Fig. 2B, tuned to a higher spatial frequency than the cell in Fig. 2A, has a non-transient, or sustained,

response component that is revealed when the onset and reversal responses are compared. (This sustained component reflects the ability of a cell to respond to standing contrast and is related to the low temporal frequency fall-off in a linear model, see Kulikowski, 1991b.) There is a clear tendency for the cells tuned to finer patterns to be more sustained.

As shown in Fig. 1C, chromatic cells usually give sustained responses: the onset response has not only a stronger sustained component, but in this case the initial burst of spikes is also greater than for contrast reversal, as can be seen in the multi-unit and field potential responses.

The point to note, then, is that the greatest difference in temporal properties is revealed when chromatic cells and achromatic cells tuned to low

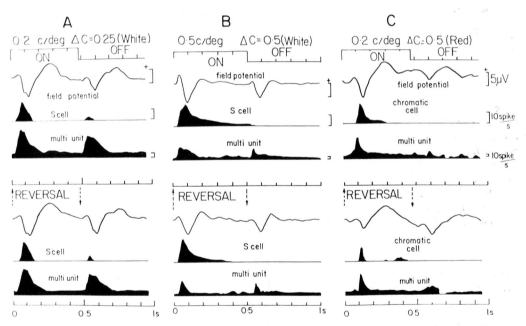

Fig. 2. Single-/multi-unit and field potential responses to stationary flashing gratings in three different sites of the striate cortex. Optimal spatial frequencies were used for the cells under investigation. In all sites grating onset was compared with contrast reversal presentation. *A*. Site of simple (achromatic) cells. Note that the corresponding onset-offset and reversal responses are virtually identical not only for the simple cell, but also for the multi-unit and field potential responses. This suggests that the cells contributing to these responses respond transiently. Low contrast makes the contribution of magno-stream cells predominant. *B*. Site of simple (achromatic) cells as in *A*, but showing preferences for higher spatial frequencies. The field potential response to grating onset is slightly larger than to reversal and both single and multi-unit responses to onset show some sustained component (evident when the corresponding reversal responses are superimposed) suggesting some contribution of non-transient cells. *C*. Site of chromatic opponent, concentric cells, similar to that shown in Fig. 1A (top). Note that the cell responds less to contrast reversal than to grating onset. The same tendency is shown in the multi-unit and field potential responses; this suggests that mostly non-transient units contribute to these responses.

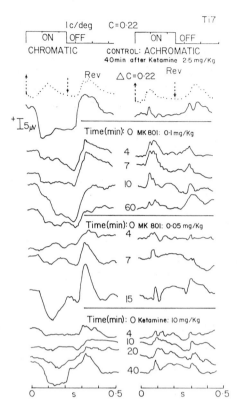

Fig. 3. The top records show visual evoked potentials recorded from the scalp of a rhesus monkey lightly sedated with ketamine. Note the similarity of the VEPs elicited by onset, offset and reversal of the achromatic 1 c/deg grating. Conversely, a substantial difference exists between VEPs to onset and offset, and onset and reversal presentations of the chromatic grating. The remainder shows the effects of the NMDA antagonists (ketamine and MK801) on the chromatic and achromatic VEPs. Note that the chromatic onset VEP is more attenuated than achromatic VEPs.

Visual evoked potential recordings

Chromatic-sustained and achromatic-transient VEPs. Fig. 3 (top) shows VEPs recorded from scalp electrodes above the striate cortex of one rhesus monkey. The VEPs were elicited by 1 c/deg chromatic isoluminant and achromatic gratings whose step change in contrast was 0.22.

One of the striking features of the VEPs elicited by 1 c/deg achromatic gratings is that both onset and contrast reversal elicit similar wave forms, thus revealing that the VEP generating mechanisms at this spatial frequency are predominantly transient. The VEP wave forms in Fig. 3 differ from potentials in Fig. 2A by being mainly positive-going which is probably due to the contributions of many visually activated extra-striate cortical areas (see Kulikowski et al., 1989b). Conversely, the onset of the chromatic grating generates a much larger VEP than the corresponding contrast reversal, clear evidence of a non-transient response. The chromatic onset VEPs resemble potentials in Fig. 2C by having

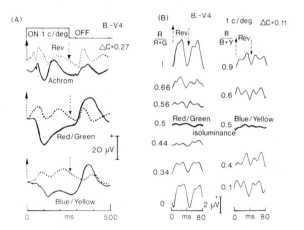

Fig. 4A. VEPs for a monkey with V4 lesions. Responses were elicited to grating onset and reversal presented at a rate of 1.9 Hz. Top: achromatic luminance modulated on-off/reversal VEPs. Middle: red/green isoluminant on-off/reversal VEPs. Bottom: blue/yellow isoluminant on-off/reversal VEPs. *B.* Reversal VEP at 12.5 Hz for different luminance ratios of red/green and blue/yellow components. There is a clear reduction in the overall VEP amplitude at isoluminance which can be best demonstrated using gratings.

spatial frequencies are compared (compare Fig. 2A and C). Nevertheless, the differences between chromatic and achromatic responses (shown by comparing onset and reversal presentations in Fig. 2) are relatively small when compared to those obtained from the scalp-recorded VEPs, of sedated monkeys (see Fig. 3, top). Part of this effect can be attributed to the effects of anaesthesia which generally reduces the onset-reversal difference (as is the case in human and monkey VEPs, see Kulikowski and Leisman, 1973, Kulikowski and Murray, 1988, and below).

dominant negativity. Similar differences between chromatic grating onset and reversal VEPs were obtained for a moderate range of spatial frequencies covering the chromatic channel in slightly sedated monkeys (Kulikowski and Murray, 1988) and fully conscious humans (Carden et al., 1985; Murray et al., 1987; Berninger et al., 1989; Kulikowski et al., 1989a; Murray and Parry, 1989). However, it should be stressed that only low-contrast and low-spatial frequency gratings allow such a clear distinction to be made between chromatic and achromatic VEPs, since higher spatial frequencies produce VEPs which resemble in shape chromatic-sustained, rather than achromatic-transient VEPs (see Russell et al., 1987, and Discussion).

The effects of NMDA antagonists on visual cortical activity. From the data presented in the above section one can conclude that the small dose of ketamine, an NMDA antagonist used to sedate animals for recording experiments, does not distort VEPs.

The remaining recordings in Fig. 3 show the acute effect of larger doses of ketamine, and another NMDA antagonist, MK801, on the onset VEPs. It is evident that ketamine or MK801 administration attenuates chromatic VEPs more than achromatic VEPs. One interesting observation is that under some conditions, the action of the NMDA antagonist produces a chromatic onset VEP that resembles achromatic-transient VEP – with similar positive onset and offset waves generated (Fig. 3, top). This can be interpreted in accord with the data of Lee et al. (1989b) that chromatic isoluminant gratings can generate residual (non-linear on-off) responses in magno-type cells.

Chromatic VEPs in the absence of visual area V4

Fig. 4A shows VEP recordings from a monkey with a bilateral V4 lesion. The shapes of the VEPs from the lesioned animal are normal but the magnitude of both chromatic and achromatic VEPs is larger than for the animal's preoperative levels. We have confirmed this observation in several lesioned animals (Kulikowski et al., 1992). It is tempting to

speculate that this may be due to removal of some inhibition of tonic V1 responses as a consequence of severing the V4 to V1 back-projection (see Dow, 1991). However, it may be simply that the postoperative skull has lower conductance. As reported by Kulikowski and Carden (1989) the chromatic VEPs before or after V4 lesion reach their maxima when the components of red-green grating are of equal luminance (close to that for human observers). The same occurs when blue-yellow gratings are used and it is seen that the maximum onset VEP (in Fig. 4A) occurs at the luminance ratio at which the smallest fast reversal VEPs are elicited.

The recordings in Fig. 4B illustrate the VEPs elicited by the 12.5 Hz reversal for various ratios of illuminants. It is clear that, as in normal humans (Kulikowski et al., 1989a) and monkeys (Kulikowski, 1991) the minimum VEP is achieved for isoluminance. The non-zero VEP at isoluminance, the physiological basis of which is thought to originate in phasic cells (Lee et al., 1989a; Kaiser, 1991), probably corresponds to the residual flicker seen by human observers under these conditions.

Perceptual significance of normal VEPs. The apparently normal chromatic VEPs of monkeys with V4 lesions prompted us to carry out some behavioural experiments on colour categorization, and our preliminary findings suggest that monkeys with V4 lesions, like normal monkeys, perceive wavelength differences according to basic perceptual categories (Sandell et al., 1979; Walsh et al., 1992).

Discussion

The main contention of this paper is that basic colour categorization can be localized in the visual cortex not earlier than V1 and not later than V2. This is understandable since the electrophysiological recordings from pre-cortical sites do not generally correlate with psychophysics, and because lesions of the secondary visual area V4 do not affect either chromatic VEPs or perceptual colour categoriza-

424

tion. Thus sites afferent and efferent to V1 and V2 can be excluded as candidates for the origin of the primary wave of the chromatic VEP. The apparently normal shape of the chromatic VEPs of monkeys with V4 lesions is consistent with another finding, namely that the source of the main negative-going wave of chromatic and fine-grating VEPs has been located close to the midline in man, i.e., at the border of V1/V2 by computing the Laplacean derivations (see Kranda and Jobert, 1989; Kulikowski et al., 1989b). The same technique revealed that the secondary negative wave has a focus several centimetres lateral, coincident with the location of area V4, which is known to be important for processing colour information (Zeki, 1980; Wild et al., 1985; Walsh et al., 1992). The data reported here then would suggest that V4's role in colour processing is post-categorical (Walsh et al., 1992). Finally, it should be noted that the mechanisms activated by chromatic borders, corners, texture, etc., may be different to those discussed here and not defined by the same spatial and temporal properties.

Conclusions

(1) Knowledge of the spatial properties of chromatic-sustained, achromatic-transient and achromatic-sustained neurons can be used to selectively activate parallel processing streams. In particular, the chromatic-sustained channel is best isolated by long, sine-wave gratings of low spatial and temporal frequency content.

(2) Global electrophysiological recordings can reveal spatio-temporal response properties of visual cortical mechanisms that correlate with observed psychophysical functions.

(3) The specificity of chromatic VEPs makes them a useful tool with which to investigate the effects of neurotoxins, surgery and pathologies on the P system.

(4) It is hypothesized that basic, perceptual colour categories are constructed by processes operating in visual areas V1 and V2.

Acknowledgements

This work has been partly supported by the Optometry and Vision Sciences Reserve Fund, Visual Science Fund, Visual Sciences Publication Support Fund (UMIST) and by grants from the Wellcome Trust and The Nuffield Foundation. We thank Dr. Stuart R. Butler, David Carden, Robert Morrisey and Keith Street for their advice and help.

References

Berninger, T.A., Arden, G.B., Hogg, C. and Frumkes, T.E. (1989) Separable evoked retinal and cortical potentials from each major visual pathway: preliminary results. *Br. J. Opthal.*, 73: 502 – 511.

Carden, D., Kulikowski, J.J., Murray, N.R.A. and Parry, N.R.A. (1985) Human occipital potentials evoked by the onset of equiluminant gratings. *J. Physiol. (Lond.)*, 369: 44P.

Crook, J.M., Lee, B.B., Tigwell, D.A. and Valberg, A. (1987) Thresholds to chromatic spots of cells in the geniculate nucleus as compared to detection sensitivity in man. *J. Physiol. (Lond.)*, 392: 193 – 213.

De Lange, H. (1958) Research into the dynamic nature of the human foveal cortex systems with intermittent and modulated light: 1. Attenuation characteristics of white and coloured light. *J. Opt. Soc. Am.*, 48: 777 – 784.

De Valois, R.L. and De Valois, K.K. (1988) *Spatial Vision. Oxford Psychology Series, Vol. 14,* Oxford University Press, Oxford.

De Valois, R.L., Abramov, I. and Jacobs, G.H. (1966) Analysis of response patterns of L.G.N. cells. *J. Opt. Soc. Am.*, 56: 966 – 977.

De Yoe, E.A. and Van Essen, D.C. (1988) Concurrent processing streams in monkey visual cortex. *Trends Neurosci.*, 11: 219 – 226.

Dow, B.M. (1991) Colour vision. In: P. Gouras (Ed.), *The Neural Basis of Visual Function,* Macmillan Press, London, pp. 316 – 338.

Dreher, B., Fukuda, Y. and Rodieck, R.W. (1976) Identification, classification and anatomical segregation of cells with X-like and Y-like properties in the lateral geniculate nucleus of Old World primates. *J. Physiol. (Lond).*, 258: 433 – 453.

Enroth-Cugell, C. and Robson, J.G. (1966) The contrast sensitivity of retinal ganglion cells in the cat. *J. Physiol. (Lond.)*, 187: 517 – 552.

Gouras, P. (Ed.) (1991) *The Perception of Colour,* Macmillan Press, London.

Hawken, M.J. and Parker, A.J. (1987) Spatial properties of neurons in the monkey striate cortex. *Proc. R. Soc. Lond.*

(Biol.), 231: 251–288.

Hicks, T.P., Lee, B.B. and Vidyasagar, T.R. (1983) The responses of cells in macaque lateral geniculate nucleus to sinusoidal gratings. *J. Physiol. (Lond.),* 337: 183–200.

Hubel, D.H. and Wiesel, T.N. (1968) Receptive fields and functional architecture of monkey striate cortex. *J. Physiol. (Lond.),* 195: 215–243.

Kaiser, P. (1991) Flicker as a function of wavelength and heterochromatic flicker photometry. In: J.J. Kulikowski, V. Walsh and I.J. Murray (Eds.), *Limits of Vision,* Macmillan Press, London, pp. 171–190.

Kaplan, E. and Shapley, R.M. (1982) X and Y cells in the lateral geniculate nucleus of macaque monkeys. *J. Physiol. (Lond.),* 330: 125–144.

King-Smith, P.E. and Carden, D. (1976) Luminance and opponent colour contributions to visual detection and adaptation and to temporal and spatial integration. *J. Opt. Soc. Am.,* 66: 69–70.

Kranda, K. and Jobert, M. (1989) Spatial sources of electrophysiological activity generated by fine pattern stimulation. In: J.J. Kulikowski, C.M. Dickinson and I.J. Murray (Eds.), *Seeing Contour and Colour,* Pergamon, Oxford, pp. 485–496.

Kulikowski, J.J. (1978) Pattern and movement detection in man and rabbit: separation and comparison of occipital potentials. *Vision Res.,* 18: 183–189.

Kulikowski, J.J. (1991a) On the nature of visual evoked potentials, unit responses and psychophysics. In: A. Valberg and B.B. Lee (Eds.), *From Pigments to Perception,* Plenum Press, New York, pp. 197–208.

Kulikowski, J.J. (1991b) What really limits vision? Conceptual limitations to the assessment of visual function and the role of interacting channels. In: J.J. Kulikowski, V. Walsh and I.J. Murray (Eds.), *Limits of Vision.* Macmillan Press, London.

Kulikowski, J.J. and Carden, D. (1989) Scalp visual evoked potentials to chromatic and achromatic gratings in macaques with ablated visual area V4. In: J.J. Kulikowski, I.J. Murray and C.M. Dickinson (Eds.), *Seeing Contour and Colour,* Pergamon, Oxford, pp. 586–590.

Kulikowski, J.J. and Leisman, G. (1973) The effect of nitrous oxide on the relation between the evoked potential and contrast threshold. *Vision Res.,* 13: 2079–2086.

Kulikowski, J.J. and Murray, I.J. (1988) Occipital potentials evoked by chromatic and achromatic gratings in sedated macaques. *J. Physiol. (Lond.),* 399: 87P.

Kulikowski, J.J. and Tolhurst, D.J. (1973) Psychophysical evidence for sustained and transient detectors in human vision. *J. Physiol. (Lond.),* 232: 149–162.

Kulikowski, J.J. and Vidyasagar, T.R. (1984) Macaque striate cortex: pattern, movement and colour processing. *Ophthalmol. Physiol. Optics,* 4: 77–81.

Kulikowski, J.J. and Vidyasagar, T.R. (1986) Space and spatial frequency: analysis and representation in the macaque striate cortex. *Exp. Brain Res.,* 64: 5–18.

Kulikowski, J.J., Dickinson, C.M. and Murray I.J. (Eds.) (1989b) *Seeing Contour and Colour,* Pergamon, Oxford, pp. 586–590.

Kulikowski, J.J., Murray, I.J. and Parry, N.R.A. (1989a) Electrophysiological correlates of chromatic-opponent and achromatic stimulation in man. In: G. Verriest and B. Drum (Eds.), *Colour Vision Deficiencies IX,* Kluwer, Dordrecht, pp. 145–153.

Kulikowski, J.J., Vidyasagar, T.R. and Carden, D. (1989c) Linear/non-linear analysis of chromatic and achromatic information. In: J.J. Kulikowski, C.M. Dickinson and I.J. Murray (Eds.), *Seeing Contour and Colour,* Pergamon, Oxford, pp. 85–100.

Kulikowski, J.J., Walsh, V. and Murray, I.J. (Eds.) (1991) *Limits of Vision,* Macmillan Press, London.

Kulikowski, J., Walsh, V., McKeefry, D., Butler, S.R. and Carden, D. (1992) Electrophysiological correlates of colour vision in normal and V4 lesioned monkeys. *Perception,* 21: 63.

Lee, B.B. (1991) Spectral sensitivity in primate vision. In: J.J. Kulikowski, V. Walsh and I.J. Murray. (Eds.), *Limits of Vision,* MacMillan, London, pp. 191–201.

Lee, B.B., Martin, P.R. and Valberg, A. (1989a) Sensitivity of macaque retinal ganglion cells to chromatic and luminance flicker. *J. Physiol. (Lond.),* 414: 223–244.

Lee, B.B., Martin, P.R. and Valberg, A. (1989b) Nonlinear summation of M- and L-cone inputs to phasic retinal ganglion cells of the macaque. *J. Neurosci.,* 9: 1433–1442.

Lennie, P., Krauskopf, J. and Sclar, G. (1990) Chromatic mechanisms in striate cortex of macaque. *J. Neurosci.,* 10: 649–669.

Livingstone, M.S. and Hubel, D.H. (1987) Psychophysical evidence for separate channels for perception of form, color, movement and depth. *J. Neurosci.,* 7: 3416–3466.

Mullen, K.T. (1985) The contrast sensitivity of human colour vision to red-green and blue-yellow chromatic gratings. *J. Physiol. (Lond.),* 359: 381–409.

Mullen, K.T. (1987) The spatial influences on colour opponent contributions to pattern detection. *Vision Res.,* 27: 829–839.

Mullen, K.T. and Kulikowski, J.J. (1990) Wavelength discrimination at detection threshold. *J. Opt. Soc. Am. A,* 7: 733–742.

Murray, I.J. and Parry, N.R.A. (1989) Generating VEPs specific to parvo and magno pathways in humans. In: J.J. Kulikowski, C.M. Dickinson and I.J. Murray (Eds.), *Seeing Contour and Colour,* Pergamon, Oxford, pp. 467–473.

Murray, I.J., Parry, N.R.A., Carden, D. and Kulikowski, J.J. (1987) Human visual evoked potentials to chromatic and achromatic gratings. *Clin. Vision Sci.,* 1: 231–244.

Russell, M.H.A., Kulikowski, J.J. and Murray, I.J. (1987) Spatial frequency dependence of the human VEP. In: C. Barber and T. Blum, *Evoked Potentials III.* Butterworths, New York, pp. 231–239.

Sandell, J.H., Gross, C.G. and Bornstein, M.H. (1979) Color categories in macaques. *J. Comp. Physiol and Psychol.,* 93:

626 – 635.

Sperling, H.G. and Harwerth, R.S. (1971) Red-green cone interactions in the increment-threshold spectral sensitivity of primates. *Science,* 172: 180 – 184.

Thorell, L.G., De Valois, R.L. and Albrecht, D.G. (1984) Spatial mapping of monkey V1 cells with pure colour and luminance stimuli. *Vision Res.,* 24: 751 – 769.

Tootell, R.B.H., Hamilton, S.L. and Switkes, E. (1988) Functional anatomy of macaque striate cortex. IV. Contrast and magno-parvo streams. *J. Neurosci.,* 8: 1594 – 1609.

Ts'o, D.Y. and Gilbert, C.D. (1988) The organization of chromatic and spatial interactions in the primate striate cortex. *J. Neurosci.,* 8: 1712 – 1727.

Valberg, A. and Lee, B.B. (Eds.) (1991), *From Pigments to Perception,* Plenum Press, New York.

Vautin, R.G. and Dow, B.M. (1985) Color cell groups in foveal striate of the behaving macaque. *J. Neurophysiol.,* 54:

273 – 292.

Walsh, V., Kulikowski, J., Butler, S. and Carden, D. (1992) The effects of V4 lesions on the visual abilities of macaques: colour categorization. *Behav. Brain Res.,* in press.

Wiesel, T.N. and Hubel, D.H. (1966) Spatial and chromatic interactions in the lateral geniculate body of the rhesus monkey. *J. Neurophysiol.,* 29: 1115 – 1156.

Wild, H.M., Butler, S.R., Carden, D. and Kulikowski, J.J. (1985) Primate cortical visual area V4 important for colour constancy but not wavelength discrimination. *Nature,* 313: 133 – 135.

Zeki, S.M. (1980) The representation of colours in the cerebral cortex. *Nature,* 284: 412 – 418.

Zeki, S. and Shipp, S. (1988) The functional logic of cortical connections. *Nature,* 335: 311 – 317.

Zrenner, E. (1983) *Neurophysiological Aspects of Color Vision in Primates,* Springer, Berlin.

T.P. Hicks, S. Molotchnikoff and T. Ono (Eds.)
Progress in Brain Research, Vol. 95
© 1993 Elsevier Science Publishers B.V. All rights reserved.

CHAPTER 35

Responses of monkey infero-temporal units in an orientation discrimination task

Rufin Vogels and Guy A. Orban

Laboratory of Neuro- and Psychophysiology, Faculty of Medicine, Catholic University Louvain, B-3000 Louvain, Belgium

Introduction

Vision provides animals with information about the lay-out of surfaces and objects in the physical world which is very important for locomotion and navigation in the world. However, visual information also is very useful in controlling adaptive behavior towards objects and other animals. In primates most of these visual discriminations are learned, i.e., the relationship between particular stimuli and behavior strongly depends on reinforcement contingencies. As such, visual discrimination behavior is not only determined by visual capacities, but also by learning and memory factors, i.e., the more cognitive capacities of the animal. It follows that the study of visual discriminations can lead to an understanding of these higher processes. In fact, a full understanding of even simple visual discriminations requires not only knowledge about sensory processing but also about these higher order factors that link the output of the early sensorial stimulus processing to the final behavioral outcome.

In order to gain understanding of the neural processes involved in visual discriminations we feel one has to follow two principles. Firstly, it is important to simplify the stimulus as much as possible. The use of simple stimuli makes it easier to determine which visual cue is controlling the behavior and the neural responses. In fact, only if one knows which visual cue is controlling the discrimination behavior one will be able to understand the cellular response prop-

erties in the context of the discrimination task. For instance, if the stimulus varies in only one dimension, one can easily determine quantitatively how well single cells are sensitive to this stimulus dimension in the context of the discrimination task.

Secondly, if one wants to understand visual discriminations it is important to appreciate that the underlying processes may well depend on the particular discrimination tasks that one uses. This is particularly important if one is interested in processes of a higher order than early visual processing. In neurobiological studies on visual discrimination thresholds one usually takes a lot of care about the stimulus but much less about the task and its implications for the processing of the sensory information. However, as already pointed out, a full understanding of a visual discrimination process also requires an understanding of the task-related processes. We will illustrate this point with an example from human psychophysics. Just noticeable differences in bar orientation can be measured with a variety of procedures ranging from orientation identification using the method of single stimuli to temporal two-alternative-forced choice methods (Vogels and Orban, 1986). The differential thresholds one obtains depend on the method one uses to measure them (Vogels and Orban, 1986), which implies that the processes underlying these tasks may well be different. In fact relatively complex mathematical formalizations about "decision processes" have been built to explain these task-

428

dependent differences in performance (e.g., Green and Swets, 1966; Johnson, 1980; Vogels and Orban, 1986). We will show that also in the monkey the performance in discrimination tasks depends on the task requirements. Hence, a careful analysis of the computational requirements of the particular discrimination task is as important as a careful analysis of the stimulus.

We measured the responses of infero-temporal (IT) single units while the monkey was performing a same-different orientation discrimination task. The stimulus and task we have chosen are inspired by the two principles we outlined above. The stimuli were square wave gratings of which the orientation served as discriminandum. We used gratings instead of a single line since with the latter stimulus one cannot be certain that only orientation is the cue controlling the behavior, i.e., changes in the orientation of a line necessarily covary with variations of the position of the endpoints. However, by randomizing across trials the phase of the square wave modulation of a grating the only cue remaining is its orientation.

The task we used is the Konorski same-different task (Konorski, 1959). In this task two stimuli are presented in succession and the monkey has to indicate whether or not the second one (S2) is the same as the first one (S1), i.e., whether or not the second grating has the same orientation as the first one. The orientation of the first grating randomly varies over trials so that the monkey is forced to compare the orientation of S2 to that of S1. This is an important point since it is the main distinction between this task and a simple discrimination task. In the latter task one stimulus, the positive one, is associated with a reward, while the other, the negative one, is not. In the Konorski task, the relationship between the stimuli (sameness or differentness) and not a particular stimulus is associated with the reward. Hence, the Konorski task requires more processing than a simple discrimination task and thus provides more opportunity to study task-related effects on neural responses. There also was a more practical reason to choose the Konorski task instead of a simple discrimination task. In the latter task one is

limited in the number of stimulus orientations one can use as discriminanda during a test, since the monkey is capable of learning only a few such orientations as positive stimuli concurrently. However, in a Konorski task one can use the full range of orientations since the reference stimulus may vary from trial to trial. This enables one to measure the tuning of single cells to the orientation of, e.g., S1 during orientation discrimination. Finally it should be noted that − in contrast to the in lesion studies frequently used matching to sample tasks − only one stimulus is presented at a given moment in this Konorski task, which makes it a lot easier to interpret the single cell responses.

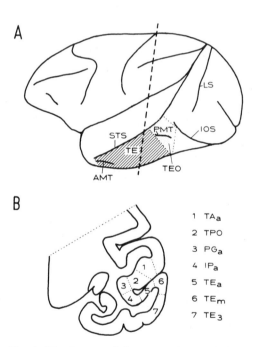

Fig. 1. Visual areas of the temporal cortex of the macaque monkey. A. Schematic lateral view of the cortex of the macaque. The borders of areas TE and TEO are based on Iwai and Mishkin (1969) and Boussaoud et al. (1991). These are only approximations since there is a large inter-animal variability. The stippled line indicates the section shown in B. Abbreviations of sulci: AMT, anterior middle temporal sulcus; IOS, inferior occipital sulcus; LS, lunate sulcus; PMT, posterior middle temporal sulcus; STS, superior temporal sulcus. B. Section showing the different areas of the superior temporal sulcus (according to Seltzer and Pandya, 1978) and area TE3.

While the monkey was performing this Konorski task we recorded single units of its infero-temporal cortex. Infero-temporal cortex is a relatively large region of the temporal lobe of the macaque brain, consisting of several distinct areas (Fig. 1): area TEO (Iwai and Mishkin, 1969; Boussaoud et al., 1991), the cytoarchitectonically defined area TE (von Bonin and Bailey, 1947; Iwai and Mishkin, 1969) and several other distinct areas confined within the superior temporal sulcus (STS, Seltzer and Pandya, 1978). The areas of the fundus and upper bank of the STS are multimodal (Bruce et al., 1981; Baylis et al., 1987), while those of the lower bank of the STS, i.e., areas TEa and TEm, and of the inferior temporal convexity, i.e., areas TE3, TE2, TE1 and TEO, are primarily visual (Gross et al., 1972; Baylis et al., 1987). In fact, area TE is the last unimodal visual area in the hierarchy of those visual areas that are part of the ventral stream thought to be involved in pattern vision, color vision and object recognition (Ungerleider and Mishkin, 1982; Maunsell and Newsome, 1987). Area TE receives its primary source of visual input from areas V4 and TEO (Desimone et al., 1980; Morel and Bullier, 1990; Baizer et al., 1991). Area TE is known to project, amongst other targets, to the polymodal areas of the STS (Seltzer and Pandya, 1978; Baizer et al., 1991), to the polymodal temporal pole (Seltzer and Pandya 1978; Moran et al., 1987), perirhinal cortical area 35 (Van Hoesen and Pandya, 1975; Webster et al., 1991), frontal cortices (Kuypers et al., 1965; Seltzer and Pandya, 1989; Ungerleider et al., 1989), the striatum (Van Hoesen et al., 1981), and amygdala (Iwai and Yukie, 1987). Given the fact that it receives projections from, e.g., parahippocampal and perirhinal cortex (Van Hoesen and Pandya, 1975; Webster et al., 1991), amygdala (Iwai and Yukie, 1987), frontal cortex (Seltzer and Pandya, 1989) and the pulvinar nuclei (Chow, 1950; Yeterian and Pandya, 1989), area TE is a good candidate to look for task-related coding of visual stimuli.

Previous research of response properties of TE neurons showed that their receptive fields are fairly large, usually bilateral and encompassing the fovea (Gross et al., 1972). Furthermore several studies investigating the receptive field selectivities of TE cells found that these neurons show shape selectivity and usually respond to much more complex stimuli than do cells in lower visual areas such as V1 and V2 (Gross et al., 1972; Desimone et al., 1984). These studies were carried out in the paralyzed and anesthetized monkey. On the other hand, studies addressing the influence of attentional factors on the responses of IT cells (e.g., Richmond et al., 1983; Moran and Desimone, 1985; Sato, 1988) use simple bars as stimuli and usually report strong responses to these simple stimuli in these behaving monkeys. In the latter studies, however, only a few stimuli are repeatedly used, and no estimate of the coding (or representation) abilities of these cells in the context of the behavioral task was obtained.

In contrast, by determining quantitatively the cells' responses to the orientation of a grating in the context of a complex task, we are able to provide an estimate of the coding (or representation) abilities of single TE cells in the context of this task. The use of the temporal same-different task further enables us to determine the contribution of non-physical task-related factors to the responses of these neurons.

In the present paper we will, after reporting some behavioral data on the temporal same-different task, describe the kind of IT unit response patterns one obtains in this behavioral paradigm. Furthermore, we will report on the sensitivity for the orientation of the grating stimulus in this task. A detailed analysis of the task-related properties of the cells shall be deferred to a forthcoming report.

Methods

Subjects

Subjects were two juvenile male rhesus monkeys, Ronnie and Adam. Ronnie had a long training history in orientation discrimination and participated in V1 recordings before the present experiment (see Vogels and Orban, 1990a, 1991). At the end of the IT recordings he was killed with an overdose of nembutal and perfused with buffered formaldehyde. Adam, who was older than Ronnie at the start of the experiment, received less extensive training than Ronnie. At the time of writing, Adam is still participating in experiments.

Recordings of the monkeys were made 5 days/week for about 3 – 5 h/day. Both monkeys were water-deprived during the experiment, i.e., they recieved dry food, which was supplemented by fruit and water during the weekend only.

Apparatus and set-up

These are similar to the one used in our previous study of area V1 responses in this task (Vogels and Orban, 1990a, 1991) and hence will only be summarized.

Square wave gratings were generated on a CRT screen by an Innisfree Picasso which was driven by a PDP11/73 microcomputer. A LED served as fixation spot and was placed laterally to the masked CRT screen. The stimulus diameter was 12°. The contrast was 80% and the fundamental spatial frequency 2 c/deg. The luminance of the display was 7 cd/m^2. The monkey and display were in a darkened separate room.

The monkey was seated in a primate chair with his head fixed by means of a head-holder cemented to the skull. Apple juice was delivered to the monkey's mouth by means of a tube connected to a solenoid of which the opening was controlled by the PDP11/73.

Eye movements were recorded by means of the scleral search coil technique. The PDP11/73 sampled and displayed the eye movements (200 Hz resolution), and compared the eye position to electronic windows set around the fixation spot and grating.

Single and multi-unit activities were recorded by means of glass-coated metal electrodes. In the early recordings of Ronnie we used elgiloy electrodes, but all other recordings were done by tungsten electrodes. No differences were noted between the two types of electrodes.

The electrode was lowered through a stainless steel guiding tube. The starting position of the electrode was 3 mm below the tip of the guiding tube, which was positioned just below the dura mater. The positioning of the guiding tube and microelectrode was done by means of a Narishige hydraulic microdrive put on top of the recording chamber. The signal from the electrode was amplified, bandpass-filtered and fed to a window discriminator and oscilloscope for monitoring. Triggered spikes were sampled by the PDP11/73 (resolution 1000 Hz) and displayed on-line in raster histograms. The unit activity together with behavioral events were saved by the computer for later off-line analysis.

Surgery

All surgery was done under ketamine anesthesia and full sterile conditions. Before training the monkeys received a scleral eye coil and head-holder. Monkey Ronnie also had a chamber implanted on the occipital lobe for area V1 recordings.

After training in the behavioral task, we implanted on the left hemisphere a recording chamber lateral to the midline centered 1 cm (Ronnie) or 1.5 cm (Adam) anterior to the auditory meatus. The chamber was tilted with respect to the temporal bone, so that we could penetrate the temporal cortex below the STS, while the guiding tube remained above the cortex of interest. This still needs histological verification in the case of monkey Adam, but worked as expected in case of Ronnie.

In order to cement the chamber to the skull, part of the temporal muscles were removed. However, the monkeys had no problems chewing or drinking. The recordings were started 2 weeks after the chamber implantation. By that time the monkeys were fully recovered from the operation.

Behavioral task (Fig. 2)

The start of a trial was marked by the onset of the fixation spot. After 1000 msec continuous fixation of this spot, a grating (S1) was presented for 350 msec in the right visual field at a eccentricity of 6.5°. After an inter-stimulus interval that could range from 300 to 800 msec a second grating (S2) was presented at the same position as S1. The monkey then had to decide whether or not S2 had the same orientation as S1 within a time period of 500 msec (Ronnie) of 600 msec (Adam). If the two gratings

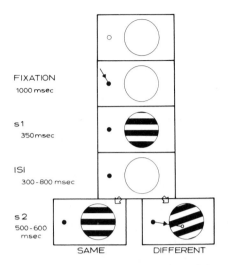

Fig. 2. The orientation Konorski task. A trial starts with the onset of the fixation spot (upper panel). When the monkey fixates the spot (second panel), a stimulus is presented after 1000 msec of fixation. This grating, S1, is shown for 350 msec (third panel) followed by an inter-stimulus interval ranging between 300 and 800 msec (fourth panel). Then a second grating (S2) is presented at the same position as S1. If S2 has the same orientation as S1 (lower left) the monkey has to continue fixating the spot for 500 – 600 msec. If S2 has a different orientation than S1 (lower right), the monkey has to make a saccadic eye movement to the grating.

ski task and then changed to measuring his orientation discrimination thresholds with a task in which the orientation of S1 did not change during a session. Then he was fully trained in the Konorski task, and this for different stimulus diameters, stimulus contrasts and positions. Monkey Adam on the other hand started with the threshold measurements in the task in which S1 was fixed during a session. Then he was trained for the Konorski task. This went very slowly probably because he had learned to ignore S1 during the threshold determination sessions. Also,

Konorski Task

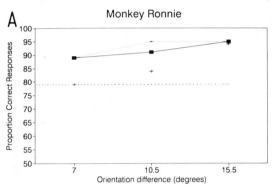

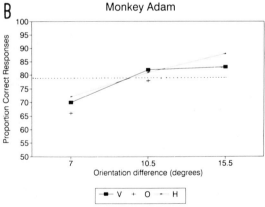

Fig. 3. Behavioral performance of the monkeys Ronnie (*A*) and Adam (*B*) in the orientation Konorski task. The mean proportion of correct responses is shown as a function of the orientation difference between S1 and S2 for three different orientations of S1. The dotted line indicates the 79% correct level, the criterion used in the threshold determinations (Fig. 4). Abbreviations: V, vertical S1 orientation; H, horizontal S1 orientation; O, oblique (45°) S1 orientation.

differed in orientation the monkey had to make a saccadic eye movement to the position of the grating within that time period. If the orientations were the same he had to continue fixation until the stimulus had disappeared. Correct responses were rewarded with drops of apple juice. No punishment in case of errors was given.

The orientation of S1 was randomly varied over trials. Each cell was tested with a standard test in which 6 (monkey Ronnie) or 7 (monkey Adam) equally spaced S1 orientations, spanning the full 180° range, were used. The orientation difference between S1 and S2 was set at 15°. The inter-stimulus interval was 300 msec. After this standard test, we occasionally tested the cell for other settings of the stimulus parameters or longer inter-stimulus intervals.

The training histories of the monkeys were very different. With Ronnie, we started with the Konor-

for his training in the Konorski task only the standard stimulus parameters were used.

During practice and the threshold determination sessions, the phase of the grating was randomized over trials. However, during the single cell recordings the phase was fixed within a single session.

Results

Behavioral data

Both monkeys had been trained for several months in the Konorski orientation discrimination task before the recordings were started. In Fig. 3 we show the proportion of correct responses as a function of the orientation difference between S1 and S2. The results are plotted for three different S1 orientations. Each curve is based on at least 600 trials. These performance levels are representative for those present during the recording sessions. Both monkeys perform rather well for a difference of 15°: the proportion of correct responses is above 85%. Monkey Ronnie's performance remains at this level for at least a difference of 7°, the smallest one tested under these conditions. For the oblique reference orientation the performance is worse at smaller

Orientation Thresholds
S1 Fixed

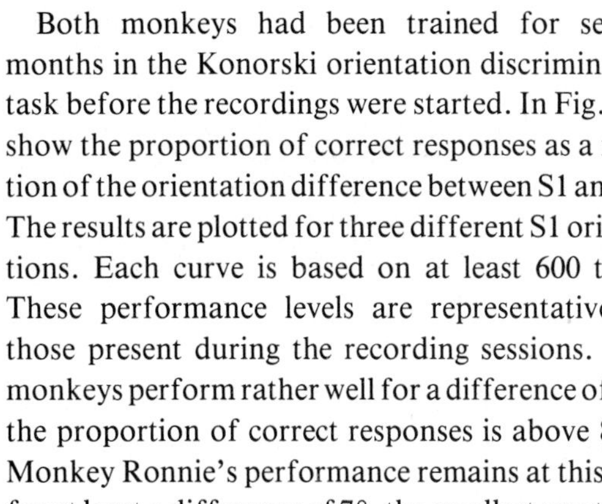

Fig. 4. Mean just noticeable differences in orientation as a function of the orientation of S1 for monkeys Ronnie and Adam. These threshold determinations were done using a task in which S1 was fixed during the sessions. Abbreviations: HOR, horizontal reference orientation; OBL, oblique (45°) reference orientation; VER, vertical reference orientation.

orientation differences. Monkey Adam in contrast performs much worse: at all orientations tested his performance drops steeply when decreasing the orientation difference.

Using the data shown in Fig. 3 one obtains 79% correct orientation discrimination thresholds of 10° and 7° for monkeys Adam and Ronnie (oblique reference orientation only), respectively. These results seem to suggest that the sensorial orientation discrimination capacity of monkeys is much worse than that of humans, which have on average just noticeable differences (jnds) in orientation of less than 3° (Vogels et al., 1984). However, in monkeys the orientation discrimination performance depends strongly on the task. In fact, monkey jnds in orientation, measured using the same stimuli as in the Konorski task, can be as low as 2°. Fig. 4 shows the jnds in orientation obtained in monkeys Adam and Ronnie more than a year before the data of Fig. 3 were gathered. These jnds were determined using a staircase method that converges at 79% correct (see Vogels and Orban, 1990a,b, for details). The only other and critical difference between the testing procedures of Fig. 3 and Fig. 4 is that during the determination of the jnds of Fig. 4 the orientation of S1 did not change during a test session. In the latter case the monkey is not forced to compare S2 to S1, i.e., a paired comparison strategy, but can solve the discrimination problem by just responding to changes in the orientation of S2, i.e., an identification strategy (see Vogels and Orban, 1986). Comparing the results obtained by Adam in the two procedures clearly indicates the difficulty this monkey had with the Konorski task: his "thresholds" in the Konorski procedure are about five times larger than those obtained with the fixed S1 procedure using the same stimuli. It should be stressed that 11 months of daily practice in the Konorski task elapsed between the two measurements. For Ronnie the difference between the two procedures cannot be appreciated very well given his relatively good performance at the smallest orientation difference used in the Konorski task. However, at the oblique reference orientation his performance in the Konorski task (Fig. 3) is much worse (7°) than expected from his

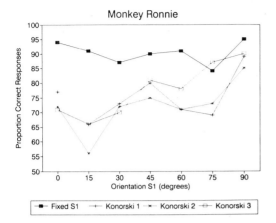

Fig. 5. The behavioral performance in the task in which S1 was fixed in the sessions (thick full line) compared to the performance in the orientation Konorski task (thin lines). In the orientation Konorski task the orientation of S1 was randomly varied over trials. The results of three different daily sessions of the Konorski task, obtained during 1 week, are shown. The orientation difference between S1 and S2 was 6°.

low jnd in orientation (1.5°) obtained in the task in which S1 was fixed in a session (see Fig. 4), confirming the observations made in Adam.

Another set of data obtained from Ronnie confirm the notion that the orientation Konorski task is more difficult than a simple orientation discrimination task. In the course of measuring his jnds in orientation with fixed S1 orientation, we repeatedly measured his performance for an orientation difference of 6° using the same task. The results of these measurements are shown by the full line in Fig. 5. Note that as expected from his low jnds in orientation (Fig. 4), his performance level was very good: on average 90% correct. Then, we started to retrain him in the Konorski task using an increasingly larger number of intermixed S1 orientations. After 1 month of this training we measured his performance for an orientation difference of 6°, but now with the same 7 S1 orientations randomly intermixed within a session, i.e., a Konorski task. The results of three of such measurements are shown by the other curves in Fig. 5. Each curve represents one daily measurement, obtained at the beginning, mid and end of a 1 week period. It is clear that even after 1 month of practice in the Konorski task, the performance level

was on average much below that obtained before in the task in which S1 was fixed. The difference in performance level between the two tasks was stable during at least 1 week of testing. At the horizontal reference orientation (90° in Fig. 4) the difference in performance between both types of tasks was very small. This may be due to the fact that in case of a different trial S2 was larger than 90°, i.e., 96° and hence outside the range of the S1 orientations. Hence, presentation of the 96° S2 orientation could readily lead to a correct response even when ignoring S1. However, it cannot be excluded that for some other, unknown, reason this monkey simply performed much better at the horizontal reference orientation in the Konorski task.

Nevertheless, these results clearly show that randomly intermixing S1 orientations and/or forcing the monkey to compare S2 to S1 leads to a dramatic reduction in average performance level. These results also explain why we used the relatively large orientation difference of 15° in the standard Konorski task during the recording sessions.

Inspection of Figs. 3 and 4 clearly shows that the overall performance level of monkey Ronnie was much better than that of monkey Adam. Not only was Ronnie more accurate in his orientation judgments than Adam, he was also much faster: average saccadic response latencies were 211 and 418 msec for monkeys Ronnie and Adam, respectively.

Unit recording data

We recorded from 489 units in 59 penetrations of IT cortex of Ronnie and we will report on the data of 469 units recorded from 37 penetrations in monkey Adam. The histology from Ronnie indicates that we recorded from the posterior part of area TE bordering anterior TEO. In some penetrations recordings may have been made from area TEm (see Fig. 1). We do not yet have histology from monkey Adam since he is still alive at the time of this writing. However, the position of his recording chamber suggests that on average the penetrations are more anterior into TE than in the case of Ronnie.

Several types of responses were encountered during the recordings while the monkey was performing the Konorski task. Some cells responded well to the presentation of the grating, but the activity of a number of cells was also affected by the monkey fixating the spot prior to the grating presentation.

We tested the significance of an excitatory response to the grating stimulus using the non-parametric Kolmogorov-Smirnov test (Siegel, 1956). With this test we compared the cumulative distribution of spike frequency for two bins of 350 msec. One 350 msec bin started 80 msec after stimulus presentation and the other one ended 80 msec after stimulus presentation. Cells for which this test was significant at at least the 0.05 significance level, were taken as grating responsive cells. We did not use a similar test to check the responses during the onset of fixation, since the latter ones were not always that well time-locked to the entrance of the monkey's eye into the fixation window. Indeed in some cells these reponses could occur prior to the fixation of the spot, just when the monkey was in the neighborhood of the fixation spot or illuminated CRT screen. Hence the presence of a response to fixation onset was judged by inspecting the post-stimulus time histograms. The same was done for inhibitory responses, for which the Kolmogorov-Smirnov test was judged to be not powerful enough.

One can roughly classify the cells according to whether or not they responded during fixation and/or during grating presentation. Furthermore one can distinguish between excitation and inhibition of the cell's response yielding three response modes: inhibition, no response and excitatory response. The proportion of cells belonging to the resulting nine categories are listed in Tables I and II for Adam and Ronnie, respectively.

It is immediately clear that the most frequently encountered category is the completely unresponsive one. Many of these unresponsive cells had a very low response rate, fired occasionally a few spikes but totally unrelated to the task or stimulus. About 50% of the other cells showed activity related to some phases of the task.

About one third of the cells responded by excitation or inhibition when the monkey fixated the LED. Fig. 6A shows such a cell that responded when the monkey entered the fixation window. It fired as long as the trial lasted, while others, like the one in Fig. 6B responded more transiently to the onset of fixation by the monkey. Others were completely inhibited during fixation (Fig. 6C). Of those cells that responded, more were excited than inhibited in this phase of the task (see Tables I and II).

About one third of the cells responded by excitation or inhibition to the grating. This is a large figure given the simplicity of the stimulus (see Discussion). Some of these cells gave vigorous sustained responses to the grating (Fig. 7A), while others responded more transiently (Fig. 7B). About one fifth of the single cells of our sample responded by

TABLE I

Proportion of cells in monkey Adam

Fixation	Grating			
	Inhibition	No response	Excitation	Total
Inhibition	1 (1)	4 (2)	3 (9)	8 (13)
No response	3 (2)	59 (16)	9 (25)	71 (44)
Excitation	7 (7)	7 (13)	8 (23)	22 (43)
Total	11 (11)	70 (31)	20 (57)	

Note: proportions of multi-unit responses ($n = 138$) are given in brackets next to the proportions for the single unit responses ($n = 469$).

TABLE II

Proportion of cells in monkey Ronnie

Fixation	Grating			
	Inhibition	No response	Excitation	Total
Inhibition	2 (3)	4 (4)	6 (13)	12 (20)
No response	2 (4)	43 (18)	14 (25)	59 (48)
Excitation	9 (6)	16 (25)	4 (10)	29 (32)
Total	13 (14)	63 (37)	24 (49)	

Note: proportions of multi-unit responses ($n = 254$) are given in brackets next to the proportion for the single unit responses ($n = 489$).

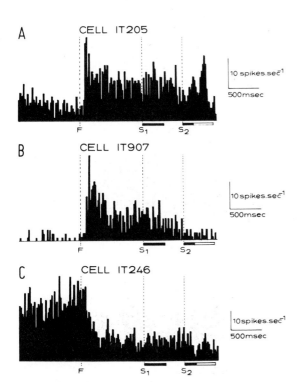

Fig. 6. Responses of three IT single units during fixation. On each histogram, F, S1 and S2 mark the onset of the fixation, S1 stimulus and S2 stimulus, respectively. The presentation of the stimuli are indicated by the horizontal filled bars. Since the end of the presentation of S2 was controlled by the monkey's saccades, the duration of S2 was variable as indicated by the partly filled bar. However, only those trials in which the saccadic response latency was longer than 180 msec were pooled. Binwidth is 20 msec.

excitation to the grating stimulus. However, about one third of the cells that responded to the grating were inhibited by it. An example of such a cell that was strongly inhibited by the grating presentation is shown in Fig. 7C. Cells activated by the grating were usually clustered together. In these cases the background "hush" responded strongly to the grating presentations. It was remarkable that these cells were usually present in a region in which the cells were difficult to discriminate and the background very active. Furthermore it should be noted that, nonetheless, neighboring cells, like two or more units recorded simultaneously with one electrode, could have dramatic different properties. For instance, usually a big spike would be totally unresponsive while a few simultaneously recordable smaller spikes would strongly respond to the grating. The median average firing rate of the (excitatory) grating responses was 22 spikes/sec (first quartile: 14 spikes/sec; third quartile: 42 spikes/sec). The median response latency was 110 msec (first quartile: 90 msec; third quartile: 150 msec).

One fifth of all single units we recorded responded both during the fixation interval and to the grating pattern. Examples of such cells are shown in Fig. 8. Some cells (Fig. 8A for an example) responded to the onset of fixation and to the grating. It should be noted that for some cells the usually transient "fixa-

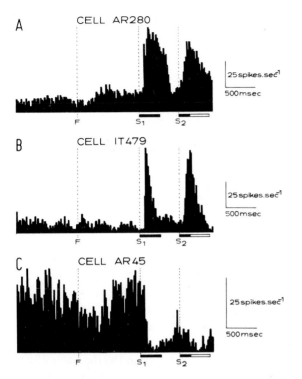

Fig. 7. Responses to the grating stimuli of three IT single units. Conventions are the same as for Fig. 6. The responses of all stimulus conditions are pooled. Hence, in case of orientation-sensitive units, the peak firing rates will be underestimated.

tion response'' was stronger than the response to the grating, while in others the reverse was the case. Other cells were inhibited by the grating but excited by the fixation (see Fig. 8B). A few cells showed transient inhibition during fixation and grating presentation. A more common type of cell was inhibited during the fixation period and responded to the grating. A nice example of the latter type is shown in Fig. 8C.

We also recorded multi-unit responses usually consisting of clusters of a few difficult to discriminate cells. The incidence of the different ''types'' of multi-unit responses are given in Tables I and II by the numbers in brackets. The main difference between the results of the single unit and multi-unit recordings was that the proportion of non-responding cells is much less for the multi-unit than for the single unit recordings. This difference

can be explained by the combination of two factors. Firstly, as already noted, many units responding to the gratings, and to the fixation also, were located in a very active region (layer?) in which the cells were usually difficult to discriminate. Secondly, when several cells were present simultaneously, the largest and most easily discriminable one was usually the one that did not respond. These two factors in combination explain at least partially the strong bias for responsive cells in the multi-unit sample compared to the single unit sample. It should also be noted that relatively more units were excited than inhibited by the grating pattern in the multi-unit sample compared to the single unit sample.

A comparison of Tables I and II learns that the proportions of the cell types were different between the two monkeys. In monkey Ronnie 83% of the cells that responded by excitation to the grating either did not respond or were inhibited during fixation. Also, 86% of the cells that responded with ex-

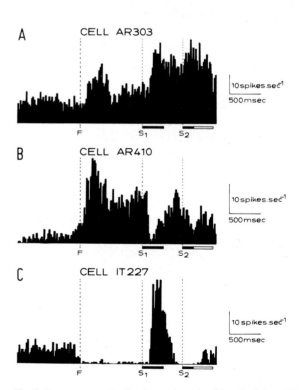

Fig. 8. Responses to the fixation and grating stimuli of three IT single units. Conventions are the same as in Figs. 6 and 7.

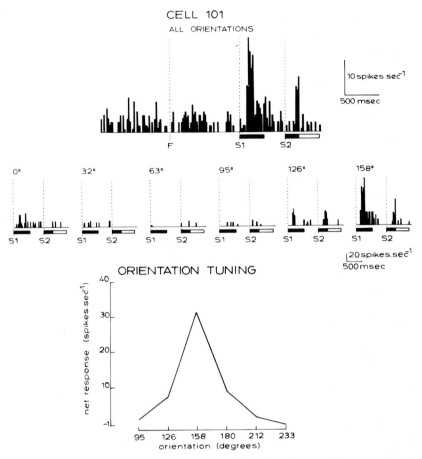

Fig. 9. Example of orientation tuning of an IT single unit. In the upper histogram, the responses to all orientations are pooled. The middle histograms show the responses as a function of the orientation of S1. The orientation of S1 is indicated in degrees at the upper left corner of each histogram. The orientation tuning curve shows the average net response (see text) to S1 as a function of the orientation of S1. The OSI was 0.72.

citation during fixation did not respond to the grating pattern or were inhibited by it. These trends towards selectivity of the responses were much smaller in monkey Adam: 60% of the cells that responded to the grating were not excited during fixation, while 64% of the cells that responded during fixation were not responding or inhibited during grating presentation. These differences between the monkeys was also present for the multi-unit sample, making it a robust finding.

Since our monkeys had to discriminate the orientation of the grating, an important variable to look at is the amount of orientation tuning of the cells

that responded to the grating. For those cells of which we had at least six trials for each stimulus orientation and which showed an excitatory response to the grating we computed the average net response strength by subtracting the average firing rate for a bin of 350 msec that ended at 80 msec after stimulus onset from the average firing rate during a 350 msec bin that started at 80 msec after stimulus onset. This was done for each orientation of S1. An example of this is shown in Fig. 9. This cell responded to the grating but not during fixation prior to the grating onset as shown in the upper histogram. The middle row of histograms displays the responses to

S1 and S2 at each of the 6 S1 orientations that were tested. The computed orientation tuning curve is shown below. Note how well this IT neuron is tuned to the orientation of the grating.

In order to have a quantitative measure of the degree of orientation sensitivity of our cells, we computed for each cell the following orientation sensitivity index (OSI):

$$OSI = \frac{\sqrt{<\Sigma[Ri \times \sin(2 \times Ai)]>^2 + <\Sigma[Ri \times \cos(2 \times Ai)]>^2}}{\Sigma[Ri]}$$

in which Ri is the net response strength at orientation Ai. This OSI index (see Batschelet, 1981, for derivation) takes into account the response strength at all tested orientations which is not the case for instance for more traditional measures of orientation bandwidth such as full width at half height. This OSI index ranges between 0 and 1, with 0 indicating no orientation tuning and 1 indicating a response at one tested orientation only. Fig. 10 shows the distribution of this OSI index for the cells of monkeys Ronnie ($n = 97$) and Adam ($n = 93$). Monkey Ronnie has more narrowly tuned cells than Adam: the median OSI indices are respectively 0.36 (first quartile: 0.22; third quartile: 0.56) and 0.21 (first quartile: 0.11; third quartile: 0.34) for Ronnie and Adam respectively. The difference between the

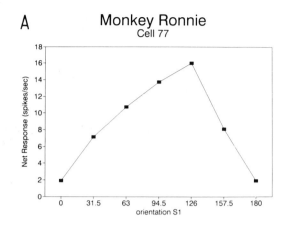

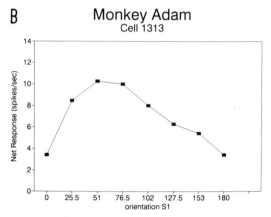

Fig. 11. Orientation tuning curves of IT units that have an OSI similar to the median OSI for monkeys Ronnie (*A*; OSI = 0.36) and Adam (*B*; OSI = 0.20). The net response to S1 is plotted as a function of the orientation of S1.

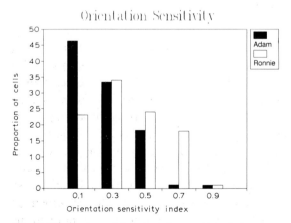

Fig. 10. Distributions of the orientation sensitivity index (see text for derivation) for the IT single units of monkeys Ronnie and Adam. Binwidth is 0.2.

two distributions is highly significant (Mann-Whitney $U = 0.00$; $P < 0.0000001$). In order to be able to appreciate better the meaning of the OSI we show in Fig. 11 the orientation tuning curves of two cells which have OSIs corresponding to the medians of the OSI distribution of each monkey. The "median cell" of Ronnie is much more sensitive for the orientation of the grating than the median cell of monkey Adam.

Finally we determined whether there was any correlation between the presence of a response during fixation and the orientation sensitivity of an unit. One might expect that units responding to the grating but not during fixation are more

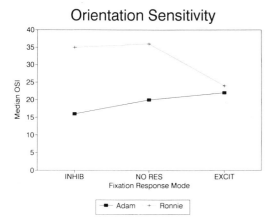

Fig. 12. The median OSI as a function of the fixation response mode for monkeys Ronnie and Adam separately. Abbreviations: INHIB, inhibitory fixation response; NO RES, no response during fixation; EXCIT, excitatory fixation response.

orientation-selective than units that respond to the grating as well as during fixation. This was indeed the case for the sample of Ronnie. In Fig. 12 we show the median OSI as a function of the response mode during fixation. For Ronnie's sample the median OSI was significantly larger for the units for which there was no response or inhibition during fixation than for the units for which there was an excitatory fixation response (Mann-Whitney $U = 485$; $P < 0.0160$). For Adam's sample there was no significant difference between the median OSIs for the different fixation response modes. Note that the median OSI for monkey Adam is similar to the median OSI for those cells of Ronnie that showed an excitatory response to the fixation.

So far we have described the responses of the IT units to the physical attributes of the stimulus. However, we also observed responses that were clearly influenced by non-physical, task-related factors. We will only briefly summarize these findings since they will be the subject of a forthcoming paper. Firstly, we observed in several instances a significant difference in the response to S1 and S2, even on those trials in which they were physically the same. An example of such a cell is shown in Fig. 8C. In this cell the response to S2 is nearly absent despite the strong response to S1. A second observation we

made was that in some cells there was an activity during the ISI that was larger than during the fixation prior to grating onset. A relatively weak example of a cell with such a "delay activity" is the one shown in Fig. 8A. The activity of this cell does not decrease after the offset of S1 to the prestimulus level. In fact during the inter-stimulus interval it keeps on firing, although no stimulus is present. Thirdly, in some cells, especially those of Ronnie, the response of S2 depended on whether or not S2 differed from S1 (Vogels and Orban, 1990b).

Discussion

The results of this investigation shows that in inferotemporal cortex of monkeys trained in a complex behavioral task many cells respond to one or several phases of the task, and are also sensitive to the stimulus dimension that is controlling their behavior. We will discuss each of these points now in detail.

The behavioral results show that the orientation Konorski task is not at all an easy task for monkeys. In fact in both monkeys we found that stimulus orientations which were easy to discriminate were nearly impossible to tell apart by the monkeys in the context of the Konorski task. This difficulty with the Konorski task can be due to two factors: the high number of reference orientations, i.e., different S1 stimuli, presented within a given session and/or the use of a paired comparison strategy. These two factors are highly related since one can only force the animal to use a paired comparison strategy by presenting several reference orientations within a given session.

The good performance in the task in which S1 was fixed and hence the monkey was not forced to compare S2 to S1 suggests that when monkeys are confronted with a task which they can solve by making either a simple discrimination of one stimulus (i.e., an identification strategy) or a temporal comparison of two stimuli (i.e., a paired comparison strategy) they choose for the former. Vandenbussche et al. have made similar observations in the case of velocity discriminations (Vandenbussche, Lauwers and

Orban, unpublished observations). This choice of strategy corresponds to the one that is computationally the simplest. This can be shown by using some recent insights from the neural computing field. Two-layer perceptrons are able to do stimulus categorization analogous to simple discrimination tasks (Rosenblatt, 1958). Indeed it is possible to model orientation discrimination accuracy in a simple orientation discrimination task using just a set of orientation-tuned input units that are properly connected to a set of output units (Orban et al., 1990). However these two-layer perceptrons are very limited with respect to the tasks they can solve (Minsky and Papert, 1969). They cannot perform an "exclusive or" (XOR) logical operation. The latter logical operation is formally identical to a same-different task in which both discriminanda are presented simultaneously. In order to perform such a XOR operation one needs three layers, i.e., an additional layer of "hidden units" connected to the input and output layer (Rumelhart et al., 1986). Our task, a temporal same-different task, is computationally even more complex since one has to bridge the time gap between the stimulus presentations. With simple multilayered neural networks one cannot solve this task. In order to solve the temporal same-different task, one needs architectures that are more complex than for a simple discrimination task.

Relatively many cells responded to the grating stimulus, a simple stimulus for a higher order visual area such as IT. Even 24% of the single units, averaged for the two monkeys, responded differently to the grating than during fixation. It should be stressed that also during fixation the unit is visually stimulated, not only by the small fixation spot but also by the illuminated CRT screen and its borders. Hence, about one quarter of the IT cells responded to a grating pattern and this at least to some degree in a stimulus-selective way.

In the past one has stressed that many IT cells need more complex patterns than, e.g., single bars in order to be activated. Especially the discovery of cells that responded well to such interesting complex stimuli as hands or faces (Bruce et al., 1981; see Desimone, 1991, for a recent review) lead to the no-

tion that many IT cells prefer complex stimuli. Nonetheless, most studies using alert monkeys use rather simple stimuli, such as light spots (e.g., Richmond et al., 1983) or bars (e.g., Richmond and Sato, 1987; Sato, 1988) and find that many cells respond to these simple stimuli. Furthermore, Gross et al. (1979) reported that a majority of the cells they recorded from in a discriminating alert monkey responded to small simple pattern stimuli, but the same stimuli did not elicit any response in the anesthetized and paralyzed preparation. The responses to these simple stimuli may be related to the behavioral significance of the stimulus.

Several studies have looked at the effect of attending to the stimulus on the responses of IT cells. And indeed some studies reported that during pattern discrimination single cells in IT are responding stronger than during pattern detection or during fixation of a spot while ignoring the stimulus pattern (Richmond and Sato, 1987; Spitzer and Richmond, 1991). However, it is not at all clear whether these effects are due to differences in attention or differences in task difficulty (and arousal) per se (Spitzer and Richmond, 1991). Also, in one study responses were observed to decrease during attention to the stimulus (Richmond et al., 1983). The results of these studies, at least those in which only one stimulus, besides the fixation spot, was presented, indicate that attention to the stimulus has not a strong effect on the excitability of IT cells. Hence, there is no convincing evidence for the hypothesis that the responses to these simple stimuli are due to the monkey giving attention to them. However, in all studies that used these simple stimuli with success in IT, the animal was trained to perform one or the other behavioral task with them. Hence, the fact that due to previous training the stimuli became behaviorally significant for the animal may have resulted in the strong responses to these stimuli in many cells. In this sense, the relatively high incidence of responses to more complex patterns or objects such as faces may well be related to the important role that these objects play in the adaptive behavior of the animal, and not to the complexity of the pattern or object per se.

This is the first quantitative study that looked systematically for orientation-tuned responses in the IT cortex of the macaque. The results of previous studies in paralyzed and anesthetized monkeys are ambiguous with respect to orientation tuning in IT: Gross et al. (1972) reported that 40% of the units were orientation-sensitive, while Desimone et al. (1984) reported that unlike striate cortical cells IT cells show little or no orientation selectivity. However, both studies used moving stimuli instead of stationary stimuli to assess orientation selectivity, and neither study gives any information on the degree of orientation sensitivity in IT cortex. We found a broad distribution of the amount of orientation sensitivity in IT cortex ranging from cells responding to only one of the tested orientations to cells responding to all orientations. On average, cells of IT seem to be more broadly tuned than those of V1: in V1 of monkey Ronnie the median width at half-height was 41° (Vogels and Orban, 1990a), while for his IT sample it was 71°.

In many other visual areas one finds cells that respond to gratings and are sensitive for their orientation: e.g., area V1 (e.g., Vogels and Orban, 1991, for a recent study using the same procedure as the present one), area V2 (Logothetis et al., 1987; von der Heydt and Peterhans, 1989) and area V4 (Tanaka et al., 1986; Logothetis et al., 1987; Desimone and Schein, 1987; Haenny and Schiller, 1988). However, given a response to a grating in one particular area does not say anything about what kind of processing of the grating pattern is going on in that particular area. In order to make some inferences of the contribution of a particular area to stimulus processing one needs to study the responses of the cells to several kinds of stimuli in the context of a behavioral task. A nice example of the need to use more stimuli to demonstrate differences between areas is the study by von der Heydt and Peterhans (1989) who reported the presence of responses to anomalous contours in V2 but not in V1. When using only gratings as stimuli this difference in processing would have been impossible to show. Measuring responses within the context of a behavioral task also shows that although responses to the physical attributes of a grating may be similar for different areas, the influence of the behavioral state can strongly differ between areas as demonstrated for areas V1 and V4 by Haenny and Schiller (1988). All this means is that observing neural responses to a simple stimulus such as a grating does not imply that the underlying neural circuit is performing a simple operation.

Given the end-position that IT has in the hierarchy of visual areas (see Introduction), it is very likely that the responses we observed are not related to a pure sensory analysis of the grating pattern. The task-related nature of many of these responses support this view. Given our current knowledge of processing in the visual areas, it is likely that a sensory analysis of the grating pattern is going on in striate cortex and prestriate areas such as V2 and possibly V4. We speculate that IT cortex categorizes the grating patterns as distinct from other patterns and objects. Since orientation is the relevant cue there will also be a categorization of the grating patterns according to their orientation, explaining the orientation-sensitive responses we observed.

In general, we propose that IT cortex categorizes the description of form, depth and color of the visual image according to its pattern, identifying it as a particular pattern or object. This can be done by having a large number of units each responsive to one, several or a specific combination of stimulus attributes computed in prestriate cortex. This network of units is supposed to be adaptive so that it can represent novel objects, or old objects in more detail if behaviorally necessary (as for instance during training for smaller orientation differences or with a larger number of S1 stimuli in our task). Evidence for this plasticity of IT responses is provided in a study by Rolls et al. (1989) who reported that the response selectivity of IT cells for faces changed when a novel face was presented to the monkey. Since some objects or patterns occur only or mostly in the context of specific tasks, like our grating patterns, these units will code for the patterns in a task-related context. This may happen by virtue of concurrent activity in other parts of the brain involved in task-related processing and which are strongly connected to IT, such as the frontal cortex (e.g., Fuster, 1980; Kubota et al., 1980) and medial temporal structures (Riches et al., 1991; Brown et al., this volume). The creation of these task-dependent responses within a network of units will lead to a more efficient and faster execution of the task in the future.

Finally we would like to return to the results of the single unit recordings presented in this paper. It is very clear that many cells respond to one or more phases of the behavioral task. The responses during fixation, however, can have several origins ranging from pure sensory responses to the fixation point or evenly illuminated CRT screen, to responses linked to the behavioral act of the fixation itself. A striking observation, also made by other researchers (e.g., Gross et al., 1972; Sato et al., 1980; Richmond et al., 1983), is that many units can be strongly inhibited by the stimulus or even during fixation. It is not so that the latter units that are inhibited by the stimulus should not participate in the task. They may well be part of the neural circuit underlying performance in this task. It is well known from simulations with artificial neural networks consisting of hidden units that can have both negative (i.e., inhibition) and positive (i.e., excitation) values, that some hidden units will be activated while others will be inhibited by the input units. This inhibition is as important for succesful performance as is the excitation. Now one should note that these cells are likely to code also for other patterns than gratings, i.e., a distributed coding, and hence those cells strongly inhibited during grating presentation are likely to be active when other patterns are presented. In fact some of the units that were inhibited by the grating responded well during fixation.

Our monkeys differed in their behavioral performance level. Interestingly enough there were also differences in the IT unit data. Two differences are notable: firstly, Ronnie's units were more narrowly tuned to orientation than those of Adam. Secondly, in Ronnie most cells that responded to the grating did not respond during fixation and vice versa. The latter trend towards stimulus specificity (fixation versus grating) was much less clear in Adam's sam-

ple of units. These two observations on neural properties may be correlated with the behavioral differences between the monkeys. Indeed the monkey with the less "selective" units, Adam, performed also worse and slower than the other monkey, Ronnie. Of course the sample size ($n = 2$) is much to small to draw any firm conclusions about this apparent correlation between behavioral performance and neural responses.

We did not show that the cells we recorded from are necessary in the performance of the task. In order to prove this, lesion experiments are necessary. That is exactly what we are doing now. Whatever the outcome of these ablation experiments, the vigorousness of the responses and the task-related effects are so impressive that they must be of some functional importance in the huge network that comprises the primate brain.

Acknowledgements

This research was supported by Grant GOA 8488-62 of the Belgian Ministry of Sciences to G.A.O. R.V. is a research associate of the National Research Council of Belgium. We thank Dr. W. Spileers for the eye coil surgery, and Dr. G. Sary and K. Lauwers for their help in training the monkeys. The technical assistance of P. Kayenbergh, G. Meulemans and G. Vanparrijs is gratefully acknowledged.

References

Baizer, J.S., Ungerleider, L.G. and Desimone, R. (1991) Organization of visual inputs to the inferior temporal and posterior parietal cortex in macaques. *J. Neurosci.,* 11: 168 – 190.

Batschelet, E. (1981) *Circular Statistics in Biology,* Academic Press, London.

Baylis, G.C., Rolls, E.T. and Leonard, C.M. (1987) Functional subdivisions of the temporal lobe neocortex. *J. Neurosci.,* 7: 330 – 342.

Boussaoud, D., Desimone, R. and Ungerleider, L. (1991) Visual topography of area TEO in the macaque. *J. Comp. Neurol.,* 306: 554 – 575.

Bruce, C.J., Desimone, R. and Gross, C.G. (1981) Properties of neurons in a visual polysensory area in the superior temporal sulcus of the macaque. *J. Neurophysiol.,* 46: 369 – 384.

Chow, K.L. (1950) A retrograde cell degeneration study of the cortical projection field of the pulvinar in the monkey. *J. Comp. Neurol.,* 93: 313 – 340.

Desimone, R. (1991) Face-selective cells in the temporal cortex of monkeys. *J. Cogn. Neurosci.,* 3: 1 – 8.

Desimone, R. and Schein, S.J. (1987) Visual properties of neurons in area V4 of the macaque: sensitivity to stimulus form. *J. Neurophysiol.,* 57: 835 – 868.

Desimone, R., Fleming, J. and Gross, C.G. (1980) Prestriate afferents to inferior temporal cortex: an HRP study. *Brain Res.,* 184: 41 – 55.

Desimone, R., Albright, T.D., Gross, C.G. and Bruce, C. (1984) Stimulus-selective properties of inferior temporal neurons in the macaque. *J. Neurosci.,* 4: 2051 – 2062.

Fuster, J.M. (1988) *The Prefrontal Cortex: Anatomy, Physiology and Neuropsychology of the Frontal Lobe,* Raven Press, New York.

Green, D.M. and Swets, J.A. (1966) *Signal Detection Theory and Psychophysics,* Wiley, New York.

Gross, C.G., Rocha-Miranda, C.E. and Bender, D.B. (1972) Visual properties of neurons in inferotemporal cortex of the macaque. *J. Neurophysiol.,* 35: 96 – 111.

Gross, C.G., Bender, D.B. and Gerstein, G.L. (1979) Activity of inferior temporal neurons in behaving monkeys. *Neuropsychologia,* 17: 215 – 229.

Haenny, P.E. and Schiller, P.H. (1988) State dependent activity in monkey visual cortex. I. Single cell activity in V1 and V4 on visual tasks. *Exp. Brain Res.,* 69: 225 – 244.

Iwai, E. and Mishkin, M. (1969) Further evidence on the locus of the visual area in the temporal lobe of the monkey. *Exp. Neurol.,* 25: 585 – 594.

Iwai, E. and Yukie, M. (1987) Amygdalofugal and amygdalopetal connections with modality-specific visual cortical areas in macaques *(Macaca fuscata, M. mulatta,* and *M. fascicularis). J. Comp. Neurol.,* 261: 362 – 387.

Johnson, K.O. (1980) Sensory discrimination: decision process. *J. Neurophysiol.,* 41: 1071 – 1095.

Konorski, J. (1959) A new method of physiological investigation of recent memory in animals. *Bull. Pol. Acad. Sci.,* 7: 115 – 117.

Kubota, K., Tonoike, M. and Mikami, A. (1980) Neuronal activity in the monkey dorsolateral prefrontal cortex during a discrimination task with delay. *Brain Res.,* 183: 29 – 43.

Kuypers, H.G.J.M., Szwarcbart, M.K., Mishkin, M. and Rosvold, H.E. (1965) Occipitotemporal corticocortical connections in the rhesus monkey. *Exp. Neurol.,* 11: 245 – 262.

Logothetis, N.K., Vogels, R. and Schiller, P.H. (1987) Neuronal activity in V1, V2 and V4 in macaque monkey performing a visual matching task. *Soc. Neurosci. Abstr.,* 13: 324.

Maunsell, J.H.R. and Newsome, W.T. (1987) Visual processing in monkey extrastriate cortex. *Annu. Rev. Neurosci.,* 10: 363 – 401.

Minsky, M. and Papert, S. (1969) *Perceptrons: an Introduction to Computational Geometry,* MIT Press, Cambridge, MA.

Moran, J. and Desimone, R. (1985) Selective attention gates visual processing in the extrastriate cortex. *Science,* 229: 782 – 784.

Moran, M.A., Mufson, E.J. and Mesulam, M.M. (1987) Neural inputs into the temporopolar cortex of the rhesus monkey. *J. Comp. Neurol.,* 256: 88 – 103.

Morel, A. and Bullier, J. (1990) Anatomical segregation of two cortical visual pathways in the macaque monkey. *Visual Neurosci.,* 4: 555 – 578.

Orban, G.A., Devos, M. and Vogels, R. (1990) Cheapmonkey: comparing ANN and the primate brain on a simple perceptual task: orientation discrimination. In: F. Fogelman Soulie and J. Herault (Eds.), *Neurocomputing - NATO ASI Series, Vol. F68,* Springer Verlag, Berlin, pp. 386 – 404.

Riches, I.P., Wilson, F.A.W. and Brown, M.W. (1991) The effects of visual stimulation and memory on neurons of the hippocampal formation and the neighboring parahippocampal gyrus and inferior temporal cortex of the primate. *J. Neurosci.,* 11: 1763 – 1779.

Richmond, B.J. and Sato, T. (1987) Enhancement of inferior temporal neurons during visual discrimination. *J. Neurophysiol.,* 58: 1292 – 1306.

Richmond, B.J., Wurtz, R.H. and Sato, T. (1983) Visual responses of inferior temporal neurons in awake rhesus monkeys. *J. Neurophysiol.,* 50: 1415 – 1432.

Rolls, E.T., Baylis, G.C., Hasselmo, M.E. and Nalwa, V. (1989) The effect of learning on the face selective responses of neurons in the cortex in the superior temporal sulcus of the monkey. *Exp. Brain Res.,* 76: 153 – 164.

Rosenblatt, F. (1958) The perceptron, a probabilistic model for information storage and organization in the brain. *Psychol. Rev.,* 62: 386 – 407.

Rumelhart, D.E., Hinton, G.E. and Williams, R.J. (1986) Learning internal representations by error propagation. In: D.E. Rumelhart and J.L. McClelland (Eds.), *Parallel Distributed Processing: Explorations in the Microstructure of Cognition. Vol. 1: Foundations,* MIT Press, Cambridge, MA, pp. 318 – 362.

Sato T. (1988) Effects of attention and stimulus interaction on visual responses of inferior temporal neurons in macaque. *J. Neurophysiol.,* 60: 344 – 364.

Sato, T., Kawamura, T. and Iwai, E. (1980) Responsiveness of inferotemporal single units to visual pattern stimuli in monkeys performing discrimination. *Exp. Brain Res.,* 38: 313 – 319.

Seltzer, B. and Pandya, D.N. (1978) Afferent cortical connections and architectonics of the superior temporal sulcus and surrounding cortex in the rhesus monkey. *Brain Res.,* 149: 1 – 24.

Seltzer, B. and Pandya, D.N. (1989) Frontal lobe connections of the superior temporal sulcus in the rhesus monkey. *J. Comp. Neurol.,* 281: 97 – 113.

Siegel, S. (1956) *Nonparametrics Statistics for the Behavioral Sciences,* McGraw-Hill Kogakusha, Tokyo.

444

Spitzer, H. and Richmond, B.J. (1991) Task difficulty: ignoring, attending to and discriminating a visual stimulus yield progressively more activity in inferior temporal neurons. *Exp. Brain Res.,* 83: 340 – 348.

Tanaka, M., Weber, H. and Creutzfeldt, O.D. (1986) Visual properties and spatial distribution of neurones in the visual association area on the prelunate gyrus of the awake monkey. *Exp. Brain Res.,* 65: 11 – 37.

Ungerleider, L.G. and Mishkin, M. (1982) Two cortical visual systems. In: D.J. Ingle, M.A. Goodale and R.J.W. Mansfield (Eds.), *Analysis of Visual Behavior,* MIT Press, Cambridge, MA, pp. 549 – 586.

Ungerleider, L.G., Gaffan, D. and Pelak, V.S. (1989) Projections from inferior temporal cortex to prefrontal cortex via the uncinate fascicle in rhesus monkeys. *Exp. Brain Res.,* 76: 473 – 484.

Van Hoesen, G.W. and Pandya, D.N. (1975) Some connections of the entorhinal (area 28) and perirhinal area (area 35) cortices of the rhesus monkey. I. Temporal lobe afferents. *Brain Res.,* 95: 1 – 24.

Van Hoesen, G.W., Yeterian, E.H. and Lavizzo-Mourey, R. (1981) Widespread corticostriate projections from temporal cortex of the rhesus monkey. *J. Comp. Neurol.,* 199: 205 – 219.

Vogels, R. and Orban, G.A. (1986) Decision processes in visual discrimination of line orientation. *J. Exp. Psychol. Hum. Percept. Perform.,* 12: 115 – 132.

Vogels, R. and Orban, G.A. (1990a) How well do response changes of striate neurons signal differences in orientation: a study in the discriminating monkey. *J. Neurosci.,* 10: 3543 – 3558.

Vogels, R. and Orban, G.A. (1990b) Effects of task related stimulus attributes on infero-temporal neurons studied in the discriminating monkey. *Soc. Neurosci. Abstr.,* 16: 621.

Vogels, R. and Orban, G.A. (1991) Quantitative study of striate single unit responses in monkeys performing an orientation discrimination task. *Exp. Brain Res.,* 84: 1 – 11.

Vogels, R., Orban, G.A. and Vandenbussche, E. (1984) Meridional variations in orientation discrimination in normal and amblyopic vision. *Invest. Ophthalmol. Vis. Sci.,* 25: 720 – 728.

von Bonin, G. and Bailey, P. (1947) *The Neocortex of Macaca Mulatta,* University of Illinois Press, Urbana, IL.

von der Heydt, R. and Peterhans, E. (1989) Mechanisms of contour perception in monkey visual cortex. I. Lines of pattern discontinuity. *J. Neurosci.,* 9: 1737 – 1748.

Webster, M.J., Ungerleider, L.G. and Bachevalier, J. (1991) Connections of inferior temporal areas TE and TEO with medial temporal-lobe structures in infant and adult monkeys. *J. Neurosci.,* 11: 1095 – 1116.

Yeterian, E.H. and Pandya, D.N. (1989) Thalamic connections of the cortex of the superior temporal sulcus in the rhesus monkey. *J. Comp. Neurol.,* 282: 80 – 97.

T.P. Hicks, S. Molotchnikoff and T. Ono (Eds.)
Progress in Brain Research, Vol. 95
© 1993 Elsevier Science Publishers B.V. All rights reserved.

CHAPTER 36

Blindsight: neurons and behaviour

Petra Stoerig and Alan Cowey

Institute of Medical Psychology, Ludwig-Maximilians-University, 8000 Munich 2, Germany, and Department of Experimental Psychology, Oxford University, Oxford OX1 3UD, U.K.

Introduction

Three classes of ganglion cells provide the retinal input to the visual system of primates. They differ both with respect to their functional and morphological characteristics. The Pα cells have large somata, large, radial dendritic trees, and thick axons. The Pβ cells have much smaller somata, small, grape-like dendritic trees, and thin axons. The Pγ cells (with some exceptions) have small somata as well, but only few long and sparsely branched dendrites. Functionally, the cell types are classified according to their receptive field size, conduction velocity, contrast gain, receptor input and wavelength specificity. On the basis of the ganglion cell input they receive, three parallel visual subsystems can be distinguished. Although the retinal ganglion cell input has not been classified for a number of retino-recipient nuclei, Fig. 1*A* provisionally illustrates these systems. The Pα system comprises the magnocellular layers of the dorsal lateral geniculate nucleus (dLGN) (Leventhal et al., 1981; Perry et al., 1984) and possibly the pretectum (Perry and Cowey, 1984); further projections to the ventral LGN, the superior colliculus, and other structures may exist. The Pβ system comprises the parvocellular layers of the dLGN (Leventhal et al., 1981; Perry et al., 1984) and possibly the retino-recipient zone of the inferior pulvinar (Stoerig et al., 1991); no other projections are presently known. The superior colliculus (Leventhal et al., 1981; Perry and Cowey, 1984), the pulvinar (Stoerig et al., 1991),

and possibly the interlaminar dLGN layers (Fitzpatrick et al., 1983) receive Pγ cell input. The Pα and the Pβ systems project predominantly to striate cortex, and then on to extrastriate visual cortex; direct projections to extrastriate cortex are sparser. Via the dLGN and, especially, the pulvinar, the Pγ system projects predominantly to the intricate network of extrastriate visual cortical areas with its numerous reciprocal connections to striate cortex and sub-cortical structures.

Anatomical consequences of a striate cortical lesion

A striate cortical lesion destroys what is probably the major source of anatomical input to extrastriate visual cortical areas (V2, V3, V4 and V5 (MT)), namely the one which arises from striate cortex itself. Its functional effect must be even more widespread for these secondary visual areas in turn have widespread projections to other extrastriate visual areas. In addition, it destroys the striate cortical input to subcortical nuclei such as the superior colliculus and the pulvinar nucleus, and causes massive retrograde degeneration of the dorsal lateral geniculate nucleus, which loses approximately 99% of its projection neurons within just 3 months (Mihailovic et al., 1975). The remaining dLGN projection neurons survive, apparently permanently, because they project directly to extrastriate visual cortical areas (Yukie and Iwai, 1981; Cowey and Stoerig, 1989). Electron

A

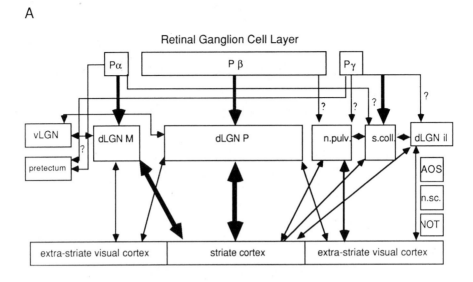

B

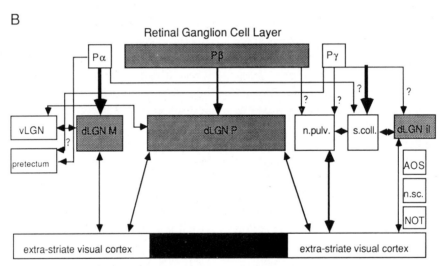

Fig. 1. *A*. A schematic view of the visual system, giving the parallel subsystems defined by their retinal ganglion cell inputs. Innervation density is indicated roughly by arrow size. For clarity the multiple projections to other nuclei have been omitted. *B*. The same view after a striate cortical lesion which causes retrograde degeneration of the dLGN and the retinal Pβ ganglion cell population. Although the three major subsystems are differentially affected, all survive at least partially. Abbreviations: dLGN, dorsal lateral geniculate nucleus; M, magnocellular; P, parvocellular; il, interlaminar; vLGN, ventral LGN; NOT, nucleus of the optic tract; n.pulv., nucleus pulvinaris; s.coll., superior colliculus; AOS, accessory optic system; n.sc., nucleus suprachiasmaticus.

microscopic analysis of surviving projection neurons, retrogradely labeled from V4, indicates that they receive a direct input from the superior colliculus and an indirect retinal input via the GABAergic geniculate interneurons (Kisvarday et al., 1991). In other words there is a sparse, retino-

(colliculo)-geniculo-extrastriate cortical pathway that survives striate cortical damage.

However, the death of the vast majority of projection neurons in both magno- and parvocellular portions of the dLGN causes transneuronal degeneration of the retinal ganglion cell layer (Van Buren,

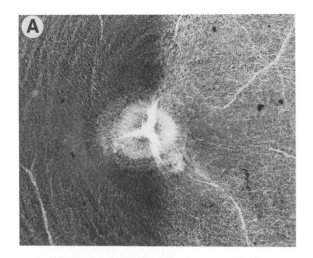

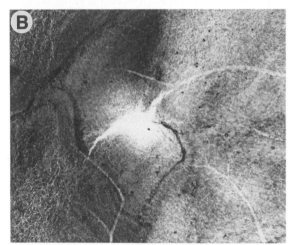

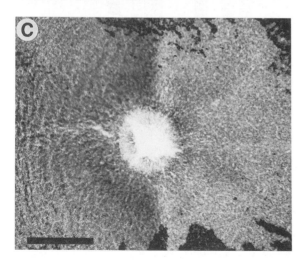

1963a,b; Cowey, 1974). Eight years after unilateral striate cortical ablation in macaque monkeys, the retinal ganglion cell population is reduced by 50–85% in the affected hemiretinae. Fig. 2A,B shows photomicrographs of the central part of the transneuronally degenerated retinae in two monkeys 8 years after unilateral removal of striate cortex. The retina was whole-mounted and Nissl-stained, and the vertical meridian is clearly distinct as a consequence of the difference in ganglion cell density between normal and degenerated sides. Fig. 2C is a similar picture from a macaque in whom one optic tract was sectioned a year earlier, leading to the loss of almost all ganglion cells. However, the overall pattern is similar in all three retinae. Note also that the line of degeneration does not bisect the fovea but falls slightly to one side of the vertical meridian, presumably reflecting the spared ganglion cells that contribute to the naso-temporal overlap and probably to macular sparing. The loss that follows striate cortical damage is substantially more pronounced in the central retina (Cowey, 1974; Cowey et al., 1989) and when the damage occurs in younger animals (Dineen and Hendrickson, 1981; Weller and Kaas, 1989). However, variation with age and duration may even be exceeded by variation between individual animals, as we have recently discovered. This is shown in Fig. 3 which gives ganglion cell density in the temporal retina of

Fig. 2. Photomicrographs, focused on the retinal ganglion cell layer, of the flat mounted and Nissl-stained retina of the right eye of three macaque monkeys. In each the fovea is in the centre and the nasal retina is to the right. In A and B the left striate cortex had been removed 8 years previously, causing retrograde transneuronal degeneration of about three quarters of the retinal ganglion cells in the central region of the nasal retina of the right eye. Note the sparing that extends about 1° on the nasal side of the vertical meridian, presumably attributable to the naso-temporal overlap. In C the left optic tract was severed about 1 year earlier and all or nearly all the ganglion cells have degenerated, leaving only amacrine cells as neuronal elements in the ganglion cell layer. Superficially the degeneration is similar in all three retinae. The dark pigmented material is histological artifact. Scale bar, 500 μm.

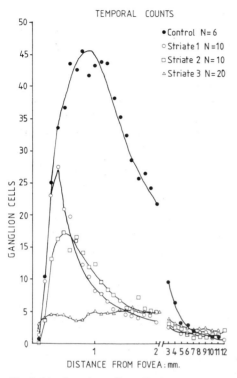

Fig. 3. Number of ganglion cells along the horizontal temporal retinal meridian. Cells were counted in 6 μm sections in 100 μm strips for the first 2 mm. For the remaining eccentricities each number is the average of three 100 μm strips at 1 mm intervals. The number of sections counted in each eye is indicated alongside each animal in the key. Numbers are not corrected for linear shrinkage, which was about 25%.

a normal rhesus macaque and in three macaques in which the striate cortex was removed at 2.5 years of age and all three animals survived for a further 30 months.

Although virtually all Pα and Pβ ganglion cells project to the magno- and parvocellular layers of the dLGN, respectively, a finding that gave rise to their being called M- and P-cells (Shapley and Perry, 1986), the two populations are not equally affected by transneuronal degeneration. The first indication of a difference came from studies using anterograde transport from the eye into the retrogradely degenerated dLGN, where autoradiographs showed that the magnocellular part of the nucleus received a substantially more prominent retinal input (Weller et al., 1979, Dineen et al., 1982), although the pro-

jection neurons in both parts of the dLGN are equally affected by retrograde degeneration. Although this is consistent with selective depletion of the parvocellular input fibres it has never been quantified and it could plausibly be argued that the magnocellular labeling is relatively so dense in the *normal* thalamus that even a large diminution is not conspicuous by autoradiography. However, there is no doubt that retinal ganglion cells are differentially affected: classification of surviving ganglion cells on the basis of morphological criteria in transneuronally degenerated retinae, which were retrogradely labeled with horseradish peroxidase from the optic nerve, showed the transneuronal degeneration to be selective for Pβ ganglion cells (Cowey et al., 1989). Interestingly, like the Pγ cells, the Pα cells are found in normal numbers in the degenerated hemiretinae. Whereas the normal retina contains about 10% Pα, 80% Pβ and 10% Pγ cells (Leventhal et al., 1981; Perry and Cowey, 1981), the selectivity of the degeneration produces an unusual ganglion cell population which consists of approx-

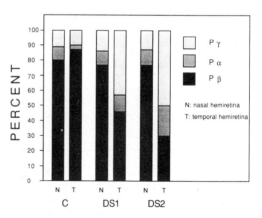

Fig. 4. The histogram shows the percentage of the three ganglion cell types classified on the basis of morphological characteristics revealed by HRP transported from the optic nerve, in four normal and two degenerated hemiretinae of macaque monkeys with long-standing striate cortical ablation. Whereas the normal proportions are approximately 1:8:1 for Pα:Pβ:Pγ cells, the degenerated retina has a ganglion cell population consisting of roughly equal proportions of the three cell classes. (Adapted from Cowey et al., 1989).

imately equal numbers of the three cell classes, as shown in Fig. 4, which summarizes the cell counts from normal and transneuronally degenerated hemiretinae.

The data show that cells of all three morphological ganglion cell classes survive the effects of a striate cortical lesion. The Pγ cell population is unaffected, indicating that there is no transneuronal retrograde degeneration of the retino-colliculo-striate cortical pathway. More surprising is the finding that the Pα cell population appears equally unaffected, despite the fact that these cells project primarily to the magnocellular layers of the dLGN. As the massive degeneration seen in these layers has no recognizable effect on their numbers, they are likely to project to extrageniculate targets as well, although the Pα cell projection to the midbrain described by Leventhal et al. (1981) and Perry and Cowey (1984) is rather small. In addition to their having additional and as yet unidentified target nuclei, it is possible that the Pα cells make contacts with dLGN interneurons and, due to their large terminal arborization, are better equipped to contact the surviving dLGN projection neurons and interneurons than the comparatively tiny Pβ cells with their much more restricted terminals (Michael, 1988). Just as interesting as the lack of degeneration in the Pα cell population is the survival of a subgroup of Pβ ganglion cells, despite the parvocellular dLGN layers being by far the most important targets of such cells. Again this implies that the Pβ cells may have one or even more additional target areas (see Fig. 1B which summarizes the anatomical effects of the lesion).

The surviving retinal ganglion cells look normal for their receptive classes, and do not show signs of being moribund (Cowey et al., 1989). However, we have recently discovered (Kisvarday et al., 1991) that the ganglion and amacrine cell layers, together with the inner plexiform layer, show conspicuously heightened GABA immunoreactivity in the transneuronally degenerated region. The physiological properties of surviving ganglion cells may therefore be unusual.

Visual function after a striate cortical lesion

In spite of the long-distance and long-term effects on the retinal ganglion cell layer, cells of all three classes survive a striate cortical lesion, implying that parts of all three subsystems survive. Are they functional? One way to answer this question is to study blindsight, i.e., the residual visual functions that can be demonstrated in the homonymous visual field defects which are caused by the striate cortical lesion. These field defects are perimetrically assessed and clinically classified with respect to their size, density and position within the visual field. Unlike relative defects where some (amblyopic) vision persists, absolute defects (or scotomata) are experienced as blind; the patients do not see the visual stimuli presented in the scotoma. Despite the experiential blindness, visual stimuli may be processed in a manner that allows the patient to respond them. Therefore, it is possible to ask whether or not the different visual functions which are usually attributed to the different subsystems can be demonstrated in the field defect, provided forced-choice behavioural responses are used which require the patients to *guess* — for example where a stimulus has been presented (Pöppel et al., 1973; Weiskrantz et al., 1974; Perenin and Jeannerod, 1978), whether or not a stimulus has been presented (Stoerig et al., 1985; Magnusson and Mathiesen, 1989), or which one of a limited number of stimuli has been presented (Weiskrantz et al., 1974; Perenin, 1978; Ptito et al., 1987; Stoerig, 1987). Alternatively, responses that are not consciously controlled even in a normal subject can be used to uncover visual processing in the blind field: measurements of pupillary responses to stimuli shown in the field defect are one example (Brindley et al., 1969; Weiskrantz, 1990); measurements of reaction times to stimuli in the normal field and their dependence on the appearance of a second stimulus in the blind hemifield are another (Marzi et al., 1986; Rafal et al., 1990), and the optokinetic response to a large patterned display moving round the head is a third (Ter Braak et al., 1971;

Heide et al., 1990). These approaches circumvent tedious guessing procedures as well as the resistance shown by some patients to doing something as apparently silly as localizing unseen stimuli.

Functions attributed to the Pγ-system

The phenomema of blindsight have most commonly been attributed to the retino-collicular pathway (e.g., Pöppel et al., 1973; Weiskrantz et al., 1974; Perenin and Jeannerod, 1978; Lepore et al., 1975; Barbur et al., 1980). Although the superior colliculus, like the pulvinar nucleus, looses its striate cortical input, a retino-colliculo-pulvino-extrastriate cortical projection remains which might mediate visual functions in the absence of striate cortex. Neurophysiological studies in monkeys have implicated the superior colliculus in the mediation of saccadic eye movements (see Wurtz and Albano, 1980, for review). A clinical investigation of a patient with a unilateral colliculectomy (Heywood and Ratcliff, 1975) and one of a patient with a lesion involving the left pulvinar (Zihl and von Cramon, 1979) support these findings, by showing that the patients' saccadic eye movement latency to the hemifield contralateral to the lesion was increased, and that spontaneous eye movements into the same hemifield were rare, less attention being paid to this side. As the Pγ ganglion cells are functionally heterogeneous, with many cells responding preferentially to moving stimuli (De Monasterio, 1978), it is not surprising that collicular cells respond well to stimulus motion. Via the pulvinar, they project to area MT (or V5) which is involved in the processing of stimulus motion. The visual responsivity of area MT that survives striate cortical ablation depends on the collicular input (Rodman et al., 1989).

On the basis of its known properties, the collicular projection is a likely candidate to mediate saccadic and possibly manual localization of targets in blind hemifields: patients and monkeys with striate cortical lesions are able to make saccades to stimuli shown briefly at different positions within the field defect. Although the accuracy is very much reduced, the correlation between stimulus and eye position is still significant (Pöppel et al., 1973; Weiskrantz et

al., 1974), as is the correlation between hand and stimulus position in manual localization tasks. Not only monkeys (Weiskrantz et al., 1977) and patients with circumscribed field defects (Weiskrantz et al., 1974) but also hemispherectomized patients (Perenin and Jeannerod, 1978) performed remarkably well, indicating that the extrastriate visual cortex of the hemisphere contralateral to the hemianopic field cannot be necessary for manual localization. Rafal et al. (1990) have recently demonstrated that a distractor signal in the blind hemifield inhibits saccades towards targets in the normal hemifield, a finding they too attribute to the retino-collicular pathway.

That it is indeed the colliculus that is involved in saccadic localization in a field defect was convincingly demonstrated by Mohler and Wurtz (1977) who produced a circumscribed visual field defect by removing a small part of striate cortex in monkeys. As had been previously demonstrated in man and monkey, the monkeys soon learned to make saccades to targets within the field defect. When they had mastered this task, the retinotopically corresponding portion of the superior colliculus was removed in a second operation, producing a collicular field defect superimposed on the cortical one. After this second operation, the monkeys did not relearn saccadic localization. A combined striate cortical and collicular ablation in monkeys also resulted in a failure to reach correctly for a 90 mm black disk (Pasik and Pasik, 1982), implying that both saccadic and manual localization are mediated via this pathway in the absence of striate cortex.

Functions attributed to the Pα system

Pα ganglion cells and cells in the magnocellular dLGN layers, which they innervate, have large receptive fields with low spatial and high temporal resolution, broadband spectral sensitivity and high contrast gain. Neurophysiological and psychophysical studies suggest that this system is involved in the processing of motion (Livingstone and Hubel, 1988; Schiller et al., 1990), high temporal frequency processing (Schiller et al., 1990; Merigan and Maunsell, 1990), and coarse stereopsis (Livingstone and Hubel,

1988). In addition, the broadband system is often equated with the luminance system whose peak photopic spectral sensitivity is around 555 nm (King-Smith and Carden, 1976) and whose smooth curve reflects summed cone activity. As the $P\alpha$ system receives little input from the short wavelength cones (Gouras, 1968), and no such input is psychophysically detectable (Lee and Stromeyer, 1989), sensitivity decreases continuously in the short wavelengths where the blue pigment has its maximal absorption.

These functions that are characteristic of the $P\alpha$ system in normal subjects can also be demonstrated in blind hemifields. Detection of fast moving stimuli (Barbur et al., 1980; Blythe et al., 1987; Magnussen and Mathiesen, 1989), low frequency spatial and high frequency bandpass temporal responses (Barbur, personal communication), and evidence for coarse stereopsis (Richards, 1973) have been described in the field defects of patients with striate cortical lesions. Under conditions that favour the luminance system, we have recently measured a hemianopic patient's increment threshold spectral sensitivity: using a Tübinger perimeter where the patient fixated a central fixation spot, a small stimulus of 44′ diameter that flickered at 20 Hz was presented for 200 msec at 10° eccentricity. Background luminance was set at 0.1 cd/m² because the high contrast gain of $P\alpha$ cells (Kaplan and Shapley, 1981; Purpura et al., 1988) makes them well-suited for twilight vision. Increment threshold spectral sensitivity was determined for nine coloured stimuli that were produced by inserting narrowband interference filters, with peak transmission spaced from 450 to 665 nm, into the projection beam of the perimeter. At the matched position in the normal hemifield, thresholds were measured by increasing stimulus luminance in steps of 0.05 log units until the patient reported just seeing the target. In the field defect, a guessing paradigm was used, and targets were presented in random order with blank trials. Both target and blank trials were signaled with a click from the perimeter shutter, and the patient responded by saying "yes" or "no". Starting with a stimulus luminance 0.2 log units above the threshold determined for the good field, it was increased in steps of 0.1 log units after each batch of 100

trials until detection became statistically significant at the 0.5% level or better. After 250 presentations with the threshold stimulus, a further 250 trials each were given at 0.1 log units more intense and less intense than the threshold stimulus. Provided the next-brighter stimulus also yielded significant detection, whereas the next-dimmer one did not, this value was defined as threshold for the blind field.

Spectral sensitivity as determined under these conditions in both hemifields is shown in Fig. 5. It resembles the spectral sensitivity of the luminance system as measured by King-Smith and Carden (1976): the plateau is a product of summed middle and long wavelength cone activity, and the curve lacks the troughs that are characteristic of colour-opponent interactions as well as the increase in sensitivity from 480 to 450 nm that indicates contributions from short wavelength cones (see also Fig. 6.). Although it cannot be ruled out that colour-opponent processes contribute to sensitivity, especially at both ends of the tested spectrum where the patient could identify the colour of the 450 and 660 nm threshold stimuli, the curve primarily reflects the sensitivity of

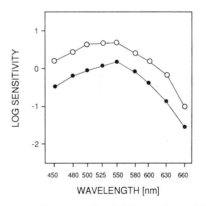

Fig. 5. Increment-threshold spectral sensitivity measured with a 44′ flickering target at 10° eccentricity at matched positions in the normal nasal (○) and the blind temporal visual field (●) of quadrantanopic patient DH with a post-geniculate vascular lesion in the territory of the posterior cerebral artery. The curves from both fields are very similar, the one from the field defect being depressed by about 0.6 log units. They resemble the sensitivity curves determined by King-Smith and Carden (1976) for the luminance system.

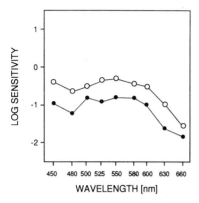

Fig. 6. Increment-threshold spectral sensitivity of patient DH measured at 10° eccentric positions in normal (○) and blind (●) portions of the visual field using stimulus conditions that favour the colour-opponent system. Curves from both hemifields show the characteristic discontinuities attributed to colour-opponent processes. Note especially the increase in sensitivity from 480 to 450 nm that indicates a contribution from the short wavelength cones.

the luminance system. It can be seen that the curve measured with the guessing paradigm in the field defect has very much the same shape as that measured with the seeing paradigm at a matched position in the normal hemifield but sensitivity is reduced by approximately 0.6 log units in the blind field.

Together with the findings mentioned at the beginning of this section, the results indicate that visual functions that are normally attributed to the Pα cell system can also be uncovered in visual field defects.

Functions attributed to the Pβ system

Like their target cells in the parvocellular layers of the dLGN, the Pβ ganglion cells have small receptive fields with high spatial and low temporal resolution (Wiesel and Hubel, 1966; De Monasterio and Gouras, 1975). They also have low contrast gain (Kaplan and Shapley, 1981), and are chromatically opponent (Wiesel and Hubel, 1966; De Monasterio and Gouras, 1975; Derrington et al., 1984), responding in opposite fashion to inputs from different cone types or combinations of cone types. These properties implicate them in the processing of wavelength,

fine spatial detail, especially at low temporal frequencies, and fine stereopsis (Livingstone and Hubel, 1984, 1988; Schiller et al., 1990). The Pβ system receives inputs from all three cone types. Colour-opponent interactions yield an uneven increment-threshold spectral sensitivity curve with characteristic troughs and peaks (Sperling and Harwerth, 1971; King-Smith and Carden, 1976; Snelgar et al., 1987; see Fig. 6).

At present, there is no indication that fine stereopsis is present in visual field defects, but it has not been tested with two alternative forced choice. There are a number of papers describing form discrimination in patients and monkeys with striate cortical damage (e.g., Weiskrantz et al., 1974; Keating, 1975; Perenin, 1978; Dineen and Keating, 1981; Pasik and Pasik, 1982), but all acknowledge form discrimination to be difficult and it is not entirely clear to what extent these findings depend on orientation discrimination, and therefore do not represent form discrimination per se. Weiskrantz (1987), in a more recent investigation of their formerly studied patient D.B. (1974), concluded that orientations were the discriminable feature when he found that the patient could not discriminate forms whose outlines had identical orientations, such as squares and rectangles. However, Dineen and Keating's (1981) rather fine grain stimuli, although not free of different orientations in their small constituent components, are more difficult to interpret in these terms, and require fine spatial resolution. Miller et al. (1980) measured spatial frequency discrimination with sinusoidal gratings in monkeys without any striate cortex; applying a criterion level of 75%, they found that acuity is reduced from better than 32 cpd to 12 cpd which corresponds to a stripe width of 2.5′. Finally, in patient DB acuity for a high contrast grating centred about 5.5° in the blind field was 1.9′, and not substantially lower than the value of 1.5′ measured at a comparable position in the intact field (Weiskrantz et al., 1974). Although it has been agreed that Pα ganglion cells and the M-pathway have a resolution that can be as good as that of the P-pathway (Crook et al., 1988; Lee, this volume), lesions of the parvocellular dLGN seriously impair acuity whereas lesions of the magnocellular layers do not (Schiller and Logothetis, 1990).

Colour-opponent spectral sensitivity. A spectral sensitivity curve, measured with the increment threshold technique under conditions that favour the colour-opponent system – a white adapting background of photopic luminance, a long presentation time, and a large target (e.g., King-Smith and Carden, 1976; Snelgar et al., 1987) – is shown in Fig. 6. It illustrates the maxima at 450, 550 and 600 nm as well as the interactive minima at 480 and 580 nm, all characteristic of colour-opponent sensitivity, and was measured at 10° eccentricity in the normal nasal half-field of one of three patients who participated in these experiments (Stoerig and Cowey, 1989, 1991). Note that the increase in sensitivity from 480 to 450 nm indicates a contribution from the short wavelength cones that is absent in curves representing the sensitivity of the luminance system (e.g., King-Smith and Carden, 1976; Fig. 5). The corresponding curve measured in the field defect is shown by filled symbols. Once again, the values for the blind field were determined by forced choice guessing, the luminance of the stimulus having been increased in steps of 0.1 log units until the performance was statistically significant at the 5% level or better and repeatable. Although sensitivity in the blind field is depressed by approximately 0.6 log units, and the variance is larger as values had to be determined in different testing sessions due to the lengthy technique, the shape of the curve is fairly normal. In all the curves that have been determined under these conditions (Stoerig and Cowey, 1991), a trough at 480 nm and an increase in sensitivity towards the short wavelength end of the visible spectrum is distinct, indicating a contribution from the blue cones which appears absent when sensitivity is measured under conditions that favour the broadband system.

The results indicate that colour-opponent channels determine threshold under the conditions just described, although the broadband system may contribute to sensitivity, especially in the middle part of the spectrum where it is very sensitive. At present it is not known what spectral sensitivity curve would

result if narrowly tuned but non-opponent wavelength channels with some combination of inputs from all three cone types were tapped. Such proprties have been described for the superior colliculus (Kadoya et al., 1971), and it may be possible to measure such a curve using a manual or saccadic response paradigm. However, visual cells are not only classified with respect to their wavelength specificity but also to their spatial summation properties, and we measured spatial summation curves in the field defects to see whether we could further specify our hypotheses regarding the neuronal substrate of sensitivity.

Spatial summation in visual field defects. The most common colour-opponent cell, referred to as Type I, has antagonistic spatial summation for white or broad-band light (which we here call intensity information), with a small receptive field centre and a larger, concentrically organized antagonistic surround region. The optimal intensity stimulus for such a cell covers, and is confined to, the receptive field centre, whereas increasingly larger stimuli progressively reduce the response of the cell by stimulating the antagonistic surround as well. For narrow-band stimuli (wavelength information), however, the cell has synergistic spatial summation: for example, an on-centre red/green cell continues to increase the discharge rate until the entire receptive field is filled with long-wavelength light (De Valois et al., 1977). Type II colour-opponent cells, which lack an antagonistic surround and also show synergistic summation for wavelength information, respond poorly to intensity information (Wiesel and Hubel, 1966; De Monasterio, 1978). To see whether it would be possible to differentiate between possible contributions of Type I or II cells to increment threshold sensitivity in visual field defects, spatial summation for wavelength and intensity stimuli was measured using conditions that favour the colour-opponent system, i.e., a white adapting background of photopic luminance, and a long presentation time (200 msec). Increment thresholds were determined at corresponding positions in normal and blind fields of five patients with post-geniculate lesions, three of the

454

patients having previously participated in the measurements of spectral sensitivity described above. Eight stimulus sizes, from 7 to 116′, were used. The intensity stimuli appeared white on the white background; the wavelength stimuli appeared red on the same white background, thus combining wavelength and intensity information. In the normal field, increment thresholds were repeatedly measured with an ascending method of limits; stimulus luminance was increased until the patient reported just seeing the target on three consecutive trials. In the field defect, a stimulus of a luminance 0.2 log units above threshold in the good field was presented in random order with blank trials. With the same procedure as described above, the patients guessed whether or not a target had appeared, and stimulus luminance was increased by 0.1 log units

after each block of trials until performance became statistically significant. This luminance was defined as threshold if the next-brighter stimulus was equally detectable, and measurements were repeated with all 16 stimuli.

The mean sensitivity at a 10° eccentric position in the intact field, derived from five measurement repetitions, shows a normal increase in sensitivity with stimulus size. An example is shown in Fig. 7. Sensitivity for the red stimuli increased linearly with stimulus size, while sensitivity for the white stimuli showed a small dip at 44′. This could be interpreted as a consequence of different spatial summation properties for both types of stimuli, and indicates a receptive field centre size of less than 44′ (Robson and Graham, 1981) at this eccentricity. Curves measured with the red targets in the field defect, based on single lengthy measurements, show a similar linear increase in sensitivity within the testable range; the maximum luminance for the red target was not sufficient to yield detection for the very small stimuli. In contrast, in all patients sensitivity for the white stimuli showed a marked dip whose position – like receptive field centre size – depends on the eccentricity of the tested retinal position: at 10° eccentricity, it is seen with the 44′ stimulus (see Fig. 7); at 30° eccentricity, it is shifted to the 69 and 116′ targets. This points to a receptive field centre size of less than 44′ at 10°, and of less than 69′ at 30° eccentricity in the blind temporal half-field, and is consistent not only with the conclusion regarding perceptive field size drawn from the curves measured in the normal nasal half-field, but also with estimates of perceptive field sizes derived from other studies. It is noteworthy that the dip is much more pronounced here in the blind than in the intact hemifield; the reason may be the severely reduced coverage of the retina by Pβ cells (Cowey et al., 1989) that would reduce interactive processes between cells, and/or an increase in surround inhibition of surviving Pβ cells that is a likely but unproven functional consequence of the increase in GABA-immunopositivity found in the retrogradely degenerated retina and dLGN (Kisvarday et al., 1991). Whatever the reason for the accentuation of the dip, the results indicate non-linear spatial summa-

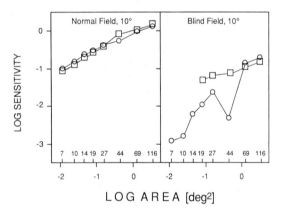

Fig. 7. Spatial summation curves measured with white (○) and red (□) stimuli on a white photopic background at 10° eccentricity in the normal and the blind field of patient BR. The two curves from the normal field which are given to the left are fairly similar, and show an almost linear increase in sensitivity with target area, with only a small indentation at 44′ with the white stimulus, indicating antagonistic interaction. In contrast, the curves from the blind field differ markedly; the curve for the red stimuli shows a similar smooth linear increase in sensitivity with stimulus size, whilst the one measured with white stimuli has a pronounced dip at 44′. This dissociation is reminiscent of the properties of Type I parvocellular dLGN neurons which combine antagonistic spatial summation for intensity with synergistic spatial summation for wavelength information, and may indicate that threshold sensitivity is mediated by these cells when it is measured under conditions that favour the colour-opponent system.

tion for intensity information complemented with linear summation for wavelength information, properties that would be expected of sensitivity mediated by the commonest colour-opponent cells.

In view of the evidence for colour-opponent processes from the spectral sensitivity curves measured under identical conditions in the same patients, the simplest hypothesis at present is that colour-opponent channels with differential spatial summation properties for wavelength and intensity information mediate threshold sensitivity in the blind field under appropriate conditions. Interestingly, spatial summation curves measured with intensity stimuli in the blind field loose the conspicuous dip when the patients respond manually (Stoerig, 1991), providing further support for parallel subsystems contributing to blindsight.

Wavelength discrimination in visual field defects. As a final function that is normally attributed to the Pβ subsystem, we tested supra-threshold wavelength discrimination in the field defects of the three patients whose spectral sensitivity curves showed that they possess colour-opponent channels, or at least channels that receive an input from all three cone types. Stimuli were matched for luminous efficiency on the basis of the spectral sensitivity curves that had been determined under identical conditions. Coloured stimuli, 116′ in diameter, were matched at 0.5 log units above the previously determined increment threshold. Each of two stimuli were presented (200 msec) in random order on the white adapting background of the perimeter. 2500 presentations were given with each pair, and Receiver-Operation-Characteristic curves were measured by varying the probability of the two stimuli. The patients were informed about the probability (see Stoerig (1987), for reasons). Three stimuli from the middle part of the spectrum were used with all patients; their peak transmissivities were approximately 550, 580 and 605 nm. The results show that all three patients were able to discriminate wavelength stimuli, albeit to a different extent. Patient BR performed significantly with the green-orange (550 – 605) pair only. Patient KK performed above chance even with the closest-spaced yellow-orange pair, but as the intensity of the orange stimulus may not have been perfectly matched with its partner for this patient, we can only conclude that his wavelength discrimination threshold in the blind field is 30 nm or better. Patient DH demonstrated the best discriminability; he was able to discriminate even luminance-matched orange and yellow, so that his wavelength discrimination is not worse than 25 nm. A residual discriminability was therefore, to a different degree, present in all patients whose spectral sensitivities showed evidence for colour-opponent processes when measured under identical conditions (Stoerig and Cowey, 1992). Previous measurements of red-green discrimination in field defects had shown that six of ten tested patients showed evidence of being able to discriminate (Stoerig, 1987). We do not know whether the patients who could not discriminate the stimuli in this previous study nevertheless had a colour-opponent spectral sensitivity.

These findings are in accordance with previous reports of evidence for wavelength discrimination in the visual field defects of totally destriate monkeys (e.g., Keating, 1979; Pasik and Pasik, 1982), although others did not find such evidence (Humphrey, 1978). Positive findings regarding the processing of wavelength information also contrast with results of spectral sensitivity measurements in bilaterally destriated monkeys, where sensitivity curves were characteristic of scotopic, rod-mediated vision, regardless of whether the monkeys were light- or dark-adapted (Lepore et al., 1975); rod-mediated vision is certainly colour-blind. In the circumscribed visual field defects of our patients, spectral sensitivity depends on the adaptation level and other experimental conditions (see above); under dark-adaptation, it shows the narrow tuning, peaking at about 500 nm, and the steep decline in the long wavelengths that is characteristic of rod absorption (see Fig. 8 and Stoerig and Cowey, 1989, 1991). In order to assess the possibility that all our results with stimuli presented in the blind field were attributable to the detection of light scattered on the intact retina, we also examined sensitivity to stimuli presented on the highly reflective, and certainly blind, optic disc. In addition, these

456

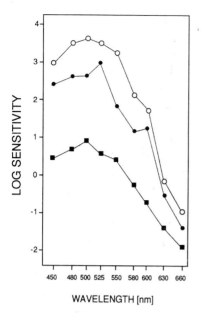

WAVELENGTH [nm]

Fig. 8. Increment-threshold spectral sensitivity measured under dark-adaptation in patient BR. The curves from both hemifields show the narrow tuning characteristic of rod vision. Increment threshold sensitivity for the detection of straylight emanating from the stimuli could also be measured under dark-adaptation; it is 2 – 3 log units lower than sensitivity in the normal field, and 1 – 2 log units lower than "blindsight" sensitivity determined at the same 10° eccentric position in the field defect.

straylight detection thresholds were determined for the tested positions in the field defect. In both cases, the patients were instructed to detect a halo, or weak light emanating from an unseen target. Results show that for the presence of the stimulus to be discernable it has to be about 3 log units more intense than a threshold stimulus in the intact visual field and about 2 log units more intense than in the field defect (see Fig. 8). The patients could therefore not detect scattered light.

Discussion

The bulk of the evidence shows that the residues of the visual system that survive striate cortical destruction and its degenerative consequences remain functional. As functions usually attributed to different subsystems can be demonstrated in the field defects, it seems likely that the remainder of all three subsystems contribute to the residual visual functions, just as all visual centres presumably contribute to visual function in the normal brain (see Fig. 1). This does not preclude the possibility that certain functional subtypes are predominantly affected by the degenerative consequences of the striate cortical lesion, or that the remaining cells may undergo specific and unusual functional changes. Visual precision and sensitivity are certainly affected, and we acknowledge that the different methods we use for testing sensitivity in the normal and blind areas of the field may underestimate the difference in sensitivity.

Indeed, the depression in sensitivity in the field defect is fairly small. The largest reduction we have so far observed was in the order of 1.5 log units when compared to the corresponding position in the normal hemifield, while the smallest was no larger than 0.3 log units. Whereas the first value was measured in a patient who was participating for the first time in this kind of threshold testing, the second was measured in one of the patients who had taken part in these experiments over a period of more than 5 years. This seems to indicate that at least in some patients, an increase in sensitivity is possible over time and with practice. The difference between patients, usually tentatively attributed to differences in their lesions and the varying extent of extrastriate cortical involvement, might eventually also become understood as a consequence of the variation in the amount of transneuronal retinal degeneration (see Fig. 4). At present, the reasons for the variability are as mysterious as the neural mechanisms responsible for the increase in sensitivity with practice.

Acknowledgements

We gratefully acknowledge the patients' invaluable contributions to our work, which was supported by grants from the Deutsche Forschungsgemeinschaft (Sto 206/4-1), the UK Medical Research Council (Grant G971/397/B) and the Oxford McDonell-Pew Centre for Cognitive Neuroscience.

References

Barbur, J.L., Ruddock, K.H. and Waterfield, V.A. (1980) Human visual responses in the absence of the geniculo-calcarine projection. *Brain,* 103: 905 – 928.

Blythe, I.M., Kennard, C. and Ruddock, K.H. (1987) Residual vision in patients with retrogeniculate lesions of the visual pathways. *Brain,* 110: 887 – 905.

Brindley, G.S., Gautier-Smith, P.C. and Lewin, W. (1969) Cortical blindness and the non-geniculate fibres of the optic tracts. *J. Neurol. Neurosurg. Psychiatry,* 32: 259 – 264.

Cowey, A. (1974) Atrophy of retinal ganglion cells after removal of striate cortex in a rhesus monkey. *Perception,* 3: 257 – 260.

Cowey, A. and Stoerig, P. (1989) Projection patterns of surviving neurons in the dorsal lateral geniculate nucleus following discrete lesions of striate cortex: implications for residual vision. *Exp. Brain Res.,* 75: 631 – 638.

Cowey, A., Stoerig, P. and Perry, V.H. (1989) Transneuronal retrograde degeneration in the retina of macaque monkeys: selective loss of Pβ cells. *Neuroscience,* 29: 65 – 80.

Crook, J.M., Lange-Malecki, B., Lee, B.B. and Valberg, A. (1988) Visual resolution of macaque retinal ganglion cells. *J. Physiol. (Lond.),* 396: 205 – 224.

De Monasterio, F.M. (1978) Properties of ganglion cells with atypical receptive-field organization in retina of macaques. *J. Neurophysiol.,* 41: 1435 – 1449.

De Monasterio, F.M. and Gouras, P. (1975) Functional properties of ganglion cells in the rhesus monkey retina. *J. Physiol. (Lond.),* 251: 167 – 195.

Derrington, A.M., Krauskopf, J. and Lennie, P. (1984) Chromatic mechanisms in the lateral geniculate nucleus of macaque. *J. Physiol. (Lond.),* 357: 241 – 265.

De Valois, R.L., Snodderly, D.M., Yund, E.W. and Hepler, N.K. (1977) Responses of macaque lateral geniculate cells to luminance and color figures. *Sensory Processes,* 1: 244 – 259.

Dineen, J.T. and Hendrickson, A.E. (1981) Age-correlated differences of retinal degeneration after striate cortex lesions in monkeys. *Invest. Ophthalmol. Visual Sci.,* 21: 749 – 752.

Dineen, J.T. and Keating, E.G. (1981) The primate visual system after bilateral removal of striate cortex. Survival of complex pattern vision. *Exp. Brain Res.,* 41: 338 – 345.

Dineen, G., Hendrickson, A. and Keating, E.G. (1982) Alterations of retinal inputs following striate cortex removal in adult monkey. *Exp. Brain Res.,* 47: 446 – 456.

Fitzpatrick, D., Itoh, K. and Diamond, I.T. (1983) The laminar organisation of the lateral geniculate body and the striate cortex in the squirrel monkey (*Saimiri sciureus*). *J. Neurosci.,* 3: 673 – 702.

Gouras, P. (1968) Identification of cone mechanisms in monkey ganglion cells. *J. Physiol. (Lond.),* 199: 533 – 547.

Heide, W., Koenig, E. and Dichgans, J. (1990) Optokinetic nystagmus, self-motion sensation and their aftereffects in patients with occipito-parietal lesions. *Clin. Vision Sci.,* 5: 145 – 156.

Heywood, S. and Ratcliff, G. (1975) Long-term oculomotor consequences of unilateral colliculectomy in man. In: G. Lennerstrand and P. Bach-y-Rita (Eds.), *Basic Mechanisms of Ocular Motility and their Clinical Implications,* Pergamon Press, Oxford, pp. 561 – 564.

Kadoya, S., Wolin, L.R. and Massopust, L.C. (1971) Collicular unit responses to monochromatic stimulation in squirrel monkey. *Brain Res.,* 32: 251 – 254.

Kaplan, E. and Shapley, R.M. (1981) The primate retina contains two types of retinal ganglion cells, with high and low contrast sensitivity. *Proc. Natl. Acad. Sci. U.S.A.,* 83: 2755 – 2757.

Keating, E.G. (1975) Effects of prestriate and striate lesions on the monkey's ability to locate and discriminate visual forms. *Exp. Neurol.,* 47: 16 – 25.

Keating, E.G. (1979) Rudimentary color vision in the monkey after removal of striate and preoccipital cortex. *Brain Res.,* 179: 379 – 384.

King-Smith, P.E. and Carden, D. (1976) Luminance and colour-opponent contributions to visual detection and adaption and to temporal and spatial integration. *J. Opt. Soc. Am.,* 66: 709 – 717.

Kisvárday, Z.F., Cowey, A., Stoerig, P. and Somogyi, P. (1991) Direct and indirect retinal input into degenerated dorsal lateral geniculate nucleus after striate cortical removal in monkey: implications for residual vision. *Exp. Brain Res.,* 86: 271 – 292.

Lee, J. and Stromeyer, C.F. (1989) Contribution of human short-wave cones to luminance and motion detection. *J. Physiol. (Lond.),* 413: 563 – 593.

Lepore, F., Cardu, B., Rasmussen, T. and Malmo, R.B. (1975) Rod and cone sensitivity in destriate monkeys. *Brain Res.,* 93: 203 – 221.

Leventhal, A.G., Rodieck, R.W. and Dreher, B. (1981) Retinal ganglion cell classes in the Old World monkey: morphology and central projections. *Science,* 213: 1139 – 1142.

Livingstone, M.S. and Hubel, D.H. (1984) Anatomy and physiology of a color system in the primate visual cortex. *J. Neurosci.,* 4: 309 – 356.

Livingstone, M.S. and Hubel, D.H. (1988) Segregation of form, color, movement, and depth: anatomy, physiology, and perception. *Science,* 240: 740 – 749.

Magnussen, S. and Mathiesen, T. (1989) Detection of moving and stationary gratings in the absence of striate cortex. *Neuropsychologia,* 27: 725 – 728.

Marzi, C.A., Tassinari, G., Aglioti, S. and Lutzemberger, L. (1986) Spatial summation across the vertical meridian in hemianopics: a test of blindsight. *Neuropsychologia,* 24: 749 – 758.

Merigan, W.H. and Maunsell, J.H.R. (1990) Macaque vision after magnocellular lateral geniculate lesions. *Visual Neurosci.,* 5: 347 – 352.

Michael, C.R. (1988) Retinal afferent arborization patterns, dendritic field orientations, and the segregation of function in the lateral geniculate nucleus of the monkey. *Proc. Natl. Acad.*

Sci. U.S.A., 85: 4914 – 4918.

Mihailovic, L.T., Cupic, D. and Dekleva, N. (1975) Changes in the number of neurons and glial cells in the lateral geniculate nucleus of the monkey during retrograde cell degeneration. *J. Comp. Neurol.,* 142: 223 – 230.

Miller, M., Pasik, P. and Pasik, T. (1980) Extrageniculate vision in the monkey. VII. Contrast sensitivity functions. *J. Neurophysiol.,* 43: 1510 – 1526.

Mohler, C.W. and Wurtz, R.H. (1977) Role of striate cortex and superior colliculus in the guidance of saccadic eye movements in monkeys. *J. Neurophysiol.,* 40: 74 – 94.

Pasik, P. and Pasik, T. (1982) Visual functions in monkeys after total removal of visual cerebral cortex. In: W.D. Neff (Ed.), *Contributions to Sensory Physiology, Vol.* 7, Academic Press, New York, London, pp. 147 – 200.

Perenin, M.T. (1978) Visual function within the hemianopic field following early cerebral hemidecortication in man. II. Pattern discrimination. *Neuropsychologia,* 16: 697 – 708.

Perenin, M.T. and Jeannerod, M. (1978) Visual function within the hemianopic field following early cerebral hemidecortication in man. I. Spatial localization. *Neuropsychologia,* 16: 1 – 13.

Perry, V.H. and Cowey, A. (1981) The morphological correlates of x- and y-like retinal ganglion cells in the retina of monkeys. *Exp. Brain Res.,* 43: 226 – 228.

Perry, V.H. and Cowey, A. (1984) Retinal ganglion cells that project to the superior colliculus and pretectum in the macaque monkey. *Neuroscience,* 12: 1125 – 1137.

Perry, V.H., Oehler, R. and Cowey, A. (1984) Retinal ganglion cells that project to the dorsal lateral geniculate nucleus in the macaque monkey. *Neuroscience,* 12: 1101 – 1123.

Pöppel, E., Held, R. and Frost, D. (1973) Residual visual functions after brain wounds involving the central visual pathways in man. *Nature,* 243: 295 – 296.

Ptito, A., Lassonde, M., Lepore, F. and Ptito, M. (1987) Visual discrimination in hemispherectomized patients. *Neuropsychologia,* 25: 869 – 879.

Purpura, K., Kaplan, E. and Shapley, R.M. (1988) Background light and the contrast gain of primate P and M retinal ganglion cells. *Proc. Natl. Acad. Sci. U.S.A.,* 85: 4534 – 4537.

Rafal, R., Smith, J., Krantz, J., Cohen, A. and Brennan, C. (1990) Extrageniculate vision in hemianopic humans: saccade inhibition by signals in the blind field. *Science,* 250: 118 – 121.

Richards, W. (1973) Visual processing in scotomata. *Exp. Brain Res.,* 17: 333 – 347.

Robson, J.G. and Graham, N. (1981) Probability summation and regional variation in contrast sensitivity across the visual field. *Vision Res.,* 21: 409 – 418.

Rodman, H.R., Gross, C.G. and Albright, T.D. (1989) Afferent basis of visual response properties in area MT of the macaque. II. Effects of superior colliculus removal. *J. Neurosci.,* 10: 2033 – 2050.

Schiller, P.H. and Logothetis, N.K. (1990) The color-opponent and broad-band channels of the primate visual system. *Trends*

Neurosci., 13: 392 – 398.

Schiller, P.H., Logothetis, N.K. and Charles, E.R. (1990) Role of the color-opponent and broad-band channels in vision. *Visual Neurosci.,* 5: 321 – 346.

Shapley, R. and Perry, V.H. (1986) Cat and monkey retinal ganglion cells and their visual functional roles. *Trends Neurosci.,* 9: 229 – 235.

Snelgar, R.S., Foster, D.H. and Scase, M.O. (1987) Isolation of opponent-colour mechanisms at increment threshold. *Vision Res.,* 27: 1017 – 1027.

Sperling, H.G. and Harwerth, R.S. (1971) Red-green cone interactions in the increment-threshold spectral sensitivity of primates. *Science,* 172: 180 – 184.

Stoerig, P. (1987) Chromaticity and achromaticity. Evidence for a functional segregation in visual field defects. *Brain,* 110: 869 – 886.

Stoerig, P. (1991) Different response paradigms yield different spatial summation curves in blindsight. *Eur. J. Neurosci., Suppl.* 4: 85.

Stoerig, P. and Cowey, A. (1989) Spectral sensitivity in blindsight. *Nature,* 342: 916 – 918.

Stoerig, P. and Cowey, A. (1991) Increment threshold spectral sensitivity in visual field defects. *Brain,* 116: 1487 – 1512.

Stoerig, P. and Cowey, A. (1992) Wavelength discrimination in blindsight. *Brain,* 115: 425 – 444.

Stoerig, P., Hübner, M. and Pöppel, E. (1985) Signal detection analysis of residual vision in a field defect due to a post-geniculate lesion. *Neuropsychologia,* 23: 589 – 599.

Stoerig, P., Cowey, A. and Bannister, M. (1991) Retinal ganglion cells that project to the pulvinar nucleus in macaque monkeys. *Soc. Neurosci. Abstr.,* 17: 711.

Ter Braak, J.W.G., Schenk, V.W.D. and Van Vliet, A.G.M. (1971) Visual reactions in a case of long-lasting cortical blindness. *J. Neurol. Neurosurg. Psychiatry,* 34: 140 – 147.

Van Buren, J.M. (1963a) Trans-synaptic retrograde degeneration in the visual system of primates. *J. Neurol. Neurosurg. Psychiatry,* 26: 402 – 409.

Van Buren, J.M. (1963b) *The Retinal Ganglion Cell Layer,* Thomas, Springfield, IL.

Weiskrantz, L. (1987) Residual vision in a scotoma. A follow-up study of "form" discrimination. *Brain,* 110: 77 – 92.

Weiskrantz, L. (1990) Outlooks for blindsight: explicit methodologies for implicit processes. *Proc. R. Soc. Lond. (Biol.),* 239: 247 – 278.

Weiskrantz, L., Warrington, E.K., Sanders, M.D. and Marshall, J. (1974) Visual capacity in the hemianopic field following a restricted occipital ablation. *Brain,* 97: 709 – 728.

Weiskrantz, L., Cowey, A. and Passingham, C. (1977) Spatial responses to brief stimuli by monkeys with striate cortex ablations. *Brain,* 100: 655 – 670.

Weller, R.E. and Kaas, J.H. (1989) Parameters affecting the loss of ganglion cells of the retina following ablation of striate cortex in primates. *Visual Neurosci.,* 3: 327 – 349.

Weller, R.E., Kaas, J.H. and Wetzel, A.B. (1979) Evidence for the loss of x-cells of the retina after long-term ablation of visual cortex in monkeys. *Brain Res.,* 160: 134 – 138.

Wiesel, T.N. and Hubel, D.H. (1966) Spatial and chromatic interactions in the lateral geniculate body of the rhesus monkey. *J. Neurophysiol.,* 29: 1115 – 1156.

Wurtz, R.H. and Albano, J.E. (1980) Visual-motor function of the primate superior colliculus. *Annu. Rev. Neurosci.,* 3: 189 – 226.

Yukie, M. and Iwai, E. (1981) Direct projection from the dorsal lateral geniculate nucleus to the prestriate cortex in macaque monkeys. *J. Comp. Neurol.,* 201: 81 – 97.

Zihl, J. and von Cramon, D. (1979) The contribution of the ''second'' visual system to directed visual attention in man. *Brain,* 102: 835 – 856.

T.P. Hicks, S. Molotchnikoff and T. Ono (Eds.)
Progress in Brain Research, Vol. 95
© 1993 Elsevier Science Publishers B.V. All rights reserved.

CHAPTER 37

Neuronal representations, assemblies and temporal coherence

Wolf Singer

Max Planck Institute for Brain Research, D-6000 Frankfurt/Main 71, Germany

The evolution of concepts

The question how the nervous system creates representations of its environment has fascinated philosophers and scientists since mankind began to reflect on its own nature. However, it is only in this last century that speculations could be replaced by precise and experimentally testable hypotheses.

Recapitulation of the concepts offered at various epochs reveals oscillations between extreme views the frequency of which increased at the same pace as progress in neuroscience. Descartes, in order to preserve unity of conscious experience assumed that all sensory signals eventually had to converge onto a single center. Because of its central location in the brain he suspected the pineal gland to be the site where the mystical conversion of physical signals into conscious experience was accomplished. The twentieth century saw the emergence of various localization theories which assigned particular functions to particular, cytoarchitectonically defined cortical areas, but all of them tacitly assumed some ultimate coordinating center endowed with the abilities of a homunculus who evaluates the distributed events. Then the pendulum swung back to more holistic views which culminated in Lashley's field-theory which treated the whole brain as a functional unit. The victory of the neuron doctrine and the technical advances in single cell recording subsequently caused a shiftback towards compartmentalization of function and emphasized the impor-

tance of individual nerve cells. The "stimulus-response" paradigm, which had been so successful in analyzing the behavior of animals and the properties of simple nervous systems has been applied to higher sensory functions and this eventually led to the discovery of cortical neurons responding selectively to particular features or combinations of features (Mountcastle, 1957; Hubel and Wiesel, 1963). In conjunction with anatomical evidence which at the time was considered compatible with serial processing of sensory signals in hierarchically arranged cortical areas, this discovery led to the proposal that not only simple features but also complex constellations of features which characterize natural objects and scenes might be represented by the responses of individual highly specialized neurons.

The discovery of hand-, face- and action-specific neuronal responses in higher visual areas of the monkey has been taken as support for the view that individual neurons with highly selective response properties emerge from serial processing of sensory signals in hierarchically arranged cortical areas (Gross et al., 1972; Desimone et al., 1984; Perrett et al., 1987). However, not all available data support such an interpretation. Cells in areas remote from primary sensory input are often less selective for particular features than those at earlier stages, the response selectivity of neurons activated by complex patterns is not exclusive, and in a particular cortical area many different cells were found to respond to the same object (see, e.g., Rolls, 1990). Moreover, it was realized that parallelism and reciprocity are a prevailing principle of cortical connectivity, which makes it difficult to assume that one particular cortical area should serve as the end stage of a hierarchical process (Felleman and Van Essen, 1991). Finally, it has been argued that there would probably not be enough cells in the brain if each of the distinguishable feature constellations would have to be represented by a specialized neuron.

For these reasons an alternative concept has been developed. It assumes that particular feature constellations are represented by matching constellations of a large number of simultaneously active neurons (Hebb, 1949; Braitenberg, 1978; Edelman and Mountcastle, 1978; Grossberg, 1980; Palm, 1982; Crick, 1984; von der Malsburg, 1985; Edelman, 1987, 1989; Abeles, 1991). Just as a particular feature can be shared by many different patterns, a particular neuron could then be shared by different representations in that it participates at different times in different "assemblies" of coactive neurons. A basic requirement for representing feature constellations or patterns by assemblies is of course, that the neuronal elements constituting a particular assembly are distinguishable as members of this very assembly. The assumption is that assemblies are formed by selective connections between the constituting elements. These connections would enable cooperative interactions between the respective neurons and, through reverberation, would stabilize the assemblies (see, e.g., Singer, 1979). Moreover, in order to allow for the generation of assemblies representing new patterns the coupling connections between the putative elements of an assembly should be endowed with adaptive synapses, the efficiency of which can change in a use-dependent way according to some kind of associative learning algorithm. This notion establishes close relations between concepts of assembly coding and associative memory networks (Palm, 1990). A related proposal is that the functional units embodying features should be local groups of reciprocally coupled neurons rather than individual cells (Edelman and Mountcastle, 1978;

Edelman, 1987, 1989). In this concept assemblies would then be constituted by sets of spatially distributed and interconnected groups rather than by distributed individual neurons.

However, it was soon realized that there was a serious limitation. As assemblies were thought to be distinguished solely by the enhanced responses of their constituents different objects could not be represented simultaneously because their corresponding assemblies would have become confounded. It was impossible to know which of the numerous active and spatially intermingled cells would actually belong to a particular assembly. To overcome this superposition problem it has been proposed that assemblies should be distinguished in addition by temporal patterning of their activity (von der Malsburg, 1985, von der Malsburg and Schneider, 1986). The suggestion was that individual neurons or groups of neurons should engage in rhythmic discharges which occur in synchrony for all members of an assembly. Assemblies coding for different figures should each engage in their own rhythm and should show no fixed phase relation between their respective synchronous oscillations. In this way simultaneously active neurons remain distinguishable as members of a particular assembly because their responses are synchronous with the responses of other cells of the same assembly but not with cells of other assemblies. In computer simulations this temporal coding principle proved to be very efficient for the solution of problems related to figure-ground segregation (von der Malsburg and Schneider, 1986; Bienenstock and von der Malsburg, 1987; von der Malsburg, 1988). Subsequently, this concept of "binding by synchrony" has been developed further and generalized to intermodal integration (Damasio, 1990) and even to integrative processes underlying phenomena such as attention (Crick, 1984) and consciousness (Crick and Koch, 1990).

Essential properties of cortical organization are compatible with these concepts of assembly coding: the distributed representation of primitive features by specialized neurons, and the grouping together of neurons with similar response properties in functional columns (Mountcastle, 1957; Hubel and Wiesel, 1963), the parallel arrangement of a large number of functionally specialized cortical areas, and the incredibly dense network of reciprocal cortico-cortical connections allowing for a very large number of combinations of different neurons and hence for the formation of very many different assemblies (for review, see Felleman and Van Essen, 1991). However, despite its attractiveness it proved difficult to obtain direct experimental support for this concept for a number of reasons: first, chances are low to record simultaneously from cells actually participating in a particular assembly, because their spatial distribution cannot be anticipated. Second, it is to be expected that interactions are difficult to detect because they are of short duration and occur at times which cannot be precisely predicted. The theory implies that assemblies are highly dynamic, rapidly changing functional entities. Moreover, because assemblies self-organize through cooperative interactions among their constituting elements, the time of their formation predictably lacks any stereotyped relation with the inducing stimuli.

The recent observation that spatially adjacent neurons in the cat visual cortex have a strong tendency to engage in highly synchronous oscillatory discharges when presented with their preferred stimulus (Gray and Singer, 1987) provided a new motivation to search for temporally structured assemblies: first, this observation indicated that feature-specific responses have a distinct temporal structure which could in principle be used for the temporal patterning of assemblies. Second, the occurrence of local response synchronization provided a legitimation for the use of multi-unit recordings when searching for correlations between responses of spatially remote groups of neurons. This was crucial in view of the predicted brevity and instability of synchronized response epochs. Using multi-unit recordings increases the number of events per time unit and thereby allows to reduce the duration of the time window required to obtain reliable data from cross-correlation analysis. Third, it was to be expected that response episodes characterized by

synchronous discharges in local cell groups should be particularly favorable for the occurrence of response synchronization among remote cell groups. The hypothesis was that the efficiency of the coupling connections should be enhanced due to spatial and temporal summation if they are active in synchrony. Thus, focusing cross-correlation analysis on response episodes associated with high local synchrony was expected to increase the prob-

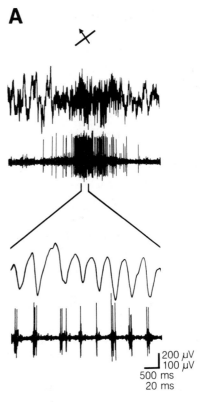

Fig. 1. Multi-unit activity (MUA) and local field potential (LFP) responses recorded from area 17 in an adult cat to the presentation of an optimally oriented light bar moving across the receptive field. Oscilloscope records of a single trial showing the response to the perferred direction of stimulus movement. In the upper two traces, at a slow time scale, the onset of the neuronal response is associated with an increase in high-frequency activity in the LFP. The lower two traces display the activity at the peak of the response at an expanded time scale. Note the presence of rhythmic oscillations in the LFP and MUA that are correlated in phase with the peak negativity of the LFP. Upper and lower voltage scales are for the LFP and MUA, respectively. (From Gray and Singer, 1989.)

ability of observing synchronization over larger distances.

Experimental evidence compatible with the concept of temporally structured assemblies

The phenomenon of local response synchronization has in the meantime been observed in several areas of the visual cortex of anesthetized (Eckhorn et al., 1988; Gray and Singer, 1989; Engel et al., 1990, 1991a) and awake cats (Raether et al., 1989), and recently also awake behaving monkeys (Kreiter and Singer, 1991) (see, e.g., Fig. 1). This supports the proposal (Edelman, 1987) that local clusters of neurons with similar response properties behave as a group consisting of tightly coupled elements. It has further been shown both in cat and monkey that response synchronization can occur also between spatially segregated cell groups within the same visual area (Gray et al., 1989; Engel et al., 1990; Kreiter and Singer, 1991). Detailed studies in anesthetized cats have revealed that in this case synchronization probability depends on the spatial segregation and feature preference of the respective cell groups as well as on the configuration of the stimuli (Gray et al., 1989; Engel et al., 1990, 1991c).

Stimuli which according to common *Gestalt-criteria* appear as single figures lead to synchronization among the responding groups while stimuli appearing as independent figures or as parts of different figures fail to establish synchrony among the groups they excite (Fig. 2; Gray et al., 1989; Engel et al., 1991c)

Furthermore, it has recently been demonstrated that two different, spatially overlapping stimuli can be represented by two independently oscillating assemblies of cells and that individual groups can switch between different assemblies depending on stimulus configuration (Engel et al., 1991c). If groups of cells with overlapping receptive fields but different orientation preferences are activated with a single moving light bar they synchronize their responses even if some of these groups are suboptimally activated (Engel et al., 1990, 1991c). However, if such a set of groups is stimulated with

two independent stimuli which move in different directions, they no longer form one coherently active assembly but split into two independently oscillating assemblies, those groups joining the same assembly that have a preference for the same stimulus. Thus, the two stimuli become represented by two spatially interleaved but temporally segregated assemblies. Groups representing the same stimulus oscillate in phase while no consistent phase relation exists between assemblies representing different stimuli (Fig. 3). However, the global aspects of the applied stimulus configurations have no detectable effect on local response parameters such as amplitude or oscillatory patterning. Thus, it is not possible to tell from the responses of individual groups whether they were activated by coherent or incoherent stimuli. Only the evaluation of phase relations between the oscillatory responses of groups provides the cue as to whether the groups are activated by one coherent stimulus or by two different, independent stimuli. These results indicate that response synchronization between simultaneously activated groups depends not only on the feature preference of the respective groups but also and to a crucial extent on stimulus configuration.

In agreement with the hypothesis of parallel processing response synchronization has also been found between groups located in different cortical areas. In the cat, interareal synchronization has been observed for field potential responses between areas 17 and 18 (Eckhorn et al., 1988), and for cellular discharges between groups in area 17 and an area specialized for motion processing (Engel et al., 1991a), and even between groups in A 17 of the two hemispheres (Engel et al., 1991b). In all these cases, synchronization depended on receptive field constellations and stimulus configurations, similar to the intra-areal synchronization.

The substrate for response synchronization

It is commonly assumed in cross-correlation studies that synchronization of neuronal responses with zero-phase lag is indicative of common input (Gers-

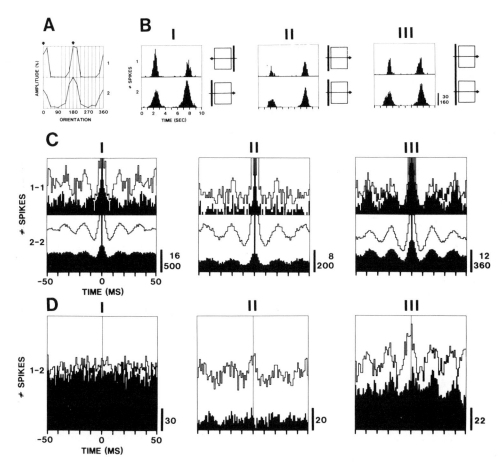

Fig. 2. Long-range oscillatory correlations reflect global stimulus properties. *A*. Orientation tuning curves of neuronal responses recorded from two electrodes (1, 2) separated by 7 mm show a preference for vertical light bars (0 and 180°) at both recording sites. *B*. Poststimulus-time histograms of the neuronal responses recorded at each site for each of three different stimulus conditions: (*I*) two light bars moved in opposite directions; (*II*) two light bars moved in the same direction; and (*III*) one long light bar moved across both receptive fields. A schematic diagram of the receptive field locations and the stimulus configuration used is displayed to the right of each poststimulus-time histogram. *C,D*. Autocorrelograms (*C*, 1 – 1, 2 – 2) and cross-correlograms (*D*, 1 – 2) computed for the neuronal responses at both sites (1 and 2 in *A* and *B*) for each of the three stimulus conditions (*I, II, III*) displayed in *B*. For each pair of correlograms, except the two displayed in *C* (*I*, 1 – 1) and *D* (*I*), the second direction of stimulus movement is shown with unfilled bars. (From Gray et al., 1989.)

tein and Perkel, 1972). It has been proposed, therefore, that the observed synchronization phenomena in the visual cortex are due to common oscillatory input from subcortical centers. This notion has received support by the discovery of pacemaker currents in thalamic neurons and corresponding oscillatory activity (Steriade et al., 1991). Moreover, it has been argued that synchronization with zero-phase lag would be difficult to achieve by reciprocal interactions between

spatially distributed neurons because of the conduction delays in the coupling connections. However, the concept of assembly coding requires that the binding-together of elements constituting an assembly is achieved through reciprocal connections between the elements of an assembly and not by common input. It is only with such a scheme of connectivity that the required combinatorial flexibility can be achieved.

Evidence is now available that response syn-

466

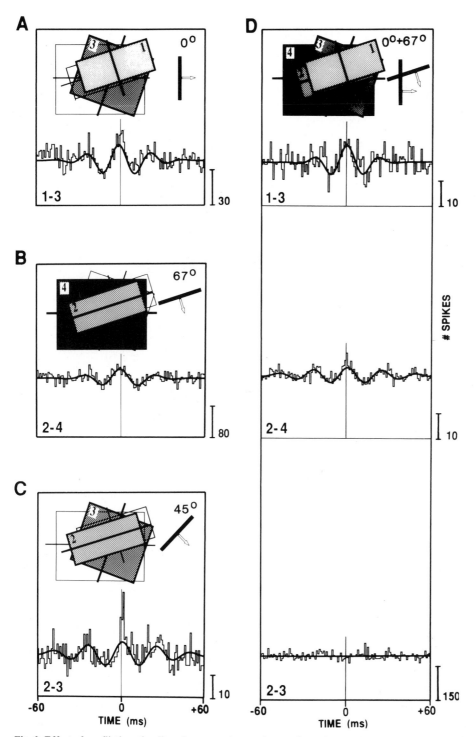

Fig. 3. Effect of conflicting stimuli on the cross-columnar interaction. We recorded simultaneously from four different cell groups that were narrowly tuned to orientation preferences of 157° (site 1), 67° (2), 22° (3), and 90° (4), as indicated in *D*. The electrode separation was 400 μm. The figure compares responses to stimulation with single light bars of 0° (*A*), 67° (*B*), and 45° (*C*) orientation with responses

chronization can be achieved by cortico-cortical connections despite considerable conduction delays. It has been demonstrated that response synchronization between cell groups in area 17 of the two hemispheres is mediated by the corpus callosum and hence by a reciprocal cortico-cortical projection that shares many features with the tangential fiber systems interconnecting cell groups within the same visual area (Engel et al., 1991b) (Fig. 4). In higher mammals signals coming from either side of the fixation point are projected to different hemispheres because of the partial decussation of the optic nerves. Neurons responding to figures extending across the vertical meridian are therefore located in different hemispheres. Following the concept of assembly coding the responses of these cells have to be bound together in the same way as those of cells located within the same hemisphere. Thus, the demonstration that callosal connections mediate interhemispheric response synchronization has two implications: it emphasizes the putative significance of response synchronization for feature binding and it proves that cortico-cortical connections can synchronize responses with zero phase lag.

Evidence for experience-dependent shaping of synchronizing connections

The theory of assembly coding implies that the structure of assemblies is determined by the functional architecture of the synchronizing connections. Therefore, these have to be selective and their functional architecture should reflect the criteria according to which particular features are grouped together rather than others. Psychophysical evidence and the electrophysiological data on synchronization probability both suggest that continuity, vicinity, colinearity, and coherent motion of

contours serve as such grouping criteria. This predicts that nearby cell groups should be coupled more tightly than distant groups and that cell groups preferring related features should be coupled preferentially. Anatomical data on the architecture of cortico-cortical connections are compatible with this postulate. In the visual cortex cells separated by less than 1 mm are interconnected by a dense network of radial axon collaterals (Fisken et al., 1975). Beyond this range connections link selectively cell groups that show a regular spacing with a periodicity of about 1 mm (Rockland and Lund, 1982). Analysis of response properties of interconnected groups suggests that these prefer similar features (T'so et al., 1986; Gilbert and Wiesel, 1989; but see Matsubara et al., 1985).

While the basic organization of cortico-cortical connections is with all likelihood determined genetically, additional shaping by an experience-dependent process is an attractive possibility for two reasons. First, the topographical arrangement of cell groups preferring particular features is not solely determined by genetic instructions but is in addition influenced by experience (Singer et al., 1981). Therefore, it would seem that the architecture of the coupling connections cannot be fully predetermined by genetic instructions either. Second, it would be advantageous if the grouping criteria could be adapted to frequently occurring feature constellations in natural scenes, and in particular to those constellations which are behaviorally relevant.

Evidence compatible with such a use-dependent selection of synchronizing cortico-cortical connections is now available. In cat, the development of cortico-cortical connections extends far into postnatal life (Innocenti and Frost, 1979; Price and Blakemore, 1985; Callaway and Katz, 1990; Luhmann et al., 1990) and data from cat visual cor-

to combined presentation of 0° and 67° light bars (D). For each stimulus condition, the shading of the receptive fields indicates the sites at which responses were elicited. The cross-correlation function (CCF) computed from the respective responses is shown with unfilled histogram bars. The thick continuous line represents the Gabor function, which was fitted to the correlogram. Note that the CCF of (2 – 3) in D reveals no correlation, i.e., the Gabor function amplitude was not significantly different from 0. Scale bars indicate the number of spikes. (From Engel et al., 1991c.)

468

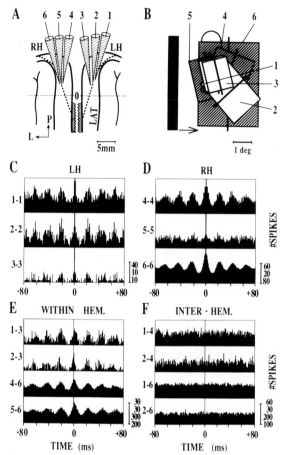

Fig. 4. Interhemispheric synchronization is absent in animals in which the corpus callosum had been sectioned. *A*. Location of the recording electrodes in the vicinity of the border of areas 17 and 18 (thick dashed line) of the RH and LH. The interelectrode spacing was 0.5 mm for the RH and 1 mm for the LH. *B*. The receptive fields of the RH (hatched) and LH (open) recordings. Thick lines, orientation preference. Circle, visual field center. All receptive fields were overlapping because the RH receptive fields extended into the ipsilateral visual hemifield. Thus, all recording sites could be co-stimulated with a single light bar. *C, D*. Autocorrelograms of the responses at the LH and RH recording sites. All correlograms were computed in a 1.5-sec window centered on the peak of the responses in the histograms (not shown). All responses show a strong oscillatory modulation in the same frequency range. *E*. Cross-correlograms between responses from different recording sites within the same hemisphere. The oscillatory responses are strongly synchronized within either hemisphere. Strong temporal correlation occurs even between electrodes separated by as much as 2 mm (1 − 3). *F*. Cross-correlograms between responses from different hemispheres. Note the absence of any temporal correlation. Cross-correlations are displayed only for those responses that showed the strongest oscillatory modulation (that is, 1 and 2 with 4 and 6). However, correlograms were also flat for all other interhemispheric combinations. (From Engel et al., 1991b.)

tex suggest that the connections attain their final specificity through an experience-dependent process (Innocenti and Frost, 1979; Price and Blakemore, 1985; Luhmann et al., 1990; Callaway and Katz, 1990). Moreover, as summarized below, recent data from strabismic cats indicate that this experience-dependent selection is based on some kind of correlation analysis.

Raising kittens with artificially induced strabismus leads to changes in the connections between the two eyes and cortical neurons so that individual cortical neurons become connected to only one eye (Wiesel and Hubel, 1965). Thus, the population of cortical neurons splits into two subpopulations of about equal size, each responding rather selectively to stimulation of one eye only.

Most strabismic animals develop normal monocular vision particularly if they are exotropic and alternate. It must be assumed, therefore, that the interactions required for feature-binding are unimpaired between cortical cells connected to the same eye. This is not the case for signals conveyed by different eyes. Psychophysical evidence indicates that strabismic subjects suppress signals coming from one eye in order to avoid double images and actually become unable to bind signals conveyed by different eyes even if these signals are made contiguous by optical compensation of the squint angle (von Noorden, 1990). This implies that in strabismics, binding mechanisms should be abnormal or missing between cells driven from different eyes. If one accepts that response synchronization is equivalent to binding and that the architecture of cortico-cortical connections determines the probability of response synchronization, two predictions follow for strabismic animals: first, response synchronization should be normal between cell groups connected to the same eye but should be very rare if present at all between cell groups connected to different eyes. Second, tangential cortico-cortical connections should extend preferentially between territories served by the same eye.

Both predictions were found to be fulfilled (König et al., 1990; Löwel and Singer, 1992) and this has several important implications. First, it corroborates the notion that tangential intracortical connections are the substrate for response syn-

469

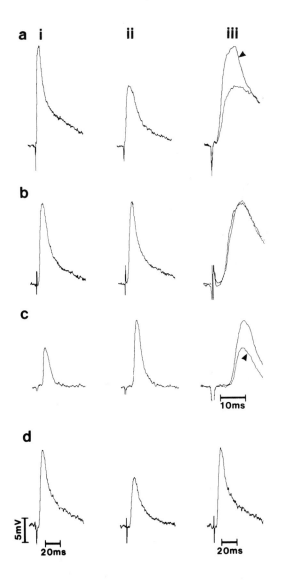

Fig. 5. Effect of depolarizing and hyperpolarizing current pulses on the induction of LTD and LTP. *a – c*. Averaged (*n* = 5, 0.03 Hz) responses to white matter stimulation recorded before (*i*) and 20 min after the tetanus (*ii*) from a cell receiving no current injection during the tetanus (*a*), in a cell hyperpolarized by − 40 mV below V$_{mr}$ (*b*), and in a cell depolarized by + 20 mV above V$_{mr}$ (*c*). Responses *i* and *ii* are superimposed at expanded time scale in *iii*. Arrows indicate the pretetanic response. *d*. The induction and the reversal of LTD. First, a tetanus was applied without current injection and caused LTD (compare the control *i* with the posttetanic response *ii*). Then a second tetanus was applied in conjunction with a depolarizing current pulse, and this caused LTP of the previously depressed response resulting in a resetting of LTD (*iii*). V$_m$ = − 71 mV in *a*, − 69 mV in *b*, − 71 mV in *c*, and − 73 mV in *d*. (From Artola et al., 1990.)

chronization. Second, it is strong support for the hypothesis that the architecture of tangential connections is shaped by experience and third, it suggests that this selection occurs according to a correlation rule. The latter conclusion is based on the plausible assumption that in strabismics, once cortical cells have become monocular, responses of cells connected to the same eye will on the average show a much higher degree of correlation than responses of cells connected to different eyes. Fourth, the close correlation between the loss of the ability to bind signals conveyed by the two eyes, the loss of response synchronization between cells driven by the two eyes, and the loss of connections between the cortical territories of the two eyes is further support for the hypothesis that the architecture of cortico-cortical connections, by determining the probability of response synchronization, determines the criteria for feature binding. Since this architecture is shaped by experience it follows, that at least some of the binding and segmentation criteria are acquired by experience, or in other terms, are learned during early life.

Synaptic plasticity of coupling connections in the adult

If selective interactions between spatially distributed cell groups in the visual cortex serve to establish neuronal representations of particular feature constellations, one is led to postulate that the connections responsible for these interactions preserve some malleability, even in the adult cortex. Otherwise, it would be impossible to modify through experience the criteria for the segmentation of patterns. Since growth and pruning of connections are probably restricted to development, changes of intercolumnar interactions in the adult need to involve modifications of synaptic efficacy of existing connections.

In accordance with this postulate, use-dependent long-term modifications of synaptic transmission have been observed in slices of the mature visual cortex (Artola and Singer, 1987, 1990). Interestingly, the conditions for the induction of synaptic

470

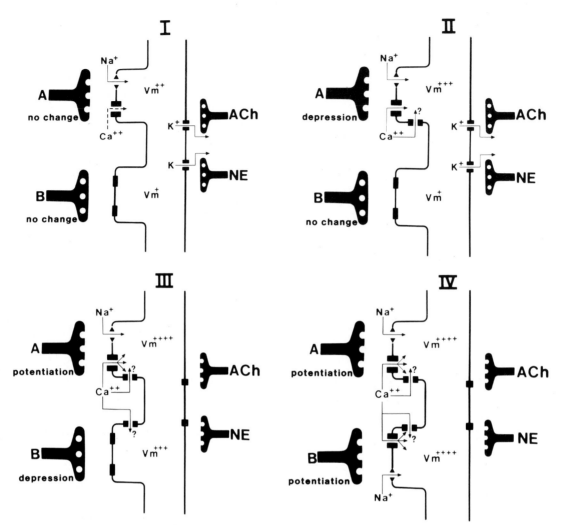

Fig. 6. Schematic representation of processes likely to be involved in activity-dependent synaptic modifications in the developing and mature visual cortex. Inputs A and B correspond to two modifiable excitatory inputs. Inputs labeled ACh and NE correspond to cholinergic and noradrenergic afferents, respectively. *I*. Input A is active while input B is inactive. Resulting depolarization is assumed to be neither sufficient to remove the Mg^{2+} block of NMDA receptors at synapse A nor to reach the threshold of the homosynaptic depression mechanism. Consequently, postsynaptic activation also fails to reach the threshold for the heterosynaptic depression process. There is no change of synapses A and B. This occurs when permissive modulatory inputs are silent (Bear and Singer, 1986). *II*. Input A is active while input B is silent. Now, depolarization is assumed to be sufficient to reach the threshold for homosynaptic depression but still insufficient to cause substantial activation of NMDA-receptor-dependent Ca^{2+} conductances. Consequently, the heterosynaptic depression threshold is not reached. Input A weakens while input B remains unchanged. In vivo this condition has been observed only after pharmacological manipulation of neuronal excitability. *III*. Input A is active in conjunction with the modulatory inputs while input B is inactive. Now input A is assumed to cause a sufficiently strong depolarization of the membrane potential to lift the Mg^{2+} block and to trigger substantial activation of the Ca^{2+} conductance of the NMDA-receptor-gated channel. As a consequence, input A potentiates and the threshold of the heterosynaptic depression mechanism is reached and synapse B weakens. The active synapse A is protected from depression because of the activation of NMDA-receptor-gated conductances at this synapse. Question marks indicate the possibility of additional activation of voltage-dependent Ca^{2+} conductances. *IV*. Afferents A and B are active simultaneously and in conjunction with permissive modulatory inputs. Inputs A and B are both assumed to cause sufficient depolarization to substantially activate the NMDA-receptor-gated conductances at their respective synapses. This protects both synapses from depression despite strong postsynaptic activation. The result is that the conjointly activated inputs A and B consolidate. (From Collingridge and Singer, 1990.)

modifications in the adult resemble in many respects those of the experience-dependent changes of cortical connectivity during development. In both cases, changes require the activation of NMDA-receptor-dependent conductances (Artola and Singer, 1987, 1990; Kleinschmidt et al., 1987; Kimura et al., 1989), and modifications are facilitated by the neuromodulators noradrenaline and acetylcholine (Kasamatsu and Pettigrew, 1979; Bear and Singer, 1986; Greuel et al., 1988; Bröcher et al., 1989). Because in vitro the activation state of pre- and postsynaptic elements can be controlled, it has recently become possible to study directly how the synaptic gain changes depend on the activation state of pre- and postsynaptic elements. Examples of such modifications and the resulting modification rules are summarized in Figs. 5 and 6. We found that there are two different thresholds for synaptic modifications, both of which appear to depend on the activation state of the postsynaptic target cell. If an input fails to reach either threshold, there is no change in synaptic gain. If the first, lower threshold is reached by an active input, synaptic gain *decreases* at the activated synapses, but there is no change at other, inactive synapses. The threshold for this homosynaptic depression mechanism is lower than that of the activation threshold of NMDA-receptor-dependent conductances. Accordingly, depression occurs even if NMDA receptors are pharmacologically blocked at the active synapses. If activation increases further, a second threshold is reached, and the active input is no longer depressed but now becomes potentiated (Artola et al., 1990). This second threshold is related to NMDA-receptor-dependent conductances and cannot be reached if NMDA receptors are blocked. If this threshold is reached, however, the active input can induce in addition to its own potentiation heterosynaptic depression of other inputs, i.e., other synapses on the same neuron become weakened if they are inactive. These inputs can in turn be protected from depression if they are also active and capable of activating NMDA-receptor-dependent conductances at their respective synapses. Thus, synapses capable of activating the NMDA-receptor mechanism have a

double competitive advantage: first, they increase their gain and are protected against heterosynaptic depression and second, they are capable of repressing other synapses if these are not sufficiently active.

Thus, the modifications occur according to an associative algorithm but the correlation rule is more complicated than that initially proposed by Hebb. It resembles in some respects the biphasic modification rule that has been proposed by Bienenstock, Cooper and Monroe (Bienenstock et al., 1982) for the self-organization of thalamo-cortical connections but it differs in that it also allows for weakening of inactive presynaptic afferents. Simulation studies indicate that a biphasic modification rule is very effective when applied in associative memory networks because it allows for error correction and learning of exceptions (Hancock et al., 1991). Available evidence indicates that intra-cortical connections are endowed with such adaptive synapses but there is still no direct proof that the connections in question actually participate also in response synchronization. If they did – and at present there is no evidence against this possibility – it would imply that binding and segmentation criteria could still be acquired or at least be modified in the adult. Recent psychophysical evidence suggests the same conclusion (Karni and Sagi, 1991). As an experience-dependent modification of the criteria for perceptual grouping is equivalent to learning, we might actually be looking at the substrate of learning when we observe use-dependent synaptic modifications of cortico-cortical connections. The reversibility of modifications would thus appear as the only difference between the developmental changes and the modifications in the adult. The developmental modifications in the architecture of thalamo-cortical and cortico-cortical connections are irreversible once growth of these pathways has come to an end while the synaptic gain changes which persist in the adult are reversible.

Concluding remarks

In conclusion then, it appears that many of the

predictions derived from the theory of temporal assembly coding are supported by experimental evidence. As far as the visual system is concerned the data on response synchronization appear without exception compatible with the hypothesis that neuronal representations of visual objects consist of assemblies of cells or cell groups that are distinguished by the synchrony of their temporally structured responses. The data are also compatible with the hypothesis that feature-specific response synchronization can serve to group features according to *Gestaltcriteria* and hence can be used as a mechanism for figure/ground segregation and scene segmentation. The criteria for the grouping of distributed features are likely to be set by the architecture of the synchronizing connections and by the gain of the respective synapses. During development, this architecture is susceptible to experience-dependent modifications. Thus, through epigenetic shaping, the grouping criteria can be adapted to the actual requirements of the environment in which the organism happens to evolve. Grouping criteria may remain modifiable in the mature system but only within the constraints of the architecture of connections. These continuing modifications are realized through activity-dependent changes of synaptic gain. In essence, these modifications strengthen connections between cell groups that are often active simultaneously, and they weaken interactions between cell groups that are only rarely co-activated. In combination, these mechanisms lead to a network that is able to evaluate relationships between spatially distributed features and to create representations for particular, frequently occurring constellations of features. These representations in turn can be used for scene segmentation because they allow for the grouping that is necessary to assign signals from spatially distributed contours to particular objects, figures and background. However, proving that natural systems actually function the way the theory of temporal assembly coding assumes will require the establishment of causal relations between the formation of synchronously active cell assemblies and perception. One way is to manipulate assemblies and to relate the modifications in the structure of assemblies to specific changes in behavioral functions. The experiments in strabismic animals can be considered as an attempt in this direction. Another possibility is to follow the dynamics of assemblies with multi-electrode recordings in awake, performing animals and to relate changes in the structure of the assemblies to changes in the animal's perception.

References

Abeles, M. (1991) *Corticonics,* Cambridge University Press, Cambridge, MA.

Artola, A. and Singer, W. (1987) Long-term potentiation and NMDA receptors in rat visual cortex. *Nature,* 330: 649 – 652.

Artola, A. and Singer, W. (1990) The involvement of *N*-methyl-D-aspartate receptors in induction and maintenance of long-term potentiation in rat visual cortex. *Eur. J. Neurosci.,* 2: 254 – 269.

Artola, A., Bröcher, S. and Singer, W. (1990) Different voltage-dependent thresholds for inducing long-term depression and long-term potentiation in slices of rat visual cortex. *Nature,* 347: 69 – 72.

Bear, M.F. and Singer W. (1986) Modulation of visual cortical plasticity by acetylcholine and noradrenaline. *Nature,* 320: 172 – 176.

Bienenstock, E. and von der Malsburg, C. (1987) A neural network for invariant pattern recognition. *Europhys. Lett.,* 4: 121 – 126.

Bienenstock, E., Cooper, L.N. and Munro, P. (1982) Theory for the development of neuron selectivity: orientation specificity and binocular interaction in visual cortex. *J. Neurosci.,* 2: 32 – 48.

Braitenberg, V. (1978) Theoretical approaches to complex systems. In: R. Heim and G. Palm (Eds.), *Brain Theory,* Springer, Berlin, pp. 171 – 188.

Bröcher, S., Artola, A. and Singer, W. (1989) Norepinephrine and acetylcholine act synergistically in facilitating LTP in the rat visual cortex. *ENA Abstr.,* 21: 18.99.

Callaway, E.M. and Katz, L.C. (1990) Emergence and refinement of clustered horizontal connections in cat striate cortex. *J. Neurosci.,* 10: 1134 – 1153.

Collingridge, G.L. and Singer, W. (1990) Excitatory amino acid receptors and synaptic plasticity. *Trends Pharmacol. Sci.,* 11: 290 – 296.

Crick, F. (1984) Function of the thalamic reticular complex: the searchlight hypothesis. *Proc. Natl. Acad. Sci. U.S.A.,* 81: 4586 – 4590.

Crick, F. and Koch, C. (1990) Towards a neurobiological theory of consciousness. *Sem. Neurosci.,* 2: 263 – 275.

Damasio, A.R. (1990) Synchronous activation in multiple cortical regions: a mechanism for recall. *Sem. Neurosci.,* 2:

287–296.

Desimone, R., Albright, T.D., Gross, C.G. and Bruce, C. (1984) Stimulus-selective properties of inferior temporal neurons in the macaque. *J. Neurosci.,* 4: 2051–2062.

Eckhorn, R., Bauer, R., Jordan, W., Brosch, M., Kruse, W., Munk, M. and Reitböck, H.J. (1988) Coherent oscillations: a mechanism for feature linking in the visual cortex? *Biol. Cybern.,* 60: 121–130.

Edelman, G.M. (1987) *Neural Darwinism: the Theory of Neuronal Group Selection,* Basic Books, New York.

Edelman, G.M. (1989) *The Remembered Present,* Basic Books, New York.

Edelman, G.M. and Mountcastle, V.B. (1978) *The Mindful Brain,* MIT Press, Cambridge, MA.

Engel, A.K., König, P., Gray, C.M. and Singer, W. (1990) Stimulus-dependent neuronal oscillations in cat visual cortex: inter-columnar interaction as determined by cross-correlation analyses. *Eur. J. Neurosci.,* 2: 588–606.

Engel, A.K., Kreiter, A.K., König, P. and Singer, W. (1991a) Synchronization of oscillatory neuronal responses between striate and extrastriate visual cortical areas of the cat. *Proc. Natl. Acad. Sci. U.S.A.,* 88: 6048–6052.

Engel, A.K., König, P., Kreiter, A.K. and Singer, W. (1991b) Interhemispheric synchronization of oscillatory neuronal responses in cat visual cortex. *Science,* 252: 1177–1179.

Engel, A.K., König, P. and Singer, W. (1991c) Direct physiological evidence for scene segmentation by temporal coding. *Proc. Natl. Acad. Sci. U.S.A.,* 88: 9136–9140.

Felleman, D.J. and Van Essen, D.C. (1991) Distributed hierarchical processing in the primate cerebral cortex. *Cereb. Cortex,* 1: 1–47.

Fisken, R.A., Garey, L.J. and Powell, T.P.S. (1975) The intrinsic association and commissural connections of area 17 of the visual cortex. *Phil. Trans. R. Soc. Lond., Ser. B,* 272: 487–536.

Gerstein, G.L. and Perkel, D.H. (1972) Mutual temporal relationship among neuronal spike trains. Statistical techniques for display and analysis. *Biophys. J.,* 12: 453–473.

Gilbert, C.D. and Wiesel, T.N. (1989) Columnar specificity of intrinsic horizontal and corticocortical connections in cat visual cortex. *J. Neurosci.,* 9: 2432–2442.

Gray, C.M. and Singer, W. (1987) Stimulus-specific neuronal osciliations in the cat visual cortex: a cortical functional unit. *Soc. Neurosci. Abstr.,* 13: 404.3.

Gray, C.M. and Singer, W. (1989) Stimulus-specific neuronal oscillations in orientation columns of cat visual cortex. *Proc. Natl. Acad. Sci. U.S.A.,* 86: 1698–1702.

Gray, C.M., König, P., Engel, A.K. and Singer, W. (1989) Oscillatory responses in cat visual cortex exhibit inter-columnar synchronization which reflects global stimulus properties. *Nature,* 338: 334–337.

Greuel, J.M., Luhmann, H.J. and Singer, W. (1988) Pharmacological induction of use-dependent receptive field-modifications in the visual cortex. *Science,* 242: 74–77.

Gross, C.G., Rocha-Miranda, C.E. and Bender, D.B. (1972) Visual properties of neurons in inferotemporal cortex of the macaque. *J. Neurophysiol.,* 35: 96–111.

Grossberg, S. (1980) How does a brain build a cognitive code? *Psychol. Rev.,* 87: 1–51.

Hancock, P.J.B., Smith, L.S. and Phillips, W.A. (1991) A biologically supported error correcting learning rule. *Neural Comput.,* 3: 201–212.

Hebb, D.O. (1949) *The Organization of Behavior,* Wiley, New York.

Innocenti, G.M. and Frost, D.O. (1979) Effects of visual experience on the maturation of the efferent system to the corpus callosum. *Nature,* 280: 231–234.

Karni, A. and Sagi, D. (1991) Where practice makes perfect in texture discriminations: evidence for primary visual cortex plasticity. *Proc. Natl. Acad. Sci. U.S.A.,* 88: 4966–4970.

Kasamatsu, T. and Pettigrew, J.D. (1979) Preservation of binocularity after monocular deprivation in the striate cortex of kittens treated with 6-hydroxydopamine. *J. Comp. Neurol.,* 185: 139–162.

Kimura, F., Nishigori, A., Shirokawa, T. and Tsumoto, T. (1989) Long-term potentiation and N-methyl-D-aspartate receptors in the visual cortex of young rats. *J. Physiol. (Lond.),* 414: 125–144.

Kirillov, A.B., Borisyuk, G.N., Borisyuk, R.M. and Singer, W. (1993) Modeling synchronized assemblies of cortical oscillators using multilayered neural networks. (In preparation.)

Kisvárday, Z.F., Martin, K.A.C., Freund, T.F., Maglóczky, Z., Whitteridge, D. and Somogyi, P. (1986) Synaptic targets of HRP-filled layer III pyramidal cells in the cat striate cortex. *Exp. Brain Res.,* 64: 541–552.

Kleinschmidt, A., Bear, M.F. and Singer, W. (1987) Blockade of "NMDA" receptors disrupts experience-dependent plasticity of kitten striate cortex. *Science,* 238: 355–358.

König, P., Engel, A.K., Löwel, S. and Singer, W. (1990) Squint affects occurrence and synchronization of oscillatory responses in cat visual cortex. *Soc. Neurosci. Abstr.,* 16: 523.2.

Kreiter, A.K. and Singer, W. (1991) Oscillatory neuronal activity in the superior temporal sulcus of macaque monkeys. *Soc. Neurosci. Abstr.,* 17: 208.1.

Löwel, S. and Singer, W. (1992) Selection of intrinsic horizontal connections in the visual cortex by correlated neuronal activity. *Science,* 255: 209–212

Luhmann, H.J., Singer, W. and Martinez-Millan, L. (1990) Horizontal interactions in cat striate cortex: I. Anatomical substrate and postnatal development. *Eur. J. Neurosci.,* 2: 344–357.

Matsubara, J., Cynader, M., Swindale, N.V. and Stryker, M.P. (1985) Intrinsic projections within visual cortex: evidence for orientation-specific local connections. *Proc. Natl. Acad. Sci. U.S.A.,* 82: 935–939.

Mountcastle, V.B. (1957) Modality and topographic properties of single neurons of cat somatic sensory cortex. *J. Neurophysiol.,* 20: 408 – 434.

Palm, G. (1982) *Neural Assemblies,* Springer, Heidelberg.

Palm, G. (1990) Cell assemblies as a guideline for brain research. *Concepts Neurosci.,* 1: 133 – 147.

Perrett, D.I., Mistlin, A.J. and Chitty, A.J. (1987) Visual neurones responsive to faces. *Trends Neurosci.,* 10: 358 – 364.

Price, D.J. and Blakemore, C. (1985) The postnatal development of the association projection from visual cortical area 17 to area 18 in the cat. *J. Neurosci.,* 5: 2443 – 2452.

Raether, A., Gray, C.M. and Singer, W. (1989) Intercolumnar interactions of oscillatory neuronal responses in the visual cortex of alert cats. *ENA Abstr.,* 12: 72 – 5.

Rockland, K.S. and Lund, J.S. (1982) Widespread periodic intrinsic connections in the tree shrew visual cortex. *Science,* 215: 1532 – 1534.

Rolls, E.T. (1990) The representation of information in the temporal lobe visual cortical areas of macaques. In: R. Eckmiller (Ed.), *Advanced Neural Computers,* Elsevier, Amsterdam, pp. 69 – 78.

Singer, W. (1979) Central-core control of visual cortex functions. In: F.O. Schmitt and F.G. Worden (Eds.), *The Neurosciences – Fourth Study Program,* MIT Press, Cambridge, MA, pp. 1093 – 1109.

Singer, W., Freeman, B. and Rauschecker, J. (1981) Restriction of visual experience to a single orientation affects the organization or orientation columns in cat visual cortex: a study with deoxyglucose. *Exp. Brain Res.,* 41: 199 – 215.

Steriade, M., Curro Dossi, R., Paré, D. and Oakson, G. (1991) Fast oscillations (20 – 40 Hz) in thalamocortical systems and their potentiation by mesopontine cholinergic nuclei in the cat. *Proc. Natl. Acad. Sci. U.S.A.,* 85: 4396 – 4400.

T'so, D.Y., Gilbert, C.D. and Wiesel, T.N. (1986) Relationship between horizontal interactions and functional architecture in cat striate cortex as revealed by cross-correlation analysis. *J. Neurosci.,* 6: 1160 – 1170.

von der Malsburg, C. (1985) Nervous structures with dynamical links. *Ber. Bunsenges. Phys. Chem.,* 89: 703 – 710.

von der Malsburg, C. (1988) Pattern recognition by labelled graph matching. *Neural Networks,* 1: 141 – 148.

von der Malsburg, C. and Schneider, W. (1986) A neural cocktail-party processor. *Biol. Cybern.,* 54: 29 – 40.

von Noorden, G.K. (1990) *Binocular Vision and Ocular Motility; Theory and Management of Strabismus,* Mosby, Baltimore, MD.

Wiesel, T.N. and Hubel, D.H. (1965) Comparison of the effects of unilateral and bilateral eye closure on cortical unit responses in kittens. *J. Neurophysiol.,* 28: 1029 – 1040.

Subject Index

486